Organization,
class and control

International Library of Sociology

Founded by Karl Mannheim

Editor: John Rex, University of Aston in Birmingham

Arbor Scientiae
Arbor Vitae

A catalogue of the books available in the **International Library of Sociology** and other series of Social Science books published by Routledge & Kegan Paul will be found at the end of this volume.

CLEGG, S. &
~~DUNKERLEY, D.~~
5/80
HJ

Organization,
class and
ntrol
.50

Organization, class and control

Stewart Clegg
School of Humanities, Griffith University, Brisbane
and
David Dunkerley
Department of Sociology and Politics, Plymouth Polytechnic

Routledge & Kegan Paul
London, Boston and Henley

First published in 1980
by Routledge & Kegan Paul Ltd
39 Store Street, London WC1E 7DD,
Broadway House, Newtown Road,
Henley-on-Thames, Oxon RG9 1EN and
9 Park Street, Boston, Mass. 02108, USA
Set in 10/11 Times by
Oxprint, Oxford
and printed in Great Britain by
Unwin Brothers Ltd
Old Woking, Surrey
© Stewart Clegg and David Dunkerley 1980

British Library Cataloguing in Publication Data

Clegg, Stewart

Organization, class and control. – (International
library of sociology).
1. Organization
I. Title   II. Dunkerley, David   III. Series
301.18'32   HM131   79-42951

ISBN 0 7100 0421 4
ISBN 0 7100 0435 4 Pbk

Contents

CONTENTS

Acknowledgments

Many institutions and people have assisted us in the production of this book. It began as a suggestion from Peter Hopkins, matured as an idea whilst Stewart Clegg was a European Group of Organization Studies (EGOS) Research Fellow and David Dunkerley a lecturer in sociology at the University of Leeds. During this period (1975–6) Stewart Clegg was the recipient of an International Institute of Management Fellowship and a Thyssen Foundation travel grant, held at the Organizational Analysis Research Unit at Bradford University's Management Centre. David Dunkerley moved to become the Head of Sociology at Plymouth Polytechnic in 1975, from whose Research Fellowship Committee he has received considerable assistance during the preparation of this volume. Meanwhile, in 1976, Stewart Clegg had moved to Griffith University School of Humanities, from whose research sub-committee's generosity the progress of the book has greatly benefited. The University Research Committee, together with the British Council, funded David Dunkerley as a Visiting Research Fellow in 1978, during which time the book was completed. Along the way we have benefited from support, advice and assistance given by Paul Barrett, Lena Bruselid, Cyril Cannon, Lynne Clegg, Geoff Dow, Jane Dunkerley, Jane Gould, David Hickson, Geoff Payne, Patricia Randall, Graeme Salaman, David Silverman, Suzanne Stanley and John Willett.

Our thanks are due to the following for permission to quote from works in which they hold the copyright: *Administrative Science Quarterly,* vols 10 and 12; Longman, G. Salaman and K. Thompson (eds), *People and Organizations;* Longman, D. Warwick, *Bureaucracy;* D. Pugh and D. Hickson, *Organizational Structure in its Context: the Aston Programme I;* HMSO, *Department of Employment Gazette;* Heinemann, J. Westergaard and H. Resler,

ACKNOWLEDGMENTS

Class in a Capitalist Society; Revolutionary Communist, vol. 5; D.
Wedderburn in P. Townsend and N. Bosanquet (eds), *Labour and
Inequality.*

Introduction

This book has a number of antecedents. Initially we began to write it shortly after completing our *Critical Issues in Organizations* (Clegg and Dunkerley, 1977). There are some continuities with our introductory remarks to this earlier collaboration. Particularly, we would draw the reader's attention to our suggestion at that time that the sociology of organizations should adopt a more historically informed perspective around the idea of 'organizations as control'. It is this theme which we have developed in this volume. In addition, in the interim between *Critical Issues* and the present text, Stewart Clegg (1979a) wrote *The Theory of Power and Organization* in which some other of the ideas presented in this volume were first developed. In particular, we would draw the reader's attention to the argument in the latter study that the sociology of organizations lacked an adequate theoretical object for its analyses. In this volume we have proposed as such an object the concept of organization as control of the labour process. 'The simple elements of the labour process are (1) purposeful activity, that is work itself, (2) the object on which that work is performed and (3) the instruments of that work' (Marx, 1976, p. 284). This concept becomes increasingly central to our argument as the book unfolds.

We begin by considering the early contributions of classical sociologists such as Comte, Saint-Simon, Spencer and Durkheim for a sociology of organizations. These writers were in a privileged position. They were witness to the emergence of the first modern forms of industrial organization and society. Compared with Max Weber, whom we discuss in Chapters 2 and 3, these writers have been somewhat neglected by organization theorists, with the exception of Alvin Gouldner (1959a). Karl Marx, for what are perhaps more apparent reasons, has suffered a similar neglect. We introduce Marx's contributions through a consideration of the historical development of the capitalist labour process in Chapter 2. In this chapter we deliberately, one-sidedly, present the development of the capitalist organization of the labour process without focusing on the concomitant domestic labour process. This is because we devote a large part of Chapter 11 to this issue. We wait until this point in order to maintain the flow of our argument. Briefly, in Chapter 3 we tend not to agree with Weber in seeing specific types of organization as a part of the general rationalization of the world. Instead we are more inclined to agree with Marx that specific types of organization were intimately connected with the rise of capitalist accumulation.

During the nineteenth century the increasing scale of industrial organizations meant that it was no longer possible for a single owner or person to control and oversee all aspects of the complex labour process. It is this changed scale of operations which Offe (1976a) refers to in making the distinction between 'task-continuous' and 'task-discontinuous' status organizations. An aid to the 'rational' development of task-discontinuous hierarchical organizations was the model of bureaucracy found in the sphere of the state and its organizational apparatus such as the army. It was these which formed the initial object for Weber's ideal type of bureaucracy. Weber regarded American scientific management or Taylorism (named after its leading proponent, F. W. Taylor) as the most extreme form of the rationalization of work because of its 'rational conditioning and training of work performances' (Weber, 1948, p. 261). In recent years, of course, since the publication of Braverman's (1974) *Labour and Monopoly Capital*, there has been a resurgence of interest in scientific management from a broadly Marxist perspective. We discuss much of this recent material in the context of scientific management's principles, precepts and practices.

Taylor was not alone in advocating what have come to be known as formal theories of administration. Others (whom we discuss) included Mooney and Reiley, Fayol, Gulick and Urwick. Formal theorists of organization were not the only writers interested in how an organization might be controlled. In explicit opposition to such theorists as Taylor were important (and in the context of organization theory) neglected figures such as Gramsci who wrote from his practical experience with the workers' council movement in Turin in 1919–20. We consider the debates that Gramsci entered into in his *Ordine Nuovo* writings from this period, as well as his later *Prison Notebooks* (Gramsci, 1971). The relationship between Gramsci's work and that of Lenin is complex and contested. We discuss them in this chapter before proceeding to a consideration of the lessons of the workers' councils for the study of organizations.

Gramsci stressed the subtle, hegemonic forms of control which capitalism had developed. One writer who subsequently contributed to the development of such controls was Elton Mayo. Mayo is best known for his association with the Hawthorne studies. We discuss these in Chapter 3. However, in this context we also stress the later work in which there is a continuity between his plea for the reconstruction of social solidarity at the level of the organization and earlier arguments for such a reconstruction at the level of society by writers such as Comte.

Mayo and Taylor as embodiments of the theories of human relations and scientific management are not merely historical curiosities, as we stress in our final chapter. Organizations, their structure and processes, are a product of a history in whose creation these figures are heavily implicated. Some of what we take for granted in contemporary organizations results from the earlier application of their theories.

Our first three chapters illuminate three key directions for the subsequent evolution of theories of organization. The first of these are the stress on organizations conceptualized in terms of ideal types. This interest clearly flows from Weber's formal model. In its use by subsequent theorists such as Etzioni (1961; 1975), Blau and Scott (1963), Gouldner (1954) and Burns and Stalker (1961) a number of further variants on the Weberian theme of typological analysis are constructed. We consider these developments in Chapter 4.

The second direction evolves from the importance placed on the 'formal' organization in the Hawthorne studies, modelled on a Paretian concept of the social system, in part as a reaction to the static, prescriptive and incomplete model of the purely formal organization. This manifests itself in the important contributions of American structural-functionalists such as Parsons (1956), Merton (1949) and Selznick (1948; 1949) to the study of organizations. We consider these writers in Chapter 5 and proceed to elaborate further developments of the systems concept, in terms of open, closed and socio-technical systems. In addition, we also consider a number of significant critiques of systems theory contributed, for example, by Silverman (1970), Elger (1975), Gouldner (1959a), Mayntz (1964) and Gunder Frank (1973). Nonetheless, the systems concept retains some utility in the work of, for example, Habermas (1976) and Wallerstein (1974a). We develop this in our final chapter.

A third key direction has been the empirical analysis of the dimensions of organization structures associated in particular with the Aston school. The researchers (Pugh and Hickson, 1976) claim to have refuted the Weberian and typological theory of organizations through the construction of an empirically grounded taxonomy generated from large-scale sampling of organizations. This work has been extremely, and deservedly, influential in recent years. It has generated a large number of replications and continuations of the original analysis of 52 British work organizations. Indeed, it has contributed significantly to an internationalization of organization theory, leading to a number of cross-national comparative analyses. However, despite these impressive and cumulative contributions, the theoretical infrastructure of this research has rarely been subject to detailed and critical scrutiny. We not only provide a detailed exposition of this research but also a contribution to its critique.

This critique was implicit in Mayntz's (1964) remarks on the level of general propositions that a systems theory of organizations might construct. She wrote:

> Once we get down to the question *which* of its features or properties a particular organization can or should keep invariant against *which* external influences, and *what kinds* of regulating mechanisms can serve this purpose, we must obviously leave the level of general propositions for all organizations and are forced to take historically specific conditions into account (Mayntz, 1964, p. 113).

If we do not, then, as in the case of the Aston researchers, we will be faced with increasingly diminishing and trivial returns for the expenditure of a sophisticated research output. The Aston school may be able to compare many organizations on a few standardized dimensions but, as Mayntz (1964) warned, it may do so at the expense of neglecting historically specific conditions.

It is precisely these historically specific conditions which seemed to form the central concern for the 'action frame of reference' which David Silverman (1970) introduced into the sociology of organizations. We discuss Silverman's works (1968; 1970; 1972; 1974a; 1974b; 1975; Silverman and Jones, 1976) in Chapter 7 in the general context of a consideration of some writers who have proposed that organizations be conceptualized as 'structures of action'. These include such influential figures as March and Simon (1958) and Simon (1957), as well as more social psychology-oriented figures such as Weick (1969). What is common to this diverse collection of writers, stretching from ethno-methodology to cybernetics, is their attempt to construct a theoretical object for organization analysis which stresses the organization as a structuring of human action.

One of the major critiques of organization theory advanced by Silverman (1970) is its tendency to reify phenomena such as the goals of the organization. In Chapter 8 the major works on goal analysis are explored, including Etzioni (1964), Yuchtman and

Seashore (1967), and Perrow (1961) as well as critiques by writers such as Albrow (1968) and Silverman (1970). One recent development in organization theory, influenced by symbolic interactionists such as Strauss *et al.* (1963), Hughes (1945; 1958; 1971) and Bucher and Stelling (1969), conceives organization goals as the outcome of a process of negotiation. This is known as the negotiated order perspective, recently proposed by Day and Day (1977). Typically, negotiated order theorists have tended to study only a limited range of organizations, concentrating mainly on hospitals. Through a reconsideration of Clegg (1975) we are able to extend this range to include construction sites as an example of negotiated orders.

If in recent years organization goals have been seen as rather more the result of a social construction and imposition of reality than a merely contingent feature, the same could be said for technology. Technology has frequently been regarded as a crucial determinant of organization structure in, for example, Woodward (1965) and Burns and Stalker (1961). In Chapter 9 we argue a contrary view which follows Child's (1972a; 1972b) argument that organization controllers have considerable discretion and power in their choice of technology. This reiterates and develops a basic theme of Marglin's (1974), which we introduced in Chapter 2. The implication of this line of argument is that technology does not 'cause' organization structure or the nature of work design. At most it places limits upon it. These limits are always constructed from within the context of the dialectical relationship of the productive forces of technology and the social relationships associated with them. Our thesis is that both technology and organization structure have developed subordinate to the needs of capital accumulation and control.

Organization theory has not only been characterized by a technological determinism. It has also, particularly since the rise of the open-systems model, been characterized by an environmental determinism in which the structure of the organization is seen to be a response to environmental pressures. The relationship between organizations and their environments has been vigorously explored in recent years by writers such as Aldrich (1975). In opposition to this, writers such as Galbraith (1969) and Child (1972a; 1972b) have stressed the ability of organization controllers, particularly of large organizations, to control and to some extent choose the environments in which they operate. Multi-national corporations are perhaps the best example of organizations having this capacity. From this realization there has developed the recent political economy perspective of writers such as Benson (1975). This perspective and the organization-environment relationship are

5

discussed in Chapter 10 and are elaborated and developed further in our final chapter.

People in organizations are frequently treated in organization theory as either sources of social psychological 'problems' or as embodiments of individual needs and dispositions. We eschew this perspective in our chapter on people in organizations in favour of one which stresses the reality of structural divisions in society: notably sexual and class divisions. These are not only of major importance in their own right but are also significantly inter-related. As practices they are in large part reproduced by organizations, particularly in their recruitment strategies and work design. There is thus a clear link between labour markets, organization structure and forms of discrimination in society, which we explore in Chapter 11. In addition, through the use of our concept of organization as control of the labour process we are able to explore the relationship between the organization's labour process and the domestic labour process. This enables us to fill in the other half of the development of the labour process which we omitted in Chapter 2.

Women in organizations, irrespective of any criteria other than their sex, are invariably less powerful than men. In Chapter 12 we explain why this should be so in terms of a general theory of power in organizations which stresses the importance of 'skill'. Skill and its distribution is related to the class structure of society reproduced in and through organizations. As we demonstrate, this entails that power and class in organizations are invariably inter-related.

Power and class form the basis for our final chapter, in which we attempt to summarize and combine much of the preceding twelve chapters in an analysis of the political economy of organizations. This is conceptualized in the framework of a theory of the state developed from writers such as Habermas (1976), Offe (1973a; 1973b) and O'Connor (1973a). Finally, we conceptualize the whole in terms of models of the dynamics of the world economy advanced by authors such as Mandel (1975) and Wallerstein (1974a).

1 Classical sociology, organizations and theory

Auguste Comte

Perhaps the most significant of the early sociological commentators for our analysis would be Auguste Comte, if only because he was the nominal founder of the discipline of sociology in 1838. Comte's work can be viewed as complementary to that of Montesquieu and Condorcet. Complementary to Montesquieu, Comte believed that he had developed his predecessor's enquiry, *The Spirit of Laws*, into a positive science through the discovery of the 'evolutionary principle'. For Comte, developing this idea from Condorcet, evolution was essentially a development of the human mind. The stage of social organization was determined by the progress of civilization. This replaced Montesquieu's principle of social determination – the role of the government – with a process of the natural evolution of civilization which culminated in industrial society. In making his analysis, Comte was not only teleologically elevating his contemporary industrial society to the beginning of analysis and the end of historical development; he was also attempting something far more concrete. This was to produce an ideological basis for the re-establishment of social order in the Restoration period after the destruction of many of the more traditional bulwarks of that order during the Revolutionary age.

From the perspective of an analysis of Comte's view of the process of industrialization, the process itself was unfolding at the time of his writing. What we have, therefore, is not an *ex post facto* analysis benefiting from the virtues that hindsight bestows, but rather an analysis of the contemporary society, or more precisely of European society during the first two decades of the nineteenth century.

The theory of history and of social change propounded by Comte is well known. Societies live and die and are replaced by new forms. Each society however, is built upon what has gone before in a truly organic manner. In the same sense that the caterpillar eventually becomes the butterfly and the tadpole the frog, so, for Comte, society evolves through distinct transitional periods. The contemporary society of which he was writing was replacing a former one. The latter, characterized by an emphasis on religious fervour and military activity, was spent. From its bankruptcy as a viable social setting the theological and military types of society were being surpassed by the industrial and scientific types, at the centre of which stood modern organizations. Religious thinking was rapidly being replaced by scientific thinking. The scientists, or those expressing scientific ideas, were emerging as the new intellectual leaders of society; it was they who were establishing themselves as the new ideologists. Moreover, Comte agreed that this new grouping was inheriting the 'spiritual power' that formerly the religious leaders had monopolized. This 'spiritual power' gave rise to beliefs, attitudes and ideas which stood at the very heart of social order.

The other transformation was the rise of the industrialist at the expense of the military man. 'Industrialist' is used here in a generic sense which includes not only the owners of capital but also financiers, managers and general entrepreneurs: 'organizers' in the general sense. The two transformations – theology to science and military to industry – are of course closely related to each other. A scientific frame of reference leads to, and in part arises from, the change from man struggling against man, to man struggling against his environment. Comte believed his positive philosophy to be such a science. The 'positive' mode of reasoning and thinking which Comte described was precisely that which he used in his own work. Thus it can be argued (cf. Aron, 1965) that Comte was an exemplification of positive thought. More especially, Comte was a theorist of a particular 'science' which he termed sociology.

Comte's contemporary society, passing from theological/military to scientific/industrial, was of necessity in a state of chaos. He believed this to be a temporary state between the two stages of social order delineated above. The *reorganization* that would inevitably arise would 'occur' not by revolution but by the sciences becoming dominant, by their synthesis and by the application of a positive political system. Sociology as a positive science could enhance the development of the emergent society. And sociology, above the other positive sciences, could realize the new social order and organization.

As a basic philosophical attitude, very little of this can be attributed solely to Comte. The observations of a new social arrangement were common amongst his contemporaries, although perhaps his original contributions can be seen in the elevation of the scientific way of thinking to the highest level, particularly the role ascribed to sociology. Furthermore, while various of the themes raised by Comte were simultaneously being discussed by his contemporaries, in many respects he was more selective. It is this selectivity that demarcates Comte as such an influential theorist.

Turning to the process of industrialization and the role of industry in the new society, we can examine what Comte took to be the important and uniquely different characteristics of the industrial society of his time. The term 'industrial society', as Therborn (1976, p. 164) argues, was an anti-feudal concept. Industrial and scientific activity are contrasted with military and clerical activity as the main preoccupations of feudal society, in Comte's analysis. Aron (1965, p. 72) notes three 'decisive' factors in Comte's writings:

1 The scientific character of industry, particularly in the way labour was organized. Custom and practice gave way to rational organization.
2 There is a previously unparalleled development of wealth and resources arising from scientific applications.
3 A new social phenomenon developed: the large-scale organization of working masses both at work (factories) and in the non-work situation (vast urban areas).

Comte took an intermediate position as to whether the evolving form had socialism or *laissez-faire* capitalism as an ideological base. For him the fundamental strength of the emergent social order lay in the ethic of what was later to be termed managerialism. He was a spokesman, in this sense, for the industrial bourgeoisie, amongst whom he allotted, in particular, a decisive role to the directors of machine industry, and increasingly to bankers. Aron (1965, p. 75) refers to this managerial ethic as characterized by what he calls the 'polytechnician-manager'. Such an individual is opposed to socialism in general terms, but approves of the tenets of capitalism only in a particular sense. For example, Comte rejected the notion of ruthless competition which is a hallmark of nineteenth-century capitalism but at the same time he favoured private ownership (particularly of concentrated wealth). Whilst there might appear to be a basic inconsistency here, it should be noted that as part of his general philosophy Comte saw individual private interests as capable of working together in harmony. In this he follows Saint-Simon in regarding the *industrielles* as a unity of both workers and owners. His work does not centre on the basic class conflict that figures so much in the writings of Marx.

From the point of view of economics, Comte believed that it was

9

necessary to over-produce. While economic theory today might question such an assumption, Comte felt that a society could advance only by experiencing this phenomenon. In other words, capitalization is a fundamental aspect of Comte's philosophy. Comte opposed any programme for transferring this capitalization from the private to the public sector. He was a committed advocate of private ownership of the means of production. This was, in part, due to the fact that he saw authority as a personal characteristic, regardless of whether the basis of this authority was social, economic or political. He argued that the possession of economic authority could only exist with a parallel possession of social authority. The two belonged together in a compatible manner. Since every society has its leaders (those with social authority) each society, *ipso facto*, has those possessing a larger accumulation of private wealth and capital. He argued that the possession of private wealth and capital should be accompanied by a sense of social duty. The rich, particularly the industrialists, managers and financiers, must display social responsibility by furthering the aims of social order.

There is a further aspect to this argument, since Comte believed that social, economic and political status did not solely determine the individual's social being. He introduces the metaphysical notion of a 'spiritual order' into his analysis. This order is beyond the temporal order that has so far been discussed. The temporal order relates closely to the exercise of authority and power in society; the spiritual order relates to the qualitative judgments made about an individual – a kind of moral assessment. Thus, from the spiritual viewpoint an individual may receive a high ranking, his position may be regarded as having a high moral worth. But simultaneously he may be ranked low from the point of view of the temporal order because he possesses minimal power in society. According to Comte the spiritual order is more praiseworthy than the temporal order: each individual should strive for ranking in the former rather than the latter.

The society of which Comte was writing should, he argued, have the spiritual order foremost in mind. Furthermore, society could ensure order and regularity only by stressing this. He argued that an emphasis on the temporal order of economic wealth and social power was insufficient for the survival of society.

Comte presents a curious analysis of industrial society, particularly when placed in the context in which he wrote. He stresses certain basic ideas: free labour, the application of science to industry (supplanting the military/theological ideologies of feudal society), the emergence of rational organization, and the emphasis on the moral worth of the individual. The importance of these ideas was to be stressed by subsequent theorists such as Marx and Weber, albeit in different contexts. However, the analysis is somewhat curious in other respects. He argued that war had no place in industrial societies, particularly in those of western Europe. He argued against imperialism and colonialism. These two points are related, since in pre-capitalist modes of production a major source of capital accumulation arose from military intervention in other societies. With an industrial society economic progress was guaranteed, he argued, through the rational (scientific) organization of work and labour.

To return to his metaphysical ideas, the 'spiritual order' was to be led by men of a scientific disposition. These were to be the sociologists, the new priests and theologians of the industrial age. It was they who would determine ideologies, legitimate the use of power, and orientate the whole of society towards its defined goals of advancement and progress. The chief task of those possessing spiritual power was, in other words, to ensure social order, harmony and unity. The possession of spiritual power was dependent upon meritocratic achievements. Indeed merit was the key to success in Comte's philosophy.

We have to recall that the period of Comte's life (1798–1857) was one of considerable social, political and economic upheaval. In all, he lived through seven very different political regimes in France. This was a period of disquiet and discontent, as witnessed by innumerable uprisings and revolts. The Industrial Revolution occurred with widespread and deep-rooted social and economic unrest. In so many respects this was a period marked by rapid social change.

Of course, Paris had a profound and central involvement in European affairs during the period of Comte's lifetime. Not only was French society experiencing more unrest and social disorder than its neighbours, Paris was also an intellectual and scientific centre. Much of the scientific development in Europe in later decades owed its existence to the scholarship in the France of Comte's time.

The French Industrial Revolution, as Hobsbawm (1975) has noted, occurred much later than its English counterpart. Whereas in England the periods of social unrest arose after the process of industrialization had taken place, in France the two occurred roughly simultaneously. It is common to point to the French Industrial Revolution occurring in the immediate post-Napoleonic era. Replicating developments in England, an industrial working class developed on a fairly large scale. However, in England this working class is argued to have migrated from rural areas (the mass movement from agriculture to industry which writers such as

Hobsbawm (1969) and Thompson (1968) discuss in detail). In France, on the other hand, the new working class was largely recruited from artisans, craftsmen and basic handicraft workers of the pre-industrial era. French industry was not characterized by the Lowry-esque factory landscape that typifies the English scene. Small enterprises were (and still are) common.

In spite of differences of this kind between developments in England and France during the period of industrialization, the social consequences were largely similar. Wages declined, employment of women and young children increased (obviously the two are related), and the increase in destitution reached alarming proportions as early as the 1830s. It is interesting to note that the rioting and social discontent that was a feature of the early part of the nineteenth century was articulated, not by these unskilled workers who experienced the greatest deprivations, but by the urban semi-skilled workers and skilled workers. The most obvious and common manifestations of discontent followed the English pattern, the systematic smashing of machines being the most frequent.

The society of Comte's time was also a bourgeois one, but comprising a bourgeoisie of relatively recent status. The domination of the self-made man was very apparent, coupled with the characteristic possessive individualism and self-energy that was a hallmark of the English entrepreneur. In accordance with Weber's thesis in *The Protestant Ethnic and the Spirit of Capitalism* (1976) many of these *nouveau-riche* entrepreneurs were either Protestant or Jewish, and their minority status in society urged them to further accumulation of capital and wealth in order to obtain an entrée into 'society'.

This briefly gives us an idea of the backcloth against which Comte was writing. One important point to reiterate is the fact that Comte was developing his ideas about 'the new society' as it was unfolding. Admittedly, he had the English experience to draw upon to some extent, but he was aware of the peculiarity of certain phenomena in France itself. We have to recognize this point and see it in relation to the writings of other writers to be examined later. These other writers were, to a much greater extent, able to stand back and interpret events; for Comte the events were very much a part of his daily existence.

In terms of his analysis of contemporary society as it was unfolding, Comte drew in part upon the ideas of economists such as Adam Smith and Jean-Baptiste Say. Comte had an ambivalent attitude towards Smith – sometimes full of praise, at other times very critical. Comte was, of course, a firm believer in an extensive societal and organizational division of labour. He recognized the economic sense of the division of labour in terms of industrial production and approved of Smith's analogy of the nation as a workshop with the work of each individual contributing to the national wealth. Equally, though, Comte saw that the extensive division of labour recommended by Smith could have dysfunctional consequences. Here the ambivalence displays itself: on the one hand, there is praise for the phenomenon as a technically elegant innovation; while on the other hand, there is strong criticism because of its social and individual human consequences.

The important point to arise from this ambivalent position is the fact that Comte owed a great deal to the work of contemporary liberal economists, as they were then defined (with Adam Smith as one of the most influential). Jean-Baptiste Say, a close follower of Smith, also had considerable influence over Comte with reference to the 'creative' functions of both entrepreneurs and workers, and thus, on the development of his view of the organic unity of the two groups. However, perhaps the most important thinker for any analysis of Comte's work is Saint-Simon.

Comte and Saint-Simon

Comte has frequently been regarded as a disciple of Saint-Simon (1760–1825). The nature of the association between the two was close. Comte was Saint-Simon's secretary for some time after 1817 and certainly injected a degree of order into his otherwise disorderly work. Comte obviously had a great respect for Saint-Simon both from an intellectual and a personal point of view (he even worked on an unpaid basis for a while). There has been a long-standing argument concerning who had the greater influence upon whom. Merely from a chronological point of view it is clear that Saint-Simon cannot have been greatly influenced intellectually, since he was almost sixty years of age when they met. However, Comte does seem to have been greatly influenced by his work. Before working for Saint-Simon, Comte expounded various Republican ideas; soon after working with him, and in later life, his work represents the views of a social élitist. Equally, many of the ideas expressed by Comte during part of his association with Saint-Simon were ideas that later reached intellectual fruition and formed the basis of his general theoretical ideas about society as delineated above.

However, there was the famous split between the two men. Although the stated cause was rather minor, it does illustrate the strained nature of their relationship. The argument concerned the publication of one of Comte's essays and whether it should be published as Comte's work or Saint-Simon's. The split left Comte a bitter man in terms of the memories of his association with Saint-Simon. He wrote to a friend:

> Now you may rest assured that henceforward I shall behave as if this man had never existed. He has done me so much harm that I shall be rendering him a service if I do nothing more than forget him. (Quoted by Manuel, 1956, p. 337).

In spite of the fraughtness of the personal side of the break-up of the association, it did mark the beginnings of Comte's recognition by the intellectual and academic communities of his time.

It is evident that Comte's ideas were strongly influenced in their development by those of his patron, as well as by those of the liberal economists. For instance, Saint-Simon and his followers made wide application of the ideas of the liberal economists, such as Say, particularly that entrepreneurs and workers both have a creative role in society. Comte also stressed this feature. Indeed, Saint-Simon's biographer, Manuel (1956) has argued that many of Comte's ideas were first mooted by Saint-Simon himself. For example, the fundamental tenets of positivism, the 'positive science of man' (sociology) and the hierarchical nature of the sciences, are said to be present in Saint-Simon's work, albeit in a confused and possibly random manner. But Saint-Simon was not a man of science, he neither knew much about the philosophy of science, nor did he work in a scientific manner. Statements that are to be found in Saint-Simon concerning positivism are perhaps too garbled to be taken meaningfully. Nevertheless, the statements are there and it is upon this evidence that his influence over Comte is argued about. It is probably the case that Saint-Simon could not help but make oblique references to positivism and to other Comtean ideas (as we now recognize them to be). They were ideas that were being widely discussed by his peers and so inevitably he could comment on them. To award them the status of ideas that were to influence the fundamental beliefs and thoughts of Comte is possibly an exaggeration of the reality, and a mistaken application of the canons of the 'history of ideas'.

Instead of looking between the lines for points of similarity, it is easier to look for points of difference between the two men. Saint-Simon, and more especially his followers, are regarded by many as among the founders of socialism. Indeed, there is an obelisk in Moscow in praise of Saint-Simon's work as one of the founders of the socialist revolution. It is no surprise that there should not be one to Comte, who, as we have seen, was not influenced by socialist ideas. On the contrary, Comte was an élitist who often spoke in laudatory terms about capitalism and capitalists. Saint-Simonian socialism has been argued to be one of the early influences in the work of Karl Marx (e.g. Bottomore and Rubel, 1963, ch. 1). What was it in Saint-Simon which could lead one to make this connection?

We have already indicated that Saint-Simon's work was lacking in systematization, but specific themes can be distinguished that enable us to understand both the man and his work. The main point we can make initially is that his work does represent a critique of the existing social order. The exact nature of this critique we shall spell out below. It was this critique that had led many commentators to regard Saint-Simon as one of the early founders of socialist thought, and as a 'critical thinker' (e.g. Marcuse, 1955). However, Marx rejected the notion that Saint-Simon was a founder of socialism, not on ideological grounds (he in fact called him a 'utopian socialist') but on historical grounds. Part of the difficulty that we see Comte trying to cope with – writing about a society whilst it was undergoing rapid change – was a much greater difficulty for Saint-Simon. As Marx pointed out, Saint-Simon was concerned with industrialization before the process had developed to a point where the problems and contradictions of the capitalist system had become apparent. For example, basic class conflict had not, during Saint-Simon's lifetime, become the ubiquitous phenomenon that it had in Marx's. Marx, then, recognized that Saint-Simon was 'on the right track', but that his critique of the *status quo* and indeed his ideas for the new society were necessarily stifled.

There exists something of a paradox in Saint-Simon. Where there is general agreement that he was a critic of the *status quo*, he was generally opposed to the French Revolution (he was 29 years of age when it occurred). His autobiography makes this point very clear: 'I did not wish to take part in it. . . . I had an aversion to destruction' (quoted in Manuel, 1956, p. 62). Like so many of his contemporaries and successors, Saint-Simon saw the social and political stability of medieval society to be attributable to the pervasive impact of religion. Furthermore, he regarded the new order of society to be one which was emerging organically from the old. The over-riding stability of medieval society was being overthrown by a number of factors such as the rise in the importance of science and technology, the growth of a bourgeoisie with an industrial base, the growth of Protestantism, and the accompanying decline in the relative importance of Catholicism.

Saint-Simon saw eighteenth-century philosophy as having had a great impact on the nineteenth century. In particular, 'Les Philosophes' had led, in Saint-Simon's eyes, to the partial breakdown of society at the time he was writing. Their interpretation of society had been destructive, but had little to offer by way of constructive alternative societal forms. Saint-Simon therefore saw his task to be creative as well as critical, constructive

15

as well as destructive.

What were the elements of this creative construction? As with his pupil, Comte, Saint-Simon's philosophy rested upon an organic social order, upon stability in the social structure, and upon slow evolutionary rather than upon rapid revolutionary change. There is little doubt from his writings that he yearned for an idealized version of the positive aspects of medieval society, particularly its emphasis upon stability. Equally, though, he recognized that times had changed and that there were limited opportunities for incorporating much of the old into the new. His work rests upon the probability of unity in society arising from a unity of thought and intellectual principles. As with Comte, although considerably less systematically, he saw knowledge (and society) passing through distinct phases: theological → metaphysical → scientific. He believed in the scientific study of society (social physiology). He observed that science had developed a moral and legitimatory function which had previously been the preserve of religion. The new élite in society for whom this legitimatory ideology functioned was an industrial/commerical/financial élite. The form of this legitimatory ideology was to be positivism, the new religion, which was to be the replacement for the role of traditional religion in medieval society. In addition, Saint-Simon believed in an élite over and beyond the temporal industrial élite. This was to be a spiritual élite of scientists.

What is interesting is that Saint-Simon was not expounding a view of society that differed in any significant way from that which had existed before. The structure would be basically similar; only those comprising the key groups in the structure would be different. Thus, scientists would replace theologians, and industrialists would replace feudal leaders. His vision proposed a bourgeois order to replace feudalism. In order to ensure stability in society, which was one of the main aims of the programme, Saint-Simon argued for a coalition between the temporal élite (the industrialists) and the intellectuals in order to produce what Gramsci (1971) was much later to call an 'hegemonic bloc'.

In summary, Saint-Simon opposed the contemporary manifestations of 'possessive individualism' (Macpherson, 1962) in the economic ideologies of his day and wished to re-emphasize the *social*. The way he did this was in terms of stressing the potential for social disorder which existed where normative order was not present. Where traditional forms of this order had broken down, particularly the legitimatory ideology of religion, he wished to create new forms of social solidarity to cement society into a new order of certainties. His solution and the basis that he proposed for a new order was in terms of a social and industrial system based upon principles of 'brotherly love' (hence Marx's remark that Saint-Simon was 'a utopian socialist'). A basically organic view of society is therefore presented by Saint-Simon. This view ensured, theoretically, the curtailment of potential and actual class conflict. This raised an interesting question, not entirely germane to our analysis here, of the extent to which Saint-Simon has been rightly labelled the founder of socialist thought. Only in one respect – centralized production planning – does he appear to have coincident interests with later socialist writers, while in most other respects his views reflect élitist, romantic, conservative thinking.

Herbert Spencer

Herbert Spencer's (1820–1903) central contribution to sociology is the analogy between society and a biological organism. Society is regarded as a social organism, in terms of its structure, functions and growth. With the linking of social change and social evolution which this entailed, it became possible to see societies as not only undergoing successive phases of growth and development, but also in some sense as competing with each other for support in differing environments, with the more successful social adaptations persisting. Spencer was to develop this view most fully, and in so doing articulated an ideology which found considerable support in the boardrooms of organizations engaged in a vigorous capitalism. While Comte and Saint-Simon were unable to make any concrete suggestions for the problems of industrial capitalism which were applicable within the context of large-scale organizations, Herbert Spencer found much more immediate acceptance. Comte and Saint-Simon proposed social theocratic ideas as the moral basis by which to renew social solidarity in the future. Spencer proposed that capitalism had already achieved perfection, but at costs which he was also prepared to recognize (see Peel, 1971). Spencer's view of his contemporary industrial society was that it was characterized by a twofold process of *differentiation* and *integration*. Society was becoming differentiated into mutually dependent elements. These integrating elements were of three types: the sustaining system, which refers to industrial and agricultural production; the distribution system which relates to forms of communication and exchange; and the regulatory system which controls society through the government and military spheres. As these systems become more differentiated, through, for instance, increases in the division of labour in the sustaining system, then the distribution system of communications also grows to integrate the whole. With the increase in the division of labour and of communications Spencer maintains that because of increased size, political authority will

17

become more centralized. All the parts of the whole, the three systems, are in an evolutionary homoeostasis or equilibrium.

Spencer used these ideas to organize his account of the emergence of contemporary industrial society. He argued that this society had emerged from an earlier form which he called 'militant society'. In counter-posing the industrial to the military, Spencer, like Comte, was proposing an anti-feudal concept. Militant society is characterized by 'compulsory co-operation' organized on the basis of an almost constant preparation for war. In such societies there exists a highly centralized authority and social control under a military-political leader. Beneath this person, Spencer noted a rigid hierarchy of power, status and property, with productive labour being the least esteemed activity. Ideologically, the hierarchy was reflected in the dominant clerical myths and beliefs and in a rigid discipline based on a scant regard for individuals.

He contrasted this society with 'industrial society', which he believed had been developing since feudal times. This society was becoming more integrated as wars became less frequent. Society becomes more voluntary and less compulsive, being essentially constituted by the mutual dependence of individuals exchanging services in an increasing division of labour. This voluntarism reaches its peak in 'modern', mid-nineteenth-century society, in which the sustaining and distributive systems develop their own regulating systems. These are independent of the state and in the case of the sustaining system of industrial and agricultural capitalism, identical with the market. Economic organization in general is conceptualized after English competitive capitalism in its most *laissez-faire* period.

> There is now no fixing of prices by the State; nor is there prescribing of methods. Subject to but slight hindrances from a few licences, citizens adopt what occupations they please; buy and sell where they please. The amounts grown and manufactured, imported and exported, are regulated by laws; improvements are not enforced nor bad processes legislatively interdicted; but men carrying on their business as they think best, are simply required by law to fulfil their contracts and commanded not to aggress upon their neighbours (Spencer, 1893, pp. 532–3).

It may be said with Therborn (1976, p. 228) that, while Spencer's evolutionary tendencies enabled him to see perfection in mid-Victorian English capitalism at the height of *laissez-faire*:

> It had never been a very accurate account of reality, even in Spencer's early days, when Engels was writing *The Condition of*

the Working Class in England, and Disraeli his *Sybil, or the Two Nations*. But it made sense to the small merchants and manufacturers of Spencer's native Derby and other new industrial cities, who were prospering with the industrial revolution and felt secure in what was indisputably the premier country of the world. . . . A model of competitive capitalism can, however, serve as an idyllic ideology in somewhat more sordid contexts. The men who paid homage to Spencer on his visits to the United States were largely the ruthless magnates of the new monopoly stage of capitalism – the Carnegies, Rockefellers, Hills and others.

As Therborn goes on to say:

But however congenial the Spencerian notion of 'the survival of the fittest' was to the victors of reckless monopolistic competition, Spencer was not truly their man (Therborn, 1976, p. 288).

The liberal tendencies of Spencer, perhaps, as Peel (1971, p. 216) has suggested, because of his direct knowledge and immediate experience of the division of labour in industry, made him well aware of the monotonous, degrading character of work, such that he could write of the cherished freedom of contract of formally free labour, that:

This liberty amounts in practice to little more than the ability to exchange one slavery for another; since fit only for his particular occupation, he has rarely an opportunity of doing anything more than decide in what mill he will pass the greater part of his dreary days. The coercion of circumstances often leans more hardly on him than the coercion of a master does on one in bondage. (Spencer, 1893, p. 610).

Spencer had no solutions for these 'social problems' of industrial capitalism, other than a limited private philanthropy to remedy the worst aspects of the worker's situation, and an optimistic support for the co-operative movement.

Today, as Parsons (1937) has said, 'Spencer is dead', killed

above all by the demise of small-scale competitive capitalism and the advent of the age of monopoly capital, in an economy dominated by big corporations. With the sharpening of international as well as internal contradictions in the new epoch, the old liberalism – pacifist, cosmopolitan and wedded to free exchange – was superseded by imperialism and social reform (Therborn, 1976, p. 230).

Emile Durkheim

Durkheim's central achievement was to spell out the elements of social explanation at a time when political and ethical philosophy, the 'science' of political economy, and the positive schools were united under the banners of individualism (Taylor *et al.*, 1973, p. 67).

Taylor and his colleagues characterize the central achievement of Durkheim as thorough-going opposition to 'analytical individualism'. In particular, this analytical individualism found its expression in the traditional political philosophies and economics of liberalism with their fiction of the 'social contract freely entered into by atomized individuals renouncing a degree of that freedom in exchange for protection by that society' (Taylor *et al.*, 1973, p. 67). They cite him to this effect:

The conception of a social contract is today very difficult to defend, for it has no relation to the facts. The observer does not meet it along his road, so to speak. Not only are there no societies which have such an origin, but there are none whose structure presents the least trace of a contractual organization. It is neither a fact acquired through history nor a tendency which grows out of historical development. Hence, to rejuvenate this doctrine and accredit it, it would be necessary to qualify as a contract the adhesion which each individual, as adult, gave to the society when he was born, solely by reason of which he continues to live. But then he would have to term contractual every action of man which is not determined by constraint (Durkheim, 1964a, p. 202).

Such an attack on utilitarian political philosophy was necessarily an attack on the presuppositions of sociologists such as Spencer, with his *laissez-faire* trust in the market. Durkheim, rather than praising the market as the ethical foundation of a natural order, was more concerned, first to delineate the role of the market as a possible source of disorder, second to specify the conditions under which order would be possible, and third, to determine the reason for its absence in contemporary industrial society.

Liberal economics rested on an assumption of egoistic individualism in the market, in which the pursuit of individual self-interest was conceptualized as having an equilibrating effect. Durkheim argued against this that on the basis purely of the market, no stable social order was possible. In *The Division of Labour in Society* Durkheim undertook to demonstrate that the organic solidarity of a division of labour and exchange required regulation from non-market phenomena: the moral community of social solidarity. Only this form of support and regulation could assure the non-contractual elements of contract and thus maintain the equilibrium of exchange. Durkheim is thus a thorough-going critic of the economic policies of *laissez-faire* (see Durkheim's (1959) 'critical conclusion' to his study of Saint-Simon).

Although Durkheim's work on *The Division of Labour in Society* was cast in an evolutionary framework, it had little in common with Spencer's evolutionism. The latter's evolutionism was developed from the utilitarian tradition represented by Jeremy Bentham and James Mill, and epistemologically is premised on pre-Darwinian Lamarckian biology (Hirst, 1975). As such it is necessarily pre-scientific and teleological, conceived as a natural philosophy rather than being based on a natural science. Its premise is a view of cosmological evolution in which all nature is conceived as subject to a common evolutionary law tending toward 'progress'. This takes the form of a transition from the simple to the complex, the homogeneous to the heterogeneous, through a process of differentiation which is homologous in all the distinct realms of nature, because it is conceived as driven by some 'fundamental necessity, some all pervading principle'. The end of progress, conceived after utilitarianism, is the greatest happiness of the greatest number. Durkheim's views were more sanguine.

Durkheim (1964b) situates himself in relation to Spencer's evolutionism, in the following terms:

> Thus although he [Spencer] claims to proceed empirically,
> the facts accumulated in his sociology seem to function prin-
> cipally as arguments, since they are employed to illustrate
> analyses of concepts rather than to describe and explain things
> (Durkheim, 1964b, p. 21).

He considers both Spencer and Comte to have proposed a 'psychologistic' concept of evolution because the principle of evolution appears to be 'some inner spring of human nature', 'some sort of instinct' which can only be 'a metaphysical entity of the very existence of which there is no demonstration' (Durkheim 1964b, p. 109). Durkheim opposes any such conception of historical necessity as 'psychologistic' because the necessity of history derives from the universal subject of history: human nature. Against this individualist account of the subject of sociology, Durkheim offers social facts, collective consciousness and social organization.

In his rejection of Spencerian and Comtean evolutionism, Durkheim did not simply repeat the evolutionary distinctions already established by sociologists such as Tönnies (1971) between the idealized past of a warm and cosy community *Gemeinschaft* and the less attractive, more individuated *Gesellschaft*. Durkheim, in

21

fact, reverses Tönnies's distinctions. Mechanical solidarity for Durkheim is based on common sentiments and beliefs among an undifferentiated population, while organic solidarity derives from the contractual relationships created by the interdependence of an extended division of labour. It was the failure of organic solidarity to emerge fully and the concommitant social disequilibrium generated by the production of egoistic individuals competing in and through a capitalist market in goods, services and labour, that gave rise to the subjects of Durkheim's major studies of *Suicide, The Division of Labour in Society* and *Professional Ethics and Civic Morals*.

Durkheim's rejection of 'analytical individualism' was elaborated in *The Rules of Sociological Method* (1964b) in his insistence on the need for the discovery of patterns of social determination which he termed 'social facts'. These were characteristically external, constraining and social 'ways of acting, thinking, and feeling that present the noteworthy property of existing outside the individual consciousness' (Durkheim, 1964b, p. 2). Of particular interest to us in this study is his claim that forms of social solidarity are such 'social facts'.

It is because of what we may term Durkheim's 'realist' epistemology (after Hirst, 1975) that he was able to analyse the contemporary development of his own society from a vantage point which he used to characterize important predecessors such as Comte as 'metaphysical' and 'utopian'. None the less, he was able to incorporate many of the important nineteenth-century writers into his own work, so that he was able to criticize, elaborate and refine many of their ideas (see Lukes, 1973). And, of course, he was in a position to evaluate critically much of this work with the benefit of hindsight, living as he did from 1858 to 1917.

His work had a curious mixture of philosophical stances. On the one hand, he was a staunch conservative, as witnessed by many of the qualitative judgments made in his work on suicide (at times this is almost a treatise in praise of poverty, since the poor had a much lower suicide rate than the rich). On the other hand, it is possible to find him having a great deal in common with Marx in his general analysis of social change. Where he differs from Marx and other socialist writers is in terms of the political nature of the movement. He also abhorred the idea of violence and violent clashes between social classes. His solution, as we shall see in more detail below, is to be found in his concept of 'organic solidarity'. The theory based upon this concept emphasized that change in society should be for the benefit of all.

Gouldner (1959b), in the introduction to Durkheim's *Socialism and Saint-Simon*, describes Durkheim as 'an uneasy Comtean'. This certainly seems to be appropriate, particularly from the point of view of the relationship between consensus and society as developed by him. But, as we saw above, the relationship between Comte's ideas and those of Saint-Simon is close, and Durkheim tended to give greater credence to the ideas of the latter. To understand Durkheim's contribution to our area of analysis we must first examine the effect Saint-Simon's work had upon him.

We need to recall Saint-Simon's analysis of the transition of society from a feudal to a bourgeois state, and the development of society based upon science and industry. In his work we see class conflict as an important feature of the early stages of development, but once the new order has been established, conflict, through being made redundant, disappears. Classes, of course, are seen to exist in the new social order, but the new fabric of society leads to stability and class harmony. Saint-Simon's emphasis upon the moral order of society accentuates in turn the integrative organic nature of the new order. This is where we see an important linkage between the two writers, both linking the extensive division of labour to the ideological community of a functioning moral order which then ensures social integration. In addition, both writers saw society in terms of ideas – society as a community of ideas, as Zeitlin (1968) has put it. In spite of the different periods in which they wrote, they both saw their task as being to define the appropriate moral system for their society. This moral system would have the function of uniting classes and occupational groups together in a common objective. Durkheim's philosophy was thus both organizational and constructive, and could hardly be seen as revolutionary or even critical.

One of Durkheim's best known ideas – that society has a reality virtually independent of those who comprise it; society being that which is greater than the sum of the parts – had already been expressed by Saint-Simon. Equally, the emphasis of Saint-Simon upon a law of progress for society (later taken up and expanded upon by Comte) was developed by Durkheim in his analysis of the evolutionary nature of social change. For both thinkers, man was subservient to society; laws of society dominated man's progress; man could merely discover what these laws were and adapt to them appropriately. Clearly, Durkheim used a different terminology and methodology in his work, but his concepts often have a 'Saint-Simonian ring' to them, for instance, in his argument that organic solidarity is replacing mechanical solidarity. Organic solidarity would represent a harmonious social existence. The harmony that Durkheim was seeking could only be achieved, as he saw it, through 'proper regulation', arguing that the 'most capable' persons ought to be the regulators, the most capable not necessarily being the most powerful. This notion of a meritocracy is, of course, very evident in Saint-Simon's work. He advocated the rejection of privilege in society, particularly privilege based upon accident of birth (a further reason why Saint-Simon is regarded as a founder socialist). Durkheim, though, did not share the same enthusiasm for this idea. If he had, he obviously would have finished up in a philosophical position much closer to socialism.

Another of Saint-Simon's ideas adopted by Durkheim relates to the commitment to an anti-individualistic position expressed in the break with 'analytical individualism'. Durkheim uses the term 'egoism', but he is clearly consistent in his views with Saint-Simon. It is interesting that although the dominant contemporary economic ideology can best be described as 'possessive individualism' (Macpherson, 1962), the societal commitment argued for by Durkheim through altruism is clearly at odds with this dominant ideology.

Related to the above point, we see a similarity in the two writers, in that both of them argue that the division of labour necessarily leads to a greater interdependence between societal members. This interdependence is the bond which unites men in an altruistic fashion. But, coupled with interdependence, there must be moral education and a moral commitment. This appeal to morality would overcome the disharmony, the turmoil, the remissness and the inertness of society. The moral commitment then can be seen as an antidote to the situation left by the decline of religious commitment.

Given the time at which Durkheim was writing, he was in a position to comment on the social effects of capitalism and industrialism to a much greater degree than his predecessors. By Durkheim's time, fundamental cracks in the fabric of capitalist society had developed; there were, for instance, frequent economic and political crises. At one point, Durkheim referred to society as being in a state of disintegration. Indeed, one of his central concepts, that of *anomie* (a state of social disorganization) relates specifically to this phenomenon and had a definite relation to his contemporary French society, as Therborn (1976) argues. In other words, the goal set by Saint-Simon in his writings had not (as yet) been achieved, and Durkheim saw it as part of his task to repeat and re-define the goal in an attempt to integrate the parts and functions of society. This integration and harmony would only occur when society was based on a system of industrial organization.

Unlike the contemporary socialist writers (and others) Durkheim saw no fundamental conflict of interests in the industrial situation. His belief in the communality of interests between occupations extended as far as a belief in the homogeneity of the interests of capitalists and workers. Like so many economists in our time, and like Saint-Simon before him, Durkheim was of the opinion that only those individuals in economically productive activities were useful individuals in society. Furthermore, he believed that those individuals should come together in relation to the common goal of determining the course of society. Therefore, there was no chance of conflict between different groups in industrial society: each group would pursue the same goals as the others. Organic solidarity could still be achieved in spite of the existence of social classes (of course, the Marxist notion of social class would deny this proposition, by definition).

To be fair to him, Durkheim did point to some societal injustices under industrialism. But he maintained that these were based upon 'structural inequalities'. We have to return, time and again, to his basic theme of the growing integration in society arising from the increasing extensive division of labour, the development of occupational guilds and associations and the necessarily more elaborate system of industrial relations pertaining in organizations. Even social classes were viewed in integrative terms, as co-operative rather than conflictual phenomena.

It is in *The Division of Labour in Society* (1964a) and in *Professional Ethics and Civic Morals* (1957) that we find Durkheim's most significant contributions to our area of study. We have already seen a number of Durkheim's ideas as developments of those of Saint-Simon. Here we can begin an examination of Durkheim's unique contribution to understanding his society and the social processes of industrialism in general.

In the earliest stages of social evolution, Durkheim saw society in homogeneous terms. Everybody in primitive society does roughly similar things, the main differentiation being based upon sexual characteristics and age. The development of society is both the cause and effect of heterogeneity of functions. The more complex society becomes, the greater the breakdown of the solidarity noted in primitive society. The development of a complex and extensive division of labour leads, or can lead, in Durkheim's view, to a new form of solidarity.

In primitive society, the solidaristic condition is referred to as the *conscience collective*. This concept represents the prevailing sentiments possessed by each individual conscience. This is the notion of mechanical solidarity, that is, 'a social structure of determined nature' associated with a system of segments, homogenous and similar to each other, as Durkheim (1964a) put it in *The Division of Labour in Society*. In complex society, this concept of solidarity has to be replaced by the notion of organic solidarity. Here, it is society that determines the collective conscience rather than the somewhat nebulous individual conscience. These relationships of social solidarity correspond to general systems of social control, and the law in particular. The transition to enacted law signifies the objective index of the progress of the division of labour; for the emergence of restitutive rather than repressive law is testimony to the decline of the mechanical social solidarity of the *conscience collective* and the emergence of organic solidarity under the increasing division of labour.

Durkheim is often viewed as the founder of the structural-functionalist movement in sociology. The notion of organic solidarity and the supremacy of society tend to reinforce this view. However, he did recognize that certain features of advanced society are dysfunctional – that is, are not solidarity-producing. Because of these negative features of society restitutive law exists to restore an equilibrium in society. In general, though, the extension of the division of labour has positive consequences.

The division of labour is a social system based upon co-operation rather than conflict. Here he introduces the word 'normally'. This is a useful device since he can then explain conflict in terms of an abnormal division of labour, a pathological form. Not only is a high level of organic solidarity achieved through the division of labour (the growth of organization and the division of labour are thus interconnected), but this also encourages the development of individuality. The argument for this is that pre-industrial society with mechanical solidarity as its predominant characteristic totally embraces the individual. Since the division of labour in society is produced by differences in functions, Durkheim argues that it also allows for differences in individual personalities, unlike the position under mechanical solidarity. Furthermore, the different functions performed by individuals allow them to develop their individual personalities.

This is clearly one of Durkheim's more questionable assumptions. Other writers start from this basis but conclude that the division of labour is the very thing that leads to social divisions and particularly to class conflict (cf. Marx). Nisbet's (1965) polemic on Durkheim suggests that it was his conservative, and at times élitist, bias that led to such a conclusion. However, we may note that Durkheim was far more interested in the position of the middle classes in society than in the plight of nineteenth-century industrial workers. Consequently, we may argue that Durkheim was probably thinking more of professionals when developing this argument.

Durkheim produces a conception of sociology which seeks to understand in a scientific manner the dysfunctions of the development of capitalist market society as these are experienced by the individuals who comprise it. His premise is that social order cannot be explained in terms of the enlightened self-interest of individuals. Indeed, on the contrary, far from accepting the utilitarian premise of the individual as a 'bundle of appetites' (Macpherson, 1962) whose happiness could be promoted by a continuous increase in the satiation of these appetites, it seemed to Durkheim that happiness could only be assured if individual appetites were limited by socially imposed norms. Without benefit of these norms the individual would be in that position which Durkheim characterized as *anomie*.

Anomie refers to a social situation characterized by either too much or too little social organization. It derives from the dissociation of individuality from the collective conscience. It finds expression in two interrelated ways. Where the collective conscience cannot reduce individual proclivities, anomie results. Where excessive individualism is encouraged beyond that necessary for the division of labour in society then norms develop which actively encourage unregulated egoistic behaviour.

Conceptualizing in this way, as Therborn points out,

> Durkheim was able to avoid dealing with 'bad' societies, for instance societies based on exploitation, or with social contradictions. Society was always good but sometimes there was too little of it. There might also be too much of it, as in the pressure of collective segments in segmental societies of mechanical solidarity, or in the pressure towards altruistic forms of suicide. Durkheim as a moralist firmly adhered to the principle of the golden mean (Therborn, 1976, p. 265).

An anomic situation would be one where the division of labour was accompanied not by reintegration but by conflict. Durkheim proposed a prescription for this diagnosis, whereby the therapy sought to procure some semblance of 'the golden mean'. In such a situation, as he argues in *Professional Ethics and Civic Morals* (1957), the reintegration of social solidarity will hinge upon the organization of individuals into occupational groups on the basis of professional ethics which do not merely integrate each group within itself but which also relate it to the totality of groups in the wider society.

As in Spencer, the Malthusian principle of population growth is postulated as the source of the disequilibrating evolutionary change, by intensifying competition between individuals for finite resources and at the same time increasing the scale of the society. The division of labour increasingly differentiates the enlarged society and lessens the increased competition of the press of numbers. At the same time, it dissolves and disrupts traditional forms of mechanical solidarity, hence the necessity for repairing

27

social solidarity through the creation of new forms of organic solidarity. With the emergence of industrial society the problem becomes acute. The old organizational forms, as far as they have survived, are no longer adequate for the changed circumstances.

In the changed circumstances of industrial society Durkheim sees a need for a particular type of organization to be created. These are secondary, mediating organizations which exist as a buffer between the individual and the state. The state, Durkheim maintains in *The Division of Labour*, will tend to grow as society grows, develops and differentiates. Durkheim reasons thus. In a society of anomic individuals whose social solidarity has been shattered by the increasing division of labour, the hapless individual, without recourse to some new form of social solidarity, will be hopelessly tyrannized and repressed by any central source of power in society. Where this power is that of the state confronting the mass of individuals, then it 'is on the mass of individuals that the whole weight of the society rests', as Durkheim (1957, p. 108) puts it. This burden of the individual must be relieved, he maintains, and as relief he proposes the establishment of 'secondary organs'. These 'will release the individual from the State and vice versa, and release the individual, too, from a task for which he is not fitted' (Durkheim, 1957, p. 109).

These 'secondary organs' will be a type of occupational association modelled on professional bodies. These associations are not conceived as purely sectional interests, but as having a social role. This role is to fill the moral vacuum left by the anarchy of the market. As Giddens (1971, p. 103) notes, 'Durkheim refrains from offering a detailed exposition of how the occupational groups would be structured', but they would not simply be trade unions or employers' associations or a revived form of the guild, but bodies having a high degree of internal autonomy within the legal supervision of the state. They would have the authority to resolve conflicts both within their own ranks and between occupational groups, and they would be the focus of social and welfare-educational activities.

These ideas reappear in organization analysis under the imprint of Elton Mayo in the 1930s and 1940s and give rise to a whole neo-Durkheimian school of organization analysis. We shall interpret this imprint as largely conservative in Chapter 3, but it is as well to acknowledge that as Eldridge (1973) and Eldridge and Crombie (1974) argue:

> One should not interpret Durkheim's corporate solution as shoring up the capitalist system. Always it is related to a concern with an equitable distribution of social goods, which he does not

think possible in a system characterized by inherited wealth and, consequently, contractual relations based on power inequalities between the parties. This brings him close to a socialist position in terms of his actual assumptions (Eldridge and Crombie, 1974, p. 135).

With reference to this point, Zeitlin (1968) has argued that Durkheim's work could have followed two different courses. The one he chose was a conservative approach which was closely related to that of Comte, with the over-riding concern with solidarity, social unity and harmony. In short, he became concerned with the problem of order and the *status quo*. The other path would have entailed an examination of the issues raised by the societal conditions of which he was aware and of which he wrote. This alternative path would necessarily have led him towards a critique of society not unlike that of Marx. He would have had to examine the phenomenon of class conflict and the relation of this to social change, and would have had to analyse the consequences of these both for the individual and for society.

Therborn (1976, p. 250) has argued that 'Durkheim and Marx had certain important traits in common'. Each of them opposed analytical individualism and 'asserted the historical and social determination of the individual'. They shared a 'fundamentally materialist approach to the study of social ideas'. In addition, as Therborn puts it,

both emphasized that the socially determined representations [*Vorstellungen*, the corresponding German word which Marx sometimes used] current within a society were not subjective illusions maintained by fraud and interest, but were derived from the objective nature of that society (Therborn, 1976, p. 251).

We can see that Durkheim was dealing with the same issues as Marx, albeit with very different solutions. Whereas Marx saw society characterized by conflict, this was merely a pathological aberration for Durkheim. The crises of capitalism that form the basis of so much of Marx's writing are examined by Durkheim and found to be moral crises, such as suicide. Instead of seeing them as inherent in the capitalist mode of production, Durkheim saw them in terms of a maladjustment among societal functions. He writes that 'in so far as labour is divided more, these phenomena seem to be more frequent. . . . From 1845 to 1869, failures increased 70%' (Durkheim, 1964a, p. 354). These were not regarded by Durkheim as a product of the economic system.

This idea of a maladjustment in functions also explains class conflict for Durkheim. The more specialization (division of labour), the more that industrial and social conflict is manifested and the less that organic solidarity is apparent. But as we saw above, all of this arises from an abnormal division of labour – a state of anomie.

Despite apparent similarities, Durkheim's analysis is distinct from those of both Comte and Marx. While Marx saw solidarity as possible only in either non-antagonistic classes or in a classless society but as impossible between antagonistic classes, Durkheim differed. He wished to produce such a solidarity without abolishing class relations. For him social conflict arose neither from social classes as it did for Marx, nor from moral decline as it did for Comte. However, like Marx, Durkheim stressed the role of planning. Marx argued the need for organization and administration once the economic system had been transformed to eliminate the structural inequalities which characterized capitalist society. Durkheim also emphasized the planning function in his analysis, but did so in a chronologically different way from Marx. His solution was in terms of planning and socio-economic regulation as a fore-runner to any structural changes. All that needed to be done was to establish the appropriate 'morality' so that changes could be brought about in order to establish a new equilibrium position (again we see the structural-functionalist emphasis here). In one respect Durkheim does go some way towards a Marxist position. He refines his original conception of the division of labour by reference to a 'forced division of labour'. This is certainly a pathological and abnormal type, and arises from the fact that in a complex society the establishment of social classes is in itself a kind of organization of the division of labour. Lower classes, through organization and consciousness, develop aspirations and realize that the possibility of achieving these aspirations is only realizable through possessing the power of higher classes. This leads to manifest conflict, which for Durkheim was a discomfort for members of the lower social classes and an activity in which they had no real wish to participate.

So, in this instance, the division of labour can lead to the opposite of solidaristic relations throughout society, and this is associated with the class structure. The concept of a forced division of labour is used because Durkheim saw industrial society as being at times based upon a division of labour in which individuals were not using their natural talents. In other words, he was the champion of a society where structural inequalities should be based upon the 'natural abilities' of individuals. Durkheim (1956), in his contributions to the sociology of education, also felt able to determine what these natural abilities were. This is very different from Marx and Engels's (1965) metaphor of the individual fishing, hunting, writing poetry and discussing philosophy as and when he chose in the future socialist society.

Certain functions in a complex society are necessarily odious, and yet Durkheim felt that some individuals have the necessary abilities for these functions or lack the ability to do anything else. An equilibrium position in society exists when there is a correspondence between the natural inequalities of ability of individuals and the structural social inequalities in society as a whole.

In spite of recognizing the prevalence of the forced division of labour in society, Durkheim maintained that the chief problem to be overcome was that of anomie. His argument, as we have already seen, rests upon the demand for subservience of the individual to society. Indeed, this was argued for even before the correspondence between natural abilities and social stratification. In his later studies, particularly in *Suicide* (1952) and *The Elementary Forms of Religious Life* (1915), this emphasis is even more pronounced.

In many ways then, a peculiar position results from the Durkheimian analysis. His account of class conflict arising from the abnormal, pathological, forced division of labour is very inadequate. What he called abnormal and pathological was, in fact, the norm; the everyday occurrence in the society about which he was writing. What for him was normal was to all intents and purposes non-existent, neither apparent nor real. It was not until towards the end of his life with the outbreak of the First World War (and the death of his son in it) that he came to realize the unreality of his ideological position.

From the point of view of 'the political and intellectual revolution' of which he was a part, we need to stress Durkheim's own emphasis: social order. Since society was the main contributor to social order, this became the deity Durkheim worshipped. Therborn (1976, p. 266) cites Durkheim's declaration in a debate at the Society of Philosophy that 'The believer bows before God, because it is from God that he believes he has his existence, and particularly his mental existence, his soul. We have the same reasons to feel the same sentiment for the collectivity'. And this was not the collectivity in the abstract, but bourgeois society in particular. This emphasis entailed the heavily conservative bias already noted. In his later work the observations made on injustices and inequalities in society became less frequent; his references to the conditions of the working masses became more intermittent and the early concepts of human dignity and freedom became historical artefacts.

While we may say that Durkheim took a Comtean position, he, in fact, moved away from Comte's solution for social order. It will be recalled that Comte assigned the regulation of societal functions to the state. Durkheim disagreed with this and argued that the Middle Age idea of the occupational guild should be re-established, adapted to the new economic order, and employed to regulat economic and industrial affairs. The guilds would also function as the moral arbiters of society. In this way, as we see in *Professional Ethnics and Civic Morals,* the anomie so characteristic of Durkheim's society would be overcome through societal regulation of the individual.

Durkheim transcends the teleology of psychologistic evolutionism. He does not replace it with the sphere of individual subjectivity as the theoretical object of his science of sociology. He concludes by producing a sociology, not of individual or human nature, but of a *social* nature which possesses a full-blown collective consciousness of its own. Within this formulation organization is conceived as having a key role, as the factor of cohesion between individual and society in and through which the phenomena of the social are made visible and given, through the effects of social organization on the individuals who are its subject.

It was at roughly the same time as Durkheim was formulating his ideas concerning the nature of social solidarity, in a context moulded by his critique of analytical individualism, that in Germany the great sociologist Max Weber (1864–1920) was struggling to apply the German historicist version of the individualist position to a study of the advent of modernity. In particular, he argued in terms of the diminishing influence of 'other-worldly' and 'religious thought' as part of the process of the 'rationalization' and 'disenchantment' of the world. He wished to demonstrate the connection between the religious ethic of Protestantism and the 'spirit' of capitalism.

2 Max Weber, Karl Marx and rationality in organizations

Max Weber and rationality

Weber (1976) organizes his investigations into *The Protestant Ethic and the Spirit of Capitalism* around the following questions: how to describe capitalism in its modern form; how to account for its emergence; and how to explain why it emerged in the West and not elsewhere in the world (Eldridge, 1972, p. 33). Weber defines 'a capitalistic economic action [as one which] rests on the expectation of profit by the utilization of opportunities for exchange, that is on [formally] peaceful chances of profit' (Weber, 1976, p. 17). Within the generic category of capitalism Weber acknowledges that nothing specifically modern could be identified in this definition which had not 'existed in all civilized countries of the earth so far as economic documents permit us to judge. In China, India, Babylon, Egypt, Mediterranean antiquity and the Middle Ages, as well as in modern times' (Weber, 1976, pp. 18–19). This is true not only of capitalism *per se*, but also of the more specific category of industrial capitalism exemplified by industrial production allied with capital accounting techniques. It is the presence of the latter that signify that the organization of enterprise is rational. When this is present with other factors such as alienable, formally free labour, then this is taken to define the distinctive characteristic of modern industrial capitalism.

These factors have only been present in certain specific conjunctures in history. What are these and why should this be so? Weber (1923) answers these questions with a list of factors which are specifically occidental. These are factors such as the geographical factor of trade connections; the special demand generated by military requirements; luxury demand; rational permanent enterprise; and the modern state, with a professional administration,

33

specialized office-holding and law based on citizenship. This law is of the specifically rational-legal type. In addition, he notes that it is only in the West that rational science exists. Rational law, rational science, the rational state, all of these are grounded in a more fundamental rationality, the underlying rationality which distinguishes that which is Western civilization:

> Western civilization is further distinguished from every other by the presence of men with a rational ethic for the conduct of life. Magic and religion are found everywhere; but a religious basis for the ordering of life, which consistently followed out must lead to explicit rationalism, is again peculiar to western civilization alone (Weber, 1923, pp. 232–3).

It is at this juncture that Weber can be related to sociologists such as Comte or Durkheim, in terms of the importance that he attaches to religion. Whereas these other sociologists take an essentially conservative view, wishing to re-create an idealized and lost social solidarity, Weber is both more realistic, pessimistic and ambivalent toward the modern phenomenon of rationality. His realism is in not proposing grandiose schemes for renewing what are now mythical forms of existence for the modern world, while his pessimism and ambivalence appear towards the end of his life with the realization that the 'absolute values' which once sanctified rational activity are no longer meaningful. Without such meaning we are condemned not to life but to existence, to being without any reason for so being.

The role of 'ultimate values' is absolutely necessary in explaining the emergence of rationality in the modern world, for, as Weber puts it:

> It is not sufficient to consider only the purely formal fact that calculations are being made on grounds of expediency by the methods which are amongst those available technically the most nearly adequate. In addition it is necessary to take account of the fact that economic activity is oriented to ultimate ends of some kind: whether they be ethical, political, utilitarian, hedonistic, the attainment of social distinction, of social equality, or of anything else. Substantive rationality cannot be measured in terms of formal calculation alone, but also involves a relation to the absolute values or to the content of the particular ends to which it is oriented (1976, p. 185).

These 'absolute values' were those of the 'Protestant ethic', which he argued had a particular 'elective affinity' with the 'spirit of capitalism'. This 'spirit' he had defined as one of 'rationality', and so the elective affinity with which he was dealing was with that between one form of rationality and another, correlated and historically antecedent form. In linking Protestantism to capitalism in this way he was making neither a novel nor a hitherto unsubstantiated relation, as Bendix (1966, pp. 55–6) is at pains to develop. Nor was he making any general and unspecific linkage between 'capitalism' and 'Protestantism'. What he sought to do was to show how a specific form of rational activity, modern industrial capitalism, as opposed to traditional capitalism, could be seen to be related to another specific form of rational activity, rational religion, and how the latter could be seen as both a precursor and correlate of specific and substantial instances of the former. These specific and substantial instances concern the rise of a modern form of industrial capital quite distinct from older more traditional and feudal forms of merchant capital among the middle-class strata who became the industrial bourgeoisie and who also happened to be predominantly Protestant, Puritan and Calvinist.

The connection is simple. The Protestant sects, in particular those which espoused Calvinism, held as a central doctrine a belief in the predestination of existence. Their lives were vessels of God's will. He had already predetermined which of His congregation would be called, would be saved, for His glory. Mere men and women could not intercede in His unknowable will. Signs of grace were taken to be present in this lonely existence of the soul. These signs were one's rigid asceticism, one's religious virtuosity, one's existence as a suitable vessel in which God might move. A particular consequence of this belief was that one attempted to work diligently and soberly in all things, including one's work. However, in contrast to what was seen as the self-indulgent excess of the unreformed church, one could not, one must not, feast on the fruits of one's labour. One must not enrich oneself materially by the results of one's labour, because to do so would be to risk one's calling. Instead one must enrich oneself spiritually, and only spiritually, through one's labour. How was one to do this? How was one to use the value, the material value, one had created, yet not damn one's existence by idle consumption? The Protestant's solution to this moral dilemma was that one invested one's surplus value back into that which gave life to existence, meaning to being. And this was one's work as one's calling. Hence the Protestant had a rational motive for exceptionally limited consumption, which could produce the primitive accumulation of capital necessary for the development of modern capitalist organization and enterprise. It was not that Calvinism 'caused' capitalism but that it provided the material preconditions for its existence in the face of the reluctance of traditional forms of capitalism to invest in new forms of industrial enterprise. As we shall see shortly, traditional capital, at least in England, displayed this reluctance.

Max Weber has been the subject of a wide number of interpretations in recent years, from perspectives as various as psychohistory (Mitzman, 1970) to historical materialism (Therborn, 1976). Given the wide range of interest in Max Weber, only a limited analysis of his thought is possible in this context. We shall be concerned primarily with discussing Max Weber's conception and method of sociology, in particular as it relates to the formation of ideal types, especially those of capitalism and organizations (see Chapter 4).

In recent years, a number of writers such as Therborn (1976), Binns (1977) and Honigsheim (1968) have stressed the centrality of marginal utility theory to Weber's analyses. These analyses were grounded in a series of methodological essays *Gesammelte Aufsätze zur Wissenschaftslehre* (1951), some of which are translated in *The Methodology of the Social Sciences* (1949), which Weber wrote between 1903 and 1906 and in which he formulated the epistemological principles of economics and history. He applied these principles in his analyses of *Economy and Society* (1968). These principles were the 'offspring of an encounter between German historicism and Austrian marginalist economics' (Therborn, 1976, p. 280).

Kant had argued that the objects of sense-experience are ordered into a system of natural laws by the in-built conceptual apparatus of the faculty of scientific reason. This reason can never know reality itself but only reality selected, organized and processed by the activity of the knowing mind. Practical reason is distinguished from scientific reason because it deals with direct intuition of the world of values. This distinction became the basis of a movement of neo-Kantian philosophers and historians, centred on Heidelberg, to establish a cultural or historical science on the basis of practical rather than scientific reason. They sought to do this in direct opposition to any naturalist conception of historical development such as that proposed by Saint-Simon, Comte and Spencer.

The distinction was based on Wilhelm Dilthey's (1883) attempt to develop the hermeneutic tradition of the *Geisteswissenschaften*, organized around the concept of 'understanding' or *verstehen* (see Outhwaite, 1975), into an historical science. It was elaborated in particular, by Heinrich Rickert, who argued against using the methods of the natural sciences in the study of historical phenomena. Instead, following Dilthey he proposed the method of *verstehen* as the key to grasping the uniqueness of cultural and historical events. Using this method Dilthey had attempted to specify a range of types of historical-cultural phenomenon.

Weber, arguing from within the *Geisteswissenschaften* was opposed to any position which wished to subsume the human sciences to science *per se* or which sought to assimilate the unique and the specific to the law-like and general. In particular, he attacked this position in economics (see Weber, 1951) and proposed that instead of conceiving of economics as a natural science to be studied through the faculty of scientific reason, it should be conceived as an aspect of culture and as such be studied through a cultural rather than a natural science. He formulated the distinction between these spheres in terms of the difference between a science of the unique and a science of the recurrent. In Therborn's (1976, p. 285) translation of Weber (1951, pp. 170f.), the cultural science, or sociology as he was later to call it, is defined thus:

> The type of social science in which we are interested is a *science of reality* (*Wirklichkeitwissenschaft*). Our aim is the understanding of the characteristic uniqueness of the reality in which we move. We wish to understand on the one hand the relationships and the cultural significance of individual events in their contemporary manifestation, and on the other the causes of being historically *so* and not *otherwise*.

At a later stage in his career he was to advance the definition of sociology as 'a science concerning itself with the interpretative understanding of social action in order to arrive at a causal explanation of its course and consequences' (Weber, 1968, p. 4). Social action, in turn, is defined as subjectively meaningful action which 'takes account of others and is therefore oriented in its course' (Weber, 1968, p. 4). The object of sociology's 'cognition is the subjective meaning-complex of action' (Weber, 1968, p. 13). This entails grasping the purposeful motives of social actors and social action, motives and purposes which are not psychologistic but are given by the cultural milieu.

Therborn (1976) has stressed the twofold significance of culture in Weber's sociology:

> The concept of culture was employed by Weber in two main ways to distinguish the kind of historical and social studies to which he was committed from the natural sciences. The first, reiterated in his early methodological writings and certainly within the historicist tradition, emphasized the decisive influence of the cultural meanings derived from historical values upon cultural scientists (historians, economists and so on), their concepts and analyses. The second, prominent in the conception of sociology within the historicist tradition, but in Weber largely derived from an interpretation of marginalist economics, focused on the determination of the objects of study of cultural scientists – social actions – by

the complexes of meaning conferred by historical values (Therborn, 1976, pp. 282–3).

This second point relates to Weber's theoretical object of analysis, which he constructs in terms of 'ideal types'. If cultural *uniqueness* is the empirical object of analysis, then, given Weber's intellectual formation, it cannot be grasped in natural law-like statements. What Weber did was to propose a method for the analysis of the culturally unique constellation of the modern economy, state and organization as it appeared in the 'age of imperialism' (Hobsbawm, 1969; see Therborn, 1976, p. 271 and Wright, 1978, for the elaboration of this point in relation to Lenin). This method consisted of constructing an ideal type of capitalism.

John Rex (1971) has stressed, as has Alan Dawe (1971), that Weber's starting point in the construction of an ideal type is that of 'relevance for value'. An ideal type is a fiction, in as much as it is not meant to represent or correspond to any real object. How could it? For Weber has already defined the real object of analysis of sociology as 'on the one hand the relationships and the cultural significance of individual events in their contemporary manifestation, and on the other the causes of their being historically *so* and not *otherwise*'. As Therborn (1976) stresses, culture is already value-laden. This unique cultural object which defines the subject of sociological investigation is itself a value. Weber puts it thus:

> The concept of culture is a value-concept. Empirical reality becomes 'culture' to us because and in so far as we relate it to value ideas. It includes those segments and only those segments of reality which have become significant to us because of this value-relevance. Only a small portion of existing concrete reality is coloured by our value-conditioned interest and it alone is significant to us. It is significant because it reveals relationships which are important to us due to their connection with our values. . . . All knowledge of cultural reality, as may be seen, is always knowledge from particular points of view . . . without the investigator's evaluative ideas, there would be no principle of selection of subject-matter and no meaningful knowledge of the concrete reality. . . . And the values to which the scientific genius relates the object of enquiry may determine, ie., decide the 'conception' of a whole epoch (Weber, 1949, pp. 76, 81–2).

Accordingly, Weber makes the question of value central to his formulation of the ideal type; such types consciously and expressly accentuate value-relevant aspects of reality in an artificial model which serves as an interpretative and explanatory scheme. By 'ideal' he is not suggesting that the content of the type is in anyway desirable. What he is referring to is a mental act of 'idealization'. The ideal type is hypothetical. What is more, the ideal type is only explanatory in a very provisional sense. It is an *as if* model, as John Lewis (1975, p. 51) puts it: 'If this were a true model, then people would be likely to behave in certain ways. They *do* in fact behave *as if* this were the case. As a model it has no other reason for being regarded as up to a point true, or likely.' And this fiction is, as Dawe (1971, p. 45) argues 'rooted in a concept of subjective meaning in which there is a fusion of the values of the sociologist and the values of the actors he studies'. The values of the bourgeois class[1] frame Weber's formulations, but he argues that once these have been formulated the *as if* nature of the suppositions can be openly and objectively studied irrespective of the value embodied in them.

In his discussion of capitalism as an ideal type of economy in *Economy and Society* it has been argued by Binns (1977) that Weber (1968) allows these values to effect an unwarranted theoretical slippage. His ideal type definition of capitalism is conceptualized not at the level of economy and society as a whole but at the level of the enterprise. In doing this he is following the method of ideal types developed from within the school of Austrian marginal economics (Therborn, 1976, p. 293). Marginalists started from the individual actor calculating how to realize his/her goals when the means to achieve them were scarce. The Marginalists then generalized from this level of the individual ideal type of the rational consumer to the level of an explanatory understanding of market regularities. Weber follows exactly the same logic applied to the individual ideal type of the rational enterprise. His definition of rational capitalist organization is an extension of the marginalist position to the enterprise, which is conceptualized as being

> organized with a view to market opportunities, and hence to economic objectives in the real sense of the word, and the more rational it is the more closely it relates to mass demand and the provision for mass needs (Weber, 1968, p. 334).

The qualities of the individual ideal type of enterprise are generalized to the structure of the economy and society as a whole (as Binns, 1977, p. 11 has argued), and in the process the idealized rationality of the part is conflated to the system. This is in terms of the equilibrium of mass demand and mass needs of the market. This equilibrium then marks the end of history and of analysis; equilibrium is marked by a mode of domination at which Weber's (1976) analysis can only despair. In his later work (see Mayer, 1956) bureaucracy appears inevitable.

The conclusion that deliverance from bureaucratic capitalism appears impossible is inevitable given the grounds of Weber's analyses. These grounds are the value relevancies of the bourgeois class. It is, as John Lewis argues:

> the logical expression – and the only logical expression – of the basic presupposition of the economy as a member of capitalist society sees things. Weber frames his model, as he himself says, on the basis of the values and desired ends developed as his own attitude towards life, as a man acting in the world of reality. This attitude was, and in his case had to be, that of a member of the upper class of the German bougeoisie. It remains the attitude today of the bourgeoisie of every land, and of those members of society who derive their ideas from the ruling class. . . . The theory of capitalism derives not from the observation of natural phenomena, but from the values and aims of a class that sees the economy as designed to serve its own interests primarily and only secondarily and as a by-product the interests of society and of the labourers (Lewis, 1975, pp. 77–8).

The historicist-idealist method of *verstehen*, allied to the marginalist conflation of individual rationality to collective rationality-in-equilibrium, 'acts as an epistemological barrier to the understanding of economic relations in capitalist society . . . it results in a mystified portrayal of the workings of the capitalist economy' (Binns, 1977, p. 12). Weber was not unaware of this. He observes that there is an unavoidable element of irrationality in economic systems. This is evident in the fact that it is not wants as such but effective demand for utilities which regulates the production of goods by profit-making enterprises. This is what Weber terms *substantive irrationality*, an unanticipated consequence of the entirely rational laws of the economy constructed on the same class point-of-view as the ideal-type of the economy. And, as he is at great pains to observe, the grounding premise of value upon which the edifice is constructed is a completely *arbitrary* and *irrational point of view*. But once embodied in the model, either as ideal type or real relations of production, irrationality becomes reason.

Weber can offer no *analysis* of how or why this transformation of rationality into irrationality takes place. All he can do in his earlier work is despair that it should be so, resigning his mature judgment to a deep *haute-bourgeois* cultural pessimism:

> Since asceticism undertook to remodel the world and to work out its ideals in the world, material goods have gained an increasing and finally an inexorable power over the lives of men as at no previous period in history. Today the spirit of religious asceticism – whether finally, who knows? – has escaped

from the cage. But victorious capitalism, since it rests on mechanical foundations, needs its support no longer. The rosy blush of its laughing heir, the Enlightenment, seems also to be irretrievably fading, and the idea of duty in one's calling prowls about in our lives like the ghost of dead religious beliefs (Weber, 1976, pp. 181–2).

By the early years of this century Weber could write that:

Already now, rational calculation is manifest at every stage. By it, the performance of each individual worker is mathematically measured, each man becomes a little cog in the machine and aware of this, his one preoccupation is whether he can become a bigger cog . . . it is horrible to think that the world could one day be filled with these little cogs, little men clinging to little jobs, and striving towards bigger ones . . . this passion for bureaucracy is enough to drive one to despair (Weber, in Mayer, 1956, p. 127).

This 'despair' is a remarkable feature when contrasted with the unreflected complacency of so much subsequent social scientific writing on organizations. Despite this, Weber's despair is of only limited value. This value-limitation is inherent in a typological construction which can only display the author's commitments. Consequently, it is important to note that Weber's despair can find only cultural expression: his analysis begins and ends at the level of cultural values. There is no way out of the hermeneutic circle in Weber's analysis nor in subsequent developments of it (see Chapters 6 and 7).

Karl Marx and capitalism

Max Weber's work has frequently been characterized as 'a debate with the ghost of Karl Marx'. This is perhaps an over-statement, as Weber never really grappled with the essential problems of historical materialism. What we may say is that he, like Marx (1818–83) before him, brought his analysis to bear upon the rise of industrial capitalism in the occident, an analysis which he presented as a positive critique of historical materialism.

What Weber's thesis concerning *The Protestant Ethic and the Spirit of Capitalism* (1976) proposes is one possible explanation of what Marx (1976) termed 'primitive accumulation', 'an accumulation which is not the result of the capitalist mode of production but its point of departure' (Marx, 1976, p. 873).

Marx is scathing about existing explanations of this process of 'primitive accumulation'.

This primitive accumulation plays approximately the same role in political economy as original sin does in theology. Adam bit the apple, and thereupon sin fell on the human race. Its origin is supposed to be explained when it is told as an anecdote about the past. Long, long ago there were two sorts of people; one, the diligent, intelligent and above all frugal élite; the other, lazy rascals, spending their substance, and more, in riotous living. The legend of theological original sin tells us certainly how man came to be condemned to eat his bread in the sweat of his brow; but the history of economic original sin reveals to us that there are people to whom this is by no means essential. Never mind! Thus it came to pass that the former sort accumulated wealth, and the latter sort finally had nothing to sell except their own skins. And from this original sin dates the poverty of the great majority who, despite all their labour, have up to now nothing to sell but themselves, and the wealth of the few that increases constantly although they have long ceased to work. Such insipid childishness is every day preached to us in the defence of property (Marx, 1976, pp. 873–4).

The problem of primitive accumulation, for both Marx and Weber, concerns the transformation of money and commodities into capital, rather than into, for example, feasting or other forms of conspicuous consumption. Weber produces a general explanation of a motive which might have contributed to this accumulation, while Marx (1976) details the 'particular circumstances' under which such a transformation of money into capital can take place. These circumstances are:

the confrontation of, and the contact between, two very different kinds of commodity owners; on the one hand, the owners of money, means of production, means of subsistence, who are eager to valorize the sum of values they have appropriated by buying the labour-power of others; on the other hand, free workers, the sellers of their own non-labour power, and therefore the sellers of labour. Free workers, in the double sense that they neither form part of the means of production themselves, as would be the case with slaves, serfs, etc., nor do they own the means of production, as would be the case with self-employed peasant proprietors. The free workers are therefore free from, unencumbered by, any means of production of their own. With the polarization of the commodity-market into these two classes, the fundamental conditions of capitalist production are present. The capitalization presupposes a complete separation between the workers and the ownership of the conditions for the realization of their labour. As soon as capitalist production stands on its own feet it not only maintains this separation, but reproduces it on a constantly extending scale. The process, therefore, which creates the capital-relation can be nothing other than the process which divorces the worker from the ownership of the conditions of his own labour; it is a process which operates two transformations whereby the social means of subsistence and production are turned into capital, and the immediate producers, are turned into wage-labourers. So-called primitive accumulation, therefore, is nothing else than the historical process of divorcing the producer from the means of production. It appears as 'primitive' because it forms the pre-history of capital, and of the mode of production corresponding to capital.

The economic structure of capitalist society has grown out of the economic structure of feudal society. The dissolution of the latter set free the elements of the former (Marx, 1976, pp. 874–5).

The basis of the process of primitive accumulation is the 'expropriation of the agricultural producer ... from the soil' (Marx, 1976, p. 576) and thus the creation of a formally free labour power, the proletariat, free to be organized into the labour process of capitalist relations of production. (A considerable debate about the relationship of primitive accumulation and industrialization has been conducted by economic historians. John Saville (1969) provides a concise summary.) What forms of organization did these social relations produce and what did they replace?

The characteristic form of organization prior to the emergence of capitalist social relations of production, at least in the economic sphere, was the guild system. This had a long and quite successful history dating from its heyday in the thirteenth and fourteenth centuries up to recent times. In contemporary society, many trades still have lengthy apprenticeships associated with them and indeed there still exist demarcation and, at times, rivalry between trades. Essentially, the guild has always been seen as a kind of protective organization for all those individuals entitled to be employed in a particular skilled trade or craft. Traditionally, both employee and employer have been guild members – a point of distinction from the trade union.

Guilds have always contained a certain paradox within them, and yet, on the other hand, there has been the traditional tripartite division within them between apprentice, journeyman and master. This constant reference to the guild's traditional status also exhibits another characteristic, that of striving to maintain the *status quo*. At all stages technological change has been resisted in order to prevent under-cutting. Work was, and some would argue still is, done in an inefficient manner so that it takes longer to complete. This inefficiency means irrationality in one sense – that is, in terms of the interests of consumers of guild skills and commodities within a capitalist market economy; but in another sense it is wholly rational, looked at from the view of the producers. A monopoly over skills brought with it a monopoly over prices, which in practice meant tight price regulation.

The distinctions within a guild appeared to be almost caste-like. As Offe (1976a) argues, progression was possible, but to move from journeyman to master was virtually impossible to achieve without the benefits of the right connections within the guild.

Changes became apparent within the guild system by the seventeenth century, although they were the manifestation of tendencies which had been accumulating since the so-called 'crisis' of feudalism in the fourteenth century (see Anderson, 1974, pp. 197–212). These tendencies were located in the sphere of agricultural production, which, by the fourteenth century, had reached a technical and ecological barrier.

> The deepest determination of this general crisis probably lay
> . . . in a 'seizure' of the mechanisms of reproduction of the
> system at a barrier point of its ultimate capacities. In particular,
> it seems clear that the basic motor of rural reclamation, which had
> driven the whole feudal economy forwards for three centuries,
> eventually over-reached the objective limits of both terrain and
> social structure. Population continued to grow while yields fell
> on the marginal lands still available for conversion at the
> existing levels of technique, and soil deteriorated through haste
> or misuse (Anderson, 1974, p. 197).

This 'increasingly precarious ecological balance', combined with demographic expansion, 'could tip into over-population at the first stroke of harvest misfortune' as Anderson (1974, pp. 199f.) records. At the same time during the fourteenth century, from the early decades onwards, there was a parallel crisis in the urban sphere, due to a decline in the availability of precious metals for currency as the European mines reached their technical and profitable limits of production. This led to wide-spread debasement and inflation of the currency.

During the first quarter of the fourteenth century, a number of concommitant factors produced a situation of spiralling inflation (through the exhaustion of the mines) in the urban sphere and because of declining population, a contraction of demand for agricultural staples, notably grain, and thus a decline in grain prices. This decline in grain prices, coupled with inflation, led to a decline in revenues of a noble stratum which had become increasingly dependent on 'urban manufactures and high cost goods produced for seigneurial consumption' which 'enjoyed a comparatively inelastic and élite clientele' and thus 'became progressively more expensive' (Anderson, 1974, p. 200). Consequently, the exploitation of the peasantry by the nobles intensified as they attempted to recuperate their surplus (after having first resorted to the type of baronial gangsterism and plunder typified by the Wars of the Roses in England) from a labour force devastated after 1348 by the plague known as the Black Death. Anderson (1974), from whom this account is taken, notes the mid-century wave of repressive legislation attempting both to batten down wages and restrict the peasantry to the land, which was repeated from England to Portugal between 1349 and 1375. A wave of peasant rebellions followed the implementation of these ordinances, 'the direct and decisive consequence' of which was 'a pervasive social alteration of the Western countryside' (Anderson, 1974, p. 204).

The limits of feudal production were ecological, because of the low level of technique, combined with a function of the amount of surface in production, which in turn was a function of the mass of disposable labour power that the lord could bring into production, as both Kula (1977) and Banaji (1977) have argued. The 'socially disposable mass of labour-time depended on the relation of forces between lord and peasant, the possibility of flight, and the relative degree of over-population' (Banaji, 1977, p. 18).

With the development of towns in the interstices of feudalism, the possibility of flight increased, as did the probability of peasant rebellion (Anderson, 1974, p. 205). The influence of these urban centres was twofold:

> For, on the one hand, it was the prevalence of these market centres that rendered a flight from serfdom a permanent possibility for discontented peasants. . . . On the other hand, the presence of these towns put constant pressure on the embattled nobles to realize their incomes in monetary form. The lords both needed cash, and, beyond a certain point, could not risk driving their peasants wholesale into vagrancy or urban employment. They therefore were compelled to accept a general relaxation of servile ties on the land. The result was a slow but steady commutation of dues into money rents in the West, and an increasing leasing-out of the demesne to peasant tenants. This process developed earliest, and farthest, in England (Anderson, 1974, p. 206).

These developments had a number of determinant effects. One was the creation of a sector of small peasant production in which the peasants disposed of the whole of their labour-time, producing a surplus with a greater elasticity than that of the manorial demesne. This was because of improvements in productivity induced through the interest of the peasantry in reducing the degree of their exploitation by maximizing the amount of their surplus, and thus relatively minimizing the amount of an expanding whole which went to the lord in the form of a fixed proportion of surplus-labour, produce or rent. The effect of this was to produce a progressive and an expanding sector which engulfed and dispossessed subsistence forms of peasant production. The reaction of the nobility to these factors (particularly as they restricted the socially available labour) was increasingly to switch 'to pasturage to supply the woollen industry that had developed in the new cloth towns, already starting a movement of enclosures' (Anderson, 1974, p. 207). On this surge of prosperity the towns which were oriented to the expanding market sector rapidly developed, securing employment opportunities outside of the guild-controlled workshops for the expropriated peasantry. By the seventeenth century, journeymen, long frustrated with their limited opportunities for advancement within the caste-like guilds, now had the material opportunity for production outside the guilds, with the rising level of demand in the urban centres. Increasingly these journeymen began to form their own societies. In some respects there is much in common between these and the present-day trade unions. For instance, the hitherto unheard of activity of the strike was engaged in by the disaffected journeymen. So, progressively running parallel to the guild system in terms of the formal relations of production, were the beginnings of the capitalist mode of production.

Despite the great homogeneity within each guild there existed enormous differences between guilds, both in terms of the level of technology and the division of labour. Indeed, to talk of technology at this stage is possibly debasing the word since most tasks required only the simplest of tools. As such, any discussion of the social relations at work is severely restricted and rather generalized (see Therborn, 1978, for such a discussion). The division within the guild was not in terms of stages of production, but rather it was based upon the total end-product. Such a division implies the existence of a small number of occupations.

The non-existence of an extensive division of labour and the employment of a simple technology combined to make the social relations at work very basic. The social relations were not based upon the production process; rather the cultural milieu of the guild itself provided the base. The high level of close contact between guild members led to primary relationships not unlike that of a community, as Durkheim was to recall. Also within the orbit of the community analogy there were the rigid divisions between the different grades.

The social fabric of guild organization, although often idealized in popular fiction, was in fact one of the causes of its downfall. The lack of mobility within the guild produced conflict; some guilds became too powerful *vis-à-vis* other guilds and other trades outside the guild system; a measure of capital accumulation occurred amongst some guild masters: markets expanded that required changes in the manufacturing process which could not be achieved through the rigid guild system.

Slowly, then, even by the sixteenth century certain cracks were appearing in the guild system. These cracks were widened by the increasing capital accumulation and the emergence of the man of capital, the new merchant capitalist.

The guild system of organization of the labour process declined with the genesis and development of merchant capitalism, that form of organization which first became apparent in England at the time of the Poor Laws. The coincidence was not accidental. The Poor Laws were the acknowledgment of the successful development of merchant capitalism (Marx, 1976, pp. 581–2). This form of organization is dominated by a new principle of economic organization: the market. Karpik characterizes the merchant economy in the following terms:

> In this society, for the first time, work and nature are assimilated to merchandise. The price mechanism becomes the basis of the table of equivalents which ensure the economic exchanges. The rationality of the entrepreneur becomes defined by an adaptation to price movements in the search for maximum profit. It is within this institutional universe that the industrial revolution based upon merchant capitalism, merchant techniques and free labour manifests its full effectiveness in the accumulation of the wealth of nations; it is achieved fully with the 'technical revolution' (Daumas, 1962) in the middle of the nineteenth century and with economic liberalism. . . . The market is an original historical creation; never before had work and nature been considered exclusively as goods, never had the economic been separated from the political, never had the individual been assigned the behaviour of *homo-economicus* (Karpik, 1977, p. 43).

Before the merchant could go to market to sell, he first had to buy labour power with which to produce his merchandise. Labour was available in two forms. On the one hand, it could be coaxed away from the guilds (thereby accelerating the guilds' decline); or on the other hand, it could be acquired from elsewhere. This involved obtaining the services of rural labour or what Marx (1976) termed expropriating the agricultural population from the land.

We should bear in mind that Marx was drawing his illustrations from the British experience, which with respect to the expropriation of the peasantry, was more bloody than in many parts of the Continent. Marx writes of the revolutionary 'prelude' that occurred at the time of the foundation of the capitalist world economy (which Wallerstein (1974a), dates at 1450–1550). During this period the development of capitalism was founded on 'a mass of free and unattached proletarians' being 'hurled onto the labour-market by the dissolution of the bands of feudal retainers' (Marx, 1976, p. 878). This led to the creation of a capitalist market in agriculture which in England was founded on the farming of sheep for wool. In the sixteenth century this 'process of forcible expropriation of the people received a new and terrible impulse' through the Reformation and dissolution of the monasteries and the conversion of 'the land into a merely commercial commodity, extending the area of large-scale agricultural production, and increasing the supply of free and rightless proletarians driven from their land' (Marx, 1976, pp. 881, 885). The land lost by the agricultural population in the making of the proletariat and the agricultural capitalist between 1501 and 1831 was reckoned to be 3,511,700 acres of common land (Marx, 1976, p. 889). The process was particularly vicious in Scotland, as Marx elaborates:

> In the eighteenth century the Gaels were both driven from the land and forbidden to emigrate, with a view to driving them forcibly to Glasgow and other manufacturing towns. As an example of the method used in the nineteenth century, the 'clearings' made by the Duchess of Sutherland will suffice here. This person, who had been well instructed in economics, resolved, when she succeeded to the headship of the clan, to undertake a radical economic cure, and to turn the whole county of Sutherland, the population of which had already been reduced to 15,000 by similar processes, into a sheep walk. Between 1814 and 1820 these 15,000 inhabitants, about 3,000 families, were systematically hunted and rooted out. All their villages were destroyed and burnt, all their fields turned into pasturage. British soldiers enforced this mass of evictions, and came to blows with the inhabitants. One old woman was burnt to death in the flames of the hut she refused to leave. It was in this manner that this fine lady appropriated 794,000 acres of land which had belonged to the clan from time immemorial. She assigned to the expelled inhabitants some 6,000 acres on the sea-shore – 2 acres per family. The 6,000 acres had until this

time lain waste, and brought in no income to their owners. The Duchess, in the nobility of her heart, actually went so far as to let those waste lands at an average rent of 2s. 6d. per acre for the clansmen, who for centuries had shed their blood for her family. She divided the whole of the land stolen of the clan into twenty-nine huge sheep farms, each inhabited by a single family, for the most part imported English farm servants. By 1825 the 15,000 Gaels had already been replaced by 131,000 sheep. The remnant of the original inhabitants, who had been flung onto the sea-shore, tried to live by catching fish. They became amphibious, and lived, as an English writer says, half on the land and half on water, and withal only half on both.

But the splendid Gaels had now to suffer still more bitterly for their romantic mountain idolization of the 'great men' of the clan. The smell of their fish rose to the noses of the great men. They scented some profit in it, and let the sea-shore to the big London fishmongers. For the second time the Gaels were driven out.

Finally, however, part of the sheep-walks were turned into deer preserves (Marx, 1976, pp. 891–2, footnotes ommitted).

This describes the 'rationalization of the world' (and its 'disenchantment') with a vengeance!

The emergence of 'rational organization'

The factory system as a mode of organizing the labour process did not develop evenly or in conjunction with the creation of the proletariat. The emergence of industrial capitalism was, both locally and globally, a process of uneven development, characterized in its early stages by the emergence of a form of organization known as the 'putting-out' system or the system of 'cottage industry'. There were a number of crucial differences between this system and its predecessor, the guild system, and its successor, the factory system. In the first place, the three systems did not develop in the simple chronological sequence suggested. There was, of course, overlapping between them – at times between all three. Their emergence was neither temporally nor spatially unilinear. They were both temporally and spatially disarticulated.

The putting-out system still involved the worker outside of the factory, normally in his own home. He owned his own tools; the merchant simply supplied the raw material and owned totally the end product. The class structure of the social relations articulated by the putting-out system was simple: there existed the entrepreneur and the worker, capital and labour. In exchange for the transformation of the raw material into the final product, the worker received a cash wage. This, together with the 'voluntary' nature of the relationship between worker and merchant, displayed a marked contrast to the guild system and at the same time, an element of similarity to the factory system. It is clear that this system heralded new forms of social relations of production, relations which became more akin to capitalistic forms over time. The 'creeping' capitalization arose from the inherent inefficiency of the system in terms of the emerging rationality of capitalism: the lack of control by the merchant-capitalist over his workers; the economic losses through waste and fraud; the uncertain nature of the labour force. The independent, voluntary status of the worker was slowly eroded in an attempt to increase the efficiency of exploitation, first, by allowing the worker to get into debt and, second, by taking away the worker's ownership of his tools. These two factors opened the way for the emergence of a class of alienable wage-labourers dependent upon the capitalist class for both a living and a livelihood. But this was yet to emerge; for the present the social relations at work did not change very much. In general, the work was home-based; and it was not until the separation of home and work occurred, with the factory system, that the social relations altered very much.

This transition from home-based to factory-based work is generally seen in terms of the development of a specialized division of labour, subsequent to technical developments, which, to achieve optimum efficiency, had to be combined with a collectivity of workers in a factory. From here it is a simple step to seeing the development of hierarchical organization as developing, quite naturally, from technical necessity.

In an important paper, 'What do Bosses Do?', Stephen Marglin (1974) has investigated 'the origins and functions of hierarchy in capitalist production' in order to argue against the commonly held view that technological developments autonomously shaped the nature of organization as it emerged in early capitalist industrialization. (This argument is not simply an academic matter of historical interpretation. In subsequent chapters, particularly Chapters 6 and 9, we shall encounter a number of contemporary organization theorists who argue that modern organization structures are determined by technology.) Marglin's argument is

> that neither of the two decisive steps in depriving the workers
> of control of product and process . . . (1) the development of the
> minute division of labour that characterized the putting-out
> system and (2) the development of the centralized organization
> that characterizes the factory system . . . took place primarily for

reasons of technical superiority. Rather than providing more output for the same inputs, these innovations in work organization were introduced so that the capitalist got himself a larger share of the pie at the expense of the worker, and it is only the *subsequent* growth in the size of the pie that has obscured the class interest which was at the root of these innovations. The social function of hierarchical work organization is not technical efficiency, but accumulation. By mediating between producer and consumer, the capitalist organization sets aside much more for expanding plant and equipment than individuals would if they could control the pace of capital accumulation (Marglin, 1974, p. 62).

Marglin (1974, p. 63) makes the point that neither hierarchy nor the division of labour originated with capitalism. Hierarchy was a feature of guild organization, although it was a different form of hierarchy from that with which we are most familiar under capitalism today. Under guild production hierarchy was linear rather than pyramidal. Not only did the master work along with his apprentice instead of simply telling him what he must do, there was also the possibility that an 'apprentice would one day become a journeyman and likely a master. Under capitalism it is a rare worker who becomes even a foreman, not to mention independent entrepreneur or corporate president' (Marglin, 1974, p. 63). In addition 'and perhaps most important, the guild workman had no intermediary between himself and the market. He generally sold a product, not his labour, and therefore controlled both product and work process' (Marglin, 1974, p. 63). The social division of labour, that is, the specialization of occupation and function, is as Marglin (1974, p. 63) says, 'a characteristic of all complex societies, rather than a peculiar feature of industrialized or economically advanced ones'. Neither is the technical division of labour peculiar to capitalism nor modern industry. For Marglin (1974, p. 64) the critical question becomes

> why the guild division of labour evolved into the capitalist
> division of labour, in which the workman's task typically became
> so specialized and minute that he had no product to sell, or at
> least none for which there was a wide market, and had therefore
> to make use of the capitalist as intermediary to integrate his
> labour with the labour of others and transform the whole into
> a marketable product.

The classic argument for the division of labour is that exemplified by Adam Smith's analysis of the pin-factory.

> In the way in which this business is now carried on, not only the

51

whole work is a peculiar trade, but it is divided into a number of branches, of which the greater part are likewise peculiar trades. One man draws out the wire, another straightens it, a third cuts it, a fourth points it, a fifth grinds it at the top for receiving the head; to make the head requires two or three distinct operations; to put it on, is a peculiar business, to whiten the pins is another; it is even a trade by itself to put them into the paper; and the important business of making a pin is, in this manner, divided into about eighteen distinct operations, which in some manufactories are all performed by distinct hands, though in others the same man will sometimes perform two or three of them. I have seen a small manufactory of this kind where ten men only were employed, and where some of them consequently performed two or three distinct operations. But though they were very poor, and therefore but indifferently accommodated with the necessary equipment, they could, when they exerted themselves, make among them about twelve pounds of pins in a day. There are in a pound upwards of four thousand pins of a middling size. Those ten persons, therefore could make among them upwards of forty-eight thousand pins in a day. Each person, therefore, making a tenth part of forty-eight thousand pins, might be considered as making four thousand eight hundred pins in a day. But if they had all wrought separately and independently, and without any of them having been educated to this peculiar business, they certainly could not each of them have made twenty, perhaps not one pin in a day (Smith, 1937, pp. 4–5).

Why should these startling increases in productivity occur? Smith's most convincing explanations stress the time that can be saved by the division of labour and 'the increase of dexterity in every particular workman' (Smith, 1937, p. 7). Marglin (1974, pp. 66–7) criticizes the time-saving argument by saying that while it implies separation of tasks and duration of activity, it does not necessarily involve the specialization of an extreme division of labour. It can, and has been, achieved without this (he cites peasant agriculture). He is equally as sceptical about 'the increase of dexterity':

Judging from the earnings of the various specialists engaged in pin-making, these were no special skills. At least there were none that commanded premium wages. In a pin manufactory for which detailed records survive from the early part of the nineteenth century, R. S. Ashton (1925) reported wages for adult males of approximately 20 shillings per week, irrespective of the particular branch in which they were engaged (Marglin, 1974, p. 69).

On this basis Marglin draws the conclusion that the skills of pin-making were not great, were quickly learned, and that the 'potential increase in dexterity afforded by minute division of tasks was quickly exhausted'. In fact, he argues, the job could just as efficiently have been done by the patriarchal exploitation of family labour, without specialization, but with the separation of tasks. Specialization, he argues, was developed by the putter-outer in order to give himself a role to play – the role of capitalist – a role which consisted of mediating between fragmented producers and the market, on the principle of divide and rule.

What evidence exists to confirm Marglin's proposition? There is only indirect evidence because, as he observes, few capitalists would publicly acknowledge that production was organized to exploit workers. Some support can be drawn from contemporary documentary evidence, however, which stresses the intentional behaviour of capitalists in ensuring their own survival by denying their workmen complete knowledge of the methods of production (the examples Marglin cites are from Boyson (1970, p. 52) and *The Spectator*, London, 26 May 1866, p. 569). In addition, he observes that in areas of organization such as coalmining, where the scarcity of raw materials and the institution of private property limited possible production, then capitalist specialization did not take hold. Also, the development of specialized wage-labourers occurred prior to the development of expensive technology in the form of machines. This specialized labour also made it much more difficult for labourers to 'steal' and illegally market the commodities they produced.

This transition from domestic to factory production is usually termed an 'industrial revolution'. The term industrial revolution, wherever it is applied, implies a number of related factors, some of which we have already discussed. It involves economic changes that transform a pre-industrial society with low productivity and zero growth rates into a society with high productivity and increased economic growth. The changes were apparent, from an economic point of view, in the industrial structure and in population and social relations. The economic changes imply a transition from a simple commodity production, developed from and retaining elements of patriarchal exploitation of family labour, to production of an impersonal kind, with a strict division of labour and the use of capital equipment. Normally it is technical knowledge, generated from the demands of capital accumulation and valorization and the relations of production, that lies at the heart of an industrial revolution in its application to the processes or forces of production and distribution (see Anderson, 1974). In particular it involves the use of machines with new sources of power, and the replacement of

53

old kinds of raw materials with new ones which are more efficient (in terms of the capitalist mode of production) and more abundant. There is a process of development from domestic production for use and the production of luxury consumer goods for exchange, to the widespread 'mass' production of exchange values, with a concommitant process of development from country to town.

These features are normally present in the transition characterized as an industrial revolution. The actual mix that occurs varies by society and historical circumstances. The ingredients themselves are not particularly distinctive – the revolution is produced by their particular combination. So the degree of development is dependent upon the actual combination of these factors rather than upon their mere existence. Even though we point to the late eighteenth century as the beginning of the English industrial revolution, it is not true to say that these factors contributing to the revolution were not present before. Prior to this time there had existed capitalist forms of production. Products had been produced for distant markets before this period. Technical knowledge had been used in the production process before. In parts of Western Europe there had been a gradual shift of population from agriculture to the towns over a prolonged period of time. But what happened in parts of England, Lowland Scotland and South Wales was that these changes developed together and on a far-reaching scale. This began a cumulative process of change and growth. Phyllis Deane (1967) argues that we cannot make the assumption that sustained economic growth becomes inevitable and irreversible in the space of a few decades. She argues that there may be more than one spurt in the process of industrialization interspersed by periods of relative stagnation. Equally she says that there may be a modest spurt followed by gradual transformation, stretching over several generations. What is critical, she argues, is to locate the changes and combinations of changes and to explain why some came to a head slowly, rapidly or erratically.

As far as Britain was concerned, there seems to have been a number of factors at work. Economic historians disagree about the actual start of the revolution in Britain. Some put it back as far as Elizabethan times. Although there was economic growth (mining, weaving, etc.) in this period it affected only a small area of the total industry and had only a minor technological influence. Equally, there was not the rapid mobilization of people that we normally associate with a revolution. It would appear that there was a difference in scale rather more than anything else.

Even if we take the end of the eighteenth century as the starting point the actual decade is in some dispute. Whatever date we take there is no dispute that between the years 1780 and 1840 the British economy changed significantly (Hobsbawm, 1969). Population trebled, the total value of economic activity quadrupled, etc. It is interesting that from the 1750s the population change was about 7 per cent per annum.

So, following Hobsbawm, we are referring to the period 1780 to 1840. This was the first period of industrial innovation when new machinery was used to make textiles and iron, when the use of steam power for industry and commerce came into its own. The period was revolutionary because there were not only structural economic transformations but also major changes in personal, social and political life. These changes became manifest in the sphere of production with the increasing division of labour on both an occupational and a regional scale.

The development of a division of labour in production necessitated a proletariat tied neither by interest nor tradition to particular skills or locales. With the development of a proletariat, the emergence of the early forms of the modern wage-paying organization are nascent, inasmuch as the dissolution of the guild system allowed the developing money capital formed by primitive accumulation to be transformed into industrial capital. This primitive accumulation developed not only from Weber's 'Protestant ethic' and medieval usury but more especially:

> The discovery of gold and silver in America, the extirpation, enslavement and entombment in mines of the indigenous population of that continent, the beginnings of the conquest and plunder of India, and the conversion of Africa into a preserve for the commercial hunting of blackskins, are all things which characterize the dawn of the era of capitalist production. These idyllic proceedings are the chief movements of primitive accumulation (Marx, 1976, p. 915).

The primitive accumulation of capital not only develops forms of organization in the centre of its genesis but also envelops its periphery while it extinguishes its past. Weber emphasizes the roots of the modern world in the world that modernity will destroy. In this he follows the analysis of Karl Marx but whereas Weber argues that modernity is the working out of the idea of rationality in the world, Marxist analysis would argue that this rationality is itself rooted in the specific organizational structures of the capitalist mode of production. Marx (1959) writes in *Capital* (vol. 3) that

> The sudden expansion of the world market, the multiplication of circulating commodities, the competitive zeal of the European nations to possess themselves of the products of Asia and the treasures of America, and the colonial system, all contributed

materially toward destroying the feudal fetters on production. *However, in its first period – the manufacturing period – the modern mode of production developed only where the conditions for it had taken shape within the Middle Ages* (Marx, 1959, pp. 332–3, our emphasis).

These remarks of Marx should not lead us to overemphasize the necessity of large-scale accumulation of capital as a prerequisite of the industrial revolution. Tribe has demonstrated that this is incorrect, citing the following example as an illustration of his thesis:

> The well-known example of Richard Arkwright's purchase of Hampton Court Estate, Locminster, in 1809 shows just how low annual investment in this 'capital intensive' industry (cotton) was. The purchase price of approximately 220,000 pounds, represented a sum equivalent to 60% of the annual investment of fixed capital in the entire cotton industry for that year, demonstrating that the money flowing around industrial enterprise was insignificant compared with the sums changing hands in the property sector. The point that must be made is that despite the relatively trivial amounts involved in industrial investment, they were of great significance because of the relations into which they were inserted. . . . On the whole, capitalists did not go in for costly mechanization, but combined credit with rented buildings and machinery, using cheap sources of labour and power (Tribe, 1975, p. 36).

What Tribe's argument suggests is that in Marx's terms 'the modern mode of production' should be the site for an analysis of the 'relations' into which capital accumulation was inserted. These were social relations of capitalism as a mode of production. Within this mode of production have developed diverse modes of organization of the labour process. From an historical materialist position it is this which would be the subject of any analysis of organizations. Study of these social arrangements involves an analysis of the historically specific and economically determined relationship of the elements of the labour process. These are, according to Marx (1976, p. 284) 'work, . . . the object on which that work is performed, and . . . the instruments of that work'. These are the material aspects of organization and correspond to production, raw materials and technology. The technology or instrument of labour includes 'in addition to things through which the impact of labour on its object is mediated, and which therefore, in one way or another, serve as conductors of activity, all the objective conditions necessary for carrying on the labour process. These do not enter

56

directly into the process but without them it is either impossible for it to take place, or possible only to a partial extent' (Marx, 1976, p. 286). How these are combined depends upon the ideology of production which derives from the more general mode of production.

We shall be concerned in particular with the capitalist mode of production, although we shall discuss how a technical practice initially developed in that context can be and has been elaborated in an alternative mode of production.

The concept of mode of production has been the subject of considerable confusion in the past (e.g., see Hindess and Hirst's (1975) and Foster-Carter's (1978) discussions). Banaji (1977) has considerably clarified this. He notes that in both the *Grundrisse* and *Capital*, Marx ascribed two distinct meanings to the term 'mode of production'. In one of these it was indistinguishable from the concept of the 'labour process' (e.g., *Capital*, vol. 3, 1959, p. 329; *Grundrisse*, 1973, pp. 586, 587), whereas elsewhere, when Marx was making 'more general statements about the various stages of social development', as Banaji (1977, p. 5) puts it, the concept of mode of production bears a broader 'and more specifically historical meaning' corresponding to the notion of a periodization, an epoch of production.

A common error in materialist analysis has been to attempt the periodization of the latter through the concept of the former. That is, that the simple category of, for example, 'wage-labour' as a possible mode of organization of the labour process has been equated with the principle of periodization of an epoch, with a mode of production *per se*, in the latter of Marx's two senses. But in terms of this latter sense, the existence of a simple category such as wage-labour cannot be taken as a defining characteristic. Several modes of organization of the labour process – several simple categories – may exist within the one mode of production. Choosing between these in order to periodize the epoch is not an arbitrary process. The epoch or mode of production is characterized by the historically concrete existence of a simple category as an abstract value-producing category; that is, as the fundamental and objective principle of the epoch's laws of motion. Thus, the mode of production is the concrete realization of specific laws of motion.

These laws of motion can be analysed at two levels: at the level of each enterprise or organizational unit, and at the level of the social totality of enterprises. At the level of the totality the analysis is of the *mode of production*, while at the level of the enterprise, the analysis is of the determinate form of historically specific *modes of organization of the labour process*. These 'posit a particular level of technique and specific historical forms of the appropriation of the objective conditions of labour' (Banaji, 1977, p. 10). The analysis of the *mode of organization* takes place within the *mode of production*. Such an analysis, which as yet does not exist, would be an historical materialist analysis of organization as a theoretical object.

It follows from the above that the capitalist mode of production entails private ownership of the means of production and the existence of a relatively sophisticated market. Either can occur without the mode of production being capitalistic. In addition, labour is performed by people without means of production who, of necessity, are obliged to sell their labour-power to those who possess such means. The owners of the means of production thus become the owners of the process of production and of what is produced. What is produced 'is geared to the accumulation of capital: products are sold for profit, the decisive part of which is invested again to yield new profits, and so on' (Therborn, 1976, p. 73). This distinguishes a more fully developed capitalist mode of production from earlier forms of market economy characterized by commercial peasant agriculture or post-guild handicraft production, which we may term petty commodity production.

In a developed capitalist mode of production people are distributed into classes as economic agents with distinct relations of production. Class relations are fundamentally and inherently antagonistic. These antagonisms can be veiled or made opaque through economic, political and ideological interventions on the part of one class interest, against another. We shall argue that *organization theory* is such an intervention.

No actual social formation or society contains only two classes. Residues of earlier classes remain embedded in the structure of the capitalist mode of production, for instance, such as the petty bourgeoisie. The petty bourgeoisie executes the roles defined by petty commodity relations of production. However, no actual social formation is or has been dominated by petty commodity production, although it remains an important residual element for many substantive analyses.

We would argue that a mode of production is an *economy-wide system*. Since the 'long sixteenth century', as Wallerstein (1974a) has argued, the economy-wide system of production has been a *world-wide system* dominated and determined (with Althusser and Balibar (1970) one might say *over-determined*), by capitalist social relations and forces of production. In such a system the private ownership of the means of production and market transactions of labour, resources and products are present and linked to each other and integrated with all production processes and sectors. They are the dominant modes of ownership and transaction. The price mechanism becomes the chief method of allocating labour and resources and the valorization of capital the motive-force. The social relations of production need not necessarily be expressed in terms of the categories of profit and formally free alienable wage labour, as Banaji (1977) has pointed out. They may be termed relations between peasants and usurers, they may produce rent, interest or surplus produce and still be integrated into capitalist relations of production. (Wallerstein 1974a also argues this point).

Since we are arguing that social relations are to a large extent determined by economic relations, it is necessary to look at this in the factory system of organizing the labour process, before we can move on to look at the social effects of economic changes. In terms of the social relations of production, the transition characterized by the term industrial revolution produced two major economic group-ings conceptualized by Marx as the classes of labour and capital, each class being defined by its social relations. The capitalist or entrepreneur differed from previous species because of his ownership (or appropriation) of the means of production. These were property and produced goods which he could dispose of as he wished. Unlike the feudal lord, the capitalist hired wage-labour bought at the market price. Once the wages had been paid, the responsibilities of the capitalist ceased, as did the rights of ownership of his labourers to their labour and its fruits. Thus the capitalist had the advantages of ownership without the respons-ibility, together with the surplus value, the profit, that this labour created. The industrial revolution produced a special kind of worker, unknown before in history. He was formally free from ties with his master but this freedom contained no rights. Theoretically, the worker could offer his services to anyone.

So, the social relations were formal and impersonal. These formal and impersonal social relations first emerged in the Lancashire cotton industry a century and a half or so ago, and in the 1830s and 1840s the factory system could still be regarded as 'novel' by some observers (see Thompson, 1968, p. 208). While some observers marvelled at the power and might of steam power, others worried at the potential power and might of the labour harnessed and related by the new technology.

> As a stranger passes through the masses of human beings which have accumulated around the mills and print works . . . he cannot contemplate these 'crowded hives' without feelings of anxiety and apprehension almost amounting to dismay. The population, like the system to which it belongs, is new; but it is hourly increasing in breadth and strength. It is an aggregate of masses, our conceptions of which clothe themselves in terms that express something portentous and fearful . . . as of the slow rising and gradual swelling of an ocean which must, at some

future and no distant time, bear all the elements of society aloft upon its bosom, and float them Heaven knows wither. There are mighty energies slumbering in these masses. . . . The manufacturing population is not new in its formation alone: it is new in its habits of thought and action, which have been formed by the circumstances of its condition, with little instruction, and less guidance from external sources (Taylor, 1842, pp. 4–6; quoted in Thompson, 1968, pp. 208–9).

The creation of these 'lower participants' of the emergent factory organization might perhaps best be viewed in terms of two opposing tendencies which accompanied the process which Marx termed an increasing rate of exploitation and which Weber termed the disenchantment and rationalization of the world.

On the one hand, the discipline of factory organization was fiercely resisted by the labourers who were either harnessed or dispossessed by it. Contemporary journals are replete with descriptions of 'agitation' in relation to Luddism, Chartism, and child labour, and for trade unions or the Ten Hour Bill (see Thompson, 1968, pp. 207–32). On the other hand, the modern form of organization through wage-labour and factory discipline was only possible given a labour force which already bowed to the hegemony of 'rational organization' or could be led to do so. It is in this connection that Weber (1976) noted the difficulties experienced by employers in the 'putting-out' industries in the seventeenth century as a result of traditional practices of the work force, such as drunkenness or the embezzlement of yarn. The hegemony of Protestantism in its 'ethic' was not confined to the organizers, but appeared also in the organized.

This argument has been advanced by Thompson (1968) in particular, and has also been stressed by Hobsbawm (1969), Wearmouth (1937), Eldridge (1972) and by Gutman (1977) for America. Thompson (1968, pp. 385–442) argues that Methodism in particular, especially during the period between 1790–1830, served as an ideological apparatus which aided the hegemonic ascendancy of capitalist rationality in the organization of work.[2] This process principally operated through the shaping of character in accord with the social structure and sentiments of capitalism: the stress on sobriety, disciplined work and authority which children received in Sunday School had a highly supportive role to play as a bulwark of the 'rational' forms of organization which the development of capitalism engendered.

Max Weber (1976) recognized that a necessary task for the development of a rational organization was the emergence of a rational worker. The major obstacles to the development of both rational workers and rational organization were traditional concepts and practices of work. Not even seemingly rational practices such as the development of piece-work systems could be guaranteed to overcome traditional inclinations in a work force which, by neither habit nor yet compulsion, did not ask

> how much can I earn in a day if I do as much work as possible? but, how much must I work in order to earn the average . . . which I earned before and which takes care of my traditional needs. . . . Wherever modern capitalism has begun its work of increasing the productivity of human labour by increasing its intensity, it has encountered the immensely stubborn resistance of this leading trait of pre-capitalist labour (Weber, 1976, p. 62).

One remedy for this 'stubborn resistance' is to intensify work further or cheapen it by reducing wages. While this may have certain attractions in tasks where no skill element is involved, it is not likely to be very satisfactory where skill is required. This is because skilled work *had* to be performed well, with care, with precision, with *skill*. Such skill is neither natural nor wholly technical: it also involves an attitude of care and concern for the practice of work itself. In short, as Weber (1976, p. 62) put it, it has to be performed as if it were a 'vocation', a 'calling', which attitude 'can only be the product of a long and arduous process of education'. This education, argues Weber, was provided by Protestantism in as much as it developed the Protestant ethic, the work ethic. Religious asceticism enabled businessmen rationally to organize for profit, confident in the belief that they were doing God's work as well as displaying their salvation in doing so. It also provided them 'with sober, conscientious and unusually industrious workmen, who clung to their work as to a life purpose willed by God' (Weber, 1976, p. 62). As Weber (1976, pp. 281f) noted, the eminent Presbyterian and author of the seventeenth-century *Christian Directory*, Richard Baxter, recommended the employment of godly servants. Anthony (1977, p. 43) has rather nicely observed, 'The engagement of God as the supreme supervisor was a most convenient device; a great part of the efforts of modern management has been aimed at finding a secular but equally omnipotent equivalent in the worker's own psyche.'

Thompson (1968, p. 395) cites Andrew Ure's (1835) *The Philosophy of Manufactures* in which it is complained that 'the main difficulty' of the factory system was the 'distribution of the different members of the apparatus into one co-operative body', and above all 'in training human beings to renounce their desultory habits of work, and to identify themselves with the unvarying regularity of the complex automation'. Ure continued:

It is therefore excessively the interest of every mill-owner *to organize his moral machinery on equally sound principles with his mechanical*, for otherwise he will never command the steady hands, watchful eyes and prompt co-operation, essential to excellence of product. . . . There is, in fact, no case to which the Gospel truth, 'Godliness is great gain', is more applicable than to the administration of an extensive factory (Ure, 1835; quoted in Thompson, 1968, p. 397).

However, as Eldridge (1972, p. 50) observes:

the congruence of values between capital and labour was of an unstable and limited kind during the period of industrialization in England . . . the element of consensus implied in the employment contract was on the basis of necessity and force and not simply a lofty view of the virtues of teamwork between masters and men.

This analysis suggests that the triumph of the formal factory organization was due not to any technological cause, in a variant of the technology determines organization argument (see Chapters 6 and 9), but was instead due to its ability to be able to organize its 'moral machinery', that is, to substitute capitalist for morally imperfect and unreliable workers' control. Ure was quite clear that the triumph of factory organization was due to discipline and supervision.

A major part of the discipline which had to be acquired was time discipline, as Thompson (1968) has stressed. The Protestant ethic was useful here as well:

The Puritan horror of waste of time helped not only to concentrate effort, to focus attention on detail, but also to prepare for the rhythms of an industrial society, our society of the alarm clock and the factory whistle (Hill, 1964, p. 130).

Herbert Gutman's (1977) work is particularly illuminating on the development of modern, rational organization time. He observes that in the United States it was not just Benjamin Franklin's contemporaries who undertook to remake the world into a rational order. The following text is extracted from a brochure prepared by The International Harvester Corporation, just before the First World War, in order to teach its Polish labourers the English language. The first lesson was this:

'*I hear the whistle. I must hurry.*'
'*I hear the five minute whistle.*'
'*It is time to go into the shop.*'

*'I take my check from the gate board and hang it on the depart-
ment board.'*
'I change my clothes and get ready to work.'
'The starting whistle blows.'
'I eat my lunch.'
'It is forbidden until then.'
'The whistle blows at five minutes of starting time.'
'I get ready to go to work.'
'I work until the whistle blows to quit.'
'I leave my place nice and clean.'
'I put all my clothes in the locker.'
'I must go home.'

Such a text barely requires commentary. It displays, in a highly
concentrated and over-determined form (over-determined by the
need for a simplified English language for an ethnic and
linguistically alien work force) the hegemonic character of
language.

Although we are here dealing primarily with these practices as
historical, it must not be thought that they are of purely historical
interest. They are not. With each expansion of industrial or
technological organization to a new periphery such as South Korea
or India, or the incorporation of previously unhabituated migrant
communities, the drama of rational discipline is enacted yet again.
Although writing of industrializing England, Pollard's (1965, p.
160) description still holds: 'there was a whole new culture to be
absorbed and an old one to be traduced and spurned'. Similarly, as
Thompson (1968, p. 57) observed, this 'entailed a severe
restructuring of working habits – new disciplines, new incentives,
and a new human nature upon which these incentives could bite
effectively'. In sociology a whole literature has developed around
this process under the concept of 'modernization' (perhaps one of
the most ideologically and value-laden of all sociological
categories).

Contemporary documentary evidence from the early period of
industrial organization suggests that successful enterprise depended
not so much on technical efficiency *per se*, but on *technological*
efficiency: the successful marriage of industrial technique and
organization of labour that Arkwright achieved and contemporaries such as Wyatt and Paul failed to achieve. This failure, it
appears, was due to an inability to *organize* (Wadsworth and Mann,
1931, p. 433; Marglin, 1974, p. 86). Further evidence that the
formal, hierarchical form of organization did not emerge as a
consequence of a technological cause can be adduced from the fact
that there was no objective technical difference between factory

and domestic production in the textile industry in the early years; the spinning jenny was the basic machine in both, well into the nineteenth century (Crump, 1931).

Marglin (1974, p. 89) finds the evidence strong enough to suggest that 'the particular forms that technological change took were shaped and determined by factory organization'. (Factory organization was also encouraged by the greater ease of detecting and punishing patent piracy in factories than in domestic production, he suggests.) As we have already noted, the introduction of this form of organization was not quiescently welcomed by the workers whose control was being eroded and overcome. Marglin (1974, pp. 96–7) suggests that where workers were still able to pursue independent labour outside of the factory they chose to do so, but that the increasing 'bias of technological change towards improvements consistent with factory organization' had eliminated these alternatives for most workers by the mid-nineteenth century, despite their agitation against them. The formal, impersonal, factory mode of organization was articulated within a mode of production whose violence towards habitual production methods was received by those who were to be organized with a mixture of agitation and acceptance of force and necessity. It is perhaps the greatest achievement of the actual emergence of the modern 'rational' form of organization that it now no longer needs the ideological legitimation of anything extraneous to its own process; it has become such an ideology in its own right, as we shall subsequently argue.

But this is to rush ahead. The victory of 'rational calculation' had first to be won. These formal, impersonal social relations did not develop overnight, but, as we have noted, began to emerge first in the cotton industry during the early course of industrialization in Britain. The development of the cotton industry in Lancashire is an almost perfect model of the double process of the initially monopolistic development of primitive accumulation subsequently determining and limiting similar development elsewhere during the first phases of the already capitalist process of production. As Mandel puts it:

> Both in each individual country and internationally, capital presses outwards from the centre – in other words, its historic birthplaces – towards the periphery. It constantly tries to extend itself to new domains, to convert new sectors of simple repro-duction of commodities into spheres of capitalist production of commodities, and to replace use values by the production of commodities (Mandel, 1975, p. 47).

At the same time as the process of the primitive accumulation of capital was developing in the cotton industry in Lancashire it was also taking place, albeit unevenly, in other parts of the world. As a precondition to the success of capital accumulation, and thus factory organization, in the emergent core countries of Western Europe, particularly the Lancashire region, it was necessary first to destroy textile production by artisans and native peasants. After the destruction of a domestic or handicraft mode of production, then a capitalist mode and organization of production could be developed. This process of the universal spread of the idea of rational organization was thus neither mystical nor inevitable – it was simply the articulation of the capitalist mode of production as a developing world economy. Some historical examples can illustrate this.

In the first instance the development of capital accumulation and factory organization in the core countries of Western Europe was able to destroy the domestic mode of production through the 'artillery of cheap prices'. Mandel cites the following cases as examples of the process:

> In Italy, at the beginning of the 1880s, half the imports still consisted of products of the manufacturing industry or semi-finished productions, and in Japan the unrestricted import of cheap cotton yarn (average price about 29.6 yen per *Kin* in 1874 and 25.5 yen in 1878). But in both cases *local machine industry* was able to take the place of local domestic industry in about ten years, i.e., the foreign products simply cleared the ground for the development of 'national' capitalism (Mandel, 1975, p. 53).

In the early stages of the development of the modern formal capitalist mode of organization and production this was the pattern simply because foreign capital was insufficiently developed to dominate the process of accumulation elsewhere. Mandel singles out two of the most important obstacles to the domination of foreign capital over this nascent capitalist accumulation:

> Firstly the extent of capital accumulation in Great Britain, France or Belgium, was not sufficient to allow this capital to engage in the establishment of factories in other parts of the world. In Great Britain, annual capital investments abroad averaged only £29 million between 1860 and 1869; they then increased in the decade from 1870–79 by 75% to £51 million a year, and then to £68 million a year in the decade from 1880–89. The second obstacle was the inadequacy of the means of communication – the uneven development of the Industrial Revolution in the manufacturing industry and in the transport industry. This effectively blocked the penetration of the

65

cheap foods produced by large-scale industry in Western Europe, not merely into the farthest villages and small towns of Asia and Latin America, but even those of Southern and Eastern Europe. Indeed, the inadequacy of transport and communications systems hindered the formation of national markets proper in Western Europe itself. Before the spread of railways, the price of a ton of coal in France varied in 1838 from 6.90 francs in the mining region of St. Etienne south of the Loire, to 36.45 francs in Paris, and even 50 francs in Bayonne and remoter Brittany.

It is thus no accident that the slowly increasing impact of the foreign capital investments of Great Britain, France, Belgium and Holland was chiefly concentrated in *foreign railway construction*, for the extension of this world-wide communications network was a precondition for the gradual extension of their domination over the internal markets of the less developed countries which had been dragged into the maelstrom of the capitalist world economy (Mandel, 1975, p. 50).

In a very potent image, one could conceive of the spread of the railway, with its destruction of local markets and the creation of one market, with its standardization of the rhythm of everyday life on the chronology of the clock and timetable, as the bearer of the rationalization of the world. However, with the development of the railways and the steamship and the full flowering of the world economy in the 'new Imperialism' of the period after the 1870s slump, foreign capital began its domination of these 'nascent capitalist economies', to culminate in the modern imperialism of the international firm. But to develop this yet would be to run ahead of our argument at this stage.

What was the nature of organization of this period in the mid-nineteenth century? Hobsbawm (1975, p. 213) writes that by 'the 1850s a factory of 300 in Britain could still be considered very large, and as late as 1871 the average British cotton factory employed 180 people, the average works manufacturing machinery a mere eighty-five'. This was not characteristic of the heavy industry of the period of *The Age of Capital, 1848–1875*, which as Hobsbawm notes 'was much larger', tending 'to develop concentrations of capital which controlled entire cities and even regions, and mobilized unusually vast armies of labour under its command'. This was particularly true of railways:

Railway companies were enormous undertakings, even when constructed and managed entirely under conditions of competitive free enterprise, as normally they were not. By the time the British railway system stabilized itself in the late 1860s every foot of rail between the Scottish border, the Pennine Hills, the sea and the River Humber was controlled by the North-Eastern Railway. Coalmines were still largely individual undertakings and sometimes quite small, though the size of the occasional great mining disasters gives some idea of the scale on which they operated: 145 killed at Risca in 1860, 178 at Ferndale (also South Wales) in 1867, 140 at Swaithe (Yorkshire) and 110 at Mons (Belgium) in 1875, 200 at High Blantyre (Scotland) in 1887. Yet increasingly, especially in Germany, vertical and horizontal combinations produced those industrial empires which controlled the lives of thousands. The concern known since 1873 as the *Gutenhoffnungshiitte A.G.* was by no means the largest in the Ruhr, but by then it had extended from iron-founding into quarrying and mining iron ore and coal – it produced practically all the 215,000 tons of iron ore and half the 415,000 tons of coal it required – and had diversified into transport, rolling and the construction of bridges, ships and a variety of machinery.

Small wonder that the Krupp works in Essen rose from seventy two workers in 1848 to almost 12,000 in 1873, or that Schneider in France had multiplied to 12,500 in 1870, so that more than half the population of the town of Creusot worked in their blast furnaces, rolling-mills, power-hammers and engineering workshops. Heavy industry produced not so much the industrial region as such as the company town, in which the fate of men and women depended on the fortunes and goodwill of a single master, behind whom stood the force of law and state power, which regarded his authority as necessary and beneficial.

For, large or small, the 'master' rather than the impersonal authority of the 'company' ruled the enterprise, and even the company was identified with a man rather than a board of directors. In most people's minds, and in reality, capitalism still meant the one-man, or rather one-family, owner-managed business. Yet this very fact raised two serious problems for the structure of enterprise. *They concerned its supply of capital and its management* (Hobsbawm, 1975, pp. 213–14, our emphasis).

It is to these two problems that we now turn. It was typical of the firm of the early half of the nineteenth century to be family owned, financed and managed, particularly in Britain. This meant that the sources of financial capital were not institutionally overlapped to any great extent with those of industrial capital. Anderson (1965) argues that the nature of the English revolution of 1640 enabled feudal landowners to transform themselves into mercantile capitalists. These mercantile endeavours developed as a parallel activity of the English ruling class to the business of ruling in the colonies and at home. And ruling was business, as the East India Company could argue:

> We are engaged, no doubt on business principles, on securing for the English people a part of that trade which has been successively the monopoly of the Portuguese, the Spaniards, and the Dutch. No doubt the produce which we bring is dear. But we have reduced the price. Had it not been for our efforts Englishmen would have to pay whatever price the Dutchmen might choose to exact. The expansion of our trade is, moreover, the expansion of English enterprise. We train seamen by the hundreds; we have, it being necessary for our trade, an armed marine which is part of the national forces, as it assuredly would be used, did needs arise, for the national defence (Rogers, 1920, p. 120).

A consequence of this was that the ruling class and its associated imperialist and mercantile institutions, saw the business of ruling as disassociated from that of industry. This was enforced by the nature of the élite educational institutions engaged in the production of what Anderson (1965, p. 63) termed a 'patrician political style . . . defined not by acts which denote skills but by gestures which reveal quintessences: a specific training or aptitude would be a derogation of the impalpable essence of nobility'. This style, on the whole, did not muddy itself with industry: the aristocracy which had previously been reliant for its wealth solely on land-ownership was now also to gain it from the investment of capital in trading ventures and speculative stocks abroad. There are exceptions, of course, particularly in the early iron and coal industry, as Rubinstein (1974) has argued, maintaining that there actually existed two quite separate sources of wealth in nineteenth-century England, in which the traditional hierarchy of status was maintained. Mercantilism sustained and maintained the feudal élite, while the owners of domestic industry tended to play a traditional, craft, subservient role. The aristocratic-mercantilist nexus tended to centre on the financial institutions of London, while the emergent industrial bourgeoise of 'muck an' brass' were concentrated in the North of England, with little or no influence in the metropolis. (It is noteworthy that this process of development was quite distinct in England. Elsewhere, especially in the United States and Germany, industrial and financial capital were interlocked almost from the beginning. It was this interconnection which enabled the massive concentration of the organic composition of capital which was evident in the US industrial dominance by 1941. Chandler (1962) argues this at length.)

It is, in view of the preceding, of no surprise that Hobsbawm should observe that:

> By and large the characteristic enterprise of the first half of the century had been financed privately – e.g., from family assets – and expanded by reinvesting profits, though this might well mean that, with most of capital tied up in this way, the firm might rely a good deal on credit for its current operations. But the increasing size and cost of such undertakings as railways, metallurgical and other expensive activities requiring heavy initial outlays, made this more difficult, especially in countries newly entering upon industrialization and lacking large accumulations of private investment capital (Hobsbawm, 1975, p. 214).

The new forms of funding were largely, apart from Britain, derived from one or other of several financial institutions. Those were either the banks or the type of financial institution known as the *credit mobilier*, or the investment type of bank known as the *banque d'affaires*, or the stock exchange.

The development of the stock exchange to its present significance was contingent upon the advent of limited liability legislation in 1856 (in Britain) in consequence of which the owners of an enterprise were no longer directly responsible for ensuring its viability. Before 1856 the situation was quite different; owners were responsible for any debts incurred by the enterprise. One consequence of this had been to limit the size of the enterprise and to maximize the amount of involvement of the entrepreneur whose personal fortune was at risk if the enterprise failed. The development of joint stock legislation, as Marx (1959) foresaw in *Capital III*, was to be of vital importance for the development of capitalism. However, Marx did not foresee that the development of 'ownership without control' or the rise of the large multi-national corporations would become as central and significant features of capitalism as they have become.

Marx actually believed that the development of joint stock legislation and the extension of credit could have a progressively destructive role to play in the capitalist mode of production. This could occur through a kind of incipient socialization of ownership as 'the abolition of capital as private property within the framework of capitalist production itself' (Marx, 1959, p. 436). He also held a contradictory view to this argument. He believed that joint stock legislation and the extension of credit raised the possibility of even greater exploitation because capital and personal assets were now legally separate: the capitalist now risked not his own savings but those of others. The existence of this freely available credit would enable the organization to achieve a growth unlimited except by its capacity to realize its capital on the market through the sale of commodities or services. This capacity, argued Marx, was limited by constant and recurrent crises of over-production and over-speculation. These led in turn, through the process of the 'little fish' being 'swallowed by the sharks and the lambs by the stock exchange wolves' (Marx, 1959, p. 440), to an increasing concentration of capitalist organizations. The existence of financial resources meant that organizations could grow through an increasingly concen-trated organic composition of capital. It is to the process of the growth of organizations and the development of systematic bodies of knowledge concerned with organization that we turn in the next chapter.

3 The emergence of an organization theory

Precursors of organization ideologies

Pre-industrial and pre-capitalist modes of production needed neither complex organizational arrangements nor complex ideological bulwarks. Traditional forms of authority were sufficient.

The size of the enterprise under the guild system and the domestic system supports this proposition. Equally, as we have seen, the early industrial enterprises were largely controlled by one individual. Such direct control required little in the way of designing improved managerial practices and, equally, the size of the organization did not warrant the development of elaborate theories. This accounts for the fact that organization theory and management theory were virtually non-existent during the early part of the industrial revolution in both Western Europe and North America. Considerable time has been spent discussing the nature of the industrial revolution and the kinds of sociological theorizing that accompanied it in order to place it in the context of later analysis. As we have seen, the basic goals of industrial entrepreneurs in the nineteenth century were centred around profit maximization and optimal output. The criterion of success in industry was the size of the personal wealth of individual entrepreneurs. The role of technology and machines was of paramount interest. It was perceived that, short of lower wages or longer hours, the installation of machinery was the one thing that could improve output, profits and personal wealth. Attention to the needs of the individual was not perceived as necessary. Authoritarianism was the 'ideology' upon which the early capitalists based their activities, as Bendix (1956) has demonstrated.

We have discussed parallel developments in the ideological sphere. Sociology emerges as a conservative critique of the market

71

effects generated by the emergence of the capitalist mode of production. These critiques have been manifested in various ways: from schemes for renewing the ideological community through a new organization of social solidarity to a *haut-bourgeois* resignation and despair. On the whole they have not been adopted much in the actual organization of the labour process, with the exception of Weber's ideal type of bureaucracy, and Mayo's neo-Durkheimian analyses of the 1930s and 1940s. In spite of this they have provided the dominant theoretical resource in the analysis of organization practice. In terms of the self-understanding of this theoretical practice, then, the analysis of organizations begins to emerge in the last years of the nineteenth century as precisely that practical and analytical individualism which characterized marginalist economic analyses of the sphere of distribution. This individualism in the analysis of the organization of production had both practical and theoretical implications. We shall discuss these in this chapter.

In the light of the industrial developments that have been discussed so far, it is obvious why most organization texts begin their analyses with the principles and practices of scientific management – the first systematic attempt to impose an ideology and a strategy upon industrial and organizational behaviour at the turn of the present century. Of course, it is perfectly feasible to trace organizational thought to an earlier date, as Wolin (1960) does, for example. In this context we are limited to a more synoptic view than this excellent source.

Since the split between political and industrial authority, between the state and civil society, did not exist to any large degree before the modern political and industrial revolutions, the main focus of thought about organizations in pre-industrial societies was upon political authority and, particularly, the ethical basis of this authority. It is possible to trace this stream of thought back as far as Plato in his discussion of justice as the aim of the 'good life'. He saw that social order was the main component of this justice, in which the state's role was that of ensuring the existence of the common good. This common good arose from the pursuit of justice and order. In *The Republic*, Plato argued that the individual, by carrying out his own functions, was the source of justice. The state was the organization. It was a manifestation of the individual realizing himself, a situation where an accord was reached between the nature of man and the demands of the state (organization).

Similar sentiments are present in the work of Aristotle, in that he also believed that the good life could be achieved through the functioning of the state. He argued, though, that the governing of the state could and should alter according to the needs and demands of the citizens of the state. The ideal situation was to be found in government with a single ruler. Recognizing that the ideal person for this ideal position was not always available, he also advocated the development of what today we would call constitutional government.

It is well documented that the ascendance of the Roman Republic and Empire brought with it a number of organization changes (see Anderson (1974) for an analysis of why these changes occurred). In particular, there was the movement away from the representative decision-making type of arrangement advocated by the Greeks towards a more bureaucratic arrangement, while the subsequent development of Christianity modified the bureaucratic nature of the Roman state, through its emphasis upon the individual and personal salvation (see Wolin (1960) for an elaboration of these themes).

From the point of view of the precursors of organization theory proper, it is perhaps the writing of Machiavelli that best displays the relationship of thinking about organizations and the ethical nature of political authority. He was much concerned with the issue of a powerful central administration in society and, for what he is best known, the strategies that can be adopted by governmental rulers in maintaining their powerful positions. Indeed many contemporary philosophers argue that it was Machievelli's emphasis upon power and the state that led to the considerable interest in political philosophy in the post-Renaissance period.

It was upon the concept of a social contract that much of this political philosophy centred. In the writing of Hobbes, for example, the idea of the social contract as a way of justifying the *status quo* in society is used. The idea of a social contract can be seen also in the writings of Locke, although in his case he rejects the idea of Divine Right which Hobbes implicitly justified. Sovereignty for him lay not in the sovereign monarch but with the general body of citizens. This body had the right to seek a new government when the existing one was considered inadequate. The notion of social contract reappears in the work of Rousseau, specifically in his delineation of 'the general will'. By this is meant that individual freedom can only be attained by the individual submitting to the general will. The assumption here is that individual objectives and state objectives are in tune with one another.

With the industrial revolution some writers and thinkers turned their attention to events within the organization. Of such writers, Adam Smith comes to mind as one of the first historically, especially through his analysis of the division of labour and the 'need' for specialization in industry. Smith's economic analysis, however, cannot be regarded as a significant fore-runner to modern organization theory. In common with the political economy of his day, Smith's main emphasis was upon the factors of production: land, labour, capital and entrepreneurship. None of these displays an emphasis upon a managerial or organizational analysis. In any case, as already indicated, the managerial function was virtually non-existent because of the prevailing structural arrangements.

Scientific management and the theory of bureaucracy mark the first major developments in the theory of organizations. Few problems of organization existed when organization was primarily through either the guild or small-scale family enterprise. Writing about these early organization forms of industrialization, Claus Offe (1976a, p. 25) has termed 'the production organization of the small craft workshop with its triple hierarchical division of master, journeyman and apprentice' a 'task-continuous status organization'. This is the type of organization which developed from the guild form of organization, in which there existed a relationship between different positions in the hierarchy 'such that there is a wide area of technical rules to which equal obedience is required from all the occupants of the positions (in the structure)'. A superordinate position would differ from a subordinate position 'merely in terms of greater mastery of the rules and greater ability, knowledge, and experience in production'. The rules that a subordinate must obey become, in their entirety, components of the role definition of a superordinate and so on, up the hierarchy. In such a situation of organization, as it was carried through to the family-owned industrial enterprise, organization could be implemented through fairly simple forms of instruction for only so long as the organizational unit remained relatively small and manageable, as Hobsbawm elaborates:

> For the basic model of the individually or family-owned and managed enterprise, the patriarchal family autocracy, was increasingly irrelevant to the industries of the second half of the nineteenth century. 'The best instruction', wrote a German handbook of 1868, 'is by word of mouth. Let it be given by the entrepreneur himself, all-seeing, omnipresent and ever available, whose personal orders are reinforced by the personal example which his employees have constantly before their eyes' (Hobsbawm, 1975, p. 216).

This advice was of only limited value once enterprises began to develop into large-scale organizations, such as those developing in the third quarter of the nineteenth century in the railways, mines and steel mills. More formal methods of organization than paternalism had to be developed, and as Hobsbawm goes on to say:

The alternative and complement to instruction was command.

But neither the autocracy of the family nor the small-scale operations of craft industry and merchant business provided much guidance for really large capitalist organization. So, paradoxically, private enterprise in its most unrestricted and anarchic period tended to fall back on the only available models of large-scale management, the military and bureaucratic. The railway companies, with their pyramid of uniformed and disciplined workers, possessing job security, often promotion by security and even pensions, are an extreme example. The appeal of military titles, which occur freely among the early British railway executives and managers of large port undertakings, did not rest on pride in the hierarchies of soldiers and officials, such as the Germans felt, but on the inability of private enterprise as yet to devise a specific form of management for big business (Hobsbawm, 1975, p. 216).

Clearly, as Hobsbawm (1975, pp. 216–17) shows, and as Weber (1948, p. 261) stated, 'No special proof is necessary to show that military discipline is the ideal model for the modern capitalist factory.' The example of the most developed form of organization, bureaucracy, the theory of which Weber found in and developed from the Prussian military forces, and which enterprises such as the British railway companies actually found in the ranks of the British Army, was to become the specific form of management of big business.

The theory of bureaucracy

Discussion of bureaucracy predates Weber's (1948) classic early twentieth-century contributions. Indeed, Albrow (1970, p. 16) has suggested that the invention of the word belongs to a M. de Gournay in 1745, who took the conventional term 'bureau', meaning both writing-table and office, and added to it a word derived from the Greek suffix for 'rule', in order to signify bureaucracy as the rule of officials. It rapidly became a standard accepted term in the conventions of political discourse, rapidly developing a pejorative tone for which in large part the novelist, Balzac, may be held responsible, with his use of the term in his novel of 1836, *Les Employés*. These French origins were soon forgotten. By the end of the nineteenth century the term was widely held to have been of Germanic origin. This attitude associated the concept with changes brought to the Prussian state after its defeat by Napoleon in 1806, and with the importance of the philosophical writings on this Prussian bureaucracy by Hegel.

Hegel conceived the governing bureaucracy of public administration as a bridge between the state and civil society. He regarded civil society as representative of particular interests, such as the various professions and corporations, while he considered the state to be the mediator of these, as the representative of the general interest. The bureaucracy was regarded as the medium through which particular interests were translated into general interests.

Bureaucracy, as a form of organization, enabled enterprises to transcend the limits of direct, extensive and formal control in commerce and business either by paternalistic owners or, in governance more specifically political, the role of traditional or charismatic persons. Simon (1952, pp. 185–94) has codified what these limits were by enumerating the preconditions for such *personal* types of organization:

1   The vertical (hierarchical) differentiation must be relatively underdeveloped, thus allowing the direct communication of orders and direct supervision of their execution.
2   The events and processes in the sphere of action have to occur within the field of vision and within hearing distance of the superior authorities.
3   Functional differentiation must also be rudimentary, not only must the majority of the actors belong to the same rank in the hierarchy, but also actors of the same rank must fulfil identical functions (Offe, 1976a, p. 27).

The advantages of the bureaucratic forms of organization were that it 'executes with the pen everything which previously would have been done by word of mouth. Hence many pens are set in motion' as the fifth edition of the *Allgemeine Deutsche Real-Encylopaedie oder Conversationslexikon* (1819, vol. 2, p. 158) put it. It was precisely this notion of *impersonality* which Weber was to develop as the cornerstone of his model of bureaucratic organization.

Weber and the theory of bureaucracy

Weber began his monumental enquiry into *Economy and Society* through a consideration of the basic concepts of sociology, in particular with reference to the concept of *verband*, or organization. The concept of organization subsumed such differing substantive entities as the state, the political party, the church or sect, and the firm. The defining characteristic of an organization was the presence of a leader and an administrative staff. These persons are ordered, *organized*, into specific types of social relationship, depending upon the type of rule to which action was oriented in the organization. Weber termed these rules the 'order' of the organization. The administrative staff of an organization has a dual relationship to this order. On the one hand, the behaviour of the administrative staff is regulated by these rules; but on the other hand, it is the task of this ruling body to see that other members adhere to the rules of the organization. Members of the organization tend to obey these rules because of their belief that they are subject to an 'order governing the organization', which was regarded by Weber as a 'structure of dominancy':

> The validity of an order means more than the existence of a uniformity of social action determined by custom or self-interest . . . the content of a social relationship [will] be called an order, if the conduct is, approximately or on the average, oriented towards determinable 'maxims'. Only then will an order be called 'valid' if the orientation towards these maxims occurs, among other reasons, also because it is in some appreciable way regarded by the actor as in some way obligatory or exemplary for him (Weber, 1968, p. 31).

This order presents features of a scene to which the actor orients his or her actions. As such, and in the tradition of an 'interpretative' sociology, it is a perceived order rather than an external thing to which the actor reacts. This concept of an order is presented in the concepts of 'convention' or 'law' in so far as:

> It is possible for action to be oriented to an order in other ways than through conformity with its prescriptions, as they are generally understood by the actors. Even in the case of evasion or disobedience the probability of their being recognized as valid norms may have an effect on action. This may, in the first place, be true from the point of view of sheer expediency. A thief orients his action to the validity of the criminal law in that he acts surreptitiously. Furthermore there may exist at the same time different interpretations of the meaning of the order. In such cases, for sociological purposes, each can be said to be valid in so far as it actually determines the course of action (Weber, 1968, p. 32).

Weber suggests that the reason why actors orient their actions toward a similarly defined order is because their individual enactments are guided by collectively recognized rules:

> Economic action, for instance, is oriented to knowledge of the relative scarcity of certain available means to want satisfaction, in relation to the actor's state of needs and to the present and probable action of others, in so far as the latter affects the same resources. But at the same time, of course, the actor in his choice

77

of economic procedures naturally orients himself *in addition* to the conventional and legal rules which he recognizes as valid, that is, of which he knows that a violation on his part would call forth a given reaction of other persons (Weber, 1968, p. 33).

An order is not merely a formal codification of conventional and legal rules, but, as we have already stressed, it is embedded in a 'structure of dominancy'. This formal structure of domination is experienced in terms of differing substantive types of rule, which make probable obedience to authority distributed substantively according to the type of rule. Different types of rule will exist in different 'orders' to which one 'orients' one's behaviour. This will thus afford a differential 'probability' that differing types of command under differing conditions of 'rule' will be obeyed. Such commands would be authorized and made legitimate by the rule. They would be 'authoritative' commands, submission to which we would call 'authority'.

It was this idea of legitimacy with which Weber classified types of organization in terms of belief: 'the foundation of all authority, and hence of all compliance with orders, is a belief in prestige, which operates to the advantage of the ruler or rulers' (Weber, 1947, p. 382). Different forms of belief in the legitimacy of authority are associated with different authority structures and hence with different organizational forms.

Weber identified three major types of belief, rule and authority. The first was that obedience was justified in terms of a belief in the sacred or extraordinary characteristics of the person giving the order. This was the type of authority which Weber termed 'charismatic'. Second, a command might be obeyed because of the weight of reverence for tradition – what Weber termed 'traditional authority'. Third, and this is the most important for contemporary organization theory, people might obey orders because they believed that the person giving the order was acting in accordance with their duties as stipulated in a code of legal rules and regulations. This form of obedience depended upon five related beliefs. Following Albrow (1970, p. 43) we can summarize these in an abbreviated form as:

1   that a legal code can be established which can claim obedience from members of the organization;
2   that the law is a system of abstract rules; these rules are applied to particular cases, and that administration looks after the interests of the organization within the limits of the law;
3   that the man exercising authority also obeys this impersonal order;
4   that only *qua* member does the member obey the law;

5   that obedience is due not to the person who holds authority
but to the impersonal order which has granted him this position.

Albrow (1970, pp. 43–4) notes that on 'the basis of these
conceptions of legitimacy Weber was able to formulate eight
propositions about the structuring of legal authority systems'.
These propositions are that:

1   Official tasks are organized on a continuous, regulated basis.
2   These tasks are divided into functionally distinct spheres,
each furnished with the requisite authority and sanctions.
3   Offices are arranged hierarchically, the rights of control
and complaint between them being specified.
4   The rules according to which work is conducted may be either
technical or legal. In both cases trained men are necessary.
5   The resources of the organization are quite distinct from
those of the members as private individuals.
6   The office holder cannot appropriate his office.
7   Administration is based on written documents and this tends
to make the office (*bureau*) the hub of modern organization.
8   Legal authority systems can take many forms, but are seen
at their purest in a bureaucratic administrative staff.

The presence of the five conceptions of legitimacy and the eight
principles of authority do not, in themselves, signify the existence of
a bureaucracy. For instance, one might have a bureaucratic administrative staff where the leadership is based not on legal-rational
precepts, but whose authoritative rule is charismatic. Bureaucracy,
in its most developed and rational form, necessarily presupposed
the previous conceptions of legitimacy and authority and can be
characterized in terms of the following characteristics:

1   The staff members are personally free, observing only the
impersonal duties of their offices.
2   There is a clear hierarchy of offices.
3   The functions of the offices are clearly specified.
4   Officials are appointed on the basis of a contract.
5   They are selected on the basis of a professional qualification,
ideally substantiated by a diploma gained through examination.
6   They have a money salary, and usually pension rights. The
salary is graded according to position in the hierarchy. The
official can always leave the post and, under certain circumstances, it may also be terminated.
7   The official's post is his sole or major occupation.
8   There is a career structure and promotion is possible either
by seniority or merit, and according to the judgment of
superiors.

9   The official may appropriate neither the post nor the resources which go with it.
10   He is subject to a unified control and disciplinary system (Albrow, 1970, pp. 44–5).

Bureaucratic organization is not a distinctively modern phenomenon, as Mouzelis (1975) recognizes in the interesting introduction to the second edition of his *Organization and Bureaucracy*, where he draws upon recent historical sociology to construct a description of the development of the bureaucratization (and on occasions de-bureaucratization) of the state. Weber (1948, p. 204) argues that bureaucracy exists 'in ever purer forms' in 'the modern European states and, increasingly, all public corporations since the time of princely absolution . . . the larger modern capitalist enterprise, the more so as it becomes greater and more complicated'. Weber advances a specific reason why this should be so:

The decisive reason for the advance of bureaucratic organiza-tion has always been its purely technical superiority over any other form of organization. The fully developed bureaucratic mechanism compares with other organizations exactly, as does the machine with the non-mechanical modes of production (Weber, 1948, p. 214).

The emergence of this form of rationality, the modern bureau-cratic organization, is 'demanded', says Weber: 'The peculiarity of modern culture, and specifically of its technical and economic basis, demands this very "calculability" of results' (Weber, 1948, p. 215). More specifically:

Today it is primarily the capitalist market economy which demands the official business of the administration be discharged precisely, unambiguously, continuously, and with as much speed as possible. Normally, the very large modern capitalist enter-prises are themselves unequalled modes of strict bureaucratic organization. Business management throughout rests on increas-ing precision, steadiness and above all, the speed of operations. . . . Bureaucratization offers above all the optimum possibility for carrying through the principle of specializing administrative functions according to purely objective considerations. Individual performances are allocated to functionaries who have specialized training and who by practice learn more and more. The 'objective' discharge of business primarily means a dis-charge of business according to calculable rules and without regard for persons (Weber, 1948, p. 215).

As we discussed in the last chapter, in his *General Economic History* (1923) Weber enumerates a number of factors which constitute this 'peculiarity of modern culture', this 'capitalist market economy', with a set of factors which include: the existence of a 'formally free' labour force; the appropriation and concentration of the physical means of production as disposable private property; the representation of share rights in organizations and property ownership; and the 'rationalization' of various institutional areas such as the market, technology and the law. In particular, rationalization of the market would depend upon the existence of an economic surplus and its exchange in monetary terms as 'normal preconditions' for this market. And in turn the market is the historical product not of reason, but of might: 'money prices are the product of conflicts of interest and compromise' (Weber, 1948, p. 211). The rationalization of work, argues Weber, is to be found in its most extreme form in the American system of scientific management which 'enjoys the greatest triumphs in the rational conditioning and training of work performances' (Weber, 1948, p. 261). These 'triumphs' are those of 'dehumanization', and derive from the 'special' virtue and 'specific nature' of bureaucratic, rational organization: 'Its specific nature, which is welcomed by capitalism, develops the more perfectly the more bureaucracy is "dehumanized" . . . this is the specific nature of bureaucracy and it is appraised as its special virtue' (Weber, 1948, pp. 215–16).

It is not surprising that Weber found this 'dehumanization' in its 'most extreme form' in 'the American system of scientific management' because this system was the apotheosis of the modern system of capitalism which was, in Weber's somewhat idealist formulation, the bearer of the underlying and defining spirit (*geist*) of modernity: rational organization. It was in this 'idealist' context that we have argued that although Weber could point toward the substantive irrationality of formal rationality in despair, he was unable to offer any systematic analysis of the process whereby this transformation occurred. In some respects Marx and Engels might appear similar. For instance, they wrote in *The Communist Manifesto* (1969) of capitalisms' progressive quality in as much as it rescued people from the 'idiocy' of rural life. On the other hand, the capitalist mode of production was seen as itself the embodiment of a fundamental irrationality. This irrationality was an immanent feature of the underlying principle of organization of the capitalist mode of production. This principle of organization was one of increasingly 'socialized' production coupled with an increasingly 'private' appropriation of profit by fewer and more concentrated elements of capital. The consequence of this process is the anarchy of the market. The importance of this divergence between Marx's and Weber's analyses of the phenomenon of rationality is crucial in comprehending the American system of scientific management. Weber can only analyse why scientific management occurred where and when it did in terms of *the irresistible advance of 'rationalization'*:

> No special proof is necessary to show that military discipline is the ideal model for the modern capitalist factory, as it was for the ancient plantation. In contrast to the plantation, organizational discipline in the factory is founded upon a completely rational basis. With the help of appropriate methods of measurement, the optimum profitability of the individual worker is calculated like that of any material means of production. On the basis of this calculation the American system of 'scientific management' enjoys the greatest triumphs in the rational conditioning and training of work performances. The final consequences are drawn from the mechanization and discipline of the plant, and the psycho-physical apparatus of man is completely adjusted to the demands of the outer world, the tools, the machines, in short, to an individual 'function'. The individual is shorn of his natural rhythm as determined by the structure of his organism: his psycho-physical apparatus is atuned to a new rhythm through a methodical specialization of separately functioning muscles, and an optimal economy of forces is established corresponding to the conditions of work. This whole process of rationalization, in the factory as elsewhere, and especially in the bureaucratic state machine, parallels the centralization of the material implements of organization in the discretionary power of the overlord. The ever-widening grasp of discipline irresistibly proceeds with the rationalization of the supply of economic and political demands (Weber, 1948, pp. 261–2).

The emergence of scientific management and the control of the labour process

In contrast to Weber's insistence on the irresistible advance of discipline and rationalization, we would wish to argue that the scientific management movement appeared when it did because of problems posed for capitalist enterprise by the organization of labour. This problem of organization was one of *control*: how 'to provide a really effective general mechanism for keeping labour hard at work' (Hobsbawm, 1975, p. 221). What scientific management provided was a bureaucratization of the structure of control that lacked any conception of a career in the Weberian sense of bureaucracy. It is indeed 'de-humanized'. No individual human potentialities would enable any particularly skilled worker to develop any creative capacities. These would remain captive and stunted. Indeed, this was a deliberate function of de-skilling (see Littler, 1978, pp. 192–4).

Hitherto, the mechanisms of control had been fairly simple, in England at least: the existence of the reserve army of the unemployed, the constant insecurity of unemployment and the misery of poverty on the negative side; and on the positive side, the existence of piece-work. It had not always been like this: 'In eighteenth-century England workers expected to get a fair day's wage in return for a fair day's work and when there was some dispute about what was "fair" in this context they expected the Justice of the Peace to arbitrate by fixing wages' (Deane, 1973, p. 219). This bargaining tended to work in the employer's favour.

> For the buyers in the labour market operated on the principle of buying in the cheapest market and selling in the dearest, though sometimes ignorant of proper cost accounting methods. But the sellers were not normally asking the maximum wage which the traffic would bear and offering in return the minimum quantity of labour they could get away with. They were trying to earn a decent living as human beings. They were perhaps trying to 'better themselves'. In brief, though naturally not insensitive to the difference between lower and higher wages, they were engaged in human life rather than in an economic transaction. . . . Increasingly, during our period (1848–75) the wage relationship was transformed into a pure market relationship, a cash-nexus (Hobsbawm, 1975, pp. 222–3, 218).

The development of the cash-nexus as the normal form of labour-control was assisted by the economic expansion of the period from 1850 to the time of the Great Depression of the 1870s, out of which, as an antidote, 'scientific management' or Taylorism, as it is sometimes called, was to emerge.

The Great Depression (arguments about the causes of which may be found in Peter Mathias's *The First Industrial Nation* (1969)) dominated the period from 1873 to the 1890s.

The Great Depression cannot be explained in purely British terms for it was a world-wide phenomenon – not simply of stagnation, because it saw extraordinary advances in the USA, Germany and Scandinavia. It marks the end of one phase of economic development (the earliest, British phase) and the start of another. Broadly speaking, the mid-nineteenth-century boom in the development of British capitalism – its second phase, after the initial consolidation of capital in the post-Napoleonic-wars period of the 1820s – was due to the initial, or virtually initial industrialization of the main 'advanced' economies outside Britain and the opening up of new areas of primary production and agriculture, based on the extension of steam technology: railways and steamships. The influx of cheap raw materials and agricultural produce enormously stimulated the mid-nineteenth-century British economy, but in the long run could only do it harm.

For one thing, the sharp reduction in costs both in industry and transport through technological innovations, while it opened up vast new areas of primary production, also caused a fall in prices. In fact, during the Great Depression, the general price level dropped by about a third; and this also meant that the general level of overseas demand declined as well, because foreign agricultural and extractive capitalists were earning less.

In addition, the benefits of the first phase of industrialization were declining. The technologies established in the earlier phases of capitalist development were not as competitive in an era when the market – at least, the domestic market – had not increased sufficiently to keep pace with the rate of production. In other words, there was a glut of production at prices the market could not readily afford, of things it did not appear to need, and at costs which the capitalist could not absorb if he was to stay in business. In fact, many of them did not. The period between 1870 and 1900 is the first great merger boom, during which many smaller firms went to the wall and an increasing concentration of capital occurred.

The picture is this: declining demand; saturated existing markets; and increasing costs of production, relatively, as less is produced and sold. The inflated super-profits of the earlier stages of capitalist development declined, squeezed between price-reducing competition and increasingly expensive and mechanized plant. This entailed increasingly large and inelastic overheads, producing a situation in which business men searched anxiously for a way out.

There were several exit-routes, pioneered at roughly the same time in different countries:

1 The creation of a high tariff protectionist economy (as in twentieth-century Australia) to protect both domestic agriculture and industrial markets; e.g., France, Germany, USA.
2 Innovations and changes in the technological basis of the economy; e.g., the rise of optics, chemistry and electrical engineering in Germany in particular,
3 Imperialism: with the depression the system of the capitalist world economy was fully cemented. The depression was one in which a 'paralysing decline of the rate of profit' was a 'root cause' (Sohn-Rethel, 1976, p. 28) due to the emergence of industrial capitalism on a global, rather than a mainly British scale.

The post-liberal era was one of international competition between rival national economies: the British, the German, the North American; a competition sharpened by the difficulties which firms within each of these economies now discovered, during the period of depression, in making adequate profits (Hobsbawm, 1975, p. 304).

Economic growth developed into economic struggle, on both the domestic and the international fronts. This struggle seemed to offer the bourgeoisie a way out of the depressed economic conditions.

In Britain the way out was primarily through the economic (and, increasingly, the political) conquest of hitherto unexploited markets in the world economy. There were two of these: the vast untapped proletarian and lower-middle-class domestic market; and the vast untapped markets of Africa, Asia and Latin America.

Each is a form of expansion of capital through strategies of *imperialism*. On the one hand, one captures, conquers and rules foreign markets on a co-operative national basis; the state preserves a sphere for its own capital to operate in. On the other hand, these capitals attempt to capture, conquer and rule the domestic markets on, initially, a competitive, but increasingly a co-operative basis. Domestic conquest primarily occurred through the growth of the mass media of communication.

4   In the USA, where this expansion of media colonization has been described by Ewen (1976), it occurred not only in the context of North American penetration of the markets and control over the raw materials of Latin America, but also the related development of a high-wages, high-profits policy of organization (also see Rose, 1975, p. 55). This was achieved through cost-cutting and demand-creation as twin strategies: first, through the strategy of industrial re-organization in a traditionally high-wage economy; and second, through the penetration of the domestic market that these high wages created via the rapidly developing mass media as a vehicle both for advertising commodities and training consumers in their consumption (see Ewen, 1976). The cost-cutting and high-wage side of the strategy was achieved through the development of mass-production methods and technology, notably the assembly line, and through 'Taylorism' or 'scientific management', as a system for its implementation and control. Taylorism developed as a way of attempting to quicken the rate of exploitation of labour in the production process, through the reorganization of the exchange relationship at work. In addition, towards the end of the century trade unionism began to expand rapidly in the USA. Rose (1975, pp. 55–6) links this rapid development, which was of the order of a 500 per cent growth in trade union membership from 1897 to 1904,

to the close of the frontier, and with it, the decreasing possibility of individualist exits from a collectively experienced situation. It was the development of unionism, in particular, which persuaded employers to turn their attention more to the problem of labour control. It became clear that employers had labour problems which required some form of intervention on their part if the 'paralysing decline of the rate of profit' was not to prove cataclysmic.

In a period in which the rate of exploitation of labour and the rate of exploitation of surplus value by capital are in decline, the type of labour control which is most readily enforced by the power of ownership is compulsion: work on the owner's terms or no work at all. Increasingly, these terms become ones in which 'the quality and intensity of the labour are here controlled by the form in which the wages of labour are paid' and so 'supervision is to a considerable extent rendered superfluous. Piece-work rates, therefore, form the groundwork of the modern system of domestic industry . . . and also of a hierarchically organized system of exploitation and subjugation' (Marx, 1974, p. 604). Marx (1974, p. 607) argued 'that piece-wage rates are the form of wages most suitable to the capitalist method of production'. As Hobsbawm summarizes the advantages, they were that piece-wages

> provided a genuine incentive for the worker to intensify his labour and thus raise his productivity, a guarantee against slacking, an automatic device for reducing the wage-bill in times of depression, as well as a convenient method – by the cutting of piece-rates – to reduce labour costs and to prevent wages from rising higher than was thought necessary or proper. It divided workers from one another, since their earnings might vary widely even within the same establishment, or different types of labour might be paid in entirely different ways (Hobsbawm, 1975, p. 219).

But there were also disadvantages:

> The trouble was that (where it was not already part of tradition) the introduction of piece-work was often resisted, especially by the skilled men, and that it was complex and obscure not only for the workers, but for employers who often had only the haziest idea of what production norms to set (Hobsbawm, 1975, p. 219).

It was Frederick Winslow Taylor who was to help them with this, through producing a body of knowledge which was both an ideological (effort-determining) and a technical (job-designing) control of the labour process, and which re-emphasized the solitary and individual nature of the worker as against the collectivist ideology of trade unionism.

F. W. Taylor

Taylor began work as an apprentice (although he came from a wealthy background; see Brown, 1977, for details), but his career developed sufficiently for him to become chief engineer of a large steel company. He was a member and subsequently president of the American Society of Mechanical Engineers. It is interesting to note that the formation of this association (at about the same times as the inception of the British Institute of Mechanical Engineers) displayed the increasing tendency for a closer examination of industrial organizations. Engineers became key people within organizations, and were instrumental in the design of both the technical and social structure of industrial organizations.

Even before his rise to eminence, Taylor had developed and espoused his ideas on management. It would appear that his techniques had been applied initially in the 1880s. But it was in 1889 that he formed his own firm specifically to use his techniques and ideas of management. Taylor is today best known for his book *Principles of Scientific Management* (1911), although his first publication was a paper he read to the American Society of Engineers in 1895, entitled 'A piece rate system, being a step towards partial solution of the labour problem'.

Taylor was the founder of 'scientific management', the time and motion study of operations which derives its claim to science from 'accurate and scientific study of unit times' (Taylor, 1903, p. 58). What the technique of scientific management does is 'aim to increase productivity by improving the performance of the workers' (Anastasi, 1964, p. 173) by taking given manual operations and collapsing them into their component smallest and simplest elements of motion. In his *Principles of Scientific Management* Taylor had three basic aims in order to increase the productivity of labour:

1   To point out, through a series of simple illustrations, the great loss which the whole country is suffering through inefficiency in almost all of our daily acts.
2   To try to convince the reader that the remedy for this inefficiency lies in systematic management, rather than in searching for some extraordinary man.
3   To prove that the best management is a true science, resting upon clearly defined laws, rules and principles, as a foundation (Taylor, 1911, p. 1).

Starting with the basic assumption that people are lazy and will attempt to get away with doing the minimum, Taylor advocated the use of an empirical approach to the management of industry. This empirical approach entailed the utilization of a number of specific techniques. These techniques could be applied to any industrial situation, since any enterprise was subject to certain basic laws in its operation. There were always certain constant and regular features in organizations. These had to be discovered empirically – through observation and experimentation – so that then the optimal performance could be achieved within the enterprise. In order to gain something of the flavour of Taylor's ideas it is useful to summarize briefly his areas of concern and recommendations.

1   *The division of labour*   Not only should there be an extensive division of labour on the shop floor (as Adam Smith had advocated a century before), this should be extended to the managerial echelons. The main function of management should be future planning. In this way it was then possible for the worker to concentrate wholly on carrying out the task. He believed that there were distinct personality types; one would lend itself well to the planning function (manager), while the other was more suitable to the doing function (worker). As well as this broad division of task, Taylor also recommended a minute division of tasks in such a way that each individual, both worker and manager, should be responsible for one function only. Taylor argued that up till then the worker had been left on his own to organize his work-life as best he saw fit. With the application of scientific methods, management could accurately specify each task.

2   *Work measurement*   Taylor advocated the use of time study in order that the optimal way of carrying out a task could be discovered. This he saw as being the essential component of scientific management. It involved measuring and studying what he referred to as 'unit times'.

Under capitalism, Taylor argued that the worker had to learn his task himself or through imitation. Both of these approaches meant that the worker often devised an inappropriate method of working. In order to overcome the inefficiency of this approach, Taylor prescribed that all tasks should be divided and that there should be a description of these tasks. Having made these descriptions, the most efficient combination of tasks could be worked out to provide for optimal efficiency. Once achieved, it was then management's task to train the worker in this most efficient *modus operandi.*

3   *Task prescriptions*   Not only should the tasks be minutely divided and the optimal method of achieving these tasks be described, the worker should also be given a clear description of what was required of him. Here Taylor stresses the planning

function of management in industrial enterprises, that tasks should be well planned in advance and that the worker be given written instructions concerning what his particular task was to be. In this way, it was argued, both the worker and manager had clearly laid down standards that facilitated work measurement.

4 *Incentive schemes* It was to be made clear to the worker that there was a price for each piece of work and that his pay was dependent upon his achieving the prescribed output. In the event of achieving a greater output then a bonus payment was operational. Taylor argued that the bonuses paid should be generous and consistent.

The example of the Dutchman, Schmidt, is often quoted as an illustration of the way in which the bonus system may operate. Through the scientific methods, Schmidt was able to receive a 60 per cent increase in his wages, achieved by shovelling 47½ tons instead of the previous 12½ tons of pig iron per day.

5 *Work as an individual activity* Taylor, unlike his human relations successors, was opposed to any kind of group activity. Part of Taylor's philosophy was that people are motivated by personal ambition and that once put into a group the individual loses his or her individual drive. The influence of the group is such as to make one less productive. He argued that female workers were particularly prone to such pressures and indeed separated them in such a way that verbal interaction was impossible. Taylorism was thus an early example of the sexist bias of organization theory (see Wolff, 1977).

6 *Motivation* We have seen that Taylor argued that self-interest was the over-riding driving force for most people. Consequently, what workers wanted was higher wages: the payment of such was the only way to increase productivity. Equally, Taylor recognized that for most individuals, work was abhorrent and was something to be avoided or got over in the shortest possible time. At one stage he argued that once the worker had completed his allotted task he should be allowed to go home, although he never put this idea into practice.

7 *Individual ability* Taylor made a distinction between the abilities of workers and managers. The basic difference, as he saw it, was that workers were unable to defer any gratification; they existed for the present rather than for any future reward. Such a view is consistent with Taylor's ideas concerning control within the enterprise that are discussed later. One method of control in

organizations is through the use of future expectations. This, of necessity, involves commitment and co-operation on the part of the individual. Taylor argued that assumptions such as these cannot be made about workers. Since their activities are closely controlled there is not the organizational commitment. Equally, the absence of any role discretion negates the possibility of organizational commitment.

8 *The role of management* We have already seen some of the distinctions that Taylor drew between worker and manager roles. The crucial thing for management was that it was forward-looking, had the ability to plan, could organize labour and could supervise effectively. He advocated authoritarian methods of management in that the organizational rules, standards, methods of working and so on should be enforced. Furthermore, the role of 'generalized wiseman' should be adopted by managers because they had the vision to understand what was good for workers.

9 *Trade unions* Predictably, Taylor was against the trade union movement, largely because he regarded trade unions as unnecessary under his system of work activity. The employers, he argued, were on the same side as the workers. Each was working towards the same goal. The widespread acceptance of the principles of scientific management would reduce, if not totally negate, conflict between workers and management. This was particularly the case in issues arising from disputes over wage rates, since scientific management itself laid down what was a fair day's pay for a fair day's work through objective rational means.

10 *The development of management thinking* It is tautological to state that Taylor, through scientific management, saw the development of management as a science. Implied in this, however, is the idea that specific laws could be derived for management practice and that these laws would relate specifically to wage rates and ways of doing work. Arriving at these laws involved management in the use of scientific method. Taylor's engineering background is of importance here since he thought that management could acquire the same scientific status as engineering.

These, briefly, constitute the main concerns and areas of activity of scientific management as espoused by Taylor. It is now possible to turn to an analysis of the validity of these ideas and to place them within an organizational context.

Braverman (1974, pp. 113–19) argues that an analysis of Taylor's work enables us to distinguish three general principles of scientific management.

90

1 The principle of dissociation of the labour process from the skills of the workers In other words, the actual task undertaken by the worker is separate from the knowledge that a worker might possess, particularly that knowledge deriving from a craft or traditional process. The labour process, therefore, is dependent upon managerial practices rather than workers' abilities.

2 The principle of the separation of conception from execution By this Braverman refers to the division under scientific management of manual and non-manual labour. As we have seen above, the organization of the work was to be solely the prerogative of management. The worker could not undertake this work because 'the possessors of labour-time (the workers) cannot themselves afford to do anything with it but sell it for their means of subsistence'. Through this process the worker is 'cheapened' and there is the utmost managerial control. For these reasons there must be the separation of conception and execution.

3 The principle of the use of monopoly over knowledge to control each step of the labour process and its mode of execution Clearly, this principle is logically derived from the previous two.

These principles and the areas of concern noted above lead us to argue that Taylor's ideas are basically concerned with control in the organization, with extracting co-operation from the work force, and the absolute reduction of conflict. In this sense, it is the case that Taylorism was the articulation, the mouthpiece, of much of what capitalist enterprises had been attempting since the genesis of capitalism. Here was a set of principles, a checklist of ideas, an inventory of guidelines that enabled management to behave in the way it did, but with an air of scientific respectability. And one of the fundamental tenets of this method was the increasing control over the work and the work force that was concentrated in management hands. (The reader may also consult Rose (1975, Part I), for a further view of Taylor.)

What is more, Taylorism, as Weber recognized, offered the most thorough de-humanization of work ever seen under capitalism. This was principally because of the fact that its 'scientific standards' of measurement of human labour-time derive from the mechanical and technological aspects of the operations being analysed. Indeed, the operative principle of scientific management is to measure the unity of labour and machinery in their productive application. This is not a unity of equals, however, for human power is to be subordinated to mechanical power:

The tool integrated into the system of machinery, becomes a

'machine-tool', a machine which incorporates social relations. Machinery is not neutral, because the machine incorporates in its mode of operation the dexterity and the skill of the individual worker who is henceforth deprived of his skill and subordinated, from the point of view of social production, to the machine, which he can only serve, set in motion, and regulate. . . . Capitalist development of machinery in the factory constitutes, on the one hand, a massive 'de-skilling' of production workers, together with a loss of autonomy in the reproduction of labour power, and on the other hand an 'over-skilling' of a small number of workers responsible for innovation, organization, regulation and repair (Palloix, 1976, p. 53).

Hence, as workers responsible for control of the 'methods' of production – the skills of the organization – these latter workers are 'Taylorized' into positions of power capacity in the formal structure of the organization.

Scientific management in context

The first stages of organizational development in the early phase of the industrial revolution were based on a relatively simple application of craft skills and ingenuity in a task-continuous setting. Those early developments which led to the growth of the textiles, railway and shipbuilding organizations typical of this first phase of British industrial development were scientifically archaic.

Yet the very scale of the railway, and the transport revolution it inaugurated, made scientific technology more necessary, and the expansion of the world economy increasingly presented industry with strange natural raw materials which required scientific processing for effective use (for example, rubber and petroleum). . . . The basic institution of science, the research laboratory – especially the university research laboratory – had also developed between, say, 1790 and 1830. Scientific technology not only became more desirable, but also possible.

The major technical advances of the second half of the nineteenth century were therefore essentially scientific; that is to say, they required at the very least some knowledge of recent developments in pure science for original inventions, a far more consistent process of scientific experiment and testing for their development, and an increasingly close and continuous link between industrialists, technologists and professional scientists and scientific institutions (Hobsbawm, 1969, pp. 172–3).

The fruits of this collaboration were to be found not only in industry based on the development of new sciences of trans-formation (Karpik, 1977) in which the institutions of the market and the laboratory became fused (e.g., optics, Zeiss; chemistry, Mond; electrical engineering, Edison), but also in the refinement of existing techniques, notably in metallurgy, which, with the development of steel alloys that were sufficiently hard and sharp to cut steel at high mechanical speeds, led to the increasing utilization of machine-tools for mass production (at first for the state in the field of armaments). Mass-production requires mass markets, and these were to be found initially in the expanding high-wage economy (because of permanent nineteenth-century US labour shortages) of the USA.

Not only was the labour in short supply, its skills, where they existed, were not pre-requisites of production on a mass scale; indeed, skilled labour was not to be encouraged in certain respects, since it was 'the best, soberest, and ablest workers' who were the most likely to form trade unions (Hobsbawm, 1975, p. 221), and hence, because of their *market power*, based on the only *resource* they owned, their *skill*, bite into the accumulation of surplus-value by organizing for a greater exchange-value. Palloix describes the factors at work in this situation:

> In the US at the end of the nineteenth century, the skilled workers, those with trade or craft training, together with those immigrants who had experience in trade-union and political activities, engaged in a political struggle which was widespread enough to form an obstacle to the valorization and accumulation of capital. At the same time there was arriving from Europe a mass of peasant immigrants who could not be incorporated just as they were into the process of production. The labour process therefore had to be modified. On the one hand they had to be adapted so as to make possible the de-skilling of the 'craft' workers, and on the other hand they had to be adapted so as to allow the employment of workers who were unskilled, or who could be very easily rendered unskilled
> (Palloix, 1976, p. 57).

The remedy to this was to be the analysis and breakdown of human skills, parallel and in addition to the developing machine process. It was in the metallurgical industry of the USA that these first systematic attempts at *organization* were conducted by Taylor.

With Sohn-Rethel (1976, p. 33) it is proposed that Taylorism, at least in its own explicit principles, albeit that its particular 'defects' have been criticized and refined (e.g., Barnes and Mundel, 1938; Hecker *et al.*, 1956; Farmer, 1923), forms the basis of technical control and domination in task-discontinuous organizations of all kinds. The stated intention of the recommendations contained in his main work, *On the Art of Cutting Metals* (Taylor, 1907), was that control of their labour-power be taken out of the hands of workers in terms of their discretionary knowledge, in order to centralize control within the organization in a few men. The impetus for his work was precisely to counter the discretionary knowledge-power which skilled labourers have in the organizational setting.

> In the fall of 1880, the machinists in the small machine shop of the Midvale Steel Company, Philadelphia, most of whom were working on piecework in making locomotive tyres, car axles, and miscellaneous forgings had combined to do only a certain number of pieces per day on each type of work. The writer, who was the newly appointed foreman of the shop, realized that it was possible for the men to do in all cases much more work per day than they were accomplishing. He found, however, that his efforts to get the men to increase their output were blocked by the fact that his knowledge of just what combination of depth of cut, feed and cutting speed would in each case do the work in the shortest time, was much less accurate than that of the machinists who were combined against him (Taylor, 1907; cited in Sohn-Rethel, 1976, pp. 33–4).

To achieve the knowledge that he required in order 'to get the men to increase their output', Taylor began his series of experiments into scientific management, the findings of which were designed

> to take all the important decisions and planning which vitally affect the output of the shop out of the hands of the workmen, and centralize them in a few men, each of whom is especially trained in the art of making those decisions and in seeing that they are carried out, each man having his own particular function in which he is supreme, and not interfering with the functions of other men (Taylor, 1907, section 126; cited in Sohn-Rethel, 1976, p. 34).

Taylor regarded the most important of his experiments as the development of slide rules which enable management, without consultation with the work force 'to fix a daily task with a definite time allowance for each man who is running a machine-tool, and to pay the man a bonus for rapid work' (Taylor, 1907, section 51). The consequence of this was to be the realization of his original intentions:

> The gain from these slide rules is far greater than that of all the

other improvements combined, because it accomplishes the original object for which in 1880 the experiments were started; i.e., that of taking the control of the machine shop out of the hands of the many workmen, and placing it completely in the hands of the management, thus superseding the 'rule of thumb' by scientific control. Under our system the workman is told minutely just what he is to do and how he is to do it; and any improvement which he makes upon the orders given him is fatal to success (Taylor, 1907, sections 52; 118; cited in Sohn-Rethel, 1976, p. 34).

At the heart of Taylor's recommendations was his realization that modern capitalism, in its attempt to maintain the long-run growth of profits had only been able to do this by increasing the organic composition of capital, such that as a primary consideration for maximal profitability, this organic composition has to be constantly operative in order to produce a sufficient volume of output. Thus, surplus value realization depends on the production and marketing of a constantly high volume of output, rather than on low wages *per se*. The mode of accumulation of surplus value has shifted from absolute to relative strategies, and in this situation, as he analysed it in *Shop Management* (1903, pp. 21–2): 'High wages and low labour cost are not only compatible, but are, in the majority of cases, mutually conditional.' This is made possible through the relation of wages to output, which in turn is made possible by the separation of mental and manual labour, such that control of both the means *and* the method of production is vested in mental labour to 'become the instrument of the domination of capital over labour' (Sohn-Rethel, 1976, p. 37).

Taylor, then, was important in his own time for the reasons stated above. He has also had a powerful impact upon the development of the industrial social sciences as well as management thinking. It is undoubtedly true that he was amongst the first to recognize how important is the social organization of an industrial enterprise. He recognized the necessity of spending both time and resources on this. What is regarded by many commentators as his significant contribution is the use he made of this recognition in the manipulation of the social resources.

Not only did his ideas achieved a wide currency, where they were applied they also did much to re-shape the structure of organizations. The more extensive division of labour, the introduction of planning techniques, the changes in occupational composition with the introduction of new specialists, and so on, all played their part in introducing new forms of work organization, or, at the very least, providing a *raison d'être* for existing organizational forms.

Scientific management, when it is being considered in the organizations literature, usually comes under the heading of a machine model of organizational functioning. By this is meant that organizations are approached by the adherents of scientific management in a mechanistic manner. Since organization theory is concerned with both the structure and process of organizations, it means that any theory must have within it an analysis of the personnel who comprise the organization and of their motivations. In the case of scientific management, the emphasis upon standardization and formalization in the organization had led to what in contemporary literature is referred to as the instrumental aspects of human behaviour. Nevertheless, there is an emphasis, as we have already seen, upon the individual as a unit of analysis, albeit in terms of the individual actions that can be undertaken to achieve optimal output.

In his analysis, Taylor presents the individual in the same way as he would an item of machinery. The worker thereby is perceived as a means of production. In just the same way that management's task is to maximize output from capital equipment, under the principles of scientific management it is also part of the managerial task to maximize the output of the human component. Pursuing this analogy, in the same way that there is no psychological involvement with capital equipment, similarly there is none with human assets; as machines are fuelled by coal, gas or petrol, so humans are regarded as being fuelled by money, in the work situation. In scientific management, there is no regard, or perhaps recognition, that the individual affects and is affected by others, his culture and the social structure. Such issues were considered irrelevant to the concerns of scientific management. As a major criticism of scientific management it is the case that both the sociological and psychological aspects of individuals in organizations were neglected.

The more fundamental point is made by Braverman (1974, ch. 5) when he remarks that the development of scientific management was coincidental with the scientific-technical revolution. More than this, though, is the fact that scientific management emerged at the time that capitalist development had reached the stage of requiring organizational changes in the functioning of industrial enterprises. Furthermore, there were, as we have already seen, fundamental changes taking place within the structure of the working classes in the industrial nations, largely arising from the development and increasing influence of trade unions.

At its base, scientific management is concerned with the question of organizational/managerial control. This is demonstrated most clearly in the way in which the production process is so tightly controlled that the possibility of employee discretion is almost non-existent. Braverman argues, however, that the over-riding importance of control, together with the separation of manual and 'mental' tasks, still enables the labour process to retain its unity.

> Production has now been split in two and depends upon the activities of both groups. Inasmuch as the mode of production has been driven by capitalism to this divided condition, it has separated the two aspects of labour: *but both remain necessary to production, and in this the labour process retains its unity*. . . . The separation of hand and brain is the most decisive single step in the division of labour taken by the capitalist mode of production (Braverman, 1974, p. 126).

Of course, the whole economic and managerial structure of capitalism facilitated this development, but scientific management gave to capitalism the 'scientific' legitimacy that it required. We can argue from this that the modern large corporation is in a line of direct descent from the early ideas of scientific management, especially those ideas emphasizing the planning function within the organization. Taylorism, in modified forms, has become the orthodox doctrine of technical control in contemporary industrial capitalism, based on the high-wages policy. And not only in capitalist organizations. As a practical way in which any management or administration can gain control over the labour process it has become the basis of organization in countries such as the USSR, and in nationalized non-productive sectors, such as hospitals in the British Health Service.

Braverman points to the decline in craftsmanship that was heralded by the rise of scientific management. To some extent he is correct, but it needs to be recalled that craftsmanship was very much in decline from the origins of the capitalist mode of production. Perhaps it is fairer to say that scientific management sounded the virtual death-knell of craftsmanship as it had been known prior to the advent of capitalism. However, as Monds (1976) and Littler (1978) have argued, job control by craftsmanship was limited in the USA and had, in fact, been eroded before the development of scientific management. The development of Taylorism was not so much from a simple craft system, but from forms of sub-contracting. This is not stressed by Braverman (1974). What is significant in Braverman's account, however, is his discussion of the separation of the individual between his craft and scientific development, where this craft basis existed. Merely by carrying out his trade, the craftsman needed to be aware of the technical and scientific developments germane to it. There was a link between technical knowledge and work. Against this, however, one might argue that as science developed at a hitherto unprece-

97

dented rate the possibility of any individual keeping abreast of relevant technical developments would have been minimal, but at the same time, subsequent scientific and technical developments were not oriented towards a unified labour process of mental/ manual labour, but were oriented more especially to its division.

The major opposition to scientific management came from trade unions. The turn of the century in most industrial or industrializing nations was a period in which trade unions grew rapidly and increased their power. The ideas of scientific management were obviously regarded as a threat by trade unionists.[1] They were obviously seen as being against the interests of workers. By the same token, the trade unions were criticized by Taylor for restrictive practices which he saw to be against the interests of workers. But the main brunt of the trade union opposition to scientific management was not in terms of the dehumanizing effects of the movement or of the work study practices as such. Rather, the primary opposition was to the decline of the craft skills and the control that previously workers had over their own work.

From scientific management to formal theories of administration

In that organization theory exists today with a body of theory coupled with an impressive amount of empirical findings (some would argue that the latter far outweighs the former), it is appropriate to talk of there being a history of organization theory. We have seen in the writings of Taylor the earliest significant contribution to organization theory (and, of course, to management thought). As with any history it is valid in the field of organization theory to talk of historical epochs. As such the writings of Taylor, chronologically and in terms of discipline development, belong to the first epoch. Also within this epoch it is possible to point to investigators such as Gulick and Urwick (1937), Mooney and Reiley (1931), and Weber (1947). This epoch is concerned with an approach to organizations that is often described as machine theory. Within machine theory there are, then, three distinct models of organization; that of scientific management described above exemplified in the work of Taylor (1911); that of the public administrators and specific management theorists (Gulick, Gilbreth, etc.); and that of a sociological input characterized initially by the work of Weber. At this stage the work of the formal theorists can briefly be examined.

The important difference between the formal theorists and Taylor lies in the focus of analysis. Taylor, as we have seen, was concerned with the worker above all else. The emphasis was upon the shop floor and with the techniques that management could employ to extract the greatest labour power and surplus value from employees. This left management in the position of having a set of principles laying down how to make its work force more productive, whilst possessing no body of knowledge that applied specifically from supervisory levels upwards in the organization hierarchy. This left a lacuna in the control of the organization structure. In this section, then, we can explore the works of those writers who took a managerial view of administration rather than one of the shop floor. As soon as scientific management principles were applied in industry it became clear that rationalization on the shop floor needed to be supplemented by rationalization throughout the whole enterprise, if the interests of profitable accumulation were to be fully serviced.

Henri Fayol

Fayol (1841–1925) is often regarded as the founder of this movement and certainly it is the case that large numbers of management writers since him have been greatly influenced by his work. To that extent, Fayol perhaps earns the title of the founder of modern management thought, particularly of what is normally regarded as the classical or universal school of management.

Coming hard on the heels of Taylor, Fayol in 1916 published his *Administration Industrielle et Generale* (see Fayol, 1949, for the English translation). Like Taylor, Fayol was trained as an engineer (in the mining industry: he worked for the French mining and metal-lurgical combine Commentry-Fourchamboult-Decazeville, first as an engineer, but from his early thirties onwards in general management), and became known as a successful administrator. A later follower of Fayol had the following to say about him:

> In the first quarter century of the scientific study of business management his is the only European figure worthy of a place beside that of F. W. Taylor. . . . Fayol showed beyond question . . . that better management is not merely a question of improving the output of labour and the planning of subordinate units of organization, it is above all a matter of closer study and more administrative training for the men at the top. Seldom in history can two men working in an identical field have differed so sharply in methods or in the details of their careers and yet have produced work which was so complementary (Urwick, 1947, p. 129).

Thus, in the same way that Taylor laid down his principles of scientific management Fayol laid down principles of management *per se*. These are: division of work; authority; discipline; unity of command; unity of direction, subordination of individual interests to the general interest; remuneration; centralization; line of authority; order; equity; stability of tenure; initiative; and esprit de corps. Of course, reading through this list one can question the extent to which the items can even be distinguished as principles. Indeed, Fayol himself is ambiguous in his writings as to what he means by these 'principles'. Some of them describe managerial activities, others lay down what managers should be doing, while again others exhort managers to behave in a certain way. They are obviously not principles in the sense of laying down precise ground-rules as to how managers should conduct their affairs to ensure the maximum efficiency. The important feature of Fayol's work, though, is that he did advocate the need for managers to learn and to be trained, and that managerial organization, just as much as 'worker organization', could be a valid subject for analysis. Also, as Urwick pointed out, the complementary nature of his work to that of Taylor is significant.

Mooney and Reiley

In their book *Onward Industry*! Mooney and Reiley (1931), two managers from General Motors, provided a conceptual framework laying down principles of management. From the point of view of the present work, their book has a certain relevance in that they attempt to provide an elaborate historical account of the genesis of management and management thought. In terms of their management principles, however, the crucial aspect of these is what they refer to as the *co-ordinative principle*. All of the other principles of management derive from this. As with Fayol, there appears to be some confusion over the use of the term 'principle' as we understand it today. What can be gleaned from their work is a set of statements showing the importance of leadership in organizations, that there must be an authority and that both of these functions require co-ordination. They proceed in the book with the 'scalar principle' – the process in organization whereby authority is co-ordinated from the top. Clearly, here they are recognizing that organizations are hierarchical both in form and structure.

In a later chapter we can see an early use of the term 'functional'. Mooney and Reiley refer to *the functional principle of organization* by which they mean that the objective of co-ordination is merely a correlation of functions. All jobs involve at least one of three functions: the determinative function (setting goals); the applicative function (acting purposively to achieve the goals); and the interpretative function (decision-making). Managers, they argue, must be aware of these functions and be prepared to discharge them where necessary. There is a complementary link here with scientific management in that Taylor suggested similar ideas in the productive system, whereas Mooney and Reiley concentrate upon administration.

One further aspect of their work relates to what they call *the staff function in organization*. They distinguish between the line and staff organization within an enterprise and show that line organization corresponds to the scalar chain referred to above and that each role in the staff organization has a certain line function which makes that role dependent upon another.

Gulick and Urwick

With these two writers we see a coming together of public administration (Gulick) and business administration (Urwick). Like other writers in formal administration, they were much influenced by Taylor and attempted to expand his ideas. They also built on the work of Fayol whom they saw as not having gone far enough in his analysis in that his principles of management did not have a wide validity. The basic aim of the work of Gulick and Urwick was to rationalize the work process by, wherever possible, bringing work together in a centralized area. In this way they argued that the division of labour within enterprises would be more effective than under other systems whilst at the same time maintaining the degree of specialization that was considered necessary for effective operation. Furthermore, such an approach would capitalize on labour-saving machinery and facilitate the introduction of mass-production techniques on a greater scale. An example of this approach can be seen in their proposals for centralized typing pools in organizations, or in the centralizing of engineering departments in manufacturing industry.

Like the other theorists of formal administration, they were also concerned to ensure that there was the greatest degree of homogeneity in individual tasks, certainly within each department. In this way, it was possible for management to combine both skills and production processes economically.

The authority relationships under this system were such that each collection of tasks brought together would be directed unitarily. In effect, this meant that there would be specialist authority positions concerned solely with the specialist departments. In short, this furthered the separation of mental and manual labour.

The primary emphasis in this work is clearly upon the division of labour. There was a recognition that the number of personnel that can be controlled by one individual is strictly limited, so that effective organization requires the existence of a division of labour in relation to authority.

There were seen to be four bases for grouping work units together in the way suggested above: the purpose to be served; the process to be used; the material to be handled (or clientele to be served); and the place where activities were to be carried out. If there was group specialization this would enable the group to strive towards a common objective, together with the fact that there was then direct accountability. The problem with this system is that no department in an organization can be autonomous in the way that Gulick and Urwick seemed to suggest. In any case the process of departmentalization leads to the existence of conflict between departments, particularly over the issue of access to scarce resources.

The general framework of the formal theorists

From this brief account of the work of some of the formal theorists of formal business and public administration (who are also dealt with in Pugh *et al.*, 1971) we can attempt to seek out the points of commonality between them and to discover what constitutes the so-called machine model of organization which developed from Taylor and scientific management.

A basic problem in this task is the fact that there is little consistency in the work of any of the writers; either between them or within them. As an illustration of this, take the notion of 'principle' that each was purportedly seeking. Mouzelis argues that there are three ways in which the term 'principle' is used by these formal theorists. Sometimes it has a descriptive connotation; it simply states the existence of a certain organization feature (e.g., the hierarchy principle). More rarely, it can express a relation between organization variables. Finally, and in its most current use, the term has a normative character: it is a guide to management action (Mouzelis, 1967, p. 92).

This semantic confusion is compounded by the fact that the validity and indeed the actual nature of the principles seem to be in some doubt. We see in the literature the principles sometimes being referred to as scientific laws with a universal validity, whereas in other cases the principles are distinguished as being merely ground rules with local application. Regarding their alleged 'scientificity' we can agree with Simon (1957). He comments on the fact that the principles are 'little more than ambiguous and mutually contradictory proverbs' (Simon, 1957, p. 240) and that, in fact, little account has been taken of the principles. They form neither a coherent conceptual pattern of determination nor an accurate description of concrete empirical reality. What has occurred, he says, has been a movement towards the study of conditions that are *conducive* to the application of principles rather than the actual application of principles themselves.

We have seen in the discussion so far that the most basic of the principles and those that appear to have an almost universal recognition by the formal theorists are those of unity of command and a hierarchy of authority. From these two, it follows that organizational authority goes hierarchically down the organization from top to bottom and that each organizational member receives instructions from only one source. Simon's response to this situation is to argue that it certainly makes sense to argue that there should be unity of command. However, consider the theoretical status of the 'unity of command'. This, in itself, does not deny the probability that 'decisional premises' can be accepted from various sources. So, empirically, for example, a worker in the production process can receive commands from one supervisor concerning productive output, whilst receiving commands from another supervisor concerning the maintenance of machinery (cf. Dunkerley, 1975, ch. 4). Hence, theoretically the concept is neither rigorous nor coherent.

Normally, it is stated in the principles that one function of the unity of command idea is to reduce, prevent or solve conflicts. This is stated in such a way as to convey the impression that this is the only means of doing so. One can think of examples, especially in the case of the armed forces, where there is obedience to all those of a certain rank and above, without there necessarily being the inherent conflict suggested by formal theorists. The 'principles' are neither universally empirically applicable nor theoretically coherent. As Simon points out, many of the concepts and principles are both ambiguous and contradictory. A small span of control is one of the recommendations that is made by a number of the writers, but this is contradictory to another principle that emerges concerning the desirability of a relatively flat organization structure in order to improve communications. Or take the bases for grouping work units that Gulick and Urwick recommend. Here, the purpose or process may, in fact, be the same activity when it is described subjectively by the individual undertaking the activity. Simon, in fact, states that there is no such thing as a single purpose organization; all that can be said is that there is a difference in degree between purpose and process. And again, clientele and place are components of the process and are normally assumed by it.

There is the further point made by March and Simon (1958) that organization analysts need to examine the economic costs of devising organization structures in the ways suggested by the formal theorists. For example, they suggest that as organizations become

103

larger and more complex the co-ordination costs become greater, whereas the advantages to be gained by specialization become smaller. Interestingly, in making the comment about 'economic costs' as a critique they themselves further exemplify the bias and interests of organization theory. Notice that they have no costs other than economic ones to enter on the debit ledger.

Clearly, there are limitations to the practical use of the principles of management and administration. One can also question the extent to which the principles have contributed to our knowledge about organizations. As Mouzelis points out:

> The principles . . . do not give the impression of a body of knowledge having a cumulative character; they rather give the image of a mosaic of principles, of definitions and redefinitions (Mouzelis, 1967, p. 94).

March and Simon see the drawbacks to the formal theories of administration in the following way:

> It is because activities are conditional, and not fixed in advance, that problems of organization . . . arise. For convenience we may make the following specifications, without interpreting them too strictly:
> (a) the times of occurrence of activities may be conditional on events external to the organization or events internal to the organization;
> (b) the appropriateness of a particular activity may be conditional on what other activities are being performed in various parts of the organization;
> (c) an activity elaborated in response to one particular function or goal may have consequences for other functions or goals (March and Simon, 1961, p. 27).

However, the principles, guidelines, concepts, etc. were not always wrong or inappropriate, given their 'control' function. Generally, they were inadequate beyond any very general level because of five factors:

1 Environmental or extra-organizational variables were largely ignored or, at most, taken as constants. Clearly a changing environment needs to be considered in terms of its impact upon the internal structure and functioning of the organization.

2 The exchanges that take place within an organization were largely ignored. An important consideration here is consideration of the influence of the wider political, legal and ideological spheres upon those individuals who are agents in the organization. The emphasis, then, was largely upon the physical component of the environment.

3   By concentrating upon homogeneity in organizations, particularly in terms of departmentalization, administrative theories have largely ignored the nature and influence of departmental interaction within organizations and the subsequent nature of conflict and co-operation.

4   The formal analysis of organizations gives rise to an impression of organizations as static entities incapable of changing through interaction with their environments.

5   The over-emphasis upon formal organization led to an almost total disregard of what was to become known as the 'informal' aspects of organizational functioning.

Although these formal theories of scientific management and administration do not have many supporters in today's ranks of social scientists concerned to analyse organizations, they have been enormously influential in shaping and structuring organizations historically, and in many cases, down to the present day.[2] Taylorism has been, and remains, the orthodox doctrine of technical control in many organizations in both capitalist countries and in Eastern Europe.

The social context of formal theorists of organization

Consider the social background of these early writers on management principles. Mooney and Reiley were managers in the expansionist General Motors in the early decades of the motor industry's development; Fayol was a manager in a conglomerate mining and metallurgical combine at the height of imperialism; Urwick was an officer in the army as well as in industry, and was also a director of the International Management Institute in Geneva, as well as heading a firm of management consultants with his colleague Brech; Gulick also shared the same bourgeois background in public administration. F. W. Taylor, the most interesting of these writers, is also the interesting exception. Taylor might well have followed in the footsteps of his father, an upper-middle-class Quaker from Philadelphia, and have taken up a career in law, after a period at Harvard. However, he did not. Instead of college he chose an apprenticeship in the firm of a family friend. This firm was the Midvale Steel Works, which he joined in 1878, rapidly becoming a foreman, then engineer, and later a consultant. Much of his success in these occupations can be credited to his period on the shop floor. It was there that he learnt the 'tricks' that he was later to oppose.

All of these men were writing in an era when the actual structures of modern organizations were being actively shaped by their managers, through the interventions of 'theories' designed and implemented by consultants such as these.

However, it is not just the bourgeoisie that has experience of organization. On those occasions when ideology has been defeated, however temporarily, and control seized, the working classes have also experienced organization as active agents rather than simply as 'the organized', more or less *under* control rather than *in* control. One neglected writer on organizations who also wrote from practical experience was Antonio Gramsci. Like Mooney and Reiley he was involved in the automobile industry, in his case Fiat of Turin, but unlike any of the other writers we have considered so far (apart from Marx) his involvement was not for capital, but for labour, resolutely defined against the hegemony which writers such as Taylor were creating. In fact, due to the nature of his involvement with the workers' struggle, in Turin 1919–21, we can dialectically contrast Gramsci's theory of organization with the standard Taylorist-bureaucratic theory which his principal ideological opponent, Olivetti, espoused. In this way we can locate organization theory as an active element in bourgeois class struggle and practice, as an instance of the bourgeois hegemony which Gramsci's knowledge, born out of the proletarian struggle, opposed. In addition we can locate the way in which the positivist nature of these theories depends upon precisely that acquiescence and passivity in organization members – the working class – which ideologically these theories seek to achieve practically. To the extent that they have succeeded then we shall see the necessity of not only a theoretical critique of positivism, but also a practical critique: i.e. one rooted in class struggle.

Antonio Gramsci

Antonio Gramsci was born in Sardinia, a poor and backward part of Italy, in 1891, and died in 1937 after a decade spent in Mussolini's prisons (for the crime of being a legally and democratically elected Communist deputy in the Italian Parliament). His childhood was one of poverty and discomforts from rickets and a hunchbacked condition, such that his life was a constant struggle against hardship (see Davidson's (1977) biography of Gramsci). Despite these obstacles he managed to acquire some schooling sufficient to win a scholarship to the University of Turin in 1911. Poor health and poverty constantly interrupted his studies until finally he was forced to suspend his registration altogether after a nervous breakdown in 1913–14, the third year of his studies. After this withdrawal he began to write for the Torinese socialist paper, *Il Grido del Popolo* (The Cry of the People), and *Avanti!* (Advance), the official Socialist Party paper. With the outbreak of war he became the editor of these.

His intellectual development was cast in the form of critical meditations on the great Italian neo-Hegelian intellectual Benedetto Croce, from a Marxist dialectical perspective which was highly anti-positivist and opposed to any determinist interpretation of historical materialism. Hence, he was opposed to any view of history which thought that socialist transformation would occur 'naturally' as a result of mechanical economic forces or of historical necessity. Initially he developed this anti-positivist position from within a Crocean-Hegelian problematic, which he was never to lose entirely, but which was subsequently and creatively mediated into a unique form of Marxism, due to the intellectual influence initially of Labriola's dialectical Marxism and, practically, the problems of the working-class struggle. It was this struggle that he reflected upon from prison in his *Prison Notebooks*. This class struggle was focused for Gramsci by the founding of *Ordine Nuovo* (A New Order) after the First World War. This was a weekly newspaper, which by 1920 had achieved a circulation of about 5,000 copies a week in Turin. Its main concern, after an early period characterized by a lack of identity and programme, became the creation of an Italian equivalent of the Russian 'soviets'. It is these that have a direct bearing on organization theory.

Ordine Nuovo defined the soviet as a democratic mass organism in which all workers would participate, irrespective of political party allegiance. These 'factory councils', as they became known, were conceived as organizations of a direct workers' democracy, possessing a revolutionary potential in the heartland of Italian capitalism – as for instance, Fiat, where they were tried. The journal, founded in May 1919, attempted to give theoretical expression and political direction to the militant and spontaneous struggle of workers in organizations such as Fiat. The struggle grew out of libertarian ideas such as direct democracy, maximum representation and workers' participation, as well as Marxist ideas about class struggle and revolution. The factory councils did not succeed, and in fact, had failed in Turin by 1920, partly as a result of their rather spontaneous nature, but also as a result of their isolation by the official Italian labour organization, and the first signs of Fascism in the press and populace. Perhaps most significantly, they were out-manoeuvred by the ideology of organization theory, in particular in the content of F. W. Taylor, and the form of Olivetti.

Gramsci and workers' councils versus Olivetti and organization theory

Adler (1977, p. 68) has argued that in 'no other case', to the best of his knowledge, 'did industrialists and Marxists reciprocally react to one another on so sophisticated a public level as was the case in post-war Italy'. The responsibility for this rests with two key individuals who were the embodiment of two opposing theoretical positions: on the one hand, Antonio Gramsci, socialist journalist and party member; on the other hand, Gino Olivetti, general secretary of *Confindustria* (the Italian industrialist employers' federation, which was founded in mid-1919). These theoretical positions were not merely speculative or idealist: they were mediated by the experience of the Bolshevik Revolution in Russia, Lenin's leadership of it and his espousal of soviets, and the wave of post-war unrest which swept over Europe and manifested itself in Turin in the 'workers councils' movement.

It is important to realize that Gramsci's view of factory councils, and in particular his attitude towards Taylorism, were not as Leninist as they have been projected to have been (Piccone, 1976). As we will argue, while Lenin's views of Taylorism lead to an uncritical and positivistic acceptance of organization theory, even in its more developed Western forms, Gramsci's analysis of Taylorism poses a completely different and far more critical perspective on the 'science of organization theory'.

Gramsci's relationship to Marxism and, in particular, Leninism is so contested and confused (see, for example, Adler, 1977; Piccone, 1976; Paggi, 1977; Anderson, 1977) by factionalist interpretations that we shall attempt to avoid becoming too engrossed in these here. What is important to us in a work on the theory of organizations is Gramsci's view of factory councils, his critique of Taylorism, and the practical acceptance of Taylorism by Lenin and its subsequent development into a theory of organizations in the USSR, which is every bit as positivist, determinant and hegemonically dominant as organization theory in the capitalist West. What this demonstrates is that the objective content of ideologies of rule and domination have an elective affinity with office-holders of power wherever that structure of power and offices remains unchallenged by its theory. Thus the theory of organizations, developed with the emergence of capitalist organizations in the West, comes to have an objective content independent of its genesis; this objective, rationalized content can become the doctrine of any group in power, be it capital or the party apparatus.

During the summer of 1919 factory councils, or workers' councils as they are sometimes known, had spontaneously formed in the Fiat factories, of which there were 30 separate plants in Turin. These councils developed out of the traditional union-defined *commissioni interne* (internal commissions). These provided for 'a functionally limited form of worker representation, primarily ensuring that existing labour contracts were rigorously adhered to and serving as a conduit within the factory for grievances' (Adler, 1977, p. 72). As such, they posed little threat to the industrial dominance of capital within the factories; they were largely integrative and accommodative, rather than oppositional and transformative institutions. 'These bodies had never been conceived as autonomous and antithetical loci of power within the factory; they were contractually prohibited from interfering with productive decisions . . . and from taking any independent action should no satisfaction be reached in dealing with management' (Adler, 1977, p. 72).

Several factors led to the transformation of these quiescent institutions in Turin in the summer of 1919. Foremost was the 'red-wave' which swept across Italy (and Europe) when previously mobilized populations, encouraged by the Bolshevik successes in Russia, demanded an immediate governmental realization of the promises of wartime propaganda. These demands were articulated in the form of mass unrest: food riots, looting, factory and land occupations; and in 1920 the longest general strike in Italy's history. Adler (1977, pp. 73–4) has noted a number of specific factors which shaped the Italian experience of workers' councils. These were:

(1) Extreme post-armistice resentment on the part of the working class against both the government and the repressive labour policy which had been promulgated during the mobilization (it should be noted that, unlike what happened in France and Germany, there had been no Italian *union sacrée* or *Burgfrieden*; Italian socialists maintained firm opposition to the war, refused to vote war credits, and constituted the only official delegation at the Zimmerwald and Kienthal conferences). (2) Manifest mass sympathy for Lenin and the Bolsheviks which led, in part, to an unsuccessful spontaneous insurrection in Torino during August 1917 (one week earlier an official Menshevik delegation visited the city and was greeted with cries of 'Viva Lenin!'). (3) Refusal or incapacity of the Italian government to contain or repress mass unrest after the armistice for fear of exacerbating an already tense domestic and international situation. (4) Initial toleration of abuses in authority by *commissioni interne* on the part of the industrialists, including the formation of officially unrecognized factory councils. (5) A growing gap between syndical leadership and the rank and file, stemming from the former's moderation and willingness to exchange salary increases for the intensified use of Taylorism and agreement to no-strike clauses.

109

It was into this gap that the workers' councils inserted themselves; and once they had appeared *Ordine Nuovo* began to provide them with a specific direction, programme and ideology as a counter-hegemony to that of the legally and 'legitimately' institutionalized (in the factory organization) hegemony of the industrialists, for whom the chief spokesman was Gino Olivetti, general secretary of *Confindustria*. As such, in Turin, he headed the most progressive industrialists in Italy. Late to industrialize, Turin had not only extremely modern plant and equipment (Fiat's factories were modelled on Henry Ford's Detroit production-line principles), but equally modern industrial relations attitudes which accepted (within 'proper limits', of course) the legitimate existence of trade unions, which they had allowed expression in the *commissioni interne*. This was a deliberate policy of containment and co-optation intended to facilitate the routinization and regularization of industrial production methods (i.e. scientific management) and to minimize conflict and strikes. Olivetti, writing in the *Bolletino della Lega Industriale* in January 1907 had noted how such institutionalization elsewhere had seemed to ensure that 'the class struggle became more calm, more civil, more orderly and more useful; conflicts broke out less frequently and the economic and moral condition of the working class in particular was elevated' (Adler, 1977, p. 78).

Combined with his progressive unionist attitudes, Olivetti was also a fervent admirer of F. W. Taylor's scientific management. This was a necessary corollary for him to the containment of conflict through the *commissioni interne* by providing the basis for an expanding production based on increased productivity which would enable the juxtaposition of higher wages and increased profits, through increasing the absolute level of wealth (see Maier, 1970). This promised an end to class conflict about the *distribution* of wealth through a stress on *production* as the creation of wealth, in which all might share in the increased surplus. With the existence of this stress on production, and the creation of an increased surplus, organizations would be organized as a Spencerian organic whole with a strictly Taylorist division of functions achieving the optimum efficiency in terms of Weberian rationality:

A modern theory says that each organ has its functions and that each function has its organ. . . . Sociologists have wished more than once to demonstrate that the laws which regulate and dominate the human body can be adapted to the social body. . . . Specialization has thus found new and important applications: for every work to be performed, for every function to exercise, for every objective to attain, one has created and creates the conditions, the ambience, the organs most adapted, so that such work may be performed, the function exercised, the objective attained in a more perfect expenditure of energy (Olivetti, *Bolletino della Lega Industriale*, IV, 4, April, 1910; cited in Adler, 1977, p. 79).

The function of management was to manage industrial capital and its social relations at work, while the function of the workers was to work in these social relations according to management's preparation of a 'pre-established plan' with which 'technically to order the factory'. If workers followed the plan, produced by the application of the scientific principles of management, then they stood to gain in wages from the increased output that would be generated. Unions should be allowed to negotiate and strike only on economic issues; the plan itself, and the planning, directive managerial functions (which were dependent upon a disciplined hierarchy in the factory, because of the theory of functional differentiation) were non-negotiable. These were the pre-war foundations of industrial organization in Turin; capitalist hegemony in the factory and over the union, and union hegemony over the rank and file. However, in the post-war period of agitation and revolutionary ferment, the union was unable to control and contain its membership, and rank-and-file discontent developed into a practical critique of the 'principles of organization' themselves through spontaneously developing occupations and self-management of the plants.

It was against the background of this explicitly Taylorist organization theory that Gramsci began to write in *Ordine Nuovo*. He realized that this organization theory not only had practical consequences such as the division of mental and manual labour, the separation and isolation of workers as individuals, and so on, but that it also had the effect of crippling the workers' consciousness, of breaking any solidarity or collective consciousness, of concentrating their consciousness on interests which were specifically bourgeois and capitalist: their *individual* output, their *individual* productivity and their *individual* wage, rather than their collective situation as a mass of de-skilled workers consciously made so by the organization theory of scientific management. Gramsci sought to counter this hegemony with that of the workers' councils movement which developed in 1919. He regarded the councils as a model of organization which could function as a medium 'through which the totality of proletarian existence – its economics and politics, its culture and social relations, its general consciousness – would be gradually transformed' (Boggs, 1976, pp. 91–2).

Writing in *Ordine Nuovo* (11 October 1919) Gramsci envisaged:

Once the councils exist, they give the workers direct responsibility for production, provide them with an incentive to improve their work, instil a conscious and voluntary discipline, and create a producer's mentality – the mentality of a creator of history. The workers will carry this new consciousness into the trade unions, which in place of the simple activity of the class struggle will dedicate themselves to the fundamental task of stamping economic life and work techniques with a new pattern; they will elaborate the form of economic life and professional technique proper to communist civilization (Gramsci, 1977, p. 101).

In September 1920 the councils took over production in Turin. At the Fiat-Centro factory they achieved almost 70 per cent of 'normal' production, despite the virtually complete absence of white-collar workers and technicians.

The central idea developed by Gramsci in his *Ordine Nuovo* writings on the councils was that of democratic participation within relatively small-scale structures. This, it was proposed, would become a '*way of life*' in which, *contra* Taylorism, 'the shop-floor workers acquire more and more skill', and in which 'the petty feelings of craft jealously that still divide them are banished forever'. Gramsci (1977, p. 96) also envisaged that there might be set up 'inside the factory, appropriate instruction departments, real vocational schools, in which every worker, rousing himself from the fatigue that brutalizes, may open his mind to knowledge of the processes of production' as a form of self-improvement. In practice, the councils were the locus of constant meetings, discussions, assemblies, educational and cultural events. From these there developed collective decision-making concerning production, intended by Gramsci as a rehearsal for a more participative democracy in society. Despite this, they never actually approximated the theoretical prescriptions developed by Gramsci from Lenin's (1947) 'The State and Revolution'.

[Gramsci] always referred to them as the 'nucleus' or 'embryo' of the fully-developed council. Of the hundreds that did emerge, most evolved out of the old union-affiliated internal commissions and these moved only gropingly towards real democratic involvement among all workers. Normally the small labour teams in a plant would elect a representative, or commissar, who would become a member of a plant-wide council of commissars, which in turn would vote to select an executive committee of 3 to 9 members. The principle of delegation held sway, but it was conditioned by open, everyday participation of most workers in the meetings, educational sessions and demonstrations (Boggs, 1976, p. 94).

The councils ran into obstacles, not least being the hostility of both the institutionalized bodies that they were effectively usurping: the employers and the unions. (The best works on this are Spriano (1975) and Williams (1975).) For instance, Gramsci's opponents on the left pointed out the danger of identifying a political institution created *after* the revolution in the USSR, with a technical, industrial *pre*-revolutionary institution.

Olivetti, for the employers, attacked the councils through an analysis of how they were functioning empirically in Russia and Germany, thus demonstrating that whatever Lenin's ideals may have been in his theoretical writings, the actual practice was quite different. Indeed Lenin did not only not carry out the programme envisaged in 'The State and Revolution' of the eligibility and revocability of every civil servant; the reduction of administrative salaries to the level of workmen's wages; and the creation of a practice whereby 'functions of control and accounting – becoming more and more simple – will be performed by each in turn' (Lenin, 1947, p. 194); he actively embraced Taylorism, the hegemonic ideology of Olivetti and his ilk, and the focus of Gramsci's opposition.

Lenin and the theory of organization

The major lacunae in Marx and Engels' writings on the nature of communism is an elaboration of the concrete principles, forms and methods of organization which would characterize the communist mode of production. Clearly it would have been possibly speculative for them to do so in advance (witness *The German Ideology*); and so the elaboration of a socialist theory of organization was left to Lenin, Leader of the October Revolution in Russia in 1917, and founder of the USSR. The compelling need for such a theory was most evident in the sphere of the state bureaucracy. As Wright notes, Lenin's view of bureaucracy was that it was 'the basic structure through which the capitalist class rules'. Because of this it 'is suited only for capitalist domination' (Wright, 1978, p. 197). His argument is that bureaucratic organization is an instrument of bourgeois coercion and control, something separated from and not accountable to the people. For this reason bureaucratic organization is both contradictory for, and unnecessary in, any future communist society.

This identification of the bureaucratic state organization as functional for capitalism but not communism leads Lenin to argue for the 'smashing' of the state in 'The State and Revolution' (1947). How is this to be done? In order to answer this, Lenin (1969) turns to Marx's analysis of the Paris Commune of 1871 as a model for the transition from bourgeois bureaucracy to communist association. Marx (1966, p. 64) had stressed that 'The working class cannot simply lay hold of the ready-made state machinery and wield it for its own purposes'. First, the administrative functions of bureaucracy had to be democratized by a workers' control, rather than a bourgeois control. The Commune provided an example of such a workers' control. Its significance lay in its worker organization rather than in its short-lived success. This worker organization functioned by staffing the administrative apparatus of the bureaucracy with elected representatives of the workers. These were subject to immediate recall and received the same wage as other workers. Lenin did not believe that a new Commune could happen overnight;

> Abolishing the bureaucracy at once, everywhere and completely, is out of the question. It is a utopia. But to smash the old bureaucratic machine at once and to begin immediately to construct a new one that will make possible the gradual abolition of all bureaucracy – this is not a utopia (Lenin, 1969, p. 297).

The result of this, he argues, would be a 'complete withering away of every form of state in general' (Lenin, 1969, p. 349). However, the state in general is not organization in general. Lenin distinguishes between the roles of *bureaucrats* and *technical experts* (Wright, 1978, pp. 202–3). These two roles are not to be confused: 'The question of control and accounting should not be confused with the question of the scientifically trained staff' (Lenin, 1969, p. 337). He includes engineers amongst these and observes that 'These gentlemen are working today in obedience to the wishes of the capitalists, and will work even better tomorrow in obedience to the wishes of the armed workers' (Lenin, 1969, p. 337). Lenin thus makes a distinction between politics and technics. Workers' control is to be political, but not technical. 'Control and accounting functions comprise the power dimension of bureaucracy, and to the extent they are democratized, bureaucratic domination is precluded. Technical functions are independent of this political dimension and therefore technically determined, subordination is not open to political challenge,' as Hearn (1978, p. 41) puts it.

Lenin's version of workers' control in the non-state sphere of, particularly, technical organizations (i.e. productive enterprises) seems to be a form of labour-hired management:

> Once we have overthrown the capitalist . . . we shall have a

114

splendidly equipped mechanism freed from the 'parasite', a mechanism which can very well be set going by the united workers themselves, who will hire technicians, foremen and accountants, and pay them all, as indeed all state officials in general, workmen's wages (Lenin, 1969, p. 299).

Lenin's democratization of work is to be only a democratization of control, not a democratization of technical expertise or of all subordination and authority in organizations (Wright, 1978, p. 203). Some such authority is always technically necessary, Lenin argued in 'The State and Revolution' (1947). Thus, he was unwilling to give more than a general image of what the structures of socialist organization would be like. To have done so would have been utopian.

It is against this background that we must consider Lenin's well-documented acceptance of Taylorism and modern capitalist technology (see Jacoby, 1973; Fleron and Fleron, 1972; Buchanan, 1976). Having no socialist guides to work from, and faced with a backward and predominantly agrarian labour force, Lenin turned to Taylorism as a theory of organization, and developed the idea of 'democratic centralism' which in theory 'demands that centralized management should constantly be combined with the broad participation of the working people in the organization of production', as Gvishiani (1972, p. 88) puts it. In theory, democratic centralism was dialectical:

Lenin always considered the strengthening of democracy in national economic management in dialectical unity with the need to strengthen centralism, i.e., unity of will in the organization and management of modern social production. While elaborating his views on the application of democratic centralism to production management, he always stressed that this principle had a dual essence, namely, that broad-based democracy in production should be combined with unity of action, personal responsibility, the execution of the functions of management at every level by a single person (Gvishiani, 1972, p. 92).

In practice, the principles of unity of action and one-man management negated any dialectical unity. This principle, deliberately counter to any collectivist or workers' council principle (which Lenin had espoused before the Revolution) was rapidly introduced, and despite opposition from several quarters, it became official policy. One-man management required absolute obedience of labour, and so, as Gvishiani (1972) observes, the most important element of labour organization by management was 'labour discipline'. Labour discipline revolves around a particular problem;

115

this was 'the problem of stimulation' or of 'how to encourage people to work'. This was resolved through introducing incentive schemes.

Lenin did not only adopt incentive schemes as persuasive forms of control. In addition, he proposed that 'the courts must be used to inculcate labour-discipline. Anyone who violated the demands of labour-discipline must be discovered, brought before the courts, and punished', as Bendix (1956, p. 193) summarized it. These were just some of a number of organization devices adopted from capitalist practice. In addition, to encourage such adoptions, the Central Institute for Labour was founded to collect and disseminate the writings of Taylor, Fayol, etc. The task of this Institute was in accord with what Lenin had defined as 'The Immediate Tasks of the Soviet Government':

> The task that the Soviet government must set the people in all its scope is – learn to work. The Taylor system, the last word of capitalism in this respect, like all capitalist progress, is a combination of the refined brutality of bourgeois exploitation and a number of the greatest *scientific achievements in the field of analysing mechanical motions during work*, the elimination of superfluous and awkward motions, the elaboration of correct methods of work, the introduction of the best system of accounting and *control*, etc. The Soviet Republic must at all costs adopt all that is valuable in the achievements of science and technology in this field. The possibility of building socialism depends exactly upon our success in combining the Soviet power and the Soviet organization of administration with the up-to-date achievements of capitalism. We must organize in Russia the study and teaching of the Taylor system and *systematically try it out and adapt it to our own ends* (Lenin, 1965, p. 259, our emphases).

It is not surprising that in such ideologically receptive ground the problem of bureaucracy was to re-appear. However, there were material reasons why the USSR should have developed Taylorist principles of functional management, discipline and incentives (in connection with this, also see Bendix (1970) on the work of the Time League), in a bureaucratic framework. Because of the war effort and the waste of millions of men in the trenches, a new proletariat had been created in the factories, composed of unskilled peasants, women, immigrants and minors. In order to use this labour force efficiently during the war, prior to the Revolution, Taylorist methods had already been adopted, particularly in the munitions plants. They were introduced under the supervision of those skilled workers who were to be the main agents in the factory committees during the events following February 1917. As such, as

Goodey (1974, p. 39) has argued, the leaders of these factory committees or workers' councils were 'closely associated from the very beginning with the attempt to build a new, centralized economic apparatus, to raise the level of productive forces'. (Other authorities such as Bettelheim (1977) support Goodey in this interpretation. It is one that runs counter to much conventional wisdom: see, for example, Brinton (1970), whom Goodey (1974, pp. 36–9) criticizes severely.) The new proletariat in the factories, on the other hand, did not wait on this democratic centralism and began seizing enterprises abandoned by their owners, the bourgeoisie who fled from the Revolution and started to socialize them for themselves, from the bottom up. It is the action of the new proletariat in thus side-stepping the workers' council movement, operating not in a centralist but in a spontaneous manner, which Goodey (1974, p. 43) credits with creating the 'objective conditions' for the further intensification of bureaucracy, rather than its withering away.

Lenin argued that the further adoption of Taylorism was necessary because of these 'objective conditions': that the revolution was in only one country in a hostile capitalist world; that Russia was under attack from this world, and fighting a civil war as well, and that the productive forces of the economy were in chaos as a result of four years of war and then revolution. 'Moreover such factors as the non-socialist relations of production between the workers and the peasants, the still existing small bourgeois and the Tsarist bureaucrat with his feudal mentality also have to be taken into consideration', as Mouzelis (1967, p. 12) argues. Any analysis of the factory committees and organization in the USSR in the immediate post-revolutionary period has also to take into account that the factory committees produced very little – not because of features *intrinsic* to them, but because of these *extrinsic* features which rendered almost any production impossible.

These factors should not delude us into thinking that it was only 'objective conditions' that changed. It is clear that Lenin did change his views between 1917 and 1921. He increasingly regarded management, as it was traditionally defined, as having a continuing major and central role to play in organization. Factory committees and trade unions decreased in importance in his thinking, to be replaced by the stress on incentives.

Ramsay (1977b, p. 7) has demonstrated how the process of direct participation by workers in management, although it has been recognized and formally reaffirmed at various stages in the subsequent development of the USSR, has remained more apparent than real. Consequently, and not surprisingly, Soviet organization theory and practice has turned increasingly to Elton

Mayo to supplement Taylor in more recent years (see Gvishiani, 1972, p. 434).

Armed with knowledge of the immediate failure of the soviets in this formative stage Olivetti, in his critique of *Ordine Nuovo's* workers' councils' schemes, stressed the failure of Lenin's proposals in the USSR through the process of an increasing Taylorization and bureaucratization of organization. Olivetti held that Soviet practice was becoming increasingly similar to the views that were held by progressive Turin employers, and thus proposed that no radical changes needed to be achieved. In short, he argued, why should there be any need for change when the 'desired' changes were already being secured by an enlightened management?

Lessons of the workers' councils for the theory of organizations

What lessons can be learned from the failure of the workers' councils for proponents of a radically alternative theory of organization? On the positive side is the fact that the councils did break the hegemony of Taylorist organization theory; that new issues and a new alternative conception of organization were raised by the workers, and that these same workers were able to manage themselves and their factories. In this latter respect Gramsci's (1977) reasoning was unfortunately in error. He argued that self-management was management of social relations of production 'ordered in a way that is determined precisely by the industrial technique being used'. His error was in arguing a thesis which suggested a necessary determination by technology, and regarding this technique 'in turn as independent (in a certain sense) of the mode of appropriation of the values that are produced' (Gramsci, 1977, p. 295). Rutigliano (1977, p. 93) has identified the error in this: 'It is not so much the capitalist organization of work that is questioned, but its direction. Therefore, it is not a matter of the relations of capitalist production, but of the management of these relations.' Thus, Gramsci makes the uncritical assumption that technology is neutral, rather than a product and producer of capitalist rationality.

Gramsci's error can be identified as almost Weberian in its conceptualization of rationality and technique as fused. Weberian theory, as Giddens (1973, p. 275) notes, draws a clear connection between 'technique, as the application of instrumental rationality to the material world, and bureaucratic organization as the application of technical reason to social activity'. Thus, Weber's concept of bureaucratization (as we argued in Chapter 2) appears as some inexorable neo-Hegelian process of rationalization 'by which the administration of things eventuates in the administration or domination of people' (Hearn, 1978, p. 42). By contrast, what Marxist theory ought to do, according to Hearn, is to distinguish between 'the rationality of technique' and 'the rationality of consciousness'. By doing this, he argues, it is possible to envisage

> the possibility of a society where the application of instrumental rationality and technical reason is confined to the material world and critical rationality or political consciousness permeates every other sphere of life to the degree that domination, whether it be rooted in the means of production or the means of administration, becomes virtually impossible (Hearn, 1978, p. 43).

This relates to a wider lesson than can be drawn from the immediate topic of the workers' councils movement, although it is implicit in them. Technology (or in Marxist terms, the forces of production) is not some autonomous variable which can automatically 'cause' revolutionary action. Perhaps the most important aspect of the workers' councils movement is the implicit denial of any such thesis. Not only did the workers' councils represent a set of material practices which denied the sole claim to rationality of any one set of principles. They also demonstrated that positivist and determinist theories of organization, which, for instance, link the necessity of a particular (Taylorized) structure of organization to a particular (Taylorist) technology, are only correct in so far as the workers remain passive and quiescent. What is more, to the extent that they do, this is not so much a law of social science as an achievement of ideological hegemony. At the same time the failure of the workers' councils movement in Turin demonstrates the inadequacy of any counter-hegemonic theory which accepts that the organization is a self-contained realm of analysis in itself. It is not. The practical failure of the workers' councils movement demonstrates this theoretical point clearly. Thus, it would seem that it is extremely unlikely, if not impossible, that a radically transformed organizational practice – the application of an alternative theory of organization – can be implemented through a social movement isolated to only the workplace, and oriented to the construction of a 'dual power' without seizing or gaining the support of the existing offices of power (e.g., the industrialists, managers, unions). This requires a thorough understanding of the distinction between technical and practical rationality which Habermas (1971) has proposed, and a realization that there is no necessary relationship between them.

Technical rationality refers to the efficient and calculated pursuit of given goals, while practical rationality refers to a process of enlightenment or of generalized reflection, defined by the fact that goals are chosen freely in the context of undistorted political

119

communication by equals who can *rationally* justify the grounds of their action and discourse. Technical rationality involves the extension of instrumentality, the growth of technique and productive forces, whereas practical rationality necessitates 'the enlargement of the sphere of action guided by social norms, formulated in and through non-distorted communication, and subject to conscious reflection' (Hearn, 1978, p. 44).

Technical rationalization expands what Habermas (1976) calls purposive rational sub-systems which lead to the more efficient functioning of society. However, it does not necessarily lead to human emancipation. There is no necessary relation between technical and practical rationality. Human emancipation is a matter of action and reflection, a practical rather than a technical reason, which rests only on the liberation of the space and time available for political discourse and critical dialogue. It is such a reason with which 'the mentality of a creator of history' (Gramsci, 1977, p. 101) must be equipped. Only with this will the domination of a technological rationality be practically opposed in a unity of cultural and organizational revolution (see Chapter 13).

Gramsci points towards such a unity in his later writings contained in the *Prison Notebooks*, in his insistence on the creative capacities of the worker even in spite of the almost total domination of technical rationalization. He does this in a reflection on the Taylorist themes which had structured the *Ordine Nuovo* movement in 1919–20. He develops a critique of Taylorist rationality which stresses that it is not as totally hegemonic as it might appear. He does this by ironically identifying the particular problems created by Taylorism:

> that 'unfortunately' the worker remains a man and even that
> during his work he thinks more, or at least has greater oppor-
> tunities for thinking, once he has overcome the crisis of adapta-
> tion without being eliminated: and not only does the worker
> think, but the fact that he gets no immediate satisfaction
> from his work and realizes that they are trying to reduce him to
> a trained gorilla, can lead him to a train of thought that is far
> from conformist (Gramsci, 1971, p. 310).

This 'train of thought' is most frequently expressed in either sabotage (see Taylor and Walton, 1971 and Brown, 1977) or in labour turnover. It was this latter factor which Gramsci stressed when he observed that:

> The instability of the labour force demonstrates that as far as
> Ford's is concerned the normal conditions of workers' competi-
> tion for jobs (wage differentials) are effective only to a limited

degree. The different level of average wages is not effective, nor is the pressure of the reserve army of the unemployed (Gramsci, 1971, p. 311).

He goes on to argue that the reasons for this turnover lie in the 'more wearying and exhausting' consumption of labour power under 'Fordism' than elsewhere. What is this Fordism?

Gramsci knew Taylorism through its introduction by Turin industrialists, such as Agnelli of Fiat and its promotion by *Confindustria* and Olivetti in the immediate post-war period. The timing is not unimportant. Everywhere in Europe among the combatants, Taylorism was introduced, albeit in an uneven development. (England was the least explicitly Taylorist in its conception, while in France Taylorism entered the arena explicitly sponsored by no less than Clemenceau in 1918: see Maier, 1970, pp. 35–45). Fordism, unlike Taylorism *per se*, belongs to the post-war period of stabilization in the late 1920s in both Europe and America. In this period, in part because of the adoption of Taylorism as a *seemingly* socialist practice in the USSR by Lenin, and its espousal by German socialists (see Maier, 1970, pp. 45–54), Taylorism had been subject to a more critical reception which helped to transform its meaning. Increasingly, in Germany in particular, it became secondary to the process of technocratic rationalization which occurred with the formation of new, huge, cartels. In addition:

> The favoured images of advanced techniques that America presented to the world were changing. The teachings of Taylorism, in its strict sense, were viewed more critically, while Fordism became the vogue. A German commentator (Briefs, 1928) explained the change as a widening of a scope; while Taylorism concerned only the management of labour, Ford's doctrines stressed reorganization of the entire productive process (Maier, 1970, p. 54).

Ford's contributions stressed the introduction of the moving assembly line, standardization, and the further enlargement of a mass market not only through low prices and high wages, but also by mass advertising and hire purchase (Ewen, 1976). The introduction of Fordism at this time served to justify the subordination of many small producers to large firms. In both Germany and Italy this rationalization 'accompanied a government shift to protectionism and a deflationary reconversion to the gold standard. In such a transition, with its own liquidity crisis, concentration of industries and pressure on wages was a logical response', as Maier (1970, pp. 56–7) argues, and was one increasingly adopted throughout Europe.

It is for these reasons – the moving assembly line dictating a pace of work determined by the capacity of the cartel to conquer the market; the standardization of wages on a standard day wage with little or no effort-bargain in the worker's hands, in a situation of 'pressure on wages' – that Fordism was 'more wearying and exhausting' as Gramsci (1971, pp. 311–12) recognized. For this reason, he argued, if it were to gain general acceptance as a rational method of organizing production, this 'cannot take place through coercion alone, but only through tempering compulsion (self-discipline) with persuasion'. What form might this persuasion take?

Basically, the form would be that of high wages; the turnover problems would be curtailed by unemployment. In fact, this turned out to be the case in the short term. In the longer term, the war economies of the Second World War acted as a kind of unintended Keynesian intervention that created conditions of full employment. The consequence of the disappearance of the 'reserve army of the unemployed' raised again the issue of 'turnover'. Organization theory, ever the efficient handmaiden of 'rational' enterprise, proposed a solution which turned out to be a form of neo-Durkheimian intervention to repair social solidarity *at the level of the organization* rather than society as a whole. This simple expediency of a shift in level proved an effective means of integrating the labour force into the capitalist state, by instilling in the labour force a sense of its corporate consciousness. The architect of this strategy was Elton Mayo. (It is interesting that during the war two distinct versions of a neo-Durkheimian strategy should have been adopted by the opposing allies; in Germany and Italy, the corporate states, in the USA the New Deal and human relations in the workplace; see Maier, 1970).

Elton Mayo

Elton Mayo's initial observations of the destruction of social solidarity by the industrial process were born of accident rather than design, by his association (from April 1928) with a series of experiments into variables affecting workers' performance which had been instituted by the management of the Western Electric Co., at their Hawthorne works, in what became known as the Relay Test Assembly Room (see Smith, 1975); but it was Mayo's wartime studies into absenteeism and labour turnover (Mayo, 1975) which contributed to the development of the 'Human Relations School'.

Mayo described the circumstances that led to his investigation as these:

Early in 1943 great public concern suddenly became manifest

with respect to the phenomenon of so-called 'absenteeism'; it was
believed that war production was seriously diminished by casual
and wilful absences of workers from their work. Many alleged
'causes' were cited – illness, difficulties of transport, family
troubles, shopping problems, and the like. It was also said
that larger earnings induced workers to take unjustifiable
weekend holidays. When the discussion was at its height –
newspapers, Congress, public meetings – we were asked by
an official agency to make a study of the situation in three
companies in a metal-working industry of great importance to
the war. These three companies work almost side by side in a
relatively small east coast industrial city. . . . On arrival in the
city we found the general alarm about absences to be as great
as elsewhere; we were offered a variety of explanations for
the occurrence of absences, based on the personal observations
of those living and working in the city.

These explanations sometimes came from company officials,
sometimes from the workers themselves or their supervisors,
sometimes from persons casually encountered. The explanations
most frequently offered were that workers were earning a
great deal of money; that, by reason of this, they tended to
take small excursions in the weekends; and that there was
much conviviality, especially during weekends. Everyone who
gave us such an explanation had one or more stories of actual
and verifiable occurrences that illustrated this claim exactly.
It was impossible, however, on the basis of these illustrations
to decide the comparative incidence or importance of these
'causes' of absenteeism (Mayo, 1975, pp. 78–9).

Mayo also conducted research into the same phenomenon in
aircraft plants in Southern California, and both of these studies led
him to conclude that the real cause of this problem was the lack of
'well-knit human groups' in the industrial organization. This was a
persistent message in Mayo's work, in which he counter-posed 'the
rabble hypothesis' of economics and administration to the
'doctrine' of human co-operation which he argued had been the
civilizing principle of the Christian church. The 'rabble hypothesis'
was what we might otherwise know these days as the doctrine of
'possessive individualism' (Macpherson, 1962), which, as Mayo
(1975) correctly observes, has developed from Hobbes to the
present day, primarily in the fields of political and economic theory.

He begins his major work on *The Social Problems of an Industrial
Civilization* by noting how a number of prominent thinkers – H. G.
Wells, Disraeli, Le Play and Durkheim – have made 'the clear
demonstration that *collaboration in an industrial society cannot be*

left to chance' (Mayo, 1975, p. 8). This analysis is made more pointedly by Mayo when he specifies the necessity of considering this problem in its relevance for administration:

> Every social group, at whatever level of culture, must face and clearly state two perpetual and recurrent problems of administration. It must secure for its individual and group membership:
> 1 The satisfaction of material and economic needs.
> 2 The maintenance of spontaneous co-operation throughout the organization.
> Our administrative methods are all pointed at the materially effective; none, at the maintenance of co-operation. The amazing technical successes of these war years show that we – our engineers – do know how to organize for material efficiency. But problems of absenteeism, labour turnover, 'wild-cat' strikes, show that we do not know how to ensure spontaneity of co-operation; that is, teamwork. Indeed, had not the emergency of war been compelling and of personal concern to every worker, it is questionable whether the technicians could have achieved their manifest success. And, now that the urgency is diminished, the outlook for continued co-operation is not good. There is no active administrator of the present who does not fear that peace may see a return of social chaos (Mayo, 1975, p. 9).

Mayo presents a bourgeois and humanist critique of scientific management, which in its insistence on the hegemonic moment, in some respects – albeit from a very different political interest – echoes Gramsci. To accept Mayo's way of formulating this problem is to miss 'both the theme of exploitation and that of the reproduction of the hegemonic strata' (Palloix, 1976, p. 63). However, Mayo's analysis is substantially correct in recommending that the most effective form of power and control in organizations is of a more hegemonic rather than a less persuasive and more coercive type.

Mayo observes that in what Offe (1976a) has termed the 'task-continuous' organizations of the craft industries of the nineteenth century that:

> The boy was thus apprenticed in some fashion to his life work and his trade, and began to acquire simultaneously technical capacity and the art of communication with his fellows. In the usual case this group changed but little during his apprenticeship. Thus through practice at his trade with the same group of persons, he learned to manipulate the objects with which he worked and to understand the attitudes and ideas of his com-

panions. Both of these are of immense importance to successful living. Dr. Pierre Janet, in fifty years of patient, pedestrian, clinical research, has shown that sanity is an achievement and that the achievement implies for the individual a balanced relation between technical and social skills. Technical skill manifests itself as a capacity to manipulate things in the service of human purposes. *Social skill shows itself as a capacity to receive communications from others, and to respond to the attitudes and ideas of others in such fashion as to promote congenial participation in a common task* (Mayo, 1975, p. 12, our emphasis).

Mayo maintains that the balance between technical and social skills has been lost in the modern world. What was has passed and will not return: 'We have in fact passed beyond that stage of human organization in which effective communication and collaboration were secured by established routines of relationship' (Mayo, 1975, p. 12). Nor is it any longer 'possible for an industrial society to assume that the technical processes of manufacture will exist unchanged for long in any type of work' (Mayo, 1975, p. 12). The 'task-discontinuous organization', in Offe's (1976a) phrase, is now the norm, in which both 'a much higher type of skill is required . . . which is based upon adequate scientific and engineering knowledge and is consequently adaptable or even creative' (Mayo, 1975, pp. 12–13). But, as Mayo goes on to observe, 'the skill required of the machine-hand has drifted downwards; he has become more of a machine tender and less a mechanic'. While considerable effort has been expended on the development of technical skills (i.e. de-skilling and hyper-skilling) 'no equivalent effort to develop social or collaborative skill has yet appeared to compensate or balance the technical development' (Mayo, 1975, p. 13). What are these social skills? In 'ordinary language', learning 'to be a good fellow', learning 'to get on with one's fellows', says Mayo (1975, p. 29). Adaptive to what? One may enquire. The answer is clear, Mayo says that:

I must not be supposed to be arguing for the placing of any limitation upon scientific advance, technical improvement, or, in general, change in industrial methods. On the contrary, I am entirely for technical advancement and the rapid general betterment of standards of living (Mayo, 1975, p. 28).

He immediately follows this with the by now familiar injunction of the necessity for 'social skills'. These social skills will help to gain the assent of members of the organization to the orders of its executives. This process is described by Mayo (1975, p. 45) in a

125

passage which he cites from Barnard (1938, p. 175) in the following terms: 'Authority depends upon a co-operative personal attitude of individuals on the one hand; and the system of communication in the organization on the other'. Social skills will, and should, be oriented to the achievement of this, and this can be realized through the establishment of 'teams' in the social organization of work, and 'interviews', the latter an instrument designed to aid 'the individual to get rid of useless emotional complications', 'to associate more easily, more satisfactorily, with other persons – fellow workers or supervisors – with whom he is in daily contact', and to develop in the worker a 'desire and capacity to work better with management'. These propositions are presented not so much as hypotheses or findings, but as assertions delivered with the conviction of one who knows their inalienable truth. Scientifically, they should be regarded with as much confidence as one would have in an ocean-going tadpole. Certainly, Mayo displays as much temerity in the face of 'evidence' as such a foolhardy amphibian. The judgment on Elton Mayo offered by Michael Rose cannot be bettered:

> Mayoism emerged rapidly as the twentieth century's most seductive managerial ideology. What, after all, could be more appealing than to be told that one's subordinates are non-logical; that their unco-operativeness is a frustrated urge to collaborate; that their demands for cash mark a need for your approval; and that you have a historic destiny as a broker of social harmony? (Rose, 1975, p. 124).

The continuity of Taylorism and the work of Mayo and what came to be known as the Human Relations School has been argued by Mouzelis in the following terms:

> One of the fundamental principles of Taylorism was the scientific selection of the worker so that there should be correspondence between his aptitudes and the requirements of the job. Already such propositions indicated what direction the movement of rationalization of work would take. As a matter of fact very soon the industrial psychologist appeared on the scene and joined the efficiency engineer in the workshop (Mouzelis, 1967, p. 97).

He stresses 'the rapid development of experimental psychology at the beginning of this century and the hostile reaction of the workers to the early attempts to put into practice the mechanistic principles of scientific management' as the major factors which hastened the spread of the Human Relations movement. The clearest link in this continuity is not Mayo's later attempt (reminiscent, ideologically, of the Durkheimian stress on social solidarity) at a re-creation of

126

social solidarity. This was conceived as a deliberate intervention in the atomization of work indicated by the emergence of theories of 'possessive individualism' (Macpherson, 1962) in the seventeenth century as an ideological buttress for the emergent market society, and completed in the labour process by Taylorism in the twentieth century. The clearest link in the continuity of scientific management and the development of the Human Relations movement is Elton Mayo's earlier work as research director of the famous Hawthorne Studies. Mayo *did not* conduct those studies. He simply popularized them (Rose, 1975, ch. 2, is particularly clear on this).

The Hawthorne studies

The Hawthorne plant of the Western Electric Company was the site of a series of experiments which began in 1924. The Hawthorne plant, situated in Chicago, was a large bureaucratic organization which employed over 40,000 people.

The research project was a company-based operation, controlled by G. A. Pennock who was a Western Electric engineer having an interest in personnel work. It was not until 1927 that Mayo was approached and became aware of the Hawthorne studies. Evidence seems to suggest that awareness was the greater part of Mayo's involvement (see Smith, 1975; Rose, 1975).

The purpose of the initial investigations was to relate different types of working conditions to the output realized under them, using an experimental situation in which independent variables such as the degree of brilliance or dimness of illumination could be systematically manipulated, and related to the dependent variable of output. The results were confusing and inconclusive, in part because the experimental situations were badly designed. It seemed that almost any variation of the independent variables, such as lighting, produced an increase in output – even when the lighting was reduced to a mere flicker! At the same time the control group was also showing increases in output, despite the fact that it was not being subject to any deliberate manipulation of variables in its physical environment. The researchers gradually came to realize that variables such as illumination *could not be treated independently of the meaning which individuals assigned to them.* (In this they can be seen as precursors of the phenomenological movement of the 1960s and 1970s, which similarly stressed the importance of the meaningful constitution of practices and actions by subjects; see Chapter 7.)

After this realization, as Roethlisberger and Dickson (1939) were to report, the researchers changed their methodological approach. Instead of searching for causal variables in the physical environment of work and the organization, they realized that the most significant variables governing output appeared not to be physical but *social*. In order to explicate this discovery the interviewers instituted a series of interviews (from which Mayo's techniques developed) as a means of exploring the complex situation they had stumbled upon.

What they had discovered was a genuine object of scientific investigation: social organization as a source of variance in the hegemonic structuring of control of social relations of production. As Mouzelis (1967, p. 99) puts it, 'the determinants of working behaviour are sought in the structure and culture of the group, which is spontaneously formed by the interaction of individuals working together'. With this realization researchers were able to develop more naturalistic methods of direct observation of work groups (e.g., Warner and Low, 1947), which were to be further developed by sociologists of an interactionist and ethno-methodological persuasion (see Chapter 7).

The distinctive conclusion which emerged from the Hawthorne studies was that economic incentives are of relatively little importance in motivating workers and increasing productivity. More important, in true Mayoite fashion, are workers' needs for social solidarity. Workers' grievances are not a rational reflection of their social relations of production, but are irrational. They can be seen to be based not on reason but on sentiment. If management cultivates these sentiments, to attend to the social and emotional needs of workers, then they may rationally expect to receive increased output and harmonious relations in return. But, of course, such outcomes cannot be left to chance. Management can consciously achieve these results by training supervisors to exercise authority in the approved (paternalistic) 'human relations' manner. Underlying neuroses in individual workers (the postulated source of grievances such as strikes, absenteeism, turnover, etc.) which, if not corrected, might develop into a disposition to support militant unions, can be dissipated by providing a quasi-clinical counselling service to which workers may 'let off steam' (see Wilensky and Wilensky, 1952).

These conclusions – that friendly, uncoercive supervision is far more important than monetary rewards in motivating people in work groups – were developed from a series of three experiments. In the first experiment (the First Relay Assembly Group) six[3] women who assembled telephone relays were moved from the factory floor to a separate room. Prior to this their output had been secretly measured. Over the first two years of the experiment the working conditions of the group were progressively changed. They were given a different payment system, based on a group bonus incentive scheme. Under the old system they had been paid on the average output of 100 workers. In the Relay Assembly Room they were paid on the average output of the group. Other factors were manipulated, such as varying rest pauses, introducing free snacks and a shortened working week. The consequence of these changes was that output increased significantly. The question that required answering was why that should be so. The obvious explanation would seem to have been the payment system, the incentives. To test this, half way through the first experiment the investigators designed a Second Relay Assembly Group. This group of five remained in the normal department and their supervision remained constant. Output increased individually by an average 13 per cent. The experiment was terminated after only nine weeks because the other workers in the department demanded the same payment system. Output then declined by 16 per cent.

A third experiment, the Mica Splitting Group had begun three months before the Second Relay Assembly Group study. In this experiment five workers were again taken out of the department, placed in an observation room and exposed to similar changes to the First Relay Assembly Group. The only exception was their payment system, which had been based on an individual piece-rate bonus. This was not altered. The results were inconclusive: output rose initially but then declined. On the average there was no increase in output over a fourteen-month period, although output rose 15 per cent in the first year. Individual variations were much greater in this group than in either of the other groups.

What was the key factor? The reporters (Roethlisberger and Dickson, 1939; Whitehead, 1938; Mayo, 1933 and Homans, (1950) had no doubt. The key variable was supervisory style.

Before we consider the objections that have been raised against this interpretation, let us first consider the criticisms that have been made of the Hawthorne experiments research design. As Rose (1975, pp. 128–9) has warned, several elementary precautions in the use of an experimental model were not followed. Random sampling was not utilized; the control group was not isolated under identical conditions to the experimental group; the experimental stimuli were not imposed singly on the experimental subjects; and the variations introduced into the experimental situation were not assessed systematically before further variations were introduced. Additionally and crucially, as Rose observes 'all these experiments occurred at different times'. They were not co-variations in a single time dimension.

Alex Carey (1967; 1976) after a thorough re-analysis of the reports of the Hawthorne experiments drew the following conclusions from the studies:

129

1   When relaxed supervision and the preferred incentive system
were introduced *together* there was no increase in output
until supervision was tightened and two (of five) operatives
sacked. Thereafter output rose rapidly.
2   When the preferred incentive system *alone* was introduced
output rose rapidly; when it was withdrawn output fell rapidly.
3   When relaxed supervision *alone* was introduced there was
no increase in output (Carey, 1976, p. 236).

In short, the data can just as much support the contrary interpretation to that which its reporters gave it, that it is not human
relations but monetary incentives which motivate! This was not the
conclusion that Roethlisberger and Dickson (1939, p. 160) arrived
at. They concluded that 'none of the results gave the slightest
substantiation to the theory that the worker is primarily motivated
by economic interest'. Instead they concluded that supervisory and
social factors were of the most significance. What can we conclude?
One conclusion might be that the Hawthorne studies were so ill-
designed and have been so inconsistently reported that the results
can equally plausibly suggest the power of both human relations and
incentives. Rose, on the basis of the Whitehead (1938) report,
suggests a third possible explanation:

> After the two unco-operative[4] subjects were replaced, one of
> their substitutes assumed a leadership style more reminiscent of
> the driving production-oriented variety than any other. The
> observer seems to have done little to check this rather different
> upset of constancy – including the constancy of his role as
> disciplinarian. If the experiments were not subject to so many
> other contaminating influences one might even conclude that the
> real 'Hawthorne Effect' centred around driving leadership
> (Rose, 1975, p. 130).

It is for the evidence of the existence of the 'Hawthorne Effect'
that these studies are considered important. This is: that individual
behaviour is modified through being the subject of investigation,
irrespective of the nature of the investigation. In addition, the
Hawthorne studies 'discovered' the informal social group which was
brought about, it was maintained, through democratic and informal
supervision. The evidence for the importance of this *informal
organization* was also drawn from the anthropological phase of their
investigations, which succeeded a period of counselling interviews
(in the Mayoite sense). W. Lloyd Warner, a functionalist anthro-
pologist who studied under Radcliffe-Brown, advised on this phase
of the study.

An Observation Room was established in which an inconspicuously sited observer noted the interactions of a group of fourteen male workers. It was quickly realized that an interesting group phenomenon was occurring. The group appeared to set some type of informal rules governing what a fair day's output was, and sanctioned 'rate-busters' who over-produced above the norm, or 'chisellers' who consistently under-produced. However, the reasons for this informal group norm may have had something more to do with the capitalist mode of production than with socio-psychological factors. The observations took place during 1932–33, the height of the Depression in the USA. Restriction of output by voluntary norms was a rational response by primarily economically oriented agents to the increasingly likely prospect of unemployment. Contrary to such an explanation, which would have provided an understanding of social action within the organization set in the context of the wider society, the observational part of the studies 'systematically suppressed . . . the potential influence of out-plant social factors on in-plant phenomena' which as Rose (1975, p. 132) argues, had been indicated by the preceeding programme of interviews. One can concur with him that 'an underlying predisposition to devalue (though not to dismiss) monetary and economic influences goes far to explain the form and course of the studies' (Rose, 1975, p. 133).

From these studies the human relations researchers developed a conceptual framework in which they made a distinction between the *formal* and the *informal* structure of the organization. The formal structure was conceptualized as the boundary condition and limiting context within which informal organization could be studied. This formal structure consisted of the rules and activities required by the organization. In addition to regarding this as a limiting condition, these researchers concentrated on the actual behaviour in the plant, and only allowed the 'environment' of the organization to affect their research inasmuch as the subjects under investigation constituted it as meaningful by including it in their definitions of the situation.

The theoretical object which they thus constituted – the common patterns of behaviour and the emergent beliefs and values of the interacting subjects – were, under the influence of a key figure in the direction of the Human Fatigue Laboratory at Harvard, where the research had originally begun, conceptualized as a *social system*. This person was A. M. Henderson, admirer of Pareto, colleague of Elton Mayo and Talcott Parsons, and indeed, with the latter, the translator of a fragment of Max Weber's work published as *The Theory of Social and Economic Organization* (1947). This social system was conceptualized as a whole, constituted by interdependent parts, where the interdependence was such that any change in one part of the system would bring changes to other parts of the system. Such changes were not conceptualized as disruptive, however, because the systems model was based on the analogy of a system tending towards equilibrium, as in an economist's model of a perfectly competitive economy. This equilibrium stems from the nature of some of the most important common beliefs and values of the interacting subjects. These are such as to enforce equilibrium. Any activity or expressed attitude which is taken to be disruptive of the group's self-regulated and self-regulating beliefs and values (the group's norms) is theorized as a threat. Because of this the behaviour of the other members of the group is conceptualized as a sanction. The strongest sanctions are group disapproval and, at worst, ostracism. Members of the group – the social system – are *in need* of the group's solidarity, and thus these sanctioning reactions tend to redress the deviation, and restore the system to its previous state of equilibrium.

Subsequent development: the elaboration of control

We can identify important subsequent streams of work which can be related to developments first made by the human relations theorists.

First, we can consider how the 'discovery' of the informal organization had certain implications for the theory of formal organization developed from Weber and the formal theorists of administration. The formal organization refers to official rules and to behaviour which is stipulated or governed by these rules. The informal organization refers to values and patterns of behaviour which are independent of these formal rules and which develop out of the interaction of persons in groups in the organization. The Hawthorne 'discovery' was that these informal rules or shared values could determine the behaviour of group members. This had certain implications, the most important being that formal and informal prescriptions need not cohere. The worker does not always behave as the formal organization logic would prescribe or suggest. In Roethlisberger and Dickson's (1939) phrase, the *logic of sentiments* of the informal organization, that is, the informal rules of the informal work group, might very well be different from, or stand opposed to the *logic of efficiency* and the formal organization's imperatives. The way in which work-group norms restrict output to an informal 'average output' for each person illustrates this. Members of the group quickly learn what the informal rules are, and what is expected of them by their colleagues. 'Rate-busters' will be subject to informal sanction, and thus group rules determine the 'proper' amount for a day's work. The existence of such informal rules and organization increase work-group solidarity, by minimizing differences within and between the group, and enabling members to achieve a greater control of their conditions of employment than would otherwise be the case, particularly in regard to the 'effort-bargain' (Baldamus, 1961) which they make in relating formal inducements to their actual contributions of effort and output to the organization.

A further consequence of the social solidarity which is generated is that the activity of the group as a group, as a source and locus of sentiments, meanings and motives for action, becomes an end in itself. As such it can have positive effects for the formal organization, as Mayo (1975) elaborated (also see Mayo and Lombard, 1944), but it can also pose *problems of organization* for management.

These problems of organization are best known in the literature as a series of dichotomies, between, for example, the formal and the informal organization or the bureaucrat and the professional. What these various formulations of problems of organization share (to be discussed in Chapter 4) is some concept of disjuncture between what the formal organization model suggests should be the case, and what actually, empirically, the case is. Prescriptions usually flow from the discovery of these discrepancies. Often these are of the order that the formal organization arrangements of management should take into account the informal organization arrangements of workers. Failure to do this is often regarded as a recipe for a 'communication breakdown'. This will occur where hierarchical communications down the organization, from management, neglect the reality of the workers' definition of the situation, or where workers do not transmit information concerning their definition of the situation because they believe it to be incorrect or illegitimate. The solution is for management to be trained ('sensitivity training') in human relations techniques. It is from this requirement that the vast and overwhelmingly ideological literature on leadership, supervisory style, group dynamics, planned change in organizations, communications problems, motivation and similar topics has developed. Champion (1975) goes into much of this literature at length.[5] Much of the literature spawned by early developments of the human relations studies is now regarded as ideological and unscientific. An early and incisive critique was made by C. W. Mills (1948), and, as Mouzelis has argued:

It was gradually realized that relationships between leadership, productivity and morale were valid only under certain conditions and that the task of further research should be to specify these conditional variables. . . . In a more general way, it was realized

133

that problems of supervision arise on all levels of the organization and that from that angle they are similar to the problem of
authority with which Weber and other theorists have dealt long
ago (Mouzelis, 1967, p. 111).

The characteristic of this approach is a stress on the effects of the
environment of the individual on the individual in the group, as the
individual perceives them in his or her definition of the situation. It
thus has what both Landsberger (1961) and Mouzelis have termed a
'psychological bias'. Mouzelis elaborates that:

The risk of such an approach is that when we take into consideration the social environment not in itself but as it is
perceived by the individual we may learn much about the
individual but very little about the environment (Mouzelis,
1967, p. 109).

In particular we may neglect the fact that many *problems of
organization* are in fact only *problems of and for management*, and
that these problems cannot be spirited away through a change of
supervisory style or the learning of social skills. They are in fact
structural contradictions inherent in the hierarchical organization
of work in terms of distinct levels of mental and manual labour, for
the private appropriation of the fruits of the collective product, and
the inegalitarian treatment and reward of organization members in
the process. These criticisms, that human relations and its
adherents emphasized harmony and neglected conflict, because of
their pro-capitalist managerial bias are common in the literature
(e.g., Kerr and Fisher, 1957; Krupp, 1961). The bias manifested
itself primarily through the key concepts of what became
functionalist systems theory; the concepts of homeostasis,
equilibrium, functional whole, etc. In addition, it conceptualized
the 'normal' state of the organization in terms of somewhat
romantic and conservative idealizations of a harmonious but dead
past. In this respect their organicism (at its most evident in Mayo,
1975) could constitute as 'pathological' states which subsequent
theorists were more likely to conceptualize as 'normal', such as
'normal strikes' (Hyman, 1975).

The theory failed to make the distinction between inter-personal
relations and social relations of production embedded within, and
deriving their meaning from, the mode of organization articulated
within a specific mode of production. There is a danger of
overstating these points of critique. Clearly, organization structures
do vary in their propensity for conflict, and useful research is still to
be done which specifies what the correlates of these variances are in
terms of the organization's structure. But, as Mouzelis (1967,

p. 116) has argued, 'future research must specify and distinguish the conditions under which communication findings are applicable, and the conditions where communications are not at fault, but where interest groups pursue in a rational and self-conscious way antagonistic strategies' (e.g., see Clegg, 1975, ch. 8). If organizational interest groups were viewed in this way, then it would be possible to regard movements such as Human Relations as important not so much in their volumes of findings, what they say, but in what they do. What the Human Relations theorists did was to produce a highly developed ideological apparatus of normative control, of hegemony, for the management of organizations. At its most developed this ideology is apparent in the literature on industrial democracy and participation within organizations which we will contrast in our final chapter with the other stream of work that we have discussed in this chapter, the workers' councils movement. From this perspective, then, the Human Relations movement has significance not as a body of scientific findings of highly dubious nature, but as part of the apparatus whereby organizations attempt to impose and maintain control of production. In this respect it is no more dead and buried than scientific management, and still plays an important role in maintaining ideological hegemony, as we shall elaborate in our final chapter.

4 Typologies of organizations

Three major directions follow from the work reviewed in the previous chapter. One follows Weber's stress on formal organization modelled around the concept of the 'ideal type', which in subsequent work re-emphasizes the importance of the informal organization but within the context of the formal organization. Another follows the Paretian elements of Mayo's thoughts through to the model of the 'social system'. The third stresses the role of technology as the key variable in the formal organization or social system. We shall consider the first direction in this chapter and consider the 'social system' perspective in the following chapter. In Chapter 9 we will consider the role of technology.

Weber's ideal type of bureaucracy

There is no doubt that the theoretical and methodological advances made by Weber in relation to the analysis and understanding of bureaucratic structures were enormous. Nevertheless, an impressive body of literature has developed suggesting that from a number of points of view Weber's analysis was deficient. This has grown into what Albrow (1970, ch. 3) has referred to as 'The Debate with Weber'.

Albrow (1970, p. 50) suggests that Weber's relative lack of interest in the question of inefficiency in bureaucracy has been the factor leading to the debate. Why, then, is there such an emphasis upon bureaucracies as efficient structures with the associated relative neglect of the factors leading to inefficiency? The intellectual influences upon Weber provide major clues to the solution of this puzzle. Albrow suggests four of these: 'These were German administrative theory; Michels; Marx; and the doyen of German economic and social historians, Gustav Schmoller.' Each in his turn

136

led to a conceptualization based upon factors of efficiency. However, the concept of a rational and efficient bureaucracy was recognized by Weber to be fraught with difficulties. As Albrow suggests:

> The concept summed up his deep ambivalence about the development of modern administration: his admiration for it as an intellectual achievement; his conviction of its inexorable advance and his fear for its encroachments on individual and national self-expression (Albrow, 1970, p. 54).

As we have already suggested, Weber's model of bureaucracy and his more general discussion of organization remained largely unchallenged until the informal organization was 'discovered' by the early human relations writers. Equally, the theorists of formal administration were able to develop their concepts, theories and principles of organization and management in a largely uncritical environment. What then comprised the nature of the critique of the formal, rational efficient model, and in what ways has the model been adjusted to account for the so-called 'Hawthorne discovery'?

At a theoretical level it has been the use of the 'ideal type' that has created the greatest controversy. It is imperative that the use of the ideal type is fully understood. As Mouzelis (1967, p. 43) has pointed out: 'Many criticisms of Weber's concept of bureaucracy are rather irrelevant, as they make the assumption that the ideal type has the same logical status as a simple classificatory model, or as an empirical model.' If that is the case, then is it proper to criticize Weber for neglecting the informal organization, the dysfunctions of bureaucracy and bureaucratic inefficiency? We can answer this only through understanding what we mean by the concept of ideal type. Following Weber (1948) it is perhaps more efficient, initially, to delineate what an ideal type is not.

1 It is not a type in the sense of being an average. Thus an ideal-typical bureaucracy is not to be equated with an average bureaucracy.

2 It is not a logical class or more usual type. A logical class – in the sense in which the word 'type' is normally used – is able to classify phenomena on the basis of common characteristics, functions or properties. Therefore, in the case of the ideal type of bureaucracy a set of definite characteristics is not being referred to such that a classification is possible.

3 The above might suggest that if an ideal type is neither an average nor a classificatory type then it is an extreme type. In the way that Weber used the concept it was not intended to have such a function.

Parsons (1937, p. 601) also points out that an ideal type is not an hypothesis; nor a thing or process; nor an average; nor a collection of common characteristics. Parsons suggests that the initial type of bureaucracy is a 'generalizing' concept (rather than an individualizing concept such as 'modern capitalism'). He states that:

> A general ideal type is such a construction of a hypothetical course of events with two other characteristics: (1) abstract generality and (2) the ideal-type exaggeration of empirical reality (Parsons, 1937, p. 605).

Friedrich perceives a number of logical objections to this view of the ideal type. He suggests that:

> Weber's concept of 'ideal types' contravenes the standards of empirical science and implies some kind of intuitional ground which appears beyond rational analysis. But Weber does not face this philosophical aspect, continuing to use the concept as if it were the outcome of empirical enquiry, whereas 'intuition' would raise entirely different methodological problems (Friedrich, 1952, p. 28).

Given these criticisms and the confusion surrounding just what constitutes an ideal type, it is profitable (following Mouzelis, 1967, p. 45) to see the way in which an ideal type is constructed. In this way it is possible to demarcate an ideal type from a theory or model. An ideal type involves:

1 Selecting empirical data and then conceptualizing them. This may involve an inductive process of considering real phenomena.

2 The selected features are exaggerated to their logical extreme. Thus, in Weber's ideal type of bureaucracy we see that formal rules exist to cover each and every possible contingency – an exaggerated logical extreme.

3 The selection and exaggeration of these features is done in such a way that the complete construct has an inter-connected logical consistency.

When this process of ideal type construction is applied to the ideal type bureaucracy, Mouzelis suggests that:

> It is the meaning of rationality, grasped in the . . . intuitive manner, which links together the various ideal characteristics and which gives consistency and logic to the whole construct. An ideally rational organization, in the Weberian sense, is an organization performing its tasks with maximum efficiency. Thus the selection and exaggeration of the various empirical elements and their inter-connections were established in such a way, that a perfectly efficient organization would result if ever such an extreme type existed in reality (Mouzelis, 1967, p. 46).

In spite of this attempt at providing clarity, the actual construct is still a matter of confusion amongst both sociologists and organization theorists. For example, Blau makes the following comments in relation to the ideal type of bureaucracy.

In part it is a conceptual scheme which calls attention to the aspect of organizations that should be included in the investigation and which supplies criteria for defining an actual organization as more or less bureaucratized. In addition, however, Weber indicates that these characteristics tend to go together, that certain historical conditions promote them (such as a money economy) and that the specified characteristics and, in particular, their combination increases administrative efficiency. They are not elucidations of concepts but statements of fact which are assumed to be correct. Whereas concepts are not subject to empirical verification, hypothesized factual relationships are. Only empirical research can ascertain for instance, where authoritarian management and impersonal detachment, singly and in combination, always promote administrative efficiency as predicted or whether they do so only under certain conditions or perhaps not at all (Blau, 1963, p. 309).

Again, Friedrich (1952, p. 28) comments that 'the profound methodological confusion associated with the notion of "ideal type" seriously affects Weber's discussion of "bureaucracy", since bureaucracy is 'supposed to be one of these nebulous entities'.

To a large extent the confusion and debate that has surrounded the use of the ideal type by Weber is misplaced. Much of the literature discussing the problem assumes that rational bureaucracy could be equated with efficiency. Thus, Mouzelis (1967, p. 46) says that 'an ideally rational organization, in the Weberian sense, is an organization performing its tasks with maximum efficiency'. Mayntz (1964, p. 97) states: 'efficiency would be higher the closer reality could be made to approximate the formal scheme. This is the basic contention of . . . Weber's ideal type of bureaucracy'. Many other writers make this assumption; and yet Albrow (1970, pp. 62–4) suggests a number of reasons why such an association between bureaucratic rationality and efficiency is not suggested by Weber. Such a response will be examined in more depth later. As empirical research has shown, the chief deficiencies of Weber's use of the ideal type construct have been in terms of the informal aspects of organization and the examination of the actual attitudes, ideologies, values and behaviour of organization members.

Traditionally such characteristics of organization members have been seen to be independent of the structure of the organization and vice versa. Indeed, although structure figures so prominently in the work of many organization theorists, it has the status of a kind of dismembered phenomenon, existing almost without regard to the members of the organization. Thus, the structure of organizations could be seen as standardized phenomena, whether these phenomena are standardized tasks, levels of authority or product types.

In the case of Weber, structure took on a somewhat different meaning from simply the existence of regularity and uniformity in the organization. Weber was concerned, *inter alia*, with how organizational members come to be controlled and directed by the way in which phenomena such as tasks, levels of authority and product types are regularized. What we see here, therefore, is the basic distinction between structure emerging as a result of negotiation and interaction and structure resulting from constraint or imposition.

Such a distinction is important for organization analysis because the official attempts by, say, senior organization members to create a distinctive organization structure is what is often taken as the structure of the organization. Such an emphasis tends to ignore the possibility that the actual behaviour and attitudes of organization members may be a product of more than the structure. Indeed, it should be stressed that the relationship between structure and behaviour is highly problematic.

Equally problematic is that for organization members there may be different perceptions of what the actual structure comprises. If it is accepted that the understanding of organization structure is important in any study of organizations, then it follows that the extent to which organizations (and their structure) differ from or are similar to one another should be questioned. Is it possible to perceive similarities between apparently diffuse organizations such as factories, churches, hospitals or armies? If structure is so important to the organization analyst, then are there universal features of structure that apply in all cases and with equal intensity? And, if there are different forms of structure that differ by type of organization; what are the consequences of these differences for organization members?

Those interested in organizations are interested in questions such as these. It has long been the task of the organization theorist to establish the characteristics of particular organizations that differentiate them from other types. Even within one type of organization – for example, industrial organizations – there are obviously differences of many kinds. And at the most general and banal level, to say that the thing that distinguishes the industrial organization from other types is the production of goods is clearly inadequate. The difficulties that exist in such classificatory exercises

140

at a common-sense level have led to the attempts to produce uni- or multi-variable classifications as illustrated below.

The attempts at classification are important especially for senior organization members in their constant striving for efficiency. In this instance the structure of the organization is designed to achieve the maximum efficiency; that is, to enable the organization to achieve its official goals. This managerial objective of discovering the most appropriate structure *vis-à-vis* the environment and goals of the organization has, not surprisingly, produced a number of classificatory exercises.

From another point of view, the classification of organizations can be seen as part of a more general sociological enterprise. Hall (1972, p. 39) for example, makes the point that 'Man must classify phenomena in order to be able to think about them'.

The classificatory schemes that exist in the literature fall into two forms: the typologies and the taxonomies. The basic difference between the two is that the former are based upon *a priori* reasoning, while the latter rely on the *a posteriori* method. Thus, 'a typology is a collection of types having certain characteristics in common but also sufficiently different to be distinguishable from one another' (Caldwell and Black, 1971, p. 66). For organizations, then, typologies refer to the descriptions of differences between organizations. As for the use of typologies in the study of organizations, Champion makes the point that:

Organizational theory is not at the level of sophistication necessary to bridge the theoretical gaps between all organizations. Consequently, many theorists have attempted to devise theories which apply to certain *classes* or *types* of organizations (i.e. those which exhibit specific characateristics in common) and not to others (Champion, 1975, p. 65).

The fact that Haas and his colleagues (1966, pp. 162–3) have been able to delineate thirty-seven different characteristics used in the classification of organization is a clear indication of the confusion that exists in this area of study.

Even if the difficulty of sifting throught the list of possible characteristics can be overcome, there is the related problem of deciding what are the most appropriate criteria. Champion (1975, p. 65) refers to the problem of distinguishing the 'right' criteria without discussing the problem of the use of the word 'right' – for example, right for whom? To state as he does that 'only through systematic research on organizations can this question be answered satisfactorily' and that 'some typologies will be more "successful" than others' is largely to ignore the definition of the term typology as being an *a priori* construct.

The greatest level of 'success' that a typology may achieve is if it is able to generate new hypotheses and if it signposts relationships that were previously not recognized. In this sense a typology is a tool, a means to an end and not an end in itself. Little is to be gained by laboriously working through the many typologies that exist in the organization literature. Rather, it is proposed to examine in detail some of the most widely quoted typologies from the point of view of their strengths and weaknesses.

Blau and Scott

The criterion used for the classification of organizations by Blau and Scott (1963) is that of 'who benefits?' or distinguishing the 'prime beneficiary' in the organization. Within any formal organization they suggest that four categories of persons can be distinguished: (1) the members or rank-and-file participants; (2) the owners or managers of the organizations; (3) the clients, or more generally, the 'public-in-contact', which means the people who are technically outside the organizations yet have regular, direct contact with it, under whatever label – patient, customer, law violator, prisoner, enemy soldier, student; and (4) the public-at-large; that is, the members of the society in which the organization operates (Blau and Scott, 1963, p. 42).

Taking each of these groups it is possible, argue Blau and Scott, to classify organizations according to which group benefits from the particular organizational activity. Thus, as Smith (1977, p. 81) puts it, 'the segment of society which consumes the output of the organization can be used to distinguish different types, the nature of members' participation and the main problems'. Blau and Scott are able to distinguish four types of organization in this way: (1) mutual-benefit associations, where the prime beneficiary is the membership; (2) business concerns, where the owners are the prime beneficiary; (3) service organizations, where the client group is the prime beneficiary; and (4) commonweal organizations, where the prime beneficiary is the public-at-large (Blau and Scott, 1963, p. 43).

Each type of organization has associated with it special and peculiar organizational problems. Thus, for example, if any organization is geared more to one group than to any of the others and thereby benefits that group more than any other, then the issues and problems being dealt with by senior members of that type of organization will differ from the issues and problems being dealt with by other organizations:

> The crucial problem in mutual-benefit associations is that of
> maintaining internal democratic processes, providing for parti-

cipation and control by the membership; the central problem for business concerns is that of maximizing operating efficiency in a competitive situation (Blau and Scott, 1963, p. 43).

The Blau and Scott typology has its main strength in the apparent logic that pervades it. In asking the question 'who benefits?' it is clear that the understanding of organizations goes far beyond what could be achieved at a common-sense level. It therefore has considerable usefulness from that point of view. But more important than the issue of usefulness is the question of relevance. Is it really important to note that different types of organization have different problems to deal with? Is it perhaps the case, as Burns has remarked, that:

> The history of sociology . . . is littered with the debris of ruined typologies that only serve as a battle-ground for that academic street-fighting that so often passes for theoretical discussion (Burns, 1967, p. 119).

This is an understandable comment, particularly since the many claims to the 'most appropriate' typology have led to the kind of brawling to which Burns points. On the other hand, the triviality and logical inconsistencies that often creep into typological schemas need to be exposed and debated.

In the case of Blau and Scott this question of relevance can be explored without, in fact, questioning either the validity or the usefulness of the scheme. A number of matters arise from this.

1   There is possibly an over-concern with the question of efficiency in this typology. Since efficiency is an implicit feature of the scheme it weakens its potential from two points of view. First, it is not made clear what is meant by efficiency: for whom is efficiency being generated and for what purposes? And second, such an emphasis suggests an ideological bias in the scheme that is not explicitly referred to or discussed.

2   Whilst being logical and having a certain elegance, the scheme, through its logical simplicity, is naive. The major emphasis, as we have seen, is upon the organization, the prime beneficiaries and the products or services. What may be called the 'political role' of organizations is overlooked through this emphasis. On the surface it may well be true to say that an organization is primarily beneficial to a certain group. But at the same time, and perhaps more insidiously, the organization may be serving some larger group such as, for example, a dominant élite within the wider society. An organization needs to be understood, not only in terms of its apparent manifest function and activity but also in terms of latent functions and activities. This may involve not only asking 'who benefits?' but

143

also two further questions with which Blau and Scott do not concern themselves: 'who does not benefit?' and 'who controls?'. The Blau and Scott typology is unable to discuss such issues.

3 Four groups are distinguished as crucial for understanding organizations in the Blau and Scott typology. The organization is concerned with the interests of such groups and operates in their interests. In essence, this means that the notion of efficiency is being categorized into these four types. That is, organizations are efficient for these four groups and these four alone. It is, though, highly questionable the extent to which it can be argued that efficiency of organizations can be related to the nature of organization structure, as we shall demonstrate in Chapter 8.

4 Following on from the last point, the relationship between the principle of 'who benefits?' and the structure of the organization requires considerably greater elaboration than is given in the Blau and Scott scheme. It would appear that implicit in their writing is the fact that goals are important in that the objectives of the organization can be largely equated with the question of who is benefiting from the organizational activities. Blau and Scott's argument is that different types of organizations have different beneficiaries and will both face, and have to solve, particular problems relevant to these beneficiaries. The structure of the organization is related to the particular problems that an organization faces. It is not a big jump to suggest that these problems correspond closely to the goals of the organization. Thus, there is the suggestion that structure and goals can be related; as we shall see in Chapter 8. This is highly problematic.

5 The universal nature of the scheme suggests that the prime beneficiaries of a particular type of organization remain constant over time. This again is highly problematic. There is no reason why the beneficiaries would remain the same and, indeed, there are many examples that come to mind where there have been significant shifts. This suggests that the model is a static one that is incapable of explaining change over time. Furthermore, it suggests that each of the four groups that may comprise the prime beneficiaries are coherent and unified. Again, this is problematic.

6 The approach used by Blau and Scott appears to ignore the fact that it is the controllers of the organization who determine the benefit that is to go to any individual or group. In the case of business concerns, the owners or managers are deciding their own interests; in each of the other types the controllers, the administrators and the managers have a large say in determining the nature and size of the benefits for the rank-and-file participants, the clients or the general public, depending upon the kind of organization. This phenomenon, together with the fifth factor mentioned above,

may give rise to conflict in organizations, particularly over the allocation of physical and social resources.

Etzioni

Etzioni's classification scheme is another attempt at producing a typology based upon a single criterion of demarcation. The initial focus in the schema is upon the inter-organizational aspects of power and control. Thus, as Pugh et al. (1971, p. 30) point out, the fundamental question for Etzioni is: 'Why do people in organizations conform to the orders given to them and follow the standards of behaviour laid down for them?' Since Etzioni argues that answers to such questions can be provided only by the use of the comparative approach, the development of a typology of organizations is important for the achievement of the task. His scheme is composed of both motivational and structural elements and relates to other areas of sociological investigation.

The key variable or criterion that Etzioni selects for the development of his typology is that of *compliance*. This, he says, 'is universal, existing in all social units. It is a major element of the relationship between those who have power and those over whom they exercise it'. The definition of compliance is 'the relation in which an actor behaves in accordance with a directive supported by another actor's power and to the orientation of the subordinated actor to the power applied' (Etzioni, 1961, p. 4). Compliance therefore relates to the obedience of an organization member and the reasons for this obedience. This is demonstrated more clearly when Etzioni refers to compliance being 'a relationship consisting of the power employed by superiors to control subordinates and the orientation of the subordinates to this power' (Etzioni, 1961, p. xv). The classification of organizations based upon their type of compliance enables Etzioni to combine the motivational and structural elements already referred to, or in Etzioni's words, the 'differential commitments of actors to organizations' and 'the kinds and distribution of power in organizations'.

Compliance is the result of two factors operating within organizations: the orientation of members towards the organization's power system (their *involvement*), and the means available for the exercise of *power*.

Within organizations there are, suggests Etzioni, three basic types of power: coercive, remunerative and normative. The differentiation between these types is through 'the means employed to make the subjects comply. These means may be physical, material or symbolic' (Etzioni, 1961, p. 5). Although it is clear that each of these types may be employed simultaneously in the same organization, Etzioni suggests that 'most organizations tend to emphasize only one means of power, relying less on the other two' (Etzioni, 1961, p. 7). The reason for this, he argues, is because the attitudes and reactions of organization members are largely determined by particular rewards or sanctions, thereby making other rewards and sanctions redundant.

Taking the three types of power, coercive power is based upon the (potential) use of physical force, the restriction of activities, restraint, etc.; remunerative power refers to the control over material resources particularly through the way in which wages are distributed, the allocation of fringe benefits, etc.; normative power depends upon what Etzioni refers to as 'the allocation and manipulation of symbolic rewards and deprivations through the employment of leaders, manipulation of mass media, allocation of esteem and prestige symbols, etc.' (Etzioni, 1961, p. 5).

The way in which organization members react to the exercise of power to which they are subject, comprises the other side of the compliance relationship. Etzioni refers to this as the members' involvement, 'the cathectic-evaluative orientation of an actor to an object' (Etzioni, 1961, p. 9). As with the power types, he distinguishes three types of involvement: alienative, for the high alienation zone; moral for the high commitment zone; and calculative for the two mid-zones (Etzioni, 1961, pp. 10–11).

Through the use of a cross-tabulation, it is clear that theoretically there are nine possible combinations of power and involvement, that is, of compliance. In fact, Etzioni argues that three of the types (1, 5 and 9) 'are found more frequently than the other six types. This seems to be true because these three types constitute congruent relationships, whereas the other six do not' (Etzioni, 1961, p. 12).

TABLE 4.1   *Kinds of involvement*

Kinds of power	Alienative	Calculative	Moral
Coercive	1	2	3
Remunerative	4	5	6
Normative	7	8	9

Source: Etzioni, 1961, p. 12.

Etzioni argues that organization effectiveness can reach its full potential when there is congruence between power and involvement. The three types of organization he refers to as coercive, utilitarian and normative are characterized as the cross-tabulation shows by the combination of power and involvement of coercive-alienative (1); remunerative-calculative (5); and normative-moral (9).

In addition to fulfilling the requirements of a typology, Etzioni argues that his classification of organizations has utility 'because compliance relations are a central element of organizational structure' (Etzioni, 1961, p. 21). Therefore, it is suggested that the scheme has value from a predictive point of view. Furthermore:

His exploration of these types is explicitly intended to make a contribution to 'middle range' theory of organizations, by filling in the 'lamentable hiatus' between case studies of single organizations and abstract generalizing about all organizations (Eldridge and Crombie, 1974, p. 47).

Turning to this application of the classification, the use of the compliance variable enables one to subdivide categories and types within the organization. An interesting example that Etzioni gives is the distinction between combat units and peace-time units within the general type 'military organization'. The two types of unit have different compliance structures, and this leads to differences in both structure and process. Thus, 'organizations that have similar compliance structures tend to have similar goals, and organizations that have similar goals tend to have similar compliance structures' (Etzioni, 1961, p. 71).

There is a relationship between the distribution of power in the organization and the compliance structure. This can be seen in the comparison between coercive and normative organizations. The coercive distinguish sharply between those exercising the power and those subject to it; the normative attempt an integration of all organization members.

At another level, compliance can be related to the cultural integration that exists within organizations. This can be demonstrated in three ways:

the degree of consensus between lower participants and organizational representatives on cultural orientations in a number of spheres; the symbolic processes reinforcing or modifying these orientations; and the processes introducing new participants to the culture of the organization and that of the lower participants' collectivities (Etzioni, 1961, p. 149).

The typology can obviously be applied in a number of organizational contexts. Salaman remarks that 'it deliberately sets out to replace and reject what he [Etzioni] classes as "common-sense" categories, such as military organizations, or unions, business organizations, and so on . . . it is directly concerned with *organizational control*' (Salaman, 1974, p. 47, our emphasis). The scheme is also interesting in terms of the questions of 'how far is it empirically true that certain organizational characteristics tend to cluster around this (or any other) key classificatory variable, and if such empirical clusterings are discernable, then why do they come about?' (Salaman, 1974, p. 47).

The emphasis so far has been upon the congruent relations between power and involvement. There are, of course, incongruent compliance types as well.

Coercive-calculative (2): this relationship occurs when an organization member who is forced (coerced) into activities that he or she feels are too lowly for him or her recognizes that the performance of these activities is necessary to achieve promotion and thereby shed the activities.

Coercive-moral (3): the best example of this relationship is where an individual is conscripted into the armed forces. In that sense an individual may feel coerced and yet performs their duty through a moral sense of commitment through higher values such as patriotism.

Remunerative-alienative (4): some aspects of industrial work reflect this relationship where an individual works purely for the wages and where he or she has a negative involvement in the organization (Beynon, 1974).

Remunerative-moral (6): the farmer in a wartime situation who makes large profits through the emphasis upon the domestic production system may experience disquiet about the circumstances in which the profits are being made.

Normative-alienative (7): the social worker who has considerable normative power at work may come to experience alienation through the normative codes to be used at work compared with the values adhered to in, say, the domestic situation.

Normative-calculative (8): professional employees are often in a situation of normative power where they comply with the exercise of power through the knowledge that the work has numerous compensations and rewards not associated with other types of work.

Another point about these incongruities is that studies of the exercise of power (e.g., French and Raven, 1959) clearly indicate that one individual may exercise different types of power in different situations. Equally, different compliance relations may exist for the same individual at different times or situation.

Etzioni presents what he calls a dynamic hypothesis that 'organizations tend to shift their compliance structure from incongruent to congruent types and organizations which have congruent compliance structures tend to resist factors pushing them toward incongruent compliance structures' (Etzioni, 1961, p. 14). In essence this is an assumption of structural balance.

Having explored Etzioni's scheme, it is necessary now to turn to some criticisms that can be levelled against it. We have seen that, at a descriptive level, the typology is elegant in that the compliance variable is associated with a number of organization characteristics. It is in terms of establishing relationships between compliance and organization structure, goals and effectiveness that the typology is suspect. As explained below, the most basic problem is that Etzioni perceives organization effectiveness operating independently of individual and organization interests and choice.

In his analysis, Etzioni makes effectiveness a key variable in that it can be demonstrated in terms of the relationship between certain organization characteristics and the compliance type. His discussion of organization goals best demonstrates his position. He remarks that an organization goal referring to order may be pursued through a structure that reflects normative compliance. This is an incongruent situation and he says of it that 'it is feasible, but not effective' (Etzioni, 1961, p. 77).

Operating within what is essentially a functionalist framework, the definition of organizations is given as 'social units oriented to the realization of specific goals' (Etzioni, 1961, p. 79). It is instructive to note the degree of similarity between this definition and that of Talcott Parsons writing a few years earlier and firmly in the functionalist mould. Where Etzioni goes beyond Parsons is in his recognition that the official goals of organizations may differ from the actual goals being pursued. In spite of this, goal pursuit and orientation figure as key concepts in the definition.

Again, following the functionalist tradition, Etzioni attempts to examine relationships in system terms, especially the relationship between the system parts. Thus, we see comments about the links between organization structure and the compliance relationship in terms of whether they are congruent or incongruent. Congruence could so easily read 'survival of the system'. He also states that relations between certain organization characteristics and the type of compliance can be discussed in terms of their effectiveness. Thus, 'The effectiveness model defines a pattern of inter-relations among the elements of the system which make it most effective in the service of a given goal' (Etzioni, 1961, p. 78).

This can be linked with Etzioni's position concerning the way in which congruent elements develop. There is a movement within the organization to develop effective combinations of structure, process and goal.

In the six ineffective types we would expect to find not only

149

wasted means, psychological and social tension, lack of co-ordination, and other signs of ineffectiveness, but also *a strain toward an effective type* (Etzioni, 1961, p. 87).

Of course there is some evidence for such a proposition. To take an obvious one, in those organizations that are committed to 'order goals' such as prisons there would naturally be ineffectiveness if the normative compliance of the prisoners was to be relied upon. (Etzioni, 1975, presents a considerable amount of evidence supporting his hypotheses.)

The basic problem rests upon the nature of causality in the inter-relationships. As we have seen, each type of compliance has a clustering of certain organizational variables resulting from the strain towards effectiveness experienced by all organizations. Here again can be seen the strong functionalist bias. It becomes impossible to discuss certain organization features and their inter-relationship. They are essentially presented as 'givens', as functional imperatives. Propositions are presented as if they were inevitable and unchangeable through intervention. Thus, industry has a re-munerative-calculative compliance type, although also experiencing elements of both coercion and alienation. This is seen as inevitable by Etzioni if the organization is to be effective through goal achievement. And yet there is no reason why this should be regarded as inevitable and beyond intervention. It is even problematic that the running of factories on these lines is effective for the organization.

Other criticisms of the Etzioni scheme may be mentioned. Perrow (1967) makes the point that difficulties arise with schemes using only one dimension or variable in their construction. The main problem is that a certain closure may arise since other important variables are not examined. As Champion (1975, p. 71) points out: 'In the general case, uni-dimensional schemes tend to be inadequate theoretically and have little explanatory value beyond certain organizational limits.' Whilst Etzioni's scheme is relatively complex using only one variable, if more variables were to be included, the complexity would increase proportionately. In addition to the problem of the number of variables is the associated problem of which variables should be used. Perrow (1972, p. 165) states that 'an adequate typology should be based upon organiza-tional characteristics that are conceptually independent of either goals or structure'. As demonstrated above, Etzioni's scheme does not satisfy this requirement in that it is very much associated with both goals and structure.

Allen (1975) has analysed Etzioni's typology from the point of view of its logical consistency. Allen is critical of the state of sociological enquiry in that, unlike many aspects of economic theory, it still has not developed the capacity for being subject to analytical treatment of a rigorous kind. He recognizes that Etzioni chose a useful key variable in compliance, especially since the probable alternative would have been legitimation. The initial problem that Etzioni has, according to Allen, is that since compliance relations are likely to be so complex the analysis tends to concentrate upon 'higher participants' and 'lower participants'.

The major problem in the analysis of the control by the higher participants is that:

> The all important thing is the classification and this is beset
> with difficulties, particularly as on Etzioni's own admission most
> organizations employ all three kinds [of power]. The question
> concerning the causal relationships between the three types of
> power is not even posed, let alone answered, in Etzioni's model
> (Allen, 1975, p. 153).

Next, Allen argues that there is a problem with the identification of the lower participants in Etzioni's scheme. Basically, lower participants are defined in terms of their involvement from the point of view of direction and intensity, the amount of performance and the degree of subordination.

Of this Allen says, 'It was necessary that Etzioni *should* define lower participants as he did in order to complete his model and not because an analysis would be defective if they were defined in any other way' (Allen, 1975, p. 156). And again, 'When faced with defining lower participants Etzioni has *either* to include among them actors who were patently not motivated by remuneration and who appeared to be motivated by the use of force *or* the influence of power systems' (Allen, 1975, p. 156). Thus, a fundamental problem is that of the inconsistency in the definition of the lower participants.

The use of the concept of involvement also raises difficulties for Allen:

> Instead of seeing alienation simply as negative involvement
> it can be recognized as a term borrowed from Karl Marx and
> referring to the attitude of work caused by the inability to
> become identified with the whole of a particular work process,
> including the disposal of the product. The point is, however,
> that the term is borrowed from Marx and not from the conceptual
> framework of which it is a part and it therefore has a somewhat
> different meaning in the hands of Etzioni (Allen, 1975, p. 160).

Etzioni's analysis of the process of the generation of alienation can be viewed as a series of sequential propositions:

1 Specialization creates dissatisfaction with work
2 The greater dissatisfaction arises among those performing the most specialized tasks
3 Industrial conflict is a function of dissatisfaction
4 There is a positive correlation between specialization and industrial conflict
5 The more efficient the productive process the more likely there will be worker-management conflict
6 The sharpest conflict in an organization involves management and the least skilled workers
7 If specialized rational action increases both productivity and dissatisfaction then there must be a positive correlation between productivity and dissatisfaction.

8 'It follows from the above propositions that the Structuralists correlate the physical work environment or organization of work (an independent variable) with satisfaction from work (a dependent variable) and conflict between management and workers (a dependent variable). . . . The above propositions . . . follow logically from Etzioni's analysis. They suggest the ludicrous conclusion that rational action results in both efficiency and inefficiency in such a way that the more efficient an organization becomes the less efficient it is' (Allen, 1975, p. 162).

Allen makes two other criticisms of Etzioni's typology that relate directly to the structuralist perspective that is adopted. In the first place, there are problems over the use of the concept of conflict.

> In the one case conflict is wholly the product of maladjustment between parts, whereas in the other case it may be this but it may also result from internal structural factors and not be amenable to remedial treatment (Allen, 1975, p. 163).

The other criticism is that Etzioni pays insufficient attention to the organization environment. The environment is not seen in causal terms; the organization is conceptually structured so as to be insulated from its environment.

Essentially what Allen has attempted to do is to lay bare the analytic framework used by Etzioni and to investigate critically the logical construction of the model. As we have seen, he finds the typology to be inadequate from a number of points of view, although he does not present an alternative. It is interesting that Etzioni himself has re-worked his analysis and has shown that while there may be problems with the internal logic of the scheme when applied to an empirical situation there is a fair level of consistency in the results. Indeed the second edition of *The Comparative Analysis of Complex Organizations* (1975) is largely a review of the empirical attempts that have been made to test the propositions by those both sympathetic and unsympathetic to Etzioni's approach.

Blau and Scott and Etzioni compared

In addition to the examination of typologies in the manner used so far, it is possible to extend the analysis by comparing typologies that have been generated for examining the same phenomenon. If one theory can be shown to relate to another theory then a theoretical continuity and advance can be established. In the case of the typologies produced by Blau and Scott and Etzioni one such exercise in linking the two was carried out by Hall, Haas and Johnson (1966). This was done from an empirical point of view but has a number of theoretical implications.

Data was obtained from 75 organizations representing the main institutional areas – economic, political, religious, etc. – and varying in size from 6 to 9,000 organization members. Data from the organizations was obtained through interviews with the top executives and through examination of records. The organizations were divided into the four types derived from the Blau and Scott typology and the three congruent types of the Etzioni typology.

Blau and Scott:
Mutual benefit: 14 – trade unions, a political party, etc.
Service: 18 – universities, hospitals, etc.
Business: 27 – banks, hotels, factories, etc.
Commonweal: 16 – post office, educational television, etc.

Etzioni:
Coercive: 11 - prison, state hospital, state school, etc.
Utilitarian: 35 – banks, restaurants, shops, etc.
Normative: 29 – church, political party, etc.

The following relationships were found between the two typologies:

TABLE 4.2

	Mutual benefit (14)	Service (18)	Business (27)	C'weal (16)
	%	%	%	%
Coercive (11)	0	17	0	50
Utilitarian (35)	43	6	89	25
Normative (29)	57	77	11	25

$\chi^2 = 52.25$; 6df; p>0.001
Source: Hall, Haas and Johnson, 1966, p. 123.

153

From Table 4.2 it is clear that there is a highly significant statistical relationship between the two typologies. As Etzioni points out, much of the clustering is to be expected. But it is somewhat surprising to discover that there are twice as many coercive commonweal organizations as either normative or utilitarian ones. It could be concluded from this that 'the public relies heavily on the government for its well-being, and that the government relies more on coercion than on other means' (Etzioni, 1975, p. 97).

It is also interesting to note the extent that normative means are used in mutual benefit organizations. Normative means are widely employed in service organizations, which again is surprising. Hall, Haas and Johnson reverse the original table in an attempt to check this finding:

TABLE 4.3

	Coercive 11	Utilitarian 35	Normative 29
	%	%	%
Mutual benefit (14)	0	17	28
Service (18)	27	3	48
Business (27)	0	69	10
Commonweal (16)	73	11	14

$\chi^2 = 52.25$; 6df; p>0.001

Source: Hall, Haas and Johnson, 1966, p. 123

The reversed Table 4.3 shows that in 73 per cent of the cases coercive organizations are commonweal and that in 69 per cent of the cases utilitarian organizations are business concerns. From this evidence, Etzioni claims that 'the compliance typology has been supported by this intra-theoretical consistency test' (Etzioni, 1975, p. 97).

We see from both Blau and Scott and Etzioni that their analyses of organizations in terms of classificatory typologies have both advantages and disadvantages. In terms of the development of organization studies they are important in that they move away from the monolithic conception of organization and bureaucracy contained in the 'classical' literature of Weber and the formal theorists of administration. In addition the typologies link some key variables to organizational efficiency.

We have already made reference to the debate over whether Weber's conception of bureaucracy in formal rational terms could be equated with efficiency. Clearly, the typological exercises distinguished do not allude to rational organization in Weber's sense, but undoubtedly efficiency is of crucial importance in the analyses.

The question of efficiency and inefficiency also figures prominently in the substantive work of Merton (1940) and Selznick (1957). In our discussion of organizations as systems in Chapter 5 the analytical frameworks of these two writers are discussed at length and from the viewpoint of systems analysis. Basically, Merton's interest was in control or the demand by 'the organization' for discipline. This produces, according to Merton, a pressure for reliability and predictability in the behaviour of organization members. Personal relationships are subsequently reduced so that, increasingly, individuals become rule-followers. Also, organizational techniques are used more extensively so that there is a reduction in flexibility. The organization is thus in the ambivalent position of being easier to control or manage, but by the same token is less adaptive to change and less capable of coping with novel problems. In many ways the organization posited by Merton corresponds closely to Weber's model of bureaucracy. Yet it is an organization that is rigid in its internal structure and inflexible in its relations with its environment. Merton, therefore, shows how, in a certain set of circumstances, Weber's construction of bureaucracy may be highly inefficient.

To summarize, Selznick's analysis shows a conception of organization that corresponds closely to that of Merton's. Selznick argues that the number of controllers, supervisors or managers in organizations needs to be increased as organizations grow in size and, therefore, have greater need for discipline within them. From this Selznick suggests that such 'controllers' may have two sets of objectives to pursue: those that are organizational and those associated with the department which the 'controller' heads. If the objectives differ, then the values affecting judgments and decisions will also vary. In turn this can be linked to the efficiency of the organization, although whether efficiency increases or decreases depends upon particular circumstances.

The work of both Merton and Selznick is important in the current context of questioning the idea of rational bureaucracy and bureaucratic efficiency. As Albrow suggests:

Neither Merton nor Selznick are concerned to point out inconsistencies in Weber's propositions on rational bureaucracy. Rather they intend to show that the formal specification of organizational structure which he outlined is insufficient as a description of how bureaucrats will in fact behave. The

155

official has characteristics as a social being beyond those which the administrative code specifies. Like other men he has interests, prejudices and fears. He forms friendships and cliques (Albrow, 1970, pp. 55–6).

What we can see here is proof of the importance of the 'discovery of the informal organization' by the Hawthorne researchers and of the Human Relations research that developed from that.

Additional organizational models

It is clear that criticisms of the ideal type model of bureaucracy abound in the literature, both from a theoretical and an empirical point of view. Equally, the typological approach employed by writers such as Blau and Scott and Etzioni suggests a critique of the monolithic bureaucratic model. The criticisms of the model have not gone unheeded, and it is interesting to note that from the organization literature has come an acceptance that different models of organization may be more appropriate in certain circumstances.

Possibly one of the best known of alternative organizational models is that suggested by Burns and Stalker (1961). The model developed from an empirical study of the Scottish electronics industry, which, among other things, attempted to explain why some industrial firms were successful while others were unsuccessful. The alternative model was labelled an 'organic' form of organization. It was found to be appropriate to changing conditions of the kind that constantly raise new problems and unforeseen requirements. Such problems and requirements cannot be automatically related to the functional roles and rules contained within the hierarchic structure of the bureaucratic organization. Organic organization is characterized by:

(a)   The contributive nature of special knowledge and experience to the common tasks of the concern.

(b)   The 'realistic' nature of the individual task, which is seen as set by the total situation of concern.

(c)   The adjustment and continual re-definition of individual tasks through interaction with others.

(d)   The shedding of 'responsibility' as a limited field of rights, obligations and methods. (Problems may be posted upwards, downwards or sideways as being someone else's responsibility.)

(e)   The spread of commitment to the concern beyond any technical definition.

(f)   A network structure of control, authority and communication. The sanctions which apply to the individual's conduct in his working

156

role derived more from presumed community of interest with the rest of the working organization in the survival and growth of the firm and less from a contractual relationship between himself and a non-personal corporation, represented for him by an immediate superior.

(g)   Omniscience no longer imputed to the head of the concern: knowledge about the technical or commercial nature of the here-and-now task may be located anywhere in the network; this location becoming the *ad hoc* centre of control, authority and communication.

(h)   A lateral rather than a vertical direction of communication through the organization; communication between people of different rank, also, resembling consultation rather than command.

(i)   A context of communication which consists of information and advice rather than instructions and decisions.

(j)   Commitment to the concern's tasks and to the 'technological ethos' of material progress and expansion is more highly valued than loyalty and obedience.

(k)   Importance and prestige attach to affiliations and expertise valid in the industrial and technical and commercial milieux external to the firm.

From this list of characteristics of the organic organization it is clear that low structure, adaptability and flexibility are its hallmarks. Nevertheless, rules and procedures exist within such organizations to the extent that a cursory examination would find it difficult to distinguish them from other (non-organic) organizations. In terms of organization practice the reality as found by Burns and Stalker is that whilst formal characteristics such as an organization chart may exist, relationships ignore them. There tends to be an emphasis on work activity rather than upon status differentials. Referring to alternative models to the bureaucratic model of organization (whether we call these organic, professional or project organizations), Thomason has pointed out that:

> The reality is such as to emphasize work roles which do not
> have precise boundaries, relationships which ignore the formal
> chart or status distinctions in favour of getting the job done,
> rules which are for the guidance of wise men but not to be
> equated with the laws of the Medes and the Persians, a degree
> of 'professionalization' of the inter-relationships and a reward
> system which reflects contribution on a continuing basis rather
> than length of service . . . but in fact it makes it more possible
> for this kind of organization to deal with changing problems
> more effectively than would the more rigid bureaucracy
> (Thomason, 1972, p. 29).

The Burns and Stalker model of an organic organization suggests not so much a rejection of the original Weber model (indeed their explication of the 'mechanistic' model demonstrates the value of such a structure in appropriate stable conditions) as a modification and refinement of it. Other writers can be labelled as being in the same tradition. Of particular interest here is the work of Alvin Gouldner (1954) and Peter Blau (1955).

Alvin Gouldner

As a result of his well-known study of a gypsum mine (a description of which is presented in Chapter 7), Gouldner (1954) was able to modify the original Weberian model of bureaucracy by suggesting three sub-classes of bureaucracy. The background to Gouldner's conclusions is of relevance. The empirical study was an attempt to test out some of Weber's ideas about bureaucracy. It will be recalled from the last chapter that Weber made much play of the fact that bureaucracies are governed by the exercise of impersonal and abstract rules. Gouldner points out, however, that the question of who makes the rules and by what process they are made, remains largely ignored in Weber's writings. Clearly such questions are important, not only from the point of view of whether, in reality, rules are arbitrarily imposed or whether they are democratically decided upon, but also from a more abstract point of view which might express an interest in the distribution of power within an organization (cf. Chapter 12). Albrow (1970) points out that it was not so much a question of Weber ignoring such vital questions, but rather the fact that his empirical reference was the civil service.

Another issue arising from Weber's analysis that Gouldner was interested in exploring, was the fact that the ends served by particular rules were not analysed. The differing perspectives that exist on the rules – depending upon whom in the organization is being asked to comment on them – is a further area of analysis largely untouched by Weber. A basic criticism that Gouldner makes, therefore, is that Weber was more concerned with structure than process.

Gouldner distinguishes three patterns of bureaucracy: mock, representative and punishment-centred. The factors associated with each of these patterns can be summarized as follows, following Gouldner (1954, pp. 216–17):

1 Who usually initiates the rules?

(a) *Mock*: The rule or rules are imposed on the group by some outside agency. *Neither* workers *nor* management, neither superiors nor subordinates, identify themselves with or participate in the establishment of the rules or view them as their own.

158

(b) *Representative*: *Both* groups initiate the rules and view them as their own.

(c) *Punishment-centred*: The rule arises in response to the pressure of *either* workers *or* management but is *not jointly* initiated by them. The group which does not initiate the rule views it as imposed upon it by the other.

2   Whose values legitimate the rules?

(a) *Mock: Neither* superiors *nor* subordinates can, ordinarily, legitimate the rule in terms of their own values.

(b) *Representative*: Usually, *both* workers and management can legitimate the rules in terms of their own key values.

(c) *Punishment-centred*: *Either* superiors *or* subordinates alone consider the rule legitimate; the other may concede on grounds of expediency but does not define the rule as legitimate.

3   Whose values are violated by enforcement of the rules?

(a) *Mock*: Enforcement of the rule violates the values of *both groups*.

(b) *Representative*: Under most conditions, enforcement of the rules entails violations of *neither* group's values.

(c) *Punishment-centred*: Enforcement of the rules violates the values of only one group, *either* superiors *or* subordinates.

4   What are the standard explanations of deviations from the rules?

(a) *Mock*: The deviant pattern is viewed as an expression of uncontrollable needs or of 'human nature'.

(b) *Representative*: Deviance is attributed to ignorance or *well-intentioned carelessness*; i.e., it is an unanticipated by-product of behaviour oriented to some other end and thus an 'accident'. This Gouldner calls a 'utilitarian' conception of deviance.

(c) *Punishment-centred*: In the main, deviance is attributed to *deliberate* intent. Deviance is thought to be the deviant's *end*. This Gouldner calls a 'voluntaristic' conception of deviance.

5   What effects do the rules have upon the status of the participants?

(a) *Mock*: Ordinarily, deviation from the rule is status-enhancing for *both* workers and management. Conformity to the rule would be status-impairing for both.

(b) *Representative*: Usually, deviation from the rule impairs the status of superiors *and* subordinates, while conformity ordinarily permits both a measure of status improvement.

(c) *Punishment-centred*: Conformity to or deviation from the rules lead to status gains *either* for workers *or* supervisors but not for both, and to status losses for the other.

159

6 Summary of defining characteristics or symptoms
  (a) *Mock*:
Rules are neither enforced by management nor obeyed by workers.

Usually entails little conflict between the two groups.

Joint violation and evasion of rules is buttressed by the informal sentiments of the participants.

  (b) *Representative*:
Rules are both enforced by management and obeyed by workers.

Generates a few tensions, but little overt conflict.

Joint support for rules buttressed by informal sentiments, mutual participation, initiation, and education of workers and management.

  (c) *Punishment-centred*:
Rules either enforced by workers or management, and evaded by the other.

Entails relatively great tension and conflict.

Enforced by punishment and supported by the informal sentiments of *either* workers *or* management.

As we shall see in more detail in the next chapter, there is a degree of similarity between Gouldner's work and that of Merton and Selznick over and above the observations already made about the latter two writers. In particular, there is a specific similarity with Merton in terms of the consequences of the exercise and existence of the rules of the bureaucracy for the maintenance of the structure of the organization. And like both writers, Gouldner was concerned with the issue of control within organizations and how control is related to the general level of equilibrium in the structure. March and Simon summarize diagrammatically Gouldner's model as in Figure 4.1.

Accounting for Figure 4.1, we can see that the original demand for control in the organization generates the use of the rules. In turn, this decreases the visibility of the power relations within work groups. The extent to which there are norms governing equality in relations interacts with this situation and thereby has an effect upon the strength of the supervisory role. The level of interpersonal tension is subsequently affected. These are the anticipated consequences of the demand for control.

Simultaneously, however, the imposition of the rules produces a clearer definition of what comprises unacceptable behaviour. There is also a tendency for the goals of the organization to be less internalized producing a reduction in the amount of fit between objectives and achievement. Given this situation, there is a need for greater and closer supervision over members. Again, this increases

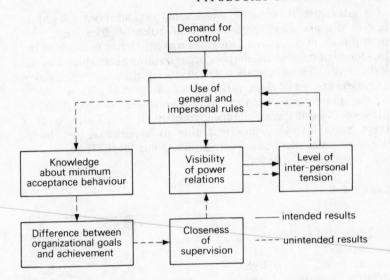

Figure 4.1
Source: March and Simon, 1958, p. 41.

the visibility of the power relations within the organization but as an unanticipated consequence of the original demand for control.

As a refinement and modification of Weber's original bureaucratic model, Gouldner's analysis is clearly important. If we examine the two main kinds of rule – punishment-centred and representative – it is clear that the former are accepted by members reluctantly in that they are seen to be imposed by an outside group and without general consent. In the case of the latter, the rules are accepted as necessary and are both legitimated and enforced by mutual agreement between all the parties concerned. Thus, in representative bureaucracies the potential for conflict is greatly reduced; and if there is rule violation this is generally explained in terms of unmalicious carelessness or ignorance on the part of members. The hallmark of the structure is not punishment but a continual process of socialization in order to reduce the potential for deviant behaviour. As Albrow (1970, p. 56) remarks, 'The two different attitudes to rules have a marked influence on the efficient working of an organization.'

We have seen that in *Patterns of Industrial Bureaucracy* (1954) Gouldner was especially concerned with the basis of rule-following in organizations. In fact, this interest arose from an earlier concern that was only to be examined at a later date: the argument over professional and bureaucratic authority and the potential for tension and conflict it generates within organizations. On the basis of a later case study using educational organizations, Gouldner (1957) distinguished the latent social roles of 'local' and 'cosmopolitan'. In this study, Gouldner was concerned to examine the incidence of conflict in complex organizations between and within individuals. These so-called latent social roles of organization members consist of three variables according to Gouldner: loyalty to the employing organization; commitment to specialized or professional skills; and reference group orientation. On the basis of these variables, Gouldner was able to hypothesize two latent organizational identities: cosmopolitan and local. These can be illustrated as in Table 4.4.

TABLE 4.4

	Cosmopolitan	Local
Loyalty	low	high
Commitment	high	low
Reference group	outer	inner

Arising from his initial interest in the analysis of conflict within organizations (as seen in the distinction between representative and punishment-centred bureaucracies) Gouldner demonstrated that organization problems can arise from these two latent identities. In the first place, when individuals are being assessed in a bureaucratic manner they are being assessed by definable criteria such as skill or competence. It is rare for a factor such as loyalty to be employed in such assessments since it can lead to organization problems when a factor such as promotion is being considered.

The concepts of cosmopolitan and local are very general categories and have little heuristic value in their own right. Consequently, Gouldner attempted a refinement of them. His empirical study of an educational organization confirmed his predictions concerning cosmopolitanism and localism. By themselves the concepts are quite sterile; they tell us little about the problems of professions in organizations nor do they add much to a modification or refinement of early concepts of bureaucracy. However, the empirical study did, in fact, suggest that three behaviour forms were associated with the concepts: differential patterns of participation; differential propensities for 'rule tropism'; and differential degrees of influence within the organization.

Briefly, what the findings indicated were that the influence increased along the scale from cosmopolitan to local; that locals participated far more than cosmopolitans (although there was even more participation at the intermediate points of the continuum); and locals tended to be higher on rule tropism than were the cosmopolitans.

Peter Blau

Blau's concern in his empirical investigation of *The Dynamics of Bureaucracy* (1955) was principally with the question of rationality in organizations. He suggests that Weber's work on bureaucracy implies a myth that rationality can come only from the top of the organization. This, of course, was the basic view of the scientific management writers as demonstrated in the last chapter. Blau argues that implicit in Weber's model (and that of the scientific managers) is the notion that an individual will behave rationally only if his work task is so structured as to deprive him of discretion and judgment, so that the prescribed nature of the role is as enforced as possible.

Two US government agencies were studied in order to test empirically the validity of such propositions. These were a federal law enforcement agency and a state employment agency. The empirical emphasis was upon the ways in which the formal regulations of the two agencies were implemented on a day-to-day basis.

Very briefly, Blau discovered that in the state employment agency there were local adjustments made to the centrally prescribed rules and procedures for finding jobs. Such adjustments were made in the interests of the unemployed and their more expeditious allocation to the available jobs. The system was such that the employment agency officials were systematically assessed on a comparative basis through the statistical records. Further, performance assessment was designed to encourage a degree of competition between the officials. In spite of this formal arrangement in the agency, Blau found that if, in fact, there was co-operation between officials and if little account was taken of the statistical recording devices, then those officials tended to be more productive than others who adhered firmly to the prescribed system of assessment. Thus, the competition that was supposed to engender efficiency was less effective in doing so than the spirit of co-operation that sometimes arose.

At a more extreme level, Blau also found that in the federal agency if there was a continuous and persistent infringement of the rules by officials, the organization as a whole tended to be more effective (that is, more likely to achieve its stated official goals). One instance can illustrate this point. It was a cardinal rule of the agency that any attempt by business managers to bribe an official should be reported immediately. If this rule was ignored officials could place themselves in a position of being able to 'blackmail' the managers if the need should ever arise. In this sense, the manager was likely to co-operate as fully as necessary because of the possibility of being reported for the attempted bribe. Here, the deliberate disobedience of the rule is highly functional for the organization and the achievement of its goals rather than being dysfunctional as might be expected.

These case studies suggest some interesting modifications that can be made to the original formal model of bureaucracy. Clearly, the impersonality of the rules combined with their actual existence indicate that dysfunctions such as lower employee morale and lower levels of productivity may pertain. This suggests that alternative organizational forms and structures may be more functional. Blau proposes that a basic condition is that control should be more decentralized in organizations. If this feature is coupled with a less authoritarian attitude the conditions exist for the individual to play a more active role in the organization, to contribute to decision-making and problem-solving, and to demonstrate his ability to behave responsibly without the need to follow rules and procedures that might not relate to every possible eventuality. It is Blau's contention that such a strategy is highly functional both for the organization and for the individual.

Blau's basic point, that rules and procedures cannot be designed to cover every possible decision, relates, in fact, to Burns and Stalker's work. Their model of organic organization was found to be most appropriate in a changing environment – where (for industrial organizations) markets, products, customers, etc. could not be relied upon to be the same over time. Blau states that 'the stable attainment of organizational objectives depends on perpetual change in the bureaucratic structure' (Blau, 1955, p. 201). It follows, therefore, that the organization member should not be made to adhere rigidly to a preconceived set of rules but should be allowed to adjust his behaviour according to circumstances as they arise.

Blau does not reject Weber's analysis out-of-hand. Indeed, his revision of the original model suggests that 'it may be preferable to follow another lead of Weber's and to conceive of bureaucracy in terms of its purpose' (Blau, 1956, p. 60). He argues that only through the creation of conditions that favour adjustive development in bureaucracies can such structures meet the challenge of a changing environment and ultimately achieve a higher level of efficiency.

Five such conditions or prerequisites for continuous adjustment can be distinguished (cf. Blau, 1955, pp. 216–9; Blau, 1956, pp. 61–6).

164

1 *Employment security* Only when individuals know that their jobs are safe will they be prepared to display initiative in their work roles. So, if the aim of the organization is to allow the individual greater freedom for discretion and judgment through decentralized control procedures, then security of tenure must prevail. Of course, there is the counter-argument that such security stifles initiative and that only in a period of uncertainty will the individual display it. Blau dismisses such a proposition as fallacious in that his view of the person is one of the individual seeking challenge, accepting change and wishing to break from established pre-ordained routines. Indeed he argues that 'insecurity generates rigidity and resistance to change' (Blau, 1956, p. 62).

2 *A professional orientation* Many occupations, through the methods of recruitment employed, ensure that those individuals who join the occupation have a particular orientation towards their work. The case of the civil service is an appropriate one for discussion here. Positions within the civil service are largely tenured, the individual can foresee a career within the structure of the one organization. This can generate an *esprit de corps*, a feeling of loyalty towards the organization that is not to be found in other organizations which lack the same benefits of security and career potential. This is what, in part, Blau refers to as professional orientation to employment (it is, as we have seen, somewhat different from Gouldner's conception of the professional with a cosmopolitan latent social identity). The other aspect of this professionalism is that 'evaluation on the basis of results achieved rather than techniques used . . . fosters a professional orientation' (Blau, 1955, p. 217). If the social cohesion that Blau has in mind can be realized in an organization, then there is likely, he argues, to be a more open attitude towards change and developments in terms of working practices.

3 *Collegial work groups* The Hawthorne studies, amongst others, have demonstrated the importance of work groups in organizations, not simply from the point of view of individual personality development but also because of the power the work group can exert over the individual in terms of the pace at which a task is performed, how the task is achieved, and so on. Successive research studies have demonstrated the need to account for group activity and pressure in order that organization objectives be met. Individuals working in groups appear to accept the norms that a group may prescribe in exchange for the security of group membership and the social relationships that are engendered by such membership. An organization problem is that work-group

cohesiveness or an *esprit de corps* mentality cannot be formally imposed; both have to emerge naturally. For this emergence to occur, the appropriate supportive conditions have to be in existence.

4 *The absence of conflict* Blau argues that the US civil service is structured in such a way as to avoid potential conflict arising between management and operating officials. This is through a procedure which he refers to as a split in managerial authority. Thus, he observes (Blau, 1956, p. 65) that 'management in government agencies, in contrast to management in private industry, controls only operations and not employment conditions'. He argues further that:

> Employees who have no reason to protect their economic welfare against the management of their own organization are more apt to maintain a professional or workmanlike concern with perfecting methods of operations and thus to contribute to continuous adjustive development in the organization. (Blau, 1956, p. 66).

5 *Evaluation by specified results* The above factors relating to professional orientations to work, the formation of cohesive work groups and the like, enable individuals to be primarily interested in their task responsibilities. As such, the goals toward which individuals are oriented should be standardized so that, as it were, everybody in the organization is moving in the same direction. The means of achieving these goals should be left to the discretion of the individual or his or her work group. Evaluation, then, is on the basis of the results, not upon the way in which the results are achieved.

> Evaluation on the basis of clearly specified results which employees are expected to accomplish in their work, encourages ingenuity and simultaneously assures the standardization necessary for effective bureaucratic operation (Blau, 1956, p. 66).

As we shall see in Chapter 13, Blau's proposals for the design of bureaucratic organizations are very much in 'the spirit of the age'. Human relations writers since the Second World War have constantly stressed the importance of work groups as a basis for task achievement; opportunities for individual and group participation are encouraged; achievement, fulfilment and actualization have become the keywords in the literature of such writers. Blau, though, was not so much concerned with individual satisfaction and the motivation to work. His concern was with devising strategies in organizations that would achieve greater efficiency, breaking with the Weberian monolithic-type structure and recognizing that different circumstances may require different structures. As Etzioni has commented:

> Blau suggests that certain external and internal factors might turn a bureaucracy into an innovating organization, interested in social change as well as in changing itself. Changes are likely to be supported by the personnel if they are aimed at satisfying organizational 'needs'. Such changes may in turn raise new needs calling for additional adjustments (Etzioni, 1969, pp. 385–6).

General problems of bureaucracy

By reference to a number of specific and well-known studies we have seen that the bureaucratic model posited originally by Weber has been subjected to a variety of modifications and refinements. Considerably more work than the above has been concerned with this topic, and for the sake of brevity it is possible for us to summarize the central issues around which the revision of the bureaucratic model have revolved. In discussing these issues, it is valuable to reiterate some of the comments made by the writers already analysed in this chapter.

1   *Individuals are not automata*   It is possibly no coincidence that one of the major criticisms levelled against the bureaucratic model is in terms of its tendency to treat individuals like cogs in a machine. Indeed, early theories of organization and bureaucracy are often referred to as 'machine theories'. There is obviously something deficient in a scheme that expects individuals to behave in a dehumanized manner within a totally impersonal environment. *Cogito ergo sum*: all individuals are at times guided in their actions by their personal values and feelings, rather than by what is defined by others as rational impersonal behaviour and attitudes. The kind of distinction that Barnard (1938) made between personal power and the power of position is pertinent here. If we neglect the personal characteristics of the individual, it follows that in a bureaucratic structure where formal rules and procedures are supposedly ubiquitous, then any individual should be able to perform any function simply by following the rules. Of course, we know this to be untrue since individuals always bring with them, to any situation or task, their own characteristics that partly determine the extent to which a task will be successfully accomplished. As we see in the work of Gouldner, Merton and Selznick, the existence of personal characteristics is partially a way of accounting for the

167

unintended results that each of their respective models of bureaucracy suggests, over and above the intended consequences of the bureaucratic model.

2 *Rules do not cover every contingency* Common-sense experience as well as the examples already quoted in this chapter suggest that it is virtually impossible for an organization to devise rules and procedures to account for every possible eventuality. As we shall see in Chapter 9, there is an increasing tendency in contemporary organizations to routinize as many tasks as possible and thereby provide rules that need to be followed for the task to be efficiently performed. Nevertheless, in every organization, particularly in the administrative component of organizations, such routinization becomes an impossibility. To suggest, as some writers have, that the bureaucratic model has this as a defining characteristic is to be misplaced in interpretation.

3 *Organizations generate the formation of informal groups* From the time of the 'discovery' of the informal group in the Hawthorne studies, the salience of informal groupings has been recognized and accounted for in organizations. Bureaucracy's 'other face', as it is sometimes termed, together with the emergence of informal group leaders, can present an organization with difficulties in the realization of its goals.

4 *Efficiency and innovation are not synonymous* Burns and Stalker (1961) have demonstrated that if an organization is to survive or develop in a changing environment, it is necessary for a more organic form of organization to exist. Bureaucracies (or mechanistic organizations, in Burns and Stalker's terminology) are slow to adapt to change whether this change be internal or external, in spite of the fact that they may have been established to generate the maximum efficiency. Once extra-organizational change occurs, the efficiency of the organization is likely to diminish.

5 *Bureaucracies are not monolithic entities* As we shall explore in Chapter 5, organizations, in systems terms, are constructed from interdependent sub-systems. Such interdependence between the parts of the system or organization tends not to be recognized in the bureaucratic model.

6 *Individuals can be decision-makers* As we have suggested in the second point, in spite of certain tendencies to routinize many organizational tasks, individuals often need to make decisions in organizations. The bureaucratic model suggests a denial of this

168

opportunity. Such individual decision-making is often regarded as anathema by bureaucratic officials.

7 *Bureaucracy is more appropriate to large organizations* As Chapter 6 will demonstrate, there is evidence to suggest that as organizations grow in size (as measured by a variety of means) there is an empirical tendency for them to become more formalized and routinized – in other words, more bureaucratized. It follows that in those organizations that are smaller and less complex, bureaucracy may not be a feasible kind of structure. Indeed, there will tend to be less need for the many characteristics that are associated with bureaucratic organizations.

These general points, together with the more substantive criticisms contained within the works of writers such as Gouldner and Blau, amount to a substantial body of criticism levelled at the formal bureaucratic model as exemplified primarily in the work of Weber and to a lesser extent in the formal theories of administration and scientific management. Such criticisms have not gone unheeded nor without reply from Weberian sociologists. It is to these that we can now turn.

The Weberians' response

The most recent, thorough and sympathetic statement of Weber's position with regard to the model of bureaucracy is that presented by Albrow (1970). He takes up the gauntlet thrown down by the critics examined above and emerges as a champion of Weber's cause. As such, Albrow's 'reply to the critics' needs to be analysed. Albrow suggests that there are two points of disagreement that can be discerned in the criticisms of Weber. He writes:

> The first is a dispute on the empirical validity (both historical and predictive) of his (Weber's) account of the nature and development of modern administrations. The second, and more important, is a rejection of his association of the ideal type of bureaucracy with the concepts of rationality and efficiency. . . . What did Weber mean by rationality and efficiency, and, in the context of bureaucracy, can those terms be used interchangeably? (Albrow, 1970, pp. 61–2).

It has been suggested earlier in this chapter that many critics equated efficiency with Weber's account of rationality. In response to this, it needs to be recalled that the concept of rationality was in no way a unitary one for Weber. Although 'rationality or a cognate term appears on twenty-three occasions even in the briefest of Weber's three essays on bureaucracy' (Albrow, 1970, p. 133),

169

Weber uses the term in at least four different ways in his writings on methodology and these four ways appear in his discussion on bureaucracy.

Albrow appears to suggest that the critics have posed the problem from the wrong point of view. We have seen in Chapter 3 that bureaucracy, for Weber, was associated with legal-rational authority. This was to be seen as a form of rationality itself, but it does not necessarily follow that legal authority was automatically associated with bureaucracy in the strictly formal, rational sense. Thus, by turning the question on its head Albrow (1970, p. 63) states that 'the problem is thus raised of explaining why Weber attributed rationality to legal authority'.

Basically, Albrow's argument is that the actual design of a rule was rational for Weber in that the intention of the formulation of the rule was rational. Furthermore, the procedure designed for applying rules was also rational in Weber's formulation. Albrow concludes that, 'It would be quite misleading to equate Weber's concept of formal rationality with the idea of efficiency' (Albrow, 1970, p. 63). On this basis, the arguments against Weber largely disintegrate.

5 Organizations as systems

The focus on the 'problems of organizations' can be said to have developed from the work done at Harvard University under the initial direction of A. M. Henderson, but usually associated with Elton Mayo. Henderson is an important link in the development of the theoretical construction of a model of the organization conceptualized as a 'social system' (See Russett, 1966). He encouraged and developed this conceptualization amongst a coterie of followers at Harvard who, like him, were of an ideologically conservative persuasion, the intellectual expression of which they found in the systems thinking of Vilfred Pareto, the Italian social scientist whose main work was *The Mind and Society* (1935).

Of the luminaries who surrounded Henderson at Harvard, among them Robert King Merton and George C. Homans, perhaps the most significant and influential figure was Talcott Parsons. Parsons' major contribution to social science has been the attempt to construct a general systems theory for analysing all elements of the social world.

Talcott Parsons

Parsons began his sociological career as a social action theorist in his first book, *The Structure of Social Action* (1937). His intention in this work, he stated, was to develop one social theory capable of explaining all social life. He attempted to do this through a laborious elaboration and elucidation of what he saw as the great convergence in social theory. This convergence, he maintained, had occurred between the works of Alfred Marshall, Vilfred Pareto, Emile Durkheim and Max Weber. Weber's work was the dominant element in this first synthesis of a 'voluntaristic theory of social action'. By the time that Parsons came to write his second major

171

work, *The Social System* (1951), it was Pareto who dominated the programme. The acknowledgment of this lies on the title page:

> The title, *The Social System*, goes back, more than to any other source, to the insistence of the late Professor L. J. Henderson on the extreme importance of the concept of system in scientific theory, and his clear realization that the attempt to delineate the social system as a system was the most important contribution of Pareto's great work. This book therefore is an attempt to carry out Pareto's intuition (Parsons, 1951, p. vii).

The programme through which this attempt was to be made was that of structural functionalism, which for Parsons (1951, p. 6) entailed 'an analysis of the functional prerequisites of the social system'.

In spite of the fact that Parsons is such a major figure in the development of social science in recent decades (if not such a major figure as he once was), it is nevertheless the case that in his work there is not a great deal of attention paid specifically to organization analysis. He has attempted to formulate a general theory of society and to provide a model of society conceptualized as a social system in which all the parts may be analysed in their functioning. As such, the theories developed and concepts used ought to be able to cast considerable light upon the construction of models of the organization and directions for organization analysis.

Parsons is rightly regarded as a structural functionalist *par excellence* as well as one of the founders of systems theory; some commentators such as Silverman (1970) do not readily distinguish between the two schools. Their closeness can be seen in the fact that the very concept of function used in the notion of structural functionalism is implicit in the systems model (see Cohen, 1970).

The definition that Parsons gives to the concept of organization is couched in terms of functionalism, in that it focuses on three functional problems that all social systems have to deal with. He defines an organization in the following terms:

> As a formal analytical point of reference, primacy of orientation to the attainment of a specific goal is used as the defining characteristic of an organization which distinguishes it from other types of social systems (Parsons, 1956, p. 63).

We can distinguish these three functional problems in this definition. In the first instance, organizations have sub-units such as individuals, groups and departments; yet in their turn organizations can be perceived as themselves sub-units of larger units such as the economy or the educational system. The basic problem, therefore, is to demonstrate the way in which organizations can integrate from one level to another higher level.

Second, the definition points to the fact that there is an orientation towards a specific goal. This implies a level of motivation on the part of 'organizations'. This being so, the problem is determining the extent to which the organization goals need to be integrated and at what level of the organization this integration occurs. In terms of his wider social theory, Parsons notes that goal orientation is a distinguishing characteristic of all social action; where he differs in his organization analysis is that the goal orientation is the primary concern of the organization and those individuals and groups that comprise it.

Third, organizations have mechanisms for solving the problem of maintaining their identity in relation to the environment, and solving the problem of acquiring support from the environment for them to survive.

These three basic problems of organizations are precisely those that Parsons states confront all social systems. To this extent, the work of Parsons should be appropriate for organization analysis, albeit at a very general level. One of the major criticisms that is often levelled at Parsons is the fact that he has not confronted the issue head-on: he has not really used the data that is available in the organization literature to test his general theory; he has not applied his general scheme to organizations in a systematic fashion; he has focused his ideas in isolation to the cognate areas of concern – indeed, some would argue that he has acted in a cavalier manner.

The main source for discussion of the general theory being applied to organizations is contained in two articles in the *Administrative Science Quarterly* (1956), whilst other references are spread rather thinly throughout his work.

Since the organization analysis is very much part of the general theory of social systems, it is appropriate that the latter should briefly be examined in order that the general concepts that have a specific relevance can be distinguished.

Parsons' general systems theory

The general approach that Parsons uses for organizations is to view them as systems in their own right, notwithstanding the fact that they are in turn part of larger systems. It is implied that this is possible because of the fact that many characteristics of organizations are similar to those of social systems in general. In fact at the organizational level many of these characteristics are more clearly discernable than at the societal level. For example, Parsons makes great play of the fact that social systems pursue goals. At the organizational level, although it is sometimes difficult to state

173

clearly what the goals are, in the case of society as a social system, such a statement is even more difficult to make. Equally, if we take another characteristic of organizations – a well-defined hierarchy of relations and authority – there is such a structure within many societies but in most of them it is much more esoteric than in organizations. Sociologists spend much of their time seeking ways to simplify the analysis of the differentiation that exists within societies; in the case of organizations this differentiation is normally spelled out very clearly at a formal level through the existence of organization charts. Again, if we take the services that organizations perform, these are almost always clearly stated as being part of the *raison d'être* of the organization. In the case of the wider social system of society such phenomena are not clearly distinguished. This raises the point that through the analysis of the services provided by an organization it is possible to adopt an open-systems perspective, which we shall consider later. Parsons advocates such a perspective, but at the societal level it is difficult to conceptualize what it would be. The kinds of system problem that Parsons maintains that every social system has to recognize and attempt to solve are again more sharply demarcated at the organizational level than at the societal level.

The idea that organizations may be seen as social systems in their own right needs some comment. If it is conceptually possible to locate organizations as social systems operating within other social systems, the immediate sub-systems in the analysis often tend to be treated as undifferentiated units. This is often the case for groups within organizations. For example, the main point of concern with the sub-system is the way in which it interacts with the larger system and the kind of relevance it has to the wider system. It follows that there is little concern with the way in which the sub-system is structured or organized. Equally, the descriptive characteristics of the sub-system are not a matter of concern.

Another point about the 'system within a system' idea is the problem of reductionism. Moving from one system to another necessarily involves moving to a different level. If the movement is to a higher level this level cannot be reduced to the properties of the lower level(s). While there is interdependence between the levels – say, between organizations and groups within organizations – there is also a high level of autonomy at the higher level.

In his general theory Parsons claims that it is possible to integrate personality systems and cultural systems into the social system. In this way much of the Hobbesian problem of order in society is solved, or so it would seem. The many disparate motivations that exist in society can be integrated into an ordered model of the social system. This integration occurs through the use of the concept of a

174

'central value system'. It is this concept which is at the centre of Parsons' theory of order (or what we have termed 'control'). Briefly, this means that there are shared orientations toward action in society, each striving for the common end. Parsons argues that this central value system forms the basis of any society. In *The Social System*, he shows how role relationships develop on the basis of shared expectations about the behaviour and attitudes of other individuals. Behaviour is thus predictable and in this way it is possible for society to persist in spite of changes in membership.

This concept of a central value system really is fundamental to the Parsonian schema. Without it the attribution of functions to system parts would be impossible. What this means is that in order to study the processes that exist in society it is first necessary to understand the values that determine the normative behaviour underlying these processes. Unless this is done, the assessments of functionality can, and normally will, be misleading.

Parsons' theory of the organization as system

Parsons argues that organizations can be viewed as systems. It therefore follows that the initial task of the organization analyst is to determine what are the values and goals of the organization. We can see from these why Parsons defines organizations in the way he does with this central notion of orientation to a specific goal.

Since the main emphasis is upon values and goals, the point of departure for organization analysis is to see the organization from a cultural and institutional point of view (wherein values and goals originate). In the language of structural functionalism the initial analysis is concerned with values in differentiated functional contexts. Organization goals must always be legitimated by organization values. In their turn the organization values are required to be consistent with societal values. The legitimacy of organization goals arises from the contribution that can be made to the functional requirements of the wider social system (society). In this way, the organization is enabled to place its goals above the goals of the sub-systems comprising the organization. Furthermore, the organizations' goals are integrated into those of the wider social system.

The integration of society's values into organization goals has other consequences. Organization roles are designed and structured in such a way that they are in harmony with the expectations that the individuals employed by the organization bring with them. These expectations are themselves the result of the joint processes of the internalization of societal norms and of socialization. Two kinds of satisfactions are present in society for individuals:

psychological satisfaction and instrumental satisfaction. At the level of the organization, the psychological satisfactions comprise features such as approval from others, recognition of task achievement and security of tenure. The instrumental satisfactions include the rewards available in organizations which are mainly of a material kind.

Four functional problems of organizations

As the values and the specific normative patterns are in accord with one another they are then able to regulate the processes through which the functional requirements of the system are met. In the general theory of social systems Parsons distinguished four functional problems or requirements that have to be solved and met in order that the system survives. The survival requirements are: the capacity to adapt, to attain the goals, to integrate the parts of the system, and to allow for latency or pattern maintenance (by which Parsons means the maintenance of the central value system and the patterns of interaction that are laid down by this system). Adaptation and goal attainment are task or instrumental in character and refer chiefly to the way in which the system relates to its environment. In the case of integration and latency requirements the emphasis is upon the internal functioning of the system. Thus, the former category relates to the efficiency of the organization or system, whereas the latter relates to its stability. These four system problems can be looked at in a little more detail to see the way in which they are appropriate in the analysis of organizations.

In the case of *adaptation*, the problem is one of ensuring that an organization acquires the necessary resources for it to function. Included as resources are human as well as material inputs. The adaptation problem also refers to the normative patterns that regulate the acquisition of these resources.

Goal attainment is largely concerned with the way in which the system or organization mobilizes its resources once they have been obtained. This mobilization is obviously performed in such a way that the goals of the organization may be achieved. It is here that decisions need to be made by the organization (or rather by its members). At this stage the power structure of the organization is of great significance. The analogy could be employed that the process of goal attainment corresponds to the political system within society.

The other two problems of *integration* and *latency* are difficult to discuss from Parsons' work, since he does not provide a systematic treatment of them in relation to organizations as social systems. This reflects the great emphasis Parsons placed on the relations

176

between the organization and its environment, to the relative neglect of the internal functioning of organizations. We can see this again in relation to the emphasis on 'boundary exchange' between the higher- and lower-level systems in Parsons' exposition. By this is meant that the organization goal at a higher-system level becomes a function.

The four problems or requirements are obviously central to the Parsonian model. It is on the basis of these that Parsons is able to construct his organizational typology. Parsons argued that organizations vary according to the type of goal(s) that they are pursuing: in other words, the function that is performed for the higher-level system of society. In this way Parsons distinguishes economic organizations (adaptation problem), political organizations (goal attainment problem), integrative organizations, and pattern maintenance organizations. Not only are different organizations functionally differentiated at the system level by being specialized to handle one or other of these functional requirements. They can also be conceptualized in terms of their internal functioning as a system composed of four separate sub-systems specialized to deal with these four functionally related requirements. Hence the fourfold paradigm is capable of a theoretically infinite regression to the 'base unit' of the individual personality system.

Whyte (1964) has pointed out that in his articles in the *Administrative Science Quarterly* the emphasis of Parsons' work is upon the 'cultural-institutional'. Indeed, he argues that this is an orientation to be seen in many of Parsons' articles. The group or individual within the organization is given very little attention. We have seen that despite the apparent limitation of the approach it is still possible to make a number of sophisticated distinctions in Parsons' work.

Three levels of analysis in organizations

In a later work *Structure and Process in Modern Societies*, Parsons (1960) goes some of the way towards a more detailed internal examination of organizations. This is done by distinguishing between what he calls the institutional, managerial and technical levels in organizations. We have seen with other approaches to organization analysis that often organizations are seen in pyramidal terms, whereby authority and influence extend from the top to the bottom of the pyramid. The scalar principles of the formal theorists of administration and the concept of hierarchy in Weber's work display this notion well. Parsons suggests that this is too simple an approach in that in most organizations there are qualitative breaks in the line structure. Once identified, it is possible then to see these managerial, institutional and technical levels in organizations.

1 *Technical* The technical level is straightforward in that it is responsible for the work of the organization. Here the vague goals of the organization are translated into action designed to achieve these goals. Essentially, this is a matter of processing, and Parsons distinguishes between the processing of objects and processing of people. The major constraint at this level in terms of functioning is the technology.

2 *Managerial* The managerial level, almost by definition, is concerned to administer the internal organization. It is responsible for obtaining the raw materials required by the technical level, and it acts as a buffer or mediator between the technical system and the customers or clients of the organization. At this level we are thinking of administrators, executives and managers, whereas at the technical level the typical personnel would be blue-collar workers, foremen and supervisors.

3 *Institutional* Parsons argues that each organization is engaged in activities that are important and functional for society as a whole. We have seen how the goals and values of the organization need to be in accord with the values of society as a whole. The institutional level is concerned to ensure that there is harmony and consistency between the organization and the wider society. As he says:

> As a technical organization . . . is controlled and 'serviced' by a managerial organization, so in turn, is the managerial organization controlled by the 'institutional' structure and agencies of the community (Parsons, 1960, p. 64).

The kind of thing that Parsons had in mind was the board of directors of an industrial organization, school governors, university councils, etc. The institutional level, therefore, is able to mediate between both the managerial and technical levels and the wider society. It is concerned with integrating the organization and its functions.

Although at a high level of generality, we can see here that Parsons is attempting an analysis of the internal structure of the organization and of the problems of integrating the organization with its environment.

Criticisms: the analysis of change and conflict

The structural functionalists in general, and Parsons in particular, have often been criticized for omission in their work of the analysis of change and conflict. Of course, it was never the intention to analyse these concepts and processes as primary concerns; structural functionalism after all is concerned with the ways in which social system parts are integrated and interdependent, not with conflict and disintegration. The emphasis is upon the concept of equilibrium in social systems.

There are two kinds of change, according to Parsons: exogenous and endogenous. The former is where the organization changes as a consequence of changes in the environment; the latter is produced from within the organization. Where there is endogenous change this arises from an imbalance (disequilibrium) between the factors of efficiency (adaptation and goal attainment) and the factors of stability (integration and latency). Normally, Parsons argues, the source of change in organizations is exogenous, a consequence of environmental change, especially from the viewpoint of changes in society's central value system. From the nature of the relation that we have already seen, if there is a change in the value system, this will necessitate a change in the organization goal which, in turn, will produce changes within the structure and process of the organization. When there is an environmental change or a change in the wider system the organization will adapt in such a way as to arrive at a new equilibrium position or a new position of stability *vis-à-vis* the environment. There are problems with such an approach. The dynamic equilibrium model has been criticized by both Silverman (1970) and Van den Berghe (1973) in similar terms. As the latter puts it:

A dynamic equilibrium model cannot account for the irreducible facts that:
1   reaction to extra-systemic change is not always adjustive,
2   social systems can, for long periods, go through a vicious circle of ever-deepening malintegration,
3   change can be revolutionary, i.e., both sudden and profound,
4   the social structure itself generates change through internal conflicts and contradictions (Van den Berghe, 1973, p. 47).

Structural functionalism as a whole suffers from these weaknesses. This is largely because of the fact that there is an orientation to the consequences of action rather than the causes. The sources of change and the causes of conflict are relatively neglected in most functionalist analyses. This can be seen quite vividly in the fact that both the organization and the environment are presented as given phenomena. It is normally the demands of the environment that are considered, while the organization merely responds to these demands. In the same way that Parsonian analysis makes it difficult to explain how societies change in a radical way, so it is virtually impossible to explain the phenomenon of an organization which is clearly deviant in terms of the central value system, as for instance, the Red Brigade in Italy or the Red Army Faction in West Germany. Such organizations are not simply a pathological outcome of insufficient or deficient socialization. They are highly organized bodies with a highly cohesive internal structure whose functioning clearly is not simply a response to the demands of the environment, but a concerted attempt to change that environment. Without entering here either into discussion of their effectivity as revolutionary strategies or as moral practices, the existence of these types of organization is a 'problem' which a Parsonian would have difficulty in analysing.

Van den Berghe (1973, p. 46) has addressed this issue in an attempted synthesis of 'functionalism' and 'dialectics' (of which Gunder Frank, 1973, has been highly critical). He notes that the consensus of certain types of organization, of which we think a revolutionary organization would be a good example, 'can precipitate the disintegration of a society' (Van den Berghe, 1973, p. 46). This kind of organization theory clearly underlies Lenin's remarks on organizational strategy – the recommendation of a revolutionary vanguard party. This suggests that we should be cautious in too hastily assuming that all organizations are necessarily 'functional'. In addition, it suggests that organizations are not necessarily consensual in themselves:

> To make value consensus a prerequisite to the existence of a social system (as Parsons does, for example) is untenable. Granting that consensus is often an important (but not a necessary) basis of social integration, one has to accept that consensus can also have disintegrative consequences, that most complex societies (*and organizations*) show considerable dissension, and that there are alternative bases of integration to consensus (e.g., economic interdependence and political coercion). Consensus, then, is a major dimension of social reality, but so are dissension and conflict. Furthermore, there is no necessary direct relation between consensus and equilibrium or integration (Van den Berghe, 1973, p. 46).

It is instructive to see the way in which Parsons (1957) uses his theoretical scheme in the analysis of a specific organization, and it is to this analysis that we can now turn. He had two objectives in this analysis: first, to explain why doctors are dominant in the mental hospital; and second, to explain why doctors are often appointed to the most senior positions within mental hospitals when in universities professors rarely succeed in achieving the top roles (in the case of the American universities anyway).

In line with his theoretical analysis, the societal values represented by the central value system are delineated as far as they impinge upon the activities of the mental hospital. One such value is the vague notion of health. The doctor is seen as an instrument in achieving this value whereas the administrator is not, at least not in a direct sense. It follows, therefore, that the doctor is placed in a much more powerful position in relation to the central value system. The problem here is that in American mental hospitals it is true that the medical profession is represented at the top level of administration, but in general hospitals this is not the case. General hospitals have the same relationship to the central value of health and yet there is this difference.

When he examines the activities of mental hospitals, Parsons seeks to discover why there is an emphasis upon custody of the mentally ill rather than therapy and cure. His explanation is that since the doctors tend to move into administration there is a disproportionate amount of the hospital resources devoted to the salaries of highly paid administrators, so that those medical personnel still concerned with medicine are relatively deprived in their resources. A consequence of this is that hospital personnel such as nurses and medical attendants have the major burden of caring for patients. The orientation of such personnel, Parsons argues, is not necessarily upon cure but rather upon custody.

What can be said about this analysis? Whyte (1964) has suggested that the analysis is both useful and sound up to a point. Some of the ideas are useful explanations but they do not appear to be novel ideas. In this case functional analysis has not illuminated many subtle points about mental hospitals. Even if the ideas were new and insightful, the range of applicability is very limited. As Whyte points out, it is all right as far as it goes when the aim is to see how the environment affects the selection of certain key personnel in mental hospitals. What, though, could the analysis contribute to a comparison of the impact upon the hospitals of two administrators? Or what would be the effects of different organization patterns in different hospitals? In Parsonian analysis the hospital would have the same relation to its environment in each case so that only the similarities between the hospitals could be noted. Parsonian analysis does not adequately explain differences between organizations.

Substantive limitations

We have already seen that there are significant drawbacks to the Parsonian model for organization analysis. There is the major problem of accounting for change and conflict within organizations and their environments. Equally, the applicability of the model in explaining the functioning of particular organizations seems to be

181

strictly limited. We can now turn to the specific limitations of the scheme.

In the first instance it is useful to examine Mouzelis' comments on this matter, since Mouzelis appears to have an affinity with Parsons' work. Indeed, he makes the point that in his view the work 'has been a very important contribution to organization theory' (Mouzelis, 1967, p. 153). He accepts that the manner of presentation is confusing, at times casual and that the scheme has a number of inadequacies. Nevertheless, he argues that the scheme has the following merits:

a I find of great value its capacity to account for different levels of analysis . . . and to point out the intricate problems of interdependence and autonomy between these levels, . . .
b Parsons takes seriously into consideration the fact that a general theory of organizations should apply to all types of organization, not only to governmental agencies and industrial enterprises. . . .
c Parsons' analysis emphasizes the need for closer links between organizational and general sociological theory (Mouzelis, 1967, pp. 153–4).

Without questioning the validity of these points, they do raise further questions concerning whether this adds up to 'a very important contribution'. We shall repeatedly see in later chapters that whilst the points made by Mouzelis are relevant they do not necessarily add up to a major contribution to our understanding of organizations.

Whyte's (1964) discussion of the difficulties of the scheme are particularly helpful. He distinguishes three main areas of concern: the scant attention to what goes on within the organization; the lack of data available to support the concepts; and the omission of features that are important for the development of organization theory.

We have already seen that Parsons' main emphasis is upon what he calls the cultural-institutional point of view. Initially, this is to be expected. However, this emphasis is maintained throughout his work. The only major departure from this is in the distinction that is made between the different levels within an organization. Here, though, little regard is taken of the technical or managerial levels as compared with the institutional level. A comprehensive analysis would involve more than an examination of the technical and managerial levels in any case. The absence of any substantive discussion of groups and roles within organizations is a major drawback to the scheme. The case of the mental hospital as an organization that has already been examined displays this limited applicability.

182

One criticism that is often levelled at organization theory is that it has too much data and not enough concepts. In the case of Parsons' intervention in the study of organizations the reverse seems to be the case. The only major reference or attempt to put data to the concepts is in relation to the work of Bales (1950) and his interaction process analysis. Superficially it would appear that such a link-up would be useful since Bales's analysis is concerned specifically with direct observation of behaviour. Whyte makes the point that all this really achieves is an acknowledgment that the two sets of concepts (Bales's and Parsons') are compatible. The major problem with this is that propositions derived from one set of concepts cannot be related to the other set of concepts.

In turn, this raises another issue: the fact that very few propositions are contained within Parsons' organization analysis. Those that do exist are so vague and general as to have little analytic value.

The third of Whyte's points is that Parsons' model contains some major omissions. Since there is little attention given to the internal functioning of the organization, it follows that little play is made of the influence of the organization structure upon individual behaviour. In fact, there is evidence that even the spatial location of individuals affects behaviour, but no account is taken of this evidence by Parsons. Whyte's (1964) case study of the ABC company vividly demonstrates this.

In each plant there was required to be both a manager and a controller who were at the same level in the hierarchy. The manager was accountable to the divisional production manager, whereas the controller reported to the divisional controller and vice-president. Whyte found that this situation led to conflict, particularly in the two largest plants that were situated in the same geographical location as the divisional headquarters. Where there was a geographical dislocation the same kind of conflict did not arise. Whyte argued that the presence or absence of conflict could be accounted for by an examination of the organization structure and location of personnel. Where the plant was close to the divisional headquarters there was considerable interaction between the plant manager and the divisional production manager, and similarly in the case of the two controllers. Thus, if there were plant level conflicts between the manager and controller it was an easy matter to get the conflict resolved at a higher level. In the case of the plant situated some distance from the divisional headquarters there was very little interaction between plant personnel and divisional personnel. A consequence of this was that the plant manager and controller were forced to arrive at a position of co-operation. As it happened in the case study the manager became dominant, but this

183

was accepted by the controller and little friction developed in their working interactions. It is clear from this brief account that structure and geography are important in determining behaviour. Other organizational characteristics such as technology and the nature of tasks have a similar influence.

One further substantive limitation in Parsons' work relates to the considerable emphasis placed upon the role of values in the scheme. Since values play such an important role in the model he used to construct an analysis of the functioning of organizations, a number of areas of neglect arise as a result.

In the first instance, there is the impression that values are all-important, that they uniquely determine, arrange and regulate everything. This sounds like the accusation of acute reification which Silverman (1970) has levelled at Parsons. Possibly so, but perhaps what is more important here is to question whether it would be better to have concentrated on *how* values arise, *whose* values they are and the general issue of *what* material interests relate, in *which* ways, to the values. Our analysis has shown the relative neglect in Parsons' discussion of the role and functions of groups within organizations. This neglect has arisen partly from the idealist over-emphasis on values. Equally, this over-emphasis has led to problems in the analysis of power within organizations. More will be said about this issue in a later chapter, but some preliminary remarks can be made at the present.

One of the system problems that an organization has to solve in order to survive is that of attaining and mobilizing resources for the achievement of the organization's goal(s). Essentially this is a question of power and thus power can be associated with goal attainment. The main problem with this approach is that it neglects to mention that power may be used for purposes other than the organizational interests. Parsons' concept is therefore very narrow in its orientation, but can be explained by the fact that Parsons is not so much interested in the distribution as in the production of power.

Most organizations have conflicting goals within them, particularly in terms of the conflict between the official and the operative goals of the organization (Perrow, 1961). Parsons' scheme assumes that such a conflict of interests does not exist. This comes back yet again to the prominence in the scheme of the role of values in setting organization objectives. This all points to the fact that Parsons' model for organizations is at best a partial model. Those areas that are explored do have some limited relevance; but the over-concentration upon certain areas of organization functioning and the great emphasis placed upon the integrative problem present a narrow and possibly one-sided view of organizations.

One defence which can be suggested for Parsons' schema in its application to organizations 'is that it involves merely the elaboration of a set of categories which are not meant to be exhaustive but to provide an essential basis for the analysis of the complexities of the real world' (Silverman, 1970, p. 58). This would be acceptable if the Parsonian enterprise were purely logical: the construction of coherent ideational models. It is not clear that it is purely logical. As Silverman (1970, p. 71) notes, in Landsberger's (1961, pp. 225–6) terms, Parsons has a tendency

> to glide, imperceptibly, from the description of a *possible* model and a definition of its various parts, to statements concerning conditions and relationships necessary and existing *if* a certain system is to be stable and then to assertions about phenomena and their relations as they actually exist.

Even if its clarity as a purely logical model were established, it is not clear what the usefulness of such a model would be for an empirical science if it were not to act as a source of research puzzles or propositions for that science. Parsons' schema has, in fact, rarely been applied (see Scott, 1959 as an exception) other than in Bales's work. It is this deficiency which led Gunder Frank (1973, p. 73) to liken functionalists (among others) to 'some proud metaphysicians' attempting to 'achieve the grand final synthesis of whole, integrated, evolving synthetic angels equilibrating on four or more synthetic pins'! Parsons, without a doubt, is the arch-metaphysician in this respect.

Other functionalist writers have made contributions to our understanding of organizations – in particular Merton and Selznick – but as with structural functionalism in general, it has been Talcott Parsons who is regarded as being of paramount importance either as an interpreter and analyst or metaphysical mystifier of social phenomena. We can see this from an analysis of the work of Merton and Selznick, but bearing in mind that their respective work on organizations preceded that of Parsons by a number of years. A major feature of both works is the fact that they have used what Allen (1975, p. 100) calls 'the Weber source'. That is, they both start their analysis from an examination of Weber's classic model of bureaucracy and develop their own models using this as a base.

Robert King Merton

In his general model of functionalism Merton is probably best known for advocating what he called theories of the middle range (Merton, 1949). The main feature of such theories is that they are able to explain the consequences of one institutional area for another. They avoid, therefore, the problem of the organic analogy in the natural system.

In terms of his organization analysis, Merton was concerned to examine the dysfunctions of organization functioning; to discover latent as well as manifest functions in the organization; and to suggest the functional alternatives to organizational arrangements.

In his article, 'Bureaucratic Structure and Personality', Merton (1940) sought to establish that changes can occur in the personality of organization members because of the impact of certain features of organization structure. The analysis develops through a series of sequential propositions in the following way. Those at the top of the organization hierarchy always make a demand for control within the organization. Such a demand is manifested in an emphasis on the reliability of behaviour on the part of organization members. This explains the need for accountability and predictability within the organization. Standardized techniques for establishing control are introduced into organizations through the techniques of scientific management and the formal theories of administration in order to achieve this predictability and control.

There are three consequences of this emphasis on the reliability of members:

1 *A reduction in personalized relationships* As we have seen, bureaucratic organizations can be seen in terms of formal sets of relationships between roles in which individuals are treated not as individuals but as role incumbents.

2 *The rules of the organization become too internalized by organization members* Whereas the rules are originally designed to achieve the goals of the organization, they can come to develop a positive value that is independent of these goals. Here, Merton distinguishes between two aspects of what he calls 'goal displacement'. In the first instance, there is a movement towards stressing the rules because they have an instrumental value. In the second place, as a result of this instrumental orientation, undesirable consequences arise that were not anticipated.

3 *The development of categorization as a decision-making technique* Here categories become restricted so that the search possibilities in problem-solving are not used to their full potential.

These three consequences combine to make members' behaviour very predictable, to such an extent that we may say that there is rigidity of behaviour. But more than this, an *esprit de corps* develops among organization members through a commonness of purpose and interests. In turn, this leads to members defending one another in the face of outside pressure. And again this tends towards more rigid behaviour. This in itself has consequences: the original demand for reliability is satisfied; the defensibility of individual action is increased; and the amount of difficulty with clients increases.

These sequential propositions have been usefully represented diagrammatically by March and Simon (1958) in the following way:

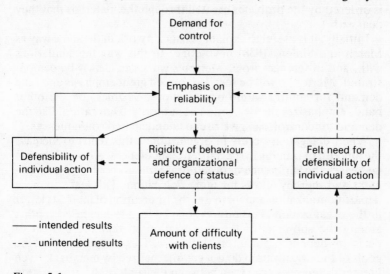

Figure 5.1

Source: March and Simon, 1958, p. 41.

This model of organization functioning clearly has a number of merits. As Silverman (1970, p. 46) has said, 'Behaviour inside organizations . . . is by no means always what it seems'. In other words, the Mertonian model shows that the actual consequences of an action may be different from the manifest intention. The major problem with the scheme is that Merton is not concerned to ask for whom problems are dysfunctional, nor does he relate the consequences of action to individual or group ends in any systematic way. Merton's model is a clear example of using a systems framework within a functionalist analysis.

Philip Selznick

Selznick's work on organizations is very much in the same mould as that of Merton, but he has made certain important changes of emphasis. In his 1943 article on 'An Approach to a Theory of Bureaucracy' Selznick draws heavily on the evidence available from the Bank Wiring Room experiment of the Hawthorne Studies. He argues that the informal structure of an organization can modify and elaborate the organization's original goals. His use of the structural-functionalist method is displayed here in the distinction he makes between goal-oriented activity and a structural element. This latter concept is the ordinary activity that individuals engage in but which is ordered by the problems created through the materials that they deal with.

Initially, it is useful to explain Selznick's work in the same way as March and Simon (1958) have done. In this way the similarities with, and differences from, Merton's work can clearly be demonstrated. Merton, it will be recalled, placed great emphasis upon the demand for control within organizations. Selznick, on the other hand, emphasizes the delegation of authority. Delegation, like the demand for control, can give rise to unanticipated consequences.

When delegation occurs in organizations this tends to increase the amount of training in specialized competences. Also, delegation decreases the difference between organization goals and achievement and thereby allows for more delegation. This leads to more departmentalization and increases the bifurcation of interests lower in the organization. This bifurcation can lead to increased conflict among the sub-units of the organization so that the content of decisions depends upon internal strategy. This is especially so if the goals of the organization do not get internalized by members. Even greater differences arise then between the goals of the organization and achievement so that there is further delegation. This very simplified model (again after March and Simon, 1958) can be represented as shown in Figure 5.2.

From this early foray into organization theory, Selznick developed his ideas further in a later paper (1948) and his book based upon empirical research, *TVA and the Grass Roots* (1949). It is in these later works that he moves away from a reliance upon the Weberian model of bureaucracy and manages more fully to develop the structural-functionalist perspective in organization analysis.

Selznick initially recognizes (together with most of his functionalist colleagues) that there exists for each organization a set of 'needs'. In the process of satisfying needs it is recognized that there may be some resistance from within the organization – the problem of recalcitrance. Individuals tend to be recalcitrant because of the diverse roles that they occupy, only one of which is an organization role. At the institutional level there is also recalcitrance because of the fact that the organization has to deal with other organizations in its environment in terms of the general rather than the specific. The general, as Merton pointed out, has little chance of covering all contingencies or all situations. Consequently, the position may be

188

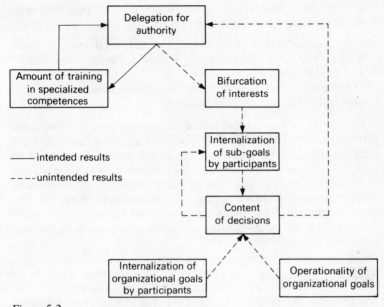

Figure 5.2

Source: March and Simon, 1958, p. 43.

that an organization is faced with a hostile environment and with friction from within. One solution to these problems is for the organization constantly to refer to its legitimacy. If the organization is to survive, the kind of response that it receives to such reference is crucial.

The empirical study of the Tennessee Valley Authority is approached with these theorectical ideas in mind. Selznick points out how the organization has to satisfy the needs of stability and goal-attainment, and this is attained through self-defensive behaviour. In common with other functionalist writers Selznick regards organizations as having to adjust to their environment and vice versa. In this way a position of equilibrium is achieved, albeit often a temporary one. There may, therefore, be both functional and dysfunctional consequences of such action. The notion of functional alternatives appears again in Selznick's work when he points out that needs often cannot be met in the culturally approved manner. It would appear from this that Selznick examines the organization from a formalistic impersonal stance with little regard to those who comprise it. On the whole this is true, except that he does make fleeting references to individual motivations to the extent that these reflect the organization needs.

189

As with other functionalist contributors the same basic problems arise. For example, as Silverman puts it:

If we analyse organizations in terms of their needs then, except teleologically, we are hardly in a position to consider the causes, as distinct from the consequences, of action; for the basic 'cause' of any act can only be that the needs of the system made it necessary (Silverman, 1970, p. 53).

Silverman's own interest in the meaning of action reflects the problem here. We have already discussed the point that causes are different from consequences. But can the meaning of an act be understood from the point of view of its consequences? It is not just in Selznick's analysis that this problem arises. Most functionalist writers manage to dodge the issue of the problem of causes. The nearest that one finds to an explanation of the process is in the distinction that Merton makes between manifest and latent functions.

Developments in systems theory

The previous two chapters have provided us with information about the development of organization theory that leaves us with a partial and very incomplete picture. The models of organization and administration derived from scientific management and the formal theories of administration are deficient in a number of ways. The conception of organization in this classical mould is one of a static structure with a single invariant objective. The model itself is prescriptive and totally oriented to the notion of productive efficiency in organizations. Such a conception of organizations is clearly inadequate when it comes to describing, analysing and understanding organizations in reality.

We have also seen that the theories derived from the human relations movement made considerable progress towards under-standing the 'other side' of organizations and producing a definition of a theoretical object of the organization for analysis. The focus of analysis on informal groups and informal interaction between individuals and groups is obviously important, but the survey research nature of the work and the piece-meal approach have done little to contribute further towards an overall conception of organizations or towards providing a theory of organizations.

Dissatisfaction with the incompleteness of these approaches and cognizance of approaches being taken in a wider sociological context led to new developments in the study of organizations. One example is the application of systems theory to organization analysis, at an abstract level. We have considered the developments of Parsons, Merton and Selznick in this sphere. It coincided with the major pieces of work and advances that were being conducted in the wider field of sociology. Mayntz has commented that 'the application of a system concept and system theory to the field of organizations proved of absolutely decisive importance', and adds that: 'It is not an accident that in countries like Germany and France, where there is less interest in abstract system theory among social scientists, organizational sociology had great difficulties taking root' (Mayntz, 1964, p. 100).

Before being able to examine further the application of system theory to organizations it is useful to look briefly at what is meant by the terms 'system' and 'system theory'. When the concept of system is used in sociology – and other disciplines such as biology and engineering – what is meant is a description of a group of phenomena that is interdependent in such a way that it carries out some task or strives to achieve a common goal. That is at the most general level. Within systems theory there are a number of concepts that require explanation. Complex systems contain within them sub-systems that normally function in an independent manner but are oriented towards the overall goal of the wider system. An examination of sub-systems is one way of understanding the overall system. Within sub-systems there are *system components* that interact with one another and which, again, tend to be interdependent. Systems do not exist in a vacuum. They always interact with and exist within a specific *environment*. The nature of this interaction means that systems both influence, and are influenced by, their environment. Recognition of this environmental factor enables us to refer to systems as being more or less *open systems*. The interaction between the system and its environment often takes the form of exchanging *inputs and outputs*, which in turn enables us to define the *system boundary*. Often, systems are designed in such a way that part of the output becomes an input; this is the notion of system *feedback*. Through such a feedback it is possible to monitor progress and behaviour.

Having distinguished these basic concepts that are used in systems theory, we can consider the way that systems theory has been worked out in particular instances.

Organizations can be viewed from either a closed- or an open-systems perspective (Thompson, 1967).

Closed-system perspective

In a closed-system model, organizations are conceptualized as self-sufficient entities insulated from extra-organizational factors. Sometimes this is achieved by arguing that the hypotheses which

191

guide theory-construction are of a general nature such as a social psychological model of human needs: e.g., Maslow's (1954) model of self-actualizing man, as developed by McGregor (1960), Argyris (1964) and Likert (1959); and thus the environment can be safely ignored. Silverman relates closed-system theory to such models, and maintains that:

> Underlying the closed-system view is the positivist assumption that objective factors, detected by the observation of the scientist, exert a direct influence upon human behaviour. Thus what is defined by the observer as expressive supervision or high reward is used to explain the action and motivations of those who are exposed to them. The characteristic feature of social action, however, is that it is motivated. It assigns meanings to situations and to the acts of others and thus the individual reacts to his definition of the situation and not to the observer's. Since it is reasonable to assume that these definitions arise in the course of both intra- *and* extra-organizational interaction, it is generally inadvisable to exclude factors outside the organization (Silverman, 1970, p. 33).

One of the most important instances of a closed-system model of the organization is the 'axiomatic theory of organizations' of Jerald Hage (1965). Hage constructs this model around axiomatic relationships between four organization goals and four organization means to achieve these goals. These goals/means relationships are similar to Parsons' four functional problems. The first goal is *adaptiveness* or *flexibility*. This is measured by the number of new programmes that the organization adopts per year and the number of new techniques it adopts in a year. Hage also suggests that flexibility may refer to adaptations to external disturbances, although new programmes and techniques can be developed on internal considerations. The second organization goal is *production*. This is gauged by the number of units produced per year and the rate of increase in the number of units produced per year. The third goal of *efficiency* is measured by the cost per unit of output in a year and the amount of idle resources in a year. The fourth and final goal is *job satisfaction*, indicated by employee satisfaction with working conditions and by the turnover rate of labour. All of these goals reflect internal organization factors, with only minimal concern paid to external considerations. They are also part of a conceptual model that 'views the organization as a system in and of itself' (Hall, 1977, pp. 50–1).

Hage generates four axiomatic organization means to these axiomatic organization ends. The first is *complexity* or *specialization*. This is indicated by the number of occupational specialities and the level of training required for them. Complexity is seen to flow from the (necessary) division of labour. The second means is *centralization* or *hierarchy of authority*. This is gauged by the proportion of jobs whose holders participate in decision-making and the number of areas in which they participate. The third organization means is *formalization* or *standardization*, and this is measured as the number of jobs that are codified in terms of things like job descriptions, as well as the range of variation allowed within jobs. The fourth means is *stratification*. This is measured by differences in income and prestige among jobs and the ease of mobility that exists between strata in the organization. All of these means are intra-organizational.

Hage develops a set of propositions and corollaries from relating these means and ends, indicated in Table 5.1.

Hage wishes to employ these intra-organizational features to produce a wholly axiomatic explanation of organizational behaviour. If organizations were wholly rational systems, peopled by automatons who were mathematically programmable, then not only would there be elegance to Hage's axioms, but there would also be utility and reality. Unfortunately for axiomatic theories of organizations, this is not the case, as Silverman (1970, p. 33) stresses, and as Hall elaborates:

> Organizations are not closed systems for the sake of being closed systems. It is at this point that the idea of rationality within the closed system must be introduced. The closed-system perspective is a way of approaching and optimizing organizational rationality – limiting means to ends (Hall, 1977, p. 51).

The results are theoretically impressive:

> The rational model of an organization results in everything being functional – making a positive, indeed an optimum, contribution to the overall result. All resources are appropriate resources, and their allocation fits a master plan. All action is appropriate action, and its outcomes are predictable (Thompson, 1967, p. 6).

However theoretically impressive they may be, one is nonetheless obliged to recall Silverman's (1970) strictures. Just how realistic is it to assume that organizations can be so rational? And if they cannot, what is the point of continuing to conceptualize them *as if* they can? As Thompson (1967) has stressed, for organizations to be as rational as possible they have to be able to 'buffer' themselves from their environment, to have what Cyert and March (1963) referred to as 'organizational slack' (of which Baran and Sweezy's (1966) 'surplus capital' could be a good example). If they

TABLE 5.1 *Major propositions and corollaries of the theory*

Major Propositions

I	The higher the centralization, the higher the production.
II	The higher the formalization, the higher the efficiency.
III	The higher the centralization, the higher the formalization.
IV	The higher the stratification, the lower the job satisfaction.
V	The higher the stratification, the higher the production.
VI	The higher the stratification, the lower the adaptiveness.
VII	The higher the complexity, the lower the centralization.

Derived Corollaries

1	The higher the formalization, the higher the production.
2	The higher the centralization, the higher the efficiency.
3	The lower the job satisfaction, the higher the production.
4	The lower the job satisfaction, the lower the adaptiveness.
5	The higher the production, the lower the adaptiveness.
6	The higher the complexity, the lower the production.
7	The higher the complexity, the lower the formalization.
8	The higher the production, the higher the efficiency.
9	The higher the stratification, the higher the formalization.
10	The higher the efficiency, the lower the complexity.
11	The higher the centralization, the lower the job satisfaction.
12	The higher the centralization, the lower the adaptiveness.
13	The higher the stratification, the lower the complexity.
14	The higher the complexity, the higher the job satisfaction.
15	The lower the complexity, the lower the adaptiveness.
16	The higher the stratification, the higher the efficiency.
17	The higher the efficiency, the lower the job satisfaction.
18	The higher the efficiency, the lower the adaptiveness.
19	The higher the centralization, the higher the stratification.
20	The higher the formalization, the lower the job satisfaction.
21	The higher the formalization, the lower the adaptiveness.

Limits Proposition

VIII	Production imposes limits on complexity, centralization, formalization, stratification, adaptiveness, efficiency, and job satisfaction.

Source: Hage, 1965, p. 300.

cannot 'buffer' they must anticipate and plan and ration their resources when the environment still impinges (Thompson, 1967, p. 19).

There are empirical data as well as these theoretical considerations which suggest that the closed-system perspective is of only limited utility. These derive from the work of Udy (1959) and Hall (1963). Udy (1959) found that 'rational' and 'bureaucratic' elements of organizations often tend to be 'mutually inconsistent within the same organization' (Udy, 1959, p. 794). Hall (1963) also found that these axiomatically derived elements of 'bureaucracy' did not cohere empirically. These findings suggest that the patterning of variables within organizations depends on more than internal conditions. This supports Silverman's (1970, p. 33) assumption.

One of the classic rebuttals of the closed-system perspective is the work of March and Simon (1958), with its stress on member participation in organizations occurring at the level of a bounded rationality which is content to *satisfice* rather than maximize, as models of fully rational *homo economicus* would have it. This is because people in organizations do not act as mathematicians might, where all the information needed to solve an equation is available because all the information needed for the actual process of organization is rarely available. Even where maximum information is available it still has to be interpreted, and as Silverman (1970) stresses, this does not rule out conflicting interpretations of the material or different definitions of the situation. (This will become apparent when we consider the social-action approach in Chapter 7.)

Additional points of criticism have also been raised by Katz and Kahn (1966). There is more than one way to produce a given outcome. Widely different means may produce a common goal or end. A closed-system model cannot take account of feedback processes.

To recapitulate this section, both theoretical and empirical considerations stress the importance of extra-organizational factors, and, from an empirical point of view, an insufficient amount of variance in organizations is explicable solely in intra-organizational terms. Yet as Hall notes:

> Despite all these shortcomings, the perspective persists in the literature and in practice, apparently for the reason that the closed-system perspective, it is a necessary component of the do. Organizations do try to maximize rationality, even if they are aware that they can attain only 'satisficing' decisions. They do try to buffer, level, and smooth out environmental fluctuations. Since organizational actions are at least partially based on a closed-system perspective, it is necessary component of the organizational analyst's repertoire, even though he recognizes that the technique will not be totally successful. Furthermore, the relationships formed by Udy and Hall and suggested by

Hage, whether positive or negative, are relationships. That is, an increase or decrease in the intensity of one internal factor is related to an increase or decrease in the intensity of another. Whether the source of the change is internal or external to the organization is thus irrelevant if the relationship is predictable. Predictable relationships are a prerequisite for theory or practice (Hall, 1977, pp. 55–6).

The development of the open-system perspective

The applications of the above concepts and paradigms have led to the existence of a natural-system or open-system model of the organization. Alvin Gouldner (1959a) is the source of this distinction. His distinctions between the *rational-system* and the *natural-system* models of organizations differentiate between what we (following Thompson, 1967; Silverman, 1970; and Hall, 1977) have referred to as closed and open systems.

Gouldner draws this distinction from an analysis of some of the authors that we have discussed in Chapters 1 and 2: Henri Saint-Simon, Auguste Comte and Max Weber. He observes that:

> Saint-Simon was probably the first to note the rise of
> modern organizational patterns, identify some of their dis-
> tinctive features, and insist upon their prime significance
> for the emerging society. . . . Saint-Simon saw with a sure
> intuition that the ground rules of modern society had been
> deeply altered and that the delicately conceived and planned
> organization was to play a new role in the world (Gouldner,
> 1959a, pp. 400–1).

Gouldner does not see a continuity of preoccupations between Saint-Simon and Comte in this respect. Whilst Saint-Simon stressed rational organization, Comte eulogized the 'natural' and 'spontaneous', argues Gouldner (1959a, p. 401). With Max Weber the 'rational' properties of organizations came into the foreground of analysis and Gouldner (1959a, p. 401) speaks of a 'convergence' in this respect between the views of Saint-Simon and Weber. This convergence leads Gouldner to the following conclusion:

> During the historical development of organizational analysis,
> two distinct approaches to the study of complex organizations
> have emerged in the work of sociologists. One of these, best
> exemplified by the work of Max Weber, is a conception of the
> organization in terms of a 'rational' model. The other, which
> can be termed the 'natural-system' model, ultimately derives
> from Comte, was later reinforced by Robert Michels, and is

now best exemplified in the work of Philip Selznick and Talcott Parsons (Gouldner, 1959a, p. 404).

The 'rational model' is similar to the closed-system model because it 'views the organization as a structure of manipulable parts' (Gouldner, 1959a, p. 405), much as Hage's (1965) axiomatic closed-system model views the organization as a structure of manipulable (because internal) variables. This is in contrast to the natural- or open-system model, which

> regards the organization as a 'natural whole' or system. The realization of the goals of the system as a whole is but one of several important needs to which the organization is oriented Its component structures are seen as emergent institutions, which can be understood only in relation to the diverse needs of the total system. The organization, according to this model, strives to survive and to maintain its equilibrium, and this striving may persist even after its explicitly held goals have been successfully attained. This strain towards survival may even on occasion lead to the neglect or distortion of the organization's goals. Whatever the plans of their creators, organizations, say the natural-system theorists, become ends in themselves and possess their own distinctive needs which have to be satisfied. Once established, organizations tend to generate new ends which constrain the manner in which the nominal group goals can be pursued (Gouldner, 1959a, p. 405).

This quotation from Gouldner serves as an extremely accurate description of the systems concerns of authors such as Parsons, Merton and Selznick, whom we have already considered. In this respect Gouldner stands midway between an open- and closed-systems approach. The stress on the closed-system model is evident in the emphasis on attempts to maintain 'homeostasis' within the organization. On the other hand, the stress on 'system needs' points, albeit in a functionalist framework, to the importance of extra-organizational factors.

Before we go on to consider the assumptions of the systems framework generally, in particular its functionalist basis, we can present in summary form the three basic assumptions of this framework which Silverman (1970) has identified. These are, first, that organizations modelled as systems can be seen to be composed of *interdependent parts* with each of the parts contributing to the survival of the whole. The parts comprise separate processes which are the focus of attention. In addition, the framework assumes that organizations have *needs for survival*, and that they can be conceptualized as *purposive systems* which behave and take actions. We can consider these in more detail.

Interdependent parts

There is a reciprocal arrangement between the parts of an organization and the whole: each gives and receives resources and problems. Silverman (1970, p. 28) illustrates this arrangement by reference to the relations between a Personnel Department and a Production Department in a manufacturing enterprise when a strike is threatened. If the Personnel Department manages to avoid the strike, its output may be seen as the input of the Production Department. If, however, the strike is averted by increasing wages, this then creates problems for the Sales Department who have to sell the product at a higher price. In turn, there may be redundancies that have to be coped with by the Personnel Department. Clearly, here is a good example of the action of one part of an organization having consequences for the whole organization. Indeed, there are also consequences outside the boundaries of the organization, such as in related enterprises, the local community, and so on.

Needs for survival

In order to survive, organizations have to satisfy certain needs. Possibly the most important of these is the need to attain the organization goals. It is important to recognize, though, that there are many organization needs, in spite of the fact that much of the literature, as seen later, tends to concentrate upon goals and goal attainment.

Purposive needs

The systems literature on organizations often makes the assumption that organizations themselves take actions, as well as the members of organizations. A reified concept of organization is often argued to be visible where one reads of 'organizations pursue goals'. (This is the basis of much of Silverman's (1970) critique). In order to avoid the risk of reductionism it would seem appropriate to avoid such statements. On the other hand, there are instances where organizations, as systems of roles and offices, do appear to act. This can be seen where the same organizational action is taken even though the organizational personnel may have changed. The fact that organizations *are* reifications is stressed by Hall (1977).

Organizations as open systems

The open-system approach to organization analysis recognizes the influences of the environment upon the interdependent parts of the organization. As we have already seen, there is a degree of reciprocity in the relationship between organizations and their environments. As Buckley's work (1967) demonstrates well, it is essential that if organizations are to be treated as systems they should be treated as open systems. Organizations interact with other organizations, associations and institutions in an interdependent manner and can be seen to be part of the sub-systems of a much wider system – that of society. We can note at this stage that while 'system' is an analytical concept, society is a term of ordinary language. Its applicability as such, in this context, may be called into question. In fact, increasingly, the notion of society as the total system becomes invalid through, for example, the influence of the multi-national enterprise.

In their social-psychological analysis of organizations, Katz and Kahn (1966) distinguish nine characteristics that they claim define an open system:

1 The importation of energy
2 The throughput
3 The output
4 Systems as cycles of events
5 Negative entropy
6 Information input, negative feedback and the coding process
7 The steady state and dynamic homeostasis
8 Differentiation
9 Equifinality.

These defining characteristics of organizations as open systems, it is maintained, move the analysis away from the 'disregard of differing organizational environments and the nature of organizational dependency on environment' (Katz and Kahn, 1966, p. 29) that exists in other organizational analyses.

In the light of these observations, it is the case that organizations are reliant upon their environments for the provision of their requirements. The concepts of *input, throughput* and *output* display the nature of an exchange of goods and services between organizations and their environments. Jaques has commented that:

> The factory operates within its larger society. It is successful as an industrial undertaking in so far as it succeeds in maintaining a connection between the new methods it is trying to develop and the central features and trends of the culture of this society (Jaques, 1951, p. 258).

It can be argued that organizations increasingly attempt to control their environments. For example, Galbraith in *The New*

Industrial State (1969) has argued that some organizations, particularly the large multi-national enterprises, attempt to determine the values of the society in which they operate. This notion appears to be accepted by management theorists, since in their writings the shaping of the economic environment is seen to be one of the organizational objectives.

In terms of the inputs to organizations there is widespread acceptance that managers do have some choice, that there is not the economic nor technical determinism that was long thought to be the case. The work of Child (1972a) develops a strategic choices model (of which more is said in a later chapter). This model suggests that managers do have choice in the strategies adopted within the organization. In spite of this proposition, attitudes and values of organization members are often determined by external factors. Values determined outside the organization do play some part in determining values within the organization. The Luton studies of Goldthorpe *et al.* (1969) provide evidence for this proposition. Of course, an open-system perspective is concerned with more than individual values and attitudes; it also has as its concern external factors such as the trade union structure, the kind of working-class movements in the past, the nature and history of the local community, and other matters.

The system environment

Since the organization environment is such a prominent feature of the open-system approach to organizations, it is interesting to see how Katz and Kahn's original formulation has been used in later work. One interesting development has been the examination of the management of rapidly changing environments. The work of Emery (1969) and Lawrence and Lorsch (1967) analyses the environmental structure in systems terms, and from this analysis arrives at measures of the rate of change of elements in the organizational environment. Lawrence and Lorsch distinguish three elements in the environment – market, research and development, and technology – and show that they can change at different rates. In such a way, it is possible for the changing environment to be more accurately analysed as well as analysing environmental feedback and organization change.

The question of organization environments has been one of concern for some time. Even before the development of open systems theory, attempts were made to analyse this relationship. The work of Woodward (1965), or of Burns and Stalker (1961), made further important contributions in this area. Their work was concerned to show that different organization structures were appropriate in different environments. In the case of Woodward, the emphasis was upon the technological environment; for Burns and Stalker features of the environment, such as product-type and rate of technical change were central.

Such work, together with that of the Tavistock researchers such as Emery and Trist (1960), is often referred to as a *socio-technical approach*. While a considerable discussion of these theories and this approach follows later, it is both relevant and appropriate at this juncture to describe what the socio-technical approach entails.

Basically, socio-technical systems take account of the technological environment of the work group. If a comparison is possible with the human relations movement, it will be recalled that the over-riding emphasis was on the informal structure. In the case of socio-technical systems the emphasis shifts towards an examination of task-related interaction. The technological environment of the work group is incorporated into the analysis. The informal aspects of interaction are still recognized by the socio-technical theorists, but they are seen to be subordinate to the task itself.

The workplace is therefore neither wholly a social system nor a technical system. There is interdependence between these two in the socio-technical system.

There are a number of points of criticism that can fairly be levelled at the application of the systems concept to organization analysis, where organizations are seen as closed, partially open, open or socio-technical systems. Before embarking on such a critique, it is worth while examining a few empirical examples to demonstrate the way in which the systems concept has been used by organization analysts.

Possibly the earliest and still one of the most widely cited works in organizational and industrial sociology is that of Roethlisberger and Dickson's *Management and the Worker* (1939). As we have seen in an earlier chapter, the research work at the Hawthorne plant was to be highly significant as the forerunner of the human relations movement. It is an equally important piece of work for another reason: it was one of the first attempts to apply a systems perspective in the analysis of organizations. Figure 5.3 demonstrates the way in which the individual can be in a state of equilibrium in the work situation. The basic proposition is that if an individual can attain a state of equilibrium then this contributes to work effectiveness.

To some extent the diagram is misleading in that it gives the impression that the Hawthorne investigators were employing a totally closed system perspective. There are two points here. First, the system concept used is not a reified one; and second, account is taken of the external environment. For example:

201

Possible sources of interference   **Responses**

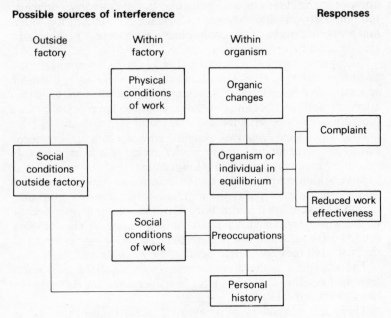

Figure 5.3   Scheme for interpreting complaints and reduced work effectiveness.

Source: Roethlisberger and Dickson, 1939, p. 122.

It is . . . possible to understand the effect upon the individual of – or the meanings assigned by the individual to – the events, objects and features of his environment, such as hours of work, wages, etc. Only then is it possible to see what effect changes in the working environment have upon the social reorganization to which the employee has become accustomed, or upon that ideal type of equilibrium which he desires. . . . The relation of the individual employee to the company is not a closed system. All the values of the individual cannot be accounted for by the social organization of the company. . . . The attitude and significance of his work is not defined so much by his relation to the company as by his relation to the wider social reality (Roethlisberger and Dickson, 1939, pp. 375–6).

The use of the systems concept can also be seen in the work of Homans (1950), which is partly based upon the Hawthorne studies. Recognizing the interdependent nature of system parts, Homans distinguished between the concepts of activity, sentiment and interaction. Activity is what individuals do; sentiments are the

202

attitudes expressed; and interaction is the contact between individuals. According to Homans, these three concepts operate as a simple system in that norms of behaviour are created that affect system performance. In more recent terminology, this might be seen as a feedback mechanism. Again, Homans points to the environmental influences that might operate since each of the three concepts may be affected by the environment. Possibly the most important part of Homans' analysis in this context relates to the restriction of output that occurred in the Bank Wiring Room. Here Homans states that it is necessary for us to understand the social environment in Chicago at the time of the depression for an adequate understanding of the phenomenon.

The question of output restriction and understanding it through a systems perspective is one examined in the British work of Lupton (1963) and Lupton and Cunnison (1964). They were concerned to examine the kinds of social factor that operate to set informal output norms in manufacturing industry. Eldridge (1973) has usefully summarized the factors operating in the organizations that each studied, which were respectively garment manufacture and electrical engineering.

TABLE 5.2

External factors	Internal factors
1 Market situation	1 Method of wage payment
(a) its stability	2 Nature of the productive system
(b) its size	3 Sex of workers
2 Relations with competitors	4 Workshop social structure
3 Location of industry	5 Degree of congruence and conflict in management-worker relationship
4 Trade union organization	
(a) national level	
(b) local level	6 Ratio of labour costs to total costs

Source: Eldridge, 1973, p. 30.

Lupton and Cunnison's work does, in fact, tend to concentrate rather more on internal than external factors. This is largely a consequence of the particular research methods used: mainly participant observation. In their discussion of this point, they make the interesting distinction between what they refer to as overlapping social systems and inclusive social systems. With regard to the former, they say that 'there are segments of other social systems which are latent in a single workshop. For instance, a man's role as a father, or as a member of a social class, may affect his behaviour in the workshop' (Lupton and Cunnison, 1964, p. 125). It is clear from this that what is required is a rigorous treatment of the factors external to the work situation of an organization. Such a treatment involves, amongst other things 'intensive interviews with the families of workers' (Lupton and Cunnison, 1964, p. 125). It is interesting that this is precisely the approach adopted by some of those using the social-action approach that is discussed below in Chapter 7.

A considerable amount of the empirical work undertaken using a systems perspective has a prescriptive flavour about it. Thus, it is clear from this work, as shown below, that the factors that influence worker productivity or managerial efficiency have been very much to the fore in these analyses. Of course, much of the work arose from industrial consultancy, and obviously the requirements of management, the sponsors and paymasters of such research, was important. At the forefront of such work has been the Tavistock Institute, which engaged in a considerable amount of consultancy. A good example of this approach can be seen in the work of Eliot Jaques (especially in *The Changing Culture of a Factory*, 1951). This account of what has come to be called the Glacier Metal Project is premised throughout with the assumption that a 'healthier' culture within industry is required, particularly in terms of the relations between workers and management. One way of achieving this is through joint consultative systems. It is interesting that Jaques's work concentrates very much on the internal structures and processes in the factory and pays only lip-service to the external environment.

The work of the Tavistock Institute is normally associated with the strides made in the development of the socio-technical system. As we have already seen, this approach stresses that industrial organizations comprise both a social and technical system, both of which require analysis. A third dimension – the economic system – is often added to these two. It has been stated that these three are interdependent and yet they have independent values of their own (Trist *et al.*, 1963, p. 6).

Initially, it was the coalmining industry in the UK that was the focus of attention of the socio-technical theorists, as seen in the work of Trist *et al.* (1963) and Dennis *et al.* (1969). Critically reviewing this work, Eldridge (1973) has suggested that because of a bias in favour of the socio-psychological system the focus of analysis tends to be the primary work group rather than the whole organization. Where the environment is specifically examined this is the environment of the 'seam society'. The whole local community which is analysed by Dennis *et al.* tends to be ignored by Trist *et al.* Again, the role of the trade union beyond its local role is largely ignored. Eldridge questions whether it is possible for work-group autonomy to be realized in the highly mechanized mining situation, even though Trist *et al.* claim that it can be. This is made possible because the researchers define a primary work group as a group with up to fifty members.

One of the most widely cited examples of the socio-technical approach is presented by Miller and Rice (1967). In an earlier volume Rice (1963) was explicitly concerned with organizations as open systems and thus with a concern for the external environment. He examines the effect that the system's components have on each other and also develops a way of measuring the success or otherwise of the organization in adapting to demands made upon it. In Rice's view, an organization is successful if it achieves its 'primary task'.

The concept of primary task is central to the later work of Miller and Rice (1967), and indeed it is here that it is developed into a viable concept. The aim of their book, through the analysis of case material, is to explore the idea that an enterprise has three forms of organization contained within it: that organization which seeks to control the performance of the task; that which seeks to gain commitment to organizational objectives; and that which seeks to regulate relations between what the writers refer to as the task and sentient systems. Basically, a sentient system is that which demands and receives loyalty from members.

The Tavistock researchers, prior to this work, seemed to make the assumption that the boundaries of the task and sentient system should coincide. In this way, there would be effective task performance and the satisfaction of human needs. This should be one of the goals in designing an organization (note the prescriptive flavour of this approach). In this later work of Miller and Rice, the approach seems to shift somewhat, particularly when they argue that:

> The organizations in which it is possible to match sentient groups to task – and so make task and sentient groups coincide – are the exception rather than the rule. What is more, a group that shares its sentient boundary with that of an activity system is all too likely to become committed to that particular system so that, although both efficiency and satisfaction may be greater in the short run, in the long run such an organization is likely to inhibit technical change. Unconsciously, the group may come to re-define its primary task and behave as if this had become the defence of an obsolescent system. The group then resists, irrationally and vehemently, any changes in the activities of the task system that might disturb established roles and relations (Miller and Rice, 1967, p. 31).

Another point about this later volume is that the notion of primary task is explored more fully. It is defined by the writers as 'the task [the organization] must perform if it is to survive' (Miller and Rice, 1967, p. 25). Silverman (1970, p. 117) points to the tautological nature of this definition, but it is made clear that the definition is not normative but descriptive and thus goes beyond what it is normally regarded a primary task ought to be. Miller and Rice follow a traditional approach in deciding what the primary task is, as our subsequent discussion of the goal approach to organization analysis displays. Such an approach is to ask the managers, the executives and the leaders of organizations what they perceive to be the organization's objectives. Such statements, however, are often misplaced and do not adequately represent the objectives being pursued by organization members.

The formal structure of organizations, according to Miller and Rice, enables the primary task to be attained. This they refer to as the task system of the organization. This is where the distinction, already noted, with the sentient system is drawn. The sentient system is essentially the informal structure of the organization, the system ensuring organization loyalty on the part of participants. There is a vaguely psychological stance here, since Miller and Rice argue that the sentient system derives from personality needs on the part of organization members – those needs that motivate individuals. Such an approach is very much in the mould of the human relations movement, in that the individual is assumed to have psychological needs to want to belong to informal groups and to engage in informal interaction. It would appear that the sentient system is non-rational: it possesses what Homans (1950) calls the 'logic of sentiment'. It follows from this that the task system follows the 'logic of efficiency'.

We have seen that a socio-technical system comprises a technical and a social system. In Miller and Rice's formulation, the socio-technical system exists where the task system operates on and influences the sentient system. It follows from this that the psychological needs of organizational members are a constraint on the design of the organization when it comes to the primary task. In this way the socio-technical system gains some meaning. As Silverman extracts from the work, it follows that the goal of analysis must be the development of solutions that take account of the technical requirements of the task and the human needs of those performing it. The 'right' organization would satisfy the task and social needs (Silverman, 1970, p. 118).

A typology consisting of three basic types can be constructed from this analysis. First, where the task and sentient system do not coincide; second, where there is a natural coincidence; and third,

206

where there is a contrived coincidence. Examples of these would be, respectively, the professional employee whose primary loyalty is to his profession; the family firm; and Trist's example of the longwall method of coal-getting.

The limitations of the systems approach

There are a number of general points that can be made about the examination of organizations as systems. Some of these are similar in form to those made about structural functionalism. Before looking at the general points, we shall refer in particular to the socio-technical approach to organizational analysis.

Silverman has pointed out that the socio-technical writers have almost all adopted the 'organic analogy':

> The deficiencies of the organic analogy as applied to social life . . . raise . . . obvious questions. Does patterned social interaction depend upon a primary task? Is social action best understood as a response to demands perceived by the observer but not necessarily by the participants? Is it useful to conceive of social forms in terms of health and pathology? (Silverman, 1970, p. 119).

To be fair to those adopting the socio-technical approach, these are abstract questions and not the kind of issue that has been their concern. Indeed, Silverman (1970, p. 118) previously recognized that they had a 'commitment to abstracted empiricism in preference to grand theory'. However, we can observe that abstracted empiricism, as a theory, has been under heavy attack in recent years, ever since Mills's (1959b) celebrated critique. A more appropriate way of examining the deficiencies in the approach is presented by Silverman (1970, pp. 121–4), when he lists some major limitations.

1   The socio-technical approach never makes clear what the status of its variables are. Thus, it is often unclear whether variables are causal or merely explanatory. Silverman calls this a failure to distinguish between the 'is' and the 'ought' type of proposition: is one left with an accurate description of the way that organizations work, or is it a formulation of the way things ought to be for effective functioning?

2   Following from this is the limitation that within the socio-technical system approach there is the regular failure of its proponents to discuss adequately the sources of the orientations of members of organizations. The question of attachment to work is normally discussed in terms of a moral or ethical attachment; the sources of the attachments, where they are discussed, seem to be

derived from vague psychological needs. The impact of external or internal features of the organization are largely ignored.

3 One of the key features of the systems approach to the study of organizations is the examination of the organization environment. In the socio-technical approach the environment, where it is considered, is the economic environment. The market demand upon economic organization seems to be the over-riding question of concern.

Comparing the natural-system model of organization with the rational model that Gouldner (1959a) distinguished, enables one to see some of the shortcomings of the systems approach. Possibly the most important of these is the fact that natural systems tend to concentrate their analysis upon the informal interactions and informal groups within organizations. In this sense, there is a neglect, certainly in comparison with the rational model (cf. Weber on bureaucracy) of the more rational and planned arrangements and structures that are characteristic of organizations. Indeed, as Gouldner points out (1959a, p. 409), rationality is also a feature of the forces that lead to the growth and maintenance of organizations. In consequence of this, there are a number of unproblematic taken-for-granted assumptions made about organizations in the natural-system mode. These assumptions include the existence and nature of the division of labour, the employment of professionals, the whole rationalistic orientation, and so on.

The relative analytical neglect of the rational features also means that in the natural-system model the focus is upon the 'forces that undermine the organization's impersonal principles and subvert its formal ends to narrower interests, rather than on those that sustain these and bolster the distinctively bureaucratic structures' (Gouldner, 1959a, p. 409). Again, in the general conduct of social affairs the role of rationality is minimized (particularly when the natural-system model stresses the impact of non-rational norms).

Gouldner also points to the limitation that arises from the emphasis upon the interdependence of the parts within an organization. This interdependence of parts is taken to be a given, since the model tends to focus upon the organization as a whole. Consequently, variations that might occur in the degrees of interdependence are not systematically examined. Gouldner's concept of 'functional autonomy' displays the fact that some parts may survive even though separated from other parts. It also shows the variation in the degree of dependence upon each other. It further moves away from the idea that interdependence is not definitionally a question of symmetry. Thus, if there is an over-emphasis upon integration and interdependence there is a neglect of the notion of functional autonomy.

208

Gouldner cites as an example of this the attempt of Talcott Parsons (1956) to define an organization in terms of its orientation to goals. It will be recalled that Parsons defines an organization as a social system which is primarily oriented toward the attainment of a specific goal. Gouldner observes that this often means 'no more than that these are the goals of its top administrators'. A more precise formulation, as he observes,

> would require specification of the ends of various people, or of the typical ends of different parts or strata within the organization. Such a specification would indicate that these ends may vary, are not necessarily identical, and may, in fact, be contradictory (Gouldner, 1959a, p. 420).

It is because the natural-system or open-system model frequently neglects this fact due to under-emphasis on the functional autonomy of the system parts that the concept of the organization which is used ends up as a reification. However, on certain occasions organizations *are* reifications: they are oriented to by people in such a reified mode that they do in fact assume a 'real' existence. As Hall puts it:

> When we hear statements such as 'it is company policy', 'Z State University never condones cheating', or 'Trans Rhode Island Airline greet you with a smile', these are recognizable as being about organizations. Organizations do have policies, do and do not condone cheating, and may or may not greet you with a smile. They also manufacture goods, administer policies, and protect the citizenry. These are organizational actions and involve properties of organizations, not individuals. They are carried out by individuals – even in the case of computer-produced letters, which are programmed by individuals – but the genesis of the actions remains in the organization (Hall, 1977, p. 27).

These reifications are not 'natural' phenomena, but the result of power differentials and practices which enable management to impose 'company policy' or 'smiles' upon the members of the organization. Where organization analysts fail to make it clear that the reification of the organization is an actuality, in terms of power within the organization, then the use of reified models of the organization is unjustified. The major reification in systems models of organizations is the tendency, particularly in Parsons (1956) and those influenced by him, to treat the organization's 'goal' as a thing-in-itself, rather than either as an 'ongoing consensus between the members of the organization' (Silverman, 1970, p. 9), or, more realistically, the capacity of management to impose its hegemony on the members of the organization. Gouldner observes that this hegemony exists as tension:

> The structure of complex organizations . . . serves to maintain and protect the parts from others within the same system, at least to some degree. Thus, organization structure is shaped by a tension between centrifugal and centripetal pressures, limiting as well as imposing control over parts, separating as well as joining them (Gouldner, 1959a, p. 423).

We have seen that systems theory concentrates heavily upon the issue of self maintenance, of maintaining a steady state. This abstract notion, when applied to organization analysis, has to be treated as a functional problem, not as something asserted implicitly in the analysis.

Using a different non-functionalist argument, Mayntz (1964) points to certain limitations of the systems approach in organization analysis. She recognizes that the approach is commendable compared with the closed view of the formal theories of administration or the very limited approaches under scientific management. In particular, the openness of the systems approach enabling an analysis of the environment is commended. The drawback with this openness, according to Mayntz, is that the interactions with the environment are necessarily selective:

> Once we get down to the question *which* of its features or properties a particular organization can or should keep invariant against *which* external influences, and *what kinds* of regulating mechanisms can serve this purpose, we must obviously leave the level of general propositions valid for all organizations and are forced to take historically specific conditions into account (Mayntz, 1964, p. 113).

Thus, systems analysis is useful in many ways but it is unable to cope with the specific instances that are necessary when making explanatory propositions. In other words, Mayntz questions the extent of the explanatory powers of systems theory. Of course, as discussed elsewhere (Clegg and Dunkerley, 1977) and developed later, the issue of the ahistorical nature of systems theory is an issue that applies to most of organization analysis.

A final limitation that has to be considered for general systems theory has already been dealt with when discussing the limitations of the socio-technical system approach; that is, the problem of the approach being prescriptive. Since efficiency of the organization is one of the objects of study in systems theory, there is little chance of the analysis being totally general. There is always a tendency, as Mayntz (1964, p. 116) points out, for systems analysis to move towards the specific case. As such the emphasis then falls upon those organizations that produce goods and services for other groups or organizations. The economic organization is therefore the prime type of organization analyzed.

As Elger (1975, p. 95) has observed, systems theories, because of their stress on the role of a consensual value system, underplay 'possible bargaining or conflict' over the ways in which organizational roles are to be performed, 'since the "maintenance" mechanisms of socialization and control are assumed to produce role-conformity. Similarly, the extent to which different patterns of experience and differential resources subvert stipulated role performance is minimized.' Of course, this stress on order and on organization members as compliant actors of prescribed roles shows a close correspondence with the interest and ideology of organization élites. It also provides a vocabulary – seemingly neutral, scientific and purged of value – with which organizations can appear to be *administered as things* rather than be ruled and exploited as resources. Hence, the socio-technical system theories identify for managers the tools that 'change-agents' can employ in their pursuit of system efficiency and survival.

Compared with the earliest sociological theories of organizations in society which we considered in Chapter 1, or contrasted with Weber's historical sociology and Marx's historical materialism, which we considered in Chapter 2, perhaps the most noticeable feature of systems theory is its almost total neglect of history and social change. In part, this results from the prescriptive framework. Managers' problems are rarely couched in terms of an historical understanding. Nor are systems theories; if they were, it is unlikely that they would be able to conceptualize administrative problems of management in terms of administrative solutions. This is to suggest that systems theory has typically been ideological, not only in its problems, but as Allen (1975, ch. 3) would argue, in its models, models essentially premised on equilibrium analyses:

> Equilibrium analysis, as it has been used by organization
> theorists, has a stability bias. The equilibrium position is seen
> to be the stable and, therefore, the desired one. This has resulted
> because equilibrium relates to the organization or whatever is
> under investigation. . . . A consequence of the use of equili-
> brium analysis has been to emphasize that a change away from
> any given equilibrium position must have negative or derogatory
> effects. It is but one logical step away to claim that change itself is
> undesirable. Thus equilibrium is equivalent to *status quo* analysis
> (Allen, 1975, p. 102).

In conclusion we can note two further points. One has been

211

proposed by Gouldner and stresses the same integrative equilibrium bias of functionalist system theories. Gouldner (1971, pp. 455–77) has argued that such theory characterizes the administration of *any* industrial society, be it the USSR or the USA, at a certain stage in its development. He terms such an administratively useful functionalist theory *academic sociology*, and proposes that its institutionalization

> is essentially a part or a special case of the more general
> development of sector autonomy. . . . It is 'instrumental' in that
> it contributes, in practical and 'applied' ways, to the efficient
> integration of different social sectors and levels. It is 'symbolic'
> in that it concerns itself with formulating a 'mapping' of the
> society that locates different social parts, symbolically con-
> necting and representing them as part of a larger social whole
> (Gouldner, 1971, p. 469).

In this context Gouldner observes the eastwards move of functionalism, and its institutionalization in the Soviet Union. Gvishiani's (1972) work on organization theory demonstrates the extent to which this systems theory is now integrated into the command apparatus of the USSR. It is in this connection interesting to note that one of the major centres of organizational analysis in Moscow is the Institute of Control Sciences!

Gouldner's observations raise the issue which Braverman (1974) addresses in his introduction to *Labour and Monopoly Capital*, that is 'the question . . . of the Soviet bloc'. The existence of both a form of organization and organization theory in the USSR which is in significant respects similar to those in the capitalist West (hierarchical organization; strong division between mental and manual labour; capitalist technology, conceptualized within a functionalist systems framework) is a sign not of the functional necessity of these structures but of decisions made concerning the process of industrialization in the USSR within the framework inherited from the developing capitalist mode of production in Russia and imported from developed examples of this mode after the Revolution (e.g., Taylorism).

Despite these generally critical remarks on systems frameworks we must not damn any application of a systems model in advance of its actual use. For instance, some contemporary neo-Marxist authors such as Habermas (1976) and Wallerstein (1974a) have attempted to retrieve and reconstruct a rational kernel from the systems shell. We shall find these useful in our final chapter.

212

6 Organizations as empirically contingent structures

Introduction

Neither the systems characterization of the organization nor the various typologies which have been constructed have developed a wholly adequate model of the organization as a theoretical object. If the open-system model leaves us in doubt as to where the organization *is*, epistemologically (that is, what could be the logical boundary of an *open* system?), the typological approach may be said to have us in doubt as to *what*, epistemologically, the organization is: is it a structure of compliance, a variable of beneficiaries or some other, or combination of some other of the many characteristics which have been taken to distinguish types of organizations? When we recall that Haas *et al.* (1966, pp. 162–3) were able to delineate thirty-seven such characteristics, it becomes obvious that the inability of organization theorists to construct any coherent or consensual theoretical object of the organization is crucial.

Personality structure and organization structure

Some of the difficulties inherent in the construction of this theoretical object have been due to the types of data and methodologies from which our knowledge of organizations has been generated. Until relatively recently the type of data used has largely been collected through *case study* analysis. We have already considered some classical case studies of organizational analysis such as those of Selznick (1949) and Gouldner (1954). Michel Crozier (1976), who is the author of the famous case study of *The Bureaucratic Phenomenon* (Crozier, 1964) has argued that the case studies method had three basic characteristics. These were the following:

213

1   *A global approach*   the approach was global because 'the main kind of reasoning was that of description and understanding and not measurement'.

2   *A mixed approach*   'it could not be sharply distinguished from a social, psychological and anthropological approach, from which disciplines it was freely borrowing methods and concepts', as Crozier puts it.

3   *An interpretative approach*   it was primarily interpretative, 'focusing on the informal, on what people experience – much more than on goals and results' (Crozier, 1976, p. 194).

Associated with this general approach was a 'dominant paradigm' argues Crozier. This was one which observed that social organization and interaction should confound the 'expected results' of 'formal goals and formal rules' (Crozier, 1976, p. 194).

Crozier goes on to identify three basic weaknesses with this case study approach:

> First, its basic questions were not focusing on organizations as units but on processes within organizations; second, its methods for generalizing its hypotheses were to go from one case to theory and back to another case, which meant great difficulty in using scientific evidence to test any kind of theory; third, it was easily associated with a kind of functionalist philosophy, based on the superiority of consensus and harmony, which gradually appeared to be too soft-headed (Crozier, 1976, pp. 194–5).

A major feature of the theoretical model of the organization as an open system was its broad conceptual scope; and it was, in part, this breadth which limited the amount of major substantive work that was able to be done on organizations, at least until this breadth could be given greater conceptual specificity. In particular, this became a major problem when researchers attempted any kind of *rapprochement* between the open- and closed-system frameworks. If lists of closed-system, intra-organizational variables, such as those of Hage's (1965) axiomatic theory, could be conceptualized, and the organization granted to be not wholly closed, then there must be some interaction between these variables and the organization environment. It was these sorts of issues which saw the emergence in the 1960s of new styles of research in organization analysis, posing new types of problems. Crozier (1976, p. 195) has contrasted the concerns of this decade with those of the case study-dominated 1950s:

The sixties have seen the emergence and progressive predominance of a hard-headed, supposedly more scientific approach; intended to produce evidence by measuring hard facts bearing specifically on the organizational phenomenon, i.e. on organizations as units. For this purpose, the main effort has been toward producing data on samples of organizations and on using statistical analyses of these data for proving or disproving hypotheses. This has meant a sharp break with social psychology and anthropology and the developments of new questions that were compatible with the new evidence; what kind of variables do affect organizations' characteristics and what kind of impact do these characteristics have on an organization's results? (Crozier, 1976, p. 195).

The key issue in this remained how to conceptualize *organization structure*, for organization structure was to be the centre of the changed problematic as the key theoretical object.

These were new problems for organization theorists. Their discipline was still very much an infant. It bore traces of its dependence on other slightly sturdier siblings such as the 'common-sense' prescriptions of management theory, or the grand theory of essentially non-empirical theorists such as Parsons. Where theory and empirical data had come together it had only been fleetingly, in case studies, as Crozier (1976) stresses. However, they were not entirely new problems for at least one other branch of the social sciences. This was psychology, particularly the psychology of *personality structure*. And, fortuitously in the right place at the right time, there developed a cross-over whereby a psychologist concerned with just these issues in personality structure came to apply the solutions developed there to problems of conceptualizing organization structure.

The psychologist's name was Derek Pugh; the place was the Industrial Administration Research Unit at what was to become the University of Aston (in 1966; it was then known as the Birmingham College of Advanced Technology); and the time was 1961. Derek Pugh and David Hickson (1976) have detailed the start of the research project which developed there as *The Aston Programme* in the interesting biographical foreword to the first volume of their collected papers (Pugh and Hickson, 1976) and how the focus of the research team concentrated on organization structure. This need not detain us here. What concerns us in this context is how they conceptualized organization structure. What assumptions did they make which enabled them to construct the key concept at the centre of their research project?

Psychologists involved in the study of personality structure encountered similar difficulties to organization theorists involved in the analysis of organization structure. In both areas of analysis there existed a large body of impressionistic and speculative data (literary excursions into the nature of personality traits, management prescriptions on the 'correct' span of control, etc.) as well as the framework of theoretical writing inherited from the founding fathers (Sigmund Freud; Max Weber). Psychologists who wished to advance a more scientific knowledge of personality were confronted with the problem of deciding which of the many personality traits were the most useful in making an analysis. That is, they had to determine which aspects of personality were the most characteristic and distinctive. And, if they were to compare one personality with another, or attempt to determine whether or not personality structure was stable over time, they had to devise some method of comparison. But what were they to compare, and how were they to compare it? Allport and Odbert (1936) found that the unabridged dictionary contains approximately 18,000 adjectives which are commonly used in the English language to describe how people act, think, perceive, feel and behave. It also contained almost four thousand words which could be taken to correspond to specific traits – words such as 'humility' or 'arrogance'. Through careful editing and the exercise of common-sense 'judgment' they were able to reduce the list to about 170 words. Although this is undoubtedly more economical than four thousand, it is still rather too many to use for scientific purposes.

Psychologists such as Cattell attempted to reduce this list further through a statistical technique known as 'factor analysis'. Cattell (1946) identified which traits appeared to be closely related to which others. After doing this, 171 traits were reduced to 35 broad clusters of traits, by combining under one trait all those which appeared to correlate highly with it. He then employed a small group of 'experienced judges' to rate a large group of adult men (not *people*) whom they knew reasonably well, on each of the 35 broad traits. It was at this stage that factor analysis was used.

Factor analysis is basically a logic of discovery. The disciplines of psychology and education have used the technique most extensively and only recently has it been used for research purposes other than the testing and measuring of abilities and attitudes. The theory of factor analysis has been stated by Fruchter as follows:

A battery of intercorrelated variables has common factors running through it . . . the score of individuals can be represented more economically in terms of these reference factors. An individual's score on a test is dependent upon two things: the particular abilities assessed by the test and the

216

amount of each of these abilities possessed by the examinee
(Fruchter, 1954, p. 44).

Measures of association – especially the Pearson product-
moment correlation coefficient – form the basis of factor analysis.
Using such measures, the inter-correlations obtained can be
manipulated through sophisticated mathematical techniques to
produce common factors. In this way concepts may be developed
for scaling purposes.

As a result of Cattell's factor analysis, the 35 traits were found to
cluster around 12 common 'factors'. This means that these 12
factors proved to be almost as good as 35 in describing personality.
The 12 factors were produced through inter-correlational analysis.

The Aston approach was simply to take this general method and
apply it to the analysis of organization rather than personality
structure. In two publications, *Writers on Organizations* (Pugh *et
al.*, 1971) and 'A Convergence in Organization Theory' (Hickson,
1966), the initial literature in which the search for structural
concepts was conducted is available to us. It covers management
theorists such as Taylor (1911), Fayol (1949) and Urwick (1947),
sociologists such as Weber (1947) and Gouldner (1954), and social
psychologists such as Argyris (1960) and McGregor (1960).

At the same time that the researchers were combing the literature
for lists of relevant concepts, they were also engaged in open
interviewing sessions with managers in a variety of organizations.
Out of these there emerged concepts of structure:

> Conversations, and the later structured interviews, were with
> managers, not workers, with administrators, not clerks, because
> organizations split activities into more and more specific
> tasks down the hierarchy and this limits the amount of informa-
> tion those at the bottom can give. What they can give would be
> different, of course: on this topic it would also be less (Pugh and
> Hickson, 1976, p. 2)

The 'experienced judges' in this research were the managers
whom they interviewed and the researchers themselves. As Pugh
and Hickson (1976, p. 2) put it, 'the concepts slowly crystallized'.
They crystallized as 'specialization of activities; standardization of
procedures; formalization of documentation; centralization of
authority; configuration of role structure' (Pugh and Hickson, 1976,
p. 2).

The next stage in the research process was to operationalize these
concepts. The process of operationism was first devised by the
physicist, Percy Bridgman (1927), to clear up the kind of confusion
that arises when a stick is half submerged in water: it looks bent and

217

feels straight. What its 'real' shape is becomes an empirical question to be settled by the operation of looking and touching. These different operations define different concepts: i.e., visual straightness and tactile straightness. These operations can be repeated on all other sticks in similar circumstances, in order to achieve comparison between sticks in terms of a standard criterion of shape. The measured object is taken necessarily to exist before the measuring instrument. This measuring instrument must not be employed in such a way as to be constitutive of the measured object, and should be capable of generalization to each and every case of the former.

To extend this measuring device to social scientific analysis of organizations would appear to be quite straightforward. One would simply generate some 'items' for data collection which appear to define the concepts one has. One would then have data on which one could perform statistical computations designed to test the statistical coherence of the items conceptualized as belonging together, as 'dimensions' of the overall concept of structure. However, this assumes that these dimensions of structure *really* exist prior to their being constituted as such by the measuring instrument. The research technique has this fallacy built into it.

One might argue that this inbuilt fallacy is unimportant, that if the technique 'works', then this is its own validation. This seems to be the assumption of the Aston researchers in that they only 'postulate' (Pugh and Hickson, 1976, p. 2) that 'the structure of any form of work organization . . . can be portrayed on these dimensions'. Certainly, the success of the technique shows that this postulate is correct: using the Aston technique any organization can be constituted as if it has these 'primary dimensions', but this does not warrant the assumption that it really does have this structure. To act as if it did would be an extremely inductive empiricism. We shall return to this question.

The Aston studies

The intention of the Aston project was to construct dimensions upon which organizations might be compared. This approach stems from the work of Lupton (1963), which stressed the necessity of taking into account 'the economic and social position of the enterprise, the technological system, and so on' (Pugh and Hickson, 1976, p. 22). Other studies had already taken this approach, such as Thompson and Bates's (1957) discussions of a wide range of technologies in extractive, manufacturing and professional organizations on their administration. The studies of Joan Woodward (1965) suggest that the technology of a manufacturing

218

firm is of primary importance in determining the firm's authority structure. Other writers had considered other important variables such as size (Acton Society, 1953; 1957; Talacchi, 1960), with which the postulated dimensions might vary.

By taking this 'variable' approach the researchers hoped to remedy some of the deficiencies with existing studies of organizations, such as those which Crozier (1976) has pointed out. In particular they wished to overcome the problems that we have already alluded to in the construction of typologies of organizations from case studies. A plethora of these have been generated from comparison of case studies with the classic Weberian typology (e.g., Gouldner, 1954; Constas, 1961; Presthus, 1961; Merton, 1949; Selznick, 1949). These studies had been extended to show that organization is influenced by behavioural factors which Weber (1947) did not consider (e.g., studies of bureaucracies in non-Western countries, such as Berger, 1956; Shor, 1960; Soemardjan, 1957; studies of the effects of professional employment in bureaucracies such as Brown, 1954; McEwen, 1956; Etzioni, 1959; Thompson, 1961 and Gouldner, 1957). However, they still remained essentially case studies. Additionally, although studies of organizations, they remained conceptualized within the framework of bureaucracy rather than the comparative analysis of organizations. Hence comparison has remained within typological variations of a unitary dimension, bureaucracy, rather than between dimensions of a postulated unitary concept, organization.

The dimensions of organization structure: variables

We have already identified the dimensions as specialization, standardization, formalization, centralization, and configuration. We will consider each of them in turn.

1 *Specialization* This refers to the division of labour within the organization. It is operationally distinguished in terms of, first, the 'number of specialisms' in the organization. This is given by a count of those functions that are performed by organization specialists. Second, it can be operationally distinguished by the 'degree of role specialization'. This is concerned with the differentiation of activities within each function. (This concept was later identified as the site of 'A Convergence in Organization Theory' by Hickson, 1966.) Another way of expressing this concept is in terms of 'role specificity' or the 'specificity of role prescriptions' (Hickson, 1966).

2 *Standardization* This dimension has two aspects upon which

scales of items can be operationalized. First we will consider 'standardization of procedures'. In the researcher's view:

> The practical problems here revolve around defining a procedure and specifying which procedures in the organization are to be investigated. A procedure is taken to be an event that has regularity of occurrence and is legitimized by the organization. A useful classification of procedures can be obtained by modifying the categories of Bales's (1950) interaction process analysis. We are thus concerned with (1) decision-seeking procedures, (2) decision-making procedures, (3) information-conveying procedures and (4) procedures for operating or carrying out decisions. Procedures are standardized when there are rules or definitions that cover all circumstances and that apply invariably. These rules would include those on how to proceed in cases not specifically covered (Pugh and Hickson, 1976, p. 31).

'Standardization of roles' is the second aspect. This is the degree to which the organization prescribes elements of the role structure in terms of a standardization of

> (1) role definition and qualifications for office, (2) role performance measurement, (3) titles for office and symbols of role status and (4) rewards for role performance. Underlying these scales is the degree to which either achievement or ascriptive attributes are taken into account (Pugh and Hickson, 1976, p. 31).

3 *Formalization* This 'distinguishes how far communications and procedures in an organization are written down and filed'. It can include:

> (1) statements of procedures, rules, roles (including contracts, agreements and so on), and (2) operations of procedures which deal with (a) decision-seeking (applications for capital employment and so on), (b) conveying of decisions and instructions (plans, minutes, requisitions, and so on), and (c) conveying of information, including feedback (Pugh and Hickson, 1976, p. 32).

In addition, a time orientation can be introduced. This would show the degree of formalization for each functional specialism in terms of a selection of documents concerned with the past, the present and the future. This is conceived of as a check of actual compared with possible occurrences:

> The degree of formalization could be gauged by seeing whether a procedure was written (and if so, on what); whether it

was filed (and if so, how); and what the source of the formalization was (a legal requirement, or, at the other extreme, an individual's unsolicited idea) (Pugh and Hickson, 1976, p. 32).

4 *Centralization* This is defined as 'the locus of authority to make decisions affecting the organization'. Two types of authority are distinguished; that deriving from formal ownership; and that deriving from expertise of knowledge. Respectively these are 'formal or institutional authority' and 'real or personal authority' (Pugh and Hickson, 1976, p. 32).

Operationally, centralization is first applied to the chief executive's position within the organization, in terms of 'his control of resources (money, people, materials, ideas and time)' and 'control of activities (identification, workflow, control and perpetuation)'. Of particular importance would be the chief executive's 'discretion for change or innovation' and the 'evaluation of the efficiency of his performance (e.g., in terms of profitability, productivity, adaptability, market standing and morale)' (Pugh and Hickson, 1976, p. 33). After the chief executive's degree of centralization has been constructed, the measure is then applied to other levels of the organization.

5 *Configuration* This dimension conceptualizes the fact that every organization has an authority structure. This is defined in terms of 'a system of relationships between positions or jobs described in terms of the authority of superiors and the responsibility of subordinates . . . commonly expressed in the form of an organization chart' (Pugh and Hickson, 1976, p. 33). What is to be compared across organizations is the shape or configuration of this structure.

This configuration can be observed at varying levels in the organization (e.g., Woodward, 1965); in varying segments or sub-units (e.g., Hall, 1962); and in addition they suggest that organizations will vary in terms of 'the number of positions in control specialists' (Pugh and Hickson, 1976, p. 34).

Performance variables

As we show below, the previous list of variables, the postulated dimensions of organization structure, form the dependent variables in the research design (see Figure 6.1). However, they are also regarded as intervening variables between specific 'contextual factors' and 'performance variables'. These performance variables concern 'the organization's success in reaching its stated goals' and are considered 'in the usual terms of profitability, productivity, adaptability, market standing, morale, and so on' (Pugh and Hickson, 1976, pp. 39–40). It is at this juncture that the researchers affirm their commitment to the basic open-system framework:

> Although the stated goals would be used to obtain relevant performance criteria, we would accept Etzioni's (1960) point that the approach would be a comparison of the organization's relative effectiveness at various times – not a comparison of its achieved goals with its stated aims; i.e., use of the system model, not the goal model (Pugh and Hickson, 1976, p. 40).

Contextual variables

Some of the contextual aspects of organizations were postulated as independent variables in the research design (see Figure 6.1). We will consider each of these in turn:

1 *Origin and history* It was postulated that differences in the origin and subsequent history of organizations might affect their present structure and effectiveness.

2 *Ownership and control* A major debate has raged over whether or not the ownership and control of organizations is a matter of importance for the organization's behaviour. It derives essentially from Burnham (1962), who argued that owner-controlled firms behaved quite differently from manager-controlled firms. Pugh and Hickson (1976, p. 36) adopt the approach to the issue used by Sargent Florence (1961), and collect information about '(1) the twenty largest shareholders, (2) the board of directors, and (3) the top management, to determine the extent to which these three spheres overlap or coincide'. From this they believe that it is possible to indicate the degree of owner control.

Alternatively, organizations could be classified according to a broad typology:

> (1) quoted firm (i.e. officially quoted on the Stock Exchange), (2) unquoted firm, (3) unquoted subsidiary of a quoted firm, (4) unquoted subsidiary of a consortium of firms, (5) subsidiary of an overseas firm, (6) co-ownership (co-operative, friendly societies, etc.), (7) public institution (nationalized undertakings, hospitals and so on), and (8) government departments (central and local) (Pugh and Hickson, 1976, p. 36).

The type of ownership and control in an organization might be expected to have an effect on centralization, in particular.

3 *Size* Size is not easily conceptualized. Pugh and Hickson (1976) conceptualize it in terms of number of employees and total net assets. Hall (1977) points out some drawbacks with a definition in terms of number of employees. First, it is only an adequate definition where the organization is composed solely of full-time employees. As he argues, it becomes more complex 'when volunteer and/or part-time personnel comprise a major part of the organization' (Hall, 1977, p. 104). He cites as an example a political party organization which can swell enormously with volunteer helpers at election time. He also points out 'a more basic issue': this is

the conceptual one, in terms of who is counted as an organization member in the first place. Again, in the case of organizations with paid employees, the issue is a rather simple one, although even here, customers, clients, and stockholders could be included within the organization. Since it has been amply demonstrated that these 'outsiders' can have an important impact on the organization, they could legitimately be included in analyses (Hall, 1977, p. 105).

Hall goes on to note that with such persons their primary interests lie outside the organization, and so they can be excluded, but that the issue is' more complicated when some non-employees are included within the organization. Examples of such organizations are prisons, colleges and universities. Are the 'clients' of such organizations members or not?

4 *Charter* This variable concerns the organization's goals and its ideology. The concept of goals is no less problematic than that of size. Do we consider the original stated goal of the organization; the current goals of the organization's élite or administration; do we accept this definition or should we infer it from what the organization does, and if so, which of the many things that the organization does should be accorded primacy? (See Silverman, 1970, pp. 9–12). What is necessary here is some specification in terms of an explicit theoretical model, for these issues are not just simply empirical. Different empirical means for ascertaining the organization's goals will very likely produce different goals.

The Aston team of researchers saw no such problems with the conceptualization of goals:

One must make a detailed analysis of the goals that an organization sets itself in order to discover its whole purpose. The basis for such an analysis is to be found in official statements, rules, records, documents and similar data. *Given the major goal*, the significant problem then is to discover the sub-goals (Pugh and Hickson, 1976, p. 37; our emphasis).

223

But, of course, the point is that the major goal is *not given*, and cannot be assumed to be, as we will argue in Chapter 8.

5 *Technology* The technology of the organization is defined as 'the techniques that it uses in its workflow activities that produce goods or services directly' (Pugh and Hickson, 1976, p. 38). They note the problems inherent in applying the concept of technology to non-manufacturing organizations, a problem which Charles Perrow (1970) was later to address (see Chapter 9).

6 *Location* This is conceptualized in terms of 'national and regional differences, with a further distinction being made between urban, urban-peripheral, and rural location' (Pugh and Hickson, 1976, p. 38)

In the research as it was actually carried out, the most significant variable in terms of location was the national dimension. One of the strengths of the Aston Programme proved to be its generalization at the cross-national level.

7 *Resources* The 'basic resources' of the organization are conceptualized as 'human, ideational, financial and material', characterized in terms of their 'quality, quantity and range' and their 'sources of supply' (Pugh and Hickson, 1976, pp. 38–9).

8 *Interdependence* This variable conceptualizes 'the relationship between one organization and other organizations and institutions in its social environment' (Pugh and Hickson, 1976, p. 39). The types of interdependence that can be considered can range from a monopoly position to one of perfect competition, and can involve relationships with factors such as 'suppliers, competitors, customers, labour unions, management organizations and political and social institutions' (Pugh and Hickson, 1976, p. 39).

The dimensions of organization structure: initial data

Data were collected in terms of the research design described beforehand, and summarized in Figure 6.1. From its inception the Aston project attempted to use what the researchers, rather misleadingly, termed 'non-personal' data. What they meant by this is that 'the data are non-personal, not about people as individuals. They are organizational' (Pugh and Hickson, 1976, p. 6). They prefer this type of data to questionnaires because they are

less obtrusive and less personally threatening to organization members. Their own feelings and experiences are not enquired

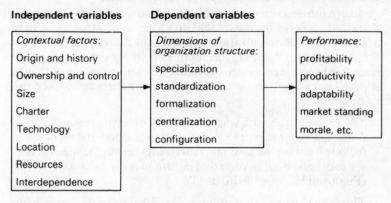

Figure 6.1   The Aston Programme variables

into. The external structure interviews ask whether there is a sales specialist, a routine of selecting personnel, a manual of procedures, a budgetary control system, a record of (production) operatives' output, and what is the ratio of supervisors to subordinates, etc. The researchers see the organization's premises and equipment, look at any manual of procedures, and may get specimens of forms and booklets. There is documentary evidence for much of what is said (Pugh and Hickson, 1976, p. 6).

It would be better to say that this data is 'non-research person personal' than that it is 'non-personal'. What the researchers are doing, as a methodological principle, is to suspend their own more skilled research judgment in the constitution and interpretation of data, and to allow the members of the organization, who produce its organizational records, to produce the data for them. Because something already exists as an objectification prior to the research act it does not mean that it is non-personal. What it does mean is that the researchers take for granted both the subjectivity of those members of the organization who produced it, and the fact of its existence. On the first point, what this entails is replacing any control that the researchers might have in an 'active' research situation with a situation in which the researcher can only accept the uncontrolled fruits of an alien activity, an alien subjectivity. There is nothing necessarily 'bad' about this – historians have to do it all the time – but without procedural checks it is certainly risky. Certainly, to elevate it to a methodological virtue when one could control the situation, seems somewhat perverse.

In addition, and this is our second point, it also condemns the researcher to the facts of the data's existence. Just because such-

225

and-such job descriptions or role prescriptions, for instance, exist, it does not necessarily mean that they are used, that they have *meaning* for the organization members, in the way they conduct themselves in, and *do*, organization. Formal organization need not necessarily be the equivalent of actual social organization, although it may be a potent resource in it. The researchers recognized this criticism:

> The project deals with what is officially expected *should be* done, and what is in practice *allowed* to be done; it does not include what is *actually* done, that is, what 'really' happens in the sense of behaviour beyond that instituted in organizational forms (Pugh and Hickson, 1976, p. 45).

This is an extremely important point. What scientific status do we attach to knowledge of a world which does not exist outside of the embodiments of management theory in documentation which has no necessary relationship to the social action which it purports to depict? Our reservations become more acute when we recall that the items which collect this strange form of data are themselves constituted from the very same management theories whose objectifications they then report. This would seem to be a perfect example of what Gadamer (1975) terms the 'hermeneutic circle'. The construction of the organization as such-and-such an organization structure is already governed by an expectation of meaning that follows from the context of what has gone before; that is, from the 'operationalization' of the data collection items from the literature of managerial theory. But it is this very same theory which is the source of the 'officially expected', that 'which *should be* done', in the work situation. These expectations are generated from the same source: formal theories of organization. The research moves in an *ideological circle*: from what formal theorists have argued organizations are like, or should be like, to what their students and readers have argued organizations should be like, in terms of intra-organizational formal procedures and rules. The research moves from formal theory to formal theory: the only difference is that the site of the formal theory changes from the ideological community of organization writers to the ideological community of organization executives. What is constant, as the researchers acknowledge, is that the research 'does not include what is *actually* done'. One may be forgiven for wondering exactly what status to attach to a knowledge of things which do not actually happen. Perhaps, like the 'sciences of transformation' (Karpik, 1977), organization theory is destined to be a science of bodies which do not really exist. Perhaps the intention is to create organizations which complete the ideological circle and thus

226

reconcile formal theory and organizational forms in actual organizations constructed on the 'structure' which 'intervenes' most effectively between 'contextual' and 'performance' factors? Certainly, the Aston studies have this potential for control.

Notwithstanding the reservations that one may have about the bases of the data, let us consider how it was collected. It was collected on a sample of 52 organizations in the Birmingham area of England. Of these, 46 were a random sample stratified by size and product or purpose. The stratification was made according to the Standard Industrial Classification of the British Ministry of Labour (as it was then called), and sampled from all organizations having more than 250 employees. The range of organizations in the sample can be gathered from Table 6.1.

All of these organizations were work organizations (largely industrial firms, as Hall, 1977, p. 99, notes) with a range of different types of ownership varying from 'independent family-dominated firms to companies owned by private shareholders, a co-operative, branch factories of large organizations' (Pugh and Hickson, 1976, p. 45).

The data was collected under the headings of the hypothesized dimensions. This data was analysed by the Brogden-Clemens coefficient (Brogden, 1949) to see to what extent the data actually represented a variable: that is, to what extent could the data be said to form a stable ordered scale of variably distributed characteristics? Once such scales have been distinguished, they can then be subject to principal components analysis (Harman, 1967) in order to identify any particular clusters of variance in the scales, which can then be refined and reconstituted into factors which summarize the variables in the original list.[1] This was done for the originally postulated list of dimensions,and as a result, a series of scales and sub-scales of measurement derived.

The data collected on the dimensions is capable of producing a visual depiction of the organization's structure, as in Figure 6.2.

The data collected on the originally posited dimensions was computed into an inter-correlation matrix which showed that several of the dimensions appeared to be highly inter-correlated, and thus might in fact be different measures of the same underlying variance. A principal components analysis of the data supported this view, and produced four principal factors accounting for most of the variance in the data (see Figure 6.3).

1 *Structuring of activities* This factor was composed of the variables of standardization, specialization and formalization. As a concept it is similar to Hickson's (1966) 'specificity of role prescription'.

TABLE 6.1   *Sample: organizations studied (n = 46)*

Number of employees		
251–500	501–2,000	2,001+
Metal manufacture and metal goods		
Components	Metal goods	Non-ferrous
Components	Metal goods	Metal automobile components
Research division	Metal goods	
Components	Domestic appliances	
Manufacture of engineering and electrical goods, vehicles		
Components	Engineering tools	Automobile components
Vehicles		
Components	Repairs for government department	Commercial vehicles
Components		Vehicles
	Automobile components	Carriages
	Engineering components	
Foods and chemicals, general manufacturing, construction		
Food	Civil engineering	Confectionery
Paper	Glass	Public civil engineering department
Toys	Printer	Brewery
Abrasives	Food	Automobile tyres
Services: public, distributive, professional		
Government inspection department	Public water department	Public education department
	Department store	Public transport department
Public local savings bank	Chain of retail stores	Bus company
Public baths department	Chain of shoe repair stores	Co-operative chain of retail stores
Insurance company		

Source: Pugh and Hickson, 1976, p. 44.

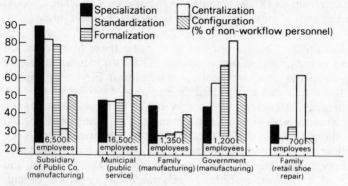

Figure 6.2 Structural profiles of five organizations
Source: Pugh and Hickson, 1976, p. 56.

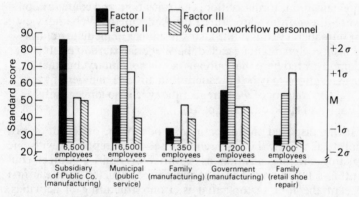

*Figure 6.3 Underlying dimensions of structure in the five organizations
in Figure 6.2*
Source: Pugh and Hickson, 1976, p. 63.

2 *Concentration of authority* This factor is 'marked by the opposition of centralization and autonomy' (Pugh and Hickson, 1976, p. 60), and encompasses organizational autonomy, centralization, percentage of workflow superordinates and standardization of procedures for selection and advancement.

3 *Line control of workflow* This factor encompasses the percentage of superordinates, the degree of formalization of role performance recording, and the standardization of procedures for selection and advancement.

4 *Relative size of supportive component* The title of this factor derives from Haas *et al.* (1963) and concerns the amount of

auxiliary, non-workflow activities in the organization. These would be occupational areas such as clerical, transport or catering.

What are the implications of identifying these four structural factors in the profile of organizations? The Aston researchers were in no doubt that these implications were radical. First, they implied that these four factors produce an empirical way of depicting any organization's structure, which 'may display all these characteristics to a pronounced degree, or virtually none at all, or display some but not others' (Pugh and Hickson, 1976, p. 61). However, this is not the most radical conclusion. They argue that they have refuted the whole typological theory of bureaucracy from Weber onwards, and replaced it with an empirically generated theory of the organization:

> In so far as the original primary dimensions of structure, specialization, formalization, centralization, and configuration were drawn from a literature saturated with the Weberian view of bureaucracy, this multi-factor result has immediate implications for what might be called the Weberian stereotype. It is demonstrated here that bureaucracy is *not* unitary, but that organizations may be bureaucratic in any of a number of ways.
> . . . The concept of *the* bureaucratic type is no longer useful (Pugh and Hickson, 1976, p. 61).

Having disposed of the dominant model of the organization as a theoretical object, the researchers resolved to replace it with one depicting the organization as a variable empirical object constituting a taxonomy. The taxonomy is constructed from the first three of the four factors; that is, from structuring of activities, concentration of authority, and line control of workflow. As a first step the researchers plotted the correlation of structuring of activities with concentration of authority, and described the results in terms of Figure 6.4.

1 *Workflow bureaucracy* What characterizes that cluster of organizations in the bottom right hand quadrant is that they were large-scale manufacturing concerns, or big businesses (such as foodstuffs, confectionery, and vehicle components firms) which were mainly independent and had a relatively highly integrated workflow. Hence they were designated 'workflow bureaucracies'.

2 *Personnel bureaucracy* Those organizations which have a high concentration of authority and a low structuring of activities are those which are grouped in the upper left quadrant. They are termed personnel bureaucracies because they bureaucratize

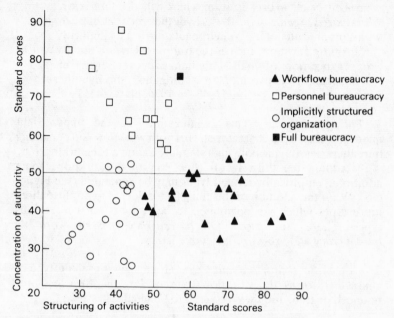

Figure 6.4 Structuring of activities and concentration of authority
Source: Pugh and Hickson, 1976, p. 114.

'everything related to employment, but not the daily work activity to the same degree'. They tend to have centralized authority which is 'usually concentrated in a controlling committee outside and above the unit itself and they are 'typically local or central government departments . . . and the smaller branch factories of large corporations' (Pugh and Hickson, 1976, p. 115).

3 *Implicitly structured organization* This is, in a sense, the residual category. This is because the organizations that are located here were the ones that had low scores on the structural dimensions. This means that they did not respond positively to the measures. Two reasons could be advanced for this:

It might be thought that this minimal structuring and dispensed authority suggests unregulated chaos. Instead this indicates that such organizations have low scores on the structural characteristics measured with the particular scales of rather overt regulation that were used. They cannot be labelled unstructured; for their structure, as far as the measures used to go, is probably

231

implicit. Such an organization is here called an *implicitly structured organization*. It was hypothesized that these organizations are run not by explicit regulation but by implicitly transmitted custom, such as the traditional means usually typical of organizations of small or medium size where ownership and management still overlap. On investigation, this hypothesis was supported (Pugh and Hickson, 1976, pp. 115–16).

4 *Full bureaucracy* This organization, in the upper right quadrant, shows the characteristics of both workflow and personnel bureaucracies, having both high standardization and centralization.

By adding the third factor, line control of workflow, some additional empirically derived types may be generated (see Figure 6.5). What the addition of this third factor does is to produce three more types which are postulated to be variants on the previous types. These are *nascent full bureaucracy, nascent workflow bureaucracy* and *pre-workflow bureaucracy*.

5 *Nascent workflow bureaucracy* These show the same type of characteristics as the workflow bureaucracy, but to a less pronounced degree, and they also tend to be smaller in size.

6 *Nascent full bureaucracy* This posseses the same type of characteristics as the full bureaucracy, but to a lesser degree.

7 *Pre-workflow bureaucracy* These are much lower on the structuring of activities than workflow or nascent workflow bureaucracies, but they have the same type of workflow bureaucracy pattern of dispersed authority and impersonal line control.

It is suggested that a developmental sequence occurs on two of the dimensions from implicitly structured organizations, through pre-workflow and nascent workflow bureaucracies to the workflow bureaucracies. These two dimensions are structuring and control. More highly structured organizations develop as the organizations become larger over time. It is suggested that this growth is related to the general development of the economy. The control dimension tends to move from line control which is exercised by the workflow personnel themselves, to more impersonal forms of control. After Woodward (1965), Touraine (1962) and Blauner (1964), this is seen as a result of developments in technology, as a result of which more and more control passes to 'procedures dictated by standardization and the new specialist who devise the procedures' (Pugh and Hickson, 1976, p. 125).

232

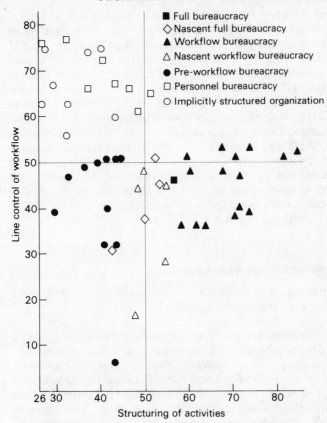

Figure 6.5   Structuring of activities and line control of workflow
Source: Pugh and Hickson, 1976, p. 117.

This development sequence is problematic. There is no indication of how or why the developmental sequence takes place, nor is it clear what the consequences of such a sequence are, other than 'bureaucracy takes different forms in different settings' (Pugh and Hickson, 1976, p. 127). The important question becomes: why? The subsequent research work begins to pose this question.

Having established the dimensional approach in the terms that we have outlined, the researchers turned to its implications for further work, and began a series of research projects relating the dimensions of organization structure to factors such as *Organizational Structure in its Context* (Pugh and Hickson, 1976, ch. 5); the

233

relation of 'Operations Technology and Organization Structure' (Hickson *et al.*, 1969; Pugh and Hickson, 1976, ch. 7), and more specifically 'Technology, Size and Organization Structure' (Child and Mansfield, 1972). In addition the research has been replicated to specific types of organization, such as 'occupational interest associations' (Donaldson and Warner, 1974); local authority organizations (Greenwood and Hinings, 1976); churches (Hinings *et al.*, 1974); educational organizations (Holdaway *et al.*, 1975); and the relationship of group and individual variables to organization structure (Pugh and Payne, 1977). The original research has not only been replicated extensively (Hinings and Lee, 1971; Inkson *et al.*, 1970), but has also been extended to the study of organizations in different cross-national contexts (McMillan, 1976). It has also been the subject of a lively methodological debate (Aldrich, 1972a; Heise, 1972; Mindlin and Aldrich, 1975).

Why do organization structures vary?

The Aston researchers answer this crucial question in terms of three factors. These are *size, technology* and *location*.

1 *Size* The relationship of size to organization structure has been developed by economists who have linked aspects of size, such as assets or annual sales, to such factors as growth, innovation, industrial structure and profitability. Perhaps the best-known example of an attempt to link size and structure is Parkinson's Law (Parkinson, 1957), which states that work expands proportionally with the time available for its completion. Following from this he argued that organizations therefore increase their number of administrators disproportionately with increases in size.

Empirical research has not extensively tested Parkinson's Law, although an early study by Terrien and Mills (1955) did support it. Subsequent research, however, has shown that this appears to be too simple a generalization. McMillan (1976) has noted how it depends on the type of organization, such as voluntary organizations, where, as Hinings *et al.* (1974) demonstrate, an increase in the number of members is related to an increase in the administrative component. As Hall (1977, pp. 108–9) notes, recent research seems to suggest that the relationship between size and the administrative component is either negative or curvilinear. Hall *et al.* (1967, p. 14) suggest that the size of the administrative component is 'greater for smaller (0–700 employees) and larger (over 1400 employees) than for those of moderate size'. However, this data comes from a small sample size, and thus although it is supported by the work of

Hawley *et al.* (1965) it cannot be taken as conclusive. However, studies by Haas *et al.* (1963) support those of Hawley *et al.* (1965) in suggesting that the relative size of the administrative component decreases as organizations become larger. This supports the view that large organizations are capable of achieving economies of scale. These are achieved as the proportion of members involved in administration decreases in relation to increases in the size of the organization (see Anderson and Warkov, 1961; Bendix, 1956, p. 22, Table 7).

The Aston studies (Child and Mansfield, 1972; Hinings and Lee, 1971) find that size is the major determinant of organizational structure, and in this respect they support the findings of Peter Blau (Blau, 1968; 1970; 1972a; 1972b; 1973; Blau and Schoenherr, 1971). Blau and Schoenherr (1971) studied 256 state employment agencies and come to the conclusion that size was the most important variable affecting the structuring of organizations. Translated into formal terms, what this entails is the following. Measuring differentiation by the number of levels, departments and job titles within an organization, Blau (1970) argued that although increasing size is related to increasing differentiation, the rate of differentiation decreases with increasing size. Administrative overheads are lower in larger organizations and the span of control for supervisors will be greater. It is because administrative overheads are inversely related to size, while the span of control is positively related to size, that larger organizations are able to achieve economies of scale. However, an anomaly exists. Size is related to differentiation. Differentiation brings increased need for control and co-ordination, which, in turn, is related to increased requirements for administrative overheads. Size and differentiation thus work at cross purposes, but, Blau (1970) concludes, the size factor is the most critical, and so he endorses the relationship between economies of scale and larger size.

There are conceptual problems with this argument. Blau (1970) makes two generalizations from his study of organizations: first, that increasing size generates structural differentiation along various dimensions at decelerating rates; second, that structural differentiation enlarges the administrative component. However, structural differentiation is defined by separate functional units, and since each would have a manager, the second generalization becomes circular, as McMillan (1976, pp. 84–5) has argued. In addition, in the first proposition, if size is held constant in a particular functional unit, with more administrative personnel the span of control will be less – it *must* become less.

Argyris has made a critical observation on Blau's (1970) work which offers an alternative interpretation:

1   Increasing the number of employees is *correlated* with structural differentiation in organizations along various dimensions *if* the organization is designed in line with traditional (administrative) management principles.

2   The prediction of decelerating rates tends to occur when, in addition to the conditions above, budgets are finite, financial constraints are strong, position openings become increasingly difficult as one goes up the hierarchy, and the marketing or service area functions of the organization are limited (Argyris, 1972, p. 14).

The Aston researchers suggest some further limitations on Blau's findings. Pugh and Hickson found that organization size was the main predictor of only *some aspects of* structure, not structure *per se*. As they put it:

Larger organizations tend to have more specialization, more standardization and more formalization than smaller organizations. The *lack* of relationship between size and the remaining structural dimensions, i.e. concentration of authority . . . and line control of workflow . . . was equally striking (Pugh and Hickson, 1976, p. 87).

Argyris (1972) argues that additional factors to that of size should also be considered. For instance, civil service organizations take the form that they do largely because of civil service regulations. The legal framework, and its specificity to the emergence of certain dominant Western capitalist conceptions of property rights and ownership is rarely, if ever, considered. Kasarda (1973) has argued that the nature of the personnel in the organization also affects its shape, so that if the members are highly professionalized, then it follows that more administrators will be needed to co-ordinate them.

Aldrich has subjected the Aston data to re-analysis, and as a result of using path analysis as a technique for testing causal models, he has suggested that size is actually a dependent variable:

The more highly structured firms, with their greater degree of specialization, formalization and monitoring of role performance, simply need to employ a larger workflow than less structured firms (Aldrich, 1972a, p. 38).

He suggests that *technology* is the major determinant of structure.

The major conclusion of the Aston researchers is that increased size is related to increased structuring of organizational activities and decreased concentration of authority. Their research has stressed the relationship between size and structure, with the implicit causal sequence being that size causes bureaucracy (e.g., Pugh and Hickson, 1976, ch. 7; Pugh *et al.*, 1969; Child and Mansfield, 1972). They have also considered the relationship between technology and structure, but have concluded that technology is a less important predictor of structure than size. This is disputed by other findings such as Aldrich's (1972a) re-analysis of Aston data. We shall now turn to this issue.

2 *Technology* Some organization theorists have argued that size is not as important as technology in explaining structure. Louis Pondy (1969) concluded that technology is a major contributor to the configuration of the administrative component of organization structure. His argument is that complex tasks performed through a high division of labour require administrative personnel to co-ordinate them, particularly where one is dealing with organizations which produce technological innovations through research and development. Pondy's data, although extremely important, are not sampled on the organization *per se*, but come from census information drawn from industry data. Notwithstanding this, his analysis provides insight into the processes leading to differential patterning of configuration of the administrative component. His findings suggest that this decreases as the organization's size increases. Where the firm is either owner-managed or controlled by partners it is less likely to add specialists to the organization. He hypothesizes that this is because these types of controller are unlikely to dilute their own personal power. This has a bearing on organizational effectiveness, conceptualized in terms of profitability. More professional and administrative specialists are related to increased profits. It need not mean that they *cause* these profits; it may just be that increased profits enable firms to employ more specialists.

Concern with issues of the relationship between technology and structure in organization theory have developed from the classic study of Joan Woodward (1965) of about 80 industrial units in the south-east Essex area of the south of England. Woodward's findings, that size is not a major factor in explaining organization structure (which Hall *et al.*, 1967 endorse) developed from her inquiries into the role of technology. She classified the organizations in her sample into a number of types. These were *small batch and unit production, large batch and mass-production*, and *process production*. This distinction was made on the basis of the technical complexity of the operations, defined as 'the extent to which the production process is controllable and its results predictable'. Through an examination of the range of organizations that she studied she found that firms with similar production systems were organized in a similar manner. Technical complexity was related to a number of organizational characteristics such as the number of levels in the organization, the spans of control of first-line supervisors, and the ratio of managers and staff to total personnel. A number of similarities was found between firms using unit and process production, which were the least, and the most complex technologies, respectively. Although staff and line personnel were sharply distinguished in mass-production firms, there was a low level of specialization among the functions of managers in the other types of organizations. She advanced some reasons for this finding which suggested that in unit production firms a smaller number of specialists tended to be employed. As a result of this relative lack of specialists, the line management had to be technically more competent. This contrasted sharply with the situation in process production. In these organizations specialists had very high status. It was because of this that it was often impossible to distinguish specialists (line) from administrators (staff), because administrators had to have some degree of technical expertise in order to grasp the complexities of process production. In addition, both process and unit production were found to be associated with relatively non-bureaucratic structure, compared to the more bureaucratized structure of mass-production. Woodward (1965) argues that this is because the central problem of the types of technology differs. The central problem of unit and process technologies is regarded as, respectively, product development and marketing. Each of these problems, she argues, requires innovation. Given this requirement, a formal bureaucratic organization might be too slow and cumbersome. In mass production technology, she argues, the control problem becomes the efficient administration and control of production, and this is seen as encouraging bureaucracy.

It is not only the central problem of the organization which is important. The number and nature of the policy decisions which arise in each type of production organization also have an effect on its structure. In unit production a relatively large number of decisions with short-term consequences are taken. The consequences of the decisions will generally only be as long as it takes to produce the 'one-off' unit. Hence, on-the-line decision-making is far more economical in time than a referral to a bureaucratic structure removed from the line. The converse is true of mass-production organization. Here, fewer decisions are taken, but these have much longer consequences in terms of time. This is because production runs will be long-lasting affairs, compared to the more 'craft' unit production. Compare, for example, the differences between a bespoke tailor and a mass-production clothing concern.

Woodward argues that these decisions usually affect only a specific management function, such as production. Hence decisions can be taken on the basis of senior management's functional responsibility. In process production, although the fewest policy decisions are made, they have longer time implications for the organization than decisions in the other forms of production organization. On this basis she argues that decision-making in such organizations will be a pooled activity, involving all the expertise that can be drawn on. This type of organization is unlikely to have a bureaucracy as a separate component. There is little point in establishing a separate administrative configuration under these technological conditions.

Since the appearance of Woodward's work, a number of models and theories have been developed which stress the role of technology. This continues the line of enquiry developing from Woodward (1965), and other seminal studies by Trist and Bamforth (1951), Walker and Guest (1952), Blauner (1964), Herbst (1962), Lodahl (1964), Mann and Hoffman (1960), Sayles (1958) and Bright (1958). Among the most significant of the more recent works on technology are Perrow's (1967) theoretical scheme; Lawrence and Lorsch's (1967) model, which links different technologies within the firm; as well as a number of studies which look at technology within particular types of organization such as welfare organizations (Hage and Aiken, 1969), and health departments (Palumbo, 1969). We shall consider some of these in the context of the more general role of technology in Chapter 9. For the remainder of this section, however, we will simply consider those works which followed from Woodward (1965) in using technology as a predictor criterion.

The major work in this area is that by Hickson *et al.* (1969) (see Pugh and Hickson, 1976, ch. 7) as part of the continuing Aston project of research into organizations. Hickson *et al.* (1969) developed a set of measures designed to operationalize and make more precise the concepts which Woodward had used. The 'objective of the research' was to test the 'proposition of the technological imperative at the organizational level of analysis' (Pugh and Hickson, 1976, p. 131).

They develop the nature of the 'technological imperative' from a review of the literature. For instance, Thompson and Bates (1957, p. 327) postulated 'that the type of technology available . . . sets limits on the types of structures appropriate for organizations', a hypothesis subsequently elaborated by Thompson (1967). They continue their review, citing Scott *et al.* (1956); Burack and Cassell (1967); Fensham and Hooper (1964); Burns and Stalker (1961); Udy (1959; 1961); and, of course, Woodward (1965). They note

239

that Woodward has been criticized for employing ill-defined concepts and inadequate data analysis (Hopkins, 1966). What these studies focus on is the role of technology in predicting structural differences; that is, to what extent technology functions as an imperative conditioning structure.

Hickson *et al.* (1969) are not concerned with technology *per se* (as Perrow, 1967, was), but, only with *operations technology*, which they define as the techniques that the organization uses in its workflow activities. This consists of a number of sub-concepts including the degree of automation of equipment, the degree of workflow rigidity, the specificity of evaluation of operations, and the degree of continuity of the units of throughput. The relationship of operations technology to structure was tested by multi-variate correlation analysis of the random sample of 46 organizations that the Aston measures were developed on (Pugh and Hickson, 1976). These results are summarized in Table 6.2.

From these results it seems that there is *some* relationship between technology and structure. However, as column 2 of Table 6.2 demonstrates, *correlations with technology are not as significant as those with size*. The data do not support the thesis of the 'technological imperative', although

a few specific configuration variables can be seen to be conspicuously correlated with workflow integration, and *not* with size or other contextual variables. These are subordinate-supervisor ratio, and the percentage of total personnel who are workflow subordinates, or who are in design, or methods or inspection (Pugh and Hickson, 1976, p. 143).

However, these results flow more from the distinction between service and manufacturing organizations, and decline in significance when this is controlled for. As column 3 of Table 6.2 demonstrates, when the 31 manufacturing organizations are extracted from the sample, there remains 'a striking lack of association between workflow integration and all three *dimensions* of organization structure' (Pugh and Hickson, 1976, p. 144). Column 4 demonstrates again the importance of size.

In order to test these findings against Woodward's findings in support of the importance of technology as a contextual independent variable, the researchers operationalized her original classification of production systems (Woodward, 1965), as in Table 6.3.

Taking the seven categories for which they had data, the researchers produced correlation coefficients between Woodward's 'technical complexity', which they re-conceptualized in variable form as a 'scale of production continuity' and the structural dimensions (see column 6 of Table 6.2), using partial correlation

240

techniques to discount the effects of size. The results still disconfirm the hypothesis that there is a relationship between technology and structure. However, there are significant correlations between a number of 'job-count' measures and technology; these are extracted in Table 6.4.

What do these inter-correlations indicate? Pugh and Hickson discuss them by noting that:

> Subordinate-supervisor ratio is a structural variable which reflects activities directly bound up with the operations tech-nology itself. This is true of the next four variables also. The relative numbers engaged on inspection and maintenance are linked to the variety of equipment and operations, which tends to be greatest in batch production. Workflow (production) control tends to decline in proportion after the batch stage, for it shows a negative linear relation, but this is complicated by the intrusion of some size effects. The transport and dispatch specialization largely reflects internal transport activities related to the workflow system. Thus these four specializations are activities visibly linked to production work (Pugh and Hickson, 1976, pp. 151–2).

From this discussion they hypothesize that *operations technology will be associated only with workflow-centred dimensions of structure*. They reconcile this with Woodward's (1965) findings, noting that:

> *The smaller the organization the more its structure will be pervaded by such technological effects: the larger the organization, the more these effects will be confined to variables such as job counts of employees on activities linked with the workflow itself, and will not be detectable in variables of the more remote administrative and hierarchical structure* (Pugh and Hickson, 1976, p. 154; italics in original).

Thus, technology matters most in small organizations and at the shop-floor level: in short, the closer the organization unit is centred on the workflow, the more effect technology will have on the struc-ture.

Child and Mansfield (1972), in a further study of 'Technology, Size and Organization Structure', studied 82 business organizations sampled on a national basis, using the Aston measures, and con-firmed the Hickson *et al.* (1969) findings, but sounded a note of caution in the discussion of their data. This was because of the possible effect on the correlations of the industry from which the organizations were sampled, in that there was a high correlation between technology and industry. The structural measures vary

TABLE 6.2   Correlation* between scales of operations technology and of size and selected scales of structure

	46 diverse organizations		31 Manufacturing organizations			
	Workflow integration	Size (log of no. of employees)	Workflow integration	Size (log of no. of employees)	Production continuity	Production continuity (size partialled out)
	(1)	(2)	(3)	(4)	(5)	(6)
Structural dimensions						
Structuring of activities	0.34†	0.69‡	0.17	0.78‡	0.41†	0.07
Concentration of authority	−0.30†	−0.10	0.00	−0.20	0.11	0.24
Line control of workflow	−0.46‡	0.15	−0.05	0.13	−0.17	—
Structural variables						
Overall role specialization	0.38‡	0.75‡	0.25	0.83‡	0.52‡	0.26
Functional specialization	0.44‡	0.67‡	0.19	0.75‡	0.34	−0.02
Overall standardization of procedures	0.46‡	0.56‡	0.19	0.65‡	0.35	0.07
Standardization of procedures for selection and advancement, etc.	−0.38‡	0.31†	0.24	0.42†	0.43†	0.29
Overall formalization (documentation)	0.17	0.55‡	0.04	0.67‡	0.27	−0.07
Formalization of role performance recording	0.41‡	0.42‡	0.00	0.45†	0.03	−0.30
Overall centralization of decisions	−0.16	−0.39‡	−0.05	−0.47‡	0.00	0.28
Autonomy of the organization	0.22	0.09	0.02	0.23	−0.07	−0.19

Configuration of structure variables:					
Chief executive's span of control	0·06	0·32†	-0·09	0·29	0·08	-0·07
Subordinate-supervisor ratio	0·35†	0·05	0·02	0·04	-0·09	—
					(0·36)	
Vertical span	0·09	0·67‡	0·15	0·77‡	0·51‡	0·26
Percentages of total number of employees:						
Direct workers	-0·18	-0·26	-0·17	-0·46‡	-0·14	0·10
Workflow superordinates	-0·53‡	-0·13	0·02	-0·31	0·13	0·33
Non-workflow personnel	0·34†	0·36†	0·22	0·53‡	0·22	-0·04
Design and development	0·45‡	-0·02	-0·08	-0·04	-0·18	—
Methods	0·38‡	0·11	0·07	0·15	-0·03	—
Inspection	0·39‡	0·02	0·07	-0·08	-0·15	—
					(0·62)	
Employment	-0·03	0·05	-0·45†	-0·03	0·04	—
Buying and stocks	-0·05	-0·04	-0·42†	-0·12	-0·10	—
Workflow control	0·27	-0·19	-0·17	-0·35	-0·44†	-0·33
Transport and dispatch	0·19	0·06	0·32	-0·18	0·45†	—
Maintenance	-0·01	0·38‡	0·05	0·13	0·20	—
					(0·46)	
Size (log of no. of employees)	0·08	—	0·30	—	0·47‡	—

*Product moment coefficients of linear correlation (r): with correlation ratio coefficients of nonlinear correlation (η) in brackets in column 5, production continuity. †Beyond 95 per cent level of confidence. ‡Beyond 99 per cent level of confidence.

Source: Pugh and Hickson, 1976, p. 141.

TABLE 6.3 *Production continuity: a further operationalization of Woodward's classification of production systems*

Woodward classification Unit and small batch: I to V Large batch and mass: V to VIII Process: VIII to X	Scale of production continuity*	Manufac-turing organi-zations (N = 31)
I Production of simple units to customers' orders	*Simple units*: units basically *single piece* not assemblies; produced one by one	0
II Production of technically complex units	*Complex units*: *assemblies*, produced one by one	0
III Fabrication of large equipment in stages	*Fabrication*: one by one; workpeople come to thᵉ unit of output (which moves about very infrequently) rather than the unit moving to different workpeople	2
IV Production of small batches	*Small batches*: equipment reset *every week* or more often, for outputs measured in *items*	11
V Production of components in large batches subsequently assembled diversely	*Large batches*: equipment reset at intervals *longer than a week* for outputs measured in items: *but items assembled diversely* (i.e. variety of assembly sequences, including assembly by unit and/or small batch methods)	3

VI	Production of large batches; assembly-line type	*Large batches*: as in V, but with *large batch assembly*	5
VII	Mass-production	*Mass*: *batch size, measured in items, is indefinite* (i.e. change of batch requires decisions on (*a*) design modification, (*b*) retooling, which are beyond the normal authority of the line production management and production planning to vary production programmes)	4
VIII	Process production combined with the preparation of a product for sale by large batch or mass-production methods	*Process*: throughputs measured by *weight or volume; but* outputs become *items at finishing stage*	0
IX	Process production of chemicals in batches	*Process*: but *ingredients* (i.e. recipes) of the throughputs *change periodically*	3
X	Continuous flow production of liquids, gases and solid shapes	*Process*: but *constant ingredients*: (i.e. recipe change beyond the normal authority of the line production management and production planning to vary production programmes)	3

*The predominant technology of an organization was assessed giving particular weight to its highest degree of 'continuity'.
Source: Pugh and Hickson, 1976, p. 146.

245

TABLE 6.4

Structural variables	Related to: Production continuity	Workflow integration
Subordinate-supervisor ratio	∩-shaped curvilinear	—
Proportion in inspection	∩-shaped curvilinear	—
Proportion in maintenance	∩-shaped curvilinear	—
Proportion in workflow (production) control	negative linear	—
Proportion in transport and dispatch	positive linear	positive linear
Proportion in employment (personnel) specialization	—	negative linear
Proportion in buying and stock specialization	—	negative linear

Source: Pugh and Hickson, 1976, p. 151

significantly between industries, according to Child and Mansfield. Given this, if technology is clearly associated with industry, which it will be, then, as they put it:

> This suggests certain problems. Either the measurements of technology employed or the framework of analysis, or both, are at least in some respects inadequate. If the differences between industries on structural variables in fact largely reflect technological differences between those industries, then it follows that the measures of technology used are not strong enough. This is likely to be the case to some degree, given the immense complexity of modern industrial technology and the simplicity and summary nature of the measures used (Child and Mansfield, 1972, pp. 390–1).

In addition, they observe that neither environmental variables nor managerial ideologies have been related to either technology or structure in any systematic large-scale study.

It would seem that despite all of the research effort expended, the relationship between technology and structure still remains provisional, although it would seem to be less important a variable than size, although of some significance when dealing with workflow-centred activity. As against Woodward (1965) the data would seem to lend support to Weber (1947), and fall in with the general results of Blau (1970) and Blau and Schoenherr (1971), they suggest the Woodward thesis of a 'technological imperative' only for delimited types of organization.

246

Some theorists, such as Argyris (1972), have criticized the technology approach on the theoretical ground that it is static and cannot account for change in the organization. If technology determines structure, what determines technology? It must change in order to change structure. It points towards Child's (1972a) thesis that the role of the 'strategic choice' of the organization's dominant coalition is vital. This re-introduces a voluntaristic element more typical of a social-action approach into what has been largely a somewhat arid positivism of the most behaviourist type, in which technological determinism has only been opposed by the determinism of size, rather than by any sustained theoretical analysis of the *processes* and *strategies* involved in any particular structure. We shall consider the concept of technology in more detail in Chapter 9.

3 *Location* The Aston programme has been extended beyond its original national boundaries. Extending it in this way enables the researchers to investigate whether or not organizations differ with the national society and culture in which they are located. Their findings suggest that certain aspects of organization structure are affected by different national settings, while some others are not (Hickson *et al.*, 1974; McMillan, 1976).

Hickson *et al.* (1974) studied 70 manufacturing organizations distributed across the United Kingdom, the United States and Canada, using an abbreviated (Inkson *et al.*, 1970) version of the measures developed at Aston. Little difference was discovered between the countries in patterns of autonomy and specialization in organizations, although there was a greater reliance on written documents in the United States. It was postulated that because the United Kingdom was more 'traditional' there was less emphasis on written documents. The relationships discovered between size, technology and structure were consistent with those found on the national sample and discussed previously. This supports the hypothesis that organizations are structurally stable across national societies. Although there are some national distinctions, it is argued that contextual constraints still persist. As they put it, 'Simply stated, if Indian organizations were found to be less formalized than American ones, bigger Indian units would still be more formalized than smaller Indian units' (Hickson *et al.*, 1974, p. 59). McMillan's conclusions support this view; in his interpretation:

> The results do not give any support to the arguments of writers who present a cultural perspective. The differences which exist on scores within any one country clearly are far greater than any differences between countries. It may be true that in this study, the Japanese units are a little more formalized, the

Swedish a little less centralized, and the British more formalized and less centralized than might be expected . . . [but] the data give convincing evidence of a common structural focus in all industrial organizations (McMillan, 1976, p. 195).

In terms of a wider debate, such findings as McMillan's support the 'logic of industrialization' argument which has been advanced by Kerr *et al.* (1973). This argues that:

The industrial society is world wide. The science and technology on which it is based speak in a universal language. Science is non-national, non-local, and although one would not say non-cultural, singularly independent of the form of government, the intermediate tradition, or the effective life of a people. . . .
The extreme discrepancies in the methods of production which now exist between more or less highly industrialized countries will tend to decrease over time, although significant differences in income levels and in the specialization of activity are likely to remain for a very long time (Kerr, *et al.*, 1973, p. 55).

Kerr and his colleagues have attempted an explanation of industrialization from a global point of view. They are able to employ a global model because of the fact, as they see it, that all societies of an industrial status have certain common features in their structures. These features, it is argued, become more and more pronounced. Underlying everything is what the authors call the 'logic of industrialization'. It is this logic that enables a description of how a society moves from pre-industrial to industrial. Indeed, they argue that the logic also enables 'the similarity of structure phenomenon' to arise. The logic has four main components that are universally applicable. These are occupational changes, societal scale, societal consensus, and the scope of industrial society.

Occupational changes   The economic changes in society that give rise to industrialization carry in their wake numerous changes in the structure of the work force. The skills and occupations associated with these skills of pre-industrial society are displaced by the new industrial system. The system itself is much more complex than the previous one and is largely dependent upon the application of science and technology. Underlying this is the driving force: scientific and technological knowledge. The new form of economy requires the utilization of these skills having a scientific/technological base. Put simply, it is the new emergent division of labour that requires a more specialized work force.

Associated with the new division of labour with its applied

248

scientific base is the ideology of change within society. The members of society must be willing and able to adapt to change, not only in terms of change of occupation, but also in terms of changes in geographical and social placement – that is, in mobility. Of course, in terms of the industrialization of a specific country the geographical dispersion arises largely from the movement from the land: the shift from agriculture to industry with its geographic movement implied. Beyond the initial stages of industrialization there is the further occupational displacement, from secondary to tertiary employment, from production to service occupations.

Since, in this view, occupation is a primary determinant of social class, it is to be expected that occupational changes (whether from agriculture to industry, or industry to non-productive occupations) will also produce changes in the social structure. Movement within the occupational structure is thus linked to social mobility, a movement away from ascribed roles towards achieved roles. The ideology of achievement, as Offe (1976a) has so clearly demonstrated, pervades the industrial world. At the individual level it affects the family, particularly in terms of the evolvement of the nuclear family and the demise of extended kin networks.

Again, the changing nature of the industrial work force has its effects upon the provision of educational facilities within society. There is a requirement for a more skilled work force, and the skills are provided through education. Furthermore, education comes to exercise a control function in society, which again hallmarks an industrial society.

In terms of the universality of the logic of industrialization, the factor of occupational changes clearly has an impact by producing a society that is differentiated, hierarchic, controlled and regulated. These characteristics are universal and independent of the specific cultural features of any particular society.

Societal scale Kerr *et al.* (1973) refer here not simply to the increasing size and complexity of a society undergoing industrialization, but also to the way in which society is organized. The emergence of the large, complex, formal organization is a good example of the scale of society. Not only does the industrial system itself give rise to such organizations, but the nature of government activity is a crucial factor here as well. Those societies that were amongst the first to industrialize (such as England, Germany and France) experienced far less government intervention than those countries industrializing later.

Paralleling the emergence of organizations is the development of regulations and laws that relate to the industrial system. Again, there is a remarkable homogeneity between societies regarding such restrictions, particularly as seen in terms of conditions of work, thereby providing further evidence of the logic of industrialization.

Societal consensus It is argued by Kerr *et al.* that the factors of occupational changes and of the increasing scale of society combined to produce an important consensus within industrial society. Whilst this consensus is pervasive, it is particularly noticeable in the way in which there is widespread agreement that scientific and technological expertise is crucial in bringing about industrial progress. Associated with this is the way in which education has a high premium placed upon it, and how the notions of social, geographical and occupational mobility are perceived as high-value goals for the society.

For the consensus on this matter to emerge there is a requirement that the work ethic is adopted throughout society. The promotion of commitment to work can arise by a variety of means varying from straight incentive systems (such as payment-by-results) to more subtle devices, including participatory measures.

The scope of industrial society Kerr *et al.* suggest that industrial society becomes a universal phenomenon. In a sense, industrialization breeds industrialization. The breaking down of rigid national barriers ensures that industrial development in one society will, in its turn, affect the development of an interacting society.

These, then, represent the common elements that enable one to analyse the process of industrialization in any society and which are universal in the changing status of a society. As the authors say,

> The logic of industrialization prevails eventually, and such similarities as it decrees will penetrate the outermost points of its universal sphere of influence. Each industrial society is more like every other industrialized society – however great the differences among them may be – than any industrial society is like any other pre-industrial society (Kerr *et al.*, 1973, p. 56).

As an analytical tool this account and explanation has many merits. However, its universal characteristics necessarily imply a high level of generality. In order to develop an explanatory description of the emergence of complex organizations in industrial society, more specific characteristics need to be delineated. In particular, it is useful to distinguish between different types of social relationship in order to analyse whether these change as a consequence of industrialization.

A convenient distinction to draw is that made by Schneider (1971) between what he calls the formal relations of production and social relations of production. The definitional distinction is that the

250

formal relations of production result from the legally and socially defined rights of individuals to have access to work and consequently to receive a share of their work input in the form of an exchange-value. The social relations of production at work differ in that they refer to the kinds of relations that occur through the association of individuals in the productive process. Clearly, as the case of advanced industrial societies shows, the nature of the technology and the extensiveness of the division of labour in society largely determine the character of the social relations at work (cf. the distinction between relations in the unit production as compared with those in mass assembly production; see Blauner, 1964). Technology and the division of labour thereby modify the 'natural' social relations that arise between individuals.

It should not be assumed that these two types of relation are mutually exclusive. It is conceivable that they both may impinge upon the same individual or group simultaneously. This is particularly the case in primary production-working both for and with the same individual. The more complex the industrial system, the less likelihood of a coincidence of the two types of social relationship. It is equally true to say that the same set of formal relations of production can have associated with them very different types of social relationship. The case of the close-knit occupational community to be found amongst coalminers, for example, can be contrasted with the highly individualized and privatized relations amongst motor car assembly workers. And yet both groups are exposed to the same set of formal relations of production (Dennis *et al.*, 1969; Goldthorpe *et al.*, 1969).

'Metaphysical pathos' and 'strategic choice' in the theory of organizations

In an important paper called 'Metaphysical Pathos and the Theory of Bureaucracy', Alvin Gouldner (1955) has touched upon issues which are immediately relatable to the linkage of the Aston group's research into organizations with the 'convergence thesis' through the cross-national comparative project undertaken by McMillan (1976). This linkage suggests that, irrespective of the cultural or political differences between nations, these differences are of less importance than the fact that all modern nations require large-scale organization, whether in the public or private sphere, whether free-enterprise capitalism, state socialism or state monopoly capitalism. The argument is found at its most sophisticated in Max Weber, who saw socialism not as an alternative to capitalism but rather as a further intensification of bureaucratic organization. He declared of socialism that 'for the time being, the dictatorship of the

251

official and not that of the worker is on the march'. Organization, it is argued, has its own logic. It is upon this logic that convergence has taken place, according to this Astonian view of the thesis.

Gouldner suggests that it is not perhaps 'logic' so much as 'sentiment' which is converging here:

> The discussions of bureaucratic organization which are heir to the Weberian analysis must be understood as being, in part, a displacement of the controversy over socialism. Weber made it clear that questions of economic choice could no longer be treated in isolation from questions of administration. . . . For many intellectuals who have erected a theory of group organization on Weberian foundations, the world has been emptied of choice, leaving them disoriented and despairing (Gouldner, 1955; 1973, pp. 338–9).

We have already argued in Chapter 2 that the source of Weber's 'cultural despair' is the epistemological framework in which he constructed his work. What Gouldner is suggesting is that this despair will infuse any theory of organizations which makes some or other element of administration, be it size, technology, location, or environment, determinant. This is important. Size, technology, etc., are not necessarily determinant. Determinancy is a feature of scientific theories about the real world, rather than the world itself. It is thus a matter of human choice and values, as Weber argued. These choices and values are, of course, not only those of the theorist, but also those of the designers of organizations. But the two choices become increasingly and inextricably linked as the designers of organizations are taught, to an ever greater degree, their principles of design through business schools and courses in organizations which themselves choose to accept the values of the theories of organization such as the Aston School (We elaborate this point in our final chapter).

> Paradoxically enough, some of the very theories which promise to make man's own work more intelligible to himself and more amenable to his intelligence are infused with an intangible metaphysical pathos which insinuates, in the very midst of new discoveries, that all is lost. For the metaphysical pathos of much of the modern theory of group organization is that of pessimism and fatalism (Gouldner, 1955; 1973, pp. 339–40).

The Aston research would seem to be a good example of the metaphysical pathos of which Gouldner writes. Bureaucracy is unavoidable. Size, if it does not cause bureaucracy, is at the very least highly conducive to it. And if the organization is not large it will not necessarily escape bureaucracy: this will depend upon its type of technology, because the smaller the organization is, the more significant technology becomes as a determinant. These conclusions support those reached by Talcott Parsons two decades earlier when he stated that 'technological advance almost always leads to increasingly elaborate division of labour and the concommitant requirement of increasingly elaborate organization'. Why should this be so?

> The fundamental reason for this is, of course, that with elaborate differentiation of functions, the need for minute co-ordination of the different functions develops at the same time. . . . There must be a complex organization of supervision to make quite sure that exactly the right thing is done. . . . Smaller and simpler organizations are typically managed with a high degree of particularism (i.e. personal consideration) in the relation of persons in authority to their own subordinates. But when the 'distance' between points of decision and of operation increases, and the number of operating units affected by decisions with it, uniformity and co-ordination can be attained only by a high degree of formalization (Parsons, 1951, pp. 507–8; cited in Gouldner, 1973, pp. 342–3).

That this is teleological in the extreme, in that autonomous things (technology) determine system needs, should be evident. That this teleology is *metaphysically pathetic* should be evident from Gouldner's (1955) discussion. Indeed, Gouldner comes to conclusions the neglect of which is perhaps the most remarkable aspect of so many of the interpretations of contemporary organization theory. These conclusions endorse those arrived at by Dreyfuss two decades earlier. In Dreyfuss' view the existence of a 'minute division of labour' is a result of managerial choices made *in the interest of control.* Where there is a high division of labour 'individual workers and employees can be exchanged and replaced at any time' (Dreyfuss, 1938, p. 75).

One of the few writers in organization theory to have made this linkage is Etzioni (1961), in particular in his discussion of Warner and Low (1947), a text which both Etzioni (1961) and Gouldner (1955) saw the significance of, but which subsequent writers, with the exception of Rose (1975), have largely overlooked. The most frequently cited sections of Warner and Low (1947) are those which Gouldner (1973, p. 345) abridges thus:

> Control problems are simplified . . . on two counts through mechanization: (1) machines are easier to control than human beings, and (2) mechanization tends to disrupt the social solidarity of the workers, who thereby become easier to control

253

than they would if they were to maintain close social relations during working hours . . . these factors tend to increase the subordination of the individual worker to management; from the management's viewpoint they are valuable means of social control over workers. . . . The routinization of jobs also simplifies control of workers in another way. The individual operative today does not have the feeling of security that the old-time craftsman derived from his special technical abilities. In most cases, today's operative is aware that only a comparatively brief training period protects him in his job from a large number of untrained individuals. The members of the supervisory hierarchy are also well aware of this fact. The psychological effect of this result of the division of labour is to intensify the subordinate position of the individual operative and to make him submit the more readily to the limitations on his behaviour required by the supervisory group (Warner and Low, 1947, pp. 78, 80, 174).

This stress on 'control' is quite consistent with the perspective that we are developing here, albeit in a different context to that of Warner and Low. In many ways their perspective in the cited passages anticipates that of Stephen Marglin (1974), as well as being consistent with the work of sociologists such as Alvin Gouldner. John Child's (1972a) stress on 'the role of strategic choice' is one of the more recent re-statements of the critique of organization theory in terms similar to those of Gouldner's (1955) 'metaphysical pathos' argument. It also explicitly addresses the Aston research. He notes of such research (in which he has also been involved, see Child and Mansfield, 1972), that 'research designed to establish statistically the presence of associations between organizational characteristics usually leave underlying processes to be inferred'. The difficulty, as he notes it, 'is that adequate explanation derives from an understanding of process, and in this regard the "fact" of a statistically established relationship does not "speak for itself". At the very least, it may mask a more complex set of direct and indirect relationships' (Child, 1972a, pp. 1–2). On this basis, and allowing for the fact that 'little understanding is afforded as to how the relationship was established and whether it is a necessary condition for the presence of other, perhaps desirable, phenomena' he proposes that 'not only is research into organization of a processual and change-oriented type still required but so equally is an attempt to offer more adequate theoretical schemes in step with the advance of empirical research' (Child, 1972a, p. 2). This theoretical inadequacy is clearly a characteristic of the Aston research (as well as that of other 'structuralist' investigators of organizations such as Blau, Hage and

Aiken, Hall, Lawrence and Lorsch). Child is quite specific about the nature of this theoretical inadequacy and about how it should be remedied:

> *Incorporation of the process whereby strategic decisions are made directs attention onto the degree of choice which can be exercised in respect of organizational design, whereas many available models direct attention exclusively onto the constraints involved. They imply in this way that organizational behaviour can be understood by reference to functional imperatives rather than to political action* (Child, 1972a, p. 2; our emphasis).

In wishing to focus on *choice* in *design,* rather than on constraints, Child (1972a) is clearly opposing what Gouldner (1955) had referred to as the 'metaphysical pathos' of organizations. To this end he opposes the typical environmental determinism of systems theory (see Chapter 5), by correctly observing that environments may be determined by choice rather than be determining *as if by nature.*

One feature of the Aston research, in contrast to much of the systems theory literature on organizations, is that it consistently opposed environmental determinism. This is evident in the cross-national studies, such as McMillan's (1976). As against an environmental determinism they have argued for a 'logic of organization' based on the internal organizational determinations of 'size' and 'technology'. We will consider Child's (1972a) objections to this type of argument.

Child (1972a, p. 5) poses as a 'fundamental problem' whether or not the concept of technology, however used, is of any value as a 'theoretical strategy'. 'Rather than concentrating upon the technological adjuncts of executing tasks, and on the technical logic whereby such tasks are linked, there would seem to be a good case for focusing upon the work itself.' This focus 'upon the work itself' would be to re-orient analysis toward what Marx termed 'the labour process'. Child (1972a, p. 5) suggests that analysis should switch to the '*planning* and *ordering* of work, together with its *meaning* to those involved'. This is not inconsistent with a more Marxist analysis of the labour process. In this perspective, rather than technology determining organization structure, it can now be

> seen as a product of decisions on workplans, resources, and equipment which were made in the light of certain evaluations of the organization's position in its environment . . . rather than the technology possessing 'implications' for effective modes of organizational structure, any association between the two may be more accurately viewed as a derivative of decisions made *by*

those in control of the organization regarding the tasks to be carried out in relation to the resources available to perform them (Child, 1972a, p. 6; our emphasis).

Child is equally critical of arguments which suggest that size determines, causes or is necessarily correlated with bureaucracy. Our argument from historical data in Chapter 2 would suggest that specialization does not automatically flow from size, and that impersonal control, rather than flowing from specialization, is part and parcel of specialization imposed in and through it precisely *as* a system of control. Hence the posited causality does not accord with the historical record, nor does it acknowledge that 'impersonal control' could be deliberate invention, rather than determined functional necessity.

The second argument that Child (1972a, p. 7) typifies is one that we would not argue against. Clearly, the direction of larger numbers of people cannot be achieved through a 'personalized, centralized style of management'. However, this does not entail that the only alternative to personalized, centralized managerial control, is 'a more decentralized system, using more impersonal mechanisms of control'. It is not. Other possibilities would include some system of workers' control (see Chapter 13). However, to our knowledge, few organization theorists have proposed, prescribed or even studied workers' control. This is in large part due to the institutionalization of industrial relations and organization theory as largely discrete discourses. By effectively delimiting the theoretical object of organization theory to some version of the organization structure/system as organizational/managerial control of the labour process, this entails that workers' control is rarely treated as part of the same theoretical and practical-empirical site of discourse.

In the structure of its argument, the thesis which correlates increased size with increased bureaucracy of formalization of structure is exactly the same as Herbert Spencer's pan-evolutionism. It will be recalled from Chapter 1 that Spencer believed that industrial society was characterized by a twofold process of differentiation and integration. As societies/organizations become larger because of an increasing (and unexplicated, hence metaphysical) division of labour, they necessarily (and tautologically) become more differentiated. The increasing division of labour occurs in production in the sustaining system. This entails increased specialization or differentiation. As the production/sustaining system of the organization becomes more complex, then the distribution system of communications ('a system of impersonal controls through the use of formal procedures' as Child (1972a, p. 7) put it) will grow to integrate the whole. *Ipso facto,* for both Spencer and the Aston researchers, 'size causes bureaucracy'. The only difference is the style in which the arguments are expressed, not the structure of the arguments.

One may object to this equation of the most primitive sociological teleology with the most sophisticated sociological research methods. While Spencer could only substantiate his case through far-fetched and discredited analogies, the Aston research is contemporary social science at its most systematic. If Spencer was killed then surely the development of scientific procedures as exemplified by the Aston project was not only a contributory factor to his demise, but also an heir to the territory which he claimed.

Empiricism

The Aston studies began by suggesting that the Weberian tradition in sociology had concentrated on only one type of bureaucratic structure. Contrary to this, through the development of scales and indices, they argued that organization structure, far from being unitary, was multi-dimensional. They arrived at this conclusion through the process of concept-formation, scale-construction, data-collection, factor-analysis and correlational induction as described earlier in the chapter. Thus, organizations vary as to specialization, formalization, centralization and configuration according to contextual variables, primarily size and technology. These conclusions are inferred from the statistical manipulation of differences between the factors which are taken to indicate real differences in organizations. These data are taken to be 'facts' which form the basis of scientific knowledge and method, from which general 'laws' of social reality can by statistically inferred (such as the correlation between size and bureaucracy). The factual and correct nature of the knowledge produced is legitimated by the judicious application of the rules of statistical inference.

The great strength of the Aston studies was that they provided a simple technique of measurement. Such a technique, like all technique, is rooted within what Habermas (1974, pp. 7–8) has termed the 'transcendental framework' of instrumental action. This transcendental framework is one of 'the system of primitive terms within which we organize all experience *a priori* and prior to all science', what Gouldner (1971) terms the domain assumptions of a discourse; these are not simply sentiments, but are ontologically grounded in concrete projects conducted under their auspices. They are thus constitutive features of any realm. The transcendental framework of instrumental action constitutes as its knowledge-guiding interest the control and manipulation of objects. Where the organization is conceived as an object, then instrumental action

257

towards it poses the possibility of control and manipulation. This has, in fact, been the objective outcome of the contingencies approach to organization structure, as can be seen in the increasing number of organization texts oriented to the *design* of organizations (e.g., Khandwalla, 1977; Galbraith, 1973). What makes design, or as we prefer, control, possible is first that the object under analysis be *objectified*. In organization theory the most sophisticated form of objectification has been through the use of operational measurement and scaling techniques.

Operational definition assumes

that empirical categories can best be defined by the operations used to observe the experiences to be included in the categories. The purpose of operational procedures is to structure these operations so that different results can be assigned numerical values. When a succession of similar operations can be performed on a succession of similar objects with each different result being assigned a different numerical value, the aggregate of all of those possible values is called a 'scale'. The 'scale', in turn, is supposed to represent a 'concept' (Willer and Willer, 1973, p. 106).

The scaling techniques used by the Aston studies (according to Levy and Pugh, 1969) were those of Guttman (1950). The Guttman scale, it has been argued, is uni-dimensional. This means that a set of items for measuring an intuitive concept (or one gleaned from a literature of intuitive concepts) can be ranked in a consistent, stable order which represents a single property or dimension.

The Guttman scaling procedure involves seeing how far responses to items deviate from the ideal scale pattern which would be given by the Guttman matrix. To use the Guttman technique it is necessary to have data in a dichotomous form. The Guttman matrix is constructed by first ordering the items in decreasing popularity (i.e., the most frequently occurring through to the least frequently occurring item) down the left hand side of a page. Responses are ordered in terms of relative scores along the top of the page (i.e., the highest scoring response through to the lowest scoring response), with the highest score next to the most popular item. The scores are added for each case. A line is constructed according to the ideal scale pattern which would place all the positive scores (1's) on one side of the stepped line, and all the negative scores (0's) on the other. The line is drawn in through the cases from the items, and continued like a flight of stairs for each case, beginning at the least frequently occurring item. If the actual distribution of the matrix was perfect, in the theoretical distribution, then all the 1's would be above the line, all the 0's below it. Invariably, there will be actual deviations from this pattern. These are called 'errors'. These are counted and used in the formula for calculating the Guttman coefficient of reproducibility:

$$\text{Coefficient of reproducibility} = 1 - \frac{\text{number of errors}}{\text{number of items} \times \text{number of respondents}}$$

The lower level of acceptability for the coefficient of reproducibility has been placed at about 0.90. Items are usually refined, removed and replaced at the pilot stage in order to achieve this coefficient. When a scale of items is constructed which scores at or above this coefficient it is claimed to represent a single property or dimension. However, Guttman (1950) did not make this claim:

> In actuality the claim of uni-dimensionality is merely a tag put on the 'scale' when the results are ordered. Although it is true, as Guttman claimed, that items which scale together will not necessarily correlate, the converse statement that items which correlate will not scale does not follow and is not true. Thus two different sets of items which correlate highly will scale together, and therefore scales differing widely in content (or dimensionality) will scale together if they correlate. Consequently the claim of uni-dimensionality simply does not hold up, even though some operationalists take the mindless position that things that correlate highly are necessarily the same. There is no guarantee in the operations of Guttman scaling that a scale will have a single dimension or even that it will have any known or identifiable number of dimensions (Willer and Willer, 1973, p. 114).

Even when the coefficient of reproducibility is satisfied on one occasion, there is no guarantee that it will be on another. The coefficient is not *necessarily* stable across time and populations. 'Each new application of the "scale" is instead simply a test of it in which the previous order may be falsified' and as the Willers go on to add:

> This is clearly a caricature of measurement. The idea of testing a yardstick against each new situation to see if it will still 'scale' is ludicrous. Guttman scaling is, in fact, not a measuring technique at all, but a technique for summarizing data by combining the responses of a population to a set of objects in such a way that, on the average and ignoring errors, an ordinal ranking is achieved. But post-factum ranking is not measurement (Willer and Willer, 1973, p. 115).

259

This is because of the critical error in organization theory use of operational definition. The instrument of measurement must not be employed in such a way as to be constitutive of the measured object, and it should be capable of generalization to each and every case of the measured object. If a scale is to be used for measurement it has to have not only the mathematical properties of a scale. It must also be capable of measuring one population after another. It must not be dependent upon the population from which it was first constructed, nor be altered by any subsequent population. This, unfortunately, is 'impossible to achieve by any empirical scaling technique. Scaling techniques are *all* dependent on particular populations for the scales they produce'. They have no validity whatsoever outside of the particular operations that constitute them. As such they are not scientific measures, 'but are simply ways of averaging and compositing which result, at most, in an overall descriptive approximate ranking for particular populations' (Willer and Willer, 1973, p. 116). At worst, what it does is simply to constitute the existence of the organization as a dimensional object through a fetishistic process of objectification.

In a scientific practice concepts are not observables and are not definable in Bridgman's (1927, p. 5) terms: 'In general, we mean by any concept nothing more than a set of operations; the concept is synonymous with the corresponding set of operations.' A concept *is* more than a set of operations and it is *not* synonymous with a corresponding set of operations. A concept cannot be observed and can only be defined in terms of other concepts. Nonetheless, in organization theory the process has been quite different to this. The whole process of theory construction has developed on the basis of a naive correspondence between objects and concepts.

We can make a number of observations about this process. The object of analysis is the self-evident existence of a class of concrete objects – organizations. Because organizations exist we can have a science of organizations. On this basis organizations as diverse as scout camps or multi-national corporations can be taken as given *as* organizations. Because there is a common-sense term, 'organization', then we may take it that any objects it corresponds to in its use as a concept (however it be employed – in common sense or a more refined discourse) have a number of constitutive features in common, such as dimensions of organization structure. Boy-scout camps and multi-national corporations can be experienced, they are both 'real'. Also, they both correspond to the concept of organization. Thus, not only are they real, they are also part of a common sphere of reality – the reality pertaining to the common sense world of objects we term organizations in our ordinary understandings. In extraordinary refinements of these understandings, through the statistical inference of factorial dimensions of the concept, we can arrive at properties through which morphology can be differentiated taxonomically. This process exemplifies a particular methodological approach known as 'empiricism'.

What is empiricism? According to the Willers (1973) it involves a system of knowledge which connects observable phenomena with observable phenomena, usually with an implicit Humean assumption of causal connection. Empiricism is not scientific. A scientific analysis is not an empiricist analysis. While science is concerned, like empiricism, with observational statements, this is not the totality of its concern. It attempts to connect observations with theoretical statements constructed in rational non-observational concepts in an isomorphism of theory and observation. This isomorphism is achieved in terms of 'laws and theories, which have been interpreted by abstractive connection to empirical events for at least some of their relevant scope'. This contrasts with empiricism which 'is concerned with empirical generalizations or causal connections of observational terms, through the observation of empirical association' (Willer and Willer, 1973, p. 20). It is this latter activity, rather than the former, which characterizes all organization theories of the Aston type.

What is entailed in this process of empirical generalization? One might, for example,[2] explain the degree of bureaucracy in an organization in terms of its observed size. We know, perhaps, of other instances in which an increasing division of labour has put stress on the communications system in an organization, and this stress has been resolved through an increase in bureaucratic controls in the organization; therefore, we may make the empirical generalization that size is associated with bureaucracy, where there is an increase in the division of labour in the organization. The division of labour became more differentiated, the organization grew bigger, and therefore more bureaucratic. This explanation uses an empirical connection in which all the terms (division of labour, organization, bureaucracy) are observational. The connection is made as a consequence of the experience of repeated observations. Explanation consists of making a general causal statement about size and bureaucracy and applying it to a particular organization. Such an explanation is a simple refinement of common-sense practices of observation and habit. Depending on one's epistemological preferences this will be seen as more or less a good or bad thing, and can generate two extremely important types of critique.

On the one hand, ethno-methodology argues that any science is necessarily grounded in common-sense assumptions and practices. From this would follow a commitment to the empirical analysis not of the objects constructed by such practices, such as dimensional models of organizations, but of the methods by which such objects are constituted. Attention would then focus on the methods that members of the collectivity of organization theorists use in producing their concept of the organization. Alternatively, attention would focus on the routine methods and understandings that members of organizations use in organizations in everyday life. Study of organizations would then be equated with the practices whereby members of organizations *do organization,* the practices through which, and in which, they construct a shared sense of what the organization is, of what the organization means. Ethnomethodology has entered into organization analysis through the contributions of phenomenological critiques of organization theory by authors such as David Silverman (1970).

Another line of critique can be developed from the realization that what passes for science is an empiricism barely distinguishable from an elaboration of common-sense practices. Rather than accepting this, and then pointing to the practical communality of science and common sense, it seeks radically to distinguish science from common sense. This is the critique developed by Louis Althusser and his colleagues from the epistemology of Bachelard. This development has yet to make any major impact on organizations as a substantive field, although Mouzelis (1975) in his introduction to the second edition of his *Organization and Bureaucracy* recognizes its potential.

The following chapter will consider the phenomenological critique of organizations developed from sociological phenomenology, ethno-methodology and interactionism.

7 Organizations as structures of action

Introduction

Hitherto the stress has been on organizations as stable, external structural, systematic constraints. On occasion this has been breached by 'action guided by images which transcend these constraints' (Bauman, 1976, p. 2) as in *Ordine Nuovo's* workers' councils experience, but such breaches have not typically been a concern of organization theory. This is not to say that this theory has been wholly deterministic and structural, but it has been preponderantly so. We encounter this determinism in the earliest formal theories of administration, most notably in Taylorism. It is also present in the human relations emphasis on the constraining influence of 'the human group' (despite its stress on needs and sentiments), particularly in studies of the function of group norms in restricting workers' output. In Weber it is evident in his stress on necessity as the basis of social action:

> To Weber the necessary was the condition of rationality. Indeed, rational action required unfreedom for it to be possible at all. It is the rules, which confront each individual cog in the bureaucratic machine with all the merciless, indomitable power of nature – the rules which make the external walls of the action safely and predictably stable – which render bureaucracy rational, which permit the bureaucrats carefully to select means for the ends, secure in the knowledge that the means will indeed bring forth the objectives they wish, or are told, to achieve. The rational action commences when the rules are 'already there'; it does not account for the origins of rules, explain why rules remain strong, or why they take on the shape they possess. The question of the origins of rules, of the origins of the environmental necessity of bureau-

263

cratic action, cannot be phrased in the language of rationality (Bauman, 1976, p. 4).

This shortcoming remains, despite the fact that organization theory allows that the rules can become 'dysfunctional' (see Merton, 1940) and that, whether functional or not, functioning or not, it can describe them with a degree of exactitude and precision (e.g., the Aston school). Indeed, organization structure itself becomes a domain of more-or-less certainty predicated upon either an immanent logic (Weber's neo-Hegelian stress on rationality which finally emerges in an unreflected and simplified form as 'size causes bureaucracy') or constraint ('technology causes bureaucracy').

Within this essentially deterministic framework little choice would be left to individuals. Indeed, it was Taylor's stated ambition to remove the element of choice from the class of manual labourers within organizations. Other writers, often working within a more social psychological or phenomenological framework, have in their various ways attempted to locate individual choice at the centre of their conceptualization of organizations. This dichotomy between choice and structure or freedom and constraint has not always been theorized, as one might expect, dialectically. The previous chapter is testament to this tendency in organization theory.

Locating choice within constraint immediately introduces uncertainty. And in the domain of social science uncertainty is invariably resisted, as Bauman (1976) has argued. There are two ways in which uncertainty can enter into organizations: through structure or through culture. An emphasis on either of these can lead to two quite distinct forms of theory. The emphasis on structure tends to minimize the scope of choice, while an emphasis on culture tends to exaggerate volitional elements.

Structure: Simon, March and Weick

The pragmatist philosophy of William James (1925) and John Dewey (1930) provided the framework for one of the most influential attempts at defining organization structure within uncertainty. This is the work of Simon (1957) and March and Simon (1958). The key to their work is a conceptualization of administrative behaviour based on habituated choice.

William James's *The Principles of Psychology,* which was originally published in two volumes in 1890, was the source of a conceptualization and discussion of 'habit' which was to have an important effect in the development of organization theory through the subsequent work of Herbert A. Simon. James stresses that among the influences of habit on individual behaviour, perhaps the most important is that it simplifies responses. This will be important not only for the individual but also for society because 'habit is . . . the enormous flywheel of society, its most precious conservative agent' (James, 1948, p. 143). Habit is articulated via consciousness. Consciousness is the process through which the individual constantly reconstructs his or her environment, while at the same time being determined by this environment. The result of this double determination, Dewey (1930) argued, was equilibrium.

Translated into organizational terms by Simon, this pragmatist emphasis produces a model of the person which stresses not a completely rational organizational actor but one who is only *habitually rational*. People attempt to be rational within the bounds of their habitual rationality rather than the bounds of objective rationality. Simon states that:

> Objective rationality . . . would imply that the behaving subject moulds all his behaviour into an integrated pattern by (a) viewing the behaviour alternatives prior to decision in panoramic fashion, (b) considering the whole complex of consequences that would follow on each choice, and (c) with system of values as criterion singling out one from the whole set of alternatives (Simon, 1957, p. 80).

Simon goes on to argue that this is an 'idealized picture'. For instance, making the picture more realistic requires recognizing that one rarely has 'a complete knowledge and anticipation of the consequences that will follow on each choice. In fact, knowledge of consequences is always fragmentary'. In addition, 'since these consequences lie in the future, imagination must supply the lack of experienced feeling in attaching value to them. But values can be only imperfectly anticipated' (Simon, 1957, p. 81). Also, although rational choice presumes knowledge of all possible alternatives, 'only a very few of all these possible alternatives ever come to mind' in actuality. In practice, in organizations, these limits to individual rationality are overcome through organization (the division of labour, standardization, hierarchy, formal channels of communication, training and indoctrination: see Simon, 1957, pp. 102–3). The organization thus functions through its structure as the definition of the situation of choice. The organization structure co-ordinates into a planned and integrated whole the web of individual meanings and choices. When the individual within the organization has to choose, the choice is made on the basis of past experience, stereotypes, prejudices and highly particularized views of present stimuli. Most frequently these choices will be routines: situations and recipes which worked in the past will be expected to work again. Where problem-solving has to be engaged in, it will be on the basis of a limited search for satisfactory, rather than optimal, solutions. This is a process of 'satisficing' as against 'optimizing'. What is satisfactory is determined through and by the organization. This is how the organization functions to define the situation of choice. It does so through the control that the organization's 'dominant coalition' has over the variables of the organization structure.

March and Simon (1958, p. 170) define the organization structure as 'those aspects of the pattern of behaviour in the organization that are relatively stable and that change only slowly'. These 'patterns of behaviour' are the satisficing behaviours already alluded to. These may involve only sequential and limited search processes rather than major innovations; a specificity of role-prescribed activity, and rules, programmes and repertoires of routinized stock-responses; a restricted range of stimuli and situations that narrow perception; organizational socialization, training and indoctrination; and the creation of a hierarchy of goals and sub-goals which form tasks and programmes which are semi-independent, in order to reduce interdependencies (after Perrow's 1972, p. 151 summary of March and Simon, 1958; Simon, 1957).

This structure exists in order to absorb uncertainty: in this way a bounded rationality may be achieved. Uncertainty is absorbed, for instance, through the use of a reified vocabulary within the organization as a way of constituting a finite organizational world out of the infinity of the possible social worlds present in any stimuli. Additionally, stimuli are channelled into the organization through the specialization of roles and functions for dealing with information, particularly at the boundaries of organizations (see March and Simon, 1958, pp. 164–71). Where there are a great many sources of information and a low degree of centralization of information, uncertainty will be greater, and thus the probability that conflict will occur will also be greater. Thus, uncertainty becomes a controllable feature of the organization's structure.

Karl Weick (1969) has developed further some of the ideas in March and Simon's (1958) and Simon's (1957) work, particularly those concerned with the organization as a constitutive agent in an uncertain environment. Just as with Simon, and March and Simon, much of what Weick has to say is explicitly concerned with the organization as a problem of social psychology (his book is titled *The Social Psychology of Organizing*). However, as with these other authors, he also has something to say about the organization as a structure of social action. To characterize this he prefers to talk about organizing rather than organizations.

He explicitly opposes the view which we discussed in the previous chapter that organization structure is the result of contingencies over which the organization has no control. Although his opposition to this view is derived from a theoretical stance which owes far more to social psychology than to sociology, he develops some similar themes to those which John Child (1972a) was later to explore.

Weick (1969, p. 28) advances as a basic proposition that rather than the organization simply reacting to its environment, it *enacts* it. This idea is developed from the same pragmatist roots as those which had earlier served as a key resource for Simon. In Weick's case these resources were the work of one of Dewey's associates, George Herbert Mead (1934) and the phenomenologist Alfred Schutz (1967). The starting point of Mead's theory is 'the recognition that the first and last "reality" is flux, process, duration, eventuation, function . . .' (Kallen, 1973, p. vii). From this phenomenological flux 'the organism creates its environment' (Mead, 1934, p. 120). Mead's dialectic of 'organism' and 'environment' expressed in terms of 'self' and 'society' becomes for Weick one of organization and environment.

For Mead neither self nor society can be reduced to the other. They are always present in an autonomous but reflexive relationship, in every experience. Mead expresses this in the dialectic of the 'I' and 'me'. 'Me' and 'I' are two aspects of the self which are also the two aspects of social reality into which we all enter as we become human through our socialization into society via language. The 'I' is a sedimentation of all the individual's previous experience of reality as a constraint upon freedom. Thus 'I' contains society in an individualized form. It is the 'I' which is aware of the social 'me' which arises through the taken-for-granted assumptions that one has of what the others assume. The 'I' and 'me' are not separable unique phenomena, with one being the seat of freedom and the other the source of constraint. They are always part of the common interdependent process of continuing action in which the 'I' creates the 'me' from the flux of process, to which it then reacts.

Weick's (1969) view is remarkably similar to this if we think of organizing in terms of the 'I–me' dialectic *vis-à-vis* an environment which corresponds to the Meadian society. This is evident in the following quotation:

> The predominant model of man adopted by organization theorists is one in which the human is essentially reactive to the environmental contingencies that occur. This environment can be inside or outside the organization, but in either case the actor essentially reacts to it as given. However, instead of adapting to a ready-made environment, it is entirely possible that the actors *themselves* create the environment to which they adapt (Asch, 1952, p. 256). Rather than talking about adapting to an

external environment, it may be more correct to argue that organizing consists of adapting to an enacted environment, an environment which is constituted by the actions of interdependent human actors (Weick, 1969, p. 27).

The actors (the 'I') create the environment to which they (as 'me's') then adapt. 'The human *creates* the environment to which the system then adapts' (Weick, 1969, p. 64). The enacted environment is always a function of what Schutz (1967) calls the retrospective glance whereby 'the coming-to-be and passing-away' of contourless flux and process is given shape and structure as discrete, separate experience. Discrete items of experience are always constituted as such retrospectively through an act of attention to that which has passed (Schutz, 1967). For Weick (1969) the environment of the organization is constituted in this way. This entails treating the organization's environment in terms of information and meaning which is more or less equivocal (i.e. uncertain). This equivocal informational environment then becomes the input into the organizing system. 'If the relevant environment for the organization is described in terms of information, then it is possible to argue that organizing is directed toward resolving the equivocality that exists in informational inputs judged to be relevant' (Weick, 1969, p. 29). Weick then attempts to develop a formal model of organizing. This is a formal model of the processes rather than the structure of organizations. It is based on the construction of a theoretical object of the formal structure of the processes whereby the organization system reduces the equivocality of its enacted informational environmental inputs. It is a socio-cultural evolution model developed from the work of Donald T. Campbell (1959; 1965a; 1965b). It proposes that there are three organizing processes. These are: enactment of an informational environment; selection of inputs to be processed from this environment; and retention of information as a feedback function for future enactment and selection.

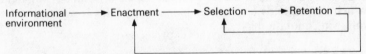

These three processes constitute a series of what Weick (1969) calls 'assembly rules' and 'interlocked behaviour cycles'. Assembly rules are 'rules for assembling the process out of the total pool of interlocked cycles that are available within the organization. These rules consist of criteria by which some sub-set of all the possible interlocked behavioural cycles relevant to the process is actually selected for application to the informational input' (Weick, 1969,

p. 72). These rules are also the' means by which the degree of equivocality in the input is registered. Weick (1969, p. 73) assumes 'that the greater the amount of equivocality present in the input, the *fewer* the number of rules that are activated to compose the process. Conversely, the smaller the amount of equivocality in the input, the greater the number of rules that are used to assemble the process.' These rules are not at this stage empirically grounded, but some examples of what they may be are given:

1　Effort: select those cycles whose completion requires the least effort.
2　Frequency: select those cycles that have occurred most frequently in the past.
3　Success: select those cycles that have been most successful in removing equivocality.
4　Permanence: select those cycles that will produce the most stable change in the input.
5　Duration: select those cycles that can be completed in the shortest period of time.
6　Availability: select those cycles that are not currently engaged in other activities.
7　Personnel: select those cycles that are 'manned' by more experienced people.
8　Relevance: select those cycles that most closely resemble content of the input.
9　Reward: select those cycles that the members regard as most rewarding.
10　Disturbance: select those cycles that will cause the least disruption in the ongoing system (Weick, 1969, pp. 72–3).

Such rules as these would seem to be a specification of what 'bounded rationality' in action might be. What the rules assemble are interlocked cycles of interstructured behaviours, in Weick's terminology. More obviously, we might refer to these as *organizational routines* which will vary from organization to organization (Weick, 1969, p. 78). They are routines because:

They consist of repetitive, reciprocal, contingent behaviours that develop and are maintained between two or more actors. Each actor uses and is used by the other person for the accomplishment of activities which neither alone could accomplish. The resolving of equivocality is assumed to be a joint activity, an activity that is accomplished by sets of actors who interlock varying sets of behaviours. Each interlocked behaviour cycle can remove some equivocality, but it is only when several different cycles are applied to the information that a sufficient degree of certainty is produced for unequivocal action to be taken (Weick, 1969, p. 91).

Finally, in a complex cybernetic model of direct (+) and inverse (–) relationships, Weick produces a model of how 'ecological change' activates the organizing process.

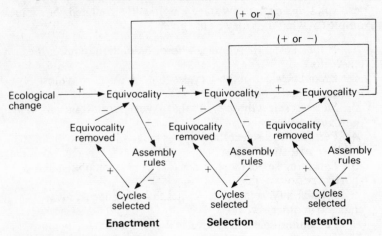

Figure 7.1   Karl Weick's model of organizing

Source: Weick, 1969, p. 93.

Weick begins by talking about meaning but ends up in a wholly deterministic and abstract system unrelated to any actual social meaning. Indeed, so far is he from a concern with meaning that his final model of the organizing process appears to have lost sight of social action entirely. What we have is an automatically functioning rational system of behaviours (albeit one which is boundedly rational) responding to changes generated from outside the system through an adaptive process. Such a model assumes a totally socialized commitment to the operative goals of the organization on behalf of its members. This becomes apparent when we are instructed how to use the model:

> The model suggests that if you can obtain two separate items of information about an organization, you should be able to predict what will happen in that organization. The two items that are crucial: (1) the degree of equivocality associated with some significant informational input that is received by some process, and (2) the use that is made of retained content. If you obtain information about the degree of equivocality in some important input, then you can predict the number of rules that will be

270

activated, the number of cycles that will be selected, the amount of equivocality that will be removed, the nature of the input to a subsequent process, and the fate of that informational input as it is processed by the subsequent process. If you obtain information about how retained content is used, then you can specify the nature of the causal relationships from retention to selection and from retention to enactment; you can predict how these two processes of enactment and selection will unfold in the future; and you can predict whether the system in which these processes are embedded will maintain a controlled existence or will show signs of disintegration. If you see that both processes have the same causal relationship to retention (i.e., both lines are plus or both lines are minus), then you would predict that productivity would decrease, absenteeism would increase, turnover would increase, morale would decrease, etc. Each of these latter items is assumed to be an indicator of disintegration (Weick, 1969, pp. 95–6).

Let us consider the last point first. Disintegration of the system is caused by the lack of systemic balance that ensues when there are conflicting demands from one sub-system, retention, on the other sub-systems. Lack of balance is indicated by amplifying feedback. Amplified feedback is any feedback that is not corrective. The system is assumed to operate in such a way that corrective feedback is always balanced (both + and –). This is because of the initial assumptions linking greater equivocality inversely to fewer rules. But social reality is not so simple nor so self-evident as Weick, at least in the later parts of his book, seems to assume. For instance, the number of assembly rules activated is a function of the amount of equivocality in the informational inputs. These are enacted. So their equivocality content is a function of their enactment, which is a function of the assembly rules used to do enactment. However, we have already defined the number of assembly rules in terms of the amount of equivocality. The whole process appears to be circular. Nor are the formulae 'number of assembly rules' or 'amount of equivocality' particularly clear. Are any ten assembly rules equivalent to any other ten? Could not ten simple assembly rules be condensed into five in another organization? Surely the number of assembly rules is quite meaningless without some specification of the work or social action involved?

Objections can be raised to the concept of equivocality also. If the amount of equivocality is always a function of enactment, then it makes no sense to speak of 'amount', for no comparative analysis is possible, although 'amount' necessitates comparisons of 'more than' with 'less than'. Each enactment is unique and serves to redefine all previous enactments as contents of experience to which no value outside of the present experiencing can be attached. Weick's originally promising model of organizing seems to lead only to either an empty formalism or a content which cannot meaningfully be compared. The environment, from being an objective determinant in earlier theories of organization, has become the enacted consequence of the decisions of the organization. As such it takes on a fantastic quality. It has no objective existence: it does not exist in laws, institutions, or material reality – except in as much as information which constitutes it as such is enacted. The environment loses all determination and becomes the ideal conditions of the organization's existence.

If this de-reifies the environment it does so at some cost. First, it implies than nothing other than an ideational environment exists. Second, it reifies the organization. It does this by assuming that the organization knows what it is doing. Implicitly, the goals of Weick's organization are crystal clear: 'Organizing consists of the resolving of equivocality in an enacted environment by means of interlocked behaviours embedded in conditionally related processes' (Weick, 1969, p. 91). The goal of the organizing is thus the reduction of equivocality. But why? To what purpose? Who determines that this is so? Explicitly no one does. Clearly the goals of the organization will be set by the institutional environment as it is interpreted by the dominant coalition in the organization. This does not imply that all members of the organization accept their imputation, nor does it suggest that they will dutifully resolve equivocality in its pursuit. They might very well further and increase equivocality in pursuit of their own sectional interests within the organization at the expense of any imputed overarching goals. As Brown (1977) has documented, sabotage is a normal, routine and widespread organizational practice. It invariably creates more equivocality than it resolves, and for certain interests in an enterprise may well be an overarching goal. What ought to flow from Weick's flirtation with a phenomenological viewpoint, but which does not, is that systems themselves only have equivocality to resolve from the perspective of their participants, and there is as much equivocality as there are different definitions of the situation and ends. The organization is not a phenomenological subject, although Weick treats it like one.

In this respect Simon's, and March and Simon's stress on 'dominant coalitions' is far more realistic. However, the stress on 'dominant coalitions' as a source of structural constraint and homogeneity within the organization needs to be developed dialectically with an emphasis on sources of diversity and heterogeneity within the organization. That the possibility of such a perspective resides in the phenomenologically oriented resources

(Schutz, Mead, Garfinkel) that Weick uses is evident from the development of David Silverman's work.

Culture: Silverman and action

David Silverman's (1970) *The Theory of Organizations* was a development of themes that he first broached in a paper in the journal of the British Sociological Association, *Sociology,* in 1968. The paper was titled 'Formal Organizations or Industrial Sociology: Towards a Social Action Analysis of Organizations'. The paper began by contrasting two approaches to organizational analysis, 'industrial sociology' and 'formal organizations'.

Industrial sociology, we are told, perceives industry 'in the context of the environment in which it exists, including the class, familial and urban structures'. Formal organizations 'is interested in all types of organizations, industrial or otherwise, and attempts to develop a general theory applicable to them all. It is less specifically "sociological" and, partially as a consequence of this, it has not given first priority to understanding the links between organizations and the wider social structure.' It is because of this neglect that Silverman proposes an 'industrial sociology' approach in preference to a 'formal organizations' approach. Mouzelis (1967) regards this as a 'bizarre' presentation because, he argues, all of the problems which Silverman points to in 'formal organizations' are also present in industrial sociology. In fact, although his initial presentation of his position is in these terms, it is not really this dichotomy which is most significant for Silverman's analyses (1968; 1970; 1972; 1975). The significant dichotomy is much more general and transcends all substantive fields of sociology.

In Silverman (1968) the dichotomy is introduced as between 'transcendental' and 'immanent' models of society (after Horton, 1966). The transcendental model views 'the problems of the system as a whole, with human action being regarded as a reflection of system needs', while the immanent model has a 'view of interaction that arises as actors attach meanings to their own actions and to the actions of others' (Silverman, 1970, p. 41). In organizational analysis Silverman (1970) terms this the dichotomy between the 'systems' perspective of structural-functionalism, and 'the action frame of reference'. More generally, this dichotomy can be located in 'the earliest debates between Positivism and Idealism' (Silverman, 1968, p. 222). What Silverman (1970) does is to use the 'idealist' side of the divide to criticize 'positivism' as it has been articulated in systems models in conventional organization theories.

The critique and the proposed alternative draw heavily upon the work of Peter Berger and his colleagues (Berger, 1966; Berger and Luckmann, 1966; Berger and Pullberg, 1966), contributions to the sociology of knowledge and upon the work of Aaron Cicourel (1964) in the sociology of methodology. What all these works have in common is a debt to the view of sociology generated by Alfred Schutz.[1]

Schutz's (1962; 1964; 1967) 'phenomenology' develops a radically subjectivist sociology which Bauman (1976) has aptly characterized as 'existentialist' because of its insistence on the self as an *active*-being-in-the-world who not only is *in* the world, but who also actively constructs the world he or she is in, as that world which has meaning for his or her self. The self, as in the pragmatism of James or the interactionism of Mead, is a social self which is both a social constructor of reality, as well as being itself socially constructed (more so in the work of Berger and Luckmann, 1966; less so in that of Schutz, 1967).

This phenomenology is implicit in Silverman's (1970, p. 5) announcement of the intention of *The Theory of Organizations*: 'I will seek to draw out the implications for study and for theory-building of a view of social reality as socially constructed, socially sustained and socially changed.' This involves a critique of reification in theories of organizations, thus developing the criticism introduced in the earlier paper:

> By treating the 'goals' and 'needs' of organizations as givens, it seems to us that we are attributing apparently human motivations to inanimate objects: in other words, we are reifying the organization. Instead of attempting to establish empirically the conception of ends and needs held by its members, we begin with *a priori* notions of an organization's 'needs' and then examine the processes through which it secures them (Silverman, 1968, p. 223).

It is through focusing on the organization as 'the outcome of motivated people attempting to resolve their own problems' (Silverman's, 1970, p. 126) definition of the theoretical object of the organization) that a number of potent critiques are made. First, that organizations can neither have needs nor goals; only people can. To speak of organizations having these is to commit an unwarranted reification. Second, that in explicitly talking of organizations *as if* they had goals or needs not only are we reifying them, we are also implicitly accepting the politically conservative value-laden views of management. Management may speak of 'the organization' but they do so in part because they are managers, seeking to foster a unitary, collective image of 'the organization' as a homogeneous, functioning whole which they consensually manage (rather than

274

control). (Fox, 1966, developed this theme.) For us to accept uncritically this way of thinking about organizations, as if they were monadic, serves to conceal the plurality and diffusely conflicting nature of the goals of different members of organizations. Phenomena such as organization charts, job descriptions, etc., rather than furnishing adequate data for building an analysis of the dimensional structure of the organization (e.g., the Aston school) are not representations of how the organizational reality actually, necessarily is, *but of how top management sees it, or thinks it should be*. To accept them as if they were depictions of what the organization is really like is to embrace managerial ideology.

Silverman (1970) develops his critique of conventional theories of organization, modelled upon the various systems analogies, in the first five chapters of *The Theory of Organizations*. In the sixth chapter he develops 'The Action Frame of Reference' as a critique of positivism. This is couched in terms of an elaboration of seven propositions which are axiomatic to his subsequent working out of the theoretical and methodological implications of the 'action' perspective. What these propositions reduce to, are the following. The familiar phenomenological distinction between natural science and social science is stated: sociology, as a social science, does not just observe behaviour (as for instance, in observing the pattern of iron filings around a magnet), but understands action. Action is meaningful, and meaning defines social reality. Meaning is institutionalized in society and is continually reproduced and changed through the routine actions of everyday life. Thus, in the tradition of the *Geistesswissenschaften* (cultural sciences) rather than the *Naturwissenschaften* (natural sciences) 'explanations of human actions must take account of the meanings which those concerned assign to their acts; the manner in which the everyday world is socially constructed yet perceived as real and routine becomes a crucial concern of sociological analysis' (Silverman, 1970, p. 127).

The 'action frame of reference' requires us to study the 'definitions of the situation' of the actors involved in the organization. These 'definitions' will be constructed by actors from the 'meaning of the social world . . . given to us by the past history and present structure of our society' (Silverman, 1970, p. 132). This meaning will be expressed in 'typifications' (Schutz, 1964), which are habituated expectations of how others will behave towards us, or of what certain abstract symbols mean. These typifications are institutionalized and thus become part of our cognitive furnishing of the world, part of that which we take for granted. As such, they are now oriented towards, as if they were objective, 'real' phenomena. Meanings thus become institutionalized as social facts. They are socially sustained through this process of reification, continually

275

recreating the fragile web of meaning in the cast-iron form of seemingly objective reality.

Because we ordinarily experience the world as if it were objectively there we forget that 'realization of the drama depends upon the reiterated performance of its prescribed roles by living actors. The actors embody the roles and actualize the drama by presenting it on the given stage. Neither drama nor institution exist empirically apart from this recurrent realization' (Silverman, 1970, pp. 133–4; quoted from Berger and Luckmann, 1966, p. 75). That which is socially constructed but objectively experienced continues to be 'realized' as such in a double sense:

> It is an apprehension of social reality as 'reality', and, at the same time, the production of this reality, in so far as individuals, taking its objective nature for granted, ongoingly act toward perpetuating and continually re-creating its objectivity. It is this knowledge which lends institutions the appearance of cohesion and harmony they enjoy; the order of the universe is in the eye of the beholder, and in the habituated action of the actor (Bauman, 1976, p. 68).

Why should individuals continually recreate these institutionally located and taken-for-granted typifications? Because of existential dread: the fear of uncertainty and chaos that lurks in the existential world. As Berger and Luckmann put it,

> The legitimation of the institutional order is also faced with the ongoing necessity of keeping chaos at bay. *All* social reality is precarious. *All* societies are constructions in the face of chaos. The constant possibility of anomic terror is actualized whenever the legitimations that obscure the precariousness are threatened or collapsed (Berger and Luckmann, 1966, p. 121).

In other words, uncertainty is an ontological condition. However, it is one which can be put to human purposes, because particular legitimations will be related to the relative power of various actors. Uncertainty can be held at bay or exploited by differentially powerful actors: 'He who has the bigger stick has the better chance of imposing his definitions' (Berger and Luckmann, 1966, p. 101; quoted by Silverman, 1970, p. 138).

Where does this lead the analysis of organizations? According to Silverman (1970, p. 147) it provides us not with a theory of organizations but with 'a method of analysing social relations within organizations'. In the context of a discussion of phenomenological deviance theory, Taylor *et al.* (1973, p. 193) observe that there are generally 'two related methodological imperatives built into a phenomenological orientation. One imperative is to give a correct representation of the phenomenon under study; the other is to show how the phenomenon is constituted or built up.' The consequence of these methodological imperatives is to turn attention away from reified conceptions of the phenomenon under investigation to the processes whereby such a reification has been constituted. The thrust will be away from deterministic theories to the study of intentional action. Silverman's discussion of 'the origin of organizations' is faithful to these imperatives. First, Silverman begins by contrasting deterministic systems theories of organizations with the action approach to the origin of organizations:

> From the Systems point of view it has been argued, in general terms, that organizations (as sub-systems of society) arise as part of an evolutionary process of internal differentiation of system parts. In order to explain the number and nature of organizations that are created at any time, it is necessary, therefore, to consider the stage of development of a society and the kind of environmental conditions to which it must adapt. An explanation in terms of the Action approach, on the other hand, would begin from the fact that organizations are created by a specific person or group. It therefore becomes necessary to ask: who are these people and what is the nature of the ends and definitions of the situation which cause them to form an organization with a particular goal? How does the pattern of expectations and type of legitimate authority within the organization relate to the stock of knowledge characteristic of the society and to the finite provinces of meaning of its founders? (Silverman, 1970, pp. 147–8).

Just as in Weick (1969), the environment of the organization has been de-reified but at the cost of reducing the environment solely to a meaningful environment of 'stocks of knowledge', 'finite provinces of meaning' and 'definitions of the situation' as they are subjectively constituted. The environment is now no longer a deterministic constraint under which people labour because the emphasis has shifted towards the active, constitutive side of people as social constructors of reality. To illustrate this perspective Silverman (1970, pp. 148–9) re-works Stinchcombe's (1965) analysis of the relationship between 'Social Structure and Organizations'. By this method he makes more explicit some of the conservative implications of the action perspective:

> Organizations reflect the prevailing meaning-structures of their time in their internal pattern of social relations. Thus organizations originating within a bureaucratized society will tend to be created with a bureaucratic structure – even when, one might

add, they are designed to overturn the political system of that society (e.g., radical political parties, trade unions). This is because the founders of organizations, whatever their aims, will usually take their ideas about efficient organization from the stock of knowledge characteristic of their society at that time (Silverman, 1970, p. 148).

Given this notion of hegemonic stocks of knowledge, it would be very difficult, for instance, to explain how radical social change might occur other than through some notion of exogenous 'stocks of knowledge' being imported into a situation – or rather, its definition – and thus changing that situation's definition. There is no conception here of how the definition may be radically shattered by transforming the situation. Situations, having been built entirely of definitions, seem to possess little solidity. However, Silverman's phenomenological project is not entirely subjective (if it were it might be a more rigorous phenomenology but at the expense of being an impossible sociology, as Bauman (1976) argues), but is instead concerned, as was Schutz (1967), with inter-subjectivity. Inter-subjectively, not all definitions of the situation are equivalent. Some are 'institutionalized expectations about the likely action of others without which social life cannot proceed' (Silverman, 1970, p. 152). These bulwarks against existential dread are 'the rules of the game'. Interestingly, Silverman maintains that these persist not because it serves the interests of a dominant class, coalition or group to make them do so, but because all groups tend to accept them 'for the time being, either because they feel they can do nothing to alter them or, more importantly, because of the rewards which stable group relations offer to all those concerned' (Silverman, 1970, p. 152). Strictly speaking, in terms of the action perspective, if all groups feel they can do nothing to alter these rules, then they can do nothing, because the situation only exists as it is defined. Therefore, if the rules persist, we can only conclude with the equilibrium analysis of both the systems theorists (derived from marginal economics) and the social psychologists March and Simon (1958), (derived from Dewey, 1930) that this persistence indicates a balance of 'inducements' and 'contributions' in members' subjective assessments.

This situation of balance may change, however. Organizational change occurs either through a change in the rules of the game or in the attachment of actors to them. Changes in the latter can, of course, produce changes in the former. Silverman explains how this may happen:

The action that occurs confirms certain expectations of the actors and refutes others. It also involves the attainment of certain ends, while suggesting to the actor that others are un-attainable. They eventually re-orientate their actions in the light of a new definition of the situation . . . while their inter-action has some sort of effect on the stock of knowledge in the organization (Silverman, 1970, p. 153).

Silverman does not produce any research results which exemplify the perspective. It is demonstrated through a presentation of existing studies. The chief one of these is his re-working of Gouldner's (1965) *Wildcat Strike*. This is done in terms of an analysis of the role system of the organization (a gypsum plant), the pattern of involvements, the definition of the situation, the actions and consequences that followed from these and the sources of change in the situation (see Silverman, 1970, pp. 155–63). From Silverman's (1970, p. 154) suggestions, this analysis and the sub-sequent chapters, one could construct an ideal-typical model of what an action perspective would do. It can be considered to consist of the following sequence:

1   What is the historical development of the role system in the organization?
2   What type of attachment do the members of the role-system have?
3   What strategies of action follow from actors' attachments and definitions?
4   What are the consequences, in terms of patterns of interaction, for the organizational 'rules of the game' in which action and meaning have been constrained?

From the re-analysis of the Gouldner (1965) materials of *Wildcat Strike*,[2] Silverman (1970) suggests a strongly historical analysis of the organization's role-system as a process development which has to be considered analytically within the context of the wider en-vironment. The environment's chief role, however, is not as a determinant of intra-organizational structure and behaviour, but as a source of meanings both for participants in action and for analysis of that action. Thus, in Gouldner's study of the gypsum plant the historical account began with an analysis of the initial equilibrium position in which the gypsum mine was in a stable situation.

The gypsum mine operated in a rural, closed community. Its role-organization depended more upon the traditional values and structure of the local community that it did upon the imperatives of rational organization. Rather than a strictly formal administration characterized by an explicit body of rules, the organization operated predominantly on implicit, contextual rules. These were analysable collectively as an 'indulgency pattern' by Gouldner. There was considerable give-and-take in management–worker relations, based on management's frequent indulgence of what would have been formally illegitimate requests or actions (borrowing or taking company equipment). These were indulged in the interests of a harmonious and peaceful existence.

This tranquil, indulgency pattern of organization was not occurring because of any specifically technological factors or environmental determinism. Although there was a general fit between the values of the organization's action system and the surrounding community, this fit was more precarious than it might otherwise have appeared to be. It depended upon a common definition of the situation which had developed historically and had never been radically re-negotiated or challenged. This was shortly to happen.

The gypsum plant was not only situated within a local, geographical and social environment. It was not an organization within the vacuum of a wholly closed system; it was part of a wider organization. While the local plant, steeped in the sleepy ways of the rural community, may not have been particularly oriented to formal, rational imperatives, the company as a whole was. Profits were not as great as they ought to be in Head Office's terms. For this reason, when the local plant manager died, rather than replacing him with another local man who could be expected to have changed little, the company brought in a manager from outside. This person was more oriented to the values of Head Office – increased profit through increased rationality – than to the settled ways of the local community. In the terms of his frame of reference and value system, the 'indulgency pattern' of organization appeared to be non-rational. A number of modernizing changes were introduced. Rules were tightened up and more strictly imposed, and modern machinery introduced.

With the dislocation of the established value-system, meanings and definition of the situation, the workers grew dissatisfied. The old certainties had disappeared. They were involved in new, more uncertain situations, because the taken-for-granted rules had been disrupted. In consequence, faced with changed definitions *and* a changed situation (redundancies were threatened), the workers expressed their grievances through demands for higher wages. These demands were expressed this way, because, given the changed definition of the situation, appeals for a restoration of the old system were clearly illegitimate, while grievances expressed in terms of wage claims were both legitimate and rational. With the settlement of the wages issue the situation appeared to have been resolved, although, as Gouldner elaborates, minor crises persisted. The situation had moved from a stable, traditional pattern of interaction, to an unstable pattern based on rules which were not legitimate in terms of the workers' previously taken-for-granted

280

meanings, attachments and definitions.

The situation was this. From a position where power appeared to be absent because organization was based far more on traditions of consent than on coercion (albeit that this persuasive element in social relationships disguised far more coercive real relationships of production) the situation had developed to one where, lacking the traditional ideological supports, organization had to be more explicitly buttressed by power. Thus, when a wildcat strike occurred, given the ideological breakdown, the manager could rely only on power to try to re-stabilize the situation. It was not a question of the situation – in terms of capitalist relations of production – ever having changed. What had changed were its ideological supports, the hegemony of definition in the situation. So the consequence of the strike, which Gouldner interpreted as an attempt by the workers to articulate their grievances, was that the manager responded by more powerfully defining the rules of the organization. A consequence of this was that even less control remained in the workers' hands, as supervision was further tightened, rules made more formal and explicit. In Gouldner's phrase, this developed into a classic 'vicious circle'; Silverman summarizes events economically in the following terms:

> Not only was each group resisting the other's demands, but the forms of reaction available to them only confirmed suspicions on both sides. Management, unable to use the informal methods of its predecessors, was forced to attempt to resolve the situation by the use of still closer supervision and of the formal channels of authority. In reply, workers resisted still more, and management reacted by once more tightening the screws. Three months after a second succession of managers, the worker walked out and, because the union official structure was unwilling to support them, a wildcat strike began. The conflict was resolved by an agreement which involved the still further bureaucratization of the factory with clearly defined functions being attached to each position and formal rules being applied to all interaction. Thus impersonal attitudes were reinforced, and both sides in time gave up the assumptions which had supported the indulgency pattern. Social relationships were now defined by the participants on a new basis (Silverman, 1970, p. 157).

The strengths of this analysis are evident. The organization is not treated as if it were a unitary, reified actor. Its class-based membership component is apparent. The action that occurs in the organization is related to structurally different interests which evolve historically over a period of closely observed time. The changes in the structure of the organization are not a result of either a technological determination (although new technology was introduced) or an environmental determination. The environment is treated as one in which differential meanings are available to different material interests (e.g., the Head Office versus the traditional 'indulgency pattern') and imposable through differential power and strategies (management can increase control while workers can resist it). As a result of the consequences of these actions, both intended and unintended, the actual enactment of the social relations of production changes. Thus the labour process, as the theoretical object of the analysis, changes from one type of informal control to one which is imposed through an increasingly formalized structure of organization.

Equally exemplary of the action perspective, in Silverman's (1970, pp. 208–10) view, is Michel Crozier's (1964) analysis of *The Bureaucratic Phenomenon*. This is because of Crozier's stress on strategies of action used by actors to minimize their dependency and increase their power within the context of a set of 'rules of the game'. Crozier shows how the dependence of production workers upon maintenance workers in a French state-owned tobacco monopoly occurs, because, in an almost wholly rationalized structure, the maintenance men control one of the last remaining uncertainties: the knowledge of how to repair broken machinery. This is a vital control over the production workers because when the machinery breaks down they cannot earn their usual pay on the output-related bonus system. Hence, the control over uncertainty which maintenance workers have gives them sufficient power to be able to expand their own region of autonomy and control, marginally, within the highly structured organization.

The so-called 'Affluent Worker' studies conducted by a team of Cambridge researchers headed by Goldthorpe and Lockwood (1968; 1969) is a further example of the social action approach to the study of organizations. In order to understand worker behaviour in the motor car and engineering factories studied, the individual definitions of the situation and the stated goals of individuals were analysed. This is clearly very different from other researchers who have emphasized the importance of factors such as technology in understanding behaviour.

Amongst the (albeit small) sample of workers studied there was found to be an overall instrumental orientation to work. Goldthorpe *et al.*'s argument is that such an orientation to work (that is, as a means to non-work ends) is indicative of the class position of the workers in the wider society. It is well documented that the 'affluent worker' sample showed few, if any, signs of embourgeoisement: for example, no obvious changes in political affiliations, in family or community patterns, or in general aspiration levels.

A number of drawbacks are evident in the Goldthorpe and Lockwood approach to understanding organizational behaviour through the social action approach. Possibly the most serious arises from the very broad generalizations that tend to be made about worker behaviour in each and every circumstance. So, as contexts vary there is no reason why reactions to work should not vary. Orientations to work are not stable phenomena, nor are they necessarily consistent within and between different groups of workers. Although Goldthorpe and Lockwood stress the extra-organizational influences upon the individual, those within the organization can be equally powerful, as studies such as Roethlisberger and Dickson's (1939) demonstrate. Organizational socialization is normally different from societal socialization. Unless the specific exigencies of the work situation are stressed the absurd conclusion is reached that all workers sharing a similar non-work situation will exhibit similar orientations to work.

Those studies which Silverman (1970) endorses have in common a concern with the *processes* rather than the *structure* of the organization. This is aptly characterized as a concern with 'the rules of the organizational game' (Silverman, 1970, p. 196). In order to understand the game one first has to learn the rules as they are understood and used by the participants. For phenomenologists, this injunction is primary. Indeed, phenomenologists would agree with Schutz:

> Each term in a scientific model of human action must be constructed in such a way that a human act performed within the life-world by an individual actor in the way indicated by the typical construct would be understandable for the actor himself as well as his fellow-men in terms of common-sense interpretations of everyday life. Compliance with this postulate warrants consistency of the constructs of the social scientist with the constructs of common-sense experience of the social reality (Schutz, 1962, p. 44).

It follows from this that any scientific account of organizational phenomena, according to phenomenological canons, ought to be one which is reducible to the meanings of the actors in the situation. However, our objectives in studying these phenomena are not necessarily the same as those of the actors who constitute the phenomena to which we then attend (see Taylor *et al.*, 1973, pp. 197-9, for a treatment of this with respect to deviancy theory). Although we would have different practical purposes, by phenomenological standards, our accounts would have to share the same common sense as lay accounts. (Thus, for instance, as McHugh (1968) makes quite clear, we could have no concepts such as 'false consciousness'). For phenomenology, nearly all theoretical concepts of sociology such as organization, its goals, rules and environment, are all second-order constructs.

That is to say, they are constructions at one order removed from any phenomenological typification, for they do not have reference to, neither are they reducible to, everyday taken-for-granted, practically constituted, intentionally created pheno-mena. Thus there is no guarantee that in extracting these second-order analytical constructs from the totality of social phenomena that they are in any sense homologous or isomorphic with the concrete reality of social existence. In one important sense, then, the process of phenomenological investigation is a radical attack upon the possibility of the very foundations of an etiol-ogical social theory itself. For it insists that sociology deals in *decontextualized* meanings and that there is no guarantee that actors in concrete settings construct their lives and the rules which govern them in a similar fashion (Taylor *et al.*, 1973, pp. 197–8).

Silverman (1970, p. 223) recognizes this phenomenological limi-tation when he states 'the nature of social life implies that the concepts employed in Sociology should not be applied without taking into account the subjective meanings of those who are being observed'. It is in obeying this imperative that Silverman suggests that the sociologist should be wary of imposing his or her own definitions on the situation studied. Thus, although sociologists may use a definition of, for example, 'authoritarian supervision', which appears to be subjectively meaningful as well as logically consistent, they ought also make their concepts conform to the canon of what has been called 'usage-adequacy' (Clegg, 1975, p. 117). If this were done, then supervision which is apparently authoritarian might be construed as something quite different:

The supervisor might see it as the only means of enforcing his wishes on a recalcitrant or uninterested work group, while the workers might interpret it as an illegitimate attempt to limit their just rights. Or, in a society where traditional authority was pre-dominant, both parties might regard such behaviour as a legitimate exercise of authority and would not think of question-ing it. It would merely be the customary act of superiors and would not be interpreted as a strategy to obtain personal ends (Silverman, 1970, p. 224).

In this 'weak' version of the canon of usage-adequacy one may detect no particular problems. Sociology at its best has always attempted to make seemingly inexplicable phenomena, meanings and situations theoretically explicable in *another set of terms*. Silver-man opposes the tendency in (positivistic) sociology to regard this other set of terms as reified social constructs, as different from, and superior to, lay constructs. This practice is characterized by what Cicourel (1964) calls 'measurement by fiat'. In *The Theory of Organizations,* apart from the implications of the phenomeno-logical project for a *theoretically* radical critique of positivist work, the implications of this stance are not fully apparent. They were to become so in Silverman's subsequent writings.

The action frame of reference: continuities and discontinuities

If the exemplary analyses of *The Theory of Organizations* were to be found in work such as that of Gouldner (1965) or Crozier (1964), reinterpreted through Berger and Luckmann (1966), a further collection of exemplaries was evident in Silverman's next excursus into organizational analysis. This was made in the course of a consideration of 'Some Neglected Questions about Social Reality' (Silverman, 1972). This new collection consisted of examples of 'ethno-methodological' enquiries made in the context of organiza-tions by Bittner (1965), Zimmerman (1971) and Sudnow (1973). We will try to construct the route from the action perspective to ethno-methodology.

The essential link is the work of Alfred Schutz (1962; 1964; 1966; 1967), in particular his appropriation of certain phenomenological terms of Husserl (1967) in the context of a discussion and critique of the Weberian approach to the issue of 'subjective meaning'. Schutz (1967) agrees with Weber (1968) that the foundation of the phil-osophy of the social sciences must be a grasp of the nature of human action as governed by subjective meanings. Schutz formulates his project in these explicitly Weberian terms:

> Never before had the project of reducing the 'world of objective mind' to the behaviour of individuals been so radically carried out as it was in Max Weber's initial statement of the goal of interpre-tative sociology. This science is to study social behaviour by interpreting its subjective meaning as found in the intentions of individuals. This aim, then, is to interpret the actions of indivi-duals in the social world and the ways in which individuals give meaning to social phenomena (Schutz, 1967, p. 6).

But he does so with phenomenological reservations.

> [Weber] breaks off his analysis of the social world when he arrives at what he considers to be the basic and irreducible elements of social phenomena. But he is wrong in this assumption. His concept of the meaningful act of the individual – the key idea of interpretative sociology – by no means defines a primitive, as he

285

thinks it does. It is, on the contrary, a mere label for a highly complex and ramified area that calls for much further study (Schutz, 1967, pp. 7–8).

This 'much further study' will be accomplished through using Husserl's phenomenological reduction of Weber's concerns as a matter already in hand. Such a use of Husserl, as both Bauman (1976) and Hindess (1977) note, is an abuse. Rather than taking Husserl's rigorous idealism, which seeks to make all phenomena subject to a 'radical investigation of sense' (Husserl, 1969, p. 5), Schutz (1967) unproblematically accepts Weber's (1968) definition of the problem of sociology without radically questioning it, or bracketing its reliance on the German idealist tradition of the *Geisteswissenschaften*. What he does is to argue that Weber's definition of the unit-act of sociological analysis was inadequate:

> Weber makes no distinction between the *action,* considered as something in progress, and the completed *act,* between the meaning of the producer of a cultural object and the meaning of the object produced, between the meaning of my own action and the meaning of another's action, between my own experience and of someone else, between my self-understanding and my understanding of another person. He does not ask how an actor's meaning is constituted or what modifications this meaning undergoes for his partners in the social world or for a non-participating observer. He does not try to identify the unique and fundamental relation existing between the self and the other self, that relation whose clarification is essential to a precise understanding of what it is to know another person (Schutz, 1967, p. 8).

In order to remedy these inadequacies Schutz (1967) insists that we turn to a 'constitutive phenomenology of the natural attitude'. This will enquire into the natural (reified) attitude which governs the common-sense or mundane world of everyday life. It will do this by showing how interacting subjects (that 'fundamental relation') experience and construct social reality. As Silverman (1972, p. 166) put it, a phenomenological sociology must 'move beyond the experience of any one person in order to reveal shared assumptions about social reality (and the activities associated with them) which generate and sustain such experiences – it must seek to understand the *process* of experiencing'. What are these 'shared assumptions'? They are 'anthropological universals' as Bauman (1976, p. 60) terms them, smuggled into this phenomenology as *a priori* factors of analysis. These consist of those stable 'background expectancies' through which actors are able to construct typifications of other persons. These inter-subjective anthropological universals are threefold. Schutz (1962) introduces these as the 'reciprocity of perspectives', the 'interchangeability of standpoints', and the 'congruency of relevances'. In other words, Schutz's phenomenology assumes *a priori* that the other will see things my way, and that I will see things the other's way, given the interchangeability of our standpoints and the fact that we have congruent relevancies. In short, as Hindess (1977) develops, there is an assumption of liberal tolerance in Schutz, that, writing as one liberal for other liberals, such things as are constitutive of a good fellow may be taken for granted. As Lassman (1974, p. 128) notes, this 'promotes a highly consensual image of the social reality of the "life world" and this image has permeated the whole phenomenological approach'. It is certainly very much at odds with Silverman's (1970) earlier concerns with an 'action perspective' as exemplified in Gouldner's (1965) analysis of *Wildcat Strike*. There the fact that the reciprocity of perspectives, standpoint of the other and the congruence of relevancies of management and the workers could not be assumed was the lynchpin of the analysis.

What continuities does this 'new direction in sociological theory' hold for analysis of organizations from an action perspective? The major continuity is in maintaining a radical distinction between natural and social science, and in refusing to treat the organization as 'real'.

> The defining processes of social life make *social* objects and forces different in kind from physical objects and forces. It would, indeed, be absurd if it were not so commonplace to treat the relations between social institutions and human behaviour in the same way as the relations between a magnet and iron filings. The reification of social phenomena – their treatment as objects – is part of the 'natural' attitude of everyday life in which the world appears as a collection of objectified typifications both solid and real. A phenomenological consciousness leads to a suspension of belief in the reality of these objects and an analysis of the social processes through which human definitions are objectivated by members. A profession, an organization or an ability range, to take three examples, are no longer treated as 'real' things, or as objects which (in the case of the first two) take actions to meet their needs; they are viewed instead as labels which members use to make sense of their activities and as ideologies used to defend their activities to others (Silverman, 1972, p. 188).

This phenomenological bracketing-out of reality is the new ingredient to the action mix. Its consequence is to make the central subject matter of a phenomenological sociology an account of members' accounts and common-sense practices. This introduces the topic of 'indexicality'. Indexical expressions refer to the objects they describe in contextual terms, and are thus bound to their occasioned use in contrast to what Garfinkel (1967, pp. 4–11) terms 'objective expression'. These are characterized as being de-contextual and typal. To say that an expression is indexical would be to say that it is relative to such contextual matters as who said it, to whom it was said, and in what kind of context, where context invokes such features as the occasion, the social relationships involved, and so on. Garfinkel argues that the substitution by sociologists of objective for indexical expressions is both an 'endless' (as necessarily reflexive) and unnecessary practice, in that indexical expressions are rational, accountable and ordered prior to any sociological reformulation (see Garfinkel, 1967, pp. 4–11; Garfinkel and Sacks, 1970; Wieder, 1974). Instead of this substitution as an 'endless' activity, ethno-methodology recommends that the process by which accounts are constructed and given, the 'glossing' activity, should become the focus of study.

This is the point at which the implications of Schutz's project become most apparent. If a phenomenological study seeks to give a correct representation of the phenomena under study (the 'descriptive imperative'[3]) and the processes by which the phenomenon is constituted (the 'constitutive imperative'[4]) the end result will be a relativistic regress which can only reach bedrock when we accept the version of what it is that they are doing that actors would ordinarily give us. We phenomenologically bracket away until we reach this common sense. Clegg (1975) has developed a critique of the conservative implications of this phenomenology in the context of a discussion of 'power' and its possible study by ethno-methodology. He comes to the conclusion that, other than at the most mundane level (which is, of course, what ethno-methodology aims for), one can say very little about power in everyday life, using phenomenology. What one can say is insignificant with respect to the ways in which power is usually conceived. An example of this would be the analysis of turn-taking in conversations as an indication of relative power. One either studies relatively trivial phenomena, it would seem, or else one is again involved in phenomenologically unwarranted reifications, such as 'power' and 'domination' (Clegg, 1975), or 'the powerful character of speech' (Silverman, 1976). It is such reifications that phenomenological bracketing seeks to avoid.

Phenomenological bracketing is simply a methodological device which seeks to set aside all judgments about the (supposed) reality of a phenomenon by suspending these judgments as a prerequisite of analysis. Once belief in the 'real' nature of the phenomenon has been bracketed, attention can switch to the ways in which any phenomenon can be treated *as if* it were real, irrespective of its actual ontological status. This necessitates that the central topic of a phenomenological sociology will be an analysis of how members' practices constitute the pervasive sense of reality (common sense) which we experience in everyday life. This is what Garfinkel (1967) referred to as 'glossing practices'. As Silverman puts it:

Phenomenologists certainly seek to *understand* common-sense interpretations of social reality but they do so in order to stand outside them more completely. They argue that only by questioning taken-for-granted assumptions about reality (phenomenological reduction) is it possible to surpass common sense. The social world is a *topic* for study but the assumptions and processes of reasoning of its members must not be used as an unexplicated resource by the observer (Silverman, 1972, p. 170).

In shifting the focus of sociological investigation to the analysis of the situated practices of everyday life, the American version of sociological phenomenology acquires its name. It is an ethnomethodology, a 'folk-methodology' (see Garfinkel, 1974). That is, it is an investigation of the everyday methods through which

situations of practical, everyday life are socially organized and, as such, are perceived, known, and treated by persons as uniform sequences of actual and potential events which the person assumes that other members of the group know in the same way that he does, and that others, as does he, take for granted (Garfinkel, 1956, p. 184).

Prime examples of such 'social organization' can not only be found in everyday practices, but also in the practices through which these may be studied (read: socially organized). This is because ethno-methodology is not an analysis of any concept or object domain, but of the ways in which all, any and every domain is constructed.

Ethno-methodological studies analyse everyday activities as members' methods for making these same activities visibly-rational and reportable-for-all-practical-purposes, i.e., 'account-able' as organizations of commonplace everyday activities (Garfinkel, 1967, p. vii).

This treatment of each and every phenomenon as problematic, as not given but as an accomplishment, has been used by Silverman (1975) in furthering his critique of reification in organization theory. He suggests that a part of the 'consensus' which 'characterizes the current state of organizational analysis' is an 'agreement

289

about the subject matter of the study of organizations'. The agreement 'rests on a commitment, shared by the spectrum of sociological perspectives, from the structural-functionalists to the symbolic interactionists, to a task of describing and explaining organizational structures and relationships' (Silverman, 1975, pp. 269, 270). A feature of this consensus 'is the non-problematic status accorded to the structures and relations which are purportedly being described and explained. The social world . . . is somehow "out there" and the role of the sociologist is to catch or to "tap" its component parts which, as it were, await explication . . . the very availability of the phenomenon and of knowledge of its features is not itself an issue' (Silverman, 1975, p. 270). The upshot of this is that 'accounts of organizational structures, which, like everyday accounts, purport to describe phenomena which exist separately from anyone attending to them, create the features of a "real", "available" world' (Silverman, 1975, p. 271).

The conclusion that Silverman would have us draw from this is that if members of organizations themselves are not attending to a phenomenon, are not involved in its practical accomplishment, then that phenomenon can not be said to be real: it does not exist unless someone thinks and acts as if it existed. And, if they do that, then it does not matter if it exists at all, because, on the old adage: 'If men define situations as real, they are real in their consequences.'

A crucial resource for this method in the context of organizational analysis is Bittner's (1965) paper on 'The Concept of Organization'.[5] This can be seen in the following quotation:

> In certain presumptively identified fields of action, the observed stable patterns of conduct and relations can be accounted for by invoking some *programmatic constructions* that define them prospectively. Insofar as the observed stable patterns match the dispositions contained in the programmes they are instances of formal organizational structure. Whereas, if it can be shown that the programme did not provide for the occurrence of some other observed patterns which seem to have grown spontaneously, these latter belong to the domain of the informal structures. . . .
> *The programmatic construction is itself a part of the presumptively identified field of action, and thus the sociologist finds himself in the position of having borrowed a concept from those he seeks to study in order to describe what he observes about them* (Bittner, 1973, p. 265, our emphasis).

In this context it is the 'borrowing' of concepts which is central to this ethno-methodological approach to organization analysis. This borrowing, in the terms of Zimmerman and Pollner (1971), is a confounding of 'topic' and 'resource', whereby 'common-sense

290

recognitions and descriptions' which are shared both by ordinary members of society and sociological investigators of it, are used as resources for the latter to study the phenomena which are 'made real' through members' practices, and thus become 'topics'. Rather than continue this confounding, whereby reified phenomena are attended to as if they were real, Zimmerman and Pollner (1971), as exemplary ethno-methodologists, would advise a displacement of analytic focus. This should shift from the presumptive 'thing-in-itself' to the practices whereby this 'thingness' is accomplished. These practices are essentially done through the use of 'rules'. These rules are not part of some external normative order, such as the fabled 'central value system' of society, but are a mundane feature of members' situated activities through which they produce the sense of the scenes they are in. The topic is 'not social order as ordinarily conceived, but . . . the ways in which members assemble particular scenes so as to provide for one another evidences of a social order as-ordinarily-conceived' (Zimmerman and Pollner, 1971, p. 83). Silverman put it in the following terms in the context of organizations:

> If one suspends belief in organizational structures as 'real things' it becomes possible to develop an alternative posture concerned with the manner in which members *use* rules to do the work of defining and interpreting actions (Silverman, 1972, p. 179).

Silverman recommends Bittner's (1973) paper as a resource for such an alternative. In particular, he suggests that studies might focus on various facets of the occasioned use of the concept of organization as a common-sense construct, instead of suppressing its resourceful character through either an operational definition or unexplicatedly assuming it. By contrast, 'the meaning of the concept, and of all the terms and determinations that are subsumed under it, must be discovered by studying their use in real scenes of action by persons whose competence to use them is socially sanctioned' (Bittner, 1973, p. 270). This does not presume that any authoritative status is attached to these socially sanctioned (i.e. managerial) accounts. Managers are merely the 'toolsmiths' of organizations, and, as Bittner (1973, p. 271) puts it, 'It seems reasonable that if one were to investigate the meaning and typical use of some tool, one would not want to be confined to what the toolmaker has in mind'. What kinds of study might be pursued? In Silverman's formulation these might be:

> (1) the manner in which the concept of organization is invoked by members to solve particular problems; (2) the meanings that problems acquire through being referred to the generalized

291

formula of action and meaning that actors refer to as 'the organization'; and (3) how behaviour is presented as 'being in accord with a rule' (Silverman, 1972, p. 179).

In addition to providing a handy instrument with which to criticize 'conventional' organizational analysis, such as that of Blau and Schoenherr (1971), which Silverman (1975) ably accomplishes, this also provides a set of methodological directions. This seems promising. What was perhaps most lacking from the development of the action framework in *The Theory of Organizations* was a consistent method whereby the general statements describing the perspective might be used in empirical research. Certainly, the endorsement of both 'participant observation' and 'grounded theory' (Glaser and Strauss, 1968) under the Mills (1959a) rubric of 'Every man his own methodologist' would be improved on by a more specific delineation. These are what Silverman (1972; 1975) provides in his new exemplaries. These examples are characterized by:

1 An attempt to examine the ways in which activities and their outcomes are displayed as-in-accord-with-a-rule such that their sensible character may be recognized, and
2 An examination of the practices and policies through which the features of the real world are provided for in the activities and accounts (both lay and professional) that routinely arise in social settings (Silverman, 1975, p. 280).

We shall discuss some examples of work in the ethnomethodological corpus which address these issues within the context of organizations.

Zimmerman (1971) researched a district office of a state Bureau of Public Assistance, paying particular attention to the everyday rationality of the record-keeping practices of the members of the organization. The task of the Bureau is to provide welfare aid. Welfare aid has to be administered in accord with the rules. Not everyone can have welfare who wants it. Intake workers have to establish a need, make a decision about the eligibility of applicants in terms of that need, and be seen to have followed the rules of the organization in doing so. After being processed by a receptionist; applicants are directed to an intake caseworker. It is this person's job to build up a documented dossier on the applicant's eligibility for welfare. What Zimmerman does, through patient ethnographic analysis, is to show how the final documented case which both indicates the approved or disapproved status of the applicant, and provides a record or justification for the action taken, i.e., its accountably 'rational character' (Zimmerman, 1971, p. 52) is the

292

result not of 'plain facts' but of organizationally located practices for producing such 'facts'. These consist of adopting what Zimmerman terms the 'investigative stance' – an attitude and practice of thorough-going scepticism. This consists of, first, evoking those 'features of a setting which are investigatable matters (can be settled by a document), and, second, in using typifications of actors and settings in order to pick holes in applicants' accounts' (Silverman, 1975, p. 287).

Thus the work of the organization, and the following of its rules, is 'brought off' through members of the organization enacting those features of a setting they will attend to, and through using documentary evidence unproblematically as a means of typifying that scene. What they produce is another documentary record, seemingly objective, seemingly like all the other documents – medical, welfare, legal records, etc. – which it is: but not in the way they assume. Rather than being literal, objective depictions of how things really are, they too are the result of organizationally situated and enacted rules embedded in members' taken-for-granted, unstated but ever present, practices. The thrust of this is that those documentary evidences, which report not so much on the 'objectively real' (there is none for phenomenologists) as on the practices which construct what passes for the objectively real, then become the basis, as official records, for subsequent sociological investigations. In this way sociologists then exemplify the very same practices as those that are embodied in the phenomena they study. By so doing, they begin to link observed features of the setting (i.e., its effectiveness in terms of case-load processing) to formal documented features that depict the structure of the setting. The former is seen as an outcome of the latter.

Sudnow (1973) made a similar study of the common-sense practices of public defenders in United States courts, and in so doing, introduced the methodologically useful notion of a 'normal' phenomenon as it is located in members' typifications. Sudnow's study is of 'normal crimes'. In the majority of criminal cases the defendant pleads guilty. This may appear to be because the police press charges only when they are confident of a conviction, but Sudnow suggests that this is not the case. What happens, he argues, is that a plea of 'guilty' is usually the outcome of a bargaining process between the public defender and the client. The bargain is that if a guilty plea is entered a lighter sentence will eventuate. However, the bargain is not struck on every occasion on which it would be legally possible. Typically, the public defender bases his offer to his client on what he takes to be 'normal crimes'. These involve typifications of many different offences and offenders, of the features of the settings in which offences occur, and of the types of victims involved. Only 'normal crimes' are subject to bargaining.

These studies by Sudnow (1973) and Zimmerman (1971; 1973), together with other studies by Garfinkel (1967) of jurors' decision-making, by Bittner (1967) of 'Police on Skid Row', and by Cicourel (1968) of *The Social Organization of Juvenile Justice* are taken by Silverman (1975) to be examples of a phenomenological approach to constructing a theoretical object for organizational analysis. In *The Theory of Organizations* this theoretical object was a concept of the organization as 'the outcome of motivated people attempting to resolve their own problems'. By the time of 'Accounts of Organizations' (Silverman, 1975) this had become the 'accounting process', as elaborated above. Correlatively, there has been a considerable reduction in focus.

The action frame of reference, particularly in its championing of work such as that by Gouldner (1965) and Crozier (1964), placed considerable emphasis on a historical perspective, on attachments and strategies, rules in organizations, and sources of variation of these. It also implied, albeit in a way which stressed subjective definition rather than objective resources, that power was a key concern of an adequate organizational analysis. Again, particularly in Gouldner (1965) and Crozier (1964), Silverman (1970) recognized the relationship of power and rules. However, by the time that Silverman (1976) conducted an empirical analysis which had originally been intended as an exemplification of the action frame of reference (see Silverman and Jones, 1976, p. 3) his intellectual interests had changed radically. Where once the writers that were being introduced into organization theory were sociologists such as Berger and Luckmann (1966), and their philosophical mentors such as Schutz (1967), with a change of interest towards more philosophical topics, these writers increasingly became replaced by quite peripheral sociological figures such as Martin Heidegger, the existential philosopher. Correspondingly, the centrality of Silverman's work to any sociology of organizations waned.

The analysis of selection interviews[6] which provides the data for 'The construction of "acceptable" selection outcomes' (Silverman and Jones, 1976, pp. 27–60) is accomplished in terms of an investigation of how candidates are judged as either 'acceptable' or 'abrasive', the two key lay terms used in producing selection decisions. The analysis displays that such terms cannot and do not stand apart from the contexts in which they are used. Indexicality is affirmed, and it can be seen that the work that the use of such terms does is to 'provide a rhetoric through which outcomes are made accountable' (Silverman and Jones, 1976, p. 60). Their use is itself grounded in a much wider collection of implicit, taken-for-granted rules, known more or less in common between candidates and

294

interviewers. The degree of 'know-in-commonness' becomes the crucial variable for a candidate's being selected. One gathers from the transcripts and the treatment of them that these rules are a feature of class practices. However, as no specific theoretical model informs the analysis (indeed, in its own terms, it would have been illegitimate if it had done so), these rules are not particularly apparent. Nor do they become so in much of the subsequent descriptive parts of the study.

In fact, *Organizational Work* is more a study of the organizational work that Silverman and Jones did in loosely composing a book around tape recordings of 'organizational work' than it is of that work itself. As such its primary themes are not those of organizations *per se* so much as a concern with how any (ethno-methodologically influenced) analysis can be accomplished. This becomes most explicit in 'Speaking Seriously' (in Silverman and Jones, 1976; also Silverman, 1974a; 1974b), which through a somewhat opaque consideration of Marx, via Heidegger, on 'exchange value', attempts to locate power and authority in the organization in language, and in the organization of language as it exists as a bureaucratic practice.

By this juncture, most people interested in organizations as a topic will probably have decided that irrespective of what Silverman (1970) usefully had to say about organizations, Silverman and Jones (1976) have little further to add. They may have much to say with respect to the complexities and problems of ethno-methodologizing, but the nature of that enterprise's displacement of the topic and replacement with the practices whereby that (or any) topic can be accomplished would seem effectively to negate any specific ethnomethodology of any concrete phenomena such as 'organizations'. Its thrust is to dissolve any notion of the organization as a theoretical object in favour of the study of 'members' practices' and the indexicality of accounts. Where, as in Clegg (1975), these have been studied in the context of a more explicit social theory than ethnomethodology allows, these practices and this indexicality *can* be related to the concerns of the earlier action frame of reference: power, rules of the game, etc. However, this is to practice something other than a 'pure' ethno-methodology.

Summary

In Weick, and March and Simon's work, the organization is modelled upon the boundedly rational practices of its members, who, arranged in a structure controlled by a dominant coalition, become the more or less structurally controllable sources of uncertainty. In Silverman these sources of uncertainty develop as a

295

result of the cultural freedom of any members of a speech community to define their situations. In his earlier work (Silverman, 1970) this is explored in the context of a broadly sociological perspective, stressing the critique of existing theories as largely positivist, determinist and conservatively-biased reifications. On the constructive side he urged that analysis should turn to a consideration of strategies and attachments, the rules of the game in which they were located, its historical development, and so on. In the later work (Silverman, 1972; 1975; 1976) this emphasis receded and the phenomenological materials that had previously formed the background of his critique became far more central and focused. The usefulness of Silverman's work for a sociology of organizations appears to vary directly with the exemplars he chooses. For our purposes, a sociology of organizations would be much nearer to Gouldner (1965) and Crozier (1964) than to Garfinkel (1967) or Heidegger (1967).

Nonetheless, certain progressive and useful points flow from both the earlier and the later work, which we will develop in subsequent chapters. We will outline them here. They concern the analysis of goals, technology, and practices.

In brief, goals, as they have ordinarily been conceived by organization theorists (in the manner which we will outline in the following chapter), are regarded by Silverman (1970) as reifications. The goal conception has been wrenched from the social practices, history and interests whereby it has been constructed. Silverman advises us to study these practices rather than to accept their reified outcomes as our phenomena of study. As Elger, a writer clearly influenced by Silverman's action frame of reference puts it:

> Such an alteration in the status to be accorded organizational goals and associated administrative designs stresses that the linkage of organizational arrangements to sponsor's goals is an accomplishment conditioned by the resources and tactics of the organizational élite in relation to bargaining with and controlling lower participants. Thus the formalized organizational arrangements indicated by job descriptions, organization charts and the like will be influenced by the involvements, perspectives and bargaining power of those members *vis-à-vis* the élite rather than being the simple product of organizational designs sponsored from above, while the avowed goals of the organization may themselves be restated as a consequence of bargaining with organizational members (Elger, 1975, pp. 97–8).

The above, and its development in the following chapter, represents a fundamental and irretrievable critique of those theories of the formal structure of organization which have been so

296

influential in organization theory (see Chapter 6). The same perspective on formal properties of organizations has led some writers to regard technology as a neutral variable and as *the* determining characteristic of organization structure. Drawing on the realization that technology cannot be considered to be a neutral variable independent of the development of organization structure, we shall develop a perspective on organizations and their theory, which stresses that these are historically locatable *practices* of production and re-production focused on the control of the labour process. By locating the theoretical object of an analysis of organizations in these terms we remain consistent with the empirical object posited by the action of *organizing*. As Eldridge and Crombie (1974, p. 22) note, the OED defines the verb 'to organize' as 'to form into an organic whole', 'to give orderly structure to; frame and put into working order, make arrangements for or get up; undertaking involving co-operation'. We shall develop our analysis of these practices in the remaining chapters.

8 Goals in organizations

The goal concept occupies an ambiguous position in organization analysis, in that it is both a central point of analysis and an ill-defined concept. For example, Gross (1969, p. 277) suggests that, 'The central concept in the study of organizations is that of the organizational goal. One might even claim that the notion of a goal is coincidental with that of an organization.' On the other hand, Georgiou (1973, p. 291) comments that 'organization theorists have faced many difficulties in conceptualizing organizational goals and understanding organizational behaviour through them'.

The difficulties attendant on the concept have been listed by Hall as:

> First, all organizations have multiple and usually conflicting goals; second, the multiplicity and conflict among goals, plus other constraints, prevent any organization from being fully effective; third, organizations that are effective for one set of constituents may be ineffective or dangerous for another (Hall, 1977, p. 67).

The idea that organizations have goals that are pursued by members is as old as the analysis of organization itself. The complex organization as it evolved in the nineteenth century and the early part of this century was clearly one that implied a set of distinctive features that demarcated it as a body of associational rather than communal relationships (McIver, 1936). Rather than individuals meeting together and engaging in shared activities on the basis of friendship, kin or community, the complex organization suggests the coming together of persons and non-human resources in such a combination that their activities constitute the rational pursuit of a goal or set of goals. The 'coming together in combination' is therefore a means of achieving such a goal or goals.

Early writings on organizations repeatedly make this point in that, it is argued, organizations need to be seen and analysed as devices for achieving or attaining goals. Weber (1947) and Michels (1949), for example, refer to the rationality that exists in and surrounds organizations: such rationality can, in part, be accounted for by the existence of organization goals and the attempts by organization members to achieve these goals. The formal theorists of administration such as Taylor and Fayol also exhibit a tendency to stress the existence and rational pursuit of organization goals. Indeed, summarizing the position of such writers, Georgiou (1973, p. 292) asks: 'How could the structure of rules be elaborated, the patterns of power determined, the labour divided, the rules devised, if there did not exist a preconceived goal, calling the organization into existence and determining its structure and operations?' As Thompson suggests, from the very beginning the organization was

an instrument, a deliberate and rational means for attaining known goals. In some versions the goals are explicitly stated: in others, the goals are assumed to be self-evident as, for example, the assumption that the goal of the private business firm is to maximize profits (Thompson, 1967, p. 397).

The mere fact of goal recognition by organization analysts, useful though the observation is, is inadequate from the viewpoint of further sociological analysis. Considerable empirical analysis has arisen from the early statements and observations but has been inadequate for a number of reasons. The over-riding one has been the apparent inability of organization theorists to agree upon the definition of goal. Merely because it is accepted that every organization has a goal or set of goals, it has often become a taken-for-granted assumption. Yet the determination of an organization's goal(s) is an empirical matter and not one to be based upon *a priori* assumptions.

Goals and definitions of organizations

We can refer to Gouldner's (1959a) argument concerning the rational and natural systems approach to organizations. With regard to goal analysis, the early statements clearly suggest that goals are the rational outcome of organization practice, that they are themselves rational phenomena, and that they contribute to the overall rationality that characterizes the modern organization. The rationality of what Georgiou (1973) refers to as the 'classical goal paradigm' was shown to have flaws through empirical investigation. The important flaws were: first, goals were often shown to be vague and/or conflicting; second, the means of goal attainment were not normally stated; and third, the relationship between the goals and organization behaviour was not fully explicated.

The alternative paradigm perceived by Gouldner in 1959 was the 'natural system' model. In this view, as we have seen in Chapter 5, the organization certainly was oriented towards goal attainment, but there was also a recognition that the needs of the organization (especially the need for survival) could be as compelling a driving force as a formal objective. Gouldner cited Parsons and Selznick as the foremost contributors to this natural system approach. These can be briefly examined from the point of view of goal analysis, but with the qualification that 'the natural system and rational models are not conflicting schemes, but stages in the evolution of the goal paradigm' (Georgiou, 1973, p. 293).

In each of his major works Selznick (1948; 1949; 1957) suggested that the goal approach to organizations was lacking in a number of important respects. The non-rational spontaneous phenomena and actions in organizations that were largely overlooked in the classical tradition but which came to be recognized as important in organization functioning meant that no organization could be planned exclusively in such a way as to cover each and every contingency.

> Plans and programs reflect the freedom of technical or ideal choice, but organized action cannot escape involvement, a commitment to personnel, or institutions, or procedures which qualifies the initial plan (Selznick, 1948, p. 32).

The recognition of the informal patterns by Selznick (and others) is clearly important because of the distinction between the organization as a formal, rational and at times clinical structure and the organization as a structure that has responded to the needs and desires of the individuals that comprise it. In Selznick's later writings, as Wolin (1960, p. 412) has observed, 'the word "organization" is reserved for what is a "technical instrument" useful in directing human energies towards a fixed goal; it is a tool, rationally designed for specific technical ends, and, like any tool, expendable'. This tool (a usage which Perrow (1972) was subsequently to elaborate) may never master all 'the non-rational dimensions' of that behaviour which falls in its compass, because 'no abstract plan or pattern can – or may, if it is to be useful – exhaustively describe an empirical reality' (Selznick, 1948, pp. 25–6). This is only to be expected; for, although the organization attempts to be rational, it also has to exist as a natural, living, peopled community (Selznick, 1948). It is precisely this factor which leads to goal-uncertainty, or rather the problem of autonomous élites maintaining *their* social values. Posing it this way, as he does, it is not surprising that Gouldner levelled the charge of a 'conservative and anti-liberal metaphysical pathos' at Selznick (Gouldner, 1955). Georgiou (1973) is somewhat more circumspect. While Gouldner (1955) regards Selznick's work as a forerunner of the natural systems model, Georgiou (1973, p. 294) argues that it is 'a restatement and re-affirmation of faith in the [goal] paradigm'. It is also, of course, a restatement and re-affirmation of, as Wolin (1960, p. 414) puts it, 'the belief that the world created by organizational bureaucracies is and should be run by élites'. Is this, perhaps, a more accurate perception of what Georgiou (1973) was to call the 'goal paradigm'?

In terms of Parsons' work the same question arises as to how committed he was to developing the natural systems approach distinguished by Gouldner. While it is true that Parsons is normally seen as the most distinguished of the sociological systems writers, it is perhaps curious that he defines organizations in the way he does: 'As a formal analytical point of reference, primacy of orientation to the attainment of a specific goal is used as the defining characteristic of an organization which distinguishes it from other types of social system' (Parsons, 1956, p. 64). Georgiou (1973, p. 294) argues that this statement 'shows his [Parsons'] fundamental accord with the goal paradigm'. This is true; but Parsons, unlike his predecessors of the classical approach, does attempt to analyse goals in relation to systems concepts. Although there are difficulties of the kind that Mohr (1973) points to in Parsons' approach (for example, the difficulties of operationalism and non-specificity and the confusion between social function and organizational purpose), it is nevertheless a systems approach in that organizations are sub-systems of a larger whole and the goals of the organization (if accomplished) become a form of input to the larger system. In addition, goals are ranged in a hierarchy, from the central value system downwards.

There are more substantive critiques of Parsons' work. Any organization has a number of outputs, and it becomes a matter of judgment to decide which outputs are to be regarded as the goals of the organization. Furthermore, in the relationship between organizations and the wider social system organization goals will often be set outside the organization itself. The acceptability of the goals to those outside the organization will itself place limits on the nature of the goals the organization élite will adopt.

The kinds of difficulty that have been suggested above were highlighted in Etzioni's (1960) paper on 'Two Approaches to Organizational Analysis'. Whereas Gouldner made the distinction between two approaches to the study of organizations and recommended that there should be an attempt to synthesize previous work, Etzioni attempted such a synthesis. The 'two approaches' are

301

what Etzioni calls the goal model and the system model, both used in the literature for the purpose of measuring organizational effectiveness.

The goal model

A great deal of the organizations literature has been concerned with defining the goals of an organization, measuring the extent to which the goals have been achieved, and thereby attaining a measure of the overall effectiveness of the organization. The prescriptive bias of this literature is evident. In essence this is what Etzioni refers to as the goal model. This is different from Gouldner's concept of the rational model in that 'the rational model is concerned almost solely with means activities, while the goal model focuses attention on goal activities' (Etzioni, 1960, p. 261). Part of the difficulty with the goal model is that too much is expected from it. The realist will recognize that stated objectives will never be achieved to the extent that the organizational élite or dominant coalition might hope them to be. Furthermore, it is a common enough observation that organizations often appear to be pursuing different goals from those they claim to be pursuing. Perhaps both of these points have greater relevance for non-production organizations where the 'output' is less tangible than for production organizations. Whilst schools and universities, prisons and hospitals or trade unions and political parties may have a specific articulated goal, the extent to which the output of the organizations can be measured is problematic. Such organizations often have qualitative objectives that are not amenable to quantitative judgment.

Organizations can be viewed as social systems in that they involve individuals and social groups in interaction. Hence, the natural systems model. Goals, on the other hand, are cultural phenomena in that they are normative and represent meanings, and might thus be more adequately studied through an action frame of reference. Etzioni suggests that generally cultural systems are more consistent than social systems. This distinction can be accounted for from two points of view:

> First of all, cultural images, to be realized, require investment of means. Since the means needed are always larger than the means available, social units are always less perfect than their cultural expectations. . . . The second reason . . . is that all social units are multi-functional units. Therefore, while devoting part of their means directly to goal activities, social units have to devote another part to other functions, such as the creation or recruitment of further means to the goal and the maintenance of

units performing goal activities and service activities (Etzioni, 1960, pp. 258–9).

One consequence of disappointed goal expectations may be to explain them in terms of the limitations of man. However, it may be a definitional problem above all else. In his explanation, Etzioni uses the metaphor of an electric light which functions at a low efficiency, in order to illustrate the point about organizations. A great deal of electrical energy may be converted into heat rather than light, making the light bulb relatively ineffective in terms of its *raison d'être*. Few individuals are overtly concerned about this; instead one tends to make a comparison between different light bulbs, thereby discovering the most effective. Effectiveness, therefore, appears to be a matter of relative rather than absolute standards. Returning to organizations, it is possible to determine whether one is more effective than another, even though neither attains high effectiveness as defined by its goals. Indeed, Etzioni makes the important point that *often the goals of an organization are not intended to be achieved.* He concludes by suggesting an alternative systems approach but sadly fails to state how this approach can lead to the different definition of organization goals.

> The goal model approach is not the only means of evaluating organizational success. Rather than comparing existing organizations to ideals of what they might be, we may assess their performances relative to one another. We would not say that practically all organizations are oligarchic; we would rather try to determine which ones are more oligarchic than others. The comparative analysis of organizations suggests an alternative approach which we refer to as the *system model* (Etzioni, 1964, p. 17).

The system model

As we have seen, the single criterion for the measurement of effectiveness with the goal model is the extent of goal attainment. The system model starts from a different premise in that the goal of the organization is not the important thing: instead, a 'working model of a social unit which is capable of achieving a goal' (Etzioni, 1960, p. 261) comprises the starting point for the analysis. From this position the extent of goal attainment of the goal model is supplanted by one of two criteria. First, that there is a 'system survival model' in that there is an allocation of resources that are either 'optimal' or 'balanced'. Second, that there is a 'system effectiveness model' by which Etzioni means 'a pattern of interrelations among the elements of the system which would make it most effective in the

303

service of a given goal' (Etzioni, 1964, p. 19).

While these suggestions sound helpful and certainly divert attention away from the over-simplified goal model of assessing effectiveness, problems still remain. With the system survival model we are not told how the optimal or balanced allocation of resources is to be achieved. Perhaps the only indication is Etzioni's statement that 'the system model requires that the analyst determine what he considers a highly effective allocation of means' (Etzioni, 1960, p. 270). But this is surely dubious. In the case of the system effectiveness model it would appear that goal attainment is still the criterion to be used. This is not a case of Etzioni contradicting his own critique because of the different concept of goal that he employs. 'An organizational goal is a desired state of affairs which the organization attempts to realize. The organizational goal is that future state of affairs which the organization as a collectivity is trying to bring about' (Etzioni, 1964, p. 6). In other words, the official objective that might perhaps be included as part of the charter of the organization is overcome; in its place is a conception of goals that arises through empirical investigation. In this sense it is possible for goal attainment to be used as the criterion for assessing effectiveness.

The chief merit, then, of Etzioni's scheme is the focus on 'real goals' and the abandoning of the 'stated goals'. Georgiou (1973, p. 295) suggests that this still enables Etzioni to focus on goals, but in such a way that he 'assimilated the system model into the goal paradigm'. Etzioni recognizes that the real goals are the result of *negotiation* and *conflict* between individuals and groups at different organizational levels; the outcome of *process* rather than formal *function*. There are, however, still difficulties with this approach. As Georgiou remarks:

> Either nothing can be said about how changes affect the ability of the organization to serve its goals as compared to an earlier state because the organization now pursues new goals, or the real goals identified by the researcher at a particular point in time become sacrosanct. A real goal, reflecting the operation of the organization at point X is transformed into the timeless, legitimate organizational goal (Georgiou, 1973, p. 296).

In addition to this, there is the general problem of the extent to which the concept of 'real goal' can be operationalized. There is a notable absence in Etzioni's work (and that of his followers) of guidelines to determine just exactly what are the real goals of an organization.

We have already seen that there is an implicit tendency in Etzioni's work to retreat to earlier thought on the goal problem, in spite of the attempt at providing the kind of synthesis that Gouldner (1959a) called for. This is evident when Etzioni (1964, pp. 78–9) states that:

> The organizational goal of private business is to make profits. The major means are production and exchange. . . . When a professional orientation dominates, this tends to 'displace' the profit goal of privately owned economic organizations (Etzioni, 1964, p. 78–9).

This statement would suggest that Etzioni is relying partly on the idea of self-evident goals. It is not always empirically the case that the 'organizational goal of private business is to make profits'. Many overseas branches of international enterprises wish to do precisely the opposite. A book loss, incurred through a policy of expensive transfer pricing of intra-corporate commodities and resources, may be the unstated, implicit, and covert goal of head office. A great deal depends on the definition of what exactly are the boundaries of the organization. In addition, as Fenlon (1978) has argued, the concept of 'profit' is not at all self-evident. Nor is it clear that the 'professional orientation' is anything other than a part of the rhetoric of professionals, including social scientists. Certainly, experience of professionally oriented, privately organized health care facilities would seem to suggest the latter.

The later work of Yuchtman and Seashore (1967) builds upon that of Etzioni and is firmly couched in a system mould. Instead of the system survival and system effectiveness models employed by Etzioni, these authors used what they call a 'system resource' model. As we have seen, Etzioni distinguished the important criterion of the optimum allocation of resources. Yuchtman and Seashore make this criterion more sophisticated by introducing the ability of the organization to acquire resources. Their emphasis is upon organization effectiveness and they see this 'in terms of its [the organization's] bargaining position, as reflected in the ability of the organization . . . to exploit its environment in the acquisition of scarce and valued resources' (Yuchtman and Seashore, 1967, p. 898). This sounds a useful development, except that, as the author points out,

> a crucial problem in this context is the determination of the relevant and critical resources to be used as a basis for absolute or comparative assessment of organizational effectiveness (Yuchtman and Seashore, 1967, p. 901).

This problem highlights the arbitrary nature of how resources are to be determined and, more importantly, shows that the concept of organization goal is still important if resource acquisition is to be a

305

measure of effectiveness. For example, there are instances where the goal of the organization is the acquisition of resources. Where, as in the majority of cases, this is not the primary organization goal, then the goals of the organization still have to be distinguished in order that resources can be established to be important in goal attainment. To a large extent, therefore, the concept of goal needs to be maintained, as Etzioni suggests.

Goals and decision-making

We have seen from the work of Etzioni and Yuchtman and Seashore that there are deficiencies in the goal concept which these authors have attempted to overcome. A further attempt has been made by Herbert Simon both individually (Simon, 1964) and with his associates (March and Simon, 1958; Cyert and March, 1963). An opposition to any monolithic approach to organizational goals has been the main contention in this work. Basically, as Mohr (1973, p. 472) points out, 'no goal is *the* goal' – that in order to understand why people do the things they do in organizations, one must take into consideration a whole host of goals *per se*. As Simon argues:

> In the decision-making situations of real life, a course of action, to be acceptable, must satisfy a whole set of requirements, or constraints. Sometimes one of these requirements is singled out and referred to as the goal of the action. But the choice of one of the constraints, from many, is to a large extent arbitrary. For many purposes it is more meaningful to refer to the whole set of requirements as the (complex) goal of the action. This conclusion applies both to individual and organizational decision-making (Simon, 1964, p. 7).

Simon is perhaps best known amongst organization theorists for his work on decision-making (cf. Dunkerley, 1972, ch. 3), yet it is interesting to see the way in which this particular focus relates to goal analysis. As he points out:

> When we are interested in the internal structure of an organization . . . either we must explain organizational behaviour in terms of the goals of the individual members of the organization, or we must postulate the existence of one or more organizational goals, over and above the goals of the individuals (Simon, 1964, p. 2).

Clearly in the process of decision-making there are certain goals that can be seen as inputs. Equally, one has to understand why some goals are selected rather than others. The reference to goals would appear to be oriented to the individual. Where Simon specifically makes reference to the goals of the organization he is careful to point out that such goals are the products of members' interactions. This then enables Simon, as we have seen, to view goals as approximating constraints on the process of decision-making. Hall suggests that Simon's approach has utility, in as much as analysis is broadened. Not only decision-making, but all organizational actions are conceived as being constrained by goals. 'Probably in the great majority of cases, goals are one, if not the only, relevant constraint' (Hall, 1977, p. 7).

In spite of this utility and the adoption by Hall of Simon's approach, the scheme is not without drawbacks. We have already seen that one of the major problems with the goal model of organization is the basic one of defining what are the goals of the organization. In Simon's scheme the problem is similar in that the constraints have to be defined. Organizations are beset by a multitude of constraints and the problem becomes one of delineating those that are relevant to goal analysis. Even where Simon attempts to clarify the situation by stating that 'the goals and constraints are appropriate to the role' (Simon, 1964, p. 13) the definitional confusion still remains.

Simon's clarification is ingenious and complex. It is grounded in his approach to organizations as structures of individual decision-making. He argues from the assumption that people usually define and judge actions not by reference to a single overarching organizational goal, but by appealing to a particular set of requirements or constraints. It is useful, he suggests, to view the constraints which are experienced by the organization decision-maker as the goal(s) of the organization. These constraints should not be interpreted as personal. They must be conceived as impersonal attributes of organization roles. If we can establish the hierarchical series of role-requirements that govern the behaviour of people in organizations, Simon suggests that then we can speak of the organization goal. However, as he recognizes, the distinction between personal and organization goals is not an easy one to maintain empirically. This is because it assumes considerable uniformity in role-conceptions among the members of an organization in any given position, such that one can expect relatively little individual deviation from the normatively given role. Although this may occur, and much of the development of formal theories of organization as they have been applied in practice has been to ensure this conformity (the increasing division of labour into de-skilled minute manual task elements), we know that the members of a given social position often have diverse conceptions of the 'proper' roles (Gross *et al.*, 1958; Reissman, 1949; Bendix, 1956). Members of organizations do not stand in a

307

one-to-one relationship with structurally-given normative expectations. Role may be defined by structural-functionalists as the structurally given demands associated with a particular position, and as such, outside the individual's meaning-constitution, but it may also be, and has been defined by symbolic interactionists (after Mead, 1934), as the member's *orientation* or *conception* of the part he or she should play in the organization.

This latter concept then gives rise to a huge literature on 'role conflicts', 'role ambiguities' and 'role stress', which are seen to occur as a result of either the incalcitrance of members or the inadequacies of role-definition in organizations (see Hickson, 1966; Clegg, 1970). A much studied aspect of this individually experienced but structurally given incapacity to produce organizational goals and individual roles in a consensual hierarchy, as Simon (1964) suggests, is the problem of *The Foreman* (Dunkerley, 1975).

One is not always able to agree with Simon when he writes that:

> Roles in organizations . . . tend to be highly elaborated, relatively stable, and defined to a considerable extent in explicit and even written terms. Not only is the role defined for the individual who occupies it but it is known in considerable detail to others in the organization who have occasion to deal with him (Simon, 1964, p. 4).

Nor would one wish to agree. This is not because one necessarily wishes to follow Silverman (1970) in placing an 'excessive stress on actor orientations, or on subjective definitions of a situation' (Rose, 1975, p. 243) as phenomenology and symbolic interactionism so often do. As Rose goes on to argue, this stress

> may suppress consideration of the underlying objective properties of the situation in which action occurs. Occasionally, some such stress may be a useful antidote to explanations which exaggerate the influence of objective features of the work situation. . . . Nonetheless, such factors do operate, if only as constraints upon possible actions . . . actors are not sovereign in defining and acting in accordance with their definitions of the situation; and subjectively rational action may be objectively irrational. . . . Misplaced sympathy for subjects may result in a sentimental exaggeration of their freedom and rationality, and indirectly assist their continued suppression (Rose, 1975, pp. 243–4),

One's opposition to Simon's rational stress on roles and goals may instead be founded on an unwillingness to support or promote further an organization theory designed in the interests of those who run and control organizations. The overt stress on goals and

308

roles as existing in a consensual hierarchy oriented towards the organization's 'effectiveness' is not only a reification in theory, but may also exist as such in practice. This does not negate the critique of reification. From our perspective, which would prefer to stress *hegemony* and *control*, rather than roles and goals, it would simply be testament to the practical efficacy of reifications aided and abetted by organization theory. We shall return to this later in the chapter, as well as elsewhere in the book.

Given the theoretical difficulties involved in maintaining the distinction between 'role-goals' and 'organization goals', and the practical problems of control (see Brown, 1977) that organizations have experienced in attempting technically to achieve this consensus, it may be better to drop such distinctions, as Simon (1964) recommends.

Charles Perrow and operative goals

Perrow's analysis of goals in organizations starts from a similar position to that of earlier writers already discussed. His initial concern is with the 'over-rationalistic' view of goals that Gouldner (1959a) pointed to. The problem with such a view is the assumed nature of the goals and the fact that such defined goals have little or no effect on the activities of personnel within the organization. Thus, the rational model suggests rational and logical goals within the managerial stratum of an organization, whereas 'the worker is seen as governed by non-rationalistic, traditionalistic orientations' (Perrow, 1961, p. 854). In effect, this means that organization goals are abstractions in that they have little relation to the activities of the organization member. For this reason, coupled with Perrow's desire to keep goals as a major feature of organization analysis, the concept of the 'operative' goal is introduced, which he contrasts with the 'official' goal(s) of the organization.

The official goals of an organization are 'the general purposes of the organization as put forth in the charter, annual reports, public statements by key executives and other authoritative pronouncements'. The operative goals 'designate the ends sought through the actual operating policies of the organization; they tell us what the organization actually is trying to do, regardless of what the official goals say are the aims' (Perrow, 1961, p. 855). Furthermore, the operative goals are shaped by

the dominant group, reflecting the imperatives of the particular task that is most critical (to the organization), their own background characteristics (distinctive perspectives based on their training, career lines, and areas of competence) and the unofficial

309

uses to which they put the organization for their own ends (Perrow, 1961, pp. 856–7).

Compared with earlier analyses Perrow's scheme is much more realistic, especially from the point of view of the operative goals referring to the ends of a particular organization group (instead of an abstracted set of organization goals). Equally, the distinction between the two types of goal enables one to see the way in which the organization can be used by groups within it to attain particular goals relevant to them. Indeed, the scheme also enables the process of goal formation to be analysed. Unlike the so-called rational model, the impact of goals upon organization activities and members' behaviour can also be examined through Perrow's distinction. The main drawback to the scheme, which Georgiou (1973, p. 297) also notes, is that there is an assumption that the goals of *any* group can determine the course an organization is likely to take, whereas the goals of powerful groups tend to prevail.

At an heuristic level the distinction between official and operative goals is an important one, if only because of the departure from the high level of abstraction often found in previous goal analyses. The distinction is grounded in actual examples. Perrow re-examines Blau's study of employment agencies (Blau, 1955) as a concrete example of the distinction between the two types of goal, and writes:

> Where operative goals provide the specific content of official goals, they reflect choices among competing values. They may be justified on the basis of an official goal, even though they may subvert another official goal. In one sense they are means to official goals, but since the latter are vague or of high abstraction, the 'means' become ends in themselves when the organization is the object of analysis. For example, when profit making is the announced goal, operative goals will specify whether quality or quantity is to be emphasized, whether profits are to be short run and risky or long run and stable, and will indicate the relative priority of diverse and somewhat conflicting ends of customer service, employee morale, competitive pricing, diversification of liquidity. Decisions on all these factors influence the nature of the organization and distinguish it from another with an identical official goal (Perrow, 1961, pp. 853–6).

From this it follows that an organization may be assessed for effectiveness through the analysis of the operative goals. It does not necessarily follow that operative and official goals are always different phenomena, but, in general, there is little relation between the imposed official goals and the emergent, and at times

310

fluid, operative goals. As Perrow (1961, p. 856) notes, 'unofficial operative goals . . . are tied more directly to group interests, and while they may support, be irrelevant to, or subvert official goals, they bear no necessary connection with them'. In this sense, it is possible to talk of the evolution of operative goals. This evolution arises through interaction within the organization; but, once evolved, the goals tend to have greater longevity than the inter-action patterns from which they evolved. The operative goals are, to a greater or lesser extent, a reflection of the official goals – the extent of the reflection being dependent upon the kinds of change produced by individuals in interaction within the organization combined with external pressures towards modification. Thus, as Hall (1977, p. 73) succinctly puts it, 'it is the combination of official goals with internal and external factors that leads to an existing set of operative goals'.

Not all groups within the organization are equally successful at influencing the evolution of operative goals. Perrow links success to task. He argues that any organization has four basic tasks to per-form: capital acquisition; the acquisition of activity legitimation; skills acquisition; and the co-ordination of the organization's activities and members with the external environment. Clearly one or two of these tasks will be dominant at any particular time; it would be rare for them all to be concurrently equally assertive. The group of individuals within the organization that is dominant (through its task being the most dominant) at any time will most probably be the group that, at that time, will be most influential in the definition of the operative organization goals.

A problem with this argument concerns what Perrow means when he argues for the changing and shifting *importance* of organization tasks. It is true to say that one task may be more prominent than another. For example, all the tasks may be carried out sufficiently well within an industrial organization. If the external economic climate shifts so that skilled personnel are difficult to acquire, the task of skills acquisition then becomes more prominent or salient. Those organization members responsible for this task may thereby become more powerful and members asso-ciated with other tasks recognize the need to relinquish some of their power within the organization. This, however, does not add up to the task of skill acquisition being more important than the other three tasks. Each task has *equal importance* but variable prominence. The mere fact that one particular task is perceived to be more salient at any particular time in no way diminishes the importance of the other tasks nor increases the importance of that task.

This criticism is compounded further, since, as suggested above, the dominant group – according to Perrow – will be the most influential in defining the current operative goals. Perrow (1961, p. 856) refers to this dominance as 'a more pervasive, thorough and all-embracing phenomenon than authority or power'. Georgiou argues against this stress on domination:

> Organizations' behaviour cannot be so fully determined by the goals of any one group. These goals are modified, conditioned and limited by the need to satisfy the demands of the other groups upon which the ostensibly dominant group is dependent to achieve its goals, or more accurately, some part of them. (Georgiou, 1973, p. 297).

One of the examples that Perrow gives to illustrate the distinction between official and operative goals is that of hospitals. In his discussion the problem described above is high-lighted. He distinguishes three groups within American hospitals: the trustees, the doctors, and the administrators. None of these groups is able to control in the sense of becoming the dominant group in the hospital. Each group is dependent upon the other groups. For one group to achieve its own operative goals it is necessary for it to use the resources of the other groups. In this way it maintains its domination.

Organization goals as abstractions

The basic property of an organization may be its functional foundation, but are the conceptions of the planners always indicative of the goals of the organization? Organizational policies are not always synonymous with organization goals. Katz and Kahn (1966, p. 259) have pointed out that 'organizational policies are abstractions or generalizations about organizational behaviour'. Policies are essentially manifestations of intent and may remain at that level because the behavioural response is lacking. All too often there is confusion because the goal is spoken of as an aim, purpose or objective, when in fact the aim may never become actualized in organization behaviour, remaining, therefore, at the level of intentionality. Before we can say that an organization has a goal, we must be in a position to give evidence of its operation. The many formulations that do not become operant may only satisfy the organization executive for the sake of official neatness or they may give the public false impressions as to efficiency. These formulations would be rationalizations or ruses rather than organization goals. 'Operancy' is the determinant that makes the difference between intended and real goals.

Etzioni (1964) distinguished between the 'stated' goals and the 'real' goals of an organization. It would seem to be necessary to add another goal distinction: 'intended' goals. There are intended goals that are neither rationalizations nor ruses, which remain at the level of intentionality until they command a response. The intended may not necessarily be stated or executed, but remain implied.

Thompson (1967, pp. 121–8) poses two questions with regard to identifying goals: (i) how can one define the goals within? and (ii) how can one discover the dominant goals? Clearly, from the intentional perspective, the answer to these questions will be dependent on whose intent generates the goal. Cartwright and Zander (1960, p. 349) point to the collectivity that characterizes the group or the organization: 'A group goal specifies a preferred state for the group as an entity and guides collective action towards achieving it.' Lazarsfeld and Menzel (1961) speak of collectivities as having two kinds of characteristics: (i) global characteristics that are factors which are inherent in the collectivity itself but which are not a statistical combination of the traits of the individuals and cannot be added together, such as organizational size; and (ii) analytical characteristics such as aggregated traits whose collective intensity can be assessed to some degree by summing or averaging. An organization goal would therefore be an analytical characteristic. One would approximate the intent level through average intensity, unanimity or majority decision in their terms. Thompson (1967, p. 28) speaks of the 'domain consensus' which connotes a certain unanimity. When we do have a case of consensus this will convey explicit or tacit agreement among members that certain behaviour provisos will be followed under certain circumstances, notwithstanding the possibility that some people might prefer other available alternatives.

One can begin to relate Thompson's (1967) ideas on 'domain consensus' to Perrow's (1961) notions of dominant operative goals, but not through Lazarsfeld and Menzel's (1961) technique of aggregation. This is likely to produce nothing more than an empiricist fiction. A more fruitful way of proceeding might be to assume that the problem involved in ascertaining the fact of some matter, such as what an organization's goals might be intended to be, is one which is concerned with the organization's 'rules of the game'. Such an account would propose that whatever intended goals are routinely imputed to be is a *conventional* arrangement, with no necessity residing in any actual mental processes. To recommend that we should theorize the possibility of 'intention' in this way is not to locate intentions as something possessed prior to an action (i.e., action oriented to achieving a goal), which somehow anticipated and predetermined the action before it was accomplished. Instead it would be to describe the grounds which would analytically be prior

313

for anyone even to invoke intention as a relevant feature of situated activity. This would be a study of conventions for using language in a particular way in a particular place and time. This use may be characterized as being grounded in knowledge of a loosely conceived corpus of 'rules', that people typically use to make sense of routine occurrences. To propose that a goal was intentional is to say that the people involved in its implementation may be defined as actors who orient their actions towards rules which all may be said to partake of in some degree.

The terms in which this discussion of whether or not, and in what ways, intention and goals might be related is influenced by recent writings in philosophy (such as Ryle, 1949; Shibbles, 1967; Melden, 1961 and Hart, 1960). In Hart's phrase, 'intention' would be a 'defeasible' concept assembled in the light of our total knowledge of past, present and future situations. Our sociological knowledge of intention would be constructed by weighing whatever some person or persons might tell us their 'intention' was, against our conventional knowledge of that 'intention' which would produce a specific type of action. Otherwise, we can only rely on our conventional rule-guided criteria for assembling 'intention'. These may vary from the explicit and conceptually rigorous systematization of an elaborated theoretical structure, to the implicit and taken-for-granted conventions of ordinary life.

Organization goals and their outcomes

Etzioni (1964, p. 6) in his definition of goal, combines the notion of intent with the attempt to realize it. We have seen how there has to be some activity that characterizes an organization goal if it is to be 'real'. Naturally, any intent carried out organizationally does not thereby constitute an organization goal. Perrow (1970, p. 134) suggests that we can infer goals from a number of 'empirical traces'. He distinguishes between types or levels of goals, according to whose point of view is being considered, such as that of the customer, the workers, the investors and the executives. The organizational programmes are initiated to satisfy major referents. These referents aid the analyst in distinguishing the major goals.

Earlier, Perrow (1968, p. 306) classified these inferred goals into two groups, according to whether their referent outcomes were internal or external to the organization. Gross (1969, p. 282) proposed a similar duality, suggesting that when we are looking for goals we look for the output in relation to the demands of external referents (output goals), and for supports with reference to the needs and wants of the internal referents in the maintenance system (support goals).

314

Gross emphasizes the activities by which the goals are recognized. Output goals are reflected in some product or service that has an outcome outside of the organization itself. Support goals are concerned with activities that have an outcome within the maintenance system of the organization itself. This twofold distinction therefore parallels that of Perrow. The two types of goal can be separately analysed in this systems framework.

When there is an intended impact of an organization outside its system the outcome is an output. (Tautologically, it must be.) For example, in the case of a food inspection agency, the intent is hygiene in, say, restaurant kitchens but its real goal is inspecting kitchens. The inspection is of primary importance to the maintenance of hygiene, which is the ultimate goal. There may be approximate goals such as making the public aware of the danger of dirty kitchens through certain publications. The question of whether a goal be primary (ultimate) or secondary (proximate) can only be decided empirically through an analysis of the organization's 'rules'. However, the real organizational programme is not synonymous with the particular output programme. The programme is a procedure designed to implement effectively the ultimate goal. The organization goal may be inspecting kitchens, but the actual mode, the labour force involved, and the resources engaged, constitute the practices which link 'intent' and 'activity', so that programmes are means created to execute the goal. Furthermore, the output goal is carried out in a situation that is anything but static. The fact can also be overlooked that participants themselves are subject to change, whether they be the 'formal' executives or the 'informal' decision-makers.

Cyert and March (1963) and Perrow (1968) discuss the situation where multiple goals are pursued all at once or in sequence. Perrow's example of the National Foundation for Infantile Paralysis shows that after the substantial elimination of the disease, the goal changed to sponsoring research into childhood diseases in general. This is what Sills (1957) refers to as goal succession. We can see this again in the case of British prisons. The Home Office Prison Rules (1964) Rule 1 states that prisoners be assisted to lead 'a good and useful life', but the existing rules stress the primacy of custodial programmes, creating conflict as to the requisite service.

Clearly, taking on new functions and following new goals will have repercussions in the internal environment of the organization. Managers who are effective according to one set of goals might very well not cope in a new situation. In the United States the struggle between the goals of those who train for the professions and those who are primarily concerned with the diffusion of knowledge has contributed to an unprecedented turnover of university presidents caught between the orientations of business-minded trustees and legislators on the one hand, the faculty and student intellectuals on the other (Perrow, 1970, p. 139).

March and Simon (1958, p. 83) refer to the support or maintenance goals as 'inducements and contributions' that evoke the participation and support of members. The objective is concerned with the conditions for adequate organizational behaviour, not necessarily for ultimate survival, as is the case for temporary organizations intent on a specific mission geared up to accept subsequent dissolution. Support goals have to do with the state or manner of functioning of the organization as a whole or departmentally in its interdependent parts – but not independently of its goods and services.

Wilavsky (1964, pp. 16–18) considers the nature of the distribution of resources and inducements. These are formally distributed to satisfy the recipients so that they may be maintained in the occupational structure. Maintenance sub-goals are created to lessen the strains of the interdependent parts of the system. These strains are created by comparisons revealing differentials in reward. So it is conceptualized that support goals require maintenance also. For instance, where there is less monetary reward there may be prestige goals, and vice versa; where there is a lack of benefits there may be a power goal and vice versa. Accordingly, the inducements-contributions literature argues that it is the balance of inducements that facilitates performance. But, what is one group's satisfying goal may be another's dissatisfying goal; this is where the sub-goals already mentioned are manipulated to offset disparities in inducements.

This 'inducements-contributions' perspective to organization goals has in fact an underlying commitment to organization membership as invariably problematic. Members lack commitment to organization goals, thus they are in need of reinforcement if organizational order is to persist. March and Simon (1958), and Simon (1957) stress the problem of divergent goals, and formulate that the achievement of these will be facilitated through a series of exchanges. The divergence of individual goals and organization goals is treated as irrational (Cyert and March, 1963, pp. 115–20; March and Simon, 1958, pp. 124–7; Simon, 1957, pp. 110—22). Individual goals, where they diverge from organization goals, can not be accounted for. They have to be taken-for-granted and controlled. Control takes the shape of rationing various resources to ensure compliance with the organizational élite's desires (March and Simon, 1958, chs 4–6). Resources are rationed through exchanges. They concentrate on the conditions under which human and material resources exchange for one another. Essentially, these theorists propose that if an exchange occurs, it must be a balanced, fair exchange, because each person involved in the exchange must have weighed up their inducements and contributions so that they subjectively balance, or are in equilibrium for the induced party. Otherwise, it is postulated, an exchange would not have occurred. This neglects that a seemingly fair exchange, and thus a goal commitment and consensus, may be underlain by a prior structure of relations which make inevitable an exchange based on a set of terms which as a rule favour the interests of one party above that of the other(s). It is in this way that Marx (1973) analyses the relations between labour and capital (see Clegg, 1977, p. 33).

Given this perspective, it is quite consistent that Likert (1961, pp. 71–6), for instance, in a similar vein, can describe 'failed' socialization (that is insufficient control) in terms of the existence of sub-organizational goals. There is no notion of rational, structural sources of opposition being generated in the normal processes of organization. Opposition is not itself structural or part of the organization, but individual and sub-organizational. Perhaps, after Taylor and Walton (1971) or Brown (1977), one might conceptualize sub-organization as subversive, as alternative attempts to reassert control by those disadvantaged by organizations. But, of course, this is admissible by definition: any goals other than those of the collectivity are already defined as 'personal', as Etzioni (1964, p. 6) makes apparent; 'the organizational goal is that future state of affairs which the organization as a collectivity is trying to bring about . . . we must carefully distinguish . . . personal goals from the goals of the collectivity'.

The analytical usefulness of goals

The discussion above has suggested that goal analysis may be analytically useful. We have seen that most activities within organizations can be related to the goals of the organization. This is so in spite of the fact that there might often be a wide discrepancy between the official and the operative goals of an organization. The whole point about organizations is that they, in part, comprise planned and co-ordinated activities. Since these activities do not occur randomly there must be some agreed-upon basis for them. In that sense the concept of goal is central to any organization analysis. It could be objected that at times the ends become transformed into means, as Merton (1940) showed in his goal displacement analysis. As Hall (1977, p. 83) remarks: 'Even when forgotten or ignored, the goal is still the basis for the organization, since the means would not have developed without it in the first place.' To a large extent Hall accepts without challenge the utility of goal analysis. He writes:

> The goal concept . . . is vital in organizational analysis. The dynamics of goal setting and goal change do not alter the fact that goals still guide what happens in an organization. If the concept of goals is not used, organizational behaviour becomes a random occurrence, subject to whatever pressures and forces exist at any point in time. Since organizations have continuity and do accomplish things, the notion that goals are abstractions around which behaviour is organized remains valid (Hall, 1977, pp. 84–5).

In spite of this forceful statement there are both general and substantive criticisms that can be levelled at the goal concept. Taking the former first, there are three general points that can be made.

First, there is a need to reinforce the point that the goals of an organization are notoriously difficult to define. From this point of view the analytical usefulness is obviously restricted.

Second, in spite of relatively recent work on goal analysis there still remains the problem of assuming a static model of organization. As we have already seen, it is a common enough observation to note that organization goals change over time. Thompson and McEwan (1958) show clearly how changes in goals occur due to the impact of 'external' forces. It is therefore unrealistic to consider the finality of goal achievement. The goals of an organization have to be continually revised and redefined, and yet in many respects the goal model is unsuitable for analysing such revisions and redefinitions.

Third, Champion (1975, p. 43) has argued that there is a tendency for goal analysis to stereotype research findings, although he does not elaborate on this point. If a comparison is made between 'ideal' and 'real' goals, there is always an assumption that the organization is under-attaining. This point is made by Etzioni (1960, pp. 257–8), who, as we have seen, suggests the systems model in an attempt to overcome the difficulty.

A substantive critique

In his paper 'The Study of Organizations – objectivity or bias?' (1968) Martin Albrow distinguishes the intellectual orientation of organization theory from the sociology of organizations. The former lays great stress upon the values of the organization and has certain clinical aspirations: the latter is more properly concerned with organizational values. He makes the point that the sociologist, in his or her traditional role, may have little or no interest in improvements in the organizations studied. Since the varying values within an organization are often the object of empirical study – and hence of description and explanation – the sociologist attempts thereby to claim a form of objectivity. This is not the place to discuss how successful the sociologist has been in this pursuit, nor to question Albrow's analytic distinction between organization theory and the sociology of organizations. A fruitful area of discussion and one highly germane to the current analysis arises from the definition of organization within the two perspectives.

We have already seen that an extensive body of literature suggests that organizations are social structures that have been formed in order to attain specific goals. From this, the division of labour, the hierarchy of authority, the rules and procedures, etc., all follow. Sociologically, Albrow argues, such a description of organizations upon which a definition is invariably based (cf. Etzioni (1960); Parsons (1956); Blau and Scott (1963)) is inadequate essentially for four reasons.

First, in many definitions of organizations there is, explicitly or implicitly, stated that there should be a *specific* goal or set of goals. This leads to problems in that different organization members and groups define the organization goals in different ways. For example, in a university, is the organization defined in terms of the specific goal of teaching or research, or for that matter of administration? Of course, the way in which such problems are solved depends upon the particular organization. Within any organization there is always a degree of flexibility in the goal interpretation. The university is an especially good example of this problem, but even in those organizations (such as business concerns) where there might appear to be a certain single-mindedness of purpose the problem still exists. The traditionally conceived conflicts between line and staff personnel in industry illustrate this point.

There is often assumed to be a close relationship between the goal of an organization and the particular form of structure that it adopts. The structure can only be designed effectively if there is a certain precision in the goal definition; that is, if it is specific. The corollary of this is that if the goal is not specific but somewhat vague and grey then the structure (the means to attain the end) will itself be vague. This is the view put forward in the orthodox goal model. In practice, as we know, the structures of organizations are relatively stable. This occurs in spite of the confusion and conflict that often arises over the goal definition. It follows from this that organization goals are not as important a determinant as the classic organizations literature suggests.

Second, it follows from the above that the rules and procedures that frequently characterize organizations do not necessarily reflect the goals of the organization. If organization structure is subject to extra-organizational influences, as the above argument suggests,

319

then likewise the rules and procedures are also subject to them. The rules, therefore, are often seen as impediments to the achievement of the goals.

Nevertheless, there is always a set of rules and procedures that is not subject to external influence in its origin or operation. For many organization members this set of rules and procedures acquires a high priority. The literature on the influence of informal organization shows that such informal patterns within the organization may aid or hinder the work of the organization according to changing circumstances. This, though, is possibly too simple a way of assessing the relationship between formal and informal aspects of organization. Furthermore, Merton (1940) has shown how the rules within complex organizations may serve other functions than the official goals of the organization.

Third, organization structures exist which are relatively stable and subject neither to external forces nor to goal conflict within the organization. In this sense, structure may be viewed as the outcome of the negotiations of different groups within the organization. It does not necessarily follow that structure has to be determined by the goals. At the level of the individual the task may be performed adequately within the organization without any reference to the organization goal (in spite of the fact that the task execution is designed with the goal in mind). The individual may be task-effective for instrumental reasons, for the satisfaction of this terminal activity itself, for the security it offers, etc.

Fourth, it follows from the above that the organization goal does not necessarily represent a common purpose for all those involved in the organization. It is conceivable that at their outset organizations have goals that are held in common by most or all organization members. But the significant changes that occur within organizations over time, affecting not only the goal but also personnel, means activities, technology and so forth, suggest that the original consensually agreed-upon goal may no longer have the mass following it once had. This also highlights the over-emphasis upon consensus with the goal approach. There can be few industrial organizations that were established in, say, the nineteenth century, that displayed a universal internal commitment to their goals. Nor does the current political economy of organizations in the industrial relations context of a state such as the United Kingdom suggest that this commitment has developed over time.

Albrow's (1968) suggestion that organization structure be viewed as the outcome of the negotiations of the different groups within the organization suggests the relevance of what has come to be known as 'negotiated order' theory. In a recent review of this theory, Day and Day (1977, pp. 126–42) have stressed that 'the negotiated order perspective calls into question the more static structural-functional and rational-bureaucratic explanations of complex organizations' (Day and Day, 1977, p. 126). This sounds promising. It is precisely this static structural functionalism, and rationalism, which critics like Albrow (1968) have objected to. In place of this, 'negotiated order' theory (associated with Strauss and Bucher and their colleagues: Strauss et al., 1963; Bucher and Stelling, 1969; and Stelling and Bucher, 1972) 'presents an interactional model involving a processual and emergent analysis of the manner in which the division of labour and work are accomplished in large organizations' (Day and Day, 1977, p. 126). In short, negotiated order theory and structural-functionalism stand to organization goals, as symbolic interactionism and structural-functionalism stand to roles. Negotiated order theory is an outcrop of symbolic interactionism applied to organization analysis, largely in the health field. In turn, these studies had an early catalyst effect in the work of Everett C. Hughes on occupations and professions (Hughes, 1945; 1958; 1971).

The basic issue which negotiated order theory addresses is highly relevant for any analysis of organizational goals. This is the problem of order, of how it is maintained and how it changes. Goals, as potent symbols of order and as means of effecting order through the control that their implementation affords (i.e., management by objectives), are one of the key elements that are subject to negotiation in organizations. Strauss and his colleagues state that:

> Order is something at which members of any society, any organi-
> zation, must work. For the shared agreements, the binding
> contracts – which constitute the grounds for an expectable, non-
> surprising, taken-for-granted, even ruled orderliness – are not
> binding and shared for all time. Contracts, understandings,
> agreements, rules – all have appended to them a temporal clause.
> That clause may or may not be explicitly discussed by the
> contracting parties, and the terminal date of agreement may or
> may not be made specific; but none can be binding forever – even
> if the parties believe it so, unforeseen consequences of acting on
> the agreements would force eventual confrontation (Strauss,
> et al., 1963, p. 148).

As Day and Day (1977, p. 126) have noted, the health field, and particularly hospitals, has been the focus of analysis. A hospital, as Perrow's (1965) earlier analysis highlighted, is characterized by multiple groups and goals, which potentially are conflictful. Ostensibly the multifarious types of staff in a hospital – for example, the medical, administrative, clerical, ancillary, catering, domestic, etc. – are all oriented to one official primary goal: this is the health

321

and well-being of the patient, usually accomplished through some notion of making the patient well, or if not well, at least comfortable. Considered through the sociological lens of negotiated order theory, this primary, official goal may not seem quite so explicitly unproblematic. The different types of occupational identities bring 'different types of training and professional socialization, varying amounts of experience, and different personal backgrounds with them and, significantly, they occupy quite different hierarchical positions in the hospital' (Day and Day, 1977, p. 129). Embodied in different occupational identities, these represent a multitude of occupational ideologies and practices 'regarding how the general tasks of patient care will be conceived, who will perform them, how they will be peformed or, in general, how the total division of labour will be carried out' (Day and Day, 1977, p. 129). Differences occur not only between different occupational categories, but also within them – thus, it is more correct to speak of an 'identity'. Psychiatrists, for instance, may be a common occupational group, but they will collectively exhibit several different ways of being a psychiatrist. These differing occupational identities (e.g., clinician, psychoanalyst, neurologist) will generate 'different conceptions of the etiology and treatment of mental illness' leading to 'situations where ideological persuasion, hierarchical position and other factors determine which groups will work together more frequently and closely, utilizing specific types of services more often than others' (Day and Day, 1977, p. 129).

From these differences there arise differences of policy and goals in the everyday accomplishment of the routines of organizational life. Bucher and Stelling (1969) demonstrate how the different perspectives of the basic science and clinical faculties in medical schools invariably lead to competition for control of resources, including control of the curriculum. Even where consensus is achieved over the official primary goals, such as etiology, treatment and organizational policy, the operative goals, which concern the implementation and assignment of tasks in their achievement, are still subject to negotiation. Thus, as Perrow (1961) recommends, operative goals can be linked to tasks so that even where official goals are the same, operative goals can distinguish what are ostensibly 'the same' type of organization.

As ethno-methodologists such as Zimmerman (1971), as well as interactionists such as Strauss *et al.* (1963) have made clear, there is little chance that formal rules can be used to resolve such conflicts. Rules are generally tacit, implicit and informal, and, where they are not, are invariably cited selectively or can be stretched or 'fudged' by persons pursuing their own vested interests. A study conducted by one of the present authors on a construction site (Clegg, 1975) can illuminate this. (Other useful instances are Navarro (1975) and Alford (1975), as Day and Day (1977) elaborate).

Construction sites are a very good example of the type of organization in which negotiation occurs. They are of relatively brief duration as organizations but have a highly refined temporality, with the structure and process of the site being inextricably linked. They also have a highly explicit official goal, the construction of a structure – be it a bridge, building, motorway or some composite project. This official goal is supported by an elaborated set of operative goals which are detailed in the organization's 'constitutional grounds'. The constitutional grounds of the organization are embodied in the construction site's contractual documents. These actually do *constitute* the organization: what is to be built, and how it is to be built, using what types of materials, over what period and at what cost. These parameters are all legally defined in the contractual documents. Given these parameters, then certain sorts of routine but negotiable activities flow from them in the enactment of the organization. Ideally, according to formal rules and recommendations (such as the Royal Institute of British Architects (RIBA) Handbook), the contractual documents ought to function as an unambiguous order for a structure which the contractor is supposed to deliver. Constructing the structure should be simply a process of obeying the orders given in the documents concerning design, specification, construction and cost for each item of the projected structure. These orders form sub-goals in the accomplishment of the formal, official goals. However, they require 'understanding' to be activated. Without these interpretative, 'glossing practices' (Garfinkel and Sacks, 1970) these orders remain mere sounds, ink marks. These 'glossing practices' are methods that members of 'natural language' communities employ to achieve objective, observable and reportable 'understanding' of a phenomenon. They are the actual implementation, the constitution-in-practice, of operative goals.

Research into construction sites suggests that the implementation of these goals is seldom trouble-free, unproblematic, or in the words of the authors of a major report on the building industry, 'effective'. In 1966 the Building Industry Communications Research Project received the results of research that it had commissioned from the Tavistock Institute into 'communications problems' in the industry. This was published as a digest titled *Interdependence and Uncertainty: A Study of the Building Industry* (Higgin *et al.*, 1966). In the introductory remarks on sampling are to be found the following comments:

In selecting projects for study we concentrated on those which

323

seemed likely to go well. No purpose was seen in criticizing projects which were obviously inefficient.

Throughout, informants have emphasized that what was observed was normal and that the contracts studied were regarded as 'good' by those concerned. Yet none of the projects studied seem to live up to expectations. The experience of the team has been of an industry in which misunderstandings, delays, stoppages, and abortive work result from failures in communications, and impressions of confusion, error, and conflict have provided the starting point for an analysis of the operational characteristics of the building process (Higgin *et al.*, 1966, p. 17).

Clearly, these construction sites would seem to be characterized by a less than clear-cut set of goals, which appears to generate 'failures in communications' and 'impressions of confusion, error and conflict'. The Tavistock researchers argued that the reason for this was a disjuncture between a 'formal' and an 'informal' system of organization, and, we may add, goals. The formal system is characteristically that which we encounter in formal texts about the building process such as the RIBA *Handbook of Architectural Practice and Management*. It stresses the independence and sequential application of tasks such as briefing, designing, design quantification, construction planning and control, manufacturing, sub-contracting, and so on. It is assumed that these tasks have a 'sequential finality' which

does not seem suited effectively to control a process characterized by the interdependence of its operations, fraught with uncertainty and requiring carefully phased decisions and continuous application of all control functions (Higgin *et al.*, 1966, p. 45).

Because of the 'uncertainties' of the building process, together with this 'interdependence', the formal, official organization with its seemingly clear-cut goals as enshrined in the contractual documents has to be modified in practice:

The characteristics of the formal system are so much in conflict with the control functions required to achieve effectiveness in the system of operations that, in practice, the formal system cannot be closely followed. Rigid adherence to the procedures of the formal system would not be possible, under normal conditions without unacceptable expenditure – particularly of time. In practice, reality forces a recognition of interdependence, uncertainty, phased decision-taking, and the continuous application of functions. It forces members of the building team to adapt themselves (Higgin *et al.*, 1966, p. 46).

Higgin and his colleagues then contrasted in an ironic manner what the formal official goals of the organization recommended, with what actually, operatively, happened.

In formal theory, design is complete at an early stage. Not only is information expected to be complete at this time, but it is also considered to be feasible in terms of 'buildability' and cost.

In practice, this is not possible, and even the formal system recognizes this by provisional items in the Bill of Quantities. But there are many other aspects of the design – not covered by provisional items – that are incomplete. This particularly applies to the design of services: the reason for this is related to the sequential manner in which the design process is usually handled. . . .

In practice, many details of services design are worked out on the job, during tours of the work after site meetings, for example. . .

In theory, the quantity surveyor preparing for full competitive tender should quantify the design in full detail. In practice, of course, he seldom, if ever, has sufficient information. He has to extemporize and include what he expects architect and client may want.

Now the formal system requires that, before Bills of Quantities are prepared, full working drawings shall be completed. According to the RIBA handbook, these drawings will embody: 'Final decisions on every matter related to design, specification, construction and cost, and full design of every part and component of the building'. Then, in heavy type, comes the warning 'any future change in location, size, shape, or cost after this time will result in abortive work'. . . . Informal practice . . . follows procedures the reverse of the formal theory. . . .

The contract, in theory, is arrived at as a result of tendering procedures which is considered to be a legally and commercially rational bargain between the client and the builder – generally the builder who can undertake the work most cheaply. This view is based on the assumption that all details of the project have been finally decided and are specified in detail in the tender documents, and that the contractor can anticipate accurately at this time what all his costs will be. This is not so and it is not surprising, therefore, that the builder's pricing and the client's acceptance of any competitive tender must always be acts of faith (Higgin *et al.*, 1966, pp. 47–8).

The idea that the contractual documents are a series of instructions, or formally complete and binding rules for constructing a structure from its detail, cannot be sustained for long

325

after one has observed a site in progress. The observations of the construction site that Clegg (1975) made supported the general impression of the Tavistock researchers. In the terms of ethnomethodology, such contractual documents are inherently *indexical*, in that apart from the use that the members make of them, and the occasions of their use, they remain potent, if unenacted, symbols. As Strauss *et al.* would put it, they exist as 'the ground for negotiation', the constitutional grounds of the organization.

Clegg (1975, pp. 238ff.) differs from the Tavistock researchers in regarding the substitution of informal operative goals for formal official goals *not* as the result of some naturally occuring 'uncertainty', but as a result of the interests and actions of differentially and structurally related members of the construction site. Because there are structural differential, but related, interests among the members of the organization (related through the potent symbols of the constitutive grounds and official goals of the organization contained in the contractual documents), they exploit the inherent indexicality of these documents to their own advantage and interests. It is this interested and creative exploitation which gives rise to what the Tavistock researchers regard as 'communication problems'. They argue that these 'problems' are the result of a collision between two entities, 'uncertainty' and the 'formal organization', in which the former as an independent variable modifies the latter, as a dependent variable. But this is to argue as if they were both something apart from the informal organization with its operative goals which, it is argued, emerges from their impact. What is the status of this 'formal' organization? Higgin *et al.* (1966) argues that it

> is not very directly manifested in actual behaviour and, if our information were based only on the behaviour of the building team on the job, we might never have become aware of the formal system in its true form. It is easily understood, however, from what people say when describing their jobs as distinct from what they do. It is even more readily understood from writings about the building process (Higgin *et al.*, 1966, p. 45).

The 'informal' organization, with its operative goals, is what people do, while in contrast the 'formal' organization is what people do not do! The formal organization comes to nothing, they argue, because of the existence of uncertainty. Their argument is causal and positivist. Uncertainty causes informal organization, because of its impact on formal organization. In contrast to this, Clegg (1975, pp. 129–30) argues that the informal organization is not a result of what uncertainty makes of the formal organization, *but that the actual informal, operative goals and organization is what*

326

members make of uncertainty and formal organization. The latter provides the constitutional (and constitutive) framework within which members *make* uncertainty out of their grasp of the indexical nature of the formal official statements and goals of the construction site organization's contractual documents.

The contractual documents are *always* indexical (see Higgin *et al.,* 1966; Clegg, 1975; and Kreiner, 1976 for documentation of this point) despite the fact that they are purportedly 'objective' (see Clegg, 1975, p. 104). On construction sites this indexicality is routinely used by the members of the organization to interpret the documents in ways which serve their own particular material interests. It is through serving these interests that operative goals function. They thus serve to link official, formal goals with structurally generated, particular interests through an analysis of power. We can elaborate this with reference to a particular instance that Clegg (1975) reports.

The exercise of power means that power must be being exercised over something or someone. Something has to be 'at issue'. On construction sites what is at issue is invariably either 'ambiguity' in the contractual documents which contain the instructions for achieving the official goal of the organization, or conflicting 'ways of seeing' these. The following dialogue (from Clegg, 1975) between Clegg (S.) and the Project Manager (P.W.) of a construction site in Northern Town in England is an instance of this:

P.W. . . . I've got a situation at the moment where the, eh, . . . the two big external ramps he's not quite certain, the architect, whether his drawing is correct or not, whether the two ramps might clash together, would I mind setting it out on the ground, so that he can see.
S. Uhmm.
P.W. All right, I mean, well there's no skin off my nose really, in doing it, but I'm not doing it now, I will do it, if he gives me a V.O. to cover it, and thereby, it means he pays me extra . . . for doing it.
S. Yeah.
P.W. By the same light he's, like all architects he draws in two dimensions, he cannot visualize in three dimensions . . . he would not agree last week at the meeting when I told him that these ramps, geometrically, must be a spiral. Something which is circular on plan, and is rising, like that, must be a spiral. He said, no it's flat, I said, no it's a spiral. So I built a model, to show him that you cannot bend plywood in two directions, and, eh, we're having a meeting this afternoon, him and the consulting engineer. Now, not only am I right, but secondly, the bill of quantities, you

327

get, various items on it, so much, . . . of, . . . a . . . description, soffit shuttering, so much per square metre, ditto circular on plan, at an enhanced rate. Now they've billed the soffit to those ramps as circular on plan. Well it might be circular on plan, but they're inclined, and the standard method of measurement which is a standard book, tells you that that's an extra item, so that they haven't allowed for it in their bill of quantities, which means now that I can submit what I call a star rate, a new rate for doing this work. And anything that's in the bill of quantities bears no relationship to it whatsoever, so as far as he's concerned he's going to be paying about fifteen quid a square metre for that now, uh, I'll have him!

What is interesting about the above is not that it re-affirms the fact that indexicality is a cardinal fact of everyday life, but the use to which this indexicality is put.

P.W. . . . well there's no skin off my nose really, in doing it, but I'm not doing it now, I will do it, if he gives me a V.O. to cover it, and thereby, it means he pays me extra . . . for doing it.

A corollary of 'understanding' seems to be that it will cost money. It is not that the details cannot be understood. They will not be understood, unless 'he gives me a V.O. to cover it'. A V.O. is a 'variation order'; that is, one which varies some element in the contractual documents. But that is not the end of the additional cost to the client. Through making an issue of re-interpreting the drawings the Project Manager is able to

P.W. . . . submit what I call a star rate, a new rate for doing this work. And anything that's in the bill of quantities bears no relationship to it whatsoever, so as far as he's concerned he's going to be paying about fifteen quid a metre for that now, uh, I'll have him!

The 'star rate' will include the 'bit of profit' which is normal, plus some 'extras' such as the 'buggeration factor':

P.W. Yeah, all right then, say I reckon, say allowing for a bit of profit it's going to cost eight quid a metre.
S. Yeah,
P.W. I'll say right, what the hell, I'll put ten quid in,
S. Yeah,
P.W. Plus, that by and large with a thing like that your, what I call, buggeration factor,
S. Hmh, huh, what the, eh, stress, the strain?
P.W. No, that, a you never know I mean, something like that, you get one job, and the radius and such might be such that you

can use three-quarter-inch plywood, cut in strips, 'cos you gotta set each one.

S.   Uhm.

P.W.   This job might be, the radius might be too sharp, and I might find it doesn't work with three-quarters, and so I've got to get some half-inch ply, I've got to use that many more bearers underneath it to stop it deflecting, you know, so you want something in for your buggeration factor.

P.W.'s gloss, as Project Manager, involves an indexical reformulation of the contractual documents in order to serve the interests of Construction Co. This interest is served by the profitable construction of the projected structure. There would appear to be no clash between this interest or operative goal, and the official goal of constructing the structure within the contractually agreed price (and anticipated profit).

In a situation where the scope of operations is limited by a contractually binding agreement, the contract, as a formal document and repository of the official goals, has a profound symbolic value. It stands as a token of the projected structure for its designers. It protects the client against unforeseen cost. But it also limits any subsequent disputes, or negotiations, within the para-meters of that documentation. Once a contract has been signed, all the major variables of cost and quality of materials which are to be used in the construction of the completed project are specified in the contractual documents. This contract becomes legally binding on the parties who are involved in it. It has frequently been observed in empirical studies of construction sites that these contracts often seem to be subject to all manner of problems of interpretation (Higgin *et al.*, 1966), often referred to as 'communication problems'. However, an alternative view of these communication problems might stress the following. In the context of this contractual situation one of the most significant means of achieving either additional profit to that contracted for, or of achieving an anticipated profit in the face of unforeseen exigencies, is to re-negotiate the terms of the contractual documents at any possible opportunity that presents itself.[1] These occasions for re-negotiation do not simply arise from 'communication problems' (although they may be seen as such) occurring because of some exogenous casual factor, such as the prevalence of 'uncertainty', but are specifically constructed as such by the Project Manager as potentially profitable issues. Thus, while the official goals con-tained in the documents formulate an unproblematic, clear, trouble-free and objectively interpretable building process, the operative goals formulate a problematic, opaque, troubled and

329

indexically negotiable building process. These are not only the operative goals of Project Managers in the situation, but of the other structurally identifiable interests such as those of the client, represented by his architect. Thus, Clegg (1975, pp. 135–51) goes on to show how the Project Manager's raising of indexicality on this occasion is grounded in a larger, current process of negotiation over a particularly critical (because potentially costly) issue concerning the interpretation of 'normal clay'. This is initially raised not by the Project Manager but the architect acting for the client organization. For the client organization, issues that may cost money are to be resisted, while issues that risk quality and design are to be raised.

These strategies are not strategies for the control of uncertainty, as organization theory (e.g., Thompson, 1967; Weick, 1969; Silverman, 1970; (Hickson *et al.*, 1971) would usually have it, but are strategies of control *of the organization as an empirical object* usually by fractions of the ruling class within it. (Sometimes workers have attempted to gain control; see Chapter 13.) Hence the conflict between the construction company, in the form of the Project Manager, and the client, in the form of the architect, on the construction site, is for control of the organization's key resource: the contract. The operative goals of the organization relate to power struggles for its control. In this way, one potent strategy may well be to attempt to challenge the official goals which legitimate one's rivals, and institute one's operative goals instead. Thus, there is no necessary correspondence between official and operative goals. Both function as ideologies-in-practice, but not necessarily in harmony.

All goals, official and operative, achieve their meaning within a set of parameters which form the operant rules of the game. To question these is not only to pose unofficial or operative goals, but is to question the legitimated framework within which goals have their meaning. Ordinarily this has happened only when either the existing legitimations appear to have failed or an alternative set of legitimations are used to challenge the normal functioning. Such a challenge would pose *radically inoperative goals* in terms of the normal legitimations. Workers' control movements, in capitalist societies, are an instance of this which we will consider in Chapter 13.

In the analysis so far it has been assumed that one of the chief functions of an organization's goal is to establish the way in which the activities of members of the organization should be structured (notwithstanding Albrow's comments on the relationship between goals and structures). Perhaps, as we have just suggested, goals could be seen differently by describing them as explanations rather than causes of action. This relates to our earlier point about 'conventions'. As explanations of behaviour goals may have the function of legitimating organization actions. We see this in Selznick's study of the Tennessee Valley Authority when he comments that one of the managerial functions was to foster 'a systematic formulation of its [the organization's] meaning and significance' (Selznick, 1949, p. 21). This legitimation is common in organizations: many actions, for example, are legitimated or justified with reference to technology or the need for innovation. In this way decisions in organizations are often presumed to be not only necessary but inevitable as well. The appeal to the goal has a function as a legitimating symbol and as an ideological tool. Elger summarizes much of this more critical perspective on goals when he observes that:

> The terms in which the goal is conceived may diverge considerably for different groups of participants, and the nature of attachment to the recognized purpose varies with the sorts of employment relationships through which participants are implicated in organizational arrangements. Thus the sponsors and controllers of organizations such as business enterprises must actively attempt to order organizational arrangements in ways they deem appropriate to their intended goals – both through the presentation of some version of the goal as having jurisdiction over organizational actions, and through techniques of implementation and control of their preferred organizational designs for goal achievement (Elger, 1975, p. 97).

This legitimatory and ideological purpose can be understood by reference to Albrow's work as previously outlined. He points out (Albrow, 1968, p. 160) that 'the goal-attainment perspective persistently minimizes conflict'. Thus, the organization's goal is designed to produce consensus and co-operation within the organization. Taking Albrow's later analysis, he argues that organizations should be viewed and studied as societies, in that what happens in society as a whole (especially the phenomenon of conflict) is as real and pervasive within organizations themselves.

Taking this theme further, we have argued that if the organizational goal is both legitimatory and ideological, then we need to question whose goal we are referring to. As Silverman suggests:

> To say that an organization has a 'goal' may be to involve oneself in some of the difficulties associated with reification — that is, with the attribution of concrete reality, particularly the power of thought and action, to social constructs. . . . It seems doubtful whether it is legitimate to conceive of an organization as having a goal except where there is an ongoing consensus between the

members of the organization about the purpose of their inter-action (Silverman, 1970, p. 9).

If 'organizations' do not have goals, but the term organization goal is widely used and understood, it means that certain (dominant) groups and individuals within the organization originate, modify and sustain the goal. This is a parallel to what Cicourel (1958) refers to as the distinction between the front and the back of an organization. He further distinguishes organizations' actions that are considered to be legitimate by outsiders and which can therefore be displayed from illegitimate practices that are kept hidden by the organization. There is a parallel here to Perrow's (1961) distinction between official and operative goals.

These official goals are 'a point of reference for actions' of other participants in the organization but not necessarily in terms of the interests of 'sponsors and controllers'. Particularistic, rather than universalistic criteria, 'such as the exercise of particular skills or the protection and extension of individual or collective rights' (Elger, 1975, p. 97) may predominate. At their strongest, such particular-istic criteria may be antagonistic to such an extent that we are dealing with what we have termed *radically inoperative goals*. This may also be true of organizationally external social units who 'will take account of the goal-relevant features of organizational arrangements while initiating bargains about such arrangements informed by their own distinctive interests' (Elger, 1975, p. 97).

Goals are much more problematic than we might have initially conceived. Before analysis of them can occur we first have empirically to discover them. They will not be necessarily consistent with what the controllers of organizations say they are. We must uncover the ethno-methodologically researchable taken-for-granteds concerning goals within which bargaining occurs. Clearly, what is 'given' and 'taken-for-granted' according to one set of participants' interests may be absolutely unacceptable according to another set of participants' interests. Elger (1975, p, 98) argues that this 'underlies the importance of examining the awareness relation-ships existing between the various groups and the ways in which these are sustained and transformed through subterfuge and sur-veillance'. The notion of 'awareness relationships' derives from the same negotiated order perspective (Glaser and Strauss, 1967) that we have discussed earlier (and which has been used in organiza-tional analysis by Wilensky, 1967 and Turner, 1971). By contrasting participants' 'awareness contexts' not only with each other but more importantly with an explicit theoretical conceptualization of the rules of the organizational game, we will have a method for relating participants' frames of reference and awareness to their structural position in organizations. We will propose such a model in Chapter 13, in terms of organizations conceived in their mode of rationality within the context of a specific mode of production.

Clearly the foregoing constitutes a formidable critique of the conventional goal approach to the study of organizations. The critique itself, however, points to an argument for the analysis of goals. In the first place, as symbols, goals serve a necessary function, especially for new or young organizations. The goal statement made by most organizations does provide a focus for the activity pursued within the organization. Indeed, such a statement can provide the legitimation and mandate that a new organization may require. A further point is that it has been suggested that conflict is as normal in organizations as in the rest of society. In that organization members and groups often compete with one another, this competition is frequently in terms of achieving their own operative goals. The justification is often through the higher-order, symbolic, official, organization goal.

Finally, if the criticisms are recognized then organization theorists should take the analysis of goals in organizations seriously. Equally the criticisms – an over-emphasis on consensus, as under-emphasis on the symbolic and legitimating functions of goals; an apparent neglect of changes in goals; and assertion of a casual link between goals and structure (and process); and a lack of historicity – need to be taken seriously as well. An analysis in terms of 'modes of rationality' attempts to address these issues, and will be taken up in our final chapter.

9 Organization and technology

The technology-organization structure link

In previous chapters we have seen a number of empirical attempts to link the concept of technology to that of organization structure. At a common-sense level such a link can be established. Organizations are social constructions whose *raison d'être* is the transformation of raw materials (both non-human and human) into a finished product through planned and co-ordinated activities. These activities, it is often argued, are shaped by the nature of the technology that an organization employs. Furthermore, the activities require not simply co-ordination but also monitoring and controlling. It is this activity that largely determines the nature of the organization structure. Thus, the link between technology and structure is supposedly formed.

The examination of the literature in earlier chapters suggests that the link is often more apparent than real. The conclusions of some of the more important studies can be examined in order to demonstrate this proposition.

The first, and for many years the most important, empirical study to examine the relationship was undertaken by Joan Woodward (1965). Her main concern was to establish the extent to which differences in the pattern of industrial organizations could be related to different principles of management. The initial stages of the investigation explored variables such as the size, complexity, reputation and relative success of the organization. No consistent pattern could be established. It was not until the organizations were classified according to the degree of technical complexity that a consistent pattern was perceived. Three types of what Woodward called production system were distinguished: small-batch and unit; large-batch and mass; and process production. Each of these production systems differed according to the amount of technical complexity. As already seen, the three types were found to be empirically related to certain structural characteristics of the organization, such as the number of levels in the management hierarchy and the ratio of administrative staff to non-administrative.

For many years Woodward's findings were the received wisdom so far as the technology-structure link was concerned. Indeed, replicated studies supported and reinforced the empirical findings (see, for example, Harvey (1968) for such support from his Canadian studies). More recently, as we have seen in Chapter 6, the Aston studies provided some reinforcement of the original findings. The definition of technology differs in the work of Hickson *et al.* from that of Woodward, but 'a residual seven variables have been identified in the tests on manufacturing industry that do have associations with technology' (Hickson, *et al.*, 1969, p. 348). Nevertheless, Pugh and Hickson (1976) suggest that size is a better predictor of organization structure than technology.

Perrow has argued that there are two features of technology that require consideration in relation to the structure of organizations. First is

> the number of exceptional cases encountered in the work, that is the degree to which stimuli are perceived as familiar or un-familiar. . . . The second is the nature of the search process that is undertaken by the individual when exceptions occur. We dis-tinguish two types of search process. The first type involves a search which can be conducted on a logical, analytical basis. . . . The second type of search process occurs when the problem is so vague and poorly conceptualized as to make it virtually unanalys-able. . . . In this case one draws upon the residue of unanalysable experience or intuition (Perrow, 1970, pp. 49–50).

Perrow suggests that these two features of technology are associated with the definition of the raw material of the organization. Thus, he argues that variations in raw materials occur according to their variability or stability. An organization strives for stability with regard to their raw material since this then minimizes activities dealing with the exceptional. If the exceptional can be minimized, then both the technology and structure of the organiza-tion will be affected, such that stability in the raw material enables the organizational roles to be more specified and prescribed. If there is uncertainty surrounding the raw material then tasks have to be more discretionary and allow for the exercise of judgment and initiative.

Perrow's ideas receive support from Hage and Aiken when they propose that:

> The more routine the organization, the more centralized the decision-making about organizational policies, the more likely the presence of a rules manual and job descriptions and the more specified the job (Hage and Aiken, 1970, p. 70).

Thus, not only does there appear to be support for the argument relating structure and technology, but it has also been suggested that if the raw material is constant and can be standardized then tightly structured roles with the minimum of discretion and initiative will be the most efficient. The refinement that Perrow suggests was, in fact, implicit in Woodward's earlier work. As we have suggested, Woodward found on the basis of her research that technology determined certain structural phenomena. This raises the interesting question of what phenomena determine the kind of technology that is to be used by an organization. Perrow would argue that different kinds of technology are considered and employed according to their efficiency with regard to a particular raw material. But Woodward also recognized this when she wrote, '. . . differences in objectives controlled and limited the techniques of production that could be employed' (Woodward, 1970, p. 202).

This body of literature, then, suggests that the technology employed by complex organizations is highly determined by a striving for efficiency. The requirement that an organization should be efficient and effective suggests a certain inexorability about technology in the sense that both 'technology' and 'efficiency' appear to be 'given' and beyond discussion. As Fox writes:

> This conventional view sees the existing design of work and job patterns, along with their profound differences of discretion, autonomy, opportunities for personal growth and fulfilment, and all associated class and status differences . . . as having been 'created' by the scientific, technological and organizational advances of the continuing Industrial Revolution. According to such a view, this technological and organizational thrust, developing in response to what was 'necessary' or 'appropriate' to the 'demands' of the prevailing economic conditions, is in itself neutral. As such, the work designs and job arrangements 'required' by this technology have been simply responses to the unavoidable exigencies of industrialization; responses to the constant search for increasing efficiency and productivity which (it would be pointed out) have benefited us all (Fox, 1976, p. 48).

Fox clearly is sceptical about the validity of linking technology and structure in the cause-and-effect manner that many writers have. Indeed there is a growing body of opinion that shares this scepticism (for a summary of this, see Dennis *et al.*, 1978). Before turning to the arguments against the proposition it is helpful to distinguish two related but analytically distinct features of the argument. In the first place, technology can be taken to mean the actual machinery and processes employed by organizations. The techniques of working derived from the technology are argued to cause the shape of jobs – the actual design of the task. A second meaning of the term refers not only to the machinery but also to the way in which work is organized, the social division of labour, the actual task allocation, and so on. Then, all of these characteristics are related to organization structure in terms of the degree of centralization, standardization and so forth, as seen in Chapter 6. Using the language of the technologists themselves, the first definition embraces the hardware alone whereas the second includes both hardware and software. Other writers have noted the distinction. For example, Fox (1974) differentiates material technology from social technology and Perrow (1972, p. 166) makes the point that technology for him does not mean 'its commonplace sense of machines or sophisticated devices for achieving high efficiency . . . but . . . its generic sense of the study of techniques or tasks'. Having made this distinction we can now turn to a critical examination of the technology-structure relationship.

The empirical evidence certainly suggests a strongly positive relationship between the two phenomena, and whilst it might be difficult to disprove the positive aspect of it the strength of the relationship is disputable. Turning to the work of Robert Blauner, who is often labelled a technological determinist in the same sense as Joan Woodward, we find the following remark:

> The most important single factor that gives an industry a distinctive character is its technology. Technology refers to the complex of physical objects and technical operations (both manual and machine) regularly employed in turning out the goods and services produced by industry (Blauner, 1964, p. 6).

The determination of the type of technology arises from the available scientific and technical knowledge, the resources of the firm in economic and engineering terms, and the kind of end-product of the organization. In terms of the last factor relating to the product, the extent to which it is standardized is crucial. From these considerations Blauner distinguishes craft technology, machine-minding technology, assembly-line technology, and process technology.

The importance of Blauner's work for the present discussion lies in the following quotation:

337

> Whereas technology *sets limits* on the organization of work *it does not fully determine it,* since a number of different organizations of the work process may be possible in the same technological system (Blauner, 1964, p. 9; our emphases).

So, in spite of Blauner suggesting a positive link between technology and structure – a norm of technological rationality – we see for the first time in the literature the suggestion that technology is not such a deterministic feature of organization structure as other writers have indicated, and that technology is possibly more appropriately to be regarded as a limiter rather than a setter of structure. More recent studies by Child (1973c) and Argyris (1972) have made similar points and indeed have taken the argument further by specifically suggesting that the relationship between technology and structure is a correlational one but not causal.

Child makes the point that if organizations are studied merely as formal structural phenomena then there is no place for the analysis of the effects of human intervention. It is not unreasonable to suggest that on occasions the structure of an organization is deliberately chosen rather than being formed in the inevitable inexorable manner suggested by the technological determinists. It is important to stress Child's point that those in powerful positions in organizations may have considerable influence over the way the organization is structured and, indeed, how work tasks are designed, notwithstanding the fact that they operate within certain constraints that are laid down by the technology, by environmental variables and so forth. In an important statement Child points out that

> When incorporating strategic choice in a theory of organization one is recognizing the operation of an essentially political process in which constraints and opportunities are functions of the power exercised by decision-makers in the light of ideological values (Child, 1973a, p. 14).

Argyris's argument is similar to that of Child but derives largely from a critique of the work of Blau and Schoenherr. At one stage of their analysis of organization structure they comment that:

> The systematic study of the formal structure of organizations, . . . reducing living human beings to boxes on organizational charts and then further reducing these charts to quantitative variables, may seem a strange procedure, but it is legitimate inasmuch as concern is with the formal structure in its own right rather than with the people in it (Blau and Schoenherr, 1971, p. 18).

338

Argyris (1972) suggests that Blau and Schoenherr are, in fact only dealing with correlations and not the type of relationships they claim to discover which are presented as immutable laws. Further, he suggests that these correlations may be little more than a reflection of the imposition of decisions made by senior organization members rather than an inevitable technological logic over which the individual is powerless. As Argyris (1972, p. 79) says, 'The formal organization is a cognitive strategy about how the designers intend the role to be played, given the nature of human beings'. Thus, Argyris is in accord with Child in suggesting that there is choice in the determination of organization structure and that the choice may reflect the specific interests of specific powerful organization members.

Clearly there are gross discrepancies in the research findings concerned with the technology-structure association. Davis and Taylor in their review of the literature argue that the discrepancies are predictable for two reasons:

> The first is that the available studies utilize fairly gross, unquantified comparative judgments of degrees of technological sophistication at the organizational level. Such gross categorization of technological sophistication makes comparison difficult and replication impossible. The second possibility . . . involves the considerable resistance to changing psychosocial assumptions operative at the system level. [Management] . . . is likely to resist . . . strongly any attempts at changing organizational form or control structure, since such modifications come (close) to touching the organizational life-space of managers themselves (Davis and Taylor, 1976, p. 410).

A possibly fruitful approach to the technology-structure relationship, at least for the purposes of empirical research, has been suggested by Davies *et al.* (1973). They have argued that the issue has tended to polarize into the 'technological determinists' on the one hand and the 'action frame of reference' writers on the other. Working within the original mould formulated by Joan Woodward, Davies *et al.* (1973, pp. 160–1) have argued for a 'concentration on variables intervening between technology and structure'. Thus, rather than isolating or dismissing technology out of hand they argue that technology may be seen as significant when viewed together with other variables, especially those of control and uncertainty. From a different perspective the general issue of the link between technology and control can now be examined.

Technology and control in organizations

It has already been established that whilst there might be a positive correlation between the type of technology employed by an organization and the type of structure the organization has, the relationship need not necessarily be a causal one. The suggestion has been made that there might be flexibility in the kind of technology employed by an organization, and that rather than determining structure it is more realistic to see technology placing limits upon it. The questions now arise of why a particular technology comes to be chosen and what is the nature of such technologies?

One argument that is gaining increasing strength is that technologies may be chosen for reasons other than those of increasing organizational efficiency, at least in a direct sense. Two recent commentaries illustrate this point.

> Machinery offers to management the opportunity to do by wholly mechanical means that which it has previously attempted to do by organizational and disciplinary means. The fact that many machines may be paced and controlled according to centralized decisions, and that these controls may thus be in the hands of management, removed from the site of production to the office – these technical possibilities are of just as great interest to management as the fact that the machine multiplies the productivity of labour (Braverman, 1974, p. 195).

> Industrial technology not only provides . . . the physical means by which decisions about the nature of his work are imposed on the individual worker, but also as formalized system . . . the means by which a general pattern of social control is maintained (Dickson, 1974, p. 34).

What is being argued by writers such as Braverman and Dickson is that technologies may be used to increase the amount of managerial control, especially that control over the individual's work and the product of his work. Why, and how, is it though, that such a view of technology has only recently been adopted? The most appealing answer lies in the fact that technology has for many years been viewed as a neutral phenomenon, especially politically neutral. As Dickson points out, the accepted view of technology

> disguises the exploitative and alienating role [it] plays within industrialized capitalist societies and leads us to accept a particular mode of technological development as being a unique, inevitable and politically neutral process (Dickson, 1974, p. 38).

The purposes of technology being presented in this apolitical sense are manifold. In the first place it does enable a specific ideology of technology to develop. As Dickson argues, if technology is not

340

politically neutral then there is clearly a great myth surrounding the actual role of technology. And again one of the important functions of any myth is to support and reinforce dominant ideology. The actual operation of such a myth can frequently be observed not only at the wider societal level but also at the organizational level. For example, the current debate about alternative sources of energy only rarely takes into account the wider issues of, say, the development of nuclear energy in terms of the desecration of aboriginal settlements in the search for uranium. At the organizational level the development of micro-processors is widely applauded without concern for the effects upon the nature and design of the industrial tasks that are created by this development and the further issue of possible widespread redundancies in a large number of industries, particularly in the telephone-communications sector. There is, instead, often a common acceptance that any technological development is inherently good and to be welcomed and that trade unions are somehow acting illegitimately and archaically if they oppose technological 'progress'. That such opposition is rationally in their interests is rarely discussed, nor that the introduction of the technology is clearly in the owners' and controllers' interests. Progress of any kind, according to the prevailing ideology, is necessarily worthy of acclaim whether it be 'progress' involving so-called urban renewal and the development of increasingly concentrated shopping centres or 'progress' involving the increasing fragmentation of organizational tasks. Since the link between technology and progress is so closely established, to oppose technology is to oppose progress – it is as outrageous as to suggest that the earth is flat. Technology, therefore, has become institutionalized: its development is seen as inevitable, natural and neutral.

This institutionalization of technology, with the mythology surrounding its role in society, is what Dickson refers to as the 'ideology of industrialization'.

It is this ideology . . . that legitimates the continued pursuit of economic growth . . . it also seeks to explain the functioning of society purely in operational terms . . . it is used to suppress the potentialities for individual and social emancipation offered by particular machines and legitimate their use towards socially-exploitative ends (Dickson, 1974, p. 40).

Dickson argues that the ideology of industrialization operates at all levels within and between societies. At the level of the organization the most obvious example is in terms of the way that the need for increased organizational efficiency is legitimated through the introduction of more fragmented work tasks. The most extreme example

341

of this fragmentation is provided by assembly-line production. In a vividly evocative account Beynon describes the assembly line at Ford's:

> On the assembly line each worker is termed an operator, he works at a particular station. He is surrounded by stacks of components and maybe a man is sub-assembling these for him. His job is to attach his components to the body shells as they come to him. Obviously the faster the line runs, the less time he has on any particular body shell, and consequently the smaller the range of tasks that he is able to do. If the line is running, for example, at thirty cars an hour he is allocated two minutes work on each car that passes him. The allocation of the two minutes work is done on the basis of the times recorded for each operation by the Works Study Department of the Ford Motor Company (Beynon, 1974, p. 135).

From such an account the ideology of industrialization in practice is illustrated. The design of motor-car production is clearly associated with a particular technology that embraces the principles and practices of scientific management described in Chapter 3. The use of technology and automation in this instance has a clearly defined control function. The prevailing ideology confidently assumes that the assembly-line method of production is the best for a particular mode of production. As previously argued, the situation is legitimated through the requirement of greater efficiency in organizations. Part of this legitimation arises through the suggestion that efficiency can be quantified in a value-free 'scientific' manner.

The quest for efficiency is not the sole determinant of the imposition of technology with deleterious effects upon the structure of work tasks, as writers like Beynon (1974) and Nichols and Beynon (1977) have described. A further consideration is the fact that certain technological forms deny to the individual at work any judgment, discretion or decision-making. If a technology can be introduced that makes redundant such creative phenomena in the work of the individual the opportunities for resistance to production methods are thereby eliminated or reduced. Since such resistance would be regarded as a cost to management the objectives of the organization should be more capable of being realized in its absence. This is an important issue for, as Fox has commented,

> The emergence of the factory system owed as much to the drive for closer co-ordination, discipline and control of the labour force as the pressures of technology (Fox, 1974, p. 179).

A similar point is made by Marglin (1974). Centralized decision-making and the development of an extensive division of labour resulted not from the alleged fact of technical efficiency but from the attempts by the owners of capital to create a central role for the manager, a role which de-skilled the worker and thereby increased the opportunities for achieving greater labour power from him. Marglin uses mostly historical evidence for his thesis, especially from the weaving industry at the time of the Industrial Revolution in England. He shows how, in that situation, the introduction of the factory method of production, with the technological change associated with it, was not a measure designed to use the technological developments as they occurred. Marglin suggests that factory production can more appropriately be viewed as an attempt by the cotton and wool merchants to control the activities of their workers. It will be recalled that the 'putting-out' system lacked the control of the factory system. There is evidence that such a process is still being used. For example, Dickson (1974, p. 34) quotes a newspaper advertisement for prefabricated (that is, factory-based) construction methods. The advertisement claimed that traditional construction site methods of production have the problem of 'the labour force [being] difficult to supervise and often unskilled' and that with factory methods of production, 'We've no problems of scattered supervision. So quality's always up to scratch' (*Sunday Times,* London, 18 November 1973).

The basic proposition, then, is that technology has been designed in such a way that the maximum control over labour is achieved and that the maximum production of goods is to some extent secondary to this consideration. The separation of maximum control from maximum production is important especially when related to the earlier proposition that there is a choice of technology in industrial organizations. The argument can be taken further than that proposed by Marglin by pointing out that the most efficient technology (in terms of the maximum production) will be chosen only if it is compatible with securing the maximum control over worker behaviour. The corollary of this is that the attempt to gain greater control may result in a less efficient or productive technological system being employed.

Consider another feature of Marglin's argument, that the new technologies associated with the industrial revolution developed after the factory system was established; that is, after the concentration of labour in factory organizations. The implication of this argument (backed up by empirical evidence from the English weaving industry) is that the factory system of production was not the product of improved, more efficient technology. As Marglin suggests, there were four factors producing pressure here:

1   The physical control afforded by the factory minimized the

level of potential waste through embezzlement.

2   The rate or speed of work could be significantly increased.

3   Technological change could be used for capital accumulation as well as for the most obvious function of immediate use.

4   Production could be organized in such a way that knowledge of the whole process rested with the owner of capital (Marglin, 1974, pp. 62–3).

Gorz goes further than Marglin by suggesting that if the exercise of control preceded the introduction of technology for greater productive efficiency then a very different technology could have developed had maximum control not been the primary objective of the introduction of the factory system. If the case of the non-capitalist countries is examined, present-day China seems closest to producing a system of production based upon maximum involvement and responsibility and the maximization of social production. As Gorz suggests:

> The minimization of skill has been a consistent policy of capitalist management, since it maximized the workers' dependence and manageability and reflected the *social* division of labour in its *technical* division. It is therefore no accident that bourgeois social relations should have re-emerged in all those so-called 'socialist' countries where the capitalist division of labour was used as a standard method (Gorz, 1972, p. 32).

We have already seen the enthusiasm with which Lenin greeted developments in scientific management and the adoption of its methods in the Soviet Union. Lenin believed that the development of technology in its capitalist form would eventually lead to the abolition of the division of labour; the outcome has, however, been a greater and more extensive division of labour both in the Soviet Union and the other East European countries such as Poland and Hungary which have adopted a similar belief in scientific management practices. Langdon Winner's book, *Autonomous Technology,* accounts for these developments in terms of the 'victory of technics over politics', by pointing out that 'technology is a new kind of conduit such that no matter which aims or purposes one decides to put in, a particular kind of product inevitably comes out' (Winner, 1977, p. 278).

Another, and equally important, aspect of the issue of technology and control in oganizations relates to the nature and purpose of organizational hierarchies. Both the division of labour and the hierarchy are basic characteristics of organizations and, indeed, Weber (1948), in describing the ideal-type of bureaucracy, noted the facilitative relationship between the two characteristics.

Hierarchy, like the division of labour, existed in many different guises before the industrial revolution and the development of complex organizations and bureaucracies. Similarly production based upon hierarchical principles was not a new or unique feature of industrialization.

Nevertheless there was a qualitative difference in the nature of hierarchy between pre-capitalist and capitalist modes of production. Marglin (1974, p. 63) has pointed to three such differences. First, that within the pre-capitalist formation the individual at the top of the hierarchy was a producer unlike his capitalist successor. Second, the hierarchy had a linear structure that enabled individuals to work their way through the pre-capitalist structure. The level of mobility through the productive hierarchy under capitalism has always been very limited. Third, the worker, especially in the guild system, sold his or her product directly to the buyer without the need for an intermediary (also see Offe, 1976a). The crucial distinction lies in the selling of his or her product rather than his/her labour, with the consequence that he/she had a greater degree of control over the work process itself as well as the product of his/her labour. Marglin develops his 'divide and conquer' argument concerning hierarchy and the division of labour through an analysis of the Tavistock researchers' work on the British coal-mining industry. Since this provides an excellent example of the impact of technology upon organizational relations it can be duplicated here.

Let us consider Marglin's basic proposition that 'the British coal industry offers an example of an industry in which the capitalist division of labour never took hold' (Marglin, 1974, p. 74). The work of Trist and Bamforth (1951) is well known in the socio-technical systems literature for its demonstration that the traditional 'board (or stall)-and-pillar' or 'hand-got' method of production was highly functional for workers and owners alike. Under this method of production the work group was responsible for the whole cycle of operations. Furthermore the work group had a direct contract with management:

> Though the contract may have been in the name of the hewer, it was regarded as a joint undertaking. Leadership and 'supervision' were internal to the group, which had a quality of *responsible autonomy* (Trist and Bamforth, 1951, p. 6).

There was not the specialization of tasks that one normally associates with the capitalist mode of production. Instead, tasks were of an interchangeable and reciprocal nature.

Eventually during the 1950s the so-called longwall method of coal-getting was introduced. This, *inter alia*, consisted of task specialization coupled with the introduction of new technology.

345

The division of labour was on a three-shift basis from cutting, through ripping to filling. Each twenty-four hours saw the completion of the cycle of operations. The longwall method, as is widely documented, was a failure, not only in economic/managerial terms of increasing productivity but also in social terms for the individual worker and the work group as a whole. According to Trist and Bamforth, the social system change that resulted from the introduction of the longwall method was largely unanticipated as, of course, was the closely related low productivity level under the new scheme. The other problem was related to supervision. Under the traditional method of coal-getting there was self-regulatory supervision; under the longwall method there needed to be supervision of groups that were responsible for only one part of the total production cycle.

In place of the specialized tasks and individual incentive schemes that partly constituted the longwall method of production, Trist and Bamforth developed a more autonomous group structure, but within the more advanced technology. This became known as the 'composite longwall' method and had the following characteristics.

> The work groups were self-selected; the group was responsible for the allocation of work between its members, but operating in terms of the objectives set by management. There was also to be some job rotation.
>
> Instead of individual incentive schemes, payment was made on a team basis.
>
> There was to be the opportunity for extending activities on a particular shift to work which under the original longwall method would have been the responsibility of the succeeding shift. So, the cutting shift might extend its activities to ripping; the ripping shift extending to filling; and the filling to cutting. Thus, as with the board-and-pillar method, a work team took over where the previous shift team had left off, regardless of what stage of the production cycle had been arrived at.

From the point of view of productivity the composite longwall method was enormously successful (20 per cent more coal being produced under this system than with the original longwall method). The large part of this success was seen to be in terms of the re-introduction of the autonomous group functioning. From the point of view of the present discussion the importance of the Trist and Bamforth study is first, that the extensive division of labour was found to be unsuitable and unnecessary with the introduction of a more complex technology; and second, that the hierarchy could be made more simple rather than complex as is usually assumed with more advanced technological innovations. (Trist and Bamforth point to the fact that the role of group regulation made much supervision redundant, and that in at least one case an overman (supervisor) was himself made redundant.)

Very similar results and conclusions have been reported by Rice (1958) as a consequence of his studies and consultancies in Indian textile mills. Later studies of the British coal-mining industry by Trist *et al.* (1963) confirm that composite autonomous work groups are more socially and economically effective, and can arise from or be designed as a consequence of a change in technology. In each case the important point to emerge is that hierarchy and division of labour are not automatically to be assumed to increase as technology advances. In terms of our earlier discussion it is also interesting to note that whilst there may be certain structural changes consequent upon technological change, these need in no way be seen as natural or neutral. As Davis and Taylor (1976, p. 403) comment, 'The group structure . . . must be consciously installed if it is to succeed'.

There is a danger in this discussion of happily reifying an atypical case. Although the above evidence clearly indicates that hierarchy and the division of labour need not be the basis of managerial control, the overwhelming weight of evidence suggests otherwise. Much of this is presented below in our analysis of reliability, but for present purposes we can refer to the work of Goldthorpe *et al.* (1968) to demonstrate the point. The three firms in their study represented rather different levels of technological advance. It is evident from the data that in automated lathe production and in process production the frequency of individual and group interaction was considerably less than in more traditional methods of production with less sophisticated technologies and which involved, in many instances, lower levels of skill. One explanation that is consistent with the developing argument here is that:

If the managers and technical system planners . . . imposed job and organizational structure which flow from the assumption that people (or parts of people) are merely parts of the machine or process, then whatever potential the technology could provide for formation of group activities would be negated (Davis and Taylor, 1976, p. 406).

So, not only a minute division of labour but also hierarchy is used as a means by which technology is imposed in organizations as an attempt to increase control. Power and control are concentrated at the top of an organizational hierarchy; both are fragmented lower in the hierarchy. Most of the evidence suggests that specific techniques of production are introduced in many organizations because of the desire to control through hierarchy. This

347

phenomenon, according to Gorz,

> appears to be a necessity that flows from production technology; but in truth it is built into production technology in so far as the latter is itself a reflection of the social division of labour (Gorz, 1972, p. 34).

The link between technology and control seems established. A major aim of technology in industrial organizations is to gain, maintain and increase control over labour in such organizations. This aim is as important and influential as the normally assumed aim of maximum production. Through the selective choice of technology made possible by the flexibility described earlier, the prevailing modes of production reinforce the existing relations of production. Through what Dickson calls the ideology of industrialization the actual nature of technological control is disguised. Its political role should by now be evident, together with the fact the division of labour and hierarchy of control introduced and reinforced by technological control are in many sense mirror-images of the social relations of production and re-production of antagonistic classes and hierarchical control in society at large.

Technology and trust in organizations

In addition to specific technologies being chosen by managements as a mechanism for increasing their control of members' behaviour, technology, in the way that it is imposed, reflects and imposes in practice the attitudes of managements towards employees. A key component of such attitudes is the extent to which organization members can be trusted; the extent to which they can be relied upon; or how confident managements feel themselves to be about their employees. In this section such ideas will be explored, together with the proposition that perceptions of trust and reliability are not simply organizational perceptions but are wider class-based assumptions made about the working class in general. The basic proposition, then, is that appeals are made to the alleged apolitical neutrality of technology and that technological change or progress may have dysfunctional consequences for the individual. Lying behind such appeals to technology are a set of assumptions concerning lower-level organization members, the working class, which provide one of the main driving-forces in the imposition of new technologies.

Our analysis of trust and reliability has been guided largely by Alan Fox's excellent study *Beyond Contract: Work, Power and Trust Relations* (1974), the first two chapters of which are summarized below. Work roles in organizations can be placed upon a continuum varying from prescribed to discretionary (Jaques, 1967) or from specific to diffuse, although there are two senses in which the terms may be used:

> In the 'task-range' sense, a role limited to one task could be seen as having the quality of specificity, whereas a role embracing a wide range of different tasks has the quality of diffuseness. . . .
> In the 'discretionary-content' sense, the behaviour called for by the role may be either specifically defined, thereby offering little choice, or diffusely defined, thereby requiring the exercise of discretion (Fox, 1974, p. 16).

In our exploration of the propositions made above we are concerned with the second sense that Fox distinguishes. The more diffuse a work role is the more the role incumbent is able to exercise judgment and control his or her own sphere of activities. We have seen from the discussion of scientific management that the degree of prescription in work roles can be almost absolute in the sense that the degree of discretion is minimal. We have also briefly seen the effects that technology has upon the design of work roles. For example, Blauner comments that production technology

> generally reduces the control of the employee over his work process. Workers are rarely able to choose their own methods of work, since these decisions have been incorporated into the machines' very design and functioning. [The assembly line] dictates most movements of the operative and pre-empts many of his potential choices and decisions (Blauner, 1964, p. 170).

Although the tendency is to regard minimum discretion as being associated with manual work (especially unskilled, assembly-line work), there is increasing evidence of the process of discretion-reduction working its way throughout organizational hierarchies. Lockwood (1958) points to the fact that a considerable amount of office work is indistinguishable from manual work in terms of its discretionary component. Also, of course, not all manual work is highly prescribed, as Blauner (1964) demonstrates with his study of printing craftsmen. In general, however, it is realistic to suggest that the discretionary component of work roles increases the further up the organizational/occupational hierarchy one looks. In order to simplify the analysis, following Fox, we can distinguish between low, medium and high discretion roles, each of which follows a particular syndrome.

The low-discretion syndrome is characterized by the individual perceiving his or her self as not being trusted; he or she is subject to close supervision; work tasks and roles are subject to close co-ordination of an imposed and standardized form. If the individual

349

fails to meet performance requirements this is interpreted as neg-
ligence or insubordination on his or her part; any conflicts that arise
are handled through group rather than individual bargaining. In
contrast, the high-discretion syndrome consists of the individual
being perceived as committed to the organization goals; close
supervision is perceived as inadequate; rather than standardized
co-ordination the role is characterized by problem-solving
relations. Inadequate performance is viewed as a personal aberration; and conflict is overcome through problem-solving
techniques or individual persuasion. The medium-discretion
syndrome contains elements of the other two.

There are, of course, a number of other factors that contribute to
the definition of the kind of discretion built into an organizational
role. Not least of these factors is the phenomenon of power.
Although power is explored in depth in Chapter 12, it is worth
noting here that high-discretion roles are invariably powerful roles.
Often the power in such roles goes unnoticed, especially since when
it is exercised it is exercised at an individual level. In the case of
low-discretion roles power is not a part of them, at least individually. In order to exercise power:

> This requires overt collective mobilization and a visible and
> usually well-publicized exercise of pressure upon the manage-
> ment concerned. This is the kind of power relationship which
> fully registers with the public, unlike that arising from high-
> discretion roles, which passes unnoticed (Fox, 1974, p. 61).

The initial link between technology and trust in organizations is a
simple one, once the distinction between different types of discretionary roles is understood. A basic feature of high-discretion
and high-trust roles is that the individual nature is emphasized (in,
say, problem-solving, the making of decisions, etc.); in the case of
low-discretion and low-trust roles, the 'other' is emphasized in
decision-making, problem-solving and the like. The working class
thus tend, in all spheres of life, but particularly at work, to be
decision-takers rather than decision-makers. One sees, therefore,
individualized and generalized roles respectively. The generalized
qualities of conformity and obedience inherent in low-discretion
roles contribute to anonymity. Hobson (1926, p. 349), who is
quoted by Fox, commented that 'all men are equal before the
machine'. This equality, this anonymity, is largely predicated by the
nature of technology, in that the technologically imposed design of
low-discretion jobs makes the individual replaceable by any other
individual. In the case of high-discretion jobs individuals are
capable of placing their own stamp upon the role through their
particular *modus operandi*. As Gouldner (1971, p. 277) points out,

'men are becoming more interchangeable, more replaceable and removable at lower costs' as a result of the fact that a 'technologically advanced civilization reduces and standardizes the skills required for wanted performances: it simplifies and mechanizes many tasks'.

We have already seen how Beynon (1974) has described the assembly-line production at the Ford Motor Company, and can use this as an illustration of the kind of low-discretion role that Fox has outlined. A further example is furnished by Bosquet in his description of a French assembly line:

Try putting 13 little pins in 13 little holes 60 times an hour, eight hours a day. Spot-weld 67 steel pressings an hour, then find yourself one day facing a new assembly-line needing 110 an hour. Fit 100 coils to 100 cars every hour; tighten seven bolts three times a minute. Do your work in noise 'at the safety limit', in a fine mist of oil, solvent and metal dust. Negotiate for the right to have a pee – or relieve yourself furtively behind a big press so that you don't break the rhythm and lose your bonus. Speed up to gain time to blow your nose or get a bit of grit out of your eye. Bolt your sandwiches sitting in a pool of oil because the canteen is ten minutes away and you've only got 40 for your lunch-break. As you cross the factory threshold, lose the freedom of opinion, the freedom of speech, the right to meet and associate supposedly guaranteed under the constitution. Obey without arguing, suffer punishment without the right of appeal, get the worst jobs if the manager doesn't like your face. Try being an assembly-line worker.

Wonder each morning how you're going to hold out until the evening, each Monday how you'll make it to Saturday. Reach home without the strength to do anything but watch TV, telling yourself you'll surely die an idiot. Know at 22 that you'll still be an assembly-line worker at 60 unless you're killed or crippled first. Be as old biologically at 40 or even 35 as a woodcutter of 65. Long to smash everything up at least once a day; feel sick with yourself because you've traded your life for a living; fear more than anything else that the rage mounting within you will die down in the end, and that in the final analysis people are right when they say: 'Aah, you can get used to anything. It's been like that for fifty years – why should it change now?' (Bosquet, 1977, p. 91).

In an autobiographical account of assembly-line working the Hungarian writer Miklos Haraszti (1977) makes the following comments:

351

The technologists would like us to adapt our movements to the rhythm and power of our machines, to pass the pieces from one hand to the other without any interruption or loss of time, in such a way that we would never deviate from the prescribed motions, even in order to obtain the desired results (p. 98).

The factory extends around me like a backdrop. I seldom perceive it as a whole, and I can hardly fit together the few details which I know. Where am I? Who am I? Is it really possible to get men in their right minds to accept this kind of life; to get them to come through a huge door, to cross these enormous workshops, to stand between neighbouring positions, to run through prescribed work, to bargain over the price of sweat, to collect a wage fixed by others, to go home and then return the next day to exactly the same situation? Is it really possible to make them believe – here, at home, everywhere – the assertions in the subtitles of this alien film, that everyone must accept what is beyond the comprehension of their senses, that we must live like this? (p. 147).

Such descriptions, of which many exist in the literature (cf. Terkel, 1975; Fraser, 1969), are not only highly evocative, they also relate an account of the perception of a lack of trust between employer and employee and demonstrate how the former can employ a particular kind of technology to achieve control over individuals that are defined as untrustworthy and unreliable. Bosquet continues his argument by suggesting that:

Technological innovations have always had a dual purpose: to make human labour as productive as possible, and also to force the worker to work to the limit of his capabilities. In the eyes of the classic boss, the need for this constraint goes without saying: the worker is suspected of idleness by definition. How could it be otherwise? Neither the product itself nor the purpose of its manufacture has anything to do with him (Bosquet, 1977, p. 95).

Not only do we see here the assumption that the lower-level organization members in low-discretion roles are idle and unreliable: there is also something of a self-fulfilling prophecy about the assumption. Specific technologies, designs of work and organizational arrangements are imposed which create high levels of disaffection and alienation among organization members. They then display the lack of commitment that management interprets as idleness and unreliability, thus re-cycling the viciousness of the situation. Furthermore, it is self-evident that the assumptions about member behaviour and their organizational consequences are

352

manifestations of further control within organizations of a more insidious kind than hitherto mentioned, through the use of technology. Thus, 'nearly all technology is designed by exercising certain assumptions about people and work' (Davis and Taylor, 1976, p. 411), and this is achieved through the fact that 'there is considerable flexibility in the design of technology' (Davis and Taylor, 1976, p. 410) as we have previously argued. In the conclusion of their review of technology, organization and job structure Davis and Taylor comment:

> The observed effects on workers . . . of technology reflect the assumptions held by the designers of the technological systems about men and social systems (Davis and Taylor, 1976, p. 412).

It is necessary for us to explore these assumptions in greater depth in order to substantiate the control, trust and technology propositions being made here. In exploring these assumptions we need also to ascertain why some jobs have discretion removed from them whilst some other jobs manage to retain individual judgment.

A common feature of much of the writing on organization behaviour since the 1960s has stressed that the design of work can be such that the tendency towards low-discretion roles in organizations can be reversed or at worst can be arrested. Much of the literature in this area comes under the aegis of the 'neo-human relations' movement as represented by writers such as Herzberg (1968), McGregor (1960) and Argyris (1957). The basic argument in these writings is that greater discretion can be given to lower-level organization members of the working class because of the move towards a 'post-industrial' system of production in which greater involvement and commitment is required of organization members for the achievement of organization effectiveness. That is, that changes in the system of production increasingly make scientific management incapable of responding to the challenge of the changes.

A great deal of this work is clearly concerned with the phenomenon of job satisfaction. The most influential technique in the industrial era for generating satisfaction has been claimed to be scientific management, in that it has been assumed that money is the prime motivating force of the individual and will produce the necessary satisfaction with work to produce the required output. As we have seen, control over the individual has been achieved through the application of technological advances that lead to tighter supervision, more minute tasks and the application of increasingly complex systems of piece-rate and incentive payments for wages.

A number of assumptions lies behind these developments that is relevant to the present discussion. As we have seen, scientific

353

management rests on the assumption that the individual is simply an operator rather than a social being. As an operator, it is possible to adjust the individual through training or incentive schemes so that his or her actions become entirely consistent with the pursuit of organization goals. The social-pychological notion of the needs of the individual rarely enter into such discussions.

When assumptions are held that a system is composed of reliable technical elements and unreliable social elements, then in order to provide total system reliability, the technical design must call for parts of people as replaceable machine elements to be regulated by the technical system or by a superstructure of personal control (Davis and Taylor, 1976, p. 412).

We see here another assumption concerning reliability and responsibility. The definition of the individual in the way described earlier may be partly attributed to the tightly defined tasks and the low level of responsibility of organization members. Where the definition of the individual is different we have seen that high discretion roles are deemed apposite. The analogy of the individual as a spare part has been used to describe the low-discretion role and the assumptions that lie behind it (Davis, 1971).

Other assumptions can be seen to be reflected in the design of work and the role of technology in it in the industrial era.

The first is that labour is a commodity to be sold by the individual and purchased by the organization. . . . A second value is that of materialism in its narrow sense, under which the end of achieving higher material comfort justifies the means required to achieve it. Lastly, . . . many managers view the typical job as a disjointed increment, an isolated event in the life of the individual. This non-careerism syndrome explains how jobs (except those for managers themselves) get to be what they are – fragmentary, unintegrated and asystemic (Davis and Taylor, 1972, p. 157).

It is widely argued that the majority of Western industrial societies are moving towards the post-industrial era (cf. Bell, 1974) in which new technologies bring with them in their wake new values in society in general and work organizations in particular. Davis and Taylor (1972, p. 162) suggest two dominant trends in this process, 'the continuing substitution of mechanical and electrical energy sources for human energy in the performance of work . . . [and] the absorption by machines of tasks and activities which are programmatic'. If such an assessment of trends is correct then it follows that human intervention at work will increasingly be of a kind requiring greater discretion than under the industrial system. Not only will these interventions be different, but the skills required and job contents will differ.

It follows further that different assumptions and values concerning the individual need to be adopted to cope with the newly-emerging structure. These assumptions are 'that the social elements are reliable, learning, self-organizing and committed elements' (Davis and Taylor, 1976, p. 412). Such values must lead to very different structures from those typical of industrialism. In essence, then, if it is valid to argue that there is a change towards a post-industrial era and if organizations are to be effective in achieving their goals under such a changed system, then there needs to be a greater involvement of individuals in their work, coupled with a higher level of commitment. The organizational arrangements based upon the principles of scientific management are incapable of achieving these levels of involvement and commitment.

In order to achieve these desired ends, a number of writers have optimistically predicted the imminent demise of scientific management systems of control; they suggest that in their place will be higher levels of trust and assumptions of reliability, much greater individual involvement, and more opportunities for expression by the individual. So long as low trust and alienation exist the potential for change as a response to technology will be inhibited. Alan Fox, at one stage, appears to be among those whose vision of the future corresponds with this view:

> The way is open for managements for whom flexibility, adaptability and problem-solving are high priorities to try to evoke high-trust commitments by, *inter alia*, enlarging the discretion of the relevant groups of employees (Fox, 1974, p. 339).

There are, of course, a number of well-documented examples of such discretion-enlargement exercises through job enrichment, the development of autonomous work groups, the use of the socio-technical concept, and so on. Such exercises, however, may be a response to the costs of low-discretion work as manifested in phenomena such as labour turnover rates, accident rates or absence rates; they may have little to do with the response of an enlightened management responding to the challenge of a changing technology. On the whole, though, the literature abounds with optimistic and at times idealistic predictions and projections. For example, Shultz and Weber, referring to the possibility of changing the design of work because of technological change, comment that:

> These assertions suggest a sharp break with the past evolution of work, and the development of working conditions likely to be more satisfying to the individuals involved. More specifically,

355

this golden era of work will bring safer and cleaner working conditions, a reduction in the physical effort required on the job, enlarged and more interesting tasks, increased professionalization of the worker, freedom from the immediate rhythm of the machine, and a greater sense of relevance to the total objective of the organization (Shultz and Weber, 1960, p. 192).

In spite of his generally optimistic view, Fox is one of the very few writers (especially in industrial sociology) who adds a cautionary note. He admits that the opportunities for greater discretion will increase and that greater trust and reliability could be placed upon those in traditionally low-discretion roles, but he adds:

Whether this movement is likely . . . to be sufficient to evoke from the employees concerned a stable identification with the company and bring to an end their collective pressures upon management decisions seems doubtful (Fox, 1974, p. 342).

We can advance a number of arguments to counter the optimism of the literature in general and go beyond the guarded caution of Alan Fox in particular. In the first instance, the exercises in job enlargement and job rotation may be far removed from the expression of greater involvement and commitment. Job enlargement does not necessarily involve skill enlargement. Perhaps somewhat facetiously we could argue that instead of doing one low-discretion job an individual might be doing five but with equal lack of judgment, trust and reliability. If we recall that job design is often a reflection of management's attempts to control through the imposition of a particular technology, then there is no reason why the felt need for control of the work force should diminish under post-industrial conditions.

It then follows that there remains a need, in the eyes of management, for the traditional systems of control, involving an extensive division of labour, hierarchy, strict supervision, elaborate systems of rules and the like, since these are the proven techniques of control. The fact of scientific management techniques being proven makes it unlikely that managements will experiment, on a large scale, with unproven techniques. To displace the traditional techniques of control could be threatening to managements as well as problematic. In any case, we can argue that the goals of managements have not changed significantly. They are still motivated in their application of managerial principles by the concerns of profit, of economic growth and of efficiency. Even if new patterns of relationships were introduced on a wide scale these structurally given and necessary motives would still exist, and with them the perceived desirability of tight employee control.

A further point to take issue with is the assumption in much of the literature that it has been only manual occupations that have been subject to the kind of control devices that have led to low discretion in occupational roles, as we have described them. It has been assumed that technology – as a mechanism for achieving this control – has been experienced only by manual and particularly unskilled and semi-skilled occupations. In other words, it is implicit in the work-humanization argument that such manual occupations would move towards white collar occupations in terms of the degree of discretion allowed for in the task. We would argue that this would hardly be a move at all. The implication that white-collar work is high-trust work is misplaced and misleading.

A prophet of the post-industrial thesis, Daniel Bell, has pointed to certain projections concerning the expansion of white-collar work as a proportion of the total labour force in the 'post-industrial society'. Here we see the idea that if white-collar work expands in the sense that more individuals are engaged in such work, then the proportion and the number of individuals involved in unskilled low-discretion manual work will decline. This is a truism. Underlying this, however, is the assumption that white-collar work is at a higher discretion level and that low-discretion roles are the exclusive preserve of unskilled or semi-skilled manual occupations. In fact, there is considerable evidence that white-collar work is increasingly becoming indistinguishable from blue-collar work in terms of the amount of work-role discretion. This is not simply a question of the classification of occupations into white-collar or manual categories (entailing, for example, the difficulties attendant upon classifying occupations such as shop assistants or policemen), but more a question of the skill requirements of various occupations.

It would be comforting to argue as Kerr and his colleagues (1973, p. 201) have done that 'the industrial order requires many new skills and ever-changing skills', and that 'the levels of skill are gradually rising'. Yet a great deal of white-collar work is purposively designed to prevent the individual exercising discretion or judgment. The amount of skill required in a considerable amount of clerical and office work is minimal for a number of reasons.

The original role of the clerk was managerial in a number of respects. Lockwood (1958, p. 22) comments that in the mid-nineteenth century 'many of the clerks . . . were performing duties which would nowadays be classified as managerial'. Since then, of course, there has been a formidable explosion in the number of clerical occupations that include 'bookkeeper, secretary, stenographer, cashier, bank teller, file clerk, telephone operator, office machine operator, payroll and timekeeping clerk, postal clerk, receptionist, stock clerk, typist, and the like' (Braverman, 1974, pp. 295–6). In addition to this increase in occupational titles there has been a significant change in the nature of the work. Comparing the work with industrial work, the closest comparison to it would be continuous-flow operations with paper documents of one kind or another being substituted for chemicals or the like.

A crucial change that has occurred since the last century has been the transformation of office work from being mental to manual. Rationalization of office work has occurred in much the same way as work on the production line. As Braverman puts it:

> With the transformation of management into an administrative labour process, manual work spreads to the office and soon becomes characteristic of the tasks of the mass of clerical workers (Braverman, 1974, p. 316).

Braverman argues that this transformation from mental to manual work occurred through the activities of management experts of the second and third generation following F. W. Taylor. The position has been reached whereby time-and-motion studies are as equally applicable to the office and the shop floor. This has been achieved largely through the impact of technology in the office in a parallel fashion to the impact of technology in the factory several decades earlier.

> As in the factory, the machine-pacing of work becomes increasingly available to office management as a weapon of control (Braverman, 1974, pp. 333–4).

Braverman continues:

> We have now described . . . the conversion of the office routine into a factory-like process in accordance with the precepts of modern management and available technology. The greatest single obstacle to the proper functioning of such an office is the concentration of information and decision-making capacity in the minds of key clerical employees. Just as Frederick Taylor diagnosed the problem of management of a machine shop as one of removing craft information from the workers, in the same way the office manager views with horror the possibility of dependence upon the historical knowledge of the office past, or of the rapid flow of information in the present, on the part of some of his or her clerical workers. The recording of everything in mechanical form, and the movement of everything in a mechanical way, is thus the ideal of the office manager. But this conversion of the office flow into a high-speed industrial process requires the conversion of the great mass of office workers into

more or less helpless attendants of that process. As an inevitable concomitant of this, the ability of the office worker to cope with deviations from the routine, errors, special cases, all of which require information and training, virtually disappears. The number of people who can operate the system, instead of being operated by it, declines precipitously. In this sense, the modern office becomes a machine which at best functions well only within its routine limits, and functions badly when it is called upon to meet special requirements (Braverman, 1974, pp. 347–8).

Environmentally there are still significant differences between office and factory work: the locations are always more agreeable for the former, as are the hours of work and often the method of payment. When the actual work itself is examined the distinction between the two sets of workers – as Braverman has vividly shown – is very blurred. Computers have been held to be the primary reason for the changes that have occurred, but the whole range of techno-logical development affecting the nature of machinery in offices needs to be considered as equally important. The imposition of Taylorism in the office coupled with factory-type instruments of control blurs the distinction further. Reverting to Fox's work, it can be asserted that a considerable proportion of white-collar occupations has shifted from being medium-discretion to low-discretion work roles. As we stated above, 'the implication of white-collar work being high-trust work is misplaced and mis-leading'. Furthermore, if the predictions of social forecasters such as Daniel Bell are correct concerning the future expansion of white-collar work, then the prediction is one of increasing low-discretion roles as a consequence of technological imposition as a means of control. And to argue as do Kerr *et al.* that skill levels are rising and must rise further is again incorrect if the analysis presented here is accepted.

This debate is both wider and more historical than organization theory suggests. It is concerned with arguments which suggest that a 'new middle class' has developed, a thesis which goes back to 1912 and Emil Lederer's *The Problem of the Modern Salaried Employee*. Lederer argued that the class structure of nineteenth-century capitalism had been modified by a growth in the numbers of salaried workers. These workers, he argued, were not characterizable in terms of a homogenous class-consciousness, nor could they be expected to accept proletarian authority, through, for instance, the trade union movement. Statistically, Lederer's thesis, with its subsequent developments, is correct. From being only 1 per cent of the employed population in 1851 in Britain, clerical workers had swelled to 12 per cent by 1961. Those workers classed as professional increased from 4 per cent in 1911 to 10 per cent by 1971. In both capitalist and non-capitalist industrial societies professional and technical workers are the fastest increasing occupational category. If all of the white-collar occupations were aggregated they would account for approximately a third of the employed population of individual industrial societies. Behind these statistics lies a theme which we will take up in Chapter 11: the sexual division of labour. Swingewood raises the question:

> Yet what is the reality behind these statistics? The service industries, for example, are largely staffed by women working as usherettes, waitresses, barmaids, hairdressers and beauticians, occupations in which pay and working conditions are poor; there are few facilities for training, no educational qualifications are required, and work is often done on a part-time basis. Indeed, of the two million sales workers and the two and a quarter million personal service workers in Great Britain nearly one-half to two-thirds are women (Swingewood, 1975, pp. 123–4).

He goes on to note that the expansion of clerical work is similarly largely due to the increasing entry of women into the labour force, so that by 1961 the percentage of women in white-collar occupations had increased to 44.5 per cent from 29.8 per cent in 1911. In addition, 'the type of work performed requires minimum training and skill (Swingewood, 1975, p. 124).

It would seem that the expansion of white-collar work in occupations has as its concomitant a spread of female employment in organizational roles equally as de-skilled as those of male industrial workers. The de-skilling thesis, it would seem, needs to be related not only to the hierarchical division of labour but also to the sexual division of labour (which we will develop in Chapter 11). We can conclude that, irrespective of the statistical increase in white-collar work, these can not be assumed to be either skilled jobs, or jobs distributed throughout the division of labour. They are predominantly low-discretion tasks occupied primarily by women within the sexual division of labour.

Low-discretion roles with their associated differential tasks of a very routinized form are prolific within organizations. We have argued that this proliferation is largely a result of the choice of technology and the application of particular principles of job design that necessarily accompany a particular technological choice. However, when we refer to a choice of technology we need to raise the following issue: who is making the choice and to what end? We have already partly answered the question by suggesting that low-discretion roles, at an individual level, are largely devoid of power. The converse – that high-discretion roles are imbued with significantly greater amounts of power – provides the clue to answering the question. Those in powerful positions have interests to preserve, not least of which is the very power to which we refer. The design of some work roles as low-discretion roles therefore arises from the powerful interests of some individuals or groups over others and the desire by the same to preserve the *status quo,* if not actually to make their positions more powerfully secure. And in referring to these powerful interests reference must need be made to class interests. This is not a new phenomenon but dates back to the origin of the factory system itself.

> The emergence of the factory system owed as much to the drive for close co-ordination, discipline and control of the labour force as to the pressures of technology. It was not long, however, before the latter were contributing their own powerful influence to the low-trust dynamic. The introduction of steam-power differentiated still more sharply between 'roles involved in the control of capital' and 'those involved in the processes of production'. By the same token, it differentiated more completely between those responsible for the decisions to produce and those engaged in production (Fox, 1974, pp. 179–80).

We have thus come full circle to the same argument presented by writers such as Marglin, Gorz and Braverman. In spite of the chronological proximity of such writers, the ideas have been in the sociological literature for some time. For example, Gouldner in 1954 commented that:

> The extreme elaboration of bureaucratic rules is prompted by an abiding distrust of people and of their intentions. . . . Rules are a form of communication to those who are seen as desirous of evading responsibilities, of avoiding commitment, and of withholding proper and full performance of obligations (Gouldner, 1954, p. 179).

Indeed Marx, writing over a century ago, recognized the division of labour as an imposition by a ruling class. The technology, the job design and the form of organization are all reflections of values and the application of practices that exist in a context wider than the particular organization, in that they are class values and class interests. We saw earlier that technology places limits upon, rather than determines, the structure of an organization and the design of work within it. Nevertheless the actual technology that is chosen is a reflection of certain attitudes and interests. Technology is not the politically neutral phenomenon suggested by some writers, since assumptions about the motives of organization members often enter into the choice of one technological system over another. The analysis is incomplete, however, without a consideration of different technological bases that underlie different organization roles. Such a consideration is rare and yet, as Perrow (1972) demonstrates, important in an analysis of the role of technology in organizations.

Perrow's main aim in analysing technology is to use it as an independent variable in the construction of an organization typology, not in the sense that Woodward produced her classification, but through using technology in a special sense of referring to tasks. His basic argument (which closely follows that of Thompson and Bates, 1957) is:

> When the tasks people perform are well understood, predictable, routine and repetitive, a bureaucratic structure is the most efficient. . . . Where tasks are not well understood, generally because the 'raw material' that each person works on is poorly understood and possibly reactive, recalcitrant or self-activating, the tasks are non-routine. Such units or organizations are difficult to bureaucratize (Perrow, 1972, p. 166).

Such a distinction is entirely consistent with our analysis presented above. Our excerpts from the works of Beynon, Bosquet and Haraszti demonstrate that assembly-line working is routine and repetitive, that the tasks are standardized and well understood. The organization of assembly-line work has this character partly because the raw materials themselves are well understood and standardized. If we take organizations at the other extreme (for example, social service departments, architects' offices or universities), here the raw material is unpredictable and not too well understood (for example, problem families, vague plans for an office complex, or first-year students, respectively). In this kind of situation, according to Perrow, there must be greater discretion allowed to individuals working in such organizations: 'more interaction is required among personnel at the same level; there must be more emphasis on experience, 'feel' or professionalization' (Perrow, 1972, p. 166). Perrow also attempts to link the extent of task routinization to the goals of the organization and points to the example of psychiatric hospitals. If the goal has a custodial nature then the degree of routinization may be high; if the goal is oriented towards treatment and cure then a more flexible structure is necessary. A detailed account of the research leading to such propositions is to be found in Perrow (1965).

The apparent simplicity of Perrow's arguments give them a seductive appeal. If only it were so simple as to say that the degree of variation in raw materials and task complexity sets limits on routinization. Of course, to a large degree what Perrow suggests is entirely valid, in that he points clearly to the reasons why some tasks are not routinized and standardized. The fact that the majority of tasks are either routinized or in the process of routinization is only partly explained by Perrow's analysis. Whether or not tasks are routinized is not a question of technological inexorability but of conscious decision by senior organization members. In making such a decision we have argued that the assumptions and values of one class are imposed upon a subordinate class.

A further weakness in Perrow's argument is his acceptance of the traditional role and status of the high-discretion occupations that are generally referred to as the professions. Although the 'futurologists' such as Bell (1974) and Galbraith (1969) predict knowledge to be the most important asset in 'post-industrial society' in the sense that the professionals and technically-based disciplines will dominate affairs, there is a growing awareness that such predictions may be incorrect. As technology becomes more sophisticated and complex the opportunities for routinizing the previously-unroutinizeable becomes greater. For example Illich has stated that:

> Science . . . could be used to simplify tools and to enable the layman to shape his immediate environment to his task. The time has come to take the syringe out of the hand of the doctor (Illich, 1973, p. 634).

Increasing standardization has taken place in the legal and accounting professions. The popularity of 'do-it-yourself' house purchase and divorce is evidence of such routinization; accountancy, largely through the effects of computers, has become more and more codified, standardized and routinized. In other words, not only clerical work but professional activities as well appear to be subject to an increasing division of labour characterized by routinization. As Braverman has put it:

> The capitalist mode of production systematically destroys all-around skills where they exist, and brings into being skills and occupations that correspond to its needs. . . . The generalized distribution of knowledge of the productive process among all its participants becomes . . . not merely 'unnecessary' but a positive barrier to the functioning of the capitalist mode of production (Braverman, 1974, p. 82).

We, together with the majority of writers in this area, can only suggest that the imposition of technology of the predominant kind which extends the division of labour in organizations, which inevitably leads to more specialized tasks, which breaks down the traditional barriers between manual and non-manual work, must

363

also breed an increasingly alienated labour force at more and more levels in the organization hierarchy.

> Capitalist control of the production process and the worker's loss of control over his labour insure that work activities develop according to the simple criteria of profitability and maintenance of secure control from the top. . . . Bureaucratic order legitimizes the totalitarian structure of production, and hierarchical authority and job fragmentation destroy class solidarity and sense of control on the part of workers, so that the functionally necessary ideology of alienated labour is reproduced (Gintis, 1972, p. 46).

This is the inevitable consequence of low-trust, low-discretion work roles. As we suggested earlier, this can lead to a vicious circle of increasing low discretion and also a self-fulfilling prophecy in the sense that managerial definitions of worker behaviour become real in their consequences. This can be illustrated as in Figure 9.1.

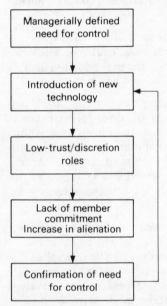

Figure 9.1   The vicious circle of controls

From the point of view of managerial behaviour such a course of action is defined as entirely rational. Within the managerial definition it is rational to introduce a form of technology that ensures tighter control in the form of supervision and discipline or more extensive use of the principles of scientific management. Such

364

a view is consistent with McGregor's 'Theory X' (1960). To argue that there should be a movement towards 'Theory Y' or towards Likert's 'System Four' (1961) – that is, to introduce more self-control at work, greater participation and industrial democracy – misses an important point. To the extent that these innovations increase the power of subordinates, management must see this as a deterioration in their power, as a reduction in their control over a work force. Where alternative strategies are introduced – that is, by not using technological development as a means of control – we need to question the sincerity of such strategies. Are they genuine attempts to give employees more control over their activities (thereby reducing the amount of employer control), or are they little short of strategies for subtly controlling a labour force that lacks commitment to the official organization goals and that experiences greater alienation as a result of traditional managerial practices? Such questions are raised in the next chapter.

10 Organizations and environments

Introduction

Throughout this volume we have alluded to the fact that organizations are not independent self-sufficient phenomena, in spite of the tendency of organization studies to treat the organization in this way. We have attempted to counter this tendency in a number of ways. The earliest analyses of organizations certainly had a macro-perspective in that writers such as Comte, Saint-Simon and Durkheim discussed the emergence of the new organizational arrangements in their contemporary society from the viewpoint of the wider societal changes taking place. This is equally true of Karl Marx, and possibly best seen in Max Weber's analysis of the Protestant ethic which took both a comparative and a historical perspective to demonstrate how the rise of capitalist organizations was tied up with the development of ideas seemingly quite 'extra-organizational'.

The general trend in organization analysis during the first three or four decades of this century moved away from a concern with such wide issues towards the study of the internal workings of organizations as in both the scientific management and human relations movements. The concern with organizations as systems acted as something of a brake on such developments, especially with the use of the 'open-system' concept. Because organizations, modelled as systems, have to exchange factors with their environments, in the form of inputs and outputs, the survival of the organization came to be seen as dependent upon boundary exchanges with its environment. From this standpoint it was argued that the environment imposes certain constraints upon the organization that can partly determine the structure of the organization. As we have seen in earlier chapters, because of this

366

determination different types of organization purportedly have different types of structure: the differences being partly attributable to different types of environment.

Even though some of the classic studies of organizations recognized and utilized this approach, it has not been until relatively recently that the systematic analysis of the organization-environment relationship has been undertaken. For example, in 1949 Selznick, in his study of the Tennessee Valley Authority, demonstrated how influential external factors could be upon the internal dynamics of the organization. His later study of the US Communist Party in 1960 followed this tradition. Studies such as these were, however, the exception rather than the rule of that time. We have seen that other studies such as Crozier (1964), Abegglin (1958) or Bendix (1956) were in large degree notable for their 'environmental' recognition. But even by the late 1960s the following criticism could be levelled at organization analysts:

> Too much sociological theory and research has been based mainly on the model of a single organization, and attention has been focused on the internal processes, by and large. . . . Having become rooted in its social and technological environment and more complex ways, organizations find themselves both constraining and being constrained by these environments in new ways. Yet investigators of formal organizations have barely begun to attack these new relationships (Smelser and Davis, 1968, p. 65).

Such criticism seemed to be taken and acted upon, in that the 1970s have seen a proliferation of attempts to understand the organization-environment relationship. As Aldrich and Pfeffer (1976, p. 80) observed, 'There is currently great interest in environmental effects and the journals are filled with papers containing the words *environment* or *inter-organizational* in their titles'.

The strong interdependence between the organization and its environment has already been partly discussed in earlier chapters. We have seen the nature of goals and how often these are reflections of interests beyond the immediate boundary of the organization. Similarly, technology has been discussed partly as a cultural phenomenon that again reflects, in its imposition, interests wider than those of the organization; for example, the suggestion that assumptions about individuals in organizations are often assumptions that are class-based. In our discussion of structures of actions we saw how orientations to work have been seen as externally determined (Goldthorpe *et al.*, 1969). In this chapter we need to be more systematic in our analysis of inter-organizational relations and

367

the relationship between organizations and their environments. The former are obviously a part of the latter and can usefully be separated for analytic purposes. In the first instance we need to be clear what the environment of organizations consists of.

The general environment of organizations

Following Hall (1977, pp. 304–12) the following conditions can be identified as the general environment of organizations: technological; legal; political; economic; demographic; ecological; and cultural.

1 *Technological conditions* Burns and Stalker's (1961) work provides a good example of the importance of technological environment on the organization structure and process. They studied twenty Scottish electronics firms which, they argued, could be distinguished on the basis of an ideal type construction into two basic types. One type they termed 'mechanistic', the other 'organic'. The mechanistic organization was similar to Weber's ideal type of bureaucracy, with a well-defined formal structure. The organic organization had no clearly defined hierarchy and was in a state of constant flux. It involved a continued re-definition of roles in the organization such that few people were sure what exactly was their actual, formal job title. People spent a great deal of time in communication and interaction with each other in the organization and acted on these as sources of information rather than instruction.

Burns and Stalker argue that neither of these is necessarily a better model than the other. It depends on the environment in which each is operative. In fact, they argue that the structure is a result of the environment. This is because, while the mechanistic structure is most suitable for organizations operating under relatively stable market conditions, and thus able to use a stable technology, the organic structure is far more flexible for an unstable environment which provides the organization with relatively unpredictable new tasks and problems. In such organic firms, in fact, it is argued that a part of the structure will often be specialized to deal with an unstable environment, such as a research and development division (for example, see Lawrence and Lorsch, 1967).

The general thinking behind this strain of organization theory is fairly simple. Hall expresses it well:

> The organization does not exist in a vacuum. A technological development in any sphere of activity will eventually get to the organizations related to it. New ideas come into circulation and become part of the environment as soon as they cease being the private property of any one individual or organization (Hall, 1977, p. 305).

As soon as these new ideas are in circulation there is an impact upon the organization. Khandwalla (1977) reports from a Canadian study that if the technological environment of an organization is complex then the management orientation in that organization will tend to be towards future planning, and there will be an emphasis upon managerial techniques to ensure the maximum utilization of resources. And, as Burns and Stalker had demonstrated earlier, where there is not a technologically complex environment the information and control systems will be much less sophisticated.

2 *Legal conditions* These aspects of the environment are amongst the most important and least studied aspect of organizations. One of the most important writers on this neglected area is Karl Renner (1969), whose work is a further development of that of Karl Marx in *Capital*.

One point which we have been developing in various ways, at various points, in each chapter, is that in essence *organization means control*. We have regarded organization as a means of extending this control. What is important to recognize is that this control is only possible given a legal framework grounded in property relations. In this legal framework, relationships which are expressed purely formally may nonetheless have decisive impli- cations for actual social relationships of organization:

In the eyes of the law, the property-subject is related to the object only, controlling matter alone. But what is control of property in law, becomes in fact man's control of human beings, of the wage labourers, as soon as property has developed into capital. The individual called owner sets the tasks to others, he makes them subject to his commands and, at least in the initial stages of capitalist development, supervises the execution of his commands. The owner of a *res* imposes his will upon *personae,* autonomy is converted into heteronomy of will. . . . Wage labour is a relation of autocracy with all the legal characteristics of despotism. The factory is an establishment with its own code with all the characteristics of a legal code. It contains norms of every description, not excluding criminal law, and it establishes special organs and jurisdiction. Labour regulations and the con- ventions valid within economic enterprises deserve just as well to be treated as legal institutions as the manorial law of the feudal epoch. . . . The right of the capitalist is delegated public authority, conferred indiscriminately upon the person who will use it for his own benefit. The employment relationship is an indirect-power relationship, a public obligation to service . . . [which] . . . differs from serfdom only in this respect, that it is

369

based upon a contract, not upon inheritance. No society has yet existed without a regulation of labour peculiar to it (Renner, 1969, pp. 34–5, 36–7).

The most important aspect of this legal framework is the way in which it reflects and buttresses class relations, which are, of course, expressed in organizations. Workers can 'exchange one individual capitalist for another' in a capitalist mode of production, but they can never escape from capital *per se,* either as employed or unemployed persons, as producers or as consumers. As Renner (1969, p. 39) puts it, 'Property, from a mere title to dispose of material objects, becomes a title to power, and as it exercises power in the private interest, it becomes a title to domination'. This title extends its sway over those subject to organization and control within an institutional framework legally fixed by the state. This may include laws governing who may do what, in terms of age, sex, nationality, skills, certification, where it may be done, in terms of environmental legislation, as well as how it may be done, to whom it may be done, when it may be done, in terms of more specific laws of both local/state and national/federal origin. Enmeshed in all this will be the employees who fill the positions in the organization:

> If a person occupies a 'position', this means that his rights and duties are closely circumscribed, the position has become a legal institution in character. . . . The position comprises the claim to adequate remuneration (settled by collective agreement or works rule), the obligation to pay certain contributions (for trade unions and insurance), the right to special benefits (sickness, accident, old age, death), and finally certain safeguards against loss of the position or in case of its loss (Renner, 1969, pp. 43–4).

A recently published paper by Edward Gross, 'Organizations as Criminal Actors', provides another example of the way in which organizations deal with the law as a contingency in their environment. Gross's basic proposition is that all organizations are inherently criminal. Elaborating on this proposition, the emphasis placed upon goal-attainment in organizations as a measure of performance and effectiveness, coupled with the uncertainty that surrounds all organizations, suggest that, if necessary, goals will be attained through criminal or illegitimate behaviour. Clearly this is an analogous position to that of the individual in many circumstances. Wherever performance is stressed there will be pressure to deviate from the legitimate means of achievement. To some extent, organizations are more likely than individuals to be involved in such activities because, first, goals are central to organizations whereas individuals are much more than goal-achieving organisms. It follows that organizations are scrutinized for their performance more often and more stringently than individuals. Second, organizations seek to 'reduce uncertainty' (i.e. increase control) as a means of achieving goals more efficiently. Third, the organizational division of labour allows for the development of sub-goals for the individual in the organization. These sub-goals become the goals to be pursued and, as indicated in Chapter 8, the overall official goals of the organization tend to be displaced. Moreover the departmentalization of organizations and their complexity create 'situations in which one part of an organization may achieve its ends at the cost of another part of an organization for which it is not responsible and which it may not even know about'.

There is little doubt that organizational crime is widespread. Sutherland's study of white-collar crime involved the analysis of the criminal behaviour of seventy top corporations in the United States. As he points out,

> Sixty per cent of the seventy larger corporations have been convicted in criminal courts and have an average of four convictions each. In many states persons with four convictions are defined as 'habitual criminals' (Sutherland, 1961, p. 25).

The ubiquity of organizational crime, and the criminogenic tendencies that Gross refers to, are not random but subject to certain organizational variations. These are, first, that the more accountability there is, the greater the probability that the organization will engage in crime. This proposition obviously relates to the emphasis placed upon goal-achievement: the more emphasis there is, the greater the likelihood of crime. Related to this is the second variation, that organizations differ in the extent to which their outputs can be measured. Economic organizations are normally capable of such measurement, whereas service organizations such as hospitals or universities are not. Third, the urge to undertake some criminal activity is inversely related to goal displacement. As Gross suggests, 'a device that reduces the need for an organization to adopt deviant means to achieve its goals is the renunciation of those goals in favour of the minimal efforts needed to keep the organization alive'. A fourth variation is that those parts of the organization having the closest contact with the organization's environment are those having the greatest pressure toward criminal behaviour. We have already argued that a changing technological environment leads to a more differentiated or organic organization structure. The departments of industrial organizations, for example, that are most exposed to the environment, such as marketing or sales (as compared with production), will be more likely to exhibit criminal behaviour. The notorious Lockheed bribes

371

scandal almost led to the collapse of the Japanese and Dutch governments; and yet the Lockheed parent company in the United States came out of the affair relatively unscathed and was in any case not considered criminally liable.

Gross's study provides a useful illustration of the way in which the legal aspects of an organization's environment is often compromised and violated, largely through the emphasis upon goal-attainment in the organization. In turn, specific organizational characteristics such as the degree of decentralization or the amount of goal displacement affect this likelihood of legal violation in the wider environment. The legal system to which Gross refers and the legal conditions distinguished by Renner all form part of the environment of the organization, which for the purposes of organization analysis may be relevant.

3   *Political conditions*   In his study entitled *The Un-politics of Air Pollution,* Mathew Crenson (1971) has shown how the differing political arrangements of two cities (East Chicago and Gary) in which one company operated (US Steel) had very important and differing implications for the organization. In East Chicago the populace successfully opposed air pollution by US Steel as early as 1942, while in Gary they did not. Whereas in Gary US Steel dominated the political environment together with one party, in East Chicago there was a plurality of both parties and firms. Hence the political environment of East Chicago made it much easier to affect the organization.

A further interpretation of this case is one which stresses the organization's control over the environment, as in US Steel's activities in Gary. This obviously produces a quite different perspective on organizations from the more conventional systems framework.

4   *Economic conditions*   Hall (1977, p. 307) has observed that 'this is the crucial variable', but one which is 'strangely neglected by most sociologists'. The economic context in which any organization operates is perhaps the most important constraint: so, for instance, if one wishes to discuss the relationship of size to some other variable, as organization structure, one will usually seek to relate changes in size itself to changes in the economy. Marx's (1974) work on the increasing organic composition of capital related to the underlying laws of motion of the capitalist mode of production is one such example of this approach. It is interesting to observe that there is little discussion in the organization's literature of this or any other aspect of Marx's work.

Hall (1977, pp. 307–8) suggests that such changes will not affect

372

all parts of an organization equally. 'In periods of economic distress, an organization is likely to cut back or eliminate those programmes it feels are least important to its overall goals.' It is because of this, he suggests, that 'changing economic conditions are, in fact, excellent indicators of the operative goals of organizations'. That is, it is assumed that an organization will eliminate its least strategically contingent operations first, as we shall see later in this chapter.

5 *Politico-economic conditions* A number of writers in recent years have pointed to changes in the politico-economic environment of organizations that have major influences upon the structure and functioning of those organizations. For our purposes in this section it is both necessary and sufficient to identify the politico-economic aspects of the organizational environment. One of the most exhaustive analyses – although bound to a particular society – has been presented by Jack Winkler in his study of 'The Corporatist Economy' (1977). Corporatism is defined as 'an economic system in which the state directs and controls predominantly privately-owned business according to four principles: unity, order, nationalism and success' (Winkler, 1977, p. 44). Winkler's overarching thesis is that the British economy has, since around 1960, pursued a corporatist trend, and that if this trend continues corporatist institutions will be well established by the late 1980s. What evidence is there for this thesis and prediction, and in what ways does the phenomenon of corporatism comprise part of the environment of organizations?

The evidence Winkler presents for his thesis is largely a descriptive account of the increasing interference by successive governments in the British economy through measures such as economic planning, investment decisions, prices and incomes policies, and state regulation of industrial relations. Through such measures the state has attempted to increase its control over economic affairs through an appeal to the national interest. This has involved a change of role for the state from its original facilitative role (for example, in terms of setting up a common currency and measurement system), through a supportive role (aiding private companies when they experience difficulties; encouraging economic demand in the economy, education and training provisions, etc.), to a directive role whereby private companies are instructed as to what they can and cannot do.

From the point of view of organization analysis such a thesis, if correct, has very significant repercussions, especially at the level of decision-making. Decision-making has always been the valued preserve of the owners and managers of capitalist organizations. We have observed in earlier chapters how decentralization may

373

occur in some organizations, but only on a piece-meal basis to the extent that the crucial decisions still rest in the hands of the owners and/or managers. From the corporatist point of view the decision-making still remains in the hands of the owners/managers but state interference places severe limits on the choice available in the decision-making process. Winkler (1977, pp. 45–6) gives the Planning Agreements System as an example of such limitation of decision choice; but the more recent incomes policy of the British Labour Government provides a more valid example in that if decisions were made by private companies to exceed the pay ceiling then the companies have been placed on a Government blacklist, thereby denying them the opportunity of gaining any further government work contracts.

As a descriptive account of changes in British capitalism Winkler's analysis is very appealing. Of course, the account is not without criticism or its critics. Westergaard, for example, questions:

> First, in what sense, if at all sensibly, can the State be said to direct: Where in fact are the sources of control over economic affairs? Next, whatever the sources of control, what are the criteria by which it is exercised: What yardsticks and operating assumptions are used to allocate resources? What finally . . . is the distributional outcome: to whose benefit, by what principles of interest and justice? (Westergaard, 1977, p. 175).

This is not the place to investigate these questions, nor to attempt an assessment of the overall validity of the Winkler thesis. Suffice it to say that the politico-economic conditions of the environment are clearly influential in guiding, if not controlling, activities that traditionally have been considered matters internal to the organization.

6 *Demographic conditions* An apposite example of demographic conditions comprising part of the organization's environment is given by the post-war 'baby-boom'. As this demographic change passed through educational organizations it had a major impact on their structure. Systems that had been designed to cope with a much lower demand and rate of growth had to adapt to changed demographic circumstances. The changes that were made in educational organizations, as for example in the tertiary sector, had a significant impact on other organizations such as work organizations. Perhaps the most evident of these was the rapid growth in certification which developed as the educational requirements of jobs increased with the greater supply of degrees, diplomas and certificates.

7 *Ecological conditions* Hall (1977, p. 309) makes a distinction between the social ecological environment and an organization's physical ecology. The former would be the number of other organizations with which any organization had contacts and relationships, as well as the type of inter-relations that these entailed. Physical ecology is an often neglected but important environmental variable (cf. Caldwell, 1977) that can include climate, geography and architecture.

8 *Cultural conditions* A substantial body of evidence suggests the importance of cultural environment on organizations. Representative of this evidence is work on French bureaucracies (Crozier, 1964); studies of Japanese factories (Dore, 1973; Abegglin, 1958); and the analysis of regional variations (Sutton, 1974). Contrary to this, we have already noted McMillan (1976) in Chapter 6. A major problem is that culture is not amenable to the type of quantitative analysis that has become characteristic of organization-environment interchanges. Thus, research in this area depends on a more 'meaning-oriented' frame of reference for organization analysis, such as that displayed in Chapter 7.

The above eight conditions comprise, in very broad terms, the general environment of organizations. Whilst these conditions provide a useful description of the environment and guide our thinking away from organizations as isolated self-sufficient phenomena, they do not provide an adequate conceptual scheme for organizational analysis. The interest in organizations and their environments over the past decade has generated a number of conceptual analytic schemes, which are summarized below.

The conceptualization of organization environments

1 *The causal texture perspective* In a relatively early paper on the relationship between organizations and environment, Emery and Trist (1965) have provided what was considered for some time to be an exhaustive and helpful conceptualization. Their analysis provides four ideal-type environments differentiated on the basis of what are referred to as qualitative dissimilarities in the 'casual texturing'. The concept of causal texture refers to the way in which environmental parts are inter-related that encourage some actions and inhibit others. The schema is firmly grounded within a systems framework, and is thus subject to the comments made in Chapter 5 with regard both to advantages and disadvantages. Two elements of the environment are considered to be significant: behaviour that is purposeful and which encourages system survival (goals), and behaviour that acts as a barrier to system survival (noxiants).

Environments can be analysed according to the pattern of these goals and noxiants, whether they are random or clustered, placid or dynamic, and whether more than one system shares the environmental profile with another. From these concepts the typology of environments can be devised: the placid-random environment, the placid-clustered environment, the disturbed reactive environment, and the turbulent environment. It is not considered necessary to elaborate this typology, largely because more recent work in the area has surpassed this exercise and largely made it redundant.

2 *The natural selection perspective* The basic argument in this perspective is that factors in the environment select characteristics of the organization in terms of how best they fit the environment. In essence this means little more than the fact that organizations attempt to achieve the best possible fit with their environments. Aldrich and Pfeffer argue that this natural selection or ecological perspective is a long-term approach and can best be seen in the attempts to produce viable typologies of organizations. We have already seen in Chapter 4 that these attempts leave much to be desired, and as such the possibility of an ecological analysis of organizations is remote. Since natural selection is by its very nature a process, it is possible to distinguish distinct stages of development.

> The first stage . . . is the occurrence of variations for whatever
> reason, planned or unplanned. . . . Variations are the raw
> material from which the selection process culls those structures or
> behaviours that are most suitable. The second stage is the
> operation of consistent selection criteria that differentially select
> some variations over others or selectively eliminate certain
> variations. . . . The third stage . . . involves the operation of a
> retention mechanism for the selective retention of the positively
> selected variations (Aldrich and Pfeffer, 1976, p. 81).

This three-stage process was in fact suggested by Campbell (1969) as a general description of evolutionary processes. The application of the process to organizations and their environments meets with difficulties. The first is the long-term perspective that is required, and the difficulties (through the limited resources) of pursuing longitudinal research except through the use of secondary material. The second is that this perspective 'focuses on outcomes involving the selective propagation of changes . . . in the structure of a large number of organizations, rather than on the route taken by any single organization in adapting' (Aldrich and Pfeffer, 1976, p. 82). Third is the fact that classificatory schemes in organization analysis are, as yet, unsatisfactory except at the most general level. Last is the fact that this perspective says nothing about the making of decisions except in so far as it suggests a model of perfect competition. To suggest, as the natural selection perspective does, that there is an optimal fit between the organization and its environment is unrealistic and makes one puzzle over Aldrich and Pfeffer's (1976, p. 79) statement that this perspective develops 'the strongest argument for an environmental perspective'.

3 *The information perspective* One of the reasons for the popularity of the information perspective on organization-environment relations is the fact that the focus on information is essentially a way for managers to reduce the uncertainty of decision-making. Put another way, the more certain one can be about decision-making and future courses of action, the more control is gained over the structure and process of the organization. Since we have consistently argued that control and organization are somewhat synonymous, it should come as no surprise to observe the appeal of this approach.

Aldrich and Mindlin (1978, p. 155) suggest that it is the *perceptions* of decision-makers about the organization's environment that are more critical in this perspective than the actual constructs of the environment. As we have already suggested, the more uncertainty there is in the environment (perceived or actual) the more the structure of the organization will be flexible or 'organic' if it (the organization) is to function objectively. Two empirical examples are sufficient to illustrate the information perspective.

Lawrence and Lorsch (1967) are often labelled the forerunners of the contingency theorists, largely because their research demonstrated that there is no optimal way to structure an organization, but that the organization analyst can best seek the most appropriate structure in a given environment. We shall see below that such reasoning may be fallacious in that a number of alternative structures may be equally viable in any one environmental setting. In many respects it is more appropriate to regard Lawrence and Lorsch's work as a contribution to the information rather than the contingency perspective (notwithstanding the fact that the two may not be absolutely independent of one another). The logic behind this suggestion lies in the fact that the writers' empirical approach involved an analysis of the *perceptions* of decision-makers with regard to environment in three rather different industries (and thus presumably with different degrees of environmental stability). The focus of attention was upon production, research and sales in the various organizations, especially the degree of integration and differentiation and its link with organization performance.

Aldrich and Mindlin succinctly summarize the results of the investigations:

> The more diversification perceived among the segments of the environments the organizations had to cope with, and the more instability perceived, the more differentiation was required among the organizational segments that dealt with specific environments in order to achieve a high level of performance. More differentiation alone was not sufficient to attain high effectiveness (Aldrich and Mindlin, 1978, p. 154).

Such results are entirely consistent with other studies in that if the perception of the decision-makers is of environments that are uncertain and dynamic, a decentralized structure makes for more effective organizations. As Burns and Stalker (1961) showed earlier, when the environment has more certainty (at least in terms of the perception of the decision-makers) a more bureaucratic and formally-structured organization is appropriate for effectiveness.

Lawrence and Lorsch's approach has been used by other researchers, although not always to the same effect (cf. Tosi *et al.*, 1973). Duncan (1972) again used the notion of perceptions and concerned himself with parts of the organization rather than the total unit. As with Lawrence and Lorsch, Duncan establishes that the degree of stability in the environment is important in terms of the production of certainty and predictability, especially as an aid to the decision-makers. The data, somewhat surprisingly, suggest that this dimension of static/dynamic is more influential than the simple/complex dimension employed as a generator of uncertainty for decision-makers (at least, in their perception).

4 *The political economy perspective* Aspects of what we are referring to as the political economy perspective appear in a number of approaches to organization-environment relations, especially in the work on strategic contingencies, resource dependencies, dialectics and exchange theory. The perspective we wish to adopt in fact incorporates many features of these approaches but, as seen below, stresses the bases of control within and between organizations. It is, though, necessary to examine the contributory approaches in order to determine which aspects are relevant to the overall perspective.

The role of strategic choice is best demonstrated by reference to Child (1972a) in his substantial critique of deterministic theories of organization. One source of such determinism is the environment. Child has distinguished three variants of environmental determinism in terms of the particular type of conditions varying and determining. These are environmental variability, complexity and illiberality.

Environmental variability 'refers to the degree of change which characterizes environmental activities relevant to an organization's operations'. This has, in turn, been seen as a function of three variables: 'the frequency of change in relevant environmental activities . . . the degree of difference involved at each change . . . the degree of irregularity in the overall pattern of change – in a sense, the variability of change' (Child, 1972a, p. 3). What is the relationship between organization and environmental variability? Child observes that writers such as Stinchcombe (1959), Burns and Stalker (1961), Hage and Aiken (1967) and Lawrence and Lorsch (1967) have concluded that the more variable the environment, the more uncertainty the organization has to cope with, so that 'the prevailing structure of organization should be adaptive, with roles open to continual redefinition and with co-ordination being achieved by frequent meetings and considerable lateral communication' (Child, 1972a, p. 3). One may observe the prescriptive tone introduced by use of the word 'should'. Do variable environments have this effect or should they? It is not clear.

Environmental complexity refers to Aldrich's (1975) heterogeneity-homogeneity variable. Lawrence and Lorsch (1967) have argued that environmental complexity entails greater boundary role specialization in the organization system. With more specialists this can increase problems of co-ordination between them. However, as Child argues, complexity need not necessarily cause uncertainty – and hence boundary specialization – because it depends, in addition, on the degree of environmental variability and the 'monitoring' resources of the environment. 'Thus, while Emery and Trist tend to link causal inter-connectedness with uncertainty, the latter would not necessarily be high if the nature of environmental sectors is changing slowly and if the order of connectedness between them is not variable' (Child, 1972a, p. 4).

Environmental illiberality as a concept is similar to Aldrich's (1975) 'domain consensus' in that it 'refers to the degree of threat that faces organizational decision-makers in the achievement of their goals from external competition, hostility or even indifference' (Child, 1972a, p. 4). The more illiberal the environment the more the organization concentrates on survival as Khandwalla (1977) has argued. Hage (1965) proposes that this will lead to more centralized decision-making and tighter controls.

These determinants appear quite acceptable *within the general framework of environmental determination.* However, it is this general framework, as well as some substantive specifications within it, of which Child has been critical. These criticisms fulfil an important corrective role in the development of organization theory, as well as forming a substantial critique of environmental determinism, in particular. In part they are generated from within the 'action framework' as discussed in Chapter 7. Child's critique stresses the role of 'strategic choice', which entails the following:

First, organizational decision-makers may have certain opportunities to select the types of environment in which they will operate. Thus, businessmen may have a choice between new markets to enter, educators may exclude certain subjects from their institution's courses, trade union officers may decide on the bounds of their recruitment policy. Second, the directors of at least large organizations may command sufficient power to influence the conditions prevailing within environments where they are already operating. . . . Some degree of environmental selection is open to most organizations, and some degree of environmental manipulation is open to most larger organizations (Child, 1972a, p. 4)

We can explore this critique in more detail. As suggested in an earlier section, Lawrence and Lorsch (1967) are frequently viewed as contingency theorists, especially with regard to their argument of there being no one best organization for any given environment. Child's argument in a later paper is that there may be a number of internal mechanisms within an organization that promote organization effectiveness, not least of which is control (Child, 1973c). Other writers (for example, Meyer, 1972) have made similar points over the choice of environment that the organization can experience. Cyert and March's (1963) suggestion that very few organizations optimize their capacity for efficiency is an indication of the 'slack' in organizations that also relates to the lack of organizational determinism apropos the environment.

An elaboration of the strategic choice approach suggested by Child is to be seen in Aldrich and Mindlin's (1978) account of the resource perspective (referred to in a less elaborate way as the resource dependence model in Aldrich and Pfeffer, 1976). This approach is firmly grounded within a political economy perspective in that 'the environment is a source of scarce resources which are sought after by a population of organizations which competes as well as shares them' (Aldrich and Mindlin, 1978, p. 156). This resource competition produces a situation where an organization may be dependent on other organizations in the environment. One can see here the similarity to the work of Yuchtman and Seashore (1967) which was discussed in Chapter 8. It will be recalled that the effectiveness of the organization was deemed to be dependent upon the success in obtaining scarce resources coupled with whether the bargaining position and autonomy could be maintained.

The resource perspective also owes much to the applications that have been made of exchange theory to organization analysis, especially from the viewpoint of the concept of dependence. Dependence of one organization A upon another B is 'directly proportional to A's *motivational investment* in goals mediated by B, and inversely proportional to the *availability* of those goals to A outside of the A–B relation' (Emerson, 1962, p. 32). Put another way,

> If A cannot do without the resource(s) mediated by B and is unable to obtain them elsewhere, A becomes dependent on B. Conversely, B acquires power over A . . . dependence is an attribute of the *relation* between A and B, and not of A or B in isolation. It is thus possible that A may be dependent upon B, while having power over C (Aldrich and Mindlin, 1978, p. 156).

It follows that an organization will be more likely to be able to determine the nature of the inter-organizational exchange, the more power that it has acquired. As the resources increase or expand the organization increases in power (through the use of these resources), since other organizations become more dependent on the resources. Blau (1964, pp. 118–25) has shown that organizations will attempt to avoid being dependent on their environments through the control over resources and through the search for alternative resources.

It should be clear that dependence and exchange are closely related. The lack of resources that figures prominently in a *dependence* relationship

> impels organizations to restrict activity to limited specific functions. The fulfilment of these limited functions in turn requires access to certain kinds of elements which an organization seeks to obtain by entering into *exchanges* with other organizations (Levine and White, 1961, p. 586; our emphasis).

Levine and White show that the organization's function partly determines the extent of inter-organizational relations, and also what kinds of exchange take place. Taking their example of organizations concerned with health education rather than organizations concerned with the restoration of health, there is a low amount of inter-organizational interaction in the former compared with a higher amount in the latter (coupled with more resources). Levine and White's approach clearly reflects the dominant sociological trend of the time of writing – structural-functionalism. Thus, it is highly *functional* for organizations to exchange with one another for the effective achievement of their goals.

381

Thompson (1967) takes the exchange notion further by suggesting that as a way of reducing uncertainty in the environment organizations engage in exchanges with other organizations and thereby operate with *negotiated* environments. As Cook (1977, p. 65) has proposed, 'Given functional specialization among organizations and a scarcity of resources organizations seek to reduce environmental uncertainty by creating "negotiated" environments'. These negotiated (and less uncertain) environments are the product of organizational exchange relations.

We can see from this analysis that at a macro-level organizations attempt to achieve control over their environments. As in earlier discussions of control within the organization, it becomes impossible to separate the attempts at control from a consideration of power. Thompson argues that:

> An organization is dependent upon some element of its task environment (1) in proportion to the organization's need for resources or performances which that element can provide, and (2) in inverse proportion to the ability of other elements to provide the same resource or performance (Thompson, 1967, pp. 29–30).

Thompson and Levine and White are in agreement here in that they both refer to 'alternative sources'. By this they mean that the process of negotiation with other organizations in the environment leads to a dispersal of the required extra-organizational capacity, thereby minimizing or reducing the power of any one environmental source. Making sure that alternative sources are available is a key element in exchange relations between organizations. As Gouldner (1959a) has argued, organizations cannot be totally autonomous in their functioning; there need to be elements of reciprocity in relations with other organizations. The nature of reciprocity is such as to reduce autonomy and thereby increase the dependence of one organization upon others. The strength of the dependence is largely a function of the power of an organization to determine its own activities and the kind, rate and terms of exchange with other organizations. 'Power may be said to derive from the central organization's control over strategic contingencies confronted by the peripheral organizations' (Benson, 1978, pp. 75–6).

Recent discussions of inter-organizational relations involving exchanges have referred to a network of exchange relations. Benson describes the inter-organizational network as consisting

> of a number of distinguishable organizations engaged in a significant amount of interaction with each other. Such interaction

may include extensive, reciprocal exchanges of resources, at one extreme, or intense hostility and conflict at the other. The organizations in a network may be linked directly or indirectly. That is, some networks may consist of a series of organizations linked together by multiple, direct ties to each other. Others may be characterized by a clustering or centring of linkages around one or a few mediating or controlling organizations (Benson, 1978, p. 71).

Benson develops his argument by suggesting that network analysis needs to focus upon the processes of resources acquisition and that in the final analysis interactions between organizations can only be explained or understood by reference to the level of resource flow. The inter-organizational network is, according to Benson, a political economy based upon the distributions of the scarce resources of money and authority. We have already indicated that power is a key phenomenon affecting the likely success of an organization in securing resources; Benson also sees the market position of the organization as a crucial feature.

Network analysis is clearly a separate kind of analysis from the kinds of perspective that we have discussed above. Possibly the dominant feature of the traditional organization-environment analysis has been that the attempts by an individual organization to remain viable and effective have been the explanatory variables. Network analysis differs in that

the locus of explanation lies in the network itself. The features of specific organizations then are determined to some degree by the tendencies of the network. Intra-organizational features become outcroppings of multi-organization networks or sets (Benson, 1977a, p. 10).

Karen Cook (1977) has extended Benson's original conception of network analysis through the use of exchange theory. Specifically she uses a general theory to analyse inter-organizational relations by seeing the general exchange relations of both organizations and organization networks at different levels. This is an approach that has been developed both by Crozier(1972) and Wassenberg (1977). Crozier, in his multi-level approach, suggests that both organizations *per se* and organization networks can be analysed from the perspective of 'games', and thereby manages to link the levels of analysis to a more general theory. Although the different games are dependently linked, this is largely at a horizontal level. As Benson (1977a, p. 11) has commented, 'Analyses which stress only the processes of exchange, negotiation or game-playing within the limits (of the boundaries of other games) fail to provide an adequate

383

grasp of social structure.'

Wassenberg makes a similar criticism when he demonstrates that traditional approaches to the dynamics of organization-environment relations neglect 'the exploration and identification of the multi-dimensionality of the relevant environment or organizations' (Wassenberg, 1977, p. 90). Wassenberg's solution to this failing is in terms of an 'institutional' approach that explores vertical as well as horizontal links between organization and environment in the network of exchanges. Such an approach, Wassenberg argues, can provide answers to 'two classic sociological questions':

1 How do transactions between organizations influence the stratification of organizations in an institutional sector (e.g., the socio-economic and politico-economic sub-systems of industrial society in times of industrial reconstruction)?

2 What structural (i.e. reciprocal, sequential, pooled interdependence) properties and what cultural (i.e. intellectual and political decision-making and evaluation) principles govern the evolution and devolution of that stratification of organizations? (Wassenberg, 1977, p. 93).

Wassenberg sees the answers to these questions in three steps that provide the kind of vertical linkages addressed above, and which come to terms with Benson's observation of failure to account for social structures.

The first step is the restoration of the concepts of power and transaction in the theory of organizations. The second step is the operationalization of the principle of bounded interdependence, legitimacy and rationality. The third step is the spelling out of the following: the anticipation of the consequences which follow when self-interested organizations choose strategies to maximize manoeuvrability in interdependent arrangements in a changing economic and political environment (Wassenberg, 1977, p. 98).

Each of the approaches used by Cook and Wassenberg in its separate way overcomes the criticism levelled by Benson (1977a) and Aldrich (1974). Aldrich's point is that the use of exchange theory has tended to emphasize organizational relations where there have been equal control and power of resources. Thus, the vertical relations among and between organizations have been relatively neglected. We have seen Wassenberg's strategy for overcoming this neglect; Cook has 'focused primarily upon power as it affects exchange relations among organizations' (Cook, 1977, p. 77) and thereby overcomes the criticism.

A second aspect of Cook's paper is important in that she suggests that work on inter-organizational relations could usefully focus on

384

the analysis of multi-organization sectors or markets. Such a focus suggests that societies themselves can be seen as inter-organizational systems and, hence, introduces a new level of analysis. 'The break [from earlier work] lies in the fact that the locus of explanation is shifted from the tendencies of the organization to the structure of networks, markets and institutional complexes' (Benson, 1977a, p. 10), in much the same way as Wassenberg has proposed. Cook concludes her paper by suggesting that

> we must begin to formulate theories which will enable us to deal with the dynamic properties of inter-organizational networks (e.g., an increase or decrease in dominance, shifts in alliances or coalitions, the formulation of mergers, the rise and fall of competitive activity, and the instigation of regulatory practices). Future theoretical development of this type will entail a commitment to the longitudinal study of inter-organizational relations.

These suggestions are well taken; and in the next section we turn to an analysis of multi-national enterprises in an attempt to move away from the often highly abstract level of inter-organizational analysis to a level having an empirical relevance in which many of the theoretical notions can be explored.

The organization and environment of the multi-national enterprise

International organizations have been a familiar part of the history of many countries of the world. The East India Companies of Holland and Britain, the Florentine Medici finance institutions, the trading organizations associated with the Roman Empire and even the Catholic Church were all organizations operating in more than one country. However, such organizations differ from what today we refer to as the multi-national enterprises for a number of reasons. Such enterprises are exclusively economic organizations, have a relatively recent history, and, indeed, as Mandel (1975) suggests, they are an organizational form associated with late capitalism. From the point of view of the present discussion the most important characteristic of the multi-national enterprise is its capacity to control and change its environment.

Following Mandel (1975, pp. 316–21) we can highlight the reasons for the development of the multi-national enterprises and in so doing can see the differences between them and more traditional and familiar economic organizations. In the first instance, it would appear that the idea of the nation-state as an economic unit is fast becoming an anachronism. This is largely because it is impossible for many companies to be profitable solely on a national basis.

385

Domestic markets have their limitations and, in any case, profitable production increasingly requires ever increasing amounts of capital. The amount that can be produced by one organization is in excess of what the domestic market can consume. Mandel gives the following examples:

> For a country like Sweden, the internal market (domestic consumption) only allows for 30% of the minimal optimum capacity of one factory producing cigarettes, 50% of one factory producing refrigerators and 70% of a brewery. Even in Canada, the domestic market is too small to permit the utilization of the minimal optimum capacity of a single plant producing refrigerators (Mandel, 1975, p. 317).

The internationalization of the forces of production have seen as a corollary the internationalization of capital. It is interesting to see the way in which one company can produce a significant number of trade movements across many countries. Ford of Europe provides an excellent example with the production of one of its most recent models, the Fiesta.

> We have a picture of carburettors being supplied to Saarlouis, Dagenham and Valencia from Ford's Belfast plant. Die-cast transaxle casings and gear components are sent from Cologne to Bordeaux; the completed transaxles are sent from there to Saarlouis, Dagenham and Valencia. These three assembly plants, each with its own stamping plant, share with Genk the supply of body stampings. All cylinder block and head castings for the 1,000 cc and 1,100 cc engines are produced in Dagenham and then sent to Valencia to be machined and assembled. Some built-up engines are then sent back to Britain for installing in Dagenham-built Fiestas (Counter Information Service, 1977, p. 29).

The overall picture of Fiesta production in Europe is as follows:

Engine:
    Castings for all engines: Dagenham, UK
    Machinery and assembly:
           1,000 cc   Valencia, Spain
           1,100 cc   Valencia, Spain
           1,300 cc   Dagenham, UK
           1,600 cc   Dagenham, UK

Body panels: Dagenham, UK
                                 Genk, Belgium
                                 Saarlouis, Germany
                                 Valencia, Spain

Transaxle gearbox
  (for front-wheel drive):

Dagenham, UK
Valencia, Spain
Saarlouis, Germany
Bordeaux, France

Other key components and sub-assemblies:
  Basildon, Dagenham, Enfield, Leamington and Treforest, UK
  Genk, Belgium
  Belfast, Northern Ireland
  Cologne, Saarlouis and Wulfrath, Germany

On first reflection such international trade movements would not appear to make much economic sense. However, when we recall that the capital investment for the Fiesta was in excess of $1 billion it is clear that such a capital outlay would be too clearly tied to the financial capabilities of any one country if it was not spread multi-nationally. The centralization of capital in one international company forces the move towards vertical integration and necessarily involves production across a number of countries. As we shall see below, this vertical integration also has important repercussions for the control of the environment in which a company such as Ford operates.

A second reason for the development of the multi-national enter-prise is the surplus profits that are generated as a consequence of capital concentration in the large oligopolies and monopolies. This is a phenomenon demonstrated by Marx (1976) in *Capital,* vol. 1. Competition and credit, he argued, produced ever-increasing capital centralization and concentration. Baran and Sweezy (1966) in their analysis of *Monopoly Capital* develop this theme further by arguing that one of the major problems of the large corporation is how to absorb economic surplus, and that one solution is to dispose of surplus abroad. (This thesis has been much criticized. See O'Connor, 1974, for instance.) So, not only does production take place beyond the national boundary; new markets are created for the products.

Mandel refers to 'technological rents' as the third cause of the multi-national development.

> In late capitalism surplus profits predominantly take the form of technological surplus profits. The reduced turnover-time of fixed capital and the acceleration of technological innovation determine a pursuit for new products and new production processes (Mandel, 1975, p. 318).

In effect the multi-national corporation has produced an international division of labour which is based upon international product differentiation. In the area of motor-car production such

387

product differentiation is clearly visible. In Europe firms such as Volvo, Mercedes-Benz and BMW have traditionally concentrated on the large luxury motor cars; British Leyland, Renault and Fiat have a larger concentration on the smaller 'family' car.

A fourth reason for the rise of the multi-national corporation is associated with its role in the third world. O'Connor (1974, p. 197) observed that 'United States, European and Japanese international corporations presently own or control between 20 and 30 per cent of the monetized resources in the underdeveloped countries'. Baran and Sweezy's argument on the absorption of economic surplus is often seen as the cause of such development. In addition the search for new sources of raw materials and energy and the more general socio-political necessity for control of such resources are other important causes. Mandel is of the opinion that capital exports to underdeveloped countries have undergone a relative decline as a result of political uncertainties. He argues that the surplus profit which would have been exported as capital to such countries 'now predominantly moves to and fro between the imperialist metropolitan countries, which further promotes the ascent of the multi-national company' (Mandel, 1975, p. 319). The role of Japanese corporations in countries as geographically dispersed as the United Kingdom, Australia and the United States in recent years would tend to confirm Mandel's observation.

Mandel suggests as a further reason for the growth of multinationals the protectionist policies that have been pursued by the advanced industrial nations. In order to get round tariff restrictions, capital rather than commodities has been exported and, as demonstrated below, this constitutes an important means of environmental control. Fluctuations in currencies provide another reason for capital rather than commodity exports and the subsequent international division of labour.

Theorists of political economy such as Mandel and O'Connor have not been the only ones to attempt to account for the phenomenon of the multi-national enterprise. It is perhaps interesting to note that many disciplines, from economics to history, have produced their own accounts, but that organization theory, which surely ought to have a central interest, has largely ignored the phenomenon. Since it would be difficult and not especially useful to analyse the many different explanations that exist in the disparate literature, it is probably most instructive to examine briefly the work of Alfred Chandler (1962). His eclectic approach incorporates case studies of the development of four corporations (Dupont, General Motors, Standard Oil, and Sears Roebuck).

There are, according to Chandler, four phases of organizational transition:

388

the initial expansion and accumulation of resources; the rationalization of the use of resources; the expansion into new markets and lines to help assure the continuing full use of resources; and finally the development of a new structure to make possible continuing effective mobilization of resources to meet both changing short-term market demand and long-term market trends (Chandler, 1962, p. 385).

Chandler seems to be broadly in agreement with Mandel as to the initial causes of multi-national growth.

The prospect of a new market, or the threatened loss of a current one stimulated geographical expansion, vertical integration and product diversification. Moreover, once a firm had accumulated large resources, the need to keep its men, money and materials steadily employed provided a constant stimulus to look for new markets by moving into new areas, by taking on new functions or by developing new product lines (Chandler, 1962, p. 15).

We can see from Chandler's analysis how the perspectives on organization and environment outlined earlier in this chapter have relevance to the multi-national enterprise. Following on from the above quotation Chandler writes:

Strategic growth results from an awareness of the opportunities and needs – created by changing population, income and technology – to employ existing or expanding resources more profitably. A new strategy required a new or at least a refashioned structure if the enlarged enterprise was to be operated efficiently.

Chandler was thus providing an analysis based upon strategic choice before writers such as Lawrence and Lorsch or Child were to see the relevance of the concept in the analysis of organization and environment. In effect, Chandler is saying that strategic choice plays a major role in the design of organization structure. The strategies available are:

the determination of the basic long-term goals and objectives of an enterprise, and the adoption of courses of action and the allocation of resources necessary for carrying out these goals (Chandler, 1962, p. 13).

Both of these basic strategies are used in the design of the multi-national organizational structure. As McMillan has put it:

Successful exploitation of strategic opportunities comes as a result of devising an organizational form which provided for top

389

management the separation of strategic or long-run decisions from the concentration on operational or day to day decisions (McMillan, 1973, p. 31).

McMillan develops this argument further by suggesting that there are typical organizational structures associated with the stages of organization development as shown in Table 10.1

TABLE 10.1

	Stage 1	*Stage 2*	*Stage 3*	*Stage 4*
Strategy product-market mix	1 Simple product line, related technology, single channel of distribution.	1 Single product line, large-scale production, product lines related by technology, one major market.	1 Diversification of product lines, new channels of distribution, accumulation of resources.	1 Complex range of products, sold in different markets, multiple channels of distribution.
Organizational structures	1 Small firm, owner-manager, single unit firm, simple communications (this is surrogate entrepreneur model of economic theory). 2 Informal control system.	1 Team management (not professional) single operating unit. 2 Increased use of rules for task co-ordination.	1 Development of operating units by geography, structure like Stage 1 or 2. 2 Centralized management to integrate operating units and adjudicate conflict at lower levels.	1 Multi-divisional product structure, headed by functional managers. 2 Divisions run as a separate profit centre with highly elaborate communications system, often used to train and test executives. 3 Highly centralized policy unit at headquarters, concentration of finance, planning, and research and development

Source: McMillan, 1973, p. 32.

From Table 10.1 it would appear that a specific model of the multi-national organization can be discerned. The typical model is one of a highly structured organization but with the flexibility to optimize from the changing environment. It is to a consideration of this environment that we can now turn by exploring the ways in which multi-national enterprises can be considered as agents of change and control in their interactions with other organizations.

1 *Multi-nationals and host governments* It must be recognized that multi-national organizations are different from the kind of organization traditionally studied by organization theorists. Their size and complexity and their capacity for capital investment in countries of their choice makes them able to control their environments in hitherto unknown ways. The fact of being independent of national governments in many instances enable them to pursue

their goals in a ruthless and unaccountable manner. Martinelli and Somaini (1973, p. 71) observe that 'the fact of belonging to a single giant enterprise weighs more than the fact of being located in a given country . . . the nation states can exercise only a "limited sovereignty" on the local branches of multi-national corporations'.

If we take the case of the relations between multi-nationals and governments it will be recalled that the corporatists have argued that the past fifteen years or so have seen a dramatic increase in the amount of state intervention in private enterprise and that this is most visible in the case of Britain. To what extent does this proposition hold good for the multi-national enterprise? The case of the Ford Motor Company's decision to build a new engine plant at Bridgend in South Wales would suggest that the corporatist argument has weaknesses. A number of European countries wanted the new engine plant; and during the summer of 1977 television viewers were subjected to newsreels of Henry Ford being wooed by various governments and prime ministers in the same fashion as that normally reserved for visiting royalty. The bids made by governments increased as the weeks crept by. In the end the British government won the day by directly providing £70 million of the required £185 million investment. The figure becomes considerably higher when the indirect contributions in the form of training grants, rates relief and so forth are considered. The irony of this is that Ford would probably have invested in Britain anyway because of the existing foundry at Dagenham, the low wage rates and the advanced engineering industry in Britain. And yet the *Financial Times* (10 September 1977) reported that, 'With the new South Wales engine plant, the biggest single investment in the UK motor industry since the 1960s, Henry Ford has demonstrated his intention to win the battle for acceptability in the most dramatic way possible.' The Ford Motor Company emerged as the Good Samaritan of South Wales with not only the press but politicians as well praising the altruistic decision. Yet if the government aid had not been as great the plant would probably have gone ahead anyway.

The same was true of the decision to build the Valencia plant in Spain. Cheap labour and legislation against industrial action ensured by a Fascist state, were the main reasons for siting the plant there, and yet the Spanish government additionally passed a statute that released Ford from abiding by the law relating to foreign ownership of investments. Further examples from countries in nearly every continent in the world can be given that demonstrate how governments have been influenced by Ford rather than the other way round.

The most blatant example of multi-national firms influencing governments in recent years has been their response to the Allende Marxist government in Chile following the national elections in 1970. The role of ITT is well documented (Sampson, 1973), but other corporations played a significant part in the eventual downfall of the government. Again Ford can be examined. Ford had made a major penetration into the Chilean economy to the extent of producing 35 per cent of the motor cars and 60 per cent of the public transport vehicles. The penetration did not end there, since Ford also suppled the spare parts for all these vehicles in the order of $156,000 worth every month before the 1970 elections. With Allende's election spare part imports were reduced by Ford to $15,000 worth each month. The public transport system virtually collapsed after a relatively short time. So did trade movement of foodstuffs, in particular, as these were trucked to market by privately, usually individually owned trucks. These trucks were largely Ford's. Although the Ford factory was nationalized it was a useless exercise because of the absence of components from other factories. Ford's role together with the combined efforts of other multi-nationals, backed by the US state through the role of the CIA, suceeded not only in destroying the Allende government, but the Chilean economy as well.

2   *Investment decision-making*   We have already suggested that there is a relationship between the strategy employed by multi-nationals and the structural arrangements within the organization on a multi-divisional basis that facilitate the attainment of the strategy (in the forms of a constellation of goals depicted by Chandler). Decision-making is the key issue in multi-nationals, since they are predominantly high-technology industries and so the stress is upon technical and managerial knowledge. Strategic decision-making (that is, involving the creation of knowledge and the allocation of knowledge) is invariably highly centralized. For the country providing the location of the headquarters of the multi-national there are considerable benefits of these highly centralized structures. Research institutes, universities, management consultancies and the like are strengthened because of their role in the creation of potentially profitable knowledge. Equally, the service organizations abound in the form of banking, insurance, communications and sub-contracting. Furthermore, as McMillan (1974, p. 41) observes, the corporate metropolis 'acts as a magnet to the most highly skilled and capable personnel'. Decision-making in the host country tends to be concerned with only day-to-day production problems.

Clearly, with such a structure, considerations of what is best for a national economy must be secondary to considerations of what is most appropriate for the international organization as a whole. As we have seen, the multi-national can obtain preferential treatment from governments, if not actually provide a powerful influence as to the nature of the political environment. The considerations involved in decision-making lead to the suggestion that multi-nationals largely create their own environments rather than passively reacting to the host environment.

3 *Economic integration* In the last two stages of the corporate development model reproduced above we shall see another way in which the multi-national corporation manages to control its environment. Although such enterprises have generally been welcomed to host countries and especially into particular regions experiencing high unemployment, the economic consequences for the host country have often been far short of successful. There are many instances of countries or regions within countries becoming almost exclusively dependent upon the multi-national corporations once it has become established. This dependence has occurred largely through the multi-national having competitive advantages over local domestic producers in the form of better credit facilities, being able to buy skilled labour at a higher price, having the ability to take over local competitors and the advantages of research and development in the home country that advantage the multi-national in product development. This is part of the process that leads to the standardization implied by the so-called 'global strategy'.

> The operations of a multi-national enterprise in any national environment generally represent a mixture of national influences. Up to a point, there is local adaptation. But anyone wandering through Volkswagen's Sao Paulo plant almost at once feels transported back to Germany; Fiat's plants in Argentina exude the atmosphere of Turin; and there is no mistaking the American origins of an IBM facility located anywhere (Vernon, 1976, p. 46).

Again we see here the way in which the multi-national organization operates without being overly concerned with the local environment in which it is situated. The homogenization to which Vernon refers is motivated by the concern of the corporation as defined by its corporate strategy. The goals of growth and profitability are the determinant factors, not whether an indigenous country is losing its national identity.

4 *Resource movement* Multi-national enterprises have sometimes been described as the new imperialists, largely through their practices of extracting as much as possible from a host country and

giving little in return. Two operations used by the multi-nationals have come in for particular scrutiny and criticisms: tax evasion and transfer pricing. Both of these practices provide further evidence of the nature of their relations with their environments. Tax evasion occurs through the multi-national taking advantage of tax havens, creating special tax treaties, using international differences in tax rates, and so on. And it does not happen only in the developing countries who, it might be thought, have less experience of dealing with multi-national companies and therefore might lose more potential tax revenue than a more developed country. The case of the British government's dealing with multi-national corporations involved in the exploration for and development of North Sea Oil provides a salutory example.

Rather than imposing a tax on the amount of oil extracted from the North Sea the Government, under pressure from the corporations involved in oil exploration, opted for a revenue tax (PRT). The argument was that an incentive had to be offered to get the corporations to undertake the massive development costs (for example, Shell claims to have invested over £1,000 million in the North Sea). PRT was set at the rate of 45 per cent (although this was increased to 60 per cent in August 1978). The agreement between the Government and the corporations was that PRT should not be paid until 175 per cent of the capital expenditure on oil exploration was written off. So, for every £100 million invested the corporations did not start paying PRT until they had earned £175 million. That in itself would suggest a disadvantage for the Government, but when other factors such as the fact of profits from one block being offset against losses from another block are considered, it would appear that the multi-nationals were able to extract a lot and give back very little. By the end of the financial year 1977–8 the Government had not received a penny in oil tax, even though one million barrels of oil *a day* were being extracted from the North Sea. If a highly developed country such as Britain is unable to realize the implications of its taxation on multi-national corporations one wonders about nations who have had less experience of dealing with them.

The other practice referred to was transfer pricing, which is a mechanism used by multi-national corporations to adjust prices of unfinished goods within the one corporation. It is a position of borrowing from Peter to pay Paul, but where Peter and Paul happen to be the same corporate body. Another feature of transfer pricing is that it can reduce the tax liability of the corporation as a whole.

Transfer pricing permits cost minimization for the global system by shifting profits earned, but not reported, in one nation to another nation with a lower tax rate. The outcome is global tax minimization, one of the key requisites for global profit maximization (Müller, 1976, p. 183).

Each of these factors demonstrates that multi-national corporations, in the singular pursuit of their corporate strategies, are able to change, manipulate and avoid their environments to a very large extent. There is no denying that they do adhere to local legislation where this does not interfere in any significant way with the achievement of their goals. Where local legislation does appear to stand in the way of the corporate strategy the legislation is either avoided or attempts are made to change it. (Exceptional cases do exist of multi-national corporations acquiescing in the face of external pressure. The success of the OPEC countries in quadrupling the price of oil in 1974 compared with 1973 prices is one of the most startling examples, but even in this instance the oil companies were hardly manipulated victims but co-conspirators and producers of not only the so-called 'oil-crisis' but also its distorted representation as such in the Western business and popular press. Not only did the oil companies not carry the cost of escalating oil prices on the oil-dependent economies they had produced; they managed to put off the price rise for a sufficient length of time to switch some of their resources; Michael Harrington, (1977, pp. 236–64), has argued these points at length, using Congressional papers to substantiate his case. It is perhaps interesting to note that it took a consortium of countries guided by common purposes to achieve what OPEC did; it is highly unlikely that a single nation-state could ever be so successful.)

Concluding remarks

Our brief account of multi-national enterprises in terms of internal dynamics and environmental control suggests a number of avenues for developments in inter-organizational analysis. Taking Cook's (1977) statement that the dynamic properties of inter-organizational networks should be explored, we can approach this from two different angles. On the one hand, work such as Chandler's (1962) demonstrates how valuable longitudinal studies of organizations can be. The strategic growth to which he refers enables us to understand the causes of organizational growth over time as well as comprehend the changing structure of organizations. The rational design of organization structure over time facilitates strategic decision-making. The increasing degree of co-ordination and control of organizational activities over time not only minimizes uncertainty and thus increases control within the organization (for example, in terms of member behaviour); it also enables the strategic decision-makers to predict demands in the environment (for example, the future market demand). The same is as true for demands for labour as for product. If the trends in the labour market can be anticipated then management can adopt an appropriate strategy to exploit the market through inducements in times of high employment and vice versa. It is as well to remember, however, that organizations operate in an imperfect situation and that total control of the product market or labour market is virtually unrealizable. To the extent that greater control of the markets is possible it can be suggested that greater structural control within the organization is also possible.

On the other hand, the example of multi-national corporations demonstrates that such organizations can strategically control the market by other means: control of their environments through tacit agreements with governments. Although, as we have seen, the corporatists argue that state intervention in the economy is systematically eroding the traditional managerial role in private enterprise, the case of the multi-national corporation suggests otherwise. Certainly the state under capitalism has attempted to ensure some stability in the market through direct fiscal measures or through indirect interventionist policies. As Chandler (1962) has shown, the strategies used by large corporations such as price fixing, take-overs and controlling the source of raw materials have been alternatives to increasing the internal co-ordination as a response to predicting market fluctuations. Thus, as we have shown in the case of the multi-national corporation, the state may even pass new laws or rescind old ones in order to facilitate the corporation's control over a market. What has become known as 'Ford's Law' in Spain is such an example. In this respect, the multi-national corporations are not unique in the history of capitalism. The expansion of the railways in nineteenth-century Britain involved changes in certain statutes to allow certain enterprises to gain monopolistic control over their environments. Such tinkering with statutes whether in the nineteenth century on a more local scale or in the late twentieth century on a national scale produces an artificial environment that facilitates corporate growth. Increasingly there are indications of nation-states combining together in an effort to stabilize and control the market for private enterprises. One such example would be the fishing rights policy adopted by member countries of the EEC. McNeil (1978, p. 72) has commented that 'the state has constantly intervened to institutionalize the struggles that evolved out of the need for discipline and control in organizations'.

These two fundamental issues have been systematically examined by the institutional economists (McNeil, 1978), especially in the work of Commons (1961: 1968). Veblen (1965) was one of the first writers to recognize that enterprises employ the state in an effort to control their environments (rather than the other way round, as argued by the corporatists). Veblen showed that the profits of industrial organizations were often as much a result of environmental control through the facilitative role of the state as a consequence of internal productive efficiency.

Commons took Veblen's ideas further through a distinction between the 'going plant' and the 'going concern'. The former relates broadly to the productive capacity of an enterprise through internal arrangements; the latter relates to profit maximization through environmental control or 'banker capitalism'. Commons argued that the state was prepared to facilitate banker capitalism in order to introduce stability into an economy. Possibly this is what Winkler (1977, p. 44) suggests when he argues that state intervention occurs because of the principles of 'unity, order, nationalism and success'; it is unlikely though, because the state is directing and controlling the enterprise according to Winkler, and not vice versa.

McNeil (1978) has made a tentative first step to understanding the organization-environment question in these terms through a reminder of Weber's contribution to the issue. We have already seen that many of the various attempts to explain the nature of the relationship between organizations and their environments have been in terms of the organization's adaptation to the environment. The natural selection perspective described by Aldrich and Pfeffer (1976) is perhaps the most extreme case. The other side of the coin to adaptation is to discover how organizations attempt to control their environments. Perrow (1972, p. 199) has commented that, 'The environment of most powerful organizations is well controlled by them, quite stable, and made up of other organizations, ones they control'. As Commons, Veblen and others have suggested, this control of the environment is facilitated by the state; the multinational enterprise examples given above provide empirical evidence for this proposition. Clearly, it is essential to recognize that industrial organizations both adapt to and dominate their environments, but 'most organizational sociologists, seeing no sinister plot to dominate, focus solely on the adaptation strategies' (McNeil, 1978, p. 66).

The emphasis upon adaptation and the relative neglect of the process of domination has arisen, according to McNeil, through the limited interpretation of Weber's analysis of organizations as rational goal-attaining structures. In this volume we have attempted to go beyond this narrow interpretation and in Chapters 2 and 3 have shown Weber's concern with the development of capitalism and the emergence of rational organization. As part of that analysis we have demonstrated the increased role of the state with the development of the rational organization.

McNeil has pointed to a number of key elements in Weber's work that have been relatively neglected and yet are valuable in understanding the relationship between organizations and their environments. In the first place he refers to the tension between market and administrative logic (McNeil, 1978, pp. 68–9). In spite of the fact that rational organization and capitalism developed simultaneously, there is a basic inconsistency between the two.

> The market logic of supply and demand for labour, commodities and capital is inherently unpredictable, yet the administrative logic of economic organizations demands a high degree of calculability. The basic problem for administration is the management of this unpredictability. . . . This tension became a source of pressure for administrative élites to dominate the environment, because the discipline of the market would quickly drive any organization that failed to produce a profit out of business (McNeil, 1978, p. 65).

In an attempt to reduce the tension to which McNeil refers organizatons strive to stabilize the uncertain elements in their environments. Organizational efficiency thus becomes a measure of how successful organizations are in controlling and dominating their environment.

A second element in Weber's work that has been distinguished by McNeil is the strategies for mobilizing power. As it has already been pointed out, no organization can totally control its environment; there is always some element of environmental uncertainty. But through the strategic choice available to it – especially to the powerful multi-national corporation – uncertainty can be minimized through '(1) internal bureaucratization and (2) stabilization of environmental forces through state regulation' (McNeil, 1978, p. 70). Both of these strategies have been examined above.

The third element is the administrative rationalities that are used as mechanisms for determining the use of power (McNeil, 1978, pp. 73–5). In the case of the multi-national enterprise a number of particular examples have been presented that demonstrate the use of power. In more general terms, Weber (1968) referred to the *rationalities* of administrative élites as being the way in which power was used. Such rationalities include 'Profit maximization, abstract legal logic through which they (managers) tap the coercive power of the state, and scientific knowledge which enhances calculability in organizational procedures' (McNeil, 1978, p. 73). It is Weberian rationalities of this kind that Karpik (1977) refers to as 'logics of action'. The logics of action describe and explain how potential power is transformed into actual power.

With the exception of Selznick's (1949) work on organizations and environment through his analysis of the Tennessee Valley Authority, the organization literature has, until comparatively recently, largely ignored the kinds of issue that McNeil has discussed from Weber's work. Of crucial importance is the attempt to account for the use of domination by organizations as a mechanism of environmental control. The somewhat cursory analysis of multi-national enterprises leads us to suggest that such accounting is of crucial importance. It is heartening, however, to note that the political economy perspective that has been described above is attempting to develop this analytic approach.

An earlier analysis by the present authors (Clegg and Dunkerley, 1977) suggested a number of areas in which organization theory displays its paucity. Among these areas were delineated the almost exclusive concern with the internal structural characteristics of organizations by recent researchers and the methodological problems of the dominant positivist tradition that has developed in organizational research. Remarkably similar criticisms have been levelled by Benson (1977b) in his preliminary account of a dialectical approach to organizational behaviour. The analysis here of the relationship between organizations and environments has been more positive than these earlier works, in that ways have been suggested for analysing the relationship that accounts for it from the point of view of strategies available to organizations that enable them to dominate *and* adapt to their environments through the exercise of power.

11 People in organizations

In general, we could say of the usual treatment of people in organizations that it has been couched at the level of individuals and individualism (Champion, 1975, provides a good example). People in organizations have been regarded as psychologically determined entities whose needs and dispositions, subject to social qualification (hence social psychology), are the source of social action. As Poulantzas says in another, yet relevant, context:

> This is a problematic of *social actors,* of individuals as the origin of *social action:* sociological research thus leads finally, not to the study of the objective co-ordinates that determine the distribution of agents into social classes and the contradictions between these classes, but to the search for *finalist* explanations founded on the motivations of conduct of the individual actors (Poulantzas, 1973, p. 295).

This chapter, and the following chapter, begin the consideration of people in organizations: not as subjectivities, as unique, individuals or social psyches, but as the bearers of an objective structure of relations of production and reproduction which are conditioned not by psychology but by history.

Men and women in organizations

The point ought not to require elaboration, but the labour process involves men *and* women. That it does require making is evident from any familiarity with the literature, which even includes volumes with such a title as *Man and Organization* (Child, 1973a). (It was against such a backdrop of sexist assumptions that Janet Wolff prepared her 'Women in Organizations' chapter for our *Critical Issues in Organizations* (Clegg and Dunkerley, 1977) as a

400

deliberate attempt to force recognition of this sorry state of affairs.) This sexism, and some of its implications for the analysis of organizations, has been commented on by Richard Brown (1976) in the context of a discussion of research on employees in industrial sociology.

Brown observes that, where they have not been ignored altogether, women in organizations have been regarded either as indistinguishable from men in any aspect relevant to their attitudes and actions at work, or as the source of problems for employers and/or the families or communities from which they come (Brown, 1976, p. 21). This neglect of the sexual division of labour is not only widespread in studies at an introductory level which deal with the psychological aspects of organizations (e.g., Schein, 1965; Tannenbaum, 1966), but is apparent in studies such as the Hawthorne experiments, which have achieved the status of classics in the genre of organization analysis. For instance, one explanation of the striking difference between the findings of the Relay Assembly Test Room experiments (where experimental activity produced increases in productivity and co-operativeness, regardless of the particular variables being manipulated in particular ways) and those of the Bank Wiring Observation Room (where workers restricted their output) was that while the employees in the former situation were females supervised by a male, in the latter situation they were all males. As Brown (1976, p. 25.6) notes, this neglect of sexual divisions in the work force has had particularly unfortunate consequences for work which developed in the wake of the Hawthorne studies. It meant that assumptions of general validity have been abstracted from famous and frequently cited studies such as Coch and French (1948) on overcoming resistance to change, and Morse and Reimer (1956) on the consequences of a re-allocation of decision-making. This is despite the fact that the employees were women. As Gouldner (1959) has argued, gender is a vital 'latent social identity'. It is for this reason that all those works which generalize from a single-sex population, be it female or male, are open to criticism. After all, gender differentiation is one of the more obvious features of the social environment.

Why should we have to draw attention to the sexual division of labour in an analysis of organization as a control process? To answer this we have to enquire into the nature of the dual labour market for men and women; women's dual role in society, and the historical development of these dual phenomena.

The dual labour market for men and women

In recent years, particularly since the civil rights movement in the

USA highlighted the confinement of most blacks to low-pay sectors of the economy, studies of the labour market in developed capitalist societies have differentiated this market into two sectors. One, which is termed the primary sector, contains relatively well-paid and stable jobs, while the other, secondary sector, contains lower paid and more insecure jobs (Barron and Norris, 1976). One feature of all the developed capitalist countries is that while women usually constitute about one third of the labour force (in the USA it is about 42 per cent), their wages usually range from, as an average, around half to nearly three-quarters of the equivalent male wages. In all of these countries the largest percentage of women workers are in unskilled jobs (Mitchell, 1971, p. 41).

We can make our discussion of this coincidence of low wages, unskilled jobs and female labour (in short, of a female secondary labour market) more specific by discussing it in the context of a specific social formation: Britain. However, although our argument takes its specificity from this instance, its general theme is universally applicable to trends in advanced capitalist societies, notwithstanding local variations.

> Women's employment has continued to be concentrated in a small number of industries and confined to a range of jobs which might be described as 'women's work'. Even where women work alongside men, they usually hold positions of lower responsibility and perform tasks of a less skilled nature . . . men are the employers, managers, top professionals, foremen and skilled workers in our society (*Social Trends,* 1974, p. 18).

Men are also the more highly paid in our society, as is shown by Table 11.1, adapted from the British New Earnings Survey 1977 (the figures relate to April 1977). The typical low-paid worker is

TABLE 11.1 (*in £*)

	10% earned less than:	10% earned more than:	Average weekly earnings
Manual occupations			
Male	48.1	98.5	154.3
Female	29.9	58.7	110.7
Non-manual occupations			
Male	51.5	133.3	227.9
Female	33.5	81.4	143.7

Source: British New Earnings Survey 1977.

female. She is also occupationally segregated. The vast majority of women workers are concentrated in a few industries. Over 50 per cent of women workers are employed in the three major service industries. In 1977 one of these, the distributive trades, accounted for 17 per cent of the female work force. Professional and scientific services (including typists, technicians, secretaries, teachers and nurses) included 23 per cent of the female employment, while miscellaneous services such as catering, hairdressing, dry-cleaning and laundering employed 12 per cent of female employees.

A quarter of all women workers are employed in manufacturing industry. Of this quarter, over a half are employed in jobs which are ranked as unskilled or semi-skilled (that is, needing between one and six months' training). Within the manufacturing sector women are concentrated in three areas. These are: food, drink and tobacco; engineering, especially electrical engineering; and textiles, clothing and footwear.

Nearly two-thirds of women work in occupations in which they are either highly over-represented or highly under-represented. In manual work they are under-represented in all skilled work, with the exception of skilled textile operators, and they are over-represented in jobs like packing. In non-manual work they are over-represented in nursing, hairdressing, as shop assistants and as cashiers, and in lower-level catering jobs (Barron and Norris, 1976, p. 48).

There is a high degree of correlation between levels of skill and levels of earnings:

Among manual workers, only one woman in eight, as opposed to nearly one man in three, works in the seven industries where men's average earnings are highest (vehicles, paper, printing and publishing, coal and petroleum, shipbuilding and marine engineering, bricks, pottery and glass, metal manufacture, and transport and communications). Yet more than a half of all women employed, compared with a quarter of men, are in the lowest paying industries: textile, clothing and footwear, distributive trades, professional and scientific services, public administration, miscellaneous services, agriculture, forestry and fishing (Davies, 1975, p. 17).

The areas in which it might be most obvious to look for women in skilled, senior, high-pay jobs would be in those industries in which women predominate. However, the obvious is not the case. As Knight (1974, p. 11) reports, in the food retailing industry, where over two-thirds of the employees were women, only 4 per cent of them were occupied in management, while 30 per cent of the much smaller number of male employees held management jobs. In engineering, women comprise 30 per cent of the work force and are almost unrepresented in management grades. As Mackie and Pattullo observe of Plessey, although it 'employs a total of 50,000 people, 15,000 of whom are women, [it] had, in 1975, 35 women in management grades out of 4,784 people'. They continue with the example of 'one of the largest national insurance companies with a staff of 6,000, of whom a third were women'. In this organization there were only '18 women above supervisor level, and none above the level of assistant controller. This meant that under 1 per cent of the female employees were in managerial posts compared to 17 per cent of the men' (Mackie and Pattullo, 1977, p. 76).[1]

The situation is not improving. Davies (1975, p. 20) has estimated that 'the opportunities for women to do skilled work are actually decreasing, while the number of women in the work force is rapidly increasing'. This can be seen in the estimate that 'the number of women classed as skilled in industry fell by a third between 1911 and 1951, and a further 8½ per cent by 1961' (Davies, 1975, p. 20). Even in those professional fields in which women have traditionally been employed, the situation is one of reverse rather than improvement. The Institute of Personnel Management's female membership dropped from 25 per cent in 1965 to 19 per cent by 1970. In 1921, 60 per cent of social workers were female. By 1960 this had declined to just over 50 per cent (figures from Mackie and Pattullo, 1977, p. 78). In both these instances, changes in the definition of the job lead to an increasing masculine influx. In personnel management, the movement from the simple elastoplast, amenities and counselling role of the personnel manager to one of tough industrial relations negotiator has lead to an increasing stress on the job as a 'male function' (Mary Niven, 'Personnel Management 1913–1963', quoted by the IPM in evidence to the House of Lords Select Committee on the Anti-Discrimination (No. 2) Bill; cited by Mackie and Pattulo, 1977, p. 78).[1]

With social work, the growth of welfare state capitalism after the Second World War created an expansion. This meant that men were recruited in large numbers for the first time and that a career structure and higher salaries were introduced to recruit them. Where equal pay for equal work has been introduced into a profession, such as teaching (as it was in 1961), then it can lead to a decline in the number of senior positions being filled by women. This has happened in teaching. It would seem that where equal pay has to be paid for equal work, employers do not necessarily provide equal access and opportunity. This is confirmed by Audrey Hunt's report to the Department of Employment on *Management Attitudes and Practices Towards Women at Work:*

A majority of those responsible for the engagement of employees start off with the belief that a woman applicant is likely to be inferior to a man in respect of all the qualities considered important (Hunt, 1975, p. 12).

This report was the result of a survey of 223 organizations. In only 1 per cent of these cases were those responsible for employment preferentially disposed towards women, while 68 per cent were negatively disposed towards hiring a woman. Women, it was reported, were only considered appropriate for 'dull repetitive work' (Hunt, 1975, p. 14). Hunt found that managers were likely to oppose the establishment of equal opportunity, regarded the male working pattern as the norm, and were disposed to thinking that women were likely to be inferior to men in appearance, ability and qualifications.

These circumstances, taken together, produce a situation in which there exists a marked tendency toward the maintenance of a dual labour market in which women are routinely underprivileged by being consigned to the secondary sector. Institutionally, this dualism is indicated by the distribution of male and female incomes into high and low wage areas; by the lack of mobility of females where structurally it could, in principle, occur (i.e. the professions); by the lack of promotional or career ladder in the vast amount of female employment; and by the lack of stability of this low-wage female employment with respect to fluctuations in the level of economic activity.

Why should this be so?

Women's orientations to work

One of the strengths of the action frame of reference which we discussed in Chapter 7 was its commitment to an explanation couched in terms of 'the ways in which social, economic and technical aspects of a worker's market and work situations are mediated by his definition of their significance'. It stressed 'the ways in which his actions must be seen as the outcome of his perceptions of the various options open to him and of which alternative best meets his priorities at the time' (Brown, 1976, p. 30). We can also apply this to *her* definitions, *her* actions, *her* perceptions of the various options open to *her,* and *her* priorities. In doing this, as Brown (1976, p. 31) suggests, the notion of 'orientation to work' may be usefully seen as the outcome of processes over time. These processes are those of the female's socialization, her choice in the labour market, her life cycle, and her adaptation and reaction to work experiences.

To be a girl in our society is quite distinct from being a boy. This is not because of biology but because of cultural determination, a fate not fixed by *being* a girl rather than a boy, but by *becoming* a culturally defined 'girl' or 'boy'. To be socialized into these gender identities is to be socialized into ideological practices of 'femininity' and 'masculinity'. Certain ways of behaving are decried for their lack of femininity and valued for their masculinity (such as being aggressive, ambitious, over-confident, intellectual). That these are clearly conventional cultural definitions has been established by cross-cultural studies by anthropologists such as Mead (1935; 1962) and Oakley (1972). These studies establish that the definition of what being female constitutes is so widely variable that in societies other than our own, such as the Tchambuli (studied by Mead, 1935) where the women are self-assertive, practical and authoritative, and where men do the shopping, carve, paint, dance and wear ornaments, one could almost mistake a description of Tchambuli femininity for one of Anglo-Saxon or Western masculinity. These counter-examples could be multiplied (see Oakley, 1972). Additionally, after reviewing a number of studies of small children in England and the USA, their treatment by their parents and experience of socialization at school, Oakley (1972, p. 86) concludes that initial similarity between boys and girls is transformed into a noticeable difference by the age of puberty. By this stage, boys have learned to become 'boys': they are assertive, active, numerate, technically inventive. Adolescence brings changes to girls' definitions of themselves. They begin to under-achieve academically, and to conform to the dominant ideological categories of femininity. These provide them with expectations about their future role in society, which for the vast majority means to expect nothing much else from life, other than marriage and home-making (also see Veness, 1962).

Janet Wolff (1977) draws some disturbing conclusions from these studies of gender, which have implications for the movement for 'equality' which have been legislated by national governments and promoted by the Treaty of Rome and the International Labour Organization. She writes:

> In our society, girls are socialized in conformity with their primary role of wife/mother, and this begins at birth. *This means that no amount of equality of pay, training or opportunities will actually make women equal with men in the work situation.* They have already learned too thoroughly to excel in the wrong qualities, and to be deficient in most of the qualities which are essential for most higher occupations. Furthermore, one of the things they have learned is not to *want* to be doctors, directors,

architects, barristers or engineers. They have not taken advantage of school or higher education to qualify themselves for the scientific, commercial or professional jobs which boys had been taught to expect and to aim for. Ten years later, an egalitarian employment policy will not do them much good (Wolff, 1977, p. 19; our emphasis).

Wolff's pessimism is justified. As one looks at the figures for pupils remaining at school past the statutory limit (16 years old) one finds that the retention rate is higher for boys than girls. In 1972 8.2 per cent of boys aged 18 remained at school; only 5.8 per cent of 18-year-old girls had made the same decision (*Social Trends*, 1973, p. 143). Boys are far more likely to gain higher-level qualifications than girls, and even when the sexes have equivalent qualifications girls are less likely to go on to university than boys (also see Mackie and Pattullo, 1977, pp. 25–38; Davies, 1975, pp. 98–114).

In part, these are realistic expectations on the part of girls. The opportunities in the labour market do not exist for girls to the same extent that they do for boys. While in recent years the number of boys leaving school to enter apprenticeship schemes has been about 39 per cent, only about 7 per cent of girls entered apprenticeships. Of these girls, over three-quarters were apprenticed as hairdressers, in which the 'training' offered is notoriously poor, and apprentices provide cheap rather than trained labour, while the boys were entering jobs in industries such as engineering, where the opportunities for acquiring a marketable skill are far greater (figures from Davies, 1975, p. 104; also see Mackie and Pattullo, 1977, pp. 96–113).

Skill is the crucial issue here. What is implied by all the above description and detail is that, irrespective of any other specific organization phenomena, women will be disadvantaged in organizations. In terms of the politics of organizations their sex already handicaps them. In the power stakes, men, irrespective of any other specific organization phenomena, will be advantaged in organizations. Women, simply by being 'women', are always outsiders. Research suggests that this is in part, at least, due to their own definitions, perceptions, priorities and actions in regarding marriage and home-making as their central life-interest, whereas men do not.

The picture requires some qualification in as much as it varies with the woman's life-cycle situation and experience. Brown (1976, p. 45) suggests that 'there are important differences in "orientations to work" between women with young or school-age children, older married women without such responsibilities, and older single, widowed and separated women; the emphasis on financial rewards is greater for the first and last category than for the middle one, whilst it was among older women that there was any interest in supervisory posts'. (He draws these inferences from 'significant differences in labour stability and turnover, absence and output as between young single, young married with children, older married and widowed or divorced women', and from a consideration of studies such as those of Lupton, 1963; Mumford and Banks, 1967; Beynon and Blackburn, 1972; Cunnison, 1966; and Jephcott *et al.*, 1962).

There is an additional factor which has to be considered in any discussion of the extent to which work is a central life-interest for women as opposed to men. We have already established that men and women rarely do the same jobs. 'Women's work' tends to be the most dull, boring and repetitive. It is therefore less likely to be a cherished central life-interest.

We have said that women's orientations to work are in some sense realistic, but they are so only given the complex interaction of a set of taken-for-granted practices of both the structure of work, labour markets and ideological values (Brown, 1976, p. 33). Within the overall configuration, we can isolate two significantly determinant factors, which are 'over-determinant' of the total situation. These are the structure of the dual labour market, which we have already discussed, and the ideological practices which maintain and reproduce it.

Ideological reproduction and the dual labour market

One should not over-stress the role of ideology too much in the production of organizations as politically sexist phenomena. To do so is to assume unwarrantedly that the ruled – in this case, women – do not rebel mainly because they accept their inferior position as justified. Therborn suggests that:

> Economic and political considerations apart, there are a number of other reasons why people do not revolt. They may be broadly ignorant of and disinterested in the form of rule to which they are subjected. They may not be aware of alternative modes of social organization, and, even if they are, they may feel powerless to affect the existing state of affairs. However, this ignorance, disinterest or lack of confidence is not simply given, as a psychological characteristic of individuals and groups. It is generated by definite social processes and forms part of the overall process of social reproduction (Therborn, 1978, p. 171).

The definite social processes of reproduction which routinely reproduce women as discriminated against, and organizations as sexist structures, relate to one simple practice employed by organizations. This practice is the use of an ascriptive characteristic (sex) as a basis for job allocation. This has the effect of confining the ascribed group or category to the secondary sector of the dual labour market for the whole of its working life. This has self-fulfilling consequences: 'the actual confinement of particular groups to the secondary sector will result in their having higher rates of labour turnover and job mobility' which create 'a vicious circle', as Barron and Norris (1976, p. 53) put it. The clearly visible social difference of sex as an ascriptive categorization device has become institutionalized and reproductive of organization practices only because of more widely embedded mechanisms of ideological reproduction.

As Therborn has stressed, 'Ideology functions by moulding personality' in a process of *subjection* and *qualification*. Ideology *subjects* the amorphous libido of new-born human animals to a specific social order and *qualifies* them for the differential roles they will play in society' (Therborn, 1978, p. 172). It does so by providing categories of *existence, possibility* and *ethics:*

1 Ideological formation tells individuals *what exists,* who they are, how the world is, how they are related to that world. In this manner, people are allocated different kinds and amounts of identity, trust and everyday knowledge. The visibility of modes of life, the actual relationship of performance to reward, the existence, extent and character of exploitation and power are all structured in class-specific models of ideological formation.
2 Ideology tells *what is possible,* providing varying types and quantities of self-confidence and ambition, and different levels of aspiration.
3 Ideology tells *what is right* and wrong, good and bad, thereby determining not only conceptions of legitimacy of power, but also work-ethics, notions of leisure, and views of inter-personal relationships, from comradeship to sexual love (Therborn, 1978, p. 172).

What mechanics of ideological reproduction tell men and women that what exists for women, what is possible for women and what is right for women is, on the whole a life inferior and in separate jobs from men in all organizations?

We have defined organization as control of the labour process. To answer our question concerning the mechanics of ideological reproduction involves an analysis of the relation of the domestic labour process and its ideological reproduction, to the non-domestic or organizational labour process and its ideological reproduction. We are dealing not only with a dual labour market in the organization of the labour process in employment. We are also dealing with a dual labour process of work itself, whereby work and its organization are seen on the one hand as work 'proper' (that is wage-labour), and on the other hand as (in both senses) *extra*-work: that is domestic – labour, as something external, outside of, additional to, and separate from, organization *per se*.

The dual labour process

Marx (1976, p. 875) argued that, 'The economic structure of capitalist society has grown out of the economic structure of feudal society. The dissolution of the latter set free the elements of the former.' In Chapter 2 we deliberately, one-sidedly, presented the development of this dissolution and evolution in terms of the organizational or wage-labour process. This was only one half of the picture. It is now necessary to sketch in the remaining half of our analysis. This analysis provides the material for drawing out the consequences for women (the neglected labour in the labour process) of the transition from feudal to capitalist social relations of production.

The feudal mode of production was centred on the family as a unit of production which was largely self-sufficient (Fussell and Fussell, 1953, p. 44). There existed obligations upon men and women through legislation such as that of the Statute of Labourers of 1349 in England (but which were to be found enacted throughout feudal Europe from 1349 to 1375) which attempted not only to batten down wages and restrict peasants to the land but also to maintain the obligation of *seigneurial* labour on the peasantry. As Davies says:

> The statutory obligation of women to turn out and work in the fields was a confirmation of the importance of women to an agrarian pre-industrial economy. But it served to make available that labour only in periods of great shortage. This might have been useful in the annual harvest, when the corn had to be gathered in quickly. But its origins lay in the Black Death of 1348–9, which reduced the population by about a third. Moreover, these women had to be forced into the labour market. There was a shortage of men to till the land, for so many had died. But many more, particularly those unencumbered with wives and children, left a particular demesne to avoid performing their workdays on the lord's land (Davies, 1975, p. 28).

Women thus provided a reserve army for agricultural production at times of crisis. This is not to say that normally they were unproductive at home. In the sixteenth century, prior to the development of capitalist rationality, the division between work and home, or the 'public office' and 'privatized hearth', made no sense (Weber, 1968). 'Family life and work life were part of the same round of activity in the same locale. Even to say people worked at home and lived at work is to impose concepts which are irrelevant to a description of feudal life', as Hamilton (1978, p. 25) has argued, noting with Laslett (1965, p. 14) that even servants and apprentices were constituted as part of the family. Of course, poor families, who constituted 90–95 per cent of the population (serfs, tenant farmers, wage-labourers), had no servants or apprentices, and, while they were far from economically viable units of self-sufficiency, wage-labour 'outside' the domestic unit was more a supplementary form of production, rather than an alternative. However, with the development of capitalist agriculture and the 'freeing' of labour from the land towards the end of the 'long' sixteenth century (1450–1650), as Wallerstein (1974a) has argued, labour became separated from 'the objective conditions of its realization – from the means of labour and the material for labour' (Marx, 1973, p. 471). With this separation the family was no longer a unit of production.

What forms of control of the labour process existed in this pre-capitalist unitary production? It was largely co-operative and traditional. In unenclosed villages people were not totally separated from the objective conditions for the realization of their own

TABLE 11.2 *Division of labour by sex in traditional rural households*

	Women's work	Men's work
Inside house	childrearing cooking cleaning household accounts cottage industrial work	lighting oven farm accounts
Outside house	wood gleaning water carrying vegetable garden poultry-dairy care poultry-dairy marketing larding haytossing weeding	wine storage cattle-feeding (varies) cattle-marketing care of agricultural implements spading ploughing scything pork slaughtering

Source: Shorter, 1976, p. 516.

411

labour; land was held in common. The compulsion to labour was one of necessity and communal tradition, which in turn, governed a rudimentary sexual division of labour which Shorter (1976, p. 516) has estimated as in Table 11.2

Although husband and wife were economically interdependent through the integration of the household and the economy (Hamilton, 1978, pp. 28–32), this economic interdependence was embedded in a patriarchally maintained subordination of women as inferiors. 'The husband was to take the active role, the wife the passive, in every point at which the household's life touched that of the surrounding world' (Shorter, 1976, p. 518). However, with the domestic unit of production 'the life of the married woman gave her a great deal of scope' (Power, 1965, p. 433), depending on the class position of the people involved. For the peasant woman proper, there was little in the way of effective limits outside the tradition and necessity governing her toil and exertions. The wife of the yeoman was less compelled to labour. In the seventeenth century:

As the division of labour became more complex and specialized the richer yeoman's wives tended to withdraw from agricultural labour, though responsibility for the dairy and catering for the farm servants who lived in and ate off their board meant that they were still very busy (Rowbotham, 1975, p. 1).

Also, during this period, the wives of craftsmen and tradesmen withdrew from production, or were obliged to withdraw by changes in the organization of production itself whereby 'women were forced out of the more profitable trades' (Rowbotham, 1975, p. 2). The reasons for this withdrawal are complex. One major reason concerned the withdrawal of bourgeois women from production entirely and into the home. This was the development of Protestantism, with its re-definition of the role of women (or, at least, wives) and the family (Hamilton, 1978, pp. 50–75; Mitchell, 1971, pp. 8–12). The culmination of this development was to be the Victorian bourgeois household, in which economically dependent and politically inferior women organized the bureaucracy of the home, with its strictly rational hierarchy of servants, rules, and career, as a rationally harmonious counterpoint to the bureaucratic tyranny of the factory and office (see Burnett, 1974, ch. 2, for some first-hand accounts of domestic service).

The dissolution of the feudal mode of production centred on the domestic economy was the result of the cyclical pattern of movement of European prices (particularly for grain staples) and its relation to the increase in the process of capital accumulation and the growth of the landless population. (This is a complex and voluminous issue which Wallerstein, 1974a, pp. 69–84, addresses in

412

detail. We can not go into this literature here.) The outcome of feudal dissolution was to produce a class of landless men and women who were to be totally dependent on selling their labour power. It was these ex-peasants who swelled into the urban centres and roamed the countryside as vagabonds (for which crime many were hanged), if they survived the frequent famines and epidemics (Wallerstein, 1974a, p. 118). Many, especially the women and babies, did not. Women were over-represented in the pauper class (Clark, 1919, p. 92; cited in Hamilton, 1978, p. 47) and in the death rates (Marshall, 1954, p. 298; cited in Hamilton, 1978, p. 47).

What were the consequences for those who did survive? If they were able to, they could sell their labour but at wages 'fixed for an age in which they were only a supplement to the living a family eked from the land' (Hamilton, 1978, p. 39). For men, this meant that work was available only at wages sufficient to reproduce themselves, not their families. For women, whose wage-labour had by tradition been extra-ordinary rather than ordinary, and by convention low-paid (Davies, 1975, p. 28; Rowbotham, 1975, p. 2), the choice was grim:

> She could sell her own labour power for half of what her husband could make. This would further endanger her children's survival through lack of supervision and withdrawal of lactation. Or she could stay at home, if indeed she had such a place, and risk starvation, for her children (Hamilton, 1978, p. 40).

Middle-class or bourgeois women thus found themselves cut-off from production and economically dependent on a man; while working-class women were forced into service, prostitution or the factory, where, like their men, they became wage-labourers, producing the appropriated surplus which enabled the luxury of bourgeois existence. However, the employment of women as wage-labour did not somehow mean that there no longer existed a domestic labour process. Working-class families still had to eat, shelter, be clothed, cleaned, etc. Women still did domestic labour. With their input into wage-labour, women simply became hand-maidens twice over: once to their husbands and families, and once to their bosses at work. The unitary labour process had become a dual labour process. This dual labour process had definite implications for the development of the organization of the capitalist labour process, which enables us to understand why women at work have been largely consigned to the secondary labour market.

The issue is clearly presented in the following:

> Capitalism left women stranded in an ambiguous situation that

was neither fully exposed to the cash-nexus nor completely freed from the older form of property ownership. The man's ownership of the *persons* of his women and children and his complete control over their capacity to produce was broken in the immediate relations of the working-class family. They ceased to be directly means of production for the man. However, their low wage was still supplementary in the commodity system. Women could not enter commodity production on the same terms as men. Like the man they sold their labour power now as a commodity. But they still worked to maintain the labour force at home. In the early years of the industrial revolution the work of women in reproducing the men's and children's capacity to labour was drastically reduced. With protective legislation and fewer hours in the factory, women workers spent more time doing housework in the family. The need for women's labour in the family, in reproducing and maintaining labour power, thus exercised a certain restraint on the direct exploitation of women's labour power in industry. But women's social usefulness was never recognized or recompensed. Instead their dependence on the male bread-winner and their work in the family reduced their capacity to organize. They were thus placed at a double disadvantage (Rowbotham, 1975, pp. 58–9).

Essentially, women's participation in the labour force became such that they were easily dispensable labour. They 'could be called upon to augment the industrial reserve army, available to be drawn into or thrown out of employment according to the needs of capital accumulation at any particular time' (Adamson *et al.*, 1976, p. 16). Not that they required much calling. Economic historians (e.g., Shorter, 1976) have stressed that industrial organization and factory labour held considerable attractions for young unmarried women whose only other source of employment was domestic service or familial bondage. Not only did they gain a measure of economic independence, but also a degree of sexual independence as well. It was in part bourgeois horror at this sexual liberation which compelled the humanitarianism of reformers like Shaftesbury in the nineteenth century. (Accounts of nineteenth-century factory work are replete with tales of factory workers', especially women's, sexual licence. One of the authors, Clegg, recalls the same folk-tales when he commenced work in a north of England textile mill in the mid-1960s.) During the eighteenth and nineteenth centuries the spread of cottage industry baptised 'rustic women' by 'an icewater bath in capitalism'. The baptism was not temporary. The trend in female employment is 'a large increase in the eighteenth and early nineteenth centuries, stabilization until the mid-twentieth, then another large rise after the Second World War' (Shorter, 1976, p. 523).

The period of stabilization, however, includes an immense dislocation: the First World War, when in all the countries involved in the war, women were enlisted into the labour force. This recruitment was paralleled by 'unprecedented rationalization in the form of the breaking down and standardization of production methods together with intensive mechanization which provided the basis on which women could be drawn as unskilled and semi-skilled workers into the munitions industries' (Adamson *et al.*, 1976, p. 20). If one were to compare the pre-1914 figures for female employment in Britain, for example, with the post-1918 figures (e.g., 1911 and 1921) then little change is visible in the employment of women. It is only through a closer consideration of the war period itself that the dislocation becomes evident. We can see this from Table 11.3.

TABLE 11.3   *Changes in women's employment, July 1914–July 1918 (in thousands)*

	July 1914	*July 1918*	*Increase or decrease*
Self-employed	430	470	+ 40
Industry	2,179	2,971	+792
Domestic service	1,658	1,258	– 400
Commerce, etc.	505	934	+429
National and local government (+ education)	262	460	+198
Agriculture	190	228	+ 38
Hotels, theatres, etc.	181	220	+ 39
Transport	18	117	+ 99
Others	542	652	+110
Total	5,965	7,310	+1,345

Source: Adamson *et al.*, 1976, p. 20.

The major change that the war economy brought was a decline in the number of women in domestic service, and, because of the administration of the war economy, a large increase in clerical jobs which women filled in commerce, national and local government. This represented a massive expansion of clerical work which became increasingly identified as women's work:

In 1851 there had been only 19 female clerks but by 1911 this had risen to 146,000. 'Clerk' in the 1850s had been a management job, but the developing needs of industry, added to the de-skilling and division of labour within the office, meant that this rapidly became another area of 'women's work'. Thus 627,000 women were drawn into commerce, national and local government between 1914 and 1918 (Adamson *et al.*, 1976, p. 20).

In both the office and the factory the increase in female employment during the First World War enabled organizations and employers to de-skill the labour process. It was during the war that Taylorism gained widespread practical application, and the structure of organizations was transformed accordingly. In Offe's (1976a) phrase, they became increasingly 'task-discontinuous' organizations. Skill and craft bases of tasks were eroded and tasks were re-constituted on a largely unskilled[2] basis, with the acceptance by the unions that this 'dilution', and female labour, would cease at the war's end.

TABLE 11.4   *Women's employment in industry, 1914–18*

	July 1914 (thousands)	July 1918 (thousands)	Increase or decrease (thousands)	% of total 1914	1918
Metals	170	594	+424	9	25
Chemicals	40	104	+ 64	20	39
Textiles	863	827	– 36	58	67
Clothing	612	568	– 44	68	76
Food, drink, tobacco	196	235	+ 39	35	49
Paper and printing	148	142	– 6	36	48
Wood	44	79	+ 35	15	32
Pottery, leather, etc.	104	197	+ 93	4	10
Government establishments	2	225	+223	3	47
Total	2,179	2,971	+792	26	37

Source: Adamson *et al.*, 1976, p. 20.

During the war, the structure of organizations was transformed, and totally new types of organization – government organizations – were created on a large scale (see Table 11.4 for the changes in women's employment by industry, 1914–18). The changes in structure were twofold. One, the organized labour process became a process organized on the basis of a considerably reduced skill component. Two, it became one operated increasingly by women (at least for the duration of the war) at lower rates of pay and lower levels of trade union organization. Indeed, women were hardly recruited to the trade union movement at all. There were only 660,000 women in unions out of a total of seven million in employment by the end of the war. The response of the labour movement, overall, was fairly simple: they resented the employment of women but recognized the wartime necessity. Their resentment was, in a sense, quite realistic. They feared that women workers would be used to de-skill the labour process and break their craft control. Thus, they ensured that women were the 'first to go' at the end of the war, such that in 1920 there were only 200,000 more women in employment than in 1913.

The consequences of the First World War on the nature and structure of employment and organizations was profound, particularly as it affected women. By 1923 the middle classes were finding it sufficiently difficult to organize their households with a bureaucratic servant structure for the government to appoint a Ministry of Labour Committee to enquire into the shortage. (The anxieties were often articulated in popular novels of the period: Miss Marple in Agatha Christie's novels constantly bemoans and has bemoaned of her 'the servant problem'.) In large part the shortage was due to aversion for the work and conditions involved. (This was not a recent aversion. It was only that since the war there existed an alternative to service; see Burnett, 1974, pp. 135–74.) A consequence of the war was that

> By the 1920s and 1930s domestic service was no longer the natural outlet for women's employment that it had been in Victorian times. Girls could now go into shop work, into the new light factory trades and into the booming area of clerical work, which already by 1931 was taking one in five of employed women; for those with higher education teaching, nursing and the minor professions were all developing. Domestic service was increasingly the refuge for the poor and ill-educated, for the over-large families where every additional child was an extra mouth to be fed, and for the daughters of normally comfortable working-class parents hit by depression and unemployment (Burnett, 1974, p. 141).

Besides the fact that servants were increasingly hard to find, the development of the bourgeois family, where the woman stayed at home and the husband went to work, had become a powerful ideological factor. In as much as the ruling ideas of any epoch are the ideas of the ruling class, those stressed, above all else, the

417

wifely, maternal, female role of women. Throughout the 1920s and 1930s, as Rowbotham (1975, pp. 123–7) details, there was a decline in feminist consciousness from the pre-war and war period. Married women were largely confined to the home and female employment was very largely of single women, most of whom worked by the end of the 1930s. What female employment there was resulted from the requirements of a depressed capitalist mode of production for a cheapened labour process: women provided a supply of cheap, unskilled, non-unionized workers. The old divisions between craftsmen and labourers were being broken down. Skilled turners and fitters were being replaced by semi-skilled assembly workers who were quite often women (Rowbotham, 1975, p. 128). The other major source of employment was in office work, which had developed as low-paid, non-unionized, clerical work for women.

Women's lack of union membership could be blamed on male trade-union official prejudice as much as women's reluctance (or difficulty, for instance in domestic service), maintains Rowbotham (1975, p. 131). One consequence of their lack of organization was that 'in contrast to male workers, women and youths worked up to 60 hours a week in non-textile factories and up to 55 hours weekly in the textile industry' (Adamson *et al.*, 1976, p. 21). For male union workers, a 48-hour week had become normal.

For those married women who were not in employment the Depression meant an intensified domestic drudgery in the face of declining income, due to wage cuts or unemployment. There were many alarming reports during the 1930s on the deterioration of women's health (e.g. Rice, 1938). The amelioration of this sordid Depression came because of the Second World War, with its full-employment war economy. Until the Second World War most female employment terminated on marriage or first pregnancy. Single women, having already been drawn into employment, could not provide a pool of labour – a reserve army – for the war effort, to replace the men who had been conscripted. The only sizable untapped reserve comprised married women, and it was the importation of two million married women into the war economy which sustained the war.

One effect of this was that patterns of employment and provision had to develop which were appropriate to the fact of these women's dual labour process: that is, their commitments to domestic labour as well as organized labour in the war effort. Structurally, this meant a major increase in part-time female employment, and a massive increase in the provision of nursery places. For the first time, the capitalist state had taken upon itself the necessity to 'socialize' a major element of the domestic labour process: child care. During the war the number of child-care places increased from only 118 full and part-time nurseries in 1941, to 1,559, catering for 71,806 children by July 1945, according to Adamson *et al.* (1976, p. 24). These nurseries were withdrawn at the end of the war, when, once again subject to the post-war ideology of motherhood, married women withdrew from the labour force. But not for long. The re-structuring of industry and the development of the Welfare State (based on intensive, cheap female labour) meant a steady growth in female employment. The rate of increase in female employment during the period 1951 to 1973 was 26 per cent, while for men it was only 1.2 per cent. By the early 1970s about 50 per cent of all married women were at work, mostly in labour market jobs *and* in the domestic labour process. This, briefly, was the development of the dual labour process.

What are its consequences for an analysis of organizations? Conceived as the organization of the labour process, this entails an analysis of the interdependent relationship of the family and its domestic labour process with the organization with its labour process. The family has been defined as 'a unit whose function is the maintenance and reproduction of labour power, i.e., that the structure of the family is determined by the needs of the economic system, at any given time, for a certain kind of labour power' (Morton, 1972, p. 53). The same author, as Hamilton (1978, p. 78) has pointed out, has argued that 'the fluctuating needs of the economy for labour power, the requirement of a family for a stable income and the need of husband and children for nurturing are in contradiction even while they act to reinforce the family'. The consequence of this contradiction is that 'Woman in her dual role as housewife and worker is the intersecting point between these increasingly contradictory forces' (Hamilton, 1978, p. 78). This dual role, is, of course, mediated through the class structure.

For instance, Epstein (1971, p. 138) has observed that full-time professional and business women often have two or more full-time servants who maintain their homes and children for them during the day. In women's careers in the primary labour market, their participation would seem to be contingent on exploitation: either their own, as unpaid domestic labour (Gardiner, 1975) or that of paid domestic labour hired on the market. Despite even these privileged examples, the participation of women in the primary labour market appears to be marked by discrimination (see Rapoport and Rapoport, 1971; Fogarty *et al.,* 1971; Wolff, 1977). The dual role is predominantly a problem for working-class women. These women's dual role becomes both the reproduction of the conditions of production (the next generation) and the nourishment and sustenance of the present generation, whilst, at the same time, out of economic necessity, entering into productive relations

419

themselves where the opportunity presents itself.

This poses two issues. How do married women work? How do working women raise children? Looked at from the other side, the requirements of the structure of production, these reduce to one question: how can married women workers serve to reproduce the labour power necessary for the continual reproduction of the conditions of production? Ideologically the problem is managed by a medium which constantly manipulates mother-child images in its further commodification of all aspects of everyday life. Structurally, during the Second World War, it was managed by state provision of nurseries on a wide scale. In the post-war boom it was managed by a growth in part-time employment, and private nurseries and child minders (see Adamson *et al.*, 1976, p. 29–30). The inadequate and *ad hoc* provision of these facilities, together with the ideological determinants, ensures that women workers are a segment of the labour force which has a high degree of voluntary labour turnover and which can, because of the ideological determinants, be more readily made to accept involuntary redundancy or be refused employment in the first place (as in the establishment of unofficial priorities in employment; e.g., married men, single men, single women, married women, in that order of priority).

Women's voluntary turnover rates are high. In large part this is characteristic of any segment of an unskilled, low-paid labour force, with no career or vocation. But it is also due to women's 'other' vocation: their tendency to leave jobs for childbirth or other reasons related to their domestic role (Hunt, 1968). Barron and Norris observe:

> *Single* women may well have lower voluntary turnover rates than married women if age is controlled for, but marital status is so clearly age-related that turnover rates for married and single women tend to converge: single women having relatively high rates because of their youth and married women having relatively high rates because of their position in the family (Barron and Norris, 1976, p. 54).

Women are also more easily made redundant or refused employment than men. This is because of the ideological determinants which stress that a woman's 'real' place is in the home, and that men are the 'real' breadwinners, although in reality (Land, 1976; also see Marceau, 1976 for French élite male business students supported by their wives) the woman's income is frequently vital to family living standards. As women also have tended to have their interests neglected by trade unions they are often not sufficiently well-organized to fight any involuntary redundancy (see Davies, 1975; Mackie and Pattullo, 1977).

It is because of these, primarily ideological, factors which stress that the domestic labour process is a woman's business (rather than a man's, or a shared affair), and that child-care be privatized rather than socialized, that women are defined, structurally, as a dispensable labour force in whom no skill need be invested because of the relative ease of replacement and recruitment. Hence, women are relatively unskilled and work in predominantly de-skilled jobs with low pay. Given the structural alternatives that women perceive are *either* these jobs *or* full-time housewifery, it is not surprising that, 'realistically', in a process of accommodation, women tend to feel caught between two equally unattractive options. Working-class women can only afford the full-time housewifery option at considerable cost to the household budget. Not only does their unpaid domestic labour contribute to keeping down the costs of their husband's labour power, and thus his wage,[3] it also maintains them in a secondary labour force, in which, as Barron and Norris (1977) elaborate, there is, as a rule neither a high degree of 'economism' nor 'solidarism'.

The structural existence of women as a secondary labour force (this analysis could also, of course, be extended to include race or ethnicity as an ascriptive categorization device) is over-determined by an ideology which stresses that what exists for a woman is to be a wife and a mother, that this ought be the possible limit of her existence, and that it is not right for her to forego these 'natural pleasures'. Ideology contradicts reality in the case of working-class women who have to work to maintain the commodity standards of reproduction to which they and their families had become accustomed in the long post-war boom. But, because of ideology and lack of structural alternatives (such as socialized child care) to that which is deemed right, possible and existent, they are consigned very largely to unskilled, low-paid jobs. In these, as part of the ideology which stresses their 'natural' role and in part as a consequence of the alienating conditions of unskilled employment, they tend to higher rates of labour turnover and thus to be a cheap, unorganized source of labour. As such, they can be called upon from the reserve army of labour at times of labour shortage (a fully employed war economy or the post-war boom) or thrown back onto it at times of crisis. Women's work force involvement historically becomes a feature of the fortunes of the world economy.

Historically, capitalist production has consistently developed its employment of women as part of the industrial reserve army of labour. At the present time of economic crisis this can be seen in terms of the differential rates of increase of female unemployment and male unemployment. In Britain, female unemployment rose by 127 per cent between 1974 and 1975 compared with 66 per cent for male unemployment (Adamson *et al.,* 1976, p. 3, citing *Society of Civil Servants Press Release 5,* February 1976, p. 2). Female labour, particularly in times of major crisis and recession, suffers most not only because of its unskilled, high-turnover nature, and the ideological determinants, but also because of cutbacks in state expenditure which result in the redundancy of state employees. In the most labour-intensive areas of state activities such as local government, health care provision, welfare and education the majority of workers are female. Hence, they will bear the burden of any direct cuts in public expenditure most severely.

What we have already discussed concerning the role and participation of women in industry is applicable to other ideologically distinguishable workers in organizations, such as black workers or 'guest' workers (Castles and Kosack, 1973; Berger and Mohr, 1975). In addition, leaving the particular ideological determinants aside, if one were to concentrate on the crucial variable of the skill of labour as it participates in organizations, then one has in the case of women and black workers a more particular, ideologically over-determined, example of a general case. The general case concerns the power of people in organizations and the explanation of its differential distribution.

If one were to make an initial assumption (which we might later wish to revise) that power in organizations were distributed pyramidally in accordance with the formal structure of the organization, then we have already seen in this chapter that women in organizations will tend to be clustered as lower-level participants. It is because of this that we have described organizations as *sexist structures.* We have stressed in this chapter how in society generally the sexual divisions of social structure overlay the class structure. This is also true of organizations. They are not only sexist structures but also class structures.

Class structure and organization structure

Sociologists generally treat the issue of differentiation among people in contemporary capitalist societies in terms of a 'class analysis' (for contemporary approaches see Poulantzas, 1975; Carchedi, 1977; Hunt, 1977; Wright, 1978; Therborn, 1978) and have done so since Marx and Engels used the concept in their various writings. However, as various observers have noted (e.g., McLellan, 1968; Swingewood, 1975), Marx and Engels' use of the term was neither wholly systematic nor clear. This confusion remains, as both Allen (1977) and Wright (1978) have recently reiterated.

Allen has clarified some problems of class analysis in a way which is related to our previous discussion of women as a secondary labour force. This stresses the existence of 'ideologically determined labour markets'. He begins

> with social relations of production and the prime division between the owners and non-owners of the means of production, or the buyers and sellers of labour power which it embodies. . . . The social relations of production in a capitalist society do not simply create the existence of a market relationship between those who are compelled to sell their labour power for sub-sistence and the owners of the means of production; they involve a process of exploiting labour power in order to extract surplus value. The market relationship and the process of exploitation are part of the same totality. The market relationship separates the worker from his labour power. It is labour power which is hired out or sold into the control of the owners of the means of production and manipulated through pressure on either its cost or its skill in order to maximize profits (Allen, 1977, p. 64).

He goes on to note that sellers of labour power 'have certain characteristics in common'. We can enumerate these:

1   Because there are many sellers (individuals) and few buyers in all markets for labour power, the balance of power lies with the buyers. The buyers are invariably organizations of one kind or another. 'A buyer of labour power can choose and discriminate between sellers; he can dispense with labour power, and, because of his proprietary control over it, he can manipulate and dilute its skill in relation to other sellers or to machines' (Allen, 1977, p. 65).

2   Notwithstanding this inferiority of sellers in relation to buyers, not all sellers are equally inferior. 'Labour power is obtained for its skill content and there are wide variations in its provision from individuals. The greater the specificity of the skill the greater the power the person who provides it has in relation to an employer.' However, we should never lose sight of the fact that this specificity can be used against the employee: 'An employer can always dilute special skills by mechanizing them in part or total', as Allen (1977, p. 66) puts it.

3   Total mechanization of skills means that people whose particular capacity as labour power was formed by these skills find their market position undercut. In other words, their labour power has been cheapened to the point of substitutability. They become redundant. They are unable to sell their skill on the market at its previous exchange-value, irrespective of the fact that the skill is still the same, with the same use-value. Their skill is no longer required because the task and work they contributed to the labour process has been reorganized. It has been reorganized because the skill can

423

be provided at a higher rate of exploitation and thus a lower cost through technological substitution. All workers who lose jobs in this way become redundant in as much as all their energies and capacities have been specialized in the market on the acquisition and development of this skill. 'All sellers of labour power . . . work in order to live . . . no seller can ignore the imperative need to subsist if their skills are discarded. People of all income levels and status are compelled to cart their skills around in varying forms when confronted by unemployment' (Allen, 1977, p. 66).

4   Sellers of labour power belong to a 'class-in-itself', as Marx put it. This is because 'selling labour power possesses common objectives which can be characterized by inferiority, helplessness, subordination, subjugation to varying extents . . . these elements are sufficiently important as determinants of behaviour to constitute a common objective position' (Allen, 1977, p. 66).

Differences in skill are not 'natural'. We already know from our analysis of the historical development of the secondary labour market for women that there are ideologically determined and segmented labour markets. Sellers of labour power are distributed 'among a multiplicity of skills involved in an even greater multiplicity of tasks' (Allen, 1977, p. 67).

These tasks collected together in an organization form the technical relations within whose structural limitations the labour process is executed. These structural limitations are a pattern of determination in which the organization's ruling élite establishes limits within which the labour process can vary. These limits establish the parameters within which specific structures or processes are possible (Wright, 1978, pp. 15–16). Thus 'structural limitation implies that certain forms of the determined structure have been excluded entirely and some possible forms are more likely than others', as Wright (1978, p. 16) puts it. In other words, to repeat the theme of Chapter 7, technology can not determine social relations except in the framework constituted by the existing social relationships. These, particularly through the actions and interests of the ruling élite in the organization, mediate between existing technical possibilities and the operant goals of the organization. It is this mediation which concretely determines the range of occupations and sub-divisions which constitute the labour process and its control. Each of these occupations and sub-divisions will have its own skill requirements, status and price. As Allen (1977, p. 67) insists, 'there is no direct correlation between skills, as technical competence, status and price, for what is a skill is ideologically determined'.

We can distinguish 'socially determined labour markets between which there is restricted mobility . . . [having] . . . comparable

424

ideologically determined skills, possessing similar prescriptions for recruitment and training' (Allen, 1977, p. 68). Within each of these markets, although there will be massive differences in types of skill, their market conditions on which they are bought and used will be comparable. One of these we have already dealt with. This is the secondary labour market, consisting primarily of groups clearly ascribed by categorization by such devices as gender, ethnicity or the statistically less significant factor of age. Working-class women were treated as an example of this secondary labour market, having high voluntary rates of turnover, in and out of an unskilled sector of jobs in which they display neither much economism nor solidarity. (It is also typical of old-age workers or 'guest' workers, as well as of young entrants to the unskilled labour force.) This secondary labour market displays some of the characteristic recruitment cycles of a 'reserve army' (see Hampton, 1978 for New Zealand; Counter Information Service, 1976 for Britain).

We can now turn to the primary labour market. When we enter organizations as employees or members we do so as more or less skilled workers. We are distributed as such according to level or rank in the organization in a hierarchy of more or less formally defined offices. This hierarchy ordinarily takes on a pyramidal form, as can be seen by the ease with which researchers (e.g., Pugh and Hickson, 1976) have empirically delineated some offices in all the organizations they have studied as being characterized by a 'concentration of authority'. This authority is usually concentrated on the basis of formally defined positions of authority in the organization. The holders of such positions comprise what Selznick (1957) has called 'dominant coalitions' and which we have referred to as a 'ruling élite' in organizations.[4]

We have established that there is a dual labour market for men and women, in which women are largely consigned to the secondary sector, while men are largely recruited into the primary sector. What we wish to establish next is whether or not they are recruited randomly into this primary sector, or whether or not they are socially determined and distributed within it.

We can broadly divide this primary male labour market into three strata (see Table 11.5), using data taken from the *Department of Employment Gazette* (1971) by Westergaard and Resler (1976, p. 78). The top stratum corresponds to what organization theorists have variously described as the ruling élite, decision-makers rather than decision-takers, or the dominant coalition in organization. In more ordinary parlance, this stratum comprises those people whom we usually meet as 'bosses'. This stratum can be regarded as a broad, socially determined labour market because of the similar prescriptions of élite recruitment, high status and pay which attach

TABLE 11.5   *Gross weekly earnings of adult full-time male employees in selected occupations, 1971*

Occupational groups (male full-time employees only, pay not affected by absence)	Median gross weekly earnings (£)	Percentages (cumulative) of employees in each occupational group having gross weekly earnings of:					
		Under £20	Under £25	£35 and more	£40 and more	£50 and more	£60 and more	£70 and more
Managers – general and divisional	69.6	—	2	92	88	75	63	50
Company chairmen and directors	66.5	3	5	85	79	64	55	43
Medical and dental practitioners	58.4	—	—	91	82	62	48	40
University academic staff	57.7	2	2	88	80	66	47	29
Managers – marketing, advert., sales	52.7	—	2	83	75	56	35	21
Managers – personnel and training	47.1	1	1	81	68	40	25	17
Architects and planners	47.2	2	3	81	69	44	24	11
Solicitors	46.2	15	22	58	54	44	29	12
Teachers in further education	44.8	1	3	84	67	33	10	2
Accountants	43.4	9	16	65	56	35	21	12
Managers – works and production	42.8	1	4	74	57	33	18	9
Engineers, scientists, technologists	41.4	1	5	71	54	28	13	6
Managers – office	40.9	2	9	65	51	32	17	9
Foremen – senior, higher level	38.1	—	3	65	41	9	2	1
School teachers	37.1	4	14	59	34	11	3	1
Office supervisors	35.1	2	10	51	23	7	2	1
Foremen and supervisors – other	33.5	2	11	43	24	7	2	1
Technicians, including draughtsmen	33.2	4	15	42	24	7	2	1
Sales supervisors	32.4	6	18	41	25	8	3	1
Clerks – senior grade	32.1	3	17	38	23	8	2	1
Sales representatives, travellers	31.4	9	25	37	24	10	4	2
Welfare workers	30.3	9	23	33	18	5	—	—
Manual workers – skilled	29.8	6	25	28	15	4	1	—
Manual workers – semi-skilled	27.7	12	36	20	10	2	—	—
Clerks – intermediate grade	25.0	16	50	10	4	1	—	—
Manual workers – unskilled	24.3	25	54	12	5	1	—	—
Clerks – routine and junior	21.4	39	73	4	1	—	—	—
Catering, domestic, service workers	21.1	44	68	7	4	1	—	—
Shop salesmen and assistants	20.4	47	81	2	1	—	—	—
Agricultural and related workers	19.9	51	81	2	1	—	—	—

Source: Department of Employment Gazette, December 1971 (pp. 1150–2, 1157–9): data from New Survey of Earnings, April 1971. (This table does not list all occupations shown in the source, but an illustrative selection from all parts of the range.)

to these jobs. Clearly there are broad differences within the stratum. The existence of private wealth in property, for instance, will tend to inflate the income and wealth of some of the groups in this stratum even further: particularly company directors, chairmen and general and divisional managers by whom the bulk of shares are owned (Blackburn, 1972). When we look at this top stratum in the context of some additional data, certain conclusions can be drawn concerning organization élites. To arrive at these conclusions we can consider some data on social status and educational background tabulated with some of these selected occupations.

It can be argued from statistics such as those shown in Tables 11.6 and 11.7 (from Warwick, 1974, p. 141), which employ indices of social status and educational background, that there would appear to be a relatively homogenous labour market of the socially and educationally privileged from which the ruling élite in upper strata positions in organizations are drawn. The major determinants of access to these most privileged jobs would seem to be a privileged background. In this case it would seem not unreasonable to argue

TABLE 11.6 *Indications of bourgeois homogeneity among members of upper strata positions in Britain by father's occupation*

Father's occupation (R.G. social class)*	Administrative class, civil service 1967	University teachers in art and social sciences 1966	Scientific officer class, civil service 1967	Top managers 1954–5	Directors 1965	Percentages British population in social classes I and II Born 1910–19	Born 1920–9	All economically active England and Wales 1966
I and II	67	60	54	72	50	67	67	18
III	23	31	39	25	40	29	28	49
IV and V	6	6	7	3	10	4	6	30
Others	3	3	—	—	—	—	—	3

Sources: This table is an extract of information from the Committee under the Chairmanship of Lord Fulton, *The Civil Service,* Volume 3(1), 'Social Survey of the Civil Service', a memorandum submitted by A. H. Halsey and I. M. Crewe, HMSO, London, 1969, Tables 3.20 and 3.22. The last column is compiled from the *Census of England and Wales,* 1966.

*The Registrar General's Social Classes: I Higher professional and managerial; II Intermediate professional and management; III Lower non-manual and skilled manual; IV semi-skilled manual; V unskilled manual.

TABLE 11.7 *Indications of bourgeois homogeneity among members of upper-strata positions in Britain by type of full-time school last attended*

Type of school	Administrative class 1967	University teachers in arts and social sciences 1966	Scientific officer class, civil service 1967	Graduate administrators in LEAs 1967	Percentages Managers of a large industrial organization 1967	MPs 1959 Con.	Lab.
LEA Modern Technical and Comprehensive Secondary	2	51	6	72	—	2	33
LEA Grammar	40		57		47	25	45
Direct grant	19	10	15	28	14		
Independent	37	22	21		36	73	22
Others	2	17	2	—	4	—	—

Sources: Drawn from Fulton Committee, *op. cit.* (see Table 11.6), Tables 3.33 and 3.35, and J. Blondel, *Voters, Parties and Leaders,* Penguin Books, 1966, Fig. 8, p. 137.

that the individual ruling élite members are very largely drawn from, intergenerationally, a ruling class which is largely self reproductive. This argument is strengthened by a consideration of Whitley's (1974) research into company directors, in which he concludes that:

> In terms of seeing directors as an elite it appears that very large industrial and financial firms do recruit their Board members from a narrow segment in the population. These directors undergo a remarkably similar educational experience and, to some extent, have similar social circles as evidenced by club membership and kinship links. They tend, in other words, to be members of the same culture, or at any rate to have the background for sharing a common culture (Whitley, 1974, p. 80).

Stanworth and Giddens, after a detailed study of the economic élite comprised by company chairmen in the UK, come to the conclusion that by the turn of the nineteenth century there had emerged among the larger industrial organizations an élite indistinguishable in background and educational experience from 'those men in the dominant positions in the spheres of politics, the civil service and the Church' (Stanworth and Giddens, 1974, p. 101). They are sceptical that this situation will be transformed by post-war reforms in education. It would seem that education is not so much a cause of social mobility but simply an avenue through which ruling class reproduction is maintained. It is the ability of the ruling class to reproduce itself as such (as empirically evidenced in Stanworth and Giddens (1974) for example), which makes it a ruling class.

The élite composition of the upper stratum of positions in organizations which Whitley (1973; 1974) identifies for company directors and which Stanworth and Giddens (1974) have identified for company chairmen, has been confirmed in a sector which these authors regarded as the least élite in British business. This sector is that of retail organizations, studied by Thomas (1978). This work shows that there is no sectoral difference in élite composition in terms of educational background. Ruling élites are routinely either recruited from the ruling class via public schools or recruited and socialized into this class's cultural ways through public schools. However, some sectoral distinctions do emerge. Retail organizations are less likely to have representatives of the traditional aristocracy on their boards, and have a smaller proportion of titled directors than other sectors (Thomas, 1978, p. 313). In this respect the financial sector is the sector in which the greatest array of titles is to be found on the boards of the major banks and insurance companies. Nor do retail organizations characteristically have

428

interlocking directorships (Thomas, 1978, pp. 313–16), as is more typical of the industrial and financial sector of the modern corporate economy (see Stanworth and Giddens, 1975). In part, this may be because of the high concentration of kinship groupings in the élite positions of particular firms (Thomas, 1978, pp. 316–18). This is characteristic of retail organizations (e.g., see Higley *et al.*, 1976; Florence, 1961), which tend to have a high concentration of ownership by shareholding and control by position (Thomas, 1978, pp. 318–22).

The picture at the top of the major organizations in the key sectors of a modern society such as the United Kingdom appears to be one in which recruitment to these positions is not all random but is in fact highly structured by class,[5] operating primarily through the avenues of the aristocracy, prestige public school education, and kinship, with education as *the* key avenue of ruling class reproduction.

In Silverman and Jones' (1976) analyses of selection interviews conducted in a large public service organization, the crucial factor that they discovered as a predictive factor in successful selection was that the candidate be 'acceptable', rather than 'abrasive'. Further work on selection interviews by Salaman and Thompson (1978) has related these personal, individual qualities to issues of class analysis. They begin their analysis by noting:

> Despite public pronouncements by the major institutions that they are seeking to recruit candidates from as wide an educational background as possible, and the claim that the emphasis is on leadership by the best qualified rather than leadership based on social superiority, there still seems proportionately to be more room at the top for the public school educated than for the state school educated (Salaman and Thompson, 1978, p. 283).

The role of selection interviews as the mediation between the class structure of the labour market and the class structure of the organization will be of central importance here. Accordingly, Salaman and Thompson's (1978) analysis is of selection interviews, drawn from data collected for officer recruitment in the British Army. As they identify, 'the results of the selection process are highly class-determined; but all parties insist that they are operating solely on the basis of [a] formal, scientific selection scheme' (Salaman and Thompson, 1978, p. 286). They demonstrate that this is possible because of the way in which the selection scheme functions. This is in terms of abstract, decontexualized qualities which are defined and described in psychological terms so that they appear *as if* they were inherent qualities of the individual *per se*. However, the authors argue that this is only an appearance. In

429

practice 'the scheme supplies a legitimation of the selection decision, but not its *basis*' (Salaman and Thompson, 1978, p. 289). This is because any selection scheme has to be interpreted just as does any formal document in organizations (see Clegg, 1975, pp. 132–51). Selectors 'use the gap between the written scheme and the activities of the applicants to interpret these activities so as to achieve a final decision that was in line with their shared preferences, while all the time appearing as mere executors of the formal selection process' (Salaman and Thompson, 1978, p. 289). In this instance they are aided in this by the categories employed by the selection scheme and the setting of the selection interview itself. The categories used in the scheme such as 'coolness' or 'social skills' are not, nor could they be, neutral. This is because

(a) certain sorts of social, educational, familial and other experiences are more likely than others to encourage the behaviour and attitudes which army officers will take as evidence of the valued qualities, (b) the selection system and procedure, and the staff who run it, are so obviously and overwhelmingly of a certain class culture that some candidates will find the situation entirely familiar, others dauntingly alien, and (c) the very qualities themselves are defined in class terms (Salaman and Thompson, 1978, p. 290).

The categories in the interview scheme are depictions of qualities 'which are more likely to be found among boys with public school education than others', and which are interpreted in ways that favour those boys who are most like the officers doing the selecting. These officers themselves are public school products. When they define seemingly innate phenomena such as 'natural leadership abilities' what they are doing is to gloss a certain style, a certain cultural hegemony, which is transmitted through public school education and the upper-class milieux generally:

The assurance of natural social superiority that underlies the social behaviour that the officers regard as natural leadership – and which therefore leads to a positive assessment under such selection qualities as 'dominance', 'coolness', and 'quality of character' – is the result of early exposure to educational and family experiences and cultures which encourage the impression of deserved and ascribed superiority – the 'right to rule' of the upper class (Salaman and Thompson, 1978, p. 297).

Failure to conform to these class qualities is seen as a subjective failure of an individual's psychology, rather than an objective class membership. This class membership colours and shapes the whole selection experience even to the setting in which it occurs. This is an old country house resonant with the milieux of upper-class county and public school life, in which those candidates not familiar with these milieux are at an immediate disadvantage.

Although Salaman and Thompson's (1978) work is an analysis of only a few interviews in one organization – the British Army – it throws some light on the processes of 'social construction' whereby at the crucial intersection of labour market and organization, 'class' is produced and used as a device for reproducing class structure. More research on a wider range of organizations is required on these processes.

Not only do we not enter organizations randomly, we are also treated differently as a result of being at different levels and in possession of different skills. Warwick (1974, pp. 118–19) relates this to the existence of ruling élite strategies of recruitment in organizations: 'the common way of ensuring or attempting to ensure the compliance of the hierarchically differentiated managers in the enterprise', irrespective of whether or not it is public or private, 'is the payment of incrementally increasing salaries and the granting of various privileges and benefits according to status. The result is of course the perpetuation of a considerable measure of inequality' (Warwick, 1974, p. 119). These privileges, benefits, etc. . . , rank together. Workers in high-status jobs tend to have higher earnings, shorter and more congenial working hours (they are less likely to be on shift work for instance), will usually have a more pleasant work environment and longer holidays in which to recuperate from work, than will those who are ranked below them (Westergaard and Resler, 1976, is invaluable on this). These work distinctions spill over into non-work situations of education and social differentiation and tend to be mutually reinforcing (Goldthorpe, et al., 1968). These distinctions can be seen from the research reported by Wedderburn (1972) in Table 11.8.

The broad mass of male manual workers, skilled and unskilled, together with service workers, shop assistants and clerks below the senior grade, all comprise a bottom stratum within which, clearly, a number of fairly distinct labour markets will operate. Despite the distinctions all workers in this stratum have much in common. They are low-paid and remain so throughout their life-cycle of participation in the labour market. They may earn slightly more in their thirties than in their twenties, but this increase declines as they enter middle and old age to a figure often less than that which they earned in their twenties. In short, they have no career, no prospects and no future. This contrasts sharply with most of the occupations in the second stratum and all of those in the top. These men typically 'have careers on incremental curves, which rise steeply during their working lives until the forties or later, with salaries at that stage

431

TABLE 11.8   *Terms and conditions of employment – per cent of establishments in which various conditions apply*

	Operatives	Foremen	Clerical workers	Technicians	Managers middle	senior
Holidays: 15 days +	38	72	74	77	84	88
Choice of holiday time	35	54	76	76	84	88
Normal working 40+ hours per week	97	94	9	23	27	22
Sick pay – employers' scheme	57	94	98	97	98	98
Pension – employers' scheme	67	94	90	94	96	96
Time off with pay for personal reasons	29	84	83	86	91	93
Pay deductions for any lateness	90	20	8	11	1	0
Warning followed by dismissal for persistent lateness	84	66	78	71	48	41
No clocking on or booking in	2	46	48	45	81	94

Source: Wedderburn, 1972, p. 177.

even on average up to nearly twice the levels reached by these men in their early twenties. The curves then flatten out and fall, but only modestly' (Westergaard and Resler, 1976, p. 82).

Sociologists argue that the key to understanding these class divisions is an understanding of the fundamental generative framework which constitutes them (Connell, 1976). In this vein, Westergaard and Resler (1976) have demonstrated that:

Private ownership of capital is the key to class division in Britain as in other capitalist countries. Taxation and public welfare provision have done little to alter the broad pattern of material inequality between classes, because the objectives and effects of public policy are limited – though they are not rigidly fixed – by the needs and influence of business in an economy where private enterprise continues to play the predominant role. Inequalities in earnings between jobs of different kinds remain marked, in much the same mould over long periods of time, because they are still – even with public employment of a substantial fraction of the labour force, and with increasing state intervention to counter inflation – determined principally by market demands in an economy directed to make capital yield a secure profit to its owners. Private capital, in other words, carries power (Westergaard and Resler, 1976, p. 107).

If 'private capital . . . carries power', then an understanding of power in organizations would seem to entail an analysis of private capital as it produces and reproduces class structure through modes of organization of the labour process.

432

12   Power and class in organizations

Power in the theory of organizations

The development of a specific concern with power in the theory of organizations is related to the post-Hawthorne 'discovery' of the informal organization (Roethlisberger and Dickson, 1939; Landsberger, 1958). Prior to this the usual focus of enquiry was the structure of formal authority, as Thompson suggests:

> The usual definitions of power are properly applicable to the internal structures of formal organizations. One reason why research workers have seldom regarded actual power in such organizations may be that the classics on bureaucracy have stressed the rational aspects of organization, with emphasis on authority to the neglect of unauthorized or illegitimate power. And it was not long ago that informal organizations were 'discovered' in bureaucracies (Thompson, 1956, p. 290).

Thompson indicts the 'classics of bureaucracy' for their neglect of 'power' to the benefit of 'authority'. As Weber's work represents the essential classics of bureaucracy for most sociologists, one might think that Weber is responsible for the neglect of 'power' in organization theory – except that Weber is so frequently cited as the source of a concern with 'power'. This seeming anomaly is explicable when one considers the context in which Weber's classics of bureaucracy were translated and incorporated into American sociology.

Weber's work on 'power' and 'authority' became available to most organization theorists through Parsons and Henderson's translation known as *The Theory of Social and Economic Organization* (Weber, 1947). In a much remarked upon footnote by Parsons (Weber, 1947, p. 152), the concept of *Herrschaft* is

433

translated as 'authority', thus preserving what Gouldner (1971) has called Parsons' 'superordinate' view of power, as if it were Weber's. This 'superordinate' concept leads Parsons to regard 'power' and 'authority' in two ways:

> either as two different stages in development, in which, for instance, power is viewed as the degenerate or the immature form of authority; or as two alternative ways in which one person or group can structure the behaviour of others. In both cases they are viewed as mutually exclusive, as if, when one exists, the other does not. . . . if it had been looked at from the standpoint of *subordination* in the social world, power and authority would more likely be viewed as dual structures, both *simultaneously* present, in subtle and continual interaction. Power, in short, exists not simply when authority breaks down, or before authority has had a chance to mature. It exists as a factor in the lives of subordinates, shaping their behaviour and beliefs, at every moment of their relations with those above them. . . . Legitimacy and 'authority' never eliminate power; they merely defocalize it, make it latent (Gouldner, 1971, p. 294).

In those studies which have followed Parsons' view of power as a 'superordinate' concept, then 'power' relates to 'authority' as something distinct, as something 'informally' rather than 'formally' developed. This becomes the theme for the development of organization-theory studies of power. For instance, Bennis *et al.* (1958, p. 144) follow this view in noting the 'formal–informal' distinction as one where 'authority is the *potentiality* to influence based on a position, whereas power is the actual ability of influence based on a number of factors including, of course, organizational position'.

This definition of the topic becomes the basis for the mainstream of organization-theory studies of power. The focus of investigation is defined in terms of deviations from the formal structure. This formal structure then appears in the analysis only in so far as it frames the initial state of rest, of equilibrium, from which the power deviation is to be measured. In itself it is not a topic for investigation or explanation. The topic becomes the *exercise* of power from within an initial equilibrium position, where that exercise is premised on the possession of some resource(s) by the power-holder.

Defining the topic in this way has at least two important consequences. First, it can lead to analyses of power which take the formal structure so much for granted that the author(s) frequently forget its existence in their zest to explicate the causal bases of power, as for instance Mechanic (1962), or Hickson *et al.* (1971).

434

Mechanic (1962) proceeds from Weber's (1968) argument that permanent officials can frequently exercise power over elected representatives because such officials have a special knowledge due to their permanency *vis-à-vis* members elected for the life of a parliament. He then extends this argument to all organizations. It is hardly legitimate to extend an argument concerned with representative government to all organizations in general. It is certainly not legitimate to do so where the critical feature of the original argument is missing. This is the case where the executive is not elected on a precarious and revokable basis, compared with a permanent administrative staff.

Mechanic (1962) also displays another representative tendency in studies of power which define it as the *exercise* of 'will' (Weber, 1947), or 'force' (Mechanic, 1962) or 'determination' (Thompson, 1956), or any similar formulation. That is that this exercise is premised on specific 'bases'. These bases have typically been conceptualized in one or other of two ways. One of these can be characterized as 'functionalist', because the bases are sought in the 'functions' of the organizational system. Examples of this can be seen in Thompson (1956) and Dubin (1957).

In a study of two USAF bomber wings Thompson (1956) argues that these bases develop 'because of the technical requirements of operations' and suggests that they include being in a 'centralized' position within the organization, and being involved in strategic 'communication'. Dubin (1957, p. 62) similarly stresses 'the technical requirements of operations' with his emphasis on a 'system of functional interdependence' in which some tasks will be highly 'essential' to the system, and are the 'exclusive' function of a specific party.

Bases of power have also been sought in specific socially sanctioned 'resources' which the individual may control, or be in some special relationship with, such that they somehow enable 'power' to be 'exercised'. A typical formulation would be that of French and Raven (1959) in which an *a priori* list of 'power resources' is constituted. The problems with any such list, no matter what its constitution may be, are apparent. Such an explanation assumes that the particular 'resources' which have a utility in one situation will have that utility in all situations. It also assumes perfect knowlege on the part of all people in being able to judge correctly the utility of all resources in all situations. Such assumptions are without warrant, and can only be guaranteed within the ideological practice of capitalist society, as Sensat and Constantine (1975) argue in their 'Critique of the Foundations of Utility Theory'. Thus, explanations premised on this assumption presume that individual utilities of different 'resources' can be

435

aggregated on a single measuring scale. This is to deny changing historical circumstances, or different societal locales. The assumption of 'resource'-based explanations of 'power' ought also to entail an exposition of how some people come to have access to these 'resources' while some others do not. The prior possession of resources in anything other than equal amounts is something which a theory of 'power' has to explain. It may presume equilibrium, but it ought to justify its presumption in some way.

Organization theories of 'power' have not warranted this assumption of equilibrium. They have presumed it. This presumption consists of the simple expedient of taking the prior and inequitable distribution of resources for granted. This is explicable when one considers the development of theorizing about power in organizations, in particular from Thompson's (1956) article onwards. A 'view' of 'power in organizations' developed as a study of variance or deviance from a presumedly unproblematic formal structure. By the late 1960s there had developed a small literature on power in organizations. There existed a general consensus on a concept of power as an 'exercise' of 'will', 'determination', etc., which was usually modelled upon Dahl's (1957) mechanical model. The formal structure of hierarchical power in the organization was rarely discussed, except in descriptive ways by writers such as Tannenbaum (1968). Increasingly the possible bases of power were modelled upon abstract concepts current in the literature, rather than specific social psychologists' lists. The most pervasive became Crozier's (1964) initially quite concrete concept of 'uncertainty', control of which he had linked to power (albeit of a marginal and discretionary type). The concept was in vogue. It had become a mainstay of the *Behavioural Theory of the Firm* as Cyert and March (1963) modelled it. It was at the centre of the cybernetic and information-theory metaphors which pervaded organization theory in its search for the definitive system analogy, a search which finds its most developed expression in Weick (1969), who seems to point toward the ultimate telos of the metaphor in a determinate physio-biology of the brain. And the concept of 'uncertainty' which was implicit in Thompson's (1956) stress on control of 'strategic communication' as a base of power becomes explicit in his *Organizations in Action* (1967).

It was at this stage in the development of the language game that a group of researchers led by Hickson attempted a synthesis of much of the available material, perhaps on the basis that with a shopping list one might as well have a recipe. They called their recipe 'A Strategic Contingencies Theory of Intra-Organizational Power' (Hickson *et al.*, 1971). We have already analysed general contingency theory in Chapter 6. We can reconsider it here through

Child's work. In an essay, titled 'Organization: a Choice for Man', Child has characterized recent perspectives on organizations in terms of their stress on 'contingencies'. In the perspective which he criticizes, the organization has to cope with contingencies which derive from 'the circumstances of environment, technology, scale, resources and other factors in the situation in which a unit is operating' (Child, 1973b, p. 237). The contingency perspective emerged from empirical enquiry into organizations which yielded statistical data on the relationships between the 'dimensions' of organizational structures, and the situational characteristics of these organizations. Child argues that contingency theory results from interpreting this data in the simplest possible way, which is to suggest that the situational characteristics predict the dimensions of the organization.

One of the specific criticisms that Child develops of this type of organization theory is that it has neglected questions of power in the organization. In an earlier article, Child (1972a) has noted a variant on the contingency approach to organization in the 'strategic contingency' approach of Hickson *et al.* (1971). This variant has proposed a 'theoretical explanation of power as the dependent variable with the aim of developing empirically testable hypotheses that will explain differential power among sub-units in complex work organizations' (Hickson *et al.*, 1971, p. 216). The concept of contingency used in this variant of the perspective is somewhat different from that in more general use in organization theory as Child (1973b) has criticized it. In the 'strategic' variant the concept of contingency is explicitly used to predict the power of a 'sub-unit' in a theoretical schema, rather than being an extrapolation from a data analysis. A sub-unit, A, is seen as being more or less contingent on the other sub-units in the organizational system. The less contingent, or dependent, a sub-unit is on these other sub-units, then, *ceteris paribus,* the theory predicts that it will be more powerful. The components of the *ceteris paribus* clause in this instance are that the sub-unit should also be highly unsubstitutable by any other sub-unit, that it should also be central to the organizational system, for which it must manage a high degree of uncertainty; these, in conjunction with contingency, predict power.

The basic idea of environmental determinism, common to this tradition of organization theory, remains in the 'strategic' variant. The unit of analysis has shifted from the organization and its environment, to the sub-unit and its environment of inputs which may come from either the wider organization, or from outside of the organization system.

437

A 'strategic contingencies' approach to power in the organization

Hickson *et al.* (1971, p. 216) claim to be offering an explanation of what has not been previously explained: 'within organizations, power itself has not been explained'. The authors of this statement make this claim from within Thompson's (1967, p. 13) 'newer tradition' which 'enables us to conceive of the organization as an open system, indeterminate and faced with uncertainty, but subject to criteria of rationality and hence needing certainty'.

The elements of this tradition derive from the functionalist approach in sociology and from the behavioural theory of the firm in economics, in particular Thompson's synthesis of these. To these ingredients are added elements of Blau's (1964) 'exchange theory'; Crozier's (1964) theoretical inter-relation of power with 'uncertainty', and Dahl's behavioural concept of power as elaborated by Kaplan (1964). It is from these ingredients, blended within the systems framework, that Hickson *et al.* produce their 'strategic contingencies' approach, as a synthesis of the two major recent traditions in the study of power: exchange and behavioural theory.

The division of labour in the organization is seen to provide the functional inter-relation of the interdepartmental system of sub-units. It is to imbalances in this interdependency that the theory ascribes power relations. In viewing the organization as composed of interdependent parts, then Hickson *et al.* (1971, p. 217) follow Thompson (1967, p. 6). Some parts are more, or less, interdependent than others. Hickson *et al.* (1971, p. 217) regard the major task element, or work, of these departments, as being 'coping with uncertainty'. The interdependent system of sub-units is an open one, whose work derives from transforming its major input, uncertainty, into more certainty than existed in its previous state. The organization is regarded as thus composed of more or less specialized sub-units, differentiated by the division of labour, but related by a need for certainty. This need leads to the system's 'essential' behaviour, which is:

limitation of the autonomy of all its members or parts since all are subject to power from the others; for sub-units, unlike individuals, are not free to make a decision to participate, as March and Simon (1958) put it, nor to decide whether or not to come together in political relationships. They must. They exist to do so. . . . The groups use differential power to function within the system rather than to destroy it (Hickson *et al.*, 1971, p. 217).

A strategically contingent system is thus composed of plural and countervailing powers which constitute the organization, an organization whose essence is limitation of the autonomy of these parts. In short, it is a traditional 'open-systems' model of the organization modified by a realization of the points that Gouldner (1967) raised. He pointed out that certain parts of a system may be relatively more autonomous than others. In this particular case their autonomy is not so great that the part may ultimately destroy the whole. The environment of the organization determines the behaviour of the organizational sub-unit, because of boundary exchanges of resources, with the resource inputs to the sub-unit being hypostasized as 'uncertainties'.

The reduction of these uncertainties is the goal of the organization. This reduction work provides the resources for sub-units to exchange with each other, and with the environment external to the organization. Given this, then one would anticipate that changes in sub-unit power might be 'caused' by factors extraneous to the sub-units (in a version of environmental determinism), which is indeed how the 'strategic contingencies' theory does explain change. For example:

> Goal changes mean that the organization confronts fresh un-
> certainties; so that sub-units which can cope or purport to cope
> with these experience increased power. Thus if institutions shift
> in emphasis from custodial to treatment goals, the power of
> treatment oriented sub-units (e.g., social service workers)
> increases only if they can cope with the uncertainties of inmate
> treatment. If they are helpless to do anything even purportedly
> effective, then they remain weak (Pennings et al., 1969, p. 420).

Such a 'strategic contingencies theory' of power explains changes in power in terms of the adaptation of a system in the face of a changed environment:

> Organizations deal with environmentally derived uncertainties
> in the sources and composition of inputs, with uncertainties in the
> processing of throughputs, and again with environmental un-
> certainties in the disposal of outputs. They must have means to
> deal with these uncertainties for adequate task performance.
> Such ability is here called 'coping' (Hickson et al., 1971, p. 219).

Changes in power are caused by a changing capacity to cope with the uncertainty caused by the systemic adaptation of sub-units to changing, or changed, environments.

Qualifications must be made when considering the question of environmental determinism within a sociological perspective. Once we allow that some members of organizations may be in a position

439

to choose the environment in which they operate, then the emphasis on the determining features of the environment diminishes. It might be that the home market is less variable than the export market, and it might be that members who manage exports are more 'strategically contingent', and hence by definition of the theory, more powerful, than these other members. This would tell us little if one crucial and unconsidered question is *who* chose to export, and how and why they chose to. As Child has pointed out,

> the directors of at least large organizations may command sufficient power to influence the conditions prevailing within environments where they are already operating. The debate surrounding Galbraith's thesis (1969) that the large business corporation in modern industrial societies is able very considerably to manipulate and even create the demand for its own products centres on this very point. Some degree of environmental manipulation is open to most organizations. These considerations form an important qualification to suggestions of environmental determinism (Child, 1972, p. 4).

Further qualifications would result from reconsidering the substantive focus on sub-units as the unit of analysis. These are those areas of an organization concerned with a specific function such as sales or production. It is assumed that these will exist as relatively autonomous, contained and identifiable areas. In attempting to argue that these sub-units behave, without at the same time suggesting how they might do so (for example, through the action of some powerful member(s) in formulating sales or other policy), one implicitly assumes that the entity reified as a 'sub-unit' somehow enacts one definition of the environment to which it then 'reacts'; or that it somehow 'picks up' the one message that the environment sends it.

If one hypothesizes that a sub-unit is a unitary and harmonious collective, speaking and acting with one voice, then one is on a sticky wicket unless one specifies clearly that one is not proposing a consensual reification. One could propose an apparently more probable and less reified hypothesis. This second hypothesis asserts that a sub-unit is a collective which is spoken for by one voice, and which over-rules competing interests, attachments, strategies and meanings. The former hypothesis opens one's theory to charges that it uncritically embraces management ideology, as Fox (1966) has suggested. In such a perspective, the sub-unit is what managers do, which means that the environment would be what managers thought important and problematic. Thus the theoretical concept of environment would be constituted by managerial definition.

This would be to refrain from explaining power in the first place.

The theory presupposes a tacit and unexplicated reliance on the very topic that it seeks to explain. This is because the theory implicitly defines both a 'sub-unit' and 'the environment' as being that which managers define them as. This concealment is then used as a resource for circular theorizing which purports to explain its own tacit assumptions. What has been assumed is the power of managers. This assumption enables the theory to talk of 'the environment' and the 'sub-unit' as if they were unitary phenomena. Thus a collective of potentially conflicting interests and world-views is regarded as one thing (a 'sub-unit'), which serves only to demonstrate the power of some members of that collective. They are able to 'speak' for it, representing it as one such thing. Any such assumption of identity in the face of difference would have to spell out how that difference was overcome in a way which the 'strategic contingency' theory does not. Such a reading without any specification or notification of the nature of the organization's stratified features, the differentia of hierarchical stratification, merely allows the theory again to assume what is to be explained. The division of labour upon which the whole argument rests may itself be the result of powerful members' definitions of what the organization and its environment are, a notion provided for in terms of Cyert and March's (1963) idea of a 'dominant coalition'.

The idea of 'dominant coalitions', ruling élites', etc. is essentially one developed in a context in which power is seen as no longer necessarily being co-terminous with ownership. These theories stress that there has been a 'managerial revolution'.

The theorists of the managerial revolution, as for example Burnham (1941), have argued that, given the 'decomposition of capital' attendant upon the separation of ownership and control, power no longer resides in ownership, but in management. The idea of a separation of ownership and control in large corporations is widely accepted among economists, and is generally held to be derived from Berle and Means' (1932) classic *The Modern Corporation and Private Property*. This book was the first attempt empirically to investigate data concerning stock ownership in the context of assumptions that shareholders were becoming less influential in the conduct of corporation affairs, and that in consequence of this the control function of ownership was being superseded by that of management.

Blackburn has been critical of these assumptions:

> If decomposition of the managerial function is scrutinized then it soon becomes apparent that it is the very specialization of the expert that constitutes the real limit on his power. The sphere of competence of the specialist is very strictly defined by his own

particular skill. Rewards and sanctions descend downwards in a hierarchical manner inhibiting the development of group solidarity among those on the same level . . . top management is constrained by the context of capitalist competition to maximize profits and to accumulate capital. The performance of each department can be evaluated in terms of its contribution to these overall goals. Increasingly sophisticated procedures in cost accounting enable top management to develop criteria for subordinating every aspect of company operations to financial control. The head office of a large corporation will employ an armoury of checking devices to ensure that its constituent divisions and departments contribute fully to the profit potential of the resources and corporations commands. Often competition between different divisions of the same corporation or the possibility of contracting out functions performed inside the corporation serve as a lever exercised by the head office over its outlying parts. Only in a company with most incompetent management will really important decisions about investment policy, product range, output, price, size of labour force, etc. escape proper central audit. The financial department will, of course, tend to have a decisive say in nearly all questions. However, the power residing with the financial expert is one which he derives from the context of the capitalist market itself and must exercise on behalf of the ultimate owners of the corporation (Blackburn, 1972, p. 178).

The theory of strategic contingencies merely takes the managerial thesis one stage further by accepting Galbraith's (1967) argument. This states that the general type of manager has disappeared only to be replaced by different departments (sub-units) of specialists, each of which pursues some key managerial function. Galbraith (1967) and Hickson *et al.* (1971) see these as the locus of power. Galbraith (1967) sees even top management as dependent on these as gatekeepers of information. This information becomes for Hickson *et al.* (1971) a key resource in terms of its degree of uncertainty. Power comes to be located in the portals of power.

Power achieves this locus through being attached to the concept of uncertainty. This concept, as we have stated, has become current in recent organization theory, largely as a result of its use by Crozier (1964), although similar related concepts have been used by Thompson (1967), and Cyert and March (1963). It has obviously become an idea in good currency. Its currency in the use that Hickson *et al.* (1971) put it to is also obscure. Besides the difficulties that Hickson *et al.* (1971) encounter in their use of the concept of 'sub-unit', the opacity that they exhibit in their use of the concept of 'uncertainty' would be sufficient to render suspect any theory based on it. For instance: 'Uncertainty may be defined as a lack of information about future events, so that alternatives and their outcomes are unpredictable' (Hickson *et al.,* 1971, p. 219).

Uncertainty is here defined as something possessed by members of organizations, rather than being something that an 'environment' might have. But, one page later we read that: 'Uncertainty might be indicated by the variability of those inputs to the organization which are taken by the sub-unit. For instance, a production sub-unit may face variability in raw materials and engineering may face variability in equipment performance' (Hickson *et al.,* 1971, p. 220). Uncertainty is now located not in members' knowledge, but in the variability of artefacts, this variability being located in the input 'environment' of the sub-unit.

In a sense which is not used in their work, one plausible interpretation of the concept of uncertainty would locate it in members' knowledge for predicting future states of affairs. If this were so, then presumably certainty would be a state of affairs in which all alternatives and all outcomes were equally and absolutely predictable. There would be no possibility of untowardness. Inexplicability, strangeness and surprise would not be possible. Were such a situation imaginable, it would conjure up a state of affairs in which a rule existed for each and every thing that might ever occur. A complete inventory of contingency procedures would exist. Uncertainty might be seen as a situation in which rules for remedying surprise had yet to be enacted. So, in this world, how would control over uncertainty confer power?

Control over uncertainty might be considered to be achieved when ruling on what causes the uncertainty, the surprise, had been made, and a course of treatment formulated, to bring the occurrence back into line as a routine. Thus, Crozier's (1964) maintenance men (who attended to machine breakdowns referred to them by the production workers) could be said to render an unexpected event into the past tense, by rendering it routine. They did this by providing a reason for it, and implementing a course of treatment. He suggests that this uncertainty conferred 'power' on these men, power which they would otherwise not have had.

In the example of uncertainty conferring power, we could claim that in a structural sense, analogous to the meaning of sovereignty which stresses it as being 'the effective source of or influence upon the exercise of political or legal power' (Marshall, 1964), the source of such power in the organization is a result of structural determinance by strategic contingencies. The inter-relationship of the organization, its structural layout, thus determines the source of sub-unit power.

Now it may seem odd that structural layout should determine the effective source of power, for one might have wanted to argue the converse. The oddity becomes clearer if one recalls that in this particular formulation, power is seen as the obverse of dependency, so that 'the crucial unanswered question in organizations is: what factors function to vary dependency, and so to vary power?' (Hickson *et al.*, 1971, p. 217).

Dependency in a system can be neither more nor less than the degree of functional autonomy and reciprocity that a unit enjoys; that is, the degree to which it is central or can be substituted for. But if at the same time, power is seen as the obverse of dependency, then power similarly is a function of functional autonomy and reciprocity.

Power in rules in organization

Power in the organization begins to look rather like a game of chess in which the pieces gain their power through their current position, rather than gaining their current position through their power to make moves according to the rules of the game. In short, the power which a piece has is defined totally in terms of its relationships. This definition entirely neglects the progress of the game in terms of its history and rules.

If power is not something that condenses in a relationship, and evaporates on its termination, what is it? To stay with the example of chess, one might say that it is a function of the relationship of pieces (units) to rules, in that rules invest a certain power in a piece, independently of its position on the board.

Imagine a game more analogous to social reality. In this game the rules are frequently changing and not at all clear. Whoever was able to exploit this uncertainty, and rule in his own interest, would in this sense have power. This is the essence of Crozier's (1964) formulation. To the extent that all pieces were able to negotiate their positions, more or less, then in a game with a fixed number of pieces, that piece which ended up ruling on the greatest number of pieces, serving its interests in preference to theirs, would be the most powerful. But obviously a piece like the Queen would start in a more privileged position than a pawn, simply because the extant rules, which are now open to interpretation, enable her to begin the sequence with more potential moves to make.

Consider the context of Michel Crozier's (1964) original formulation of the 'control of uncertainty confers power' hypothesis. The factory described by Crozier is a plant of a state monopoly organization which mass-produces cigarettes. The monopoly controls the sales of the factory's output. Almost every activity

444

seems to be encapsulated by constraints of a technical or organizational nature. For instance, the organization's output goals and mechanization processes are fixed, and the majority of petty decisions have been centralized or are rigidly standardized. The task of the factory was basically to combine 350 employees and 45 machines in four limited functions: (1) preparation of raw material; (2) maintenance and setting of machines and buildings; (3) utilization of man-machine combinations for output in several parallel production segments; and (4) allocation of jobs among employees (Crozier, 1964, p. 66).

The organization 'lives a perfectly colonized, deprived life even as a manufacturing sub-unit', as Koot (1976, p. 205) puts it. It cannot determine its own mode and pace of mechanization. It cannot acquire additional income through sales, as this is not one of the functions in its control. The accounting system does not welcome innovations which will require capital investment, as it lacks the funds to commit to this purpose. Thus, the organization cannot reorganize its basic technology. Within the organization there is not even any control on the allocation of jobs. At a national level the monopoly faces union pressure which prevents the plant engaging in any autonomous personnel policy measures. Output norms, workload and pay rates are all fixed at a national level. In short, for people working in the organization 'the daily problems of running the plant are completely boring' (Crozier, 1964, p. 126). The plant is an almost completely routinized and de-skilled production unit paralleled by an almost completely routinized clerical task structure for monitoring and controlling the situation. This is the management's task.

In many respects, as Crozier (1964, p. 59) suggests, the organization 'appeared precisely to represent the ideal type in the Weberian sense'. However, this was not the case in *all* respects. There were areas of variance from the formal bureaucratic structure. Somewhat surprisingly, even in this highly structured, rigid organization some of the rank and file workers, notably the maintenance men, have the capacity to be able to exercise an illegitimate 'parallel power' which they use in their own interests against those of supervisors and production workers. They are able to do this because their capacity for power is vested in the de-skilled and piece-rate payment nature of production workers' jobs compared with skilled maintenance work which is paid on a fixed salary. Production workers' interests are in a continuous flow of work in order to maximize their earnings under the bonus system. Any machine failure or breakdown lessens their earnings because the flow of production is interrupted. Only the maintenance men have the necessary skill for repairing the machines. This gives them

445

a situational skill advantage which becomes the basis of a local plant dependence upon them by both management and workers. Crozier did not claim that maintenance men were the most powerful members of the industrial bureaucracy, because of their undoubted success in controlling, in an almost monopolistic manner, discretionary areas of their tasks. What he suggests is that there is an existing context of organization rules which constitute the formal power structure. Within this there exist areas of uncertainty which groups or individuals are capable of controlling. Indeed, individuals or groups can, and do, control these areas. So the areas become key resources by means of which individuals and groups procure less dependence for themselves, within the power structure (Crozier, 1964, pp. 150–65).

The concept that transforms 'less dependence' into 'power' (albeit of a local and contextually bound type – as Crozier (1964) himself recognizes, and as Hickson *et al.* (1971) do not), is derived from Dahl's (1957) operational definition of power. This is that the power of a person A over B is the ability of A to ensure that B does something he would not have done otherwise.

Dahl argues that three necessary conditions have to exist in order for us to say that there has been an exercise of power. These are, first, that there is a time lag between the actions of the actors said to be exercising power and the responses presumed to signify its exertion. Second, the two actions must be connected. Third, the actor exercising power must be able to get the other party or parties to do something that they would not otherwise have done (Dahl, 1957, pp. 204–5). Dahl uses these conditions in the following example of his 'bedrock idea of power':

> Suppose I stand on a street corner and say to myself, 'I command all automobile drivers on this street to drive on the right hand side of the road'; suppose further that all drivers actually do as I 'command' them to do; still most people will regard me as mentally ill if I insist that I have enough power over automobile drivers to compel them to use the right hand side of the road. On the other hand, suppose a policeman is standing in the middle of an intersection at which most traffic ordinarily moves ahead; he orders all traffic to turn right or left; the traffic moves as he orders it to do. Then it accords with what I conceive to be the bedrock idea of power to say that the policeman acting in this particular role evidently has the power to make automobile drivers turn right or left rather than go ahead (Dahl, 1957, pp. 202–3).

We want to extend this discussion of Dahl in order to point to an underlying unity between the seemingly different concerns of Dahl

446

(1957) and Crozier (1964). Crozier indicates this difference by placing his own work in a context assuredly not that of Dahl's; 'the theory of bureaucracy – that theory in terms of which sociologists since Max Weber have been considering the processes of organization' (Crozier, 1964, p. 175). This 'underlying unity' concerns the way in which power, like uncertainty, depends for its behavioural possibility upon an unexplicated concept of 'rule'. This concept may be found in the very tradition that Crozier (1964) claims to continue, but in fact waives in favour of Dahl's (1957) behaviourism. Having described 'the underlying unity' in more detail, we will argue that the same theme of 'rule' can be seen to underlie 'exchange'-based explanations of power. We will argue further that the concrete explanations of exchange theory are as neglectful of the concept of power as are those of the seemingly different behavioural tradition.

All that would appear to mark off the efforts of, for example, a passer-by from those of a policeman in conducting the flow of traffic, would be that the passer-by, unlike the policeman, is not able to alter what automobile drivers actually do. The bystander, in willing the traffic to proceed as it was, would be patently not exercising power, although he might be said to be 'connected', and his behaviour might follow that of some passing motorist.

Retaining the same example, let us alter some of its conditions. Suppose that the bystander, disguised as a policeman, were to attempt to control traffic, and the traffic obeyed. Meanwhile, the policeman, disguised as a bystander, attempts to exercise his earlier power, but fails. Motorists merely mock his policing pretensions, and are disposed to regard his behaviour as psychotically disturbed.

We would be tempted to explain the traffic control behaviour in terms of motorists' response to what they presumed, in each case, were a policeman and a psychotic. The 'normal' identity of the two agents is not in question, rather we attend to the way in which their actions were labelled as either responsible or psychotic, according to the typifications that motorists have of police uniformed traffic controllers and madmen. The uniform acts as a symbol which displays a role. The role serves as a shorthand expression for what every motorist knows: motoring is a rule-guided activity, and policemen represent the power of the rules. The rules would be the basis of the policeman's power, and not Dahl's three necessary conditions, which are mere occurrences within the rules. Policemen have a certain power because motorists recognize them as embodying certain rules. Just like pieces in a chess game.

Consider the traffic policeman again. Let him control a traffic light system. We might account for the movement and non-movement of traffic in terms of a correlation between the effects of red and green lights. Although we might say that the traffic policeman caused the traffic to stop and go, we would in effect mean that both the policeman and the motorists know that there are rules which govern traffic movement in such situations. Thus, we could formulate the traffic behaviour in terms of the following rules: red lights mean stop; green lights mean go. Just as with Crozier's maintenance men and production workers, we can similarly say that the behavioural outcome is only possible because of some underlying rule(s) that people use in constituting their actions. The manifestation of power is enabled by an underlying rule.

We can make similar observations about exchange and power. Consider the example of the Mafia. The Mafia control a local commodity market in which all exchanges between the Mafia and its suppliers of materials are conducted on the Mafia's terms. Other markets are available, as are potential competitors of the Mafia in the existing market. None the less, there are no movements in or out of any markets, We might account for the absence of movement into the market in terms of a correlation with monopoly control procedures such as aggressive trade wars, takeovers, and trusts. Although we might, in shorthand, say that the Mafia thus caused members of some of the other organizations not to sell in that market, while causing members of some of the other organizations not to sell in any other market, we would in effect mean that both the Mafia and those other organizations know that there are rules governing, for example, access to monopoly markets. In this situation what is obvious is that the monopolist constructs the particular substantive instances of them. The exchanges that occur are made possible by people constituting them according to some underlying rule(s). The exchanges that do not occur are made impossible because people similarly constitute them, this time by 'exclusion rules'.

Rules are not simply a property of actors exercising power, but are constitutive of relations between them. And these relations are of differential power and interest. It would be a mistaken assumption to argue from resources as 'things in the world', such as control over uncertainty, to power as something determined by responses to these resources. Doubtless Dahl is correct in that power is sometimes relational, but not in the Newtonian way that he (and implicitly, those who accept his definition) assumes it to be. Its relational aspect is constituted by an assumption on the part of each party that the other knows that there *are* rules, which does not necessarily entail knowing *the* rules.

Crozier's (1964) discussion of rules is almost entirely within the context of the usual interpretation given to Weber (1968) on rules; that is, as the formal codifications of bureaucracy. Had he interpreted Weber on this topic in terms of 'enacted' rules, a legitimate interpretation, then his discussion of power as a concept at both the discretionary level, and at the level of the structure of the organization, could have been made in the same terms. These terms would remain relevant to the meaningful context in which people work.

Crozier (1964) deploys Dahl's (1957) concept of power in a context which is concerned to develop insights about the different ways in which organization members define their situations, and the limits on their rationality in doing so. His indebtedness to Simon (1957) and March and Simon (1958) provides the concept of 'bounded rationality':

> Such an approach allows us to deal with the problems of power in a more realistic fashion. It enables us to consider, at the same time, the rationality of each agent or group of agents, and the influence of the human relations factors that limit their rationality (Crozier, 1964, p. 150).

His analysis focuses on the ways in which members of an organization can manipulate their situations in such a way as to maintain or enlarge their areas of discretion within the conditions of membership, which are set by a 'controlling group' (Simon, 1957) or an 'organizational coalition' (Cyert and March, 1963). They achieve this manipulation through the use of strategies to protect their interests as they perceive them. Their perceptions are located in the prevailing values of members of the French bureaucracy, which in turn are seen as 'reflecting' French society. Action is seen as situational, resulting from meaningful and bounded rationality, which includes a varying commitment to the system of interactions, structured as it is by the rules in which it operates.

What Hickson *et al.* (1971) do is to take both a similar concept of power (deriving from Kaplan, 1964), and a similar stress on uncertainty. Where they differ from Crozier (1964) is in their neglect of the structural and cultural forms of power to which Crozier makes reference.

Hickson *et al.* (1971) manage to ignore prior questions of 'rules of the game' which effectively structure the types of issues (and hence outcomes) that arise for power to be manifested. They do this because they write in the tradition of an exchange theory allied to a behavioural concept of power, in a functionalist systems framework. The implications of the systems framework and the behavioural concept of power have been considered. What remains is to show how Hickson *et al.* (1971) make Dahl's (1957) implicit notion of an exchange explicit. They do so by making Dahl's (1957) concept of a 'social relationship' one which is determined by the

449

'division of labour'. This division of labour creates the inter-dependent relationships which then determine 'power relations' (Hickson *et al.*, 1971, p. 217). The exercise of power is then explicitly related to the author of exchange theory, Blau (1964), in terms of which 'sub-units can be seen to be exchanging control of strategic contingencies one for the other' (Hickson *et al.*, 1971, p. 222), in order to acquire power through the exchange.

Rules in exchange

The underlying assumption of an exchange theory such as that of Blau (1964) is that each party to a potential exchange has something which the other(s) also value and want. A typical exchange would be where each party preferred the other(s) to make the greatest contribution, but would himself be willing to do so rather than discontinue the exchange. Although both actors have shared interests, they diverge on grounds of self-interest. Although both want the exchange to persist, neither wants to make the greatest contribution. While the parties concerned profit from an exchange they have an interest in maintaining it, although self-interest leads them to wish to benefit most from any exchange.

Blau's exchange theory stresses the tendency of any participants to try to control the behaviour of others in their own interests. Sometimes only very partial control can be effected, where both have valuable resources to contribute. On some other occasions one party may have nothing immediate to offer. Blau (1964) suggests that such a person in need has several strategies open to him in principle; he can force the other to help him; he can get help from someone else, or he has to do without the valued resource. If he cannot adopt any of these solutions, he has no option other than to submit to power, on the assumption that he cannot do without the required good or service.

Power is distinguished from sheer coercion. In the latter, the powerless party would not have a choice. He would be unable to opt for punishment, or withdrawal of facilities, as a sanction for non-compliance. A man thrown into prison would be physically coerced, unless he had voluntarily resigned his freedom in order to save his life. Had he done the latter, then this could be construed as an exchange. Where there is no robbery there must be fair exchange, in however tautologous a sense.

One can make a number of criticisms of this perspective. First, although exchange theories provide us with a way of seeing exchanges occurring, they have nothing to say about the rules governing exchange processes, nor how these operate, nor how they have developed. Second, as Heath argues:

Where the account is unsatisfactory . . . is that it equates power with the ability to secure submission and compliance (following the Weberian tradition) and thus makes power a product of the *extreme* case where there is a 'unilateral exchange' of services. . . . But surely we do not want to restrict the concept of power to such unusual and bizarre situations, which seem virtually to be ones of slavery (Heath, 1976, p. 25).

Exchange-based theories may provide some insight into some aspects of power, but how significant are these in themselves? The insights that they can obtain are on the surface level of appearances, on power as manifested in the outcomes of particular exchanges. Exchange-based theories ignore the 'deep structure' of these appearances as this exists in the particular issues over which power is displayed. Such a deep structure might be uncovered by research premised on Bachrach and Baratz's critique of 'pluralist' models. This critique argues that any such model

takes no account of the fact that power may be, and often is, exercised by confining the scope of decision-making to relatively 'safe' issues. . . . The model makes no *objective* criteria for distinguishing between 'important' and 'unimportant' issues arising in the political arena. . . . Can a sound concept of power be predicated on the assumption that power is totally embodied and fully reflected in 'concrete decisions' or in activity bearing directly upon their making? (Bachrach and Baratz, 1971a, p. 378).

What such a critique recommends is research premised on a theoretically elaborated model of the relationships between particular issues – which arise for power to be exercised over – and the institutional areas in which they occur. In short, it demands an account of the rationality of power in whatever arena is under study, a rationality under whose domination issues become transparently a 'ruled' phenomenon. Such a perspective would not propose that the power displayed in any one exchange was a chance outcome of that exchange alone, in which resources might be utilized which have no power in another setting; but would instead attend to their prior differential institutionally defined value.

The community power debate and organization theory

One of the most surprising features of the previously cited literature is the way it has developed in isolation from such debates in political science. A consequence of this has been the uncritical application of a concept of power which has been subject to extensive criticism.

This is the critique of Dahl's (1957) concept of power by writers such as Bachrach and Baratz (1971a, 1971b). One writer on the role of power in organization theory who has addressed this literature is Abell (1975).

Abell attempts to circumvent three particular problems in his discussion of power. First, he attempts to break with the tradition which he terms the 'control of resources' approach. Second, he proposes to study 'decision-making' rather than rely on a 'reputational approach' to data collection. Third, he proposes a two-stage model of the organization as a 'bargaining and influence system' in which it is proposed to incorporate Bachrach and Baratz's (1962) argument that 'what is and what is not open to bargaining is itself related to the concept of power' (Abell, 1975, p. 11).

Abell (1975, p. 13) rejects the use of 'resources' or 'bases' as an 'operational definition' of power (on grounds similar to those employed earlier). Instead he proposes that one should first detect the power or influence of a group or person, and then provide an explanation of this power in terms of resources. The distinction between power and influence that Abell makes is quite specific, and serves the purpose of attempting to incorporate Bachrach and Baratz's (1962) critique of Dahl's concept of power into organizational analysis.

Abell (1975, p. 15) argues that if we can obtain data on people's 'initial preferred outcomes' to a decision, and observe the 'ability of A to modify B's preferred outcomes in a bargaining/influence situation all other influences "held constant" then this will give us the influence of A over B in securing B's "modified preferred outcomes"'. The 'bargaining power' of A will then be 'his ability to obtain his preferred outcomes, when facing competing preferred outcomes, in a bargaining situation, all other bargaining power held constant', determined by the 'final bargained outcome'. But although this approach does not simply aggregate 'bases' or 'resources' and does not depend on a simple assumption of an initial equilibrium, it is still not really satisfactory. The 'initial preferred outcomes' that people will have are in a sense arbitrary. They will depend upon *when* the researcher has defined the bargaining sequence as beginning. Nor is an 'initial preferred outcome' as unproblematic as it might at first sight seem to be. What constitutes an initial preferred outcome may be the very problem that we wish to address, rather than its solution. To the extent that the possibilities of a person's existence and participation in an organization will be circumscribed within the dominant 'theorizing power' of the organization's 'form of life' (Clegg, 1975), then surely a very significant form of power will be the members' inability to see beyond the actuality of presence? In Marcuse's (1964) phrase, they will be one-dimensional people embedded within the unthought consensus of everyday life.

The presuppositions of organization theory of power

If one knew nothing of organizations in contemporary capitalist society, yet one was willing to absorb what knowledge one could from the existing scholarly texts on the topic, what picture of power would these present?

One might be led to think that organizations are composed of 'behaviours' (Lawrence and Lorsch, 1967, p. 3), which belong to something called a 'sub-unit', which occupies a space in a 'system' (Hickson *et al.*, 1971, p. 217). These sub-units are engaged in a permanent struggle with each other as each tries to control more aggregated 'bases' of 'power' than the others (Butler *et al.*, 1974; Hickson *et al.*, 1971). Sometimes these behaviours and sub-units form 'coalitions' with others of their kind, from inside or outside the same system. Coalitions are usually not very stable, and change over specific issues (Benson, 1975; Butler *et al.*, 1974).

As with much science fiction which features alien beings, one finds no explanation of the Hobbesian assumption that there exists some innate need for power. Sub-units, like Daleks, just happen to be like that. And if we recognize human beings inside the Dalek shell, or inside the sub-unit – well, it must just be that it is somehow *in* human nature to strive for power like that. None of our scholars tells us otherwise.

The assumption of a power struggle as a principle of the system fulfils the same function in organization theory as does the principle of unfettered competition in economic models of price equilibrium (after Macpherson, 1973, pp. 184–91). These economic models are premised on the assumption of a freely competitive market for resources and commodities in which there exists a division of labour and exchange of products and labour. It is assumed that each individual in this market would rationally try to maximize his or her gains (or minimize the real costs). Where both a division of labour and an exchange of commodities and labour exist, then it would follow that competition would determine prices for everything in a determinate system which tended to equilibrium (as Lipsey, 1963, demonstrates).

Organization theory rephrases these assumptions but without substantially altering the problematic of 'equilibrium' which they animate. In organization theory the equilibrium is achieved through the creation of 'dependencies'.

On the assumption of a freely competitive power struggle in the organization's market (its 'bargaining zone' in Abell's phrase), in which, as in economic theory, each individual tried to maximize his or her gains (or minimize the real costs), where the division of labour creates exchanges, then it would follow that control of scarce 'resources' or 'bases' of exchange, would maximize dependencies for everyone (as in Hickson *et al.*, 1971). And, where power is defined as the obverse of 'dependency', then we would have achieved a theory of power in a determinate system which tended to equilibrium as in economics, or in organization theory as Hickson *et al.* (1971) render it.

Such a model is premised on a market model whose motive force is a series of ontological assumptions which

> treat the maximization of utilities as the ultimate justification of a
> society, [which] is to view man as essentially a consumer of
> utilities. It is only when man is seen as essentially a bundle of
> appetites demanding satisfaction that the good society is the one
> which maximizes satisfactions (Macpherson, 1973, p. 4).

This is a distinctively different concept of being from that which is found in the tradition of political theory, as it is seen in Plato's *Republic,* for instance. Here the good society is that in which men are free to use and develop their natural abilities, attributes and capacities. In this version of power, for it to be exercised, the person must have access to whatever means are necessary in order that he or she may use and develop natural attributes, capacities and abilities. To the extent that this access is denied, or limited and transferred to others, this power is diminished (Macpherson, 1962, p. 56). This conception of being leads to a quite different concept of power from that which has previously been sketched. While the obverse of being exercising power in these formulations may be being 'dependent', in the older formulations being 'free' is opposed to being under power.

Adopting this latter view has some important consequences for our theorizing. It concentrates our thought on the theoretically and practically prior conditions for the exercise of power. The essence of this view of power is to see it as 'potential' or 'capacity' for future action, including any specific exercise of power. In ordinary language, it would be the type of power meant when we say that someone 'has power', or when we speak of someone 'being in power'.

To abstract this latter concept is to distract our attention from the underlying social relations that grant to some positions in organizations more or less capacity to exercise power than others. Instead it focuses our attention on the exercise after any prior structuring of capacity has occurred. Power is seen simply as the exercise of an ability, taken after any accretion or diminution of capacity has occurred.

This concept of power does not stipulate access to whatever means are necessary to *exercise* this capacity; instead it abstracts the whole question of capacity out of consideration. Power is power over others only after some exercise moves the state of play from some point taken as an initial state of rest. There is no specification of how the rules of play have developed, nor of how they might grant a greater capacity to one set of players over the others. This has the ideological function of preserving the structural framework of social relations as something outside, and prior to, theoretical enquiry into power. Thus, this structural framework cannot enter into any explanation of how the exercise of power can create a 'variance' from 'authority'.

The remainder of the argument seeks to open a space whereby this may be possible.

Organization theory re-presents the ontological assumptions of the market theory which developed as a justification for liberal-democratic society from Hobbes onwards (and is still being developed by contemporary theorists of the right). Marx came to refer to its economic doctrine as 'vulgar' political economy. One might refer, after the same manner, to 'vulgar' organization theory. Rowthorn (1974) has detailed the ontological assumptions of vulgar political economy as *subjective individualism, naturalism and exchange*. By showing how these premise vulgar organization theory, much as they do vulgar political economy, it is possible to suggest an alternative way of seeing organizations which enables us to provide a basis for connecting discussion of power with that of 'domination' and 'autonomy'.

We have discussed the subjective individualism of organization theories whose seemingly structural concepts such as a sub-unit have to be regarded as being premised, methodologically, on individual managers' power. For Weber (1968) individual social actions are motivated neither by an insatiable desire for power nor for certainty, but by collectively recognized and publicly available social rules which orient individual social actions in rationally structured ways. He notes that these rules, in so far as they form social actions, are 'without exception . . . profoundly influenced by structures of dominancy' (Weber, 1968, p. 941), which do not

utilize in every case economic power for [their] foundation and maintenance. But in the vast majority of cases, and indeed in the most important ones, this is just what happens in one way or another and often to such an extent that the mode of applying economic means for the purpose of maintaining domination, in turn exercises a determining influence on the structure of dominancy. The crucial characteristics of any form of domination, may, it is true, not be correlated in any clearcut fashion with any particular form of economic organization. Yet the structure of dominancy is in many cases both a factor of great economic importance and at least to some extent a result of economic conditions (Weber, 1968, p. 942).

Power as a particular type of social action is constructed and acted out by individuals as a ruled enactment. Such enactments occur in the context of an economically conditioned structure of domination. The individual is a 'bearer' of a particular rationality in which an 'objective principle' is regarded as a 'concrete object' which 'governs the domination', as Simmel (1971, p. 116) put it (also see Clegg, 1975, pp. 63–5). The individual is essentially a social being, who, as a bearer of social relations, is ruled and dominated in the last instance by economic power. This economic power is embedded and displayed within the framework of a 'structure of domination' which is articulated through different types of 'rule'. Domination thus concerns, and grants, the prior capacity to be able to 'exercise' power at all.

There is no room in such a sociology for the *naturalist* and *ahistorical* tendencies that find their expression in current versions of the organization as a natural system. Contrary to this view is one which poses an understanding of the organization as a locus of the domination of a specific form of life. This is that of the juncture of materials with practices which relate and tie these to each other. These materials comprise not only the organization's site, plant, capital and raw materials, but also its labour. Within organizations constituted under a capitalist form of life it is the case that this labour is also regarded descriptively as just another commodity to be exploited (Macpherson, 1973, p. 10). The basis of the organization is the 'labour power' (Marx, 1973, p. 154), the 'capacity for labour' of the individuals who collectively comprise the creativity of the organization. Some of these members control not only their own creativity, their own capacity for labour, but also that of other members through the formal distribution of domination. Those members who have less than full control of their labour power will have a consequently limited capacity to exercise power because of their relative loss of freedom.

This implies a different perspective on 'membership' from that which is typically found in such organization theory formulations as those of March and Simon (1958) or Barnard (1938). These stress the conditions under which human and material resources exchange for one another, and formulate these in terms of 'inducements' and 'contributions'. If an exchange occurs, the theory proposes that it must be a fair exchange because each person involved in the exchange must have weighed up their inducements and contributions so that they subjectively balance, or are in equilibrium for the induced party. Otherwise an exchange would not have occurred. This neglects that a seemingly fair exchange may be underlain by a prior structure of relations which make inevitable an exchange based on a set of terms which as a rule favour the interests of one party above that of the other(s). It is in this way that Marx (1973) analyses the relations between labour and capital. This analysis proposes a theoretical understanding of the social relations which are entered into in organized employment and production.

Marx (1973) argues that what the worker sells to the capitalist in return for his wages is his labour power. Marx maintains that this cannot be a fair exchange. If it were, the capitalist would quickly have no money left. This would be because if the capitalist did not share in the labour then all the money would soon pass to the labourer. Where there existed profit there could be no fair exchange. What might appear on the surface to be a just exchange 'inducing' the 'contribution' of organizational membership will in fact have to be an unjust and exploitative exchange if the organization as the capitalist's instrument for materializing profit is to remain in being in the long run. Exploitation concerns the way in which under the institution of the market the capacity concept of power is organized as a form of domination which provides the framework within which power may be exercised. In capitalist organizations exploitation is the material basis of capital's domination of labour as a class (as Cole's (1957) introduction to Marx reiterates concisely). Capital, with its functionaries in management, has a greater prior capacity for an exercise of power because its very existence is premised on the diminution of the power of labour (also see Macpherson, 1973, pp. 43–5).

Profit, or surplus value minus costs, which Marx (1973, pp. 194–207) defines as those of constant and variable capital, is the organization standard whereby the creativity of current labour and the determinations of past labours are mediated. Current labour is organized around the organization's location in a mode of production and the strategies by which surplus value is to be accumulated, be it through either absolute, relative or indirect accumulation (see O'Connor, 1974). The relative profitability of each of these strategies will depend upon the juncture of the organization's location in a mode of production and the past history it represents, with the current costs of commodities, including labour, and the present possibilities of the world economy as a social formation.

457

Power in context in organizations

Power has been typically formulated as a variance from formal structure in organization theory. This version of power is still in need of explanation, even if one rejects current attempts at such explanations. Discrediting the explanations does not always remove the problem to be explained. How might a variance from the formal structure of domination within an organization be achieved?

Variances from a formal structure of domination might be explained by means of a model which affords a mediation between the different levels of structures. Let us consider the structure of the world capitalist economy as a social formation.

It has recently been argued by Immanuel Wallerstein (1974a, 1974b, 1976a, 1976b) in the field of comparative history, that the only sensible unit of comparative analysis for macro-sociological enquiry, is the *world system*. He arrived at this position through a consideration of the question: 'What are the appropriate units to study if one . . . purports to analyse the process of social change in a modern world?' (Wallerstein, 1974a, p. 3). His difficulties in arriving at an answer to this question centred on the 'concept of stages of development', and 'criteria for determining stages, and comparability of units across historical time' (Wallerstein, 1974a, p. 6). As he puts it:

> The crucial issue when comparing 'stages' is to determine the units of which the 'stages' are synchronic portraits (or 'ideal types', if you will). And the fundamental error of ahistorical social science (including ahistorical versions of Marxism) is to reify parts of the totality into such units and then to compare these reified structures (Wallerstein, 1974b, p. 389).

An instance of this practice to which he refers is the acceptance of society as an empirical entity, on the assumption 'that the unit within which social action principally occurs is a politico-cultural unit' (Wallerstein, 1976a, p. 345), and the compounding of this empirical fallacy by conceptualizing each unit, as characterized by a specific stage or model: e.g., feudal, capitalist, or socialist. Such a way of thinking creates what has been a major problem for historical analysis of post-revolutionary Russia and China: can a stage of development be skipped? Can a society catapult from a feudal to a socialist mode and by-pass the capitalist model? Wallerstein argues that these questions are

> only logically meaningful if we have 'stages' that 'co-exist' within a single empirical framework. . . . If we are to talk of stages, then – and we should talk of stages – it must be stages of social

systems, that is, of totalities. And the only totalities that exist or have historically existed are mini-systems and world-systems, and in the nineteenth and twentieth centuries there has been only one world system in existence, the capitalist world economy (Wallerstein, 1974b, pp. 389–90).

What is a world economy?

As a formal structure, a world economy is defined as a single division of labour within which are located multiple cultures . . . but which has no overwhelming political structure. Without a political structure to redistribute the appropriated surplus, the surplus can only be redistributed via the 'market', however frequently States located within the world economy intervene to distort the market. Hence the mode of production is capitalist (Wallerstein, 1976a, p. 348).

This concept of a capitalist world system has as a fundamental premise the demonstration of a single division of labour which we can regard as

a grid which is substantially interdependent. Economic actors operate on some assumption (obviously seldom clear to any individual actor) that the totality of their essential needs – of sustenance, protection and pleasure – will be met over a reasonable time-span by a combination of their own productive activities and exchange in some form. The smallest grid that would substantially meet the expectations of the overwhelming majority of actors within these boundaries constitutes a single division of labour. . . . What was happening in Europe from the sixteenth to the eighteenth centuries is that over a large geographical area going from Poland in the northeast, westwards and southwards throughout Europe and including large parts of the Western Hemisphere as well, there grew up a world economy, for which men produced largely agricultural products for sale and profit. I would think the simplest thing to do would be to call this agricultural capitalism. . . . Capitalism was from the beginning an affair of the world economy and not of nation-states (Wallersten, 1974b, pp. 397, 399, 401).

The units of comparative analysis within this world economy are regional specializations occurring in specific and different areas of the world economy (Wallerstein, 1974b, p. 400).

This regional specialization comes about by the attempts of actors in the market to avoid the normal operation of the market whenever it does not maximize their profit . . . capital has never allowed its aspirations to be determined by natural boundaries in a capitalist world economy . . . thus . . . one cannot reasonably explain the strength of the modern world system primarily in terms of a genetic-cultural line of argumentation, but rather in terms of a structural role a country plays in the world economy at that moment in time (Wallerstein, 1974b, p. 403).

Within this concept of only one social system – the modern capitalist world economy – within which social change can be studied, Wallerstein (1974a, p. 7) proposes that 'sovereign states . . . be seen as one kind of organizational structure among others within this single social system'. This notion of organizational structures within one social system is also relevant for the general analysis of organizations. This analysis has frequently foundered either on the epicyclical complexities and sterility of a modern systems theory (e.g., Weick, 1969) which sees all organizations as systems of systems within systems, without regard to problems either of boundaries or of distinctiveness in the way of the organizations functioning (the work it is designed to do, its labour) or on the microscopic retailing of the work members of organizations do in socially constructing their sense of the setting they are in, without taking account of 'the significance of interactional patterns within a structural or societal context' (Lassman, 1974, p. 141). In addition, one can criticize both 'cognitivist' and 'systems' theory for their neglect of an historical perspective (e.g., see Martins' 1974 critique).

Reconceptualizing organizations in the world system

We may begin the reconceptualization of organizations as structures of regional dominance and subordination within a social sytem which is a world system, i.e., 'one that has boundaries, structures, member groups, rules of legitimation, and coherence', whose 'life is made up of the conflicting forces which hold it together by tension, and tear it apart as each group seeks eternally to remould it to its advantage'. Such a system 'has the characteristics of an organism in that it has a life span over which its characteristics change in some respects and remain stable in others . . . its structure . . . being at different times strong or weak in terms of the internal logic of its functioning' (Wallerstein, 1974a, p. 347). This reconceptualization would be one way of addressing what some recent critics have regarded as a key failing of organization theories that 'they are both unhistorical and ethnocentric' (McCullough and Shannon). As they elaborate it:

> The point is really that all the organizations compared and
> classified in different countries or regions by organizational

analysts in terms of their memberships or prime beneficiaries, bases of compliance or structural characteristics, etc. may be themselves organized in relation to a nation state and to a global balance of power involving competing nations. Nations themselves may not even be the most significant organizing feature of a modern world economy. New alignments and power blocs continuously emerge and it is these which globally determine the total organization of organizations in such a way that they may be structurally connected despite the lack of apparent immediate contact required by organizational analysis. The image shifts, broadly speaking, from a sea on which ships collide or coalesce without their shockwaves extending much beyond, to a planetary constellation in which all movements are inter-related by gravitational laws (McCullough and Shannon, 1977, p. 75).

This requires further elaboration. Let us begin with the concept of the organization, as it was developed by Weber (1968) in his analysis of legal-rational bureaucracy. Where the basis of the organizational power structure is of the rational-legal type then this rationality, 'in the vast majority of cases, and indeed in the most important ones' can be seen to 'utilize . . . economic power for its foundation and maintenance' (Weber, 1968, p. 942). Such 'economic power' as a 'concrete object' is the realization of the 'objective principle' of a

> legal norm . . . established by agreement or by imposition, on grounds of expediency or value rationality or both, with a claim to obedience, [to those] . . . who stand in certain social relationships or carry out forms of social action within the order governing the organization have been declared to be relevant (Weber, 1968, p. 217).

These social relationships are constituted through the possession of differential skills ('technical knowledge . . . by itself, is sufficient to ensure . . . a position of extra-ordinary power') for the organization and its staff; while 'in addition to this, bureaucratic organizations, or the holders of power who make use of them, have the tendency to increase their power still further by the knowledge growing out of experience in the service' (Weber, 1968, p. 225).

Weber's model of a bureaucracy, providing its employees with a bureaucratic career through the grades of the organization, depicts a particular type of organization which Offe (1976a) has termed a task-continuous status organization, in which both functional and hierarchical differentiation coincide. As a result of the increasing 'denaturalization' and mechanization of the effort required for work through the increasing application of technique to technology,

461

the division of labour has become increasingly specialized. Specialization is defined as 'the increasing *difference* between the requirements operating at one position and those at another position' (Offe, 1976a, p. 24). A consequence of this increasing specialization of skill is the development of a 'task-discontinuous status organization'. This emerges parallel to the rational-legal hierarchy of office, on the principle of 'functional differentiation'. Offe notes that 'hierarchical differentiation and functional differentiation both produce status systems' which 'in the course of industrial development can become independent of one another' (Offe, 1976a, p. 24).

This model of a 'task-discontinuous status organization' has a particular relevance for a discussion of power in organizations. What people bring to bear on their participation in organizations is their special skill or skills (Allen, 1975). Offe (1976a) suggests that over a period of time functional differentiation based on skill can produce a task-discontinuous status organization which becomes independent of the authority structure of the organization. We have argued earlier in this chapter that power in organization theory has typically been formulated as 'a variance from the structure of formal authority'. A connection between these separate arguments can be constructed.

Task-discontinuous status organization

In the task-continuous status organization there exists a relationship between different positions in the hierarchy 'such that there is a wide area of technical rules to which equal obedience is required from all the occupants of the positions [in the structure]' (Offe, 1976a, p. 25). A superordinate position would differ from a subordinate position 'merely in terms of greater mastery of the rules and greater ability, knowledge and experience in production'. The rules that a subordinate must obey become, in their entirety, components of the role definition of a superordinate, and so on, up the hierarchy. Offe typifies this organizational structure as 'the production organization of the small craft workshop, with its triple hierarchical division of master, journeyman and apprentice'. In such a structure, power clearly derives from ownership and control of the means of production, and, overlying this, knowledge of the methods of production. This type of organization is not typical of the modern large-scale organization, and presents no particular problems for analysis of power. In this situation power derives from ownership and control of the key resources of production: means and method.

The origins of this type of organization lie in the development of different labour processes as landmarks in the history of capitalism, from simple forms of co-operation to the fully socialized labour of the modern organization. These have been investigated by Palloix, who writes of the principle of co-operation that it

> lies in the co-ordination of labour processes based upon *crafts* ('craft' here being given both a social and a technical definition), processes co-ordinated under the control of the owner of capital, who takes into his own hands the power to select and design particular use values. This co-ordination of labour processes based upon crafts reproduces in a modified way the hierarchical productive organization of artisanal production, characterized by the relationship between the master craftsman and journeyman (the primary relationship) and between apprentice and adult workers (the secondary relationship) (Palloix , 1976, p. 51).

As a further stage in the development of organization structures of social relationships, 'the principle of manufacture amounts to an extension of the principle of simple co-operation, with an initial dissolution of the preceding labour process based upon crafts' (Palloix, 1976, p. 51). With the transition to manufacturing, new forms of work, still based on craft skills, are produced: 'the *artisan* becomes a *worker* with profound ensuing effects on social relationships arising from the process of technical dequalification and hyperqualification of labour power within manufacture as a result of fragmentation of tasks' (Palloix, 1976, p. 52). This signals the emergence of what Offe (1976a) termed the task-discontinuous organization.

Task-discontinous status organization

This form of organization is based on an increasing differentiation between mental and manual labour. This distinction does not mean a separation in terms of descriptive criteria of a bio-physiological character such as 'natural movements' *v.* 'thought' or 'hand work' *v.* 'brain work', etc., as Poulantzas (1975, pp. 234–5) clarifies. Nor does the division betwen manual and mental labour coincide with that between productive and unproductive labour. For both Sohn-Rethel (1978) and Poulantzas (1975) it is the subordination of science to capitalist relations of production which is decisive. Sohn-Rethel (1978, p. 111) characterizes this in the formulation, 'Medieval handicraft began with the personal unity of head and hand; Galilean science established their clearcut division'. Poulantzas describes its conditions of continuing existence:

> This division is thus directly bound up with the monopolization of

463

knowledge, the capitalist form of appropriation of scientific discoveries and of the reproduction of ideological relations of domination/subordination, but the permanent exclusion on the subordinated side of those who are deemed not to 'know how' (Poulantzas, 1975, p. 237).

The important division is between those who produce or apply, who conceive and execute the knowledge which both technically and socially reproduces these ideological relations of domination and subordination, and those who are reproduced as ideologically dominated and subordinated. (Some strata may, of course, be both superordinate and dominated, as we will shortly elaborate.)

Part of this ideological domination and subordination, as we have developed in Chapter 8, consists of the ruling class fractions in the organization constituting the 'goals' of the organization. This is the attempt by the organizational rulers to counteract the subjectivity of labour within the 'limits defined by the wage-contract in the sphere of exchange and by the objective of valorization in the sphere of production' (Brighton Labour Process Group, 1877, p. 18). Effective ways of achieving this subjection include the economic constraint of the threat of the withdrawal of work, and thus wages, from recalcitrant wage labour; the use or threat of violence for failure to conform; and the threat of ideological excommunication, which is the 'threat or risk that no one will listen to a given discourse, except as a revealing symptom calling for therapy or repression' (Therborn, 1978, p. 175). Mayo's refusal to hear the discourse of class struggle as anything other than a symptom of neurosis is such an example. However, this subjection can also be achieved through what Marx (1974, p. 456) termed 'the *fetishistic character* which attaches to the products of labour, as soon as they are produced in the form of commodities'. In its extreme forms we are dealing here with questions of corporate or strata identity. The production of the organization as a corporate image embodied in uniforms, standardized furnishings, letterheads, images, etc. (the example of the multi-national hotel chain, for instance, the Holiday Inn or Hilton, which is always objectified as the same irrespective of where it may be) is an example of this fetishism. 'We try harder' becomes the fetishized form of existence for all members of an organization bearing that corporate slogan, such that their social existence is conditioned by their corporate subjection. This may be further divided on the basis of strata, as most obviously it is in the army, with its fetishism of rank and hierarchy. The production and reproduction of the organization goal as a fetish conforms exactly to Marx's description of the fetishism of commodities:

We are concerned only with a definite social relation between human beings, which, in their eyes, has here assumed the semblance of a relation between things. To find an analogy, we must enter the nebulous world of religion. In that world the products of the human mind become independent shapes, endowed with lives of their own, and able to enter into relations with men and women (Marx, 1974, p. 45).

The most effective forms of subjection in the organization are not only ideological but also practical: they are ideological practices, such as Taylorism, human relations, or dimensional re-design of organization structures. At their most subtle these practices will be at their most opaque, as in the literature of 'industrial democracy' (see Chapter 13).

The subjection of manual to mental labour occurs in the process of the capitalist division of labour. It is articulated through the process of de-skilling. De-skilling represents a loss of control by the worker over a given task because of a re-design of the job by which the task is accomplished. As a concept it refers us to the distinction between conditions of craft control, in which the worker is essentially the controller of his instruments of labour, and those of machine control, where the worker is subordinated to the pace, rhythm, etc. of the machine to which he or she is appended. The process of de-skilling is the historical process of the transition from a more or less craft type of control to one which is more or less a machine type of control. De-skilling does not mean that the worker loses total control: this is impossible, for as long as workers are involved in the labour process (see Brown, 1977). What is entailed is that the control function which previously skilled workers exercised passes from them in conditions of job re-design to 'higher' levels in the job hierarchy. Control becomes less and less the task of those who fill the places designed as de-skilled work, and becomes more and more a specialist skill-in-itself at a higher level in the organization. All those tasks which require some special skill for their operation, after the process of job re-design, are divided up into separate tasks. What craft skill (based on apprenticeship) remains or is still required is distributed to as few specialized workers as possible. (These workers would, for instance, be Crozier's (1964) maintenance men.) The remaining unskilled or semi-skilled tasks are separated out from each other so that they can be distributed into different jobs.

The de-skilling thesis, in an embryonic and somewhat apocalyptic form, is present in *The Communist Manifesto*:

With the development of industry the proletariat not only increases in number; it becomes concentrated in greater masses,

465

its strength grows and it feels that strength more. The various interests are more and more equalized, in proportion as machinery obliterates all distinctions of labour, and nearly everywhere reduces wages to the same low level. The growing competition among the bourgeois . . . makes their livelihood more and more precarious: the collision between individual workmen and individual bourgeois takes more and more the character of collision between two classes (Marx and Engels, 1969).

This simplistic two-class model has been refuted countless times by sociologists ever since Weber (1947) first introduced the idea of status into class analysis and this analysis became analysis of stratification. Clearly the refutations are in many respects correct. An immense immiserized proletariat and a tiny wealthy property-owning bourgeoisie have not become the only two polar classes in subsequent capitalist development. An increasingly large middle stratum has inserted itself into the dichotomy of a binary class structure of owners/non-owners of the means of production. This development has been intrinsic to the capitalist mode of production and the development of the labour process and its organization appropriate to it. Other discussions (e.g., Carchedi, 1977; Poulantzas, 1975; Palloix, 1976; Crompton and Gubbay, 1977 and Wright, 1978) and commentaries on the key texts of Carchedi (1977) and Poulantzas (1975) such as, for example, Johnson (1977) or Hunt (1977) have all stressed the complexity of any contemporary identification of social classes in relations of production in the organization of the labour process. Despite the many subtle (and sometimes seemingly scholastic) differences between these authors, we will outline as simply as possible some key points which are relevant for the argument we are developing here.

The labour process is that process by which raw materials or other inputs are transformed into products which have a use-value. As such, any labour process comprises three elements: the human activity or labour power which is put to work; the object, raw materials, unfinished product or activity which is worked upon, and the means or techniques of production by which labour acts (after Palloix, 1976, p. 46). The capitalist labour process is one in which this combination takes on a specific class character determined by the production not just of use-values, but of use-values subordinated to the production of self-expanding value: the process of valorization. This entails the production of commodities having not simply a use-value but also an exchange-value. Through the production of exchange-value, that class which owns and controls the means of production, which in the capitalist mode of production in its pure model (as found in Marx's *Capital*) is the class of capitalists, by virtue of its ownership and control, retains the right to the surplus produced. This surplus, although legally owned and retained by the capitalists, is not produced by either the individual capitalist or the collective class of capitalists (who are defined by their relation to the means of production: one of ownership and control). The surplus is produced by the class of labourers who neither own nor control their means of production. It is because they do not possess any means of production that they are obliged to sell their individual labour power to the class of capitalists who do own and control the means of production. In return for their labour power they receive its market price, its exchange-value. As Marx (1973) argued, and as we have discussed earlier, any such exchange could not be a fair exchange.

Marx (1959) wrote only an incomplete fraction on classes, which would seem to argue that classes can be identified by the source of their income. Seemingly, surplus value defines capital, while exchange-value defines labour (Marx, 1959, pp. 885–6). Carchedi (1977, p. 3) has developed this 'pure' model of the capitalist mode of production much further than this simple identification of income with class. He follows Lenin in defining the concept of classes as large groups of agents differing from each other: (1) by the place they occupy in a historically determined system of social production; (2) by their relation (in most cases fixed and formulated in law) to the means of production; (3) by their role in the social organization of labour; and (4) consequently, by the share of social wealth going to a class, by the mode of acquiring this wealth, and by the wealth's origin.

Looking at capitalist production relations in terms of the role or function of labour and capital, the means of production, Carchedi derives four elements in the dichotomous relations of production:

1   The producer/non-producer relationship: This corresponds to production/appropriation of surplus value, or exploited/exploiter.

2   The non-owner/owner relationship: By this category Carchedi (1977, pp. 50–1) means not legal but real economic ownership of the means of production. This real ownership is a capacity associated with the process of surplus-value appropriation.

3   The labourer/non-labourer relationship: Johnson (1977, p. 202) explains this clearly: 'While it is the case that all producers are labourers it is not the case that all labourers are producers (of surplus value).'

4   The relations of distribution: These are seen as a consequence of the other three, and involve: the share of social wealth going to a class; the mode of acquiring it, and its origin. This distinguishes revenue from wages, and surplus value from labour power.

467

Carchedi (1977) argues that in a pure model of the capitalist mode of production the working class would correspond to those who were producers/exploited/non-owners/labourers/wage-earners, while the capitalist class would be non-producers/exploiters/owners/non-labourers/revenue receivers. These are the 'pure' definitions of the capitalist mode of production which come into combination in the capitalist labour process.

Capital, by virtue of its power of ownership and control, initiates the labour process. It does this through purchasing the commodities that it needs to assemble in order to initiate the production process. This entails that there are available on the market means of production and labour power in the form of commodities (i.e., it entails the development of the pre-conditions for capitalist relations of production: formally free labour, the market, etc.). The continuing availability of these in the form of exchange relationships is reproduced by their combination in the capitalist production process in which the product takes the form of commodities which must be exchanged for money. There is a continuing reproduction of commodities by and through commodity forms of production. These commodity forms of production (wage labour, means of production, objects of production) are combined into relations of production within the general process of production. These relations of production 'are the various aspects of the control of the labour process by capital. In order that the capitalist mode of production be hegemonic, capital must establish its own specific form of control over labour within production' (Brighton Labour Process Group, 1977, p. 4). The specificity of capital's forms of control is given by the necessity of valorization: that is, of a surplus value producing process *as well as* a labour process. Thus, the capitalist production process is a process in which the production of surplus value dominates the production of use-values. This domination has taken the form of a unity of the processes of valorization and the labour process on the basis of the development of specific forms of organization (of the labour process). This development is a transition from *formal* to *real* subordination of the labour process *per se* to the necessities of the capitalist labour process. The specificity of the capitalist labour process is visible in the particular development of organization as control of the labour process:

> Capital assembles means of production and labour power and sets them to work, but it does so in a way that is determined by the object of valorization, of maximizing surplus-value production, and as far as possible eliminates all other potentially conflicting objectives. Capital *needs* real control of the labour process precisely because the formal separation of labour from the means

of production is cancelled in reality by the material form of labour process in which labour and materials and instruments combine. Capital needs to have control over the form of this combination, because whatever the instruments and materials (e.g., whatever the technology) there is always more than one way of effecting the combination and there is always the possibility of the process being informed by some objective other than that of valorization and potentially in conflict with it (e.g., the objective of healthy and safe working conditions, or of a socially useful product). The development of the productive forces that is the basis for the real subordination of labour to capital is a development of both objective conditions of labour, and of the social combinations of labour. The capitalist labour process cannot be specified on the basis of its technological components. But also note that it cannot be specified on the basis of the relations established within it between the *individual* worker and the instruments of production. It can only be specified as a *particular form of social organization of labour*, a form which is a specific form of coercion and the realization on an adequate basis of the objective of valorization (Brighton Labour Process Group, 1977, p. 6).

This particular form of social organization has undergone a development from formal to real subordination. The first stage of capitalist development is the formal subordination of labour to capital. This involves the subordination of the labour process to the surplus value process but without any accompanying revolution in the technical conditions (or forces) of production. Marglin (1974), whom we discussed in Chapter 2, presents an analysis of the emergence of capitalist control and organization at this stage, which after Karpik (1977) we may call 'merchant capitalism'.

The second stage brings the adaptation of the labour process to the surplus value producing process through a continuous revolution in the division of labour associated with the institutionalized application of science and technology. This is the development of 'industrial capitalism', in which there develops a real subordination of labour to capital, 'the adaptation of the labour process pure and simple to the surplus value producing process, its becoming a technically divided and scientifically organized process along the lines dictated by the need to create an ever-increasing mass of surplus values' (Carchedi, 1977, p. 55). Increasingly, under such conditions, the product is no longer that of an individual but becomes the outcome of what Marx refers to as the 'collective labourer'.

Under the formal subordination of labour to capital the pro-

469

duction of surplus was increased extensively through increasing the social labour time devoted to production through the historical prolongation of the working day in the early nineteenth century, or in more recent times, by intensifying the social labour time devoted to production. This is done by systematically removing slack, empty or pause periods from the working day by fixing the exertion of labour power to the routinized rhythm of machinery largely (apart from sabotage: see Brown, 1977) out of the workers' control.

The employment of machinery through the conscious application of science and technology leads to the development of the collective labourer and the complex labour process. In this complex labour process surplus value is produced not so much by intensifying social labour time as by increasing the productivity of labour by developing the productive forces of technology, and by moving into large-scale production. This is the development of Taylorist scientific management which enables a number of profound developments to occur. These are:

1   The increasing fragmentation of work.
2   The real separation of constant from variable capital, of labour from the conditions of labour, of means from actual labour of production.
3   The development of a collective, co-operative complex labour process. This complex labour process has a dual nature. First, it is increasingly dominated by the requirement of valorization which results in the increasing fragmentation of work: as Braverman (1974, p. 81) puts it, this enables the labour power capable of performing a process to be 'purchased (and reproduced) more cheaply as dissociated elements than as a capacity integrated in a single worker'. Second, the complex labour process is increasingly co-operative. A wide range of occupations are integrated into the surplus value producing process, 'even though they do not do manual work, even though they are not directly engaged in the production of use-values' (Carchedi, 1977, p. 56). We are confronted by the paradox that while the labour process becomes increasingly capitalist and antagonistic, it also becomes an increasingly co-operative form of the division of labour, including in this the function of co-ordination of the fragmented parts.

With the emergence of the real subordination of labour to capital and the technical division of labour the labour process becomes increasingly complex. Carchedi (1977, p. 58) elaborates the nature of this complexity in terms of its increasingly collective nature. He refers to this as the emergence of the 'collective worker', a process which he analyses in functional terms:

470

With the introduction of the technical division of labour within the labour process, this process becomes increasingly complex; from a process in which the individual labourer produces the whole commodity, to one in which the final outcome, the commodity, is produced by an ensemble of people organized as a collective labourer; as collective labour-power. The labour-process is sub-divided in a number of fractional operations, i.e. fractional units logically determined by a certain technical division of labour. As a first approximation, we can say that each one of these operations is performed by different agents of production. This implies that the function performed by an agent taking part in the labour process always has a specific content which is determined by the technical division of labour . . . all functions share one common feature: that of being functions to be performed within the complex labour process (Carchedi, 1977, p. 58).

In this process, the given functions of the collective worker, or in our terms, of the organized labour process, will be determined by the technical division of labour. We do not wish here to introduce a further version of technological determinism, but will argue in Chapter 13 that this technical division of labour is determined by the functions of capital in as much as they mediate contradictions in the world economy. Before we can elaborate on this, we have first to show how these functions of capital, which Carchedi (1977) calls 'the global capitalist', emerge, so that there exist functions to mediate. Having done that, we can extend our analysis through the various functions of capitalist production and reproduction in the contemporary phrase of monopoly capital, incorporating the role of the state, in order to show how this development not only de-skills labour, as Braverman (1974) argues, but can also generate new capacities for limited kinds of power within organizations. This analysis will needs be at a very general and broad level of abstraction.

In Carchedi's (1977) third stage of monopoly capitalism, the role of the capitalist is sub-divided into fractional operations in such a way that the functions associated with the appropriation of surplus value become collectivized in 'the global capitalist' (as they did in the 'collective worker' under the second stage of industrial or 'private' capitalism). A separation occurs between legal and 'real' ownership in the power to dispose of the means of production. The global functions of capital are dispersed to agents who do not themselves own the means of production. 'This dispersal involves the growth of a complex organizational structure which performs collectively what under "private" capitalism was the function of the individual, personified capitalist', as Johnson puts it in his commentary. This provides an explanation of the process of bureaucratization:

> The bureaucratization of the enterprise expressed the dualistic structure of the labour and surplus value producing processes. On the one hand, it is the result of the increasing co-operative nature of the labour giving rise to the work of *co-ordination unity*, which is the function of the collective labourer and, therefore, compatible with working-class membership. On the other hand, bureaucratization involves the extension of the *global function of capital*; that is to say, the work of *control and surveillance* in respect of surplus value appropriation performed by a large number of non-owner functionaries (Johnson, 1977, p. 204).

We can also look at those types of unproductive organization which are not state-owned, such as capitalist commercial enterprises but conform to the type of 'professional' organization such as a large legal, accounting, or banking concern. In as much as these organizations have a division of labour, then they also have collective workers in them who, although unproductive, do not fulfil the functions of capital. What do these collective workers do?

> The production process in the unproductive enterprise is the unity of the labour process and the process connected with the appropriation of (share in) the surplus value produced elsewhere. Here the workers are economically oppressed (direct appropriation of labour) rather than exploited (appropriation of labour in the form of value) and are the agents through which the capitalist appropriates surplus value (Carchedi, 1977, p. 68).

The unproductive capitalist production process thus forms a unity of the labour process *per se* with the surplus labour producing process, but dominated by the latter. Taking only the functions of the collective worker in this process, we can arrive at the following definition of such workers in both productive and unproductive capitalist organizations:

> To perform the function of the collective worker means to take part in the complex, scientifically organized labour process (i.e., in the production of use values, either material or not) as a part of the collective labourer, as agents through which capital in the productive sphere produces and appropriates directly surplus value (economic exploitation) or through which capital in the unproductive sphere participates in the sharing of the surplus value produced in the productive sphere of the economy (economic oppression) (Carchedi, 1977, p. 68, emphasis removed).

472

The 'capital' in this definition is not the personified capitalist, but the global function of capital, the global capitalist. The phenomenon which marks the emergence of the global capitalist and the collective worker has often been treated in the organization literature under the topic of the separation of ownership and control. This global capitalist may be identified with the functions of the non-owner/non-labourers/non-producers/exploiters/revenue receivers where the ownership of the firm and its control are not vested in the same agents. Marx related this development to the emergence of joint-stock companies:

> Stock companies in general – developed with the credit system – have an increasing tendency to separate this work of management as a function from the ownership of capital, be it self-owned or borrowed. . . . The mere manager who has no 'title whatever to the capital, whether through borrowing it or otherwise, performs all the real functions pertaining to the functioning capitalist as such, only the functionary remains and the capitalist disappears as superfluous from the production process' (Marx, 1959, pp. 387–8).

It is the joint-stock institution which permitted the passage from individual capitalist ownership to socialized capitalist ownership and the development of the global capitalist. A further consequence of the emergence of stock companies has been the increasing dispersion of stock. This has not led to the dispersal of power, but an actual concentration of the power of 'real ownership' which parallels the dispersion of share ownership. This is because the corporation system allows an increase of the power sphere of capitalist owners, who are now able to control larger economic units with a reduced proportion of legal ownership.

De Vroey (1975) has extended this discussion by using some distinctions similar to Carchedi's (1977), but made by Bettelheim (1976). Three levels of ownership are distinguished: possession; ownership as a relation of production or economic ownership; and legal ownership. Possession 'designates the ability to put the means of production to work. It thus pertains to the management of capitalist factories' (De Vroey, 1975, p. 3). Economic ownership is what Carchedi (1977) refers to as 'real' ownership: the capacity to organize labour power in concert with raw materials, plant, tools, etc., and to set the rate and intensity of work. Economic or real ownership is often linked to legal ownership, although it is analytically distinguishable from it (see Barratt-Brown, 1968; Domhoff, 1967; Mills, 1959a; Baran and Sweezy, 1968). The separation of ownership and control contains a twofold dimension. First, as Marx (1959) and, much later, Dahrendorf (1967) have

473

argued, it refers to the separation of ownership and management, a process of functional or role differentiation. This is a separation between the agents holding actual 'possession' and those having the capacity of 'real' or 'economic ownership'. The second dimension entails a dissociation between legal ownership and ownership as a relation of production, or, in Carchedi's (1977) term, 'real' ownership. De Vroey makes an interesting point:

> The two aspects do not necessarily occur in parallel. For example, one may conceive of a corporation whose main stockholder is a family owning 10 per cent of the total stock, with the remaining stock widely dispersed among small holders. If this family is active in management, the case exhibits a high degree of stock dispersion but no separation of ownership and management. And of course, the opposite situation is also very conceivable. This would be the case where there is very little dispersion of stock but at the same time no participation of the chief owners in management (De Vroey, 1975, p. 4).

Where the global function of capital is separated from the legal ownership of capital, not all of those performing this function will have the real ownership of capital. Some part of managerial/supervisory workers will perform this function without having this real ownership, while yet another, third part, will perform the functions of both the collective worker and the global functions of capital. These workers, those who have a contradictory location, are those workers whom Carchedi (1977) terms the new middle class. (We shall not at this stage consider the role of the state and its employees; i.e., non-capitalist organizations, but will do so in the following chapter.)

The process of the emergence of the collective worker, together with the development of the global capitalist, leads to the fully task-discontinuous organization which Offe (1976a) identifies. It is based on an increasing differentiation between mental and manual labour. This differentiation is achieved first by reducing the area in which the workers' skills can be used and developed. In particular it is achieved by progressively limiting that part of the worker's activity which consists of preparing and organizing work in the customary way. This has the effect of eliminating the workers' understanding of the whole of the labour process. Without this overall comprehension, the worker loses control over the methods of production. On the other hand, this differentiation is achieved through up-grading mental labour over and above manual labour, by what Palloix (1976, p. 52) terms the 'hyper-qualification' of a small majority. To this mental labour falls the tasks appropriated from the collective manual labour. These are: 'to systematize the

474

fragmentation of work' and 'to adapt each tool, which previously was used for many purposes, to new narrower uses, in such a way as to increase their efficiency' (Freyssenet, 1974, p. 36).

The result of this separation and differentiation of mental and manual labour is that the owner of capital, because of his owner-ship of the means of production, is thus able to extend this control over the methods of production, and hence the producers, He is able to do this by the systematic de-qualification and hyper-qualification of the skills involved in the organization of the labour process. Organizationally, the consequence of this is the emergence of the task-discontinuous status organization. In this type of organization, the relationship between hierarchically ordered positions is basically *not* an essential component of a superordinate position. This is a situation of functional differentiation, which Offe describes as one where the 'task areas' of positions 'and the technical knowledge and abilities required for their fulfilment no longer coincide: at any rate there is not the smallest element of the role definition of the lowest member of the organization's status hierarchy which is common to all the other positions' (Offe, 1976a, p. 25).

It is the existence of this type of task-discontinuous organization which has been the impetus for those studies of Crozier (1964), Mechanic (1962) and others into the power of 'lower participants' given by control of uncertainty, because the structure of such an organization

> results in a relationship between 'below' and 'above' such that some of the decisions that have to be made in the lower position are not fully covered by the commands and controls from above – they therefore have to be left to the independent decision of the workers (Offe, 1976a, pp. 26–7).

Analysis of the changing formal organization of the military is the example which Offe cites from Simon (1952, pp. 155–94) to demonstrate that there are necessary preconditions for direct, extensive formal control. These are:

1 The vertical (hierarchical) differentiation must be relatively underdeveloped, thus allowing the direct communication of orders and direct supervision of their execution.
2 The events and processes in the sphere of action have to occur within the field of vision and within hearing distance of the superior authorities.
3 Functional differentiation must also be rudimentary; not only must the majority of the actors belong to the same rank in the hierarchy, but also actors of the same rank must fulfil identical functions (Offe, 1976a, p. 27).

Power in task-discontinuous status organizations

An extremely important point concerning the analysis of power in organizations flows from these simple preconditions. We may in general define power as the ability to exercise control over resources which, when agents engage in or refrain from practices, produce effects on other agents; in the instance of organizational analysis these will be those practices that are the visible structure of social relationships, and changes in these, which are the organization. This power is expressed in organizations through the control of the means and methods of production. The most extensive and basic form of power is ownership and control of the organization. Zeitlin (1974) demonstrates that a majority (60 per cent) of large US corporations are controlled by ownership interests, notwithstanding that they are extensively managed by functionaries. Work by Scott and Hughes (1976) and Nyman and Silberston (1978) reveals strikingly similar data for Scotland and for England.

Additionally, as Francis (1977, p. 2) argues, recent data suggest 'more structural possibilities for groups of institutions to exercise control' than the theorists of managerialism had argued (e.g., Burnham, 1941). This is suggested by recent research on patterns of interlocking directorships by Levine (1972) for the USA, Scott and Hughes (1976) for Scotland, Stanworth and Giddens (1975) and Whitley (1973) for England. Crompton and Gubbay have argued that even where this separation between 'possession' and 'real' ownership has occurred, it may not be of sociological significance:

> The evidence of similarities in social class background, educational experiences and social relations between managers and shareholders suggests that even though there may be some characteristic areas of difference or conflict of outlook there are likely to be common general beliefs and attitudes. The two groups are equally wedded to the instrumental and moral value of company profitability and the principle of production for profit as such, together with an associated corpus of conservative ideas (Crompton and Gubbay, 1977, p. 66).

Some authors, such as Galbraith (1969), whose ideas of the techno-structure stand behind the strategic contingencies thesis, have argued that managers have other goals than profitability. They may well have so, but do they characteristically sacrifice the goal of profitability where there is a conflict with these goals? Crompton and Gubbay think not:

> It is apparent that managers' central goal is the pursuit of profit, even if this is 'only' a necessary means to other goals that are

positively embraced. We certainly do not wish to suggest by this that the managers of the modern corporation simply select the policy which yields the best short-term profit. Rather, long-term profits are characteristically sought, which requires an extremely complex evaluation of alternatives, using partial and inadequate calculative techniques applied to imperfect knowledge of a situation which is only subject to limited control by the firm . . . any . . . conflict (between managers and shareholders) is *within* a consensus about the supreme importance of long-term profitability (Crompton and Gubbay, 1977, p. 67).

This last point comes out strongly in Pahl and Winkler's (1974, p. 115) research. They conclude that although the powers of conception and execution may be functionally distinct from both labour and capital *per se*, it does not mean that the interests of the managers may be *either* those of labour *or* capital. The 'profitable allocation of capital' as the ground rule of the system of functional relationships entails that the interests of the managers are, in the long run, those of the owners of capital. Indeed, as Carchedi (1977) stresses, the managers' existence as the functions of global capital not only entails the work of *co-ordination* of the fragmented task-structure, but also the work of *control and surveillance* in respect of surplus value appropriation:

The possibility of effective long-term profit is enhanced by the creation of corps of experts in the firm and procedures for checking and pooling their evaluations, which is in turn facilitated by the development of a body of theory and techniques prescribing rational managerial decision-making. From the point of view of management there are threats to profitability from a number of different directions: price and quality competition in the product market, price rises in the factor market – particularly for labour, availability and cost of credit or share yield demand in the capital market, and danger of take-over or forced merger. The best way to cope with these threats to *profitability as such* is to plan, calculate and organize methodically to *maximize* long-term profit; the controllers of the modern corporation are characteristically devoted to that cause (Crompton and Gubbay, 1977, p. 67).

With reference to the second dimension of the separation of ownership and control, that is the dissociation between legal ownership and possession, the dispersion of stock is not an obstacle to concentrated control. Quite the contrary, in fact. Dispersion of stock favours the centralization of capital because 'the greater the number of shareholders and the smaller the size of the average shareholding,' as Gilbert (1972, p. 17) has argued, 'the smaller is the proportion of the entire voting stock which is in practice needed to exercise effective control'.

The real economic owners, the bourgeoisie, monopolize 'the power of assignment and disposition of the means of production' and are able 'to use this power for its specific class interests, i.e., to produce and realize surplus-value' (De Vroey, 1975, p. 5) either directly, through the fusion of possession/real/legal ownership, or their mediation through a separation of possession and real ownership in the form of the managerial stratum, identifiable through its primary functions of control and surveillance.

Possession is not as broad a category as legal ownership; but in the USA, according to Smith and Franklin (1974), only 1 per cent of the households owned 54 per cent of corporate stock in 1969; in the UK during 1964–9, according to Glyn and Sutcliffe (1972, p. 53), only 0.4 per cent of the adult population held 68 per cent of the total value of shares on the average; in France in 1970 0.8 per cent of households held 24 per cent of stockholding incomes (De Vroey, 1975, p. 5), and in Belgium in 1964 47 per cent of the corporate wealth was owned by 0.5 per cent of taxpayers (Duvivier, 1972). (Figures from De Vroey, 1975, p. 5.) These figures almost certainly under-represent the degree of concentration of legal ownership because of the existence of institutional devices such as trusts and holding companies. However, they indicate quite clearly that there is a ruling class in the major capitalist countries which owes its rule to economic ownership of the means of production. This will be even more concentrated if we restrict membership of this class simply to those having possession of these organizations. The separation of ownership and control does not mean the demise of the ruling class, but is itself a consequence of capital accumulation which makes possible its further development precisely through the *depersonalization* of bureaucratization:

> The progressive *depersonalization* of property, brought about by the development of the great modern 'limited liability' company, implied the emergence as *a subject* of *the object* of property itself, i.e., the complete emancipation of property from man himself, with the result that the firm seemed to acquire an independent life of its own as though it were nobody's property, transforming itself into an entity in itself with similar characteristics to those of the state (Colletti, 1972, p. 98).

The similarity of characteristics of this transformed entity to those of the state should not be surprising, because, as Mouzelis (1975, introduction) outlines, the state was not only the first political structure of the modern world, it was also the bureaucratic

478

model for subsequent political structures, among which the modern large-scale organization is premier.

The most basic and extensive power in organizations is vested in the fusion of possession/legal/real ownership. Where there is a separation of possession from legal ownership, then possession is clearly more powerful as it entails actual economic control.

The growth of firms which develops contingent to the introduction of joint-stock companies presented organizations with problems of management which were not evident when the enterprise was still small enough to conform to the model of the preconditions for formal, direct and extensive control. The implications of this for an analysis of power in organizations are quite clear. Historically, we can point to power in the organization as something flowing quite 'naturally' from the ownership and control of the means and methods of production. As organizations have grown in size, and become qualitatively differentiated in terms of their specialist skill composition, control through direct ownership, coercion and command – on a primitive military model – becomes less and less feasible or practical. In its place has developed

a complex structure of roles defined in functional terms. The functions include exchanges in factor and product markets for labour, goods and capital and the supervision of labour, all of which are subject to monitoring, evaluation, directions to innovate, planning and control for the purpose of achieving accumulation of capital. Such functional elements would include personnel management, market research and analysis, quality control, investment management, marketing, research and development, design management and so on; these functions are co-ordinated and controlled by financial and general management according to company strategy as determined by major shareholders and top managers. These various functions are organized in different ways in different firms (Crompton and Gubbay, 1977, p. 70).

These functions, collectively known as the labour function, are the carrying out under the control of capital of tasks specified by capital, in a complex labour process defined by the social relations of production (antagonistic class relations) in which the task-operations are embedded. Within this organization in its historical development from task-continuous to task-discontinuous status structure there is a 'progressive alienation of the process of production from the worker' which 'to the capitalist . . . presents itself as the problem of management' (Braverman, 1974, p. 58, de-italicized).

479

Implications for analyses of power in organizations

At various stages throughout this chapter we have attempted to connect the wider argument concerning the development of the labour process to an area of specific substantive concern: power in organizations. For example, it has been suggested that it is only with the emergence of task-discontinuous organizations that the type of problem which has typically been characterized as 'power in organizations' becomes apparent. This is the existence of unauthorized and informal sources of control over methods of production as a special skill uncontrollable at other levels of the organization. Examples of this are Crozier's (1964) maintenance men or Mechanic's (1962) 'lower participants'. Worked out to its fullest, the logic of this argument leads to the strategic contingencies position exemplified by Hickson *et al.* (1971). This chapter has suggested some of the specific historical conditions for the applicability of theory such as 'strategic contingencies', and in so doing raises some questions about the scientific generalizability of such theory. It suggests the need for a greater historical reflexivity on the part of organization researchers. At the same time, it points towards what may be a more generalizable and adequate explanation of power in organizations.

Power, when it is exercised, is exercised over issues. Given this, then the crucial point is to determine which issues in the world economy (as it is constituted by or impinges upon the organization) are critical for the organization. (This, of course, implies the corollaries of non-criticality and non-issues.) Once we have determined what these are we can establish which management function(s), group(s) or skill(s), within or without of the organization, are responsible for the domain in which they occur. Clegg (1979a) has suggested that a critical issue will be one which effects organizational control of the labour process within the context of the hegemonic domination of the ground rules (the objective organizing principle) in which the organization labours.

This introduction of a structural, contextual *and* analytical perspective into organization research is central to the argument. We would propose research designs in the future which are sensitive to the suggestion that macro-structural phenonema have an important and differentiating function. In particular we would propose that a critical issue within organizations involved in the immediate reproduction of the capitalist mode of production will be one which effects the ideal of profitability as it is manifested in the organization's mode of rationality. As Pahl and Winkler (1974, p. 115) put it, 'In a capitalist society, effective economic power lies with those who have the ability to conceive and carry through schemes for the profitable allocation of capital.'

The major exercise of formally warranted power in the organization will affect issues that affect the rational functioning of the control of this objective organization principle. That is, power will be exercised to re-assert control. Thus, individual power relations are only the visible tip of a structure of control, hegemony, rule and domination which continues to appear to be *the* natural convention. It is only when control slips, taken-for-grantedness fails, routines lapse and problems appear that the overt exercise of power is necessary. And that is exerted in an attempt to re-assert control.

If we were to have a theory of 'significant issues' in the organization, we would implicitly have a theory concerning the functioning of power. The position(s) that 'exercised' power over 'significant issues' would then be the position that had the effective functioning power to act on issues. (In French and Raven's (1959) terms there would be a disjuncture between formal and expert power.) They would have this ability because they had a specific capacity in a task-discontinuous organization. This capacity would be that of a particular skill (Mulder, 1974, also relates skill to power), specialized to deal with that issue or issues, and which was critical to the probability of controlling these. (These skills might not exist within the capacity of the labour power that is the organization; in such a case they would have to be hired on either a consulting or employee capacity.) Thus, although everything occurs so as to make it appear that power is either an individual property or relationship between individuals, it is in fact a social relationship determined by the mediation of the organization with the environment of the world economy that this mediation constitutes and the critical issues that the organization's functioning engenders.

V. L. Allen (1975, p. 218) adds a 'further comment on the relationship between skills and power in a capitalist society'. These are that the relationship between them

is reinforced by the operation of the market mechanism, whereby prices are given to skills according to their scarcity value. Scarcity here is an ideologically based term, contrived to satisfy the ideological needs of the society. But it has a measurable quality, with the consequence that the prices accorded to some skills are determined, within a given range, by the ability of their practitioners to restrict their distribution. . . . In a capitalist society as a whole, skills, and the power they give rise to, are distributed in a pyramidal fashion with that of the owners of the means of production at the apex and that of employees distributed hierarchically below (Allen, 1975, p. 219).

The power that employees have over and above, or outside of, the formal structure, is a capacity which is only possible within the framework of hegemonic domination to which they would first have to submit – the possibility of an issue would have to be framed within the dominant theorizing power for it to be ruled admissible. An alternative means of formulating issues might be through radical action which openly challenges the theorizing power of the dominant hegemony (see Allen, 1975, pp. 233–47).

Where the formal structure of domination within the organization and the functioning of power no longer cohere, as a result of the historical development of the organization's skill structures, then we could anticipate that unless contradictions persist unchecked – which they very well might – a political process of incorporation into the structure of the organization would be in process, whereby this coherence would be re-established. This structure of domination is itself a power-phenomenon, which, in the next chapter, we will suggest we might begin to understand through an analysis of the organization's 'selection rules', in the comparative and historical context of the world-economy system. When we compare the degree of inequality of domination which different organizations are able to achieve *vis-à-vis* their competitors and the generalized resource of the state, we shall be comparing political units within a larger system. We shall conceptualize these organizations as political units of structured selectivity rules which afford differential controls of both an intensive and extensive type, organized around those issues which are critical or significant for that mode or modes of rationality through which the organization operates. This will enable us to see organizations as total power phenomena. In this model there is no sense in splitting off intra-from inter-organizational power, or the organization system from other systems. Intra- and inter-organizational power are features of the same phenomenon: organizational control. Organization control is not a feature of an isolated organizational system and its environment, but a sedimented structure of selection rules for dealing with one system: the world system.

In Chapter 3 we developed our analysis of practices of control and surveillance of the functions that we can now term the collective worker, in terms of scientific management and human relations practices. Through reconsidering these in the perspective suggested here, we can develop the control perspective further in our final chapter on 'The Political Economy of Organizations'.

13　The political economy of organizations

Control: a perspective

Early attempts at control, from the creation of a moral machinery, through the development of piece-work, to the introduction of scientific management and human relations, although they all have implications for the structure of organizations, were oriented to individuals and groups within organizations, rather than to organizations *per se*. Although they were developed initially in the sphere of productive enterprise as means of controlling the capitalist labour process, they are capable of extension both beyond productive organizations and capitalist societies. While the example cited in Chapter 3 of Lenin's use of Taylorism justifies the correctness of the first assertion, changes in the structure of nursing in the British Health Service demonstrate the latter. In the late 1960s the whole structure of nursing in Britain was transformed by the implementation of the Salmon Report. This recommended that a hierarchical structure of nursing grades be established as part of the management of a modern hospital, to be implemented through the process of writing job descriptions for the new grades in the hierarchy. The job descriptions re-defined the nurse's role at the various levels, and removed many elements of both mental (ward supervision) and manual (physically moving patients, emptying bed-pans) labour from the nurse's role, removing them either to a superordinate or subordinate, such as a higher-graded nursing post, or to porters or auxiliary staff. The process whereby this re-design was achieved was one of individual jobs being re-designed on criteria of efficiency not too far removed from those which can be found in scientific management's re-design of jobs. The objective consequences are exactly the same: the hyper-qualification of mental labour, the hiving off of mental from manual labour and the down-grading of manual labour to a less professional auxiliary status.

In the instance both of a non-productive non-profit-making organization such as a nationalized hospital and a 'socialist' country such as the USSR an apparatus of control initially developed under the dictates of capital accumulation and labour exploitation can take on an effectivity unlimited by the occasion of its genesis.

Most Marxist analysis of organization is of the capitalist labour process. One of the great strengths of the theories of organizations is that they are not limited solely to a discussion of capitalist organizations. They attempt to refer to all organizations *per se* (even if sometimes this seems to have more of an ideological task of making the capitalist labour process seem more opaque than the task of rendering other labour processes more transparent). However, there are ways of connecting organizations in the sphere of capitalist production to organizations in other spheres by a method other than just comparative analysis of their structure as a formal homology. This can be achieved through a comparative analysis of the political, ideological and economic *processes* which inter-connect organizations. Johnson has suggested a way in which this process can be conceived which involves an extension of the perspective we have been developing here. He suggests that:

> The sphere of circulation, entailing the reconversion of commodities into money capital, can be considered a specifically economic process of reproduction which itself arises out of those production relations specific to commodity production. In this 'sphere' we are concerned with the mechanisms by which surplus value is *realized* rather than *appropriated*. The development and differentiation of such mechanisms with the development of monopoly capitalism involves an extension of the institutional place of capital beyond the direct functions of surveillance and control in appropriation to include the institutions and organizations of commercial and banking capital and their functions in the process of realization – as an aspect of the separation of economic ownership and possession (Johnson, 1977, p. 216).

This development is a further refinement of the development of intra-organizational control of the Taylorist scientific management type or of the Mayo human relations type. These latter types of control are at the level of production relations and concern the appropriation of surplus value directly. This entails direct surveillance and control of labour in the labour process, in order to increase productivity and to lower costs. The process of realization also involves control and surveillance, but less directly. The mechanisms of control which develop in the process of the realization of surplus value, as a necessary adjunct to its production, entail a further complexity in the process of organization.

Within any specific organizations involved in the production of surplus value there develop

> large administrative divisions entirely concerned with the accounting of value; in checking and controlling the flow of stock and cash at each point in the process. Such internal systems of control, ensuring an upward flow of management information, are supplemented by mechanisms of value allocation which meet the requirements of external agencies concerned with securing credit, raising capital, distributing surplus, etc., which centre on the empires of banking, insurance, state taxation, etc. There has emerged then a labour process – the work of a mass of people – producing nothing but increasingly elaborate mechanisms of control associated with realization of capital and its enlargement (Johnson, 1977, p. 217).

The consequences of these forms of control are greater than a process of technical rationalization *per se*. Technical rationalization and the requirement of co-ordination are obviously crucial here, but should also be considered in terms of capital concentration and, in Johnson's term, concerned with the 'accounting of value'. It is precisely these developments which have generated those evident differences in organizations which Marx's analysis did not cover. The division of labour amongst different occupational groups in organizations has multiplied enormously. The development of new skills has led to a much greater range of occupations, and thus a considerably more differentiated and specialized organization structure of skills. Of particular significance would be the emergence of a heterogeneous middle-class stratum of managers, technicians, clerks, etc. While Marx did envisage 'the constant increase of the middle classes' in Volume Two of *Theories of Surplus Value* (1969), the type of middle classes he envisaged were composed largely of domestic servants and the relatively uncomplex category of commercial wage-workers – the type of clerk characterized by Dickens in many of his novels. In the twentieth century domestic servants have disappeared from the homes of all but the most wealthy, to be replaced by female domestic labour – the housewife – supported by commodities produced by an expanded capitalism: irons; vacuum cleaners; washing machines; dishwashers, etc. We have discussed this in Chapter 11.

Perhaps the most obvious difference between organizations today and those of Marx's era is that so many of them exist as a result of the expanded role of the state, as either state or public agencies or as nationalized enterprises. For example, in 1975 23 per cent of the employed population of the United Kingdom were employed by national or local government, while another 8.8 per cent were employed in state-owned enterprises such as coal, steel, gas, electricity or the post office (*British Labour Statistics Yearbook* 1975, p. 216).

State enterprises can be subdivided into capitalist and non-capitalist organizations. Following Carchedi (1977, p. 128) we can refer to these as capitalist state activities (CSA) and non-capitalist state activities (non-CSA). An example of a non-CSA organization would be a state hospital, while an example of a CSA organization would be a state-owned steelworks whose goal is primarily profit-oriented, i.e., as Carchedi (1977, p. 129) puts it, they 'spend their money in order to increase it'. This is in contrast with a non-CSA organization which does not do this. These, on the contrary, 'spend the money allocated to them basically in order to meet needs' (Carchedi, 1977, p. 129). While the former are oriented to the production of surplus values, the latter are not. Their orientation is to the production of use-values.

It can be argued with Carchedi that there is no difference between a CSA organization and a privately organized enterprise. He employs the example of a state-owned steelworks. In such an enterprise legal ownership is vested in the state, which is to say in that class which dominates the state apparatus and which in this instance executes administrative management by rule application (Therborn, 1978). In a capitalist society this will be the bourgeoisie as a whole. To continue with Carchedi's distinctions, as far as real ownership is concerned, he argues that

> it belongs to the managers, both in the joint-stock and in the state-owned enterprise. In both forms of enterprise, it is the manager who is the non-labourer/exploiter/non-producer/real owner . . . opposed to the labourer/exploited/non-owner/producer (Carchedi, 1977, p. 130).

Why does he draw this conclusion? His answer relates to what is being done by the labour process which is being organized in each instance:

> Both behave according to the laws of capitalist competition and accumulation, both produce commodities in order to produce surplus value rather than use-values, both re-invest the surplus value produced according to criteria of profitability rather than of the customers' needs to be met, in short, *both advance money in order to increase it* (Carchedi, 1977, p. 130).

Both the private capitalist enterprise and the state-owned enterprise are similar organizations of the labour process. Their similarity resides in them both being 'production for and of surplus

486

value' (Carchedi, 1977, p. 130). We can compare such productive organizations with unproductive ones, such as a bank (either state or private). In Carchedi's terms;

> Both of them are production *for* profit, because in both cases the capitalist has advanced money in order to increase it. But only the former process is also production of surplus value; the latter is not, since here we have only a formal transformation (Carchedi, 1977, p. 131).

Thus, we can define the unproductive state or capitalist organization 'as production for, but not of, surplus value' (Carchedi, 1977, p. 131). This would be achieved, for instance, through advancing loans to productive organizations at interest rates. We can compare either of these types of organization with basically different ones: those which advance money not in order to increase it but in order to meet needs. Carchedi suggests the following example:

> Take, to begin with, a private and a state hospital. The former is a capitalist (productive) enterprise: it provides use-values (health services) only as a means to produce surplus value. The latter is basically concerned with meeting needs, e.g., it tends to expand when the number of patients grows (at least in principle, i.e., disregarding the government's investment policy, etc.); the former, on the other hand, might or might not expand if the number of patients grows, depending on the profitability . . . of doing so. *The latter is neither production of surplus value nor production for surplus value.* It is this type of activity which we define as the non-CSA (Carchedi, 1977, p. 131).

This is important for organization analysis for the following reason. Hospitals producing use-values only, not surplus values, might be expected to develop quite different operations, activities, skills, specialisms and structures from those developed by parallel hospitals within the same society whose labour process is premised on production only for surplus value. We have here, irrespective of the usual organization theory variables of size or technology, an independent variable capable of structurally explaining why widely differing labour processes should emerge in a profit-oriented surplus value producing hospital compared with a public use-value oriented hospital. The former, we would hypothesize, will functionally specialize on profitable illnesses (those of the wealthy which are not statistically uncommon), while the latter, by exclusion, will tend to develop in ways far less connected to the market's effective demand, but oriented to the actual demand: i.e., human (rather than specific class) needs. The former produces capitalist commodities; that is, treatment and service defined as a unity of both exchange-value and use-value, in which the exchange-value aspect is dominant. In contrast to this, the non-CSA 'spends its money not in order to increase it but in order to meet needs. Its production process is neither for nor of surplus value' (Carchedi, 1977, p. 133). The commodities and services it produces possess a unity of both exchange- and use-values. Take, for instance, schooling or health care. These are both use-values, and inasmuch as they produce healthier or more educated workers, then, up to a point, they also have an exchange-value, in that such workers as commodities on the labour market usually command a greater exchange-value than sick or uneducated workers. Thus, Carchedi (1977, p. 133) can argue that because the emphasis in the non-CSA is on use- rather than exchange-value, 'the extraction of surplus labour[1] is not the primary reason for the provision of the non-CSA's services', while it is exactly opposite for unproductive capitalist enterprises. In the CSA the surplus labour producing process dominates the labour process and the exchange-value dominates the use-value. For both of these the opposite is true for the non-CSAs.

Despite these differences we should remember that in the vast majority of cases the nature of the commodity or service produced, whether as one use-value or another, is a matter of indifference to the labourer, as indeed it is whether he or she is oppressed by a CSA organization, a non-CSA organization, or a capitalist organization in the private sphere. All of this organization takes place in a structure which is embedded in the structure of capitalist economic criteria. Theories of organization used in any of these spheres have been developed in a context in which use-values are produced just as if they were capitalist commodities. Just as a state employee such as a primary school teacher is a labourer, defined by non-ownership of the means of production and paid the equivalent of his or her labour power's value, so also the school head teacher and the authority which employs them fulfil the role of the global functions of capital, 'those whose function is to oversee the labour process in its despotic organization, who ensure that labour is provided continuously and at the required speed, with the needed degree of efficiency and skill, etc.' (Carchedi, 1977, p. 68).

Within capitalist organizations the fact of competition between many organizations (at least in the competitive sector) leads to precise calculation within them and to a partial rationality in the reduction of production costs. Although there is no objective social mechanism in the state sector by which the non-CSAs can constantly reduce costs, they are governed by the principle of an 'allocation economy'. This produces a 'permanent wastage of resources to the extent that all individuals active in it have a material interest in increasing these allocations' (Mandel, 1975, p. 579). The reason for this material interest is simple: in an allocation economy any savings on expenditure lead to a reduction in allocations. In terms of the dynamics of power and status within organizations, increased or large allocations are potent resources, of both a material and symbolic nature. Hence the need for the global functions of capital to control the costs of the labour process and the ambiguous and contradictory location of those state personnel charged with this control, but at the same time seeking to increase their allocation. Mandel (1975, p. 579) argues that the allocation principle, whereby expenditures are under a constant and automatic inflationary pressure, 'governs all public administration in a commodity-producing society'.

We can conclude this section on state organizations by saying that little objective differences exist between state employees and non-state employees at the level of relations of production. The only difference is that in the state sector wages are received which are produced in the productive sphere of the economy, and are paid by the state after a part of the surplus value which originates in the productive sphere has been expropriated by the state and re-allocated among the various unproductive sectors of the economy. (This can have decisive political and economic consequences, as we argue below.)

The functions of the state can, in part, be identified with this expropriation, which, in Marxist usage, is never identified with the general, but a particular, interest. Modern analyses (see Frankel, 1978 and Esping-Andersen *et al.*, 1976) rely almost axiomatically on a repudiation of any theory of the state as a neutral arbiter of class (or other) interests. This is a rejection of the liberal perspective which views the state as a pluralist mechanism which responds to competing interests, with agencies, programmes and legislation as an outcome. The model is primarily behavioural (e.g., Dahl, 1961). The state is regarded as a neutral channel through which different stimuli are registered. These stimuli are in turn mediated through the channels of political parties (e.g., Lipsett, 1960). A further version of this perspective regards the state agencies as open to influence and control in competitive battles between different interest groups over scarce resources (McConnell, 1966).

Ranged against these liberal views of the state are those which derive from the works of Marx and Engels. The earliest writings by Marx on the state date from 1842–3; these he developed in the context of a *Critique of Hegel's Philosophy of the State* (1970) and 'A Contribution to the Critique of Hegel's Philosophy of Right' (1975). Hegel (1967) had developed a theory of the state as the universal synthetic institution created through a series of mediations between civil and political society. Marx and Engels (1965), developing Marx's (1970) earlier critique of Hegel, argued that the state 'is nothing more than the form of organization which the bourgeois necessarily adopt both for internal and external purposes, for the mutual guarantee of their property and interests' (Marx and Engels, 1965, p. 59). It is this theme which Lenin develops when he defines the state as the oppression of one class by another in 'The State and Revolution' (Lenin, 1947). Later analyses by Althusser (1971) and his associate Poulantzas (1973) take this theme but give it a distinctive structuralist twist. This is derived from the centrality in their work of a particular conception of Marx's *Capital* (see Althusser and Balibar, 1970). In this interpretation *Capital* is an analysis of the concept of a 'pure' mode of production as an abstraction. In actual instances, the capitalist mode of production, which is the subject of *Capital,* develops in an uneven articulation. This necessitates the existence of an institution concerned with the maintenance of the mode of production's overall cohesion and equilibrium. The state is the institution that fulfils this political function. The state is still conceptualized as oppressive, not simply because it supports the ruling class interest, but as Wolfe (1974, p. 136) puts it, 'because it is responsible for the cohesion of an entire system within which dominant classes dominate' (also see S. Clarke, 1977 and Bridges, 1974). It is for this reason that Althusser (1971), to whom we will turn later, stresses that the key feature of the state is its reproductive character; that is, its ability to be able to reproduce the conditions of production. This leads Althusser to stress the role of ideology, in particular the ideological state apparatus, which we criticize below.

A further variant of economic structuralism defines the state in terms of the economic functions which the state must perform to 'temporarily resolve economically determined contradictions' (Esping-Andersen *et al.*, 1976, p. 188). These functions would be, for instance, the neo-Keynesian one of maintaining aggregate effectived demand in order to avert realization crises of monopoly capitalism (e.g., Baran and Sweezy, 1968). The state fulfils functions that the individual capital units cannot. Both these political and economic functions would have to be incorporated into an analysis of what the state does.

Wolfe (1974) has stressed the problems with both the earlier, critical perspective, which stresses the state's 'instrumentalist' (Esping-Andersen *et al.*, 1976, p. 188) role of representing dominant class interests and with the structuralist/functionalist view.

The problems with the latter are evident from our analysis of Lenin's view of the state in Chapter 3. If the most important thing about the state is the functions it fulfils, then these functions can be filled by different interests. Hence, the technocratic rationality of the state in its purely functional form can be 'seized', taken over, by a proletarian class interest as opposed to a bourgeois class interest. But this is to negate the dialectical relationship between form and content, between technical reason and practical reason. As Wolfe (1974, p. 138) puts it: 'The capitalist state is repressive, because its basic form is to exercise oppressive power by the minority over the majority. A meaningful socialist revolution does not simply pour a new liquid into the glass; it abolishes the glass and replaces it with a new form.' In other words, technical reason conceived independently as a pure function 'protects rather than cancels the legitimacy of domination, and the instrumentalist horizon of reason opens on a rationally totalitarian society' (Marcuse, 1964, p. 159). The history of the Soviet state would seem to lend credence to this view.

There are additional problems with this view of the state. If the state functions always as the institutional source of capitalist cohesion in a capitalist society, there is little point in attempting to gain any concessions or reforms from it; they will always (in the long run, of course!) be in the best interests of capital. This induces either a fatalistic acceptance of the state or a utopian belief in the possibility of somehow radically 'smashing' it totally. How one would do this is not clear.

What *is* seemingly clear with this perspective is what the state is. It is, in Althusser's (1971) terms, composed of repressive and ideological state apparatuses. While the former include institutions such as the police and the armed forces, the latter incorporate almost everything that maintains the cohesion of (capitalist) social formations. Ernesto Laclau has pointed to the absurdity of this position in which

> [if] the reformism of trade unions and social-democratic leaders constitutes a factor of cohesion . . . consequently those leaders would be State functionaries; socialist parties would be divided between a State wing and a revolutionary wing and also, *reductio ad absurdum,* the mind of every individual would be schizo-phrenically divided between a State half, tending to the cohesion of the social formation and an anti-State half, tending to its disruption (Laclau, 1975, p. 100).

This is not very helpful. If we are to accept Carchedi's (1977) argument we really need to know what exactly the state is, and what it does. In short, we need to know the answer to the question Göran Therborn (1978) has posed: *What Does the Ruling Class Do When it Rules?* Therborn's answer is as follows. The state is composed of a system of apparatuses as 'a type of formal organization . . . distinguished by its specific functions' (Therborn, 1978, p. 37). What

491

are these? Therborn says that they are 'coercive defence, political governance (by supreme rule-making), administrative management (by rule-application), and judicial regulation of a given social formation' (Therborn, 1978, p. 37). These are to be conceived 'as a formally bounded system of structured processes within a global system of societal processes'. Within this perspective,

> if we conceive of organizations as processes formally structured by specific mechanisms of input, transformation and output, we can relate them directly to the ever-advancing social processes of reproduction and change, which provide the inputs and receive the outputs. The class character of an organization may then be determined in the way in which the input, transformation and output processes are traversed and shaped by the class struggle (Therborn, 1978, p. 38).

Much of the recent interest in the theory of the state has been in terms of the output processes of ideological reproduction, usually couched in terms of Gramsci's concept of *hegemony* (Gramsci, 1971). Because we wish to reject Althusser's (1971) conflation of the concepts of the state and ideological reproduction through hegemony, we will first turn to a consideration of Gramsci, with particular reference to organizations, the role of intellectuals and the concept of hegemony, before considering the Althusserian concepts of ideological reproduction.

Gramsci, intellectuals and organizations

Williams, one of the earliest English-speaking commentators on Gramsci's work, formulates the concept of hegemony, in the most general terms, as

> a 'moment' in which the philosophy and practice of a society fuse or are in equilibrium; an order in which a certain way of life and thought is diffused throughout society in all its institutional and private manifestations, informing with its spirit all taste, morality, customs, religions and political principles, and all social relations, particularly in their intellectual and moral connotation (Williams, 1960, p. 587).

He observes that Gramsci 'explicitly states' that hegemony is the 'normal form of control', and that 'force and coercion' only become 'dominant at times of crises' (Williams, 1960, p. 591). Femia regards hegemony in Gramsci similarly, as

> the predominance obtained by consent rather than force of one class or group over other classes . . . attained through the myriad ways in which the institutions of civil society . . . shape, directly

and indirectly, the cognitive and affective structures whereby men perceive and, evaluate problematical social reality (Femia, 1975, p. 31).

In an echo of Bachrach and Baratz (1962) he says that 'Gramsci eventually came to view hegemony as the most important *face* of power' (Femia, 1975, p. 31, our emphasis).

Merrington develops the relationship between power and hegemony further, noting that:

> The concept of hegemony is thus linked to Gramsci's aim to re-define the nature of power in modern societies in more compre-hensive terms, allowing for the articulations of the various levels or instances of a given social formation, political, cultural or ideological in the determination of a specific power structure (Merrington, 1972, p. 152).

In a letter to his sister-in-law, Tatiana, dated 7 September 1931, Gramsci explicitly connects the process whereby hegemony func-tions with the role of 'the intellectuals'. His letter outlines some proposed research concerning the concept of the state conceived as

> a balance between political society and civil society, by which I mean the hegemony of one social group over the entire nation, exercised through so-called private organizations like the Church, trade unions, or schools. For it is above all in civil society that intellectuals exert their influences (Gramsci, 1975, p. 204).

Intellectuals are formed out of and reflect back upon 'the original terrain of an essential function in the world of economic produc-tion' (Gramsci, 1971, p. 5) inhabited, historically, by distinct social groups which create, as well as themselves, 'organically, one or more strata of intellectuals which give it homogeneity and an aware-ness of its own function not only in the economic but also in the social and political fields' (Gramsci, 1971, p. 5). Gramsci cites as an example of such a social group the process whereby the 'capitalist entrepreneur creates alongside himself the industrial technician, the specialist in political economy, the organizers of a new culture, of a new legal system, etc.'. An élite amongst these entrepreneurs

> must have the capacity to be an organizer of society in general, including all its complex organism of services, right up to the State organism, because of the need to create the conditions most favourable to the expansion of their own class; or at the least they must possess the capacity to choose the deputies (specialized employees) to whom to entrust this activity of organizing the general system of relationships external to the

business itself. It can be observed that the 'organic' intellectuals which every new class creates alongside itself and elaborates in the course of its development, are for the most part 'specializations' of partial aspects of the primitive activity of the new social type which the new class has brought into prominence (Gramsci, 1971, pp. 5–6).

The intellectuals thus have a crucial role in Gramsci's thought, because they are the custodians of 'the sphere of ideology' by which means 'consciousness is mediated in capitalist society, preserved and protected behind the whole complex of institutions, private and public, which legitimize bourgeois dominance, rendering its values and definitions universal because accepted as the definitive values of society as such' (Merrington, 1968, p. 154). When this situation exists, there is an equilibrium between 'leadership' or 'direction' based on consent, and 'domination' (*dominazione*) which is based on coercion. Gramsci characterizes this as an 'historical bloc', the situation of class hegemony. This is mediated by the intellectuals as agents promoting ideological and political unity, a unity which universalizes a particular class rule.

The achievement of hegemonic functioning through an historical bloc becomes the normal mode of the functioning of power. It is only in moments of crisis, when control, which is ordinarily structured in and through hegemony, slips or fails, that power has to be directly exercised in order to attempt to restore this control. Such an exercise of power signals not the presence of a strong capacity for power, but instead indicates that this exercise of power flows from a position of weakness. This position is one in which hegemony has failed and so power is exerted in an attempt to re-assert the 'normal' situation of control.

The absence of the exercise of power does not mean the absence of power. It signals the presence of a far more subtle and powerful power – the power of a capacity for any further action. Anderson expresses this clearly with respect to the political system:

In the political system, a . . . structural (non-additive and non-transitive) relationship between ideology and repression, consent and coercion, prevails. The normal conditions of ideological subordination of the masses – the day-to-day routines of a parliamentary democracy – are themselves *constituted by* a silent, absent force which gives them their currency: the monopoly of legitimate violence by the State. Deprived of this, the system of cultural control would be instantly fragile, since the limits of possible actions against it would disappear. With it, it is immensely powerful – so powerful that it can, paradoxically, do 'without' it: in effect, violence may normally scarcely appear within the

494

bounds of the system at all (Anderson, 1977, p. 43).

In an organization the situation is similar, although complicated by the extension of civil and legal rights such as unemployment benefits and other forms of social welfare, and legislation restricting the right of management directly to coerce workers by withdrawing jobs from them as a specific discriminatory practice against particular individuals. This does not limit the fundamentally coercive nature of the labour–capital relationship, however, whereby labour has to sell itself to capital as the owner and controller of the means of production in order to work, and thus indirectly to live. Nor does it limit the capacity of capital to choose not to reproduce itself in ways which are socially useful if it can reproduce profit more rapidly in alternative ways. And, if these alternative ways involve unemployment for particular workers, through shifting investments into overseas production, or non-productive property speculation, then nothing exists to prevent capital from doing this.

Much of the time the power of capital does not have to be exercised to be present. It is present in the absence of its exercise, because this exercise is grounded in a structural 'capacity' which frequently obviates the necessity of this exercise. This capacity is visible in the routine practices of everyday life. Westergaard and Resler (1976, pp. 141–277) are among the few writers on power (along with Pahl and Winkler, 1974; Parry and Morris, 1974; and Clegg 1975) who have stressed the importance of these as 'certain social mechanisms, principles, assumptions . . . taken for granted' (Westergaard and Resler, 1976, p. 142). As they note, these typically 'favour the interests of this or that group *vis-à-vis* the rest of the population. The favoured group enjoys effective power, even when its members take no active steps to exercise power . . . simply because things work their way in any case' (Westergaard and Resler, 1976, pp. 142–3). No mystery surrounds these 'mechanisms and assumptions'. In a capitalist society, they are 'those, in the first instance, of private property and the market . . . which largely determine the living conditions of the people and the use of resources'. These

> clearly favour the interests of capital: they confer power on capital in a very real and tangible sense. But the proof of that power is not to be found only, or even chiefly, in the fact that capitalists make decisions. It is to be found in the fact that the decisions which both they and others – including government – make, and the sheer routine conduct of affairs even without definite decision-making, in the main have a common denominator: an everyday acceptance of private property and market mechanisms. . . . *Power is to be found more in uneventful*

495

routine than in conscious and active exercise of will (Westergaard and Resler, 1976, pp. 143–4, our emphasis).

Ordinarily, as Westergaard and Resler demonstrate, capital does not maintain order in its domain through the remote threat of coercion. It has no need to for most of the time. It is in order to understand this that Gramsci's work becomes important for any analysis of power in organizations.

Gramsci's focus is on the role of superstructural elements in the dense social formations of the capitalist West. These have become so institutionalized that, even in moments of severe structural crisis in the economic sphere (such is the opacity and embeddedness of a people's ordinarily available ways of theorizing), the consequences of crises in the economic system remain more or less taken for granted. Little effort is expended in critique or counter-strategy, because the weapons of critique are not readily available. Unemployment, inflation, or wage-cuts can come to be accepted as normal, as natural, as something which could not have been otherwise, as their sense is constituted in and through hegemonic forms of theorizing.

The dominant institutional domain and hegemony of the ideological apparatus at a particular moment becomes regarded as the 'universal moment', the 'organizing principle' (in Habermas' (1976) phrase) of our being and time as it permeates throughout civil society.

Any concrete social formation does not contain just one hegemony, but many. Nevertheless, we can point to the dominance of a particular form at different historical moments. For instance, Catholicism or Protestantism may each have had a hegemonic function in society; their importance has receded, but still retains a specific effectivity (e.g., Ulster), in the face of new forms of technocratic rationality. The concept of hegemony is thus not necessarily tied to class, as was the strictly Marxist concept of ideology, although one would expect that the dominant hegemony would be. The formal domination of a world-view expressed in and through the concept of hegemony could act in ways that cut across class lines. Despite this relative autonomy, we will maintain that the relation of hegemony to a mode of production must be of particular interest.

A considerable and, for the non-specialist, sometimes bewildering debate surrounds the concept of mode of production in Marxist literature (see Foster-Carter, 1978). We can begin to conceptualize the concept of mode of production by beginning with the concept of the 'labour process'. The labour process consists of the conscious, purposeful activity of people, directed to transforming, modifying and adapting natural objects to their needs. In order to do this, they employ means of production which include both objects of labour and instruments of labour. Objects of labour are the raw materials or natural phenomena which are the object of the labour process. The instruments of labour mediate between labour as a process and those objects it transforms, modifies and adapts. In a broad sense, all material conditions of work, such as land, production, buildings, roads, etc., are instruments of labour. The objects and instruments of labour together form the means of production. The means of production and the labour power of people setting them in motion compose the productive forces of society, or the 'forces of production'. The productive forces reflect the relationship between people and nature.

In the process of production, people also inevitably enter into certain social relationships of production with each other. In order to produce they must use 'means of production'. These means of production may be the property of all of the labourers, some of the labourers, or none of the labourers: they may belong to a class of non-labourers. Whoever the means of production belong to will ordinarily own what is produced, the product. A 'mode of production' is thus composed of a number of invariant material elements which are capable of being combined in any number of ways. These elements are labourers, non-labourers, and means and products of production. These elements, combined as factors of production, can be seen as a twofold relation: the relation between the labourer and the means of production; the relation between non-labourers and the product of the first relationship. As Poulantzas puts it:

> The determination of a mode of production by the economic in the last instance, and of the articulation and index of dominance of its instances depends precisely on the forms which the combination in question takes on (Poulantzas, 1973, p. 27).

What are the other elements of social practice in addition to the economic? Althusser (1969, p. 167) would answer that they were, in addition, political, ideological and theoretical. Now, it is possible to separate these out analytically and apportion them, or sub-divide them, within the context of any particular social formation. Additionally, it is possible to analyse them in their interdependency and contradiction within a specific region and any pre-given complex structured whole.

Within the 'complex whole' of society, as Althusser (1969, p. 205) argues, the 'relations of production' are not the pure phenomena of the forces of production; they are also the conditions of its existence. Taken together with some other later work of Althusser's (1971) this concept of the 'super-structure' leads to a conceptualization of 'hegemony', which, when theorized as a reflexive moment of the mode of (re)-production, in specific instances, can illuminate the concept of domination as an element of both the structural, political, ideological, and theoretical functioning of material life.

Althusser (1971, p. 128) argues that the reproduction of labour power is not simply in terms of a concern for material conditions. Skills clearly have to be reproduced; but equally, through socialization, 'it is in the forms and under the forms of ideological subjection that provision is made for the reproduction of the skills of labour power'.

Althusser calls these forms *ideological state apparatus*, and contrasts this form of *subjection* with that which functions through the *repressive state apparatus*. The contrast is one of functioning primarily through ideology or violence, which is institutionally located, for example, in the family or the police. (This is not to say, for instance, that family life is only ideological and not violent. It often is.) Unfortunately, apart from his brief allusion in the previous citations, he nowhere discusses the role and functioning of ideology in the institutional area of specifically capitalist institutions: that is, the production and reproduction of material life through capitalism's organizational functioning. The difficulty of doing so is, of course, due to Althusser's appending the ideological apparatus as a necessary part of the state. While evident links exist between state and industry at the empirical level (e.g., see Martin, 1977, ch. 10 for a convenient summary), and one can argue whether, theoretically, the state in capitalist society is a capitalist state or not (see the Poulantzas-Miliband debate in Urry and Wakeford, 1973), it would seem that:

> To suggest that the relevant institutions are actually part of the State System does not seem to me to accord with reality, and tends to obscure the difference in this respect between these political systems and systems where ideological institutions are indeed part of a State monopolistic system of power. In the former systems, ideological institutions do retain a very high degree of autonomy; and are therefore the better able to conceal the degree to which they do not belong to the system of capitalist power (Miliband, 1969, p. 59).

With this in mind, let us refer only to ideological apparatus, rather than state ideological apparatus. We can conceive of more or less distinct institutional areas: the family, education, the economy and so on. Within, and cutting across, these different and distinct institutional areas will be numerous organizations. These organizations have become the 'real-object' of an autonomous discipline, the administrative science of organization theory based on the partially rational properties of organizations.

As Marcuse (1971, p. 136) observes, 'the main basis of this rationality is abstraction . . . the reduction of *quality* to *quantity*'. The qualities of the person are disregarded in favour of their quantification as factors of production having a specific value. The bureaucracy is built up on this basis: it is materially supported by virtue of the specific value accruing from the appropriation of labour power. This appropriation may be immediate, where the bureaucracy is supported within a profit-oriented enterprise on the basis of deductions from that enterprise's surplus value, or it may be mediated, the primary mediator in modern capitalist society being the state.

The service that bureaucracy provides has to be seen analytically as the service of the irrational ideal of profitability whose rule and domination provide the 'framework of the calculable chances of gain in private enterprise, i.e. in the context of the *profit* of the individual entrepreneur or enterprise' (Marcuse, 1971, p. 136). What service is provided, and who is serviced, depends upon the employer's calculation of the gain in value likely to accrue from their employment as formally free quantities of labour. As Schroyer (1972, p. 114) notes: 'What Weber would call 'rationalization' can now be seen as a special type of rationalization – that which can increase value production.' As such, it may be said to have 'hegemonic functioning'. (Also see Cohen, 1972).

This rationalization is that which is operative and functioning in and through the everyday routines and rule of production. It is because of this constant re-constitution and reproduction of the routine in, through and by production, and the practices that are production – from the most authoritative executive action to the most habitual reflex of the production worker – that the mode of production is 'directly encountered, given and transmitted from the past' and remade in the present.

In any work situation the people engaged in that work will usually be encountered doing more than just 'that work'. Another way of putting this would be to say that the hegemony of 'work' is not absolute. Normal work frequently includes practices of sabotage, theft, cultural discussion, politics and a myriad of other aspects of life. In this way one may point to elements of religious, cultural or political hegemony in any specific work setting.

If one were to focus empirically on any particular work settings, then with regard to these one could analytically concentrate on any of a number of co-terminous hegemonic elements. Not all hegemonic practice will be equivalent. Within the business organization of the modern firm, for instance, one can quite clearly relate the enterprise's hegemonic functioning to its material functioning within the content of the capitalist mode of production. While labour, as the primary and determinant practice within any mode of production, is the source of material transformation, the continued possibilities of the reproduction of this practice in an evolving sense (in terms of its contradictions and order) will require the objective principle of a particular hegemony in dominance. Hence, we may speak of patterns of hegemonic dominance and subordination within the specific practices of work in the organization at any one time and space.

In some instances, there exists a reflexive reciprocity between the mode of production and hegemonic dominance. Here, the 'linguistic labour' (Clegg, 1975) of hegemony will be a reflexive feature of the reproduction of the setting. In this case, the hegemony will 'reproduce the conditions of production at the same time as it [is] produced' (Althusser, 1971, p. 123).

It is on such occasions as this, where the theorizing power of hegemony reflexively re-constitutes the mode of production of its own practice independently of the conscious knowledge of particular agents engaged in production, that we believe we may refer (in the sense of Clegg, 1975) to the concept of a 'form of life'. This is the ground of specific human practices exhibited in the unity of a mode of production reflexively reproduced through the hegemonic dominance of unreflected, reified convention. It should be quite clear that this may refer to theoretical, just as much as material, production and practice. In either case, the production of material or ideal artefacts, it is, in Gramsci's phrase, 'the intellectuals' who produce and reproduce the raw material of hegemony.

These intellectuals are distinctly related to particular institutional domains of the ideological apparatus, with a particular domain being dominant at different moments in the development of a mode of production in different social formations. Gramsci observes, for instance, that one reason for twentieth-century American capital's ascendancy is that it does not have the leaden burden of 'great historical and cultural traditions' to support. It is because

these preliminary conditions existed, already rendered rational by historical evolution, [that] it was relatively easy to rationalize production and labour by a skilful combination of force (destruction of working-class trade unionism on a territorial basis) and persuasion (high wages, various social benefits, extremely subtle ideological and political propaganda) and thus succeed in making the whole life of the nation revolve around production. *Hegemony here is born in the factory and requires for its exercise only a minute quantity of professional political and ideological intermediaries* (Gramsci, 1971, p. 285, our emphasis).

Hegemony in the factory is born out of specific practices devised by an intellectual cadre and mediated by management. This cadre is that of the administrative and organization sciences.

Analysis of power in organizations needs to specify both those practices and the intellectual production of these, which maintain hegemony as the normal functioning of a situation. It is in these instances, rather than those of crisis, that power is least visible in the structure of the organization. Historically, power in organizations has consisted of the ability to control means and methods of production. More abstractly and generally, we can say that power is the ability to exercise control over resources which, when subjects engage in practices, produce effects on other subjects. In this instance the practice that we are concerned with is that practice which is the visible structure of social relations of production and changes in these, in the organization.

Reconceptualizing structure

Clearly, in any empirical analyses we shall be confronted with a vast diversity of visible structures of social relations of production. Analytically we require some way of conceptualizing an order in this diversity. As is evident, the production or discovery of such an order requires a form of reductionism achievable only by 'isolating social facts from the historical situation' (Karpik, 1977, p. 41). We are concerned with the social fact of the structure of social relations of production in the organization. This structure can be conceived of as a history-in-the-present composed of 'remnants and ruins inherited from the past . . . realities which are still living although they were born in distant ages . . . categories of phenomena which have not yet reached historical maturity and which are juxtaposed with others still being formed' (Karpik, 1977, p. 41). The structure of the organization is a sedimented social fact, a sedimented social reality. As such, following Offe (1976b), we can conceive of it as a set of sedimented (i.e., historically laid-down and superimposed) selection rules. These sedimented selection rules constitute those phenomena that the structure attends to as matters requiring regulation; what we may term its enacted environment (after Weick, 1969). Habermas defines these sedimented selection rules, which can be conceptualized as structure, as determining

what is thematized, what – with what priority and by which means – is actually publicly regulated, etc. The relatively stable administrative patterns of helping and hindering are objectively functional for capital realization, that is, they are independent of the professed intentions of the administration. They can be explained with the aid of selection rules, that predetermine the consideration or suppression of problems, themes, arguments and interests. (Habermas, 1976, p. 60).

This conception of visible, diverse structure being underlain by rules offers us a form of reductionism which Karpik (1972) has termed a logic of action, and Clegg (1975) a mode of rationality. The difference in terminology requires elaboration in this context.

First, we are proposing that organization theory become more historically sensitive and less empiricist in its theory construction. We cannot simply take this entity – the organization – for granted as a real empirical phenomenon which our data simply reports on. We must construct an explicit and theoretical model of our object of analysis which is related to the historical development of our concrete empirical object of organizations. In doing this we may find that if we wish to say anything other than the most general things about empirically visible aspects of its structure (e.g., size, centralization, etc.) our faith in the category of *the* organization may have been premature. Perhaps, after all, there are types of organization which cluster not at the level of empirically given variation, but at the level of specificity within an overall macro-structural context.

Second, in particular we are proposing that the concept of the organization's mode of rationality affords a basis for such enquiry, through research which aims to construct abstract models. In this sense the work of Karpik (1973; 1977; 1978) and his colleagues on 'logics of action' clearly exemplifies this approach. It is not for the sake of either superfluity of terms or peculiar idiosyncrasy that we use the term 'modes of rationality' rather than logics of action. There are two good reasons. One is that it enables one to construct an important continuity with the work of Weber (1968) and the critique of Marcuse (1971) on 'rationality' which is lost in the appellation 'logic of action'. The other reason is that, to be strict, one is not proposing a logical model, nor a model of the logic of action. Action remains as it is, on the surface. What one is doing is to construct a possible abstract model (a mode, not a determinant logic) not of action but of the rationality which can be demonstrated through de-constructing that action. The abstraction 'mode of rationality' is itself conceptualized within the abstraction of the mode of production. The mode of rationality is the analytical form-ulation of sedimented selection rules. These rules are the means by which owners and controllers of the means of production orient their practice towards the hegemonic domination of some objective principle, which, in the last instance, will tend to be conditioned economically by the mode of production. When we are dealing with institutional spheres constituted in the immediate production of surplus value, the mode of production and hegemonic domination have, in the long run, a necessary reflexive relationship between them which provides the reproduction of the ground rules of the mode of production. These have been recently specified for the capitalist mode of production by Hindess and Hirst;

> Capitalist relations of production define a mode of appropriation of surplus labour which works by means of commodity exchange. Capitalists buy means of production and items of personal consumption from each other. They buy labour power from labourers in exchange for wages. With these wages the labourers buy items of personal consumption from capitalists and must then sell their labour power for a further period in order to be able to buy further means of personal consumption. Appropriation of surplus labour here depends on a difference between the value of labour power and the value that may be created by means of the labour power. Surplus labour takes the form of surplus value. This appropriation of surplus labour presupposes that means of production are in the hands of the capitalists, since otherwise there is no necessity for the labourers to obtain means of consumption through the sale of their labour power. Thus capitalist relations of production define a mode of appropriation of surplus labour in the form of surplus value, and a social distribution of the means of production so that these are the property of non-labourers (capitalists), while the labour power takes the form of a commodity which members of the class of labourers are forced to sell to members of the class of non-labourers (Hindess and Hirst, 1975, p. 10).

In spheres other than those concerned with the institutional area of the economy the level of domination is only contingently determined by the mode of production. This allows subjects considerably more choice, theoretically, at the surface level of social practice and action. None the less, this freedom, like all freedom, is conditioned, and one can hypothesize rules which condition the selection of strategies of action.

Organization structure and mode of rationality

With the growth in size of organizations and the development of task-discontinuity, coercive domination through direct control or command becomes less feasible or practical. The balance of power shifts from domination by coercion and command, to the other side of Gramsci's dual perspective, domination by hegemony.

Offe (1976a, p. 28) recognizes this in terms of 'normative orientations': 'As both hierarchical and functional differentiation proceeds, the compliance which results from the effects of formal control has to be supplemented by *additional* normative orientations.' Simon (1952, p. 193) adds that 'unless a subordinate is himself able to supply most of the premises of a decision, and to synthesize them adequately, the task of supervision becomes hopelessly burdensome'.

These normative orientations, which (following Gramsci) we shall refer to as domination by hegemony, function as both principle and substance of specific organization structures. As principle, they operate at the general bedrock level of mode of production/ hegemonic domination as a form of life, as the ground rule of domination. Within this general context, they may be seen in substance in the organization as a structure of sedimented selection rules. Conceiving of these as a possible combination, we can develop an abstract mode of rationality of the development of organization structure.

This model of the organization derives from an earlier analysis of language-in-use, which treated conversation materials collected in an organization as the surface manifestation of a deeper, underlying mode of rationality (see Clegg, 1975). In the context being developed here, the organization structures can be conceived in terms of the selection rules which can be analytically constructed as an explanation of its social action and practice (its surface detail, what it does). These rules, collected together, may be conceived of as a mode of rationality.

The types of selection rules indicated in Figure 13.1 are not mutually exclusive but are found in combinations in specific organizations. Analytically, they are separable, while empirically, they may be found co-existent. The schema is neither a necessary nor a sufficient list, but simply an abstract model, which indicates some of the major rule-governed interventions which have been made in the organization of the labour process in the capitalist mode of production.

In the section which follows, we wish to illustrate this abstract schema through a possible history. This possible history constructs an ideal type which, by definition, we shall never meet in reality. It condenses and concentrates certain determinate features of organizations conceived as modes of rationality which we have argued are crucial for an understanding of how the structure of organization of the labour process has developed. In reality we are more likely to meet not only concrete organizations with these past histories still actively sedimented in their constitution, but also different types of organization 'stalled' at one point in time in their development, yet still suspended in the same space in which there are other organiza-

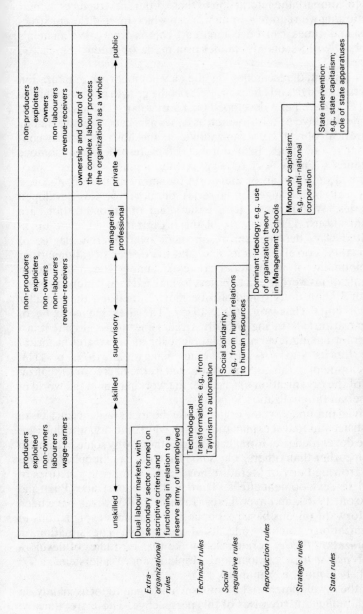

Figure 13.1 *The main types of sedimented selection rules available to organizations and their structural location*

tions belonging to another time altogether. Because we wish to be able to compare the interaction of these different structures in their functioning we require a framework in which these different structures and times can be compared. This is where Wallerstein's (1974a) 'world-economy' model of a mode of production can be utilized.

Sophisticated researches on the development of organization structures (Pugh and Hickson, 1976) or the growth of firms (Child *et al.*, 1975) have been developed on a particular set of assumptions. The perspective of this research assumes as a basic premise that its theoretical object is 'organizations' in the abstract, which contextually, one finds in a number of more-or-less autonomous 'societies'. These societies are co-terminous with the space occupied on the map of the world by autonomous nation states. They can be arranged in a series of more- or less-developed societies. Within these, as a basic agent of rationalization, are organizations. The structure of the organization, in some unexplicated way, becomes the result of its own inherent degree of rationality, correlated to its size, and the degree of rationality or development of its national context. 'Simply stated, if Indian organizations were found to be less formalized than American ones, bigger Indian units would still be more formalized than smaller Indian units' (Hickson *et al.*, 1975). The idea seems to be of organizations all tracing 'broadly parallel lines of development in a quadrant having level of development for its y-axis and historical time for its x-axis' (Hopkins and Wallerstein, 1977, p. 111). Development in this context is indicated by the degree of formalization of the organization's structure: the working out in the world of Weberian rationalization.

Given this imagery, the organization theorist's task is clear: it is to construct and to test explanations as to why some organizations are more developed (i.e. formalized) than others, why some became so much earlier than others, why some have not caught up. A diverse and growing body of literature now exists, comprising theories of 'the late-development effect' (Thurley, 1975), constructs (Pugh and Hickson, 1976), and hypotheses (Francis, 1977), which have been put forward on this basis as possible or plausible explanations of organization structure and its development. The situation in organization theory is remarkably like that in studies of development *per se* (for comparison, Hopkins and Wallerstein, 1977, pp. 111–12 may be examined).

In the development field, criticism has begun to focus mainly on the paradigmatic premises of this perspective. These are 'that the globe consists of relatively autonomous "societies" developing in relation to one another along roughly the same path although with

506

different starting times and at different speeds' (Hopkins and Wallerstein, 1977, p. 112). If one were to substitute 'organizations' in this sentence for 'societies', it would not be a parody of organization theory but an accurate depiction of some of the work of its major practitioners. Hopkins and Wallerstein note that in the place of these developmentalist models there is emerging a 'world-system perspective'. It is worth quoting them in full on this perspective:

> The premise is that the arena within which social action takes place and social change occurs is not 'society' in the abstract, but a definite 'world', a spatio-temporal whole, whose spatial scope is coextensive with the elementary division of labour among its constituent regions or parts and whose temporal scope extends for as long as the elementary division of labour continually reproduces the 'world' as a social whole (whether on an expanding, contracting, or unchanging scale). Specifically, this arena of modern social action and modern social change has been and continues to be the modern world-system, which emerges in the sixteenth century as a European-centred world economy. This 'world-system' has since grown through cycles of expansion and contraction in its geographical scope (and now encompasses the globe), in its productive capacity (capital formation), in its integration as a whole (world-scale interdependence), and in its penetration and organization of social relations ('commodification' and class-formation). Throughout, it has operated 'spatially' as an ever-present division of centres and hinterlands, or as we shall say 'cores' and 'peripheries', united and reproduced through processes of capital accumulation and unequal exchange, and 'temporally' in a fundamentally cyclical fashion, such that its 'growth' (as registered by secular trends) has occurred and continues to occur in 'waves' (as registered by accelerating, then decelerating, trend 'rates of growth'). The phases of its cycles, then, like the zones of its division of labour, are not only the continuous consequences of social action, but also very real conditions of such actions and very real constraints on their outcomes (Hopkins and Wallerstein, 1977, p. 112).

Within this world economy it has been proposed that 'sovereign states . . . be seen as one kind of organizational structure among others within this single social system' (Wallerstein, 1974a, p. 7). We have argued in the previous chapter that this notion of organizational structures within one social system is also relevant for the general analysis of organizations.

This analysis has been almost wholly premised on organizations located in, or modelled on those located in, the core of the world economy. Organization theory, to the best of our knowledge, contains little or no reference to, for example, the organization of the labour process in Africa, in the sphere of the colonial economy, the concession-owning economy or the economy of the labour reserves (Amin, 1974). There is an important and growing literature on these topics (e.g., Gutkind and Wallerstein, 1976; Magubane, 1975). The labour reserves of South African mining are just as much a formal organization (of the labour process) as the wage-labour organization of an English Midland factory. But in organization theory, neither the wage-labourer and his/her household nor the reserve-labourer ever enter into the analysis. The analysis is always of the superstructure of control erected on top of the complex labour process, rather than the formal organization (of the labour process) in its entirety.

Not only has organization theory never explicitly addressed the question 'formal organization of what?' and answered '. . . the labour process', it has been largely core-centric. When it has not, it has analysed only those types of organization forms developed in the core. There is insufficient space for us to pursue this point much further here. To do so would need at least another volume. It is clear, using Wallerstein's world-system perspective, that just as we find systematic differences in state political structures according to their position in the international division of labour, so we might also expect to find systematic differences in the formal organization of the labour process according to its location in core, periphery or semi-periphery. In fact, in the development literature these differences are widely recognized, even if their interpretation is hotly contested around the notion of whether, for instance, coerced labour is a pre-capitalist survival in the modern world, or an intrinsic feature of a capitalist mode of production internationally divided among a capitalist world economy, and thus a normal form of control outside of the core states. Hopkins and Wallerstein (1977, p. 139) would argue the latter, as does Wallerstein (1974a).

Returning to our initial theme that organizations themselves (irrespective of their world-economy location) may be regarded as historically and temporally complex sedimented structures, then the crucial question becomes: what determines their structuration in similar modes of rationality, such that we can address similarities underlying evident differences? We have suggested that the construction of an abstract schema through a possible history may be useful. The purpose of this history is to show how the sedimentation has developed at the mediate level of the mode of rationality within the context of the mode of production. The purpose of these sedimented rules, it will be argued, is to maintain control of the labour process. The organization of the labour process thus becomes the site of a specific struggle between labour and capital. Marx, of course, was well aware of this struggle but he did not develop an analysis of the strategies followed by capital to accommodate and forestall worker resistance.[2]

To reiterate what has already been stated: power in organizations derives from control of the means and methods of production. This twofold resource base allows the possibility of worker control of methods of production within a context in which capital still controls the means of production. It is in such a situation that strategically contingent workers (Hickson *et al.*, 1971) or workers with a degree of control of uncertainty (Crozier, 1964) have a strictly limited potential for a small, minor but relative degree of control over and above that formally granted them. But such marginal elements of control must be seen in the context of the capitalist mode of production.

Within the capitalist mode of production the economy is both the dominant and determinant structural level, over and above the ideological and political levels.

Within this economy, labour faces capital individually as citizen and consumer, while capital confronts the individual as that which controls the possibilities of his or her employment. Labour gains short-term, individualistic personal income from the exchange; while capital gains, in return for this labour, control not only over it *per se,* but also over all it makes possible: production, commodities, distribution, technologies, etc. Control over these domains is grounded in the institutions of 'private property' (for early Marxist discussion of which one can consult Engels, 1969), which provide

a general normative pressure and a potentially vast network of supporters (in formal as well as informal positions) who can be mobilized to protect the existing social and material arrangements. Also, definite 'support structures' are formally organized and charged with the responsibility of preventing disruption of the system: judicial, administrative and police branches of the State. They function both explicitly (by legal directives, e.g., to protect private property and prerogatives of the owners and managers of private property) and implicitly (by a set of assumptions underlying policies and operations with respect to business enterprises) to maintain the position of employers in autonomous private properties and their rights to operate their firms without 'undue interference' from workers, consumers, or the general public. In particular, the police and courts of the capitalist state operate to guarantee that, should ideology and persuasion fail, the structure of socio-economic relations and the configuration of constraints outlined above would be maintained 'by other means': namely 'legitimized force' (Baumgartener *et al.*, 1977, p. 6).

These constraints are, of course, historically *conditioned*. In the earliest stages of real subordination they were largely of a Taylorist, neo-Taylorist and formal administrative theory type, tempered by the even more compulsive power of the reserve army of the unemployed. In Chapter 3 we developed an analysis of how the unity of an alienating labour process indicated, in particular, by high rates of labour turnover and an ever-ready reserve army of the unemployed was broken by the full employment of the Second World War. Taylorist interventions in the labour process in the nature of rules of technical practices, or *technical rules*, were now no longer sufficient in themselves. By placing these interventions of technical rules in the context of Mandel's (1975) work, we can gain some important insights using our control perspective on organizations.

Mandel (1975) has argued that capitalist development is conditioned by fundamental movements, which he calls 'long waves'. These determine the general character of a whole era as one of relatively fast or slow accumulation. Accumulation depends on the rate of profit. A heightened rate of profit leads to a relatively fast period of accumulation. The relationship of fast to slow periods of accumulation is one of succeeding cycles of 'long waves of accelerated and decelerated accumulation determined by long waves in the rise and decline of the rate of profit' (Mandel, 1975, p. 129). The expansionary, accelerating phase of a long wave occurs when the rate of profit is 'triggered' by 'triggering factors'. These are factors which lower the organic composition of capital or raise the rate of surplus value. As these factors are exhausted then the rate of profit begins to fall because of unfavourable changes in either the organic composition of capital or the rate of surplus value. The long wave moves back into expansion when the rate of profit is once again lifted radically by a further combination of factors. Mandel identifies four specific factors 'which render possible a sudden increase in the average of profit'. These are:

1 A sudden fall in the average organic composition of capital, for example as a result of the massive penetration of capital into spheres (or countries) with a very low organic composition.
2 A sudden increase in the rate of surplus value, due to a radical defeat or atomization of the working class. . . .
3 A sudden fall in the price of elements of constant capital, especially of raw materials . . . or a sudden fall in the price of fixed capital. . . .
4 A sudden abbreviation of the turnover-time of circulating

capital due to perfection of new systems of transport and communications, improved methods of distribution, accelerated rotation of stock, and so on (Mandel, 1975, pp. 114–15).

Mandel argues that if several of these factors exist in a situation in simultaneous and cumulative over-determination, there will be a rise in the long-run rate of profit and a 'revolution in production technology'.

Rowthorn (1976, p. 63) has argued that Mandel is mistaken in thinking that such a shift should be sudden. What is significant, he argues, is that it be *radical*. The subordination of the working class, laying the foundation of conditions for expansion after the First World War, was not sudden, it was radical. It took about 20 years, from 1929 to the late 1940s to be accomplished, as Rowthorn (1976, pp. 63–4) argues. He cites the effect of 'depression, Fascism, wartime integration and the Cold War' as contributory factors. Mandel, he argues, over-stresses the role of Fascism 'in his search for a *sudden* shift in the balance of power' (Rowthorn, 1976, p. 63). This leads Mandel to under-emphasize 'more subtle versions of control which, at one level, rest on consent rather than coercion and incorporate trade unions as junior partners in capitalist society'. As he goes on to say, although built slowly, such mechanisms 'play a central role in making possible a sustained accumulation of capital' (Rowthorn, 1976, p. 64).

We are in agreement with Rowthorn (1976) on this and would single out one in particular from Mandel's (1975) list of specific factors contributing to a revolution in technology as having a bearing upon the analysis of organization structures. This is a radical increase in the rate of surplus value, due to a radical defeat or atomization of the working class.

Such a defeat or atomization is, in part, effected in and through organizations and has effects on organization structures. If we attach a leading role to this and the other specific factors which Mandel mentions, then we have the basis of an adequate explanation of transformations in organization structures through, first, class struggle (looked at in this context from the side of the ruling class), and second, through the technological reconstruction such struggle can assist (see Chapter 9). We will consider in this context the factor of radical working-class defeat or atomization, taking into consideration Rowthorn's (1976) remarks that we need to stress more subtle types of control. We shall do this by relating to our earlier discussion of Gramsci. This will enable us to develop a perspective on control in organizations which is related to the class struggle.

Types of hegemonic control

From human relations to work humanization

The individual enterprise is not the overall economy. At the economic level, the capitalist mode of production is characterized by an industrial cycle of the successive acceleration and deceleration of accumulation, as Mandel (1975, ch. 4) argues. The fully-employed war economy followed by the economy of the long post-war boom would pose particular problems for the organization and control of the labour process at the level of the specific enterprise. As we have already argued in Chapters 3 and 11, it would specifically withdraw the coercive domination of the reserve army of the unemployed. In these circumstances we would anticipate that the balance of domination would fall on the hegemonic side of the equation. Elton Mayo's (1975) wartime studies were an attempt to restore domination in a situation marked by the absence of the coercive aspects of unemployment. The latter was not a strategy that was available during the full employment of the Second World War. Mayo's 'hegemonic' answer to the control of labour has been adopted by the so-called progressive elements in industry through the process of 'work humanization' (Maher, 1971). This work humanization or neo-human relations has a direct lineage from the early Hawthorne experiments, but equally can be seen as 'an adaptation of Taylorism to new conditions of struggle in production, with the aim of *preserving* the profitability of capital, rather than a *radical revolution* of the labour process' (Palloix, 1976, p. 63).

Hofstede (1977) has referred to the humanization of work as a part of the 'third industrial revolution' (the other two being concerned with mechanization and cybernation, respectively), in that structural changes have taken place in the organization of work that have provided greater opportunities for autonomy, discretion, challenge and intrinsic satisfaction. These kinds of change have been spurred on by the writings of psychologists such as Herzberg *et al.* (1959), Herzberg (1966), McGregor (1960), Likert (1961) and Argyris (1957; 1962; 1964). The International Labour Office (1977) has compiled a bibliography on work humanization that contains over 2,000 references; Taylor (1976) has shown that the number of references to work humanization doubled in each five-year period of the years 1957 to 1972. The specific forms of work humanization such as job enrichment and job rotation have been the subjects of experiments both in the USA (Texas Instruments, Polaroid, IBM, Chrysler, Ford and General Motors) and in Europe (Volvo, Saab, ICI, Philips, Fiat, Olivetti). Clearly the scale of the phenomenon has been large. But to what extent do the experiments and innovations represent a challenge to the industrial *status quo*? Are they an indication that scientific management has failed? As Braendgaard has put it:

> What more effective proof of the fallacy of Marxist propositions about the inevitability and persistence of worker alienation in capitalist society could one ask for? This wave of reforms, which apparently has been successful in terms of both economic and human standards, should thus definitely end allegations of capitalist wickedness and prove that competition in a capitalist market is no impediment to the achievement of human values at work. But is this really an adequate appraisal of what has been accomplished? (Braendgaard, 1978, p. 2).

If Hofstede is correct in referring to an 'industrial revolution' when describing the increased participation and emphasis upon intrinsic rewards, the first point to make is that this has been a revolution initiated for and not by the labour force. The changes that have occurred have been almost totally management-imposed changes, brought about largely through the increasing costs of scientific management (absenteeism, turnover, reduced productivity, poor quality, etc.). Work humanization has been an attempt to raise employee morale, 'to make good the damage caused by management's own work design' (Fox, 1976, p. 22). These *social regulative* rule-guided interventions have developed in response to contradictions generated by technical rule interventions such as Taylorism or automation.

Furthermore, Vilmar (1973) has referred to the neo-human relations techniques as 'pseudo-strategies' in that there is only a pretence to overcome the perceived problems. These problems are the very phenomena that have dehumanized work: dependence and exploitation; psycho-physical suffering at work; and external control. Work humanization has never attempted to overcome the issue of dependence and exploitation, nor the problem of psycho-physical suffering. The main thrust has been directed at the issue of external control. Yet, even in the empirical cases that seek to demonstrate the employee's greater control over his/her work environment, the setting of work goals and standards are still beyond his or her grasp.

At another level, the work humanization movement can be questioned because of the economic climate in which it was introduced. As the world economic recession bit deeper during the first half of the 1970s the enthusiasm for the humanization of work waned. Braendgaard (1978, p. 9) comments that 'the prospect for humanizing changes now that we have economic crisis and unemployment with us are . . . quite bleak'. One can see a reversion to the previously dominant emphases upon productivity and competition. The innovations of the 1960s did not, in fact, challenge the Taylorist division of labour into a hierarchy of mental and manual skills: they were neo-Taylorist rather than anti-Taylorist and conform strictly to Mayo's (1975) intention not to negate a Taylorist division of labour, but to attempt to preserve it through new forms of 'persuasion' in changed conditions of control.

Hunnius (1977, p. 20) has pointed out that 'in the majority of cases where job enrichment has been introduced by management . . . the enterprise has been in financial difficulties of some kind'. This is precisely the point made by Ramsay (1977a) in introducing the concept of 'cycles of control'. Whether these difficulties have been the long-term effects of Taylorism or have been caused by wider economic matters is an empirical question. The point that Ramsay (1977a, p. 481) makes is that 'worker participation has not evolved out of the humanization of capitalism . . . but has appeared cyclically'.

Ramsay presents an historical account of the cycles of control with respect to Britain. These cycles are traced back over a century and show that interest by management in participation 'corres-pond[s] to periods when management authority is felt to be facing challenge' (Ramsay, 1977a, p. 481). The principal cycles that Ramsay distinguishes originate with profit-sharing schemes in the 1860s and pass through the period of the introduction of the Whitley Councils after the First World War, the period of joint consultation during and immediately after the Second World War, and then through to the more contemporary cycles of productivity bargaining, work humanization and discussion of industrial democracy in the 1960s and 1970s. Ramsay concludes that certain trends can be discerned from such an historical analysis of participation schemes:

(a)   They seem on each occasion to have arisen out of a managerial response to threats to management authority . . . the initiative is management's and the consequence is, if significant at all, to nullify pressures to change the *status quo*, not to stimulate its reform.
(b)   Each time the schemes emphasize almost without exception a consensual unitary philosophy, and bear related hallmarks of management ideology (Ramsay, 1977a, p. 496).

Ramsay demonstrates that increasingly the state has been extremely active in innovating new forms of control through co-determination, worker participation and so on. This, as we have repeatedly demonstrated, is not a novel role for the State to play. We can elaborate this point with reference to discussions of the capitalist state.

The capitalist state did not develop in some abstract space. It evolved out of feudal society and forms of the feudal state (see Anderson, 1974). Feudal society had its own highly organized form of economic life known as mercantilism. It was because of the existence of this highly regulated set of economic activities of state control and protection that early political economists of capitalism such as Adam Smith argued for free enterprise. The development of absolute states at the end of the Middle Ages was constructed around a bureaucratic apparatus and organization devoted to the contrivance of monopoly profits through the sale of rights to trade under princely protection. This right to trade became an exclusive property right vested in guilds, who could demand that the coercive power of the state be legitimately used against those who infringed the guilds' monopoly privileges. The zenith of this system occurred in Tudor England. The life of Tudor people was everywhere constrained by monopoly:

> It is difficult for us to picture to ourselves the life of a man living in a house built of monopoly bricks, with windows (if any of monopoly glass; heated by monopoly coal (in Ireland monopoly timber), burning in a grate of monopoly iron. His walls were lined with monopoly tapestries. He slept on monopoly feathers, washed himself with monopoly soap, his clothes in monopoly starch. His hat was of monopoly beaver, with a monopoly band. Out of monopoly glasses he drank monopoly wines and monopoly spirits; out of pewter mugs made from monopoly tin he drank monopoly beer made from monopoly hops kept in monopoly barrels or monopoly bottles, sold in monopoly-licensed alehouses. He shot with monopoly gunpower made from monopoly saltpetre. He travelled in monopoly sedan chairs or monopoly hackney coaches, drawn by horses fed on monopoly hay. He tipped with monopoly farthings (Hill, 1969, p. 38).

The activities of the state were often virtually indistinguishable from organized crime and banditry and, in fact, during the millenium from AD 700 to 1700 prince and plunderer were often the same. By the seventeenth century the state created monopolies in order to sell them, including monopolies for licensing which gave permission to break the law (McCullough and Shannon, 1977, p. 80). As they put it, 'the state acutally traded in the sale of exemptions from its own legal restrictions'.

By the eighteenth century, with the development of the productive forces of capitalism outside the guilds, some power and regulatory authority was necessary to create free enterprise and the lack of regulation. This creation of free trade was the first historical action of the capitalist state. As Polanyi (1957, p. 139) observes, there was no continuous development from a lack of government intervention through to a fully developed welfare state apparatus: *laissez-faire* was an artificial creation of the state.

The state, as has historically been its role, even in its advocacy of *laissez-faire* policies, has been an active agent intervening in conditions of control in organizations (see Taylor, 1972). In general the state intervenes in modern organizational processes by establishing a framework in which conflicts between labour and capital can be, depending on political complexion, outlawed or contained (within which range there is an enormous empirical variation). As we have seen, Ramsay (1977a) has observed how one social-regulative class of intervention sponsored by the state, that of reforms calling for participation, has been a cyclical occurrence, varying with the fortunes of the world economy. At times of full employment and high wages, calls for 'participation' have generally increased. The development of Mayoite strategies during the Second World War may be noted in this context. The rise and fall of the fortunes of work humanization practices similarly have followed this pattern. Baumgartener *et al.* have observed that:

> [Participation schemes are] attempts to blur the social differentiation between capitalists/managers and workers by making workers (typically, their trade union representatives) into capitalists/managers. Profit sharing/ownership participation, in particular, is intended to interest workers in the profitability of their enterprise, and thus achieve at the aggregate level the same effect in improved motivation, attentiveness, and sense of responsibility that job enrichment programmes try to accomplish at the micro-level (Baumgartener *et al,* 1977, p. 27).

These experiments are clearly intended to change the surface structure of power relationships between management and labour whilst leaving the underlying structure of social relationships and hegemony intact. Indeed, what is lost by management hierarchically will be more than gained hegemonically, to the extent that 'interest' is generally attached to the profitability of the enterprise. 'Incorporation' (see Ramsay, 1977a) has a long and successful history.

From work humanization to workers' control?

Following Habermas (1976), it is possible to speculate whether or not the introduction of a new 'objective' or 'organizing' principle, in the form of demands for a genuine self-management and liberation of work, could introduce a contradiction which might be the locus of new legitimation problems or even crises for organizations? To the extent that these could, as an unanticipated consequence, contradict the existing icon of domination – that of 'private goals of profit maximization' (Habermas, 1976, p. 73), then out of a *public* (rather than *exclusive*) participation and the interests of those workers engaged in it, as possible bearers 'of the generalizable interests of the population' (Habermas, 1976, p. 73), there could develop

> the moderation of cyclical economic crises to a permanent crisis that appears, on the one hand, as a matter *already* processed administratively and, on the other hand, as a movement *not yet* adequately controlled administratively (Habermas, 1976, p. 93).

The introduction of democratic principles to organizations may have the dangerous potential of articulating non-individualist senti-ments. It is because of this that strategies of social-regulative rules, for capital rather than for labour, have to be subordinated to hegemonic domination. That is, the theoretical practice of these rules, the ways in which they are constituted in organizational practice, has to be subordinated to the ground rule of an 'objective principle' of private interests of profit maximization rather than one of publicly generalizable interests of participation and account-ability. If this is not the case, then there exists an objective con-tradiction of principles which threatens the reproduction of the mode of production at the organization level.

Ideas of industrial democracy, of worker participation, of work humanization, etc., come dangerously near to resonating with the sentiments of the 'alternative dominant ideology' (Allen, 1975, p. 233) of collectivism, which, in its reasoning on organization, emerges from the theory and practice of the Soviets which were articulated in Lenin's and Gramsci's writings (discussed in Chapter 3). We can now consider the further development of these alter-native concepts of organization, in order to elucidate precisely how and why demands for a genuine self-management or liberation of work could introduce contradictions which might lead to new legitimation problems for organizations.

That we can pose this as a probability is to question any views which would stress only 'the domination of our form of life' (Clegg, 1975, p. 151) without recognizing the existence of contradictions. It is well documented in studies of British working-class life (e.g., Hill, 1976; Nichols and Armstrong, 1976), for instance, that workers are not subject to any total hegemony. Ideological repro-duction may just as readily be radical as conservative. Parkin (1972) has argued that not only is there a dominant value system with a correspondingly subordinant and accommodative counterpart, but that there is also a radical one which can be the source of opposition. It has been suggested by Blackburn (1967) that the dominant ideology coexists in a state of uneasy tension with radical ideas in the working class. At times of crisis the latter can surface. As normal hegemony breaks down, then radical alternatives become possible. The workers' control movement, in its various forms, provides both a practice and a theory for aiding our reflection on radical alternatives.

The difficulty in assessing workers' control strategies is in determining whether there is genuine self-management or merely a 'pseudo-strategy'. Certainly it is the case that many writers suggest that self-management can operate effectively within the existing framework of capitalism; others, possible more realistically, have observed that self-management is a means to an end and can never be genuine whilst capitalism exists. These two views of self-management can be expressed as the difference between 'participation' and 'workers' control' respectively. The former represents much of the work of the neo-human relations researchers to which we have already referred; the latter involves considerably more control of the work situation and the transfer of power to the labour force, especially over the making of decisions that affect the work situation. We can explore both of these views in terms of the demands for a genuine control over work: that is, where the demands have led to schemas operating within a capitalist framework, and those in a non-capitalist framework. Following Coates (1975, p. 91), 'it seems sensible for us to speak of "workers' control" to indicate the aggressive encroachment of trade unions on management powers in a capitalist framework, and of "workers' self-management" to indicate attempts to administer a socialized economy democratically'.

Workers' control under capitalism

We have already seen in considerable detail that efforts to produce genuine workers' control under capitalism have been made throughout this century, and have examined the factory councils' brief career in relation to Gramsci around 1920 in Turin. The factory committees, or Internal Commissions, in fact have a history of development dating from 1906, when they were originally established as grievance committees. The important point is that, unlike the management-sponsored commissions, they were the product of genuine demands by workers. Delegates were democratically elected from the various shops to the factory committee. The committees were a direct challenge to management in that they demonstrated the workers' knowledge and competence of the process of production; the workers showed that hierarchical forms of authority could effectively be substituted by self-initiated discipline. Tornquist (1973, p. 382) has suggested that 'the factory committee . . . has the two important functions of altering work psychology from that of the wage-earner to that of the producer and of transforming relations in the work place towards workers' management'. Of course, for Gramsci industrial democracy was an evolutionary phenomenon: the factory committee through increasing strength, could alter the relations of production and move towards socialism. But the outcome of Gramsci's strategy is well known.

> In April, 1921, 5,000 revolutionary workers were laid off by Fiat, the factory councils were abolished, real wages were reduced. At Reggio Emilia something similar probably happened. The workers, in other words, were defeated (Gramsci, 1957, p. 42).

We see here an attempt at workers' control operating under capitalism which, derived from a genuine worker movement for a system by and for the working class, was defeated by the dominance of capital. Let us turn to more recent attempts employing a similar ethos, but again working within capitalism.

Since the early 1970s there has developed in Britain a new worker co-operative movement, new in the sense that the co-operative movement in Britain can be traced back to the early nineteenth century, although the 'Rochdale Pioneers' of 1844 are more often cited as the first significant feature of the movement. The occupation of Upper Clyde Shipbuilders (UCS) in 1971 heralded a large number of sit-ins and factory occupations. Mills (1974) enumerated 102 different occupations between July 1971, and March 1974, most of which were motivated by the threat of redundancy through factory closure. Given the large number of occupations, it is not unreasonable to refer to the phenomenon as a 'movement'. With the benefit of hindsight we can now see that the vast majority of these occupations were doomed to failure for much the same reasons as Gramsci's factory committees. One factor which prevailed in each of the British sit-ins was that the companies were experiencing profound economic difficulties largely as a result of the worldwide recession. If these companies were unable to cope with the situation with the assistance of finance capital, the prospects for groups of workers, operating often with little more than their redundancy payments, were very slim. Not all of the occupations suffered this fate, however. There are a few notable exceptions that can be examined that provide us with some evidence of the possible opportunities that exist for workers' control within a capitalist framework.

It has been well documented, especially in the press, that the most successful of the factory occupations owed their success to a sympathetic government and especially a sympathetic Secretary of State for Industry, Tony Benn. At the time of the election of the

Labour Government in 1974, British companies were experiencing their most severe liquidity crisis in forty years. One result was the ever-increasing number of manufacturing company bankruptcies. Inspired by the activities of UCS workers and the threat of redundancy becoming a *fait accompli,* 250 motor cycle workers of the Norton Villiers Triumph (NVT) factory at Meriden in 1973 occupied the factory and eventually established the Meriden co-operative. The story of this struggle has been adequately recounted by Fleet (1976). Very briefly, the upshot was that with considerable financial backing from the government (a grant of £750,000 and a low-interest loan of £4.2 million for 15 years) the factory was re-established as a viable concern. A further, but much smaller, injection of capital was made available later. The commercial viability of the plant is demonstrated by an increasing work force (all members of which, incidentally, receive equal pay) and by the fact that the market absorbs every motor cycle produced. In terms of the organization of the plant, organizers and co-ordinators (who are appointed by the shop-steward directors) have replaced foremen. As Fleet has remarked:

> As a consequence of . . . democratic and egalitarian arrangements they have achieved an enthusiasm amongst the workers, with every man his own inspector, which has meant good productivity at high quality and the minimum of rectification work. Job enlargement and rotation have become quite commonplace and flexibility of labour means that bottlenecks can be overcome quickly (Fleet, 1976, p. 105).

In spite of the success of the Meriden venture it must be stressed that this is the show-piece of the workers' co-operative movement and could only have succeeded with the significant government financial assistance. Support for this proposition is afforded by the worker take-over of the Fisher-Bendix factory on Merseyside. There had been a long occupation of the factory that had started in January 1972. Government capital was not forthcoming until 1974. During that period the co-operative was constantly on the verge of collapse; this, though, was inevitable, since the workers 'were proposing to run a factory which nobody had made to pay in 13 years of operations' (Eccles, 1976, p. 153). Even with the government aid (£3.9 million, of which £1.8 million went directly to the Receiver) the factory was in a precarious position. Furthermore, the workers were unable to gain the same degree of control of the factory as their counterparts at Meriden. Although there was a strategy employed to prevent the reassertion of managerial control (the two convenors became the sole directors),

There was a certain amount of fudging of the organization structure, which was scarcely surprising in view of the speed with which the co-operative proposal had developed. . . . What was clear was that day-to-day operations would be under the control of professional managers (Eccles, 1976, pp. 157–8).

A third venture which again eventually received government aid was the *Scottish Daily News* newspaper in Glasgow. Of all three of the co-operatives this was the one most fraught with problems and possessing the greatest potential for eventual failure. Whilst all three examples represent companies operating on the open market and hence subject to powerful market forces, the *Scottish Daily News* was subject to the most severe market influences. The technology of newspaper production enables little variation in work design (whilst this may sound like an extreme form of technological determinism, the fact should be recognized that there are effectively only two manufacturers of printing presses in Great Britain and both produce a remarkably similar product), and the nature of the product – the physical newspaper – is largely pre-determined (again the choice being between the tabloid product associated with the popular press or the broadsheet associated with the quality press of the *Guardian, The Times* and the *Daily Telegraph*). The recent history of the British press was one of contraction, with national dailies and weeklies disappearing (*Reynolds News,* the *News Chronicle,* the *Daily Sketch* and the *Sunday Pictorial* being the main casualties). The probability of launching a successful mass circulation newspaper with a left-wing bias was extremely low.

The story of the *Scottish Daily News* as told by Allister Mackie (1976), the original chairman of the Action Committees, is a moving one and yet, to a large extent, a predictable one. The central problem related to membership of the Executive Council of the co-operative: the constitution permitted election '*by* the employees, but not necessarily *from* the employees' (T. Clarke, 1977, p. 374). This feature of the constitution enabled Robert Maxwell, a 'left-wing' millionaire and publisher, eventually to take complete control of the newspaper. At this point Mackie (1976, p. 139) has suggested that 'the co-operative was dead; the newspaper lasted only another seven weeks'.

In assessing the results of the workers' co-operative movement of the early 1970s in Britain it should be pointed out that from its conception it had little support from any quarter except the government. Even the left-wing press was sceptical. For example, the *Socialist Worker* (July 1974) in an editorial stated

You cannot build islands of socialism in a sea of capitalism, and workers' management of a commercial concern operating in that sea deprives the workers of the strength of union organization directed against management.

Again, Mandel, writing in *International* (1975) said:

> The fundamental principle underlying self-management . . . is unrealizable in an economy which allows the survival of competition. . . . It is thus to deceive the workers to lead them to believe that they can manage their affairs at the level of the factory. In the present economic system, a whole series of decisions are inevitably taken at higher levels than the factory.

These arguments are hardly novel. Marx, too, was sceptical of a co-operative movement:

> The co-operative system will never transform capitalist society. To convert social production into one large and harmonious system of free and co-operative labour, general social changes are wanted, changes of the general conditions of society, never to be realized save by the transfer of the organized forces of society, viz., the state power, from capitalists and landlords to the producers themselves (Marx, 1974, p. 90).

As we have seen, the co-operatives are subject to the enormous pressures of the market as well as being beholden to the whims of government. Furthermore, the workers involved in the factory occupations were not politically motivated. 'Little explicit political consciousness was exhibited whatsoever; an abundance of motor-cycle and craft consciousness was displayed, but that is a different matter' (T. Clarke, 1977, p. 375). Let us instead turn to the position in those societies where there have been 'changes of the general conditions of society'.

Workers' self-management under socialism

The many different guises under which socialism appears in different societies makes it impossible to generate universal statements about the operation of workers' self-management under socialism. Consequently two different forms of Socialist State will be examined which form something of a continuum from a highly centralist position (USSR) to a highly decentralized position (Yugoslavia). The third example (China) differs significantly from these two through the use of widely different criteria for operation.

Yugoslavia   Although we have said that Yugoslavia represents the other end of a continuum from the centralist Soviet position, the worker-managed organization in Yugoslavia in fact emerged from the Soviet pattern. It is significant that the majority of the literature on comparative forms of workers' control points to the Yugoslav system as being the closest to a perfect model that could be achieved in an imperfect world (see, for example, Blumberg, 1968; Wachtel, 1973; Vanek, 1972 and Pateman, 1970).

The basic structure of the Yugoslav model is that the market system has replaced the centralized planning bureaucracy of the USSR, and that, at the level of the factory, authority has been decentralized to the factory workers. This decentralization in the form of the workers' councils is maintained in spite of the professional management employed. As Ramsay has commented:

> The theory is an evolutionary one. Yugoslav self-management in tandem with community participation and rising educational standards, should progressively raise the objective potential and subjective political efficacy of the worker as the years go by. Dangers of expert domination should thus recede after a few years whilst the experience and enormous incentive of direct control should enable the unrealized productive potential of the worker to be unleashed (Ramsay, 1977b, p. 10).

This is the theory; but what of the practice? The enthusiasm of Western liberals for the Yugoslav system is possibly misplaced for a number of reasons. First, the professional managers appear to have increased their control over individual enterprises, management boards and workers' councils (Hunnius, 1977, p. 296; Obradovic, 1975). Second, Yugoslav workers appear to be increasingly instrumental in their orientation to work. Their involvement and participation in the meetings of workers' councils seem increasingly to be limited to matters affecting them at a personal level. Involvement on matters concerned with production or finance seems to have declined quite dramatically (Obradovic, 1975; Kolaja, 1965). Burt (1972, p. 152), for example, cites a 1968 Slovenic study showing that 72 per cent of workers were concerned with matters relating to their private incomes, whereas only 5 per cent were interested in the self-management operation itself.

Two accounts of the Yugoslav system as quoted by Ramsay (1977b) suggest that the system, in spite of its Western apologists, has indeed had an evolutionary component but that the end of this evolution has been greatly displaced from the original.

> With obvious sorrow in their voices, several workers told the researcher of the era of festivity (dancing, embracing, etc.) when the company's siren would announce that a production plan had not only been realized but surpassed. People no longer felt pride in such accomplishment or in their production heroes. Those

523

individuals who began to gain status were technocrats (Adizes, 1971, p. 292).

The expectation when workers' management was introduced was that this scheme of organization would lead to a democratic, equalitarian distribution of influence, in which the workers and worker' councils would have the greatest influence, while line and staff were perceived merely as executive organizations subordinate to the workers themselves. *Just the opposite seems to have occurred* (Rus, 1970, p. 151).

It would be interesting to speculate on the nature of cause and effect in the Yugoslav economy. Not only has there been a shift in workers' orientations towards the desire for extrinisic over intrinsic rewards (and the related decline of interest in the self-management system), the whole Yugoslav economy appears to have taken a turn towards capitalism. The familiar characteristics of high inflation rates, high unemployment, industrial unrest and dependence on foreign capital are all visible in the Yugoslav economy (Adizes, 1971; Warner, 1975). It would, of course, be unrealistic to attribute such characteristics solely to the form of self-management in Yugoslavia, but undoubtedly the particular structure of the phenomenon and the kinds of change that have taken place within it are all symptomatic of a form of self-management that, traditionally, is more characteristic of Western capitalism than socialism.

USSR   In Chapter 3 we presented an account of Lenin's theory of bureaucracy that, *inter alia,* suggested the form of self-management in the early history of the USSR. We made the point that self-management was perceived as a way of democratizing the administrative functions of the bureaucracy through the introduction of the commune. Furthermore, we demonstrated that the increasing influence of Taylorism in the Soviet Union led to an increased role for the enterprise director, so that by the early 1920s the so-called Production Conferences were the chief mechanisms for participation. Stalin's influence reduced the degree of participation in the Conferences in the 1930s, and they disappeared as effective organs by the beginning of the Second World War. Not until 1957 were the Production Conferences revitalized. In 1958 they were renamed Permanent Production Conferences and, by law, there had to be both management and union support for, and participation in, them. Further legislation in 1970 and 1971 affirmed the commitment to participation, although 'the power of the director seems little challenged (though less directly coercive than under Stalin) and his authority has been repeatedly re-emphasized alongside the

524

calls for greater worker involvement' (Ramsay, 1977b, p. 7).

Clearly, neither Yugoslavia nor the Soviet Union has achieved the form or level of self-management that might be expected in a socialist society. There is, however, another approach that has been adopted in China that not only offers a useful contrast with the two already examined, but contains an implicit critique as well.

China The prevailing form of workers' self-management and participation in China today can really be understood only through an historical analysis of the events which have led to the present. The history of China since 1949 is largely the history of struggles between three different ideological groups: the revisionists who see technology as the dominant force in society; the radicals or Maoists who reject the revisionist argument and the obsession with material incentives as a motivating force; and the ultra-left whose emphasis is upon 'voluntarist zeal [which] can only bring disillusion and collapse, thus leaving victory to the right' (Ramsay, 1977b, p. 14).

Immediately after Mao's victory in China the main stress was upon greater direct representative democracy coupled with an emphasis upon modernization through the rationalization of consciousness. Gray (1974, pp. 31, 33) has commented that at this time the rationality of consciousness and rationality of technique were in 'a dialectical relationship of growth of production, institutional change, developing socio-political consciousness and cultural advance. Each element feeds the others . . . in a sense *literally* dialectical – it is dialogue, its motive force depends on the community's discussion of past experience in relation to present choices'. In effect, the emphasis was upon the avoidance of those developments such as technical specialization and bureaucratic élitism and centralization which inhibit critical discourse. The radical Maoist approach clearly stands apart from that of Lenin or Weber with regard to modernization, since consciousness and technique, urban and rural, industry and agriculture, manual and mental labour are all combined.

This approach to modernization declined in the early 1950s when the model of bureaucracy and administration employed by the Soviet Union was officially adopted. The Soviet model appeared to offer an accelerated means of achieving industrialization. The result was a break from emphasizing participation, initiative and consciouness. 'One-man management replaced dialogue and the industrial sector increasingly exhibited an unresponsive bureaucratic structure' (Hearn, 1978, p. 46).

Towards the end of the 1950s the ideological break between China and the Soviet Union led to the reaffirmation of dialectical development. Production was to be increased through socialist co-operation. The Great Leap Forward marked the complete rejection of the Soviet model. Its aim was to move from 'centralized to decentralized decision-making, from one-man factory management to greater roles for the party committees and greater initiative by the workers, from the extensive use of material incentives to increased reliance on social responsibility' (Nee and Peck, 1975, p. 50). Bettelheim (1974) comments that one of the central themes was an attack on the division of labour through the 'triple combination' (of cadres, technicians and workers) and the 'two participations' (workers in management and vice versa). Clearly, élitism was under attack through the politicization of the bureaucracy.

For many reasons, the Great Leap Forward failed. Andors (1971, pp. 411–31) has suggested that one of the most crucial reasons was the continued influence of the revisionists. The structures involving a lessening of participation, material incentives and hierarchical control had proved too entrenched to displace. With the failure of the Great Leap Forward the revisionists re-asserted their influence and the process of bureaucratization appeared to be following precisely that predicted by Max Weber in his work on socialism and bureaucracy. Ramsay (1977b, p. 15) states that '1961–64 found a reimposition of Bolshevik solutions, including labour discipline, regulations impressed from above, management autocracy and individualistic material incentives'.

The next phase, commencing in late 1965 and continuing into 1966, was that of the Great Proletarian Cultural Revolution. Essentially the Cultural Revolution was an ideological debate concerned to expose and reverse the revisionism of the previous phase. Its aims were: 'first, to eradicate the élitist tendencies sustained in consciousness and, second, to infuse this now politically purified consciousness into the administrative apparatus' (Hearn, 1978, pp. 46–7). The Cultural Revolution, in other words, was a transformation of consciousness. The radical Maoist line thus reasserted itself; production and revolution were once again combined. As King (1977, p. 364) has pointed out, 'The Chinese cultural revolution with its anti-bureaucratic idealism and activism arrived at the very moment when Western intellectuals were eagerly searching for an alternative to the bureaucratic "capitalism" of the West or the bureaucratic "socialism" of the East.' What was the alternative form of organization that emerged from the Cultural Revolution?

Possibly the easiest way to answer the question is through the use of the Maoist slogan 'Politics takes Command'. Organization is, according to the Maoists, a contradictory phenomenon and is thus constantly subject to conflict. But conflict has a desirable effect, it is functional. 'Revolution is without guilt; rebellion is justified.'

The institutional organization of the factory varied considerably from one factory to another (Macciocchi, 1972; Goldwasser and Dowty, 1975; Davies, 1976) and in any case such organization does not

> constitute the relations of workers' control in themselves. Any form of organization, irrespective of formal democratic structure, can become riddled with the wormholes of renewed authoritarianism and managerialism. Only the political activity and consciousness of the people, who give the institutions life, can ensure that the spirit of the Anshan Constitution is maintained (Ramsay, 1977b, p. 16).

Broadly, three institutional levels can be distinguished: the Party Committee; the Revolutionary Committee; and the Workers' Management teams. The political leadership is given by the Party Committee. Officially it has the ultimate authority in the enterprise. It is elected by Party members, although the work force as a whole endorses its membership (Bettelheim, 1974).

The Revolutionary Committee is the administrative organ, often concerned with the crucial decision-making in the factory. A revised version of the triple combination exists with the 'three-in-one combination' which, as King (1977, p. 367) observes, is 'best seen as a decision-making structure which allows multi-perspectives of different organizational units, vertical as well as horizontal, to be expressed through the participation of their reprsentatives'. Bettelheim (1974, p. 40) showed in a survey of Shanghai that 49 per cent of the members of Revolutionary Committees were also Party members, and that 70 per cent of Party committee members were also on Revolutionary Committees.

The third level of the Workers' Management teams is composed solely of production workers. Their concern is with ideology and general welfare conditions. During the period between the cultural revolution and 1973, when trade unions were rejected, the workers' management teams combined the union functions with their other duties.

What emerges then is an organization structure which in many ways is the antithesis of the Weberian model. Following King (1977) we can describe this structure as anti-hierarchical; anti-functional specialization; anti-expert; anti-administrative professional; and anti-administrative routine.

Part of the attack on the division of labour during the period of the Great Leap Forward was manifested in the so-called 'two participations'. This notion was reactivated after the Cultural Revolution by means of participatory management systems. One of these – the role shifting system – entails the requirement of organization leaders adopting rank-and-file roles on a regular basis. In the

Maoist jargon this involves a process of 'from the masses, to the masses'; it requires leaders to 'squat at a spot'; its aim is to prevent a 'mandarin spirit', 'commandism' and 'aristocracy arrogance'. The other system – group-based decision-making – involves the familiar techniques of worker participation in management.

Unlike the many types of workers' control and self-management we have examined in this section, the organization structure that emerged after the Cultural Revolution was 'an organization of, for, and by the masses' (King, 1977, p. 369). This is a reflection of the fact that the Paris Commune was the model upon which post-Cultural Revolution organization was based. The similarity can be seen from the perspective that

> the masses were the real masters of the Paris Commune. While the commune was in being the masses were organized on a wide scale and they discussed important state matters within their respective organizations . . . they made proposals or advanced critical opinions on social and political matters great and small. . . . This revolutionary enthusiasm and initiative was the source of the commune's strength (Cheng, 1966, p. 24; quoted by Hearn, 1978, p. 47).

But as quickly as the ideas motivating the adoption of the Paris Commune model emerged, so with the same speed they were abandoned. This points to one of the most basic problems in China: the continuing influence and counter-influence of the radicals and the revisionists; in other words, the trends and pressures in Chinese society both for centralism and democracy, for discipline and freedom. The preservation of Leninism in Maoist thought is, of course, a contributor to the dilemma. The doctrine of politics in command necessitated the provision of time for political discussion and criticism. In terms of productivity this is surplus time. At the factory level time has been made available; the question-mark hangs over the relation to the centralized Party. Hearn comments that

> the recurring process of establishing and, in turn, subjecting to massive attack a strong, centralized Party may constitute a method for making surplus time during which the rationalization of consciousness can proceed and, if necessary, catch up with the rationalization of technique . . . it is perhaps the only way by which the contradictory demands of democracy and centralism can be reconciled (Hearn, 1978, p. 50).

The period immediately after the Cultural Revolution was, then, a period designed to accommodate the two rationalities of technique and consciousness. Productive efficiency thus became a matter of

maximizing 'the ability of the working class to increase its domination of the means of the production and minimize the possiblity of
revisionist slippage back toward further ruling class domination'
(Gordon, 1976, p. 29). Productive efficiency at that time was not a
question of speed or precision.

Hearn (1978, p. 51) concludes that 'China so far has been able to
avoid the unaccountable, highly regimented organizational forms
that emerged in Russia during a comparable period of development. The creation of a non-élitist socialist bureaucracy has not
been accomplished, but it remains a real possibility'. Similarly
Whyte (1973, p. 163) has commented that 'claims that China has
found a route to modernization without bureaucratization . . . must
be treated sceptically'. And Ramsay (1977b, p. 18) has suggested
that the organizational arrangement 'whilst revealing a deep-seated
stress on worker involvement and control, also gives plentiful
indication of channels through which managerialism, autocracy and
apathy could re-emerge'.

These conclusions, scepticisms and predictions largely came
about. Although the revisionists were routed by 1975, the death of
Mao, the arrest of the 'Gang of Four' and the coming to power of
Hua Kuo-feng all combined to produce a swing back to the revisionist line. Indeed, its era of 'politics takes command' seems to
have been supplanted by an era of 'production takes command'.
This, though, is unsurprising: it is what has occurred after each
major upheaval, since in each case such as the Great Leap Forward
or the Cultural Revolution the initial revolutionary emphasis has
been accompanied by economic slump. The revisionists, the
'experts', the 'pragmatists', or whatever epithet one chooses, have
returned to power on the strength of their claim of economic stimulation. This is precisely what happened again after the confluence of
the events of the mid-1970s. And, again, this political change
resulted in organizational changes which subsequently affected the
opportunities for workers' self-management.

Ramsay (1977b) has monitored some of the changes that have
occurred in China since the rise to power of Hua. First, an increased
emphasis upon managerial authority, discipline and rules can be
noted (*People's Daily,* December 1976). This emphasis is a mixture
of revisionism and radicalism. The Party committees in the enterprise have been given a more prominent role and the Chairmen (but
not other members) of the Revolutionary Committees are now
more powerful in the sense of being able to intervene in more
matters of a day-to-day nature in the factories. the corollary of these
changes is that the opportunities for worker participation have been
reduced. Second is the fact that Lenin's statements about Taylor
and scientific management, especially the requirement for rules and

discipline, have been reproduced favourably (*Peking Review*, 14, 1977).

Third, there seems to be an increasing approval of Western technology and science. The *People's Daily* in May 1977 had this to say, 'We want to learn all that is genuinely good and useful either in the political, economic, scientific and technological fields. . . . This is a scientific approach of Marxism'. This resembles very closely the Soviet model (see Gvishiani, 1972). If Western technology is adopted one wonders at the extent to which the adoption of Western work design and organization can be avoided.

The fourth point is that material incentives are being introduced very much on the Soviet model. Again, the *People's Daily* (March 1977) said that 'bourgeois material incentives, though inherently bad, are inevitable'.

For the purposes of descriptive elegance our discussion of the workers' control literature has been divided between capitalism and socialism. For analytical elegance such a division is inappropriate. In both cases we have clearly seen that the relations of production have a profound effect upon the type and quantity of production. Workers' control and self-management movements show that to separate economic relations from other relations is problematic (see, for example, our discussion of the 'base' and 'superstructure' in this context). Ramsay (1977b, p. 2) asserts that 'relations of production are also *forces* of production'. But, as we have argued in this chapter, the state is one of the relations of production. The evidence on workers' control in both types of society displays clearly that workers' control is largely dependent upon certain political achievements (for example, through gaining state sympathy or gaining actual control of the political process and institutions). Consistent with our overall argument, control over work involves more than simply changing the structure of work relations, more than a technical rationality; it involves an accommodation with the state, a practical rationality. The very act of accommodation involves new relations between the state and the relations of production.

Yet both general examples of workers' control suggest the correctness of Abercrombie and Turner's (1978) thesis that dominant ideologies function not so much as a control over subordinate classes but as a control of the dominant class. The workers' control literature affords evidence that the subordinate classes are not incorporated into the dominant ideology. It is this which leads us to develop some distinctions between *types of control* and *types of workers,* and to relate the two in terms of Figure 13.1. Different types of control can become functionally specialized on different types of workers, as we elaborate in the following section.

530

Types of hegemonic control and types of worker

Friedman (1977) has suggested that the two strategies which we have termed *technical* and *social regulative rules* may be applied to the labour process not only in different moments of the world economy, particularly as its rhythm has been modulated by two world wars, but also selectively, to different elements in the labour process. Technical rules will tend to be applied to those workers who are more peripheral to the labour process (less strategically contingent), while social regulative rules will tend to be applied to those workers who are more central (more strategically contingent) to the labour process. This differential strategy arises as a way of handling inflexibilities generated by contradictions within each intervention into the labour process.

On the one hand, Taylorist technical rules could not be applied universally. Not everyone could be de-skilled, nor could everyone be a high-wage labourer. In both spheres differentials would have to be preserved for the strategy to work. Second, the 'affluent worker' is not necessarily a happy worker (e.g., see Nichols and Beynon, 1977). Finally, neither is he or she necessarily a very satisfactory worker in a situation which demands flexible workers with a degree of discretion. It is precisely these types of worker, those who are more strategically contingent, that capital will attempt to control through more subtle hegemonic domination: that is, though social regulative rules as a form of control.

The division of the work force can be carried further through the intervention of *extra-organizational rules.* Those skills which are not strategically contingent – generally those with low status, relatively low pay and low job entrance requirements – can be further distinguished by capital from the rest of the labour process. This has the effect of minimizing the possibility of Labour's developing a collective consciousness of itself *for* itself. In this way the contradictory possibility that 'participation' might become a collective and liberating catch-word would be minimized.

This has been achieved by Taylorizing unstrategic skills in the organization. Because of their low social definition in the labour market such unstrategic skills tend to attract the most socially disadvantaged groups in the labour force. These are those groups which are sexually and racially discriminated against: women and ethnic minorities such as blacks or recent migrants (see Chapter 11). It has frequently been observed that management will often actively encourage these divisions by over-qualifying not only managerial skills but also other strategically contingent skills; or by locating administration and research tasks only where white male native-born workers can easily get to them (see Friedman, 1977, p. 54;

Gordon, 1972, ch. 4; Edwards *et al.*, 1972, chs 8–9; Wolff, 1977; Mackie and Pattullo, 1977; and Berger and Mohr's (1975) magnificent *A Seventh Man*). There is substantial evidence, as Friedman (1977, p. 54) argues, 'from several countries concerning the more volatile unemployment levels for blacks, immigrants and women', citing Hill *et al.* (1973, pp. 52–4); Edwards *et al.* (1972, chs 8–9); and Castles and Kosack (1973, ch. 3) as evidence. These extra-organizational rules relate to the structure of the secondary labour force that we analysed in Chapter 11.

We are postulating that social regulative rules will tend to be more specifically aimed at workers structurally located in the new middle class which Carchedi (1977) identifies; those workers in contradictory supervisory positions who fulfil functions both of the collective worker *and* the global capitalist. Hypothetically, if our thesis is correct, we would expect to find that controls on the working class will tend largely to be of either technical rules or extra-organizational rules. Extra-organizational rules, of the dual labour market type, will function through the development of secondary labour markets largely at the level of relatively unskilled workers. Technical rules, as forms of control, will tend to be developed principally in relation to technological transformations such as Taylorism or automation which increase the amount of surplus (either labour or value depending on whether the organization is a non-CSA or not) that can be accumulated from skilled workers. It is this phenomenon of interventions by technical rules in the labour process which can generate the limited discretionary powers of decision-making identified by Crozier (1964), for instance, with respect to maintenance workers. These discretionary powers are historically sedimented in residual craft skills which escaped rationalization by scientific management. However, the machinery in the cigarette factory studied by Crozier (1964) might very well have been automated in the meantime, in which case, if Crozier had repeated his study more recently, he might very well have produced an analysis of the 'politics' of organizational decision-making which stressed the discretionary powers given by automated technology to computer personnel (at least before their production on the market in sufficient quantities made them more available and thus less relatively skilled resources).

The development of actual organization studies of decision-making in organizations would seem to lend support to this hypothesis. Hickson *et al.* (1978, p. 2) have observed 'an interesting history of the study of decision-making as this has related to organization theory'. They noted that 'computer and electronic data processing issues were disproportionately represented' (Hickson *et al.*, 1978, p. 3) in the literature. They also noted that there appeared to be two 'waves' of study of these. One was of wholly American studies, set off by Cyert *et al.'s* (1956) 'classic account of a long-drawn-out computer purchase' and terminated by Cyert and March's (1963) *A Behavioural Theory of the Firm*. This American wave then seemed to recede, only to be replaced in the early 1970s with a mainly European wave emanating from Britain, Canada, Germany and Scandinavia (e.g., Pettigrew, 1973; Pugh *et al.*, 1976; Witte, 1972; Lund, 1976; and March and Olsen, 1976).

The reasons for these national and geographical shifts are quite clear. They are related to the uneven development of the 'third technological revolution' (Mandel, 1975) in the world economy of the capitalist mode of production. This occurred in America during the late 1950s and early 1960s, such that, by the middle of the 1960s, a McGraw Hill Company survey revealed that 21,000 of 32,000 American manufacturing establishments employing over 100 people were using some automatic control and measurement devices and data-handling systems. In 1963 roughly one-third of the investment in machinery in the USA was on automatic or advanced technology (Mandel, 1975, p. 194). This development did not peak until later in Europe, hence the national and geographical shift in its study, related to the earlier acceleration of technological innovation in the American context, and the monopolization of this by the leading American firms such as IBM. This acceleration enabled such firms to earn what Mandel calls 'technological rents'. These are surplus profits derived from this monopolization of technical progress, that is:

> from discoveries and inventions which lower the cost price of commodities but cannot (at least in the medium-run) become generalized throughout a given branch of production and applied by all competitors, because of the structure of mono- poly capital itself: difficulties of entry, size of minimum in- vestment, control of patents, cartel arrangements, and so on (Mandel, 1975, p. 192).

This identifies the form of organization which Karpik refers to as 'technological capitalism', based on 'the rapid renewal of products created by research operations integrated within the production system' (Karpik, 1977, p. 53, italics removed). The development of technological capitalism and other forms of monopoly capitalism necessitates a further kind of intervention in organizations which we can call 'strategic rules.'.

Strategic rules are an intervention in the spheres of both produc- tion and circulation, while social regulative rules and technical rules are an intervention only in the production of commodities, and not their circulation. As such, they are a one-sided intervention in

533

commodity production with very definite implications for commodity circulation, which necessitates these further forms of intervention of the type of strategic rules.

Any organization based on a type of mass-production premised on a high concentration and centralization of the organic composition of capital necessarily has to harness its labour power to its machine power for the maximum utilizable time because of the peculiarities of a modern plant economy. The more that such a modern plant is utilized by the organization below its rated capacity, then the greater will be the unit cost of its output. Hence, in terms of the production process, economy is achieved and the greatest surplus potentially produced, when maximal production is achieved. But:

> Between the increase of output and the capacity of the markets
> no intrinsic correlation exists, since they are governed by
> economic laws of a heterogenous nature, the one related to
> socialized labour, the other by origin to individual labour, the
> one as a law of the labour process, the other as a law of property
> relations (Sohn-Rethel, 1976, p. 31).

The consequence of this is that although it is necessary in some instances to make use of social regulative and technical rules in order to maintain productivity, these interventions by themselves are sometimes neither necessary nor sufficient.

First, let us consider some occasions on which such interventions are not necessary. One class of such instances indexes a determinate absence from this picture. It can be appreciated that the previous analysis of the need for such strategies holds most true for developed market economy social formations, in which the national proletariat, on the average, will form part of an international labour aristocracy. (Obviously there will be gross wage differences within any given social formation.) In low-wage, less developed social formations – the periphery and semi-periphery of the world economy – hegemonic forms of domination will recede in importance. It is for this reason that a large number (Vernon (1973) estimated it at 187) of US, European and Japanese international firms have established themselves in these more peripheral regions. These enterprises are there precisely because of the reduced cost of the labour process, the possibility of multi-factor supply for core production (in the USA, etc.), and the frequently observed phenomenon of transfer pricing. These firms, as both Karpik (1977) and Adam (1975) have argued, tend to be large technological enterprises. In terms of their control of the labour process, what is not assured by wages which in the local context are considered to be high wages, coupled with a large reserve army of the unemployed, can frequently be assured by the policies of the domestic state. This assured quantity is the existence of a compliant work force asserting no power.

We can now consider the case of organizations primarily operative in the core states of the world economy. For certain types of these organizations, primarily monopoly capitalist organizations, control of the labour process in itself, while it is absolutely necessary, is not sufficient. For these firms such interventions have to be buttressed and supported by strategic rules which intervene in the market, as Sohn-Rethel argues:

> The discrepancy between the new economics of production and the old economics of the market needs to be taken care of by artificial means. It is this that lies at the root of private planning as an indispensable strategy of large-scale modern business. But it is a remedy which does not, of course, eradicate the underlying discrepancy but only allows its further growth. I am inclined to regard the duality of two economics as the root of monopoly capitalism from its very inception. Production that for structural rules cannot, without undue economic loss, obey the rules of the market must necessarily attempt to obtain control of the markets (Sohn-Rethel, 1976, p. 32).

The 'underlying discrepancy', as Sohn-Rethel elaborates in his book, *Intellectual and Manual Labour* (1978) is, in fact, the source of a fundamental contradiction. Considerably more automation of production than has occurred in the capitalist world could be carried out. (Ideological offensives in Australia, conducted through the August 1978 editions of *The Australian* newspaper, suggest that this is the case and that we are being ideologically prepared for an impending material reality.) The reason that such automation has not gone as far as it might does not simply lie in the cost of introducing it 'but the fact that the extension of automation beyond certain limits is bound to defeat the end of the whole process, which is to maximize profits' (Sohn-Rethel, 1978, p. 174). Without sufficient wage-labourers, commodity production cannot be increased indefinitely. Not only does there come a point where the commodification of everyday life can clearly go no further, there can also come the point when the expulsion of living labour from the labour process can go no further. Somewhere between the last labourer and the last commodity lies the last contradiction. In the meantime, as Sohn-Rethel (1978, p. 174) says, 'It is safer and easier for monopoly capital to scan the world for cheap and willing labour still available for exploitation'. And, as he goes on to say, 'to develop the full potentialities of automation will probably be a task remaining for socialism'.

535

The development of organizations in both the state and private spheres gives rise to whole strata of non-producers/exploiters/non-owners/revenue-receivers who fulfil, amongst other types of task, the functions of operating extensive controls of, and in, the organization. These agents do not necessarily have the decisive material interest of ownership (in the legal terms of possession) of the means of production which they control. This then poses the problem of how they are to be controlled? How can they be trusted to do what is 'right', only what is 'possible', and attend only to what 'exists' for capital? (Which is not to say that they always do. No hegemony is ever total.)

The definition of what exists, what is right, and what is possible is the role of the dominant ideology. We agree with Abercrombie and Turner (1978, p. 147) that 'the apparatus of transmission of the dominant ideology is not very efficient' when aimed at the subordinate class. That is why we have stressed forms of hegemony in organizations oriented at workers constructed in terms other than 'dominant ideologies'. Similarly, we agree with them that dominant ideologies are typically directed at the dominant rather than the subordinate class. However, we cannot agree with them that there is no well-marked dominant ideology in late capitalism.

We can begin by reconsidering our original model of task-continuous organizations. Here there was no divorce between ownership and control. The ideology which had been dominant in feudal times, and in early capitalism, recognized this in the stress that it put on the inheritance and accumulation of property (Abercrombie and Turner, 1978, p. 166). As ownership and control were consolidated in the material basis of individual property rights, the dominant ideology stressed these. This ensured secure channels for the maintenance and expansion of the feudal manor and family firm, giving rise to 'a superstructure of political, legal and moral beliefs which grasped at the level of ideas, this functional requirement' (Abercrombie and Turner, 1978, p. 164). This was expressed in 'a relatively stable marriage system, clear laws of inheritance, principles of legitimacy, adoption and remarriage' backed up by 'a psychology of guilt which inhibited illicit sexuality, disregard of parents' wishes for suitable mates, respect for the (economic) needs of the family' (Abercrombie and Turner, 1978, p. 164). Institutionally these supports were borne by Catholicism and systems of honour.

Although Catholicism and honour are still of importance today, they are not as dominant in as many organizations as they once were (although, for instance, unpublished research by Michael Cass, of the Department of Sociology at the University of Queensland, demonstrates that religious belief is the best predictor of success in some Australian federal government departments). Sociologists such as Westergaard and Resler (1976) have stressed the continuity of the themes of this dominant ideology of *early* capitalism in *late* capitalism. However, although this is clearly still of considerable importance, it ignores, and cannot be expected to function effectively for, the changed conditions of ownership, control, possession and expanded state employment of today. Indeed, as Abercrombie and Turner (1978, p. 162) argue, 'the ideology of owners of small capitalist firms in the private sector is frequently in opposition to the beliefs and interests of large capitalist enterprises, multi-national firms and the state industries'.

What, if any, communality of ideological reproduction in a dominant ideology can we establish for the dominant classes of contemporary capitalism who control, but do not own, means of production? In terms of our schema in Figure 13.1, what are the *reproduction rules* of late capitalism and where are they located?

Marceau and her colleagues answer this question for us. In a paper entitled 'Business and the State: Management Education and Business Elites in France and Great Britain' they argue that:

> In both countries after 1945, and with growing momentum in the 1950s and 1960s, following significant changes in industrial structure and concentration, a new form of ideology legitimating business decision-making structures and managerial practices developed. This was institutionalized in a series of schools new in Europe – such as the Henley Administrative Staff College and the Business Schools at London and Manchester (Marceau *et al.*, 1978, p. 130).

These business and management schools have become the institutional site for the reproduction of the contemporary dominant ideology of late capitalism, which stresses above all else, *rational* methods: of marketing, finance, forward planning, of design of organization structures, etc. Modelled on business schools in America (e.g., Harvard), and fused in the 'white heat of the technological revolution, these new institutions increasingly come to serve as the basis for managerial recruitment in the advanced sectors of the state and economy. Marceau *et al.* (1978) relate the growth of business/management education in the postwar period to a number of factors in addition to the decisive separation of ownership and control. These include the role of increased foreign competition, linked to loss of empire (which deprived organizations of both privileged markets and cheap raw materials), increased foreign investment in industry and commerce, increasing concentration of capital and technological reconstruction, aided and abetted by the state. In addition, there was the example of American practice.

Recruitment to these schools and centres has been of two types. Either students have been recruited at the undergraduate or post-graduate level, or they have been recruited through short-term in-service post-experience courses for middle or senior 'level managers. The in-company type of training is preferred by business because it is more controllable, in the organization's terms, than courses conducted according to the more formal and general intellectual criteria of the academies (Marceau *et al.*, 1978).

However, because of our view of ideological reproduction, developed from Gramsci (1971), we are inclined to believe that the most important aspect of the business schools, and of management education generally, is not so much their relative success as channels of élite reproduction (as Marceau *et al.* (1978) stress), but their role in reproducing ideology as well as middle-class careers. This ideology is what people do at these institutions, which is to learn the rational science and techniques of modern management, among which will be the organization theory we have criticized in this book. By providing concepts of 'the organization', for instance, which are absolutely independent of any political economy, but related only to presumed universal systems of structures of organizations, and by stressing the universal applicability of these 'rational precepts' (which on closer inspection are not always so ideologically pure as they might seem) these schools produce, on the whole, sound and reliable ruling-class functionaries who have complex rules built into them' (Perrow, 1972, p. 27). The point barely requires elaboration. It has been made any number of times before (e.g., Allen, 1975; Clegg, 1975; 1979a; Clegg and Dunkerley, 1977; Benson, 1977; Heyderbrand, 1977) and was identified particularly clearly by Mills, writing over twenty years ago, when he observed that:

> The demand of the bureaucracies has been not only for intellectual personnel to run the new technical, editorial and communication machinery, but for the creation and diffusion of new symbolic fortifications for the new and largely private power these bureaucracies represent. (Mills, 1956, p. 153).

He continues by displaying how organization ideologies are supported and justified.

> The whole growth of ideological work is based on the need for the vested interests lodged in the new power centres to be softened, whitened, blurred, misinterpreted to those who serve the interests of the bureaucracies inside and to those in its sphere outside (Mills, 1956, p. 154).

Much of the ideological work of organization theory represents such a softening, whitening, blurring and misrepresentation. In our discussion of technology and organizations in Chapter 9 we showed how technology is presented as an inevitable, apolitical and rational phenomenon – yet behind this veneer exists an over-riding ideology expressed in terms of 'rationality'. The concept of rationality employed can be equated with what is reasonable. And yet this is to miss the importance of the distinction made by Weber (1947) between formal and substantive rationality. The former refers to organizational procedures or *means* such as the practice of scientific management, whilst the latter concentrates upon the *ends* of organizational practice. By neglecting the latter in favour of the former organization theory achieves ideological work. As we elaborated, this can be seen in the way in which the concept of technology is presented in the organization literature as an example of formal rationality. The analysis of goals in organizations is also constructed in terms of formal rationality. We have attempted in Chapters 8 and 9 to present an analysis that includes discussion of substantive rationality.

The reproduction rules offered by the business schools are not free of contradictions. They do not provide a total hegemony. This never exists. Inasmuch as a great deal of the curriculum of management education requires its students to keep abreast of the social sciences, such as sociology, then this knowledge (which includes Marx as well as Mayo, Gramsci as well as Taylor) may itself be the source of contradictions and change. At its best sociology provides a demystification of the world which is essential for any informed action.

Mandel has argued that the tendencies towards the greater co-operative socialization of labour in large organizations, together with its higher qualifications as a result of developments not only in technology, but also in higher education, 'inevitably clash sharply' with hierarchical forms of organization and control. He regards this educational extension as an 'Achilles Heel of Late Capitalism'. Rather more, we might argue, it could become a Trojan Horse:

> For the more that labour becomes objectively socialized and dependent on conscious co-operation, the more that immediate shortages disappear, and the higher are the educational level and average qualification of the typical producer – all the more intolerable will be the direct organizational and technical sub-sumption of labour under capital become to the mass of wage-earners, and with it their social and economic subordination.
>
> The crisis of capitalist relations of production thus finds logical expression in a crisis of the authority of the entrepreneur and of

the structure of the enterprise (Mandel, 1975, p. 584).

With such a 'crisis of authority', prevailing mystifications may be more critically examined. That such mystifications exist has been empirically well documented by sociologists. For instance, it has been amply demonstrated at the level of the workplace by Nichols and Armstrong (1976) and Beynon (1974). Mystification is not the sole prerogative of the workplace. It also occurs at the level of the organization structure, as Burrage (1973) has shown with regard to the design of public corporations in Britain. He argues that these have been based upon a professional and intuitive model expressing a cultural preference rather than a consideration of alternative models. In this instance the rationality has been very partial indeed.

As a parallel to intensive control developments (technical, social regulative and extra-organizational rules), capitalism develops extensive control of the *selectively relevant* features of the market, through reproduction rules, which also serve as controls of senior and middle management, as constructed by managerial market analysis, simulation models, etc.

In addition to these types of rule, which we have already outlined, some organizations will attempt to develop strategies which 'co-opt' the state to their interests. We can refer to these as 'state rules'.

The state and organizations

For capitalist organizations operating on the market, the state exists as a potential source of protection (see McCullough and Shannon, 1977) from the operation of this market. Polanyi (1957) describes two central features of the market system. These are, first, that greater profit accrues to those organizations that possess larger amounts of resources. It is because of this that there is a continual pressure toward monopolization and the creation of privileged access to resources. In addition, however, the market system is dynamic and creates risks and uncertainties for any specific organization, since new areas of demand and new profit opportunities can be continually exploited, often undercutting and disadvantaging existing organization profit centres. Hence organizations continually attempt to control those contingencies which are strategic for its profit-centred activity, in order both to protect and increase their advantages. This leads organization actors

> to avoid the normal operation of the market whenever it does not maximize their profit. The attempts of these actors to use non-market devices to ensure short-run profits makes them turn to the political entities which have, in fact, power to effect the market – the nation states (Wallerstein, 1974a, p. 403).

The general functions of the state have been identified by Mandel (1975, p. 475) as:

1 Provision of those general conditions of production which cannot be assured by the private activities of the members of the dominant class.

2 Repression of any threat to the prevailing mode of production from the dominated classes or particular sections of the dominant classes, by army, police, judiciary and prison system.

3 Integration of the dominated classes, to ensure that the ruling ideology of the society remains that of the ruling class, and that consequently the exploited classes accept their own exploitation without the immediate exercise of repression against them.

Engels (1959) conceptualized the state as an ideal total capitalist operating in a sphere in which there are many competing and contradictory claims made upon its budget and policies by different competitive interests, organized as lobbies (representing particular sectional interests), employers' associations and monopolies (e.g., ITT – see Sampson, 1973). Any state tariff, tax, policy, budget devaluation, revaluation, or decision

affects competition and influences the overall social re-distribution of surplus value, to the advantage of one or other group of capitalists. All groups of capital are therefore obliged to become politically active, not just to articulate their own views to collective class interests, but also to defend their particular interests (Mandel, 1975, p. 480).

These interests tend towards securing increasing favourable state interventions, in the socialization of costs, risks and losses, in an increasing number of organizations (e.g., British Leyland and Rolls Royce in the UK). Mandel cites some direct examples of this tendency as:

the increasing use of state budgets to cover research and development costs and of state expenditure to finance or subsidize nuclear power stations, jet aircraft and large industrial projects of every sort. Indirect examples are the provision of cheap raw materials by the nationalization of the particular industries producing them, which thereby make concealed subvention to the private sector. State capital thus acts as a prop for private capital (and in particular for monopoly capital) (Mandel, 1975, p. 480).

Additionally, the state provides, through guarantees and subsidies, opportunities for the profitable investment of capital in the armaments industry, overseas aid, the environment industry,

TABLE 13.1 Examples of sectoral/fractional analysis using the British social formation

	non-capitalist state activities sector (non-CSA)	capitalist state activities sector (CSA)	monopoly sector	competitive sector	residual labour power sector
Industrial capital organizations	Industrial Reorganization commission	Nationalized steel industry	Major motor engineering, shipbuilding, etc. firms	Petty commodity producers, e.g., motor vehicle repairs	Navvies; migrant labour; female labour
Merchant or commercial capital organizations	Retail industries Training Boards	Post Office Retailing; Milk Marketing Board	Major retail stores, e.g. Debenhams, etc.	Corner shops; small services, e.g. window cleaners	Primarily female labour
Finance capital organizations	State Insurance Schemes	Dept. of Trade and Industry loans; Bank of England	Major banks; Lloyds, etc.	Pawnshops, moneylenders, etc.	Family, private loans, exchanges, redistributions; charity; petty theft
Technological capital organizations	Technical Colleges, Polytechnics, etc.	Nationalized chemical companies, e.g., ICI	Major drug companies; e.g., Boots		Migrant labour; female labour
Agricultural capital organizations	Agricultural Colleges; Agricultural support schemes, e.g., EEC Common Agricultural Policy		British Sugar Corporation	Market gardeners	Seasonal labour, drawn from migrant, female young and old workers
Extractive capital organizations	Mining Colleges	National Coal Board	Major mining firm: e.g., Rio Tinto Zinc	Petty commodity extraction, e.g., regional markets in peat, tin, etc.	Migrant labour

and infra-structural works, as Mandel (1975, p. 485) writes. Finally, the state is both a capitalist state, structurally, in capitalist societies; it is also staffed over-whelmingly by members of the capitalist class (Miliband, 1969), and it draws its planning information from the capitalist class and their organizations (Mandel, 1975, pp. 496–7). In summary, one could say that the state is not only automatically a source of vital extra-organizational hegemony, it is also the site of a constant battle between different organizations of capital and labour, for control of the resources it has available to it. This leads us to adopt a perspective on the state as a formal organization which focuses on its structure, as that of other organizations, as an object of class struggle. As Esping-Andersen and his colleagues put it:

> The capitalist class attempts to create state structures which
> channel working-class political activity in ways that do not
> threaten capitalist political dominance and objective interests.
> Working-class challenge makes the success of such attempts
> problematic. A political class struggle perspective on the state
> tries to locate the state within the dialectical relationship between
> class dominance and systemic constraints (Esping-Andersen *et
> al.*, 1976, p. 190).

Organizations, state and non-state sectors

Successful co-optation of the state by organizations can have decisive consequences, as will be argued next. It is for this reason that we seek to maintain a distinction between different types of organization: CSA; non-CSA; competitive, monopoly, etc. In doing this we are following work from the Frankfurt school on political economy.

Despite the expanded role of the state in production and repro-duction, some authors (O'Connor, 1973a; 1973b; Habermas, 1976; Offe, 1973a; 1973b; 1975a; 1975b 1976b; 1976c; Offe and Ronge, 1975) have argued that it is important to retain the analytical dis-tinction between state and civil society, or the public and private sectors. Both O'Connor and Offe have argued in their work that it is necessary to conceive of late capitalist social formations in terms of a sectoral analysis. O'Connor (1973a) divides the USA into three sectors: a monopoly sector, a competitive sector, and a state sector. Offe (1973a, 1973b) would also see a fourth sector which he identifies as consisting of 'residual labour power'. Within each of these sectors there exist diverse forms of organizational modes of rationality. A sectoral analysis enables one to begin a structural, holistic analysis of organizations, in which one can begin by deter-mining which organizations are subject to the 'rationality' of market, neo-market and non-market forces. Within each of these sectors, cross-cutting the analysis, will be different ruling 'fractions' of capital: for instance, merchant, industrial, financial and techno-logical (after Karpik, 1977; 1978). In addition, we can add extrac-tive and agricultural capital to this list. The list is not exhaustive but may be a useful aid for analysis.

Some examples of cases yielded by this cross-cutting analysis are provided in Table 13.1. Actual organizations will cross-cut and combine categories in many instances. Frankel (1978, p. 33), who provides a very useful summary of this literature, argues that with this sectoral distinction one can examine 'the important quantita-tive and qualitative scale of operations and relations of production which differentiate – whether it be agricultural, manufacturing or circulation processes'. At the same time it enables us to understand why, for instance, an industrial capitalist organization in the competitive private sector which only employs perhaps 50 workers has very different relations of a political and economic nature with the state sector from that of a monopoly sector industrial capitalist organization such as General Motors. Organizations such as the latter may be simultaneously involved directly or indirectly not only in finance, industrial and merchant capital operations and invest-ments but, since British Leyland has been taken over by the state, the CSA sector. In addition it draws our attention to the distinctive role of the state non-CSA organizations, which although hier-archically controlled by similar rules to those of CSA state and the other sectors, functions in a different mode of rationality.

We can briefly summarize the sectoral distinctions. This summary is not a replacement for empirical research but a necessary preparation for analysis of actual modes of rationality.

Non-CSA sector: Depending on constitutional structure, and level of historical development, this may be located at any of central, federal, regional, or local units of organization. Workers are not governed directly by market conditions, but indirectly by dependence on revenue from public funds (raised by taxation from surplus value) derived from private capital and wage-earners. Labour-intensive, largely drawn from secondary labour markets, hence low wage levels predominate in unskilled labour. Weak unions.

CSA-sector: Virtually indistinguishable from monopoly sector except greater state control over wages. Production dictates vary from political/administrative decrees to neo-market forces.

Monopoly sector: Characterized by highly organized sales

544

markets, capital intensive production, national and international operations, relatively high wage-levels, passed on in the form of price increases. Price makers not takers. Strong unions.

Competitive sector: Not price makers but price takers, dependent to varying extents upon capitalist accumulation in the CSA and monopoly sectors. Local or regional organizations, largely because of technical and administrative blocs imposed by CSA and monopoly sector and subjection to the 'laws of the market'. Lower wages paid, usually because of low levels of union organization faced with many small capitals.

Residual labour power sector: Most removed from exchange relation, most dependent on 'market forces'. Comprises low level of union organization amongst pensioners, migrants, students, female domestic labourers out of wage employment, the unemployed, prisoners, mental patients, drafted soldiers, welfare 'clients', etc. Maintained by state allocations of finances, private pensions, super-annuation, charity and petty theft. Source of cheap labour in expansionary periods, easily dispensable in recession. Secondary labour market.

The significance of these distinctions lies in the political, ideological and economic divisions between CSA, non-CSA, monopoly, competitive and residual sectors, which aid our understanding of the differing mode of both worker rationality (Hyman, 1975; 1978) and organization rationality.

Let us first consider modes of worker rationality. The degree of class organization will decrease from the CSA sector and monopoly sector, through the non-CSA, competitive to residual labour power sector. The exception to this in the non-CSA sector is obviously the police and military – many capitalist states have prevented workers in the repressive state apparatuses from unionizing. Workers' control strategies would seem to have been largely confined to 'failed' organizations in the competitive sector. Thus, they have tended to occur in the sector where their survival is most precarious.

Different worker strategies will have a more or less specific effectivity depending on the sector in which they are exercised. Hyman (1978, p. 334) has developed an analysis of modes of trade union rationality which suggests that strikes normally serve three separate functions: 'they are a means of withdrawal from the work situation; a display of aggression; and a calculative attempt to obtain alterations in the work situation or the employment relationship'. They will vary in the relative degree of intensity of each of these on different strike occasions and at different moments in the

545

career of any specific strike. When we consider a strike in these terms and locate it in terms of the categories delineated by Table 13.1, then we shall be able to assess the degree of rationality of the strategies followed (which collectively comprise the workers' mode of rationality) in terms of the mode of rationality dominant in each category of the analysis. For instance, we may expect to see considerably greater use made in the future in the monopoly sector by unions of challenges to corporate rationality and profits through 'social audits' (see Fenlon, 1978). Similarly, such strategies are likely to be counter-challenged by schemes by monopoly capital for not only 'profit-sharing' but 'loss-sharing' as well. It is unlikely that this strategy could become very widespread or effective in either the competitive or residual sector. Neither could it work in the state sector which is governed by an allocation economy, at least in the non-CSA organizations.

The organization will be the site of contradictory rationality. We could reconsider Gouldner's (1965) analysis of the gypsum plant in terms of the contradiction between competing worker and organization modes of rationality, as Hyman suggests:

> At one level, workers may object to the speeding-up of their jobs. At another level, managers may argue that their company will go bankrupt if productivity is not increased: they may accept that workers' expectations are indeed frustrated, yet insist that these expectations are in the situation not realizable and hence not rational. This was the situation in the plant described by Gouldner: management felt obliged to tighten discipline because of acute market pressures and in order to achieve maximum output from expensive new machinery; the firm could not survive while maintaining traditional managerial leniency. At yet another level, however, it might be argued that an economic system in which competitive pressures compel an intolerable deterioration in work conditions is itself a 'remediable' source of deprivation. It may be suggested that to the extent that workers striking against speed-up have pursued these different levels of analysis of their situation, so their action is based on a higher or lower level of rationality (Hyman, 1978, p. 335).

Both the organization, embodied in its management, and the workers were pursuing what were in their own terms quite coherent modes of rationality. However, when these are taken together in unity they represent a fundamental and antagonistic contradiction of principles of action, rules of functioning and modes of rationality. Overall, there is only a partial rationality characterized by an opposing balance of forces. The outcome – the organization structure – is always a comprise, always a partial, never a total, rationality; always a result of practical, never wholly technical reason.

This makes our analysis of reproduction rules clearer. Their function is to disguise and mystify the organization as practical, partial, political reason, by presenting it as if it were the outcome of a total, technical reason: the 'logic' of industrialization, the causal outcome of 'size' or 'technology', etc. Clearly these variables matter. But not totally or wholly. Nor are they 'independent' variables. They are tactics and resources in political struggle open and available to controllers of the means of production and reproduction. Their value as such depends solely on the strength of opposing forces: both ideological, political and economic. This can only be assessed in concrete situations, not conjecturally.

Additionally, as Hyman suggests, analysis in terms of modes of rationality is particularly relevant in aiding our understanding of conflicts between different groups of workers such as demarcation disputes:

> Given the insecurity of employment with which ordinary workers are faced, it is perfectly natural for them to attempt to establish some form of property rights in their jobs by drawing a demarcation line around it (Hyman, 1978, p. 336).

However, as he goes on to add, this limited mode of rationality is unlikely to be successful in the long run. Divisions among workers which are emphasized in this way can be easily used by employers to exploit workers further. Indeed, in the long run, the workers' mode of rationality always has to be defined in terms of collectivism rather than division, because it is their collective position as defined by their employment status 'which condemns them to permanent insecurity' (Hyman, 1978, p. 336). On the other hand, in the short run, it is the divisions which give individual workers low-level discretionary powers in the organizations, as we outlined in Chapter 12. On those workers who benefit from these divisions, in particular, will fall the competing pressures of contradictory modes of rationality.

Not only can we consider the balance of power within any of the specific categories such as are suggested in Table 13.1. We can also consider the overall balance of forces between the five sectors in particular. For instance, if the state sector grows disproportionately to the monopoly and competitive sectors, particularly the non-CSA, or the residual labour power sector (with its drag on aggregate effective demand and drain on the re-allocative priorities of the welfare state in terms of increased clients, or on the warfare state in terms of increased military), this threatens the ability of the state to reproduce its output functions of ideology and welfare benefits yet still maintain a given, legitimated level of taxation-inputs. In such a situation of increased output, either a decline in quality of outputs measured in cost terms, or a decrease in the cost of providing the outputs (that is, the transformation process) must occur if the input factor of taxation is not to increase.

Either a decrease in output (i.e., welfare benefits) or an increase in inputs (taxes) has the potential to lead to legitimation crises. On the one hand, the residual labour power sector may cease to accede to a situation in which their actual (or real, through state-induced inflation: see Gamble and Walton, 1976) income in benefits declines. On the other hand, the middle-stratum in the class structure and the organizations, particularly in the competitive sector, may cease to accede to continuing, accelerating taxation, as witness the growing orchestration of the 'tax-revolt' from California's 1978 'proposition thirteen' to media campaigns in Australia (*The Australian,* July 1978). Either way the capitalist state faces potential crisis: either a fiscal crisis or a legitimation crisis. And if it tries to resolve it by cutting its own expenditures, particularly in the non-CSA, then it can only serve to exacerbate the underlying contradictions. This is because the non-CSA, although a drain on revenue because of its labour-intensity, provides considerable employment. Cut that through cuts in public expenditure and one cuts aggregate effective demand, and creates often highly educated and unemployable workers whose skills are not readily transferable, and so have to enter employment at a much lower status-level than would otherwise have been the case. Teachers in particular have suffered these cuts in Britain (over-determined in part by demographic changes). An unemployed, unemployable or under-employed intelligentsia is the precondition for a radicalized, alienated intelligentsia like that which produced historical figures such as Marx (Therborn, 1976).

Within sectors, returning to this level of analysis, there can also arise potential contradictions. It has been argued by Habermas (1976) that the monopoly sector in the post-war expansionary period immunized itself from the possibility of widespread conflict with a revolutionary potential by monetizing class relationships. It did this through granting wage rises to unions on the one hand, while on the other hand simultaneously raising prices. The consequences of this have been outlined by Habermas (1976, p. 36). One consequence has been increasingly disparate wage increases where the monopoly sector has led the way, with a consequent sharpening of wage disputes in the non-CSA as workers in this sector found their wages declining against the average. Where they lacked a strong union organization they were unable to counter this decline effectively.

In Britain this has led to the development of stronger public-sector unions such as NUPE (National Union of Public Employees), who have been prepared to use the withdrawal of their labour as a bargaining weapon. In January/February 1979 this caused an extremely effective widespread dislocation of public services such as sanitation, refuse-disposal, hospital catering and laundry services, schools, etc. Workers in these sectors had become particularly low-paid because their wages had been held back not only be wages and incomes policies but also by cuts in public expenditure. These cuts were the implementation of monetarist economic policies which bodies such as the IMF, with the support of the Treasury, had advocated as remedies against inflation. These policies produced a sharp decline in real earnings for workers in the UK. This has been further exacerbated by a permanent inflation channelled through monopoly-sector price rises and wage demands chasing each other in a spiral. The consequence has been the temporary redistribution of income to the disadvantage of workers in the non-monopoly sector, particularly in the non-CSA and residual labour power sectors. A further consequence of this inflation has been an escalation in commodity costs, which in turn produces a permanent crisis in government finances, together with an increasing public poverty due to cut-backs in expenditure on public education, health, housing and transport.

Public-sector decline occurs in the context of decline in specific sectoral and regional areas of economic development, notably the decline of certain regions of older industrial production or of exhausted extractive or agricultural capital. Regional and industry support schemes have provided increasingly inadequate adjustments by the state to these growing disproportionalities (see Holland, 1976). The decline of these sectors, particularly export-oriented industries, extractive and agricultural production, has effects on the balance of payments and thus the overall fiscal crisis. The crisis seemingly becomes resolvable only through either more of the same policies, such as further cuts in expenditure, tougher wage policies, or further loans from the IMF or World Bank. The combination of these have thus far only served to exacerbate the underlying crisis, as Gamble and Walton (1976) have argued.

These crises at the level of the overall system of the nation state, when conceptualized within the context of not only organizations as political structures, but states themselves as such potential structures within the world system, can lead us to understand how organizations may attempt to maintain *social integration* (through the types of intervention rules we have discussed so far), but still be victims of *system contradictions* outside of their control. In such circumstances they seek to co-opt the only other powerful political structure available. This structure is that of the state.

549

System contradiction

To borrow a distinction first made by Lockwood (1964) and more recently re-stated by Habermas (1976), no necessary coherence exists between social and system integration. In the sphere of the production of commodities, social integration in the form of technical, social regulative, reproductive and extra-organizational rules may assure that no overt crises or conflicts occur, despite the contradictions of private appropriation of socialized production. But this sphere of social integration, while it occurs in production, and thus at the basis of the capitalist system, is the sphere in which crisis manifests itself. Crisis becomes manifest through phenomena such as over-production, unemployment, short-time, wage cuts, etc. This crisis is generated by contradictions which define the necessary, but not sufficient, objective conditions which precipitate crisis, and which are located in the world-economy system of the market. While intensive control is an attempt to maintain social integration, this social integration is itself structurally related to the degree of system integration, with system, rather than social integration, being determinant of the relation (Parkin, 1976, also makes use of this distinction). Hence, organizations having the structural facility to be able to do so, attempt to intervene in the processes of system integration through extensive control.

The argument is this. The state in capitalist society must try to fulfil two basic but contradictory functions. These are 'accumulation' and 'legitimization'. On the one hand, the state must try to maintain or create the conditions in which profitable accumulation is possible, but on the other, the state, just like the individual organization, must try to maintain hegemonic domination. Thus, it has to maintain 'legitimacy' through retaining the loyalty, apathy or acquiescence of economically exploited and socially oppressed classes, while at the same time it aids their further exploitation. The state cannot afford to neglect the profitable accumulation of certain key organizations: to do so is to risk drying up the source of its own power, the surplus production capacity of the economic system, the taxes drawn from this surplus and the labour that produces it.

We can discuss the process at both the system and organization level. At the system level:

> Although the state has socialized more and more capital costs, the social surplus (including profits) continues to be appropriated privately. Private ownership and control of the means of production permits private businessmen to appropriate a large part of the social surplus themselves. The socialization of costs and the

private appropriation of profits creates a fiscal crisis or 'structural gap' between state expenditures and state revenues. In other words, there is a tendency for state expenditures to increase more rapidly than the means of financing these expenditures (O'Connor, 1973b, p. 82).

This has particular implications at the organizational level within those sectors of the world economy which are in decline, such as regions like the United Kingdom. Within the context of the national economy there may be a number of highly strategic and key enterprises. These organizations will be strategic because of their centrality to the processes of accumulation and legitimation. Let an example suffice to illustrate the issue. British Leyland is central to both the accumulation and legitimization functions of the British state. It was until recently a major source of surplus in the economy, while it still remains a major employer. Precisely because of its centrality to the surplus production capacity of the economy *and* its central legitimation function as a major employer, and because it is the only national motor company in the country, the state has been caught in the contradictory position of having to subsidize the ailing enterprise on a major and long-term scale. However, although the organization is structurally central (one might even say strategically contingent) to the British economy, it is a peripheral and weak enterprise on the world economy. Hence the state's intervention, through strategic rules, is absolutely necessary for the domestic economy, in terms of both accumulation and legitimation, but can hardly affect the structurally weak position of the enterprise on the world economy because of the development of regional dislocations, historically, on a world (rather than local) scale. The generalization of demands for state intervention in strategic rules, in terms of increasing state subsidies of social capital (accumulation) costs and social expense (legitimation) costs, by individual organizations, while it may lead to stabilization of its individual structure, has the potentiality for profound dislocation at the national state structure level, with the likelihood of increasing 'structural gaps' in revenues and expenses. Again, at this level, hegemonic domination becomes imperative in persuading labour as a class to accept the social costs of the re-structuring of capital – hence the centrality of the social contract in recent British politics.

The 'social contract' has been seen by some observers (e.g., Winkler, 1977) as a version of corporatism (which we have discussed in Chapter 10 in the context of a discussion of organizations and their environments). Corporatism has been seen in terms of the state extending its effective control over business policy, profits,

prices, investments, wages, salaries, welfare: in short, as Westergaard (1977, p. 171) says, 'control . . . over the key variables
hitherto subject to determination by business policy and market
forces'. The social contract, in this context, represents an attempt to
achieve national economic order and unity in the pursuit of the
goals of a counter-inflationary and capital reconstruction policy,
through establishing institutions which are

> singular, non-competitive, hierarchically ordered, sectorally
> compartmentalized, interest associations exercising representa-
> tional monopolies and accepting (*de jure* or *de facto*) govern-
> mentally imposed or negotiated limitations on the type of leaders
> they elect and on the scope and intensity of demands they
> routinely make upon the state (Schmitter, 1974, pp. 99–100).

A number of writers, such as Warren, have suggested that the
political incorporation of the working class is a necessary political
requirement for the reconstructing of capital accumulation at new
levels of profitability in order to minimize the share of value in the
form of wages going to workers. This was much easier for social
democratic parties to achieve than conservative parties, he argues
(Warren, 1972, p. 13), because of their greater legitimacy to trade
unions as working-class parties. Once in office, and with corporatist
policy in process, he notes that social democratic parties have
increasingly become efficient, technocratic managers of the
capitalist state, rather than a socialist alternative. Nothing that has
occurred anywhere in Western Europe or Australia since 1972
would seem to disprove this thesis.

Esping-Andersen *et al* (1976, p. 197) have argued that corporatism 'is an internally contradictory mode of incorporating the
working class'. It depends upon the incorporated union leaders
retaining legitimacy in both their organization role as trade union
leaders and in their role as state policy makers. To the extent that
popular pressures from union members are in conflict with the
requirements of state policies (e.g., wage demands over and above
government-imposed percentage norms) these union leaders will be
subject to a role conflict. Which of two mutually contradictory set of
expectations will they legitimate?

> Here lies the contradictory quality of corporatism: If the leader-
> ship of the incorporated working-class organizations is suf-
> ficiently isolated from the working class so that state planning is
> insulated from popular pressures, then that leadership will tend
> to gradually lose legitimacy and thus cease to function as a means
> for integrating the working class. If, on the other hand, the
> leadership maintains close ties to the working class and remains a

legitimate instrument of real working-class organizations, then corporatist planning will be hampered by the constant pressure for accommodation with mass demands (Esping-Andersen *et al.*, 1976, p. 197).

If the leadership loses legitimacy then the incorporation will cease to function as effectively. This is because the union movement will not be contained by the actions of the discredited leadership. It is unlikely that new leadership would follow the same illegitimate policies. If the leadership retains legitimacy then it raises the spectre of class struggle to a 'presence' in the actual administration of the state: the supposedly neutral, liberal instrument. This spectre materialized in Britain in early 1979.

The organizational level may yet aid in the precipitation of systemic contradictions which could transform the structure of organizations as we take them for granted at the present.

Figure 13.2 re-presents our initial model together with the dynamic aspect of 'articulation' which we have discussed. Some examples of these and the state's cohesive and feedback function are depicted.

In summary, we may say that the organization will construct itself as the type of organization that it can analytically be conceived to be, by its selectivity concerning those aspects of its position in the world economy that it will attempt to control, or secure control of. As its most selective it will attempt to generalize both its intensive and extensive control, while at least selective it would be a victim of forces beyond its control – the quaint model of perfectly competitive enterprise. At its most developed we shall be dealing with the organization structures of metropolitan monopoly capitalism and metropolitan states. The possibilities of selectivity are clearly features of any structure's position and its historical development within the world economy (see Mandel, 1975, ch. 2).

We can conclude our study of organizations by reconsidering the concept with which we began reflection on organizations. This is the concept of rational bureaucracy developed by Max Weber (1968) in an analysis of the state. What is the use of this concept for analysis of the state in late capitalism?

It still retains some effectivity in the understanding of the purely *technical rationality* of the state: the allocation of resources in routinized, rule-bounded ways; interpreting regulations, etc. However, the thrust of our contribution has been to stress that this purely technical rationality is, and can only ever be, a *partial rationality*.

This is particularly the case in the non-CSA sector. Goods and services such as housing, education, health care or transport are

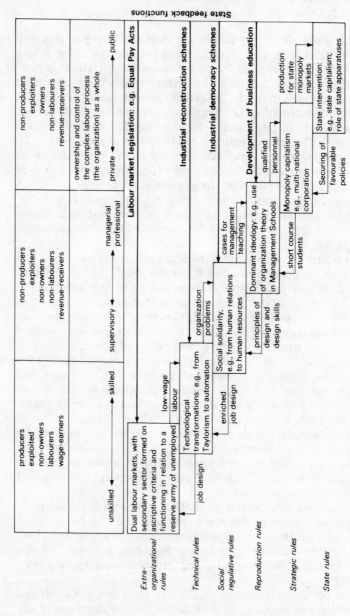

Figure 13.2 *Examples of the main types of sedimented selection rules available to organizations, their structural location and articulation*

qualitative goods which have not proved reducible to the technical rationality of impartial rules and techniques. Their allocation, provision, quality, etc. do not depend on a purely formal rational bureaucracy neutrally interpreting rules and regulations. This is because the quality, allocation, provision, etc. of these use-values is the result, not of reason, but of might. Rather than acting as purposefully rational organizations, state organizations, particularly in the non-CSA sector, are characterized by a reactive avoidance of responsible rational planning in the face of competing and contradictory pressure and conflicts.

In the face of crisis, the contradictory role of both successfully maintaining accumulation and simultaneously retaining legitimacy, without producing a crisis of practical reason, appears almost impossible. As we enter into the last years of this century it will be surprising if this possibility can be achieved without a massive shift in the balance of overall, systemic hegemonic domination, either to a genuine legitimacy of rule or an intolerable burden of repression. We hope for the former, but fear for the latter.

Notes

2 Max Weber, Karl Marx and rationality in organizations

1 Mommsen (1974) notes Weber speaking of himself as 'we bourgeoisie'; Lewis (1975, p. 52) says of Weber's sociology that 'it comprises the outlook, the prejudices, the values, of a typical member of the upper class of the German business community'.

2 But as both Anthony (1977) and Gutman (1977) argue, it is not a total hegemony. For instance, it could infuse radical labour movements in nineteenth-century America (Gutman, 1977) as much as it had fired Winstanley's Diggers in seventeenth-century England. As Anthony (1977), p. 49) suggests:

> The ideology of work could develop in two directions. The first, the 'respectable' direction, is the development taken by the Protestant ethic as it is delineated by Max Weber. This stresses work in relation to business, enterprise, and political feedom. The second, the radical direction, sets the line of development which ends in socialism and communism. The Levellers exemplify the first direction, Winstanley's Diggers the second.

3 The emergence of an organization theory

1 The development of scientific management was uneven. In the U.S.A. it accelerated during the First World War as a way of securing extra production. However, it had been developing there since the 1880s. Both Fiat of Italy and Renault of France had introduced it before the war. Littler (1978) argues that it did not develop in Britain until the inter-war period, while Brown (1977, chapters VII and VIII) would seem to locate it earlier. Littler's (1978) definition of scientific management is 'stricter' which may explain the seeming discrepancy.

2 We have not, in this text, considered the immediate causes of Taylorism's decline in *academic* (as opposed to 'practical') esteem. As Rose (1975, Part II) states at length this was due, in Britain at least, to the development of industrial psychology as an autonomous and far

more sophisticated practice than Taylorism. The responsibility for this rested largely with the pioneering work of C. S. Myers (1921) and the institution of the National Institute of Industrial Psychology and The Industrial Fatigue Research Board (1918), which in 1929 became The Industrial Health Research Board. A detailed consideration of this history is outside the scope of this sociological contribution to organization theory.

3 Five operatives, and one layout operator.

4 Their unco-operativeness consisted chiefly of 'low output and behaviour' (see Carey, 1976, p. 235).

5 We do not. Their importance, as ideology, should not be neglected however. Carey (1976, p. 233) refers to this.

6 Organizations as empirically contingent structures

1 The Aston project's 'Scaling and Multivariate Analyses in the Study of Organizational Variables' (Levy and Pugh, 1969), is the basis of Chapter 8 of Pugh and Hickson (1976), and may be studied by those who wish to pursue the methodological issues further. One interesting point is that although the paper on 'Dimensions of Organization Structure' (see Chapter 4 of Pugh and Hickson, 1976) mentions using the Brogden-Clemens coefficient for scaling, the Levy and Pugh (1969) article only mentions using Guttman's (1950) scaling methods.

2 What follows is deliberately modelled on Willer and Willer (1973, pp. 20ff.).

7 Organizations as structures of action

1 *Not* Schultz (as in Schultz and Cresara, 1951) as Argyris (1972, p. 62) seems to think. As Silverman has nowhere in any of his work ever referenced Schultz (or Cresara), one can only speculate as to the thoroughness of Argyris' reading of Silverman. Certainly if Argyris had been familiar with the work of *Schutz* (or had troubled to follow up Silverman's references to him) he would surely not have made the ill-informed remarks about 'typical actors' and 'typical motives' which he does. Argyris (1972, pp. 62–3) seems to regard these as empirically locatable phenomena rather than theoretical constructions! Argyris' reading of Silverman on the uninvoked Schultz is the most 'bizarre' account we have discovered in our research for this book.

2 It should be pointed out to the reader that we are not following either Gouldner (1965) or Silverman's (1970) re-analysis exactly here. Our thrust is to illuminate the concern with rules that can be drawn out of both their interpretations. This will lead us to make somewhat more of the power relationships involved than Silverman (1970) did. It will also, because of the stress on rules in the context of power, allow us to make some critical comments on the continuity of Silverman's (1970) action perspective and his later, more explicitly ethno-methodological stress (e.g., Silverman and Jones, 1976).

3 Term taken from Phillipson and Roche (1971), as used in Taylor *et al.* (1973).

4 Ibid.

5 This was reprinted in the Open University textbook *People and Organizations* (Salaman and Thompson, 1973). The volume, *People and Organizations,* and the associated Open University course of the same title, partly through the influence of Silverman (who was a member of the course team), did much to develop a more sociologically pheno-menological action perspective on organizations. At the same time, through the influence of David Hickson, Charles McMillan and Arthur McCullough, who were then colleagues at the University of Bradford, and Charles Perrow, a selection of more conventional structure-oriented papers was also included. These two emphases were not integrated in either the course or the text, which was an adequate reflection of the field of organizational analysis at that time. It is partly through this Open University course, for which *The Theory of Organizations* was a set text, that Silverman's (1970) 'action framework' has been influential in teaching, if not in research.

6 A part of the Open University *People and Organizations* course is concerned with a similar issue to that of David Silverman and uses a similar methodology. Through the use of filmed selection interviews for British Army officers, the Ford Motor Company (UK) and the BBC, the course team is able to demonstrate the way in which various aspects of selection systems (e.g., their design, interpretation and applications) are closely bound with and even derive from the socio-cultural attributes of those doing the selecting. Thus, in the British Army interviews the qualities of an individual applicant that demonstrate his identity with discipline, tradition and military values are valued, coupled with the personal qualities of leadership, ease of adaptation to a stratified organizational life, and the like. With Ford, the selectors stress the need for qualities in the applicants that demonstrate commitment to organizational values and culture. Of course, the applicants are aware of this situation and present themselves accordingly. We discuss the British Army selection interviews reported by Salaman and Thompson (1978) in Chapter 11.

8 Goals in organizations

1 What constitutes a 'possible opportunity' is complex. Not all opportunities are taken. Whether or not they are depends on the 'state of play' in the organization, the currently prevailing interpretations of the rules, etc. Clegg (1975) goes into this in detail.

11 People in organizations

1 This situation is not unique to Britain. For example, according to figures presented by the Australian Bureau of Statistics, only 2.1 per cent of all employed women in Australia in November 1977 were in the adminis-

trative, executive and managerial category, as compared with 8.1 per cent of all men employed.

2 Not only was the reorganization largely on a rationalized and de-skilled basis. 'All protective legislation was put aside, and women were exposed to dangerous and heavy trades, with disastrous effects on health' (Rowbotham, 1975, p. 111). One account of these dangers is contained in Rosina Whyatt's autobiography of a munitions-factory worker (Burnett, 1974, pp. 125–32).

3 A considerable debate has ensued in recent works on women's domestic labour, concerning whether or not women's domestic labour is productive of the value of labour power (Secombe 1974; 1975; Coulson *et al.*, 1975; Gardiner, 1975; 1977; Himmelweit and Mohun, 1977; Adamson *et al.*, 1976). The debate is confused and confusing. The balance of it at the present time would appear to be that domestic labour does not create value because it is not related to the market. It produces use-values, not exchange values.

4 Giddens (1974) has identified three primary dimensions involved in the study of élites: their recruitment, structure and power. We deal with their recruitment in this chapter, while we deal with their power in the following chapter. In the final chapter we shall argue that the distinct élites in organizations are increasingly achieving a high degree of structural integration, irrespective of their degree of social integration, through the hegemonic functioning of organization theory as a moral discourse of 'reproduction rules': one which grants its initiates common ideas and a common moral ethos conducive to overall solidarity. (The idea of a moral discourse is suggested by Giddens' (1974, p. 5) notion of 'moral integration'.)

5 That this 'varies not with different societies but with different modes of production' is argued by Therborn (1978), who demonstrates considerable bourgeois similarity between the ruling class of all the major capitalist societies, compared to, for instance, the far greater proletarian homogeneity of the USSR. To the extent that the research we have cited (and the class structure of organizations requires considerably more research) displays commonalities across organization élites in terms of a common class background, then we can argue that the ruling élite of organizations is predominantly restricted to persons from a ruling background.

13   The political economy of organizations

1 The direct appropriation of labour.

2 In this connection, it is worth noting Friedman's (1977) observation of the usual tendency for Marxist analyses to distinguish between 'spontaneist' struggles within the labour process – what Lenin (1956) calls 'trade union consciousness' – and the more strategic 'socialist consciousness' arising from conjunctural analysis of 'the sphere of the relations between *all* the various classes and strata and the state and government' (Lenin, 1956, p. 98). As Friedman (1977) also goes on to note, even analyses such as that of Braverman (1974) have missed the

element of resistance within the labour movement to the current organization of the labour process. In contrast to this 'fatalist' view (common to Lenin, as well, of course, in his equation of Marxism and Taylorism) he cites the work of recent labour historians in America (Montgomery, 1974; Stone, 1974) and in Britain (Hinton, 1973, ch. 2).

Bibliography

ABEGGLIN, J. C. (1958), *The Japanese Factory*, Chicago, Free Press.

ABELL, P. (1975), *Organizations as Bargaining and Influence Systems*, London, Heinemann.

ABERCROMBIE, N. and TURNER, B. S. (1978), 'The Dominant Ideology Thesis', *BJS*, 29, pp. 149–70.

ACTON SOCIETY TRUST (1953, 1957), *Size and Morale, I and II*, London, Acton Society.

ADAM, G. (1975), 'Multinational Corporations and Worldwide Sourcing', in H. Radice (ed.), *International Firms and Modern Imperialism*, Harmondsworth, Penguin, pp. 89–104.

ADAMSON, O., BROWN, C., HARRISON, J. and PRICE, J. (1976), 'Women's Oppression under Capitalism', *Revolutionary Communist*, 5, pp. 2–48.

ADIZES, I. (1971), *Industrial Democracy: Yugoslav Style*, New York, Free Press.

ADLER, F. (1977), 'Factory Councils, Gramsci and the Industrialists', *Telos*, 31, pp. 67–90.

ALBROW, M. C. (1968), 'The Study of Organizations – objectivity or bias?' in J. Gould (ed.) *Penguin Social Sciences Survey*, Harmondsworth, Penguin, pp. 146–67.

ALBROW, M. C. (1970), *Bureaucracy*, London, Pall Mall.

ALDRICH, H. E. (1972a), 'Technology and Organizational Structure: a re-examination of the findings of the Aston Group', *ASQ*, 17, pp. 26–42.

ALDRICH, H. E. (1972b), 'Reply to Hilton: seduced and abandoned', *ASQ*, 17, pp. 55–7.

ALDRICH, H. E. (1974), 'The Environment as a Network of Organizations: theoretical and methodological implications', paper presented at ISA, Toronto, Canada.

ALDRICH, H. E. (1975), 'An Organization–Environment Perspective on Co-operation and Conflict in the Manpower Training System', in A. R. Negandhi (ed.), *Inter-Organization Theory*, Kent, Ohio, Kent State University Press

ALDRICH, H. E. and MINDLIN, S. (1978), 'Uncertainty and Dependence: two perspectives on environment', in L. Karpik (ed.), *Organization and*

561

Environment, London, Sage, pp. 149–70.

ALDRICH, H. E. and PFEFFER, J. (1976), 'Environments of Organizations', in A. Inkeles, J. Coleman and N. Smelser (eds), *Annual Review of Sociology,* 2, 1976, Palo Alto, Calif., Annual Reviews Inc., pp. 79–105.

ALFORD, R. R. (1975), *Health Care Politics: Ideological and Interest Group Barriers to Reform,* University of Chicago Press.

ALLEN, V. L. (1975), *Social Analysis,* London, Longman.

ALLEN, V. L. (1977), 'The Differentiation of the Working Class', in A. Hunt (ed.), *Class and Class Structure,* London, Lawrence & Wishart, pp. 61–80.

ALLPORT, G. and ODBERT, H. S. (1936), 'Trait Names: a psycholexical study', *Psychological Monograph,* 47, pp. 1–171.

ALTHUSSER, L. (1969), *For Marx,* London, Allen Lane, The Penguin Press.

ALTHUSSER, L. (1971), *Lenin and Philosophy and other Essays,* London, New Left Books.

ALTHUSSER, L. and BALIBAR, E. (1970), *Reading Capital,* London, New Left Books.

AMIN, S. (1974), *Accumulation on a World Scale,* 2 vols, New York, Monthly Review Press.

ANASTASI, A. (1964), *Fields of Applied Psychology,* New York, McGraw-Hill.

ANDERSON, P. (1965) 'Origins of the Present Crisis', in P. Anderson and R. pp. 26–54.

ANDERSON, P. (1965) 'Origins of the present crisis', in P. Anderson and R. Blackburn (eds), *Towards Socialism,* London, Fontana.

ANDERSON, P. (1974), *Passages from Antiquity to Feudalism,* London, New Left Books.

ANDERSON, P. (1977), 'The Antinomies of Antonio Gramsci', *New Left Review,* 100, pp. 5–80.

ANDERSON, T. and WARKOV, S. (1961), 'Organizational Size and Functional Complexity', *ASR,* 26, pp. 23–8.

ANDORS, S. (1971), 'Revolution and Modernization: man and machine in industrializing society, the Chinese case', in E. Friedland and M. Selden (eds), *America's Asia,* New York, Pantheon, pp. 393–444.

ANTHONY, P. D. (1977) *The Ideology of Work,* London, Tavistock.

ARGYRIS, C. (1957), *Personality and Organization: The Conflict between System and the Individual,* New York, Harper & Row.

ARGYRIS, C. (1960), *Understanding Organizational Behaviour,* London, Tavistock.

ARGYRIS, C. (1962), *Interpersonal Competence and Organizational Effectiveness,* London, Tavistock.

ARGYRIS, C. (1964), *Integrating the Individual and the Organization,* New York, Wiley.

ARGYRIS, C. (1972), *The Applicability of Organizational Sociology,* Cambridge University Press.

ARON, R. (1965), *Current Trends in Sociological Thought,* Harmondsworth, Penguin.

ASCH, S. E. (1952), *Social Psychology,* Englewood Cliffs, N.J., Prentice-Hall.

ASHTON, T. S. (1925), 'The Records of a Pin Manufactory – 1814–21', *Economica,* November, pp. 281–92.

BACHRACH, P. and BARATZ, M. S. (1962), 'Two Faces of Power', *Am. Pol. Sci. Rev.*, 56, pp. 947–52.

BACHRACH, P. and BARATZ, M. S. (1971a), 'Two Faces of Power', in F. G. Castles, D. J. Murray and D. C. Potter (eds), *Decisions, Organizations and Society,* Harmondsworth, Penguin.

BACHRACH, P. and BARATZ, M. S. (1971b), *Power and Poverty,* Oxford University Press.

BALDAMUS, W. (1961), *Efficiency and Effort,* London, Tavistock.

BALES, R. F. (1950), *Interaction Process Analysis,* Cambridge, Mass., Harvard University Press.

BANAJI, J. (1977), 'Modes of Production in a Materialist Conception of History', *Capital and Class,* 3, pp. 1–44.

BARAN, P. A. and SWEEZY, P. M. (1966), *Monopoly Capital,* New York, Monthly Review Press.

BARAN, P. A. and SWEEZY, P. M. (1968), *Monopoly Capital,* Harmondsworth, Penguin.

BARNARD, C. I. (1938), *The Functions of the Executive,* Cambridge, Mass., Harvard University Press.

BARNES, R. M. and MUNDEL, M. E. (1938), 'Studies of Hand Motions and Rhythm Appearing in Factory Work', *The University of Iowa Studies in Engineering,* 12, Ames, Ia.

BARRATT-BROWN, M. (1968), 'Who Controls the Economy?', in K. Coates (ed.), *Can the Workers Run Industry?* London, Sphere Books.

BARRON, R. D. and NORRIS, G. M. (1976), 'Sexual Divisions and the Dual Labour Market', in D. L. Barker and S. Allen (eds), *Dependence and Exploitation in Work and Marriage,* London, Longman, pp. 47–69.

BAUMAN, Z. (1976), *Towards a Critical Sociology,* London, Routledge & Kegan Paul.

BAUMGARTENER, T., BURNS, C. R. and DEVILLE, P. (1977), 'Work, Politics and The Structuring of Social Systems', paper presented to the International Conference on Possibilities for the Liberation of Work and Political Power, Dubrovnik, February.

BELL, D. (1947), 'Adjusting Men to Machines', *Commentary,* 3, pp. 79–88.

BELL, D. (1974), *The Coming of Post-Industrial Society,* Penguin.

BENDIX, R. (1956), *Work and Authority in Industry,* New York, Wiley.

BENDIX, R. (1966), *Max Weber, an intellectual portrait,* London, Methuen.

BENDIX, R. (1970), *Embattled Reason: essays on social knowledge,* New York, Oxford University Press.

BENNIS, W. G., BERKOWITZ, N., AFFINITO, M. and MALONE, M. (1958), 'Authority, Power and the Ability to Influence', *Human Relations,* 11, pp. 143–56.

BENSON, J. K. (1975), 'The Interorganizational Network as a Political Economy', *ASQ,* 20, pp. 229–49.

BENSON, J. K. (1977a), 'Innovation and Crisis in Organizational Analysis', *Sociological Quarterly,* 18, pp. 3–16.

BENSON, J. K. (1977b), 'Organizations: a dialectical view', *ASQ,* 22, pp. 1–21.

563

BENSON, J. K. (1978), 'The Interorganizational Network as a Political Economy', in L. Karpik (ed.), *Organization and Environment*, London, Sage, pp. 69–102.

BERGER, J. and MOHR, J. (1975), *A Seventh Man: The story of a migrant worker in Europe,* Harmondsworth, Penguin.

BERGER, M. (1956), 'Bureaucracy East and West', *ASQ,* 1 pp. 518–29.

BERGER, P. (1966), *Invitation to Sociology,* Harmondsworth, Penguin.

BERGER, P. and LUCKMANN, T. (1966), *The Social Construction of Reality: A Treatise in the Sociology of Knowledge,* New York, Doubleday.

BERGER, P. and PULLBERG, S. (1966), 'Reification and the Sociological Critique of Consciousness', *New Left Review,* 35, pp. 56–71.

BERLE, A. A. and MEANS, G. C. (1932), *The Modern Corporation and Private Property,* New York, Macmillan.

BETTELHEIM, C. (1974), *Cultural Revolution and Industrial Organization in China,* New York, Monthly Review Press.

BETTELHEIM, C. (1976), *Economic Calculation and Forms of Property,* London, Routledge & Kegan Paul.

BETTELHEIM, C. (1977), *Class Struggle in the USSR: first period 1917–1923,* Hassocks, Sussex, Harvester Press.

BEYNON, H. (1974), *Working for Ford,* Harmondsworth, Penguin,

BEYNON, H. and BLACKBURN, R. M. (1972), *Perceptions of Work,* Cambridge University Press.

BINNS, D. (1977), *Beyond the Sociology of Conflict,* London, Macmillan.

BITTNER, E. (1965), 'The Concept of Organization', *Social Research,* 32, pp. 239–55.

BITTNER, E. (1967), 'The Police on Skid-Row: A Study of Peace Keeping', *American Sociological Review,* 32, 699–715.

BITTNER, E. (1973), 'The Concept of Organization', in G. Salaman and K. Thompson (eds), *People and Organizations,* London, Longman, pp. 264–76.

BLACKBURN, R. (1967), 'The Unequal Society', in R. Blackburn and A. Cockburn (eds), *The Incompatibles,* Harmondsworth, Penguin.

BLACKBURN, R. (1972), The New Capitalism', in R. Blackburn (ed.), *Ideology in Social Science,* London, Fontana, pp. 64–186.

BLAU, P. M. (1955), *The Dynamics of Bureaucracy,* University of Chicago Press.

BLAU, P. M. (1956), *Bureaucracy in Modern Society,* New York, Random House.

BLAU, P. M. (1963), 'Critical Remarks on Weber's Theory of Authority', *Am. Pol. Sci. Rev.,* 57, pp. 305–16.

BLAU, P. M. (1964), *Exchange and Power in Social Life,* New York, Wiley.

BLAU, P. M. (1968), 'The Hierarchy of Authority in Organizations', *ASR,* 33, pp. 453–67.

BLAU, P. M. (1970), 'A Formal Theory of Differentiation in Organizations', *ASR,* 35, pp. 201–18.

BLAU, P. M. (1972a), 'Interdependence and Hierarchy in Organizations', *Social Science Research,* 1, pp. 1–24.

BLAU, P. M. (1972b), Reply to M. W. Meyer's 'Some Constraints in Analyzing Data on Organizational Structures', *ASR,* 36, pp. 304–7.

BLAU, P. M. (1973), *The Organization of Academic Work*, New York, Wiley.

BLAU, P. M. and SCHOENHERR, R. (1971), *The Structure of Organizations*, New York, Basic Books.

BLAU, P. M. and SCOTT, W. (1963), *Formal Organizations: a comparative approach*, London, Routledge & Kegan Paul.

BLAUNER, R. (1964), *Alienation and Freedom*, University of Chicago Press.

BLOOD, C. L. and HULIN, M. R. (1967), 'Alienation, Environmental Characters and Worker Responses', *J. Applied Psychology*, 51, pp. 284–90.

BLOOM, R. and BARRY, J. R. (1967), 'Determinants of Work Attitudes among Negroes', *J. Applied Psychology*, 51, pp. 291–4.

BLUMBERG, P. (1968), *Industrial Democracy: the Sociology of Participation*, London, Constable.

BLUMER, H. (1947), 'Sociological Theory in Industrial Relations', *ASR*, 12, pp. 271–8.

BOGGS, C. (1976), *Gramsci's Marxism*, London, Pluto Press.

BOSQUET, M. (1977), *Capitalism in Crisis and Everyday Life*, Hassocks, Sussex, Harvester Press.

BOTTOMORE, T. and RUBEL, M. (1963), *Karl Marx: Selected Writings in Sociology and Social Philosophy*, Harmondsworth, Penguin.

BOYSON, R. (1970), *The Ashworth Cotton Enterprise*, Oxford University Press.

BRAENDGAARD, A. (1978), 'Cultural-Normative Change or Interest Politics in Disguise? Two Different Interpretations of Recent Efforts in Work Humanization?' Paper presented at EIASM Seminar on Cultural and Normative Change in Organizations, Brussels, 20–21 April.

BRAVERMAN, H. (1974), *Labour and Monopoly Capital*, New York, Monthly Review Press.

BRIDGES, A. (1974), 'Nicos Poulantzas and the Marxist Theory of the State', *Politics and Society*, 4, pp. 162–90.

BRIDGMAN, P. (1927), *The Logic of Modern Physics*, London, Macmillan.

BRIGHT, J. R. (1958), *Automation and Management*, Boston, Harvard Business School.

BRIGHTON LABOUR PROCESS GROUP (1977), 'The Capitalist Labour Process', *Capital and Class*, 1, pp. 3–42.

BRINTON, M. (1970), *The Bolsheviks and Workers' Control 1917–1921: the State and Counter-Revolution*, London, Solidarity.

BROGDEN, H. E. (1949), 'A New Coefficient: Application to Biserial Correlation and to Estimation of Selective Efficiency', *Psychometrika*, 14, pp. 169–82.

BROWN, G. (1977), *Sabotage*, Nottingham, Spokesman Books.

BROWN, P. (1954), 'Bureaucracy in a Government Laboratory', *Social Forces*, 32, pp. 259–68.

BROWN, R. (1976), 'Women as Employees: some comments on research in industrial sociology', in D. L. Barker and S. Allen (eds), *Dependence and Exploitation in Work and Marriage*, London, Longman, pp. 21–40.

BUCHANAN, H. R. (1976), 'Lenin and Bukharin on the Transition from Capitalism to Socialism: the Meschersky controversy 1918', *Soviet Studies*, 28, pp. 66–82.

BUCHER, R. and STELLING, J. (1969), 'Characteristics of Professional Organizations', *Journal of Health and Social Behaviour*, 10, pp. 3–15.

BUCKLEY, W. (1967), *Sociology and Modern Systems Theory*, New York, McGraw-Hill.

BURACK, E. H. and CASSELL, F. (1967), 'Technological Change and Manpower Developments in Advanced Production Systems', *Academy of Management Journal*, 10, pp. 293–308.

BURNETT, J. (1974), *Useful Toil: Autobiographies of Working People from the 1820s to the 1920s*, Harmondsworth, Penguin.

BURNHAM, J. (1941), *The Managerial Revolution*, New York, Day.

BURNHAM, J. (1962), *The Managerial Revolution*, Harmondsworth, Penguin.

BURNS, T. (1967). 'The Comparative Study of Organizations', in V. H. Vroom (ed.), *Methods of Organizational Research*, University of Pittsburgh Press, pp. 119–35.

BURNS, T. and STALKER, G. M. (1961), *The Management of Innovation*, London, Tavistock.

BURRAGE, M. (1973), 'Nationalization and the Professional Ideal', *Sociology*, 7, pp. 253–72.

BURT, W. J. (1972), 'Workers' Participation in Management in Yugoslavia', *Bulletin of the International Institute for Labour Studies*, 9.

BUTLER, R. J., HICKSON, D. J. and MCCULLOUGH, A. E. (1974), 'Power in the Organizational Coalition', paper presented to the World Congress of Sociology, Research in Organizations Section, Toronto, Canada, August.

CALDWELL, M. (1977), *The Wealth of Some Nations*. London, Zed Press.

CALDWELL, R. G. and BLACK, J. A. (1971), *Juvenile Delinquency*, New York, Ronald Press.

CAMPBELL, D. T. (1959), 'Methodological Suggestions from a Comparative Phsychology of Knowledge Processes, *Inquiry*, 2, pp. 152–182.

CAMPBELL, D. T. (1965a), 'Ethnocentric and other Altruistic Motives', in D. Levine (ed.), *Nebraska Symposium on Motivation*, Lincoln, University of Nebraska Press, pp. 283–311.

CAMPBELL, D. T. (1965b), 'Variation and Selective Retention in Socio-cultural Evolution', in H. R. Barringer, G. I. Blankstein, and R. Mack (eds), *Social Change in Developing Areas*, Cambridge, Mass.; Schenkiman, pp. 19–49.

CAMPBELL, D. T. (1969), 'Variation and Selective Retention in Socio-cultural Evolution', *General Systems*, 16, pp. 69–85.

CARCHEDI, G. (1977), *On the Economic Identification of Social Classes*, London, Routledge & Kegan Paul.

CAREY, A. (1967), 'The Hawthorne Studies: a radical criticism' *ASR*, 32, pp. 403–16.

CAREY, A. (1976), 'Industrial Psychology and Sociology in Australia', in P. Boreham, A. Pemberton and P. Wilson (eds), *The Professions in Australia*, St Lucia, University of Queensland Press.

CARTWRIGHT, D. (1965), 'Influence, Leadership and Control', in J. G. March (ed.), *Handbook of Organizations*, Chicago, Rand McNally, pp. 1–47.

CARTWRIGHT, D. and ZANDER, A. (1960), 'Individual Motives and Group Goals', in D. Cartwright and A. Zander (eds), *Group Dynamics* (2nd edition), New York, Row Peterson, pp. 403–7).

CASTLES, S. and KOSACK, G. (1973), *Immigrant Workers and Class Structures in Western Europe*, Oxford University Press.

CATTELL, J. (1946), *Description and Measurement of Personality*, New York, World Press.

CENTERS, R. J. and BUGENTAL, D. E. (1966), 'Intrinsic and Extrinsic Job Motivations Among Different Segments of the Working Population', *J. Applied Psychology*, 50, pp. 193–7.

CHAMPION, D. J. (1975), *The Sociology of Organizations*, New York, McGraw-Hill.

CHANDLER, A. D. (1962), *Strategy and Structure*, Cambridge, Mass., MIT Press.

CHENG, C. S. (1966), 'The Great Lessons of the Paris Commune', *Peking Review*, 15 April.

CHILD, J. (1972a), 'Organization Structure, Environment and Performance: the Role of Strategic Choice', *Sociology*, 6, pp. 1–22.

CHILD. J. (1972b), 'Organization Structure and Strategies of Control', *ASQ*, 17, pp. 163–77.

CHILD, J. (ed.) (1973a), *Man and Organization*, London, Allen & Unwin.

CHILD, J. (1973b), 'Organization: A Choice for Man', in J. Child (ed.), *Man and Organization*, London, Allen & Unwin, pp. 234–57.

CHILD, J. (1973c), 'Strategies of Control and Organizational Behaviour', *ASQ*, 18, pp. 1–17.

CHILD, J., FRANCIS, A., KIESER, A., NYMAN, S. and SILBERSTON, A. (1975), 'The Growth of Firms as a Field of Research', *The University of Aston Management Centre – Working Paper Series*, 30.

CHILD, J. and MANSFIELD, R. (1972), 'Technology, Size and Organization Structure', *Sociology*, 6, pp. 369–93.

CICOUREL, A. (1958), 'The Front and Back of Organizational Leadership', *Pacific Sociological Review*, 1, pp. 54–8.

CICOUREL, A. (1964), *Method and Measurement in Sociology*, New York, Free Press.

CICOUREL, A. (1968), *The Social Organization of Juvenile Justice*, New York, John Wiley.

CLARK, A. (1919), *Working Life of Women in the Seventeenth Century*, London, Dulton.

CLARKE, S. (1977), 'Marxism, Sociology and Poulantzas' Theory of the State', *Capital and Class*, 2, pp. 1–31.

CLARKE, T. (1977), 'Industrial Democracy: the institutionalized suppression of industrial conflict?' in T. Clarke and L. Clements (eds), *Trade Unions Under Capitalism*, Harmondsworth, Penguin, pp. 351–82.

CLEGG, S. (1970), 'Role Stress and Role Recipe: Concept and Construct: An Empirical Study in a Hospital Group' (Parts One and Two), B.Sc. (Hons.) thesis, University of Aston in Birmingham.

CLEGG, S. (1975), *Power, Rule and Domination: A Critical and Empirical Understanding of Power in Sociological Theory and Everyday Life*, London, Routledge & Kegan Paul.

567

CLEGG, S. (1977), 'Power, Organization Theory, Marx and Critique', in S. Clegg and D. Dunkerley (eds), *Critical Issues in Organizations*, London, Routledge & Kegan Paul, pp. 21–40.

CLEGG, S. (1979a), *The Theory of Power and Organization*, London, Routledge & Kegan Paul.

CLEGG, S. (1979b), 'The Sociology of Power and the University Curriculum', in M. Pusey and R. Young (eds), *Ideology, Domination and Knowledge*, Canberra, ANU Press.

CLEGG, S. and DUNKERLEY, D., eds (1977), *Critical Issues In Organizations*, London, Routledge & Kegan Paul.

COATES, K. (1975), 'Democracy and Workers' Control', in J. Vanek (ed.), *Self-Management: economic liberation of man*, Harmondsworth, Penguin, pp. 90–109.

COCH, L. and FRENCH, J. R. P. (1948), 'Overcoming Resistance to Change', *Human Relations*, 1, pp. 512–32.

COHEN, J. (1972), 'Max Weber and the Dynamics of Rationalized Domination', *Telos*, 14, pp. 63–86.

COHEN, P. (1970), *Modern Social Theory*, London, Heinemann.

COLE, G. D. H. (1957), Introduction to *Capital* by Karl Marx, vol. 1, translated from the fourth German edition by Eden and Cedar Paul, London, Dent, Everyman.

COLLETTI, L. (1972), *From Rousseau to Lenin: Studies in Ideology and Society*, London, New Left Books.

COMMONS, J. R. (1961), *Institutional Economics*, vols 1 and 2, Madison, Univeristy of Wisconsin Press.

COMMONS, J. R. (1968), *Legal Foundations of Capitalism*, Madison, University of Wisconsin Press.

CONNELL, R. W. (1976), *Ruling Class, Ruling Culture: Studies of Conflict, Power and Hegemony in Australian Life*, Cambridge University Press.

CONSTAS, H. (1961), 'The USSR – from Charismatic Sect to Bureaucratic Society', *ASQ*, 6, pp. 282–98.

COOK, K. S. (1977), 'Exchange and Power in Networks of Interorganizational Relations', *Sociological Quarterly*, 18, pp. 62–82.

COULSON, M., MAGAS, B. and WAINWRIGHT, H. (1975), 'The Housewife and her Labour Under Capitalism – a Critique', *New Left Review*, 89, pp. 59–72.

COUNTER INFORMATION SERVICE (1976), *Crisis: Women Under Attack*, London, CIS Anti-Report no. 15.

COUNTER INFORMATION SERVICE (1977), *The Ford Motor Company*, London, CIS Anti-Report no. 20.

CRENSON, M. A. (1971), *The Un-Politics of Air Pollution: a Study of Non-Decisionmaking in the Cities*, Baltimore, Johns Hopkins Press.

CROMPTON, R. and GUBBAY. J. (1977), *Economy and Class Structure*, London, Macmillan.

CROZIER, M. (1964), *The Bureaucratic Phenomenon*, London, Tavistock.

CROZIER, M. (1972), 'The Relationship between Micro- and Macrosociology, a Study of Organizational Systems as an Empirical Approach to Problems of Macrosociology', *Human Relations*, 25, pp. 239–51.

CROZIER, M. (1976), 'Comparing Structures and Comparing Games,' in G.

Hofstede and M. S. Kassem (eds), *European Contributions to Organization Theory*, Assen, Van Gorcum, pp. 193–207.

CRUMP, W. B. (1931), *The Leeds Woollen Industry, 1780–1820*, Leeds, Thoresby Society.

CUNNISON, S. (1966), *Wages and Work Allocation*, London, Tavistock.

CYERT, R. M. and MARCH, J. G. (1963), *A Behavioural Theory of the Firm*, Englewood Cliffs, N.J., Prentice-Hall.

CYERT, R. M., SIMON, H. A. and TROW, D. B. (1956), 'Observation of a Business Decision', *Journal of Business*, pp. 237–48.

DAHL, R. A. (1957), 'The Concept of Power', *Behavioural Science*, 2, pp. 201–15.

DAHL, R. A. (1961), *Who Governs?*, Yale University Press.

DAHRENDORF, R. (1967), *Class and Class Conflict in an Industrial Society*, London, Routledge & Kegan Paul.

DAUMAS, M. (1962), *Histoire générale des techniques*, Paris, PUF, vol. 1.

DAVIDSON, A. (1977), *Antonio Gramsci: towards an intellectual biography*, London, Merlin Press.

DAVIES, C., DAWSON, S. and FRANCIS, A. (1973), 'Technology and other Variables: Some Current Approaches in Organization Theory', in M. Warner (ed.), *The Sociology of the Work-Place*, London, Allen & Unwin, pp. 149–63.

DAVIES, K. (1976), 'Notes on Factory Management', *China Now*, 67, p. 15.

DAVIES, R. (1975), *Women and Work*, London, Arrow.

DAVIS, L. E. (1971), 'Job Satisfaction Research: the Post-Industrial View', *Industrial Relations*, 10, pp. 176–93.

DAVIS, L. E. and TAYLOR, J. (1972), *Design of Jobs*, Harmondsworth, Penguin.

DAVIS, L. E. and TAYLOR, J. (1976), 'Technology, Organization and Job Structure', in R. Dubin (ed.), *Handbook of Work, Organization and Society*, Chicago, Rand McNally, pp. 379–419.

DAWE, A. (1971), 'The Relevance of Values', in A. Sahay (ed.), *Max Weber and Modern Sociology*, London, Routledge & Kegan Paul, pp. 37–66.

DAY, R. A. and DAY, J. V. (1977), 'A Review of the Current State of Negotiated Order Theory: an Appreciation and a Critique', *Sociological Quarterly*, 18, pp. 126–42.

DEANE, P. (1967), *The First Industrial Revolution*, London, Allen & Unwin.

DEANE, P. (1973), 'Great Britain', in C. M. Cipolla (ed.), *The Fontana Economic History of Europe*, 4 (1), *The Emergence of Industrial Societies*, London, Fontana, pp. 161–227.

DENNIS, N., HENRIQUES, F. and SLAUGHTER, C. (1969), *Coal Is Our Life*, London, Eyre & Spottiswoode.

DENNIS, S. M., GILLESPIE, D. F. and MORRISEY, E. (1978), 'Technology and Organizations: Methodological Deficiencies and Lacunae', *Technology and Culture*, 19, pp. 83–92.

DE VROEY, M. (1975), 'The Separation of Ownership and Control in Large Corporations', *Review of Radical Political Economics*, 7, pp. 1–10.

DEWEY, J. (1930), *Human Nature and Conduct*, New York, Modern Library.

BIBLIOGRAPHY

DICKSON, D. (1974), 'Technology and the Construction of Social Reality', *Radical Science Journal*, 1, pp. 29–50.

DILTHEY, W. (1883), *Einleitung in die Geisteswissenschaften*, Leipzig.

DOMHOFF, G. (1967), *Who Rules America?* Englewood Cliffs, N.J., Prentice-Hall.

DONALDSON, L. and WARNER, M. (1974), 'Bureaucratic and Electoral Control in Occupational Interest Associations', *Sociology*, 8, pp. 47–57.

DORE, R. (1973), *British Factory, Japanese Factory*, Berkeley, University of California Press.

DREYFUSS, C. (1938), *Occupation and Ideology of the Salaried Employee*, translated by E. Abramovitch, New York, Basic Books.

DUBIN, R. (1957), 'Power and Union Management Relations', *ASQ*, 2, pp. 60–81.

DUNCAN, R. (1972), 'Characteristics of Organizational Environments and Perceived Environmental Uncertainty', *ASQ*, 17, pp. 313–27.

DUNKERLEY, D. (1972), *The Study of Organizations*, London, Routledge & Kegan Paul.

DUNKERLEY, D. (1975), *The Foreman*, London, Routledge & Kegan Paul.

DUNLOP, J. T. (1950), 'A Framework for the Analysis of Industrial Relations: two views', *Industrial and Labour Relations Review*, 3, pp. 383–93.

DURKHEIM, E. (1915), *The Elementary Forms of Religious Life*, London, Allen & Unwin.

DURKHEIM, E. (1952), *Suicide*, London, Routledge & Kegan Paul.

DURKHEIM, E. (1956), *Education and Sociology*, Chicago, Free Press.

DURKHEIM, E. (1957), *Professional Ethics and Civic Morals*, London, Routledge & Kegan Paul.

DURKHEIM, E. (1959), *Socialism and Saint-Simon*, London, Routledge & Kegan Paul.

DURKHEIM, E. (1964a), *The Division of Labour in Society*, New York, Free Press.

DURKHEIM, E. (1964b), *The Rules of Sociological Method*, New York, Free Press.

DUVIVIER, P. (1972), 'La repartition de la fortune mobilière en Belgique', *Courrier Hebdomadaire du CRISP*, Brussels, 561.

ECCLES, T. (1976), 'Kirby Manufacturing and Engineering', in K. Coates (ed.), *The New Worker Co-operatives*, Nottingham, Spokesman Books, pp. 141–72.

EDWARDS, R. C., REICH, M. and WEISSKOPF, T. E. (1972), *The Capitalist System*, Englewood Cliffs, N.J., Prentice-Hall.

ELDRIDGE, J. E. T. (1972), *Max Weber: The Interpretation of Social Reality*, edited and with an introductory essay by J. E. T. Eldridge, London, Thomas Nelson.

ELDRIDGE, J. E. T. (1973), *Sociology and Industrial Life*, London, Nelson.

ELDRIDGE, J. E. T. and CROMBIE, A. D. (1974), *A Sociology of Organizations*, London, Allen & Unwin.

ELGER, A. J. (1975), 'Industrial Organizations, a Processual Perspective', in J. B. McKinley (ed.), *Processing People: Cases in Organizational Behaviour*, London, Holt, Rinehart & Winston, pp. 91–149.

EMERSON, R. (1962), 'Power-Dependence Relations', *ASR*, 27, pp. 31–41.

EMERY, F. E. (ed.) (1969), *Systems Thinking,* Harmondsworth, Penguin.

EMERY, F. E. and TRIST, E. L. (1960). 'Socio-Technical Systems', in C. W. Churchman and M. Verhulst (eds), *Management Science, Models and Techniques,* vol. 2, Oxford, Pergamon, pp. 83–97.

EMERY, F. E. and TRIST, E. L. (1965), 'The Causal Texture of Organizational Environments', *Human Relations,* 18, pp. 21–31.

ENGELS, F. (1959), *Anti-Dühring: Herr Eugene Dühring's Revolution in Science,* 2nd edition, Moscow, Foreign Languages Publishing House.

ENGELS, F. (1969), 'The Origin of the Family, Private Property and the State', in *Karl Marx and Frederick Engels, Selected Works,* vol. 3, Moscow, Progress Publishers.

EPSTEIN, C. (1971), *Woman's Place,* University of California Press.

ESPING-ANDERSEN, G., FRIENLAND, R. and WRIGHT, E. O. (1976), 'Modes of Class Struggle and the Capitalist State', *Kapitalistate,* 4–5, pp. 186–220.

ETZIONI, A. (1959), 'Authority, Structure and Organizational Effectiveness', *ASQ,* 4, pp. 43–67.

ETZIONI, A. (1960), 'Two Approaches to Organizational Analysis', *ASQ,* 5, pp. 257–78.

ETZIONI, A. (1961), *The Comparative Analysis of Complex Organizations,* New York, Free Press.

ETZIONI, A. (1964), *Modern Organizations,* Englewood Cliffs, N.J., Prentice-Hall.

ETZIONI, A. (1969), *A Sociological Reader on Complex Organizations,* New York, Holt, Rinehart & Winston.

ETZIONI, A. (1975), *The Comparative Analysis of Complex Organizations,* 2nd edition, New York, Free Press.

EWEN, S. (1976), *Captains of Consciousness: advertizing and the social roots of the consumer culture,* New York, McGraw-Hill.

FARMER, E. (1923), 'Time and Motion Study', *Industrial Fatigue Research Board,* Report No. 14.

FAYOL, H. (1949), *General and Industrial Management,* London, Pitman.

FELDMAN, H. (1937), *Problems in Labor Relations,* New York, Macmillan.

FEMIA, J. (1975), 'Hegemony and Consciousness in the thought of Antonio Gramsci', *Political Studies,* 23, pp. 29–48.

FENLON, G. (1978), 'The Political and Ideological Implications of Corporate Information Disclosure: the British Worker's Challenge to Corporate Profits', MA Thesis, Department of Government, University of Essex.

FENSHAM, P. J. and HOOPER, D. (1964), *The Dynamics of a Changing Technology,* London, Tavistock.

FLEET, K. (1976), 'Triumph Meriden', in K. Coates (ed.), *The New Worker Co-operatives,* Nottingham, Spokesman Books, pp. 88–108.

FLERON, F. and FLERON, L. J. (1972), 'Administration Theory as Repressive Political theory: the communist experience', *Telos,* 12, pp. 63–92.

FLORENCE, P. SARGENT (1961), *Ownership, Control and Success of Large Companies,* London, Sweet & Maxwell.

FOGARTY, M., RAPOPORT, R. and RAPOPORT, R. (1971), *Sex, Career and Family,* London, Allen & Unwin.

FOSTER-CARTER, A. (1978), 'The Modes of Production Controversy', *New Left Review,* 107, pp. 47–78.

FOX, A. (1966), *Industrial Sociology and Industrial Relations*, Research Paper 3, Royal Commission on Trade Unions and Employers Associations, London, HMSO.

FOX, A. (1974), *Beyond Contract: Work, Power and Trust Relations*, London, Faber & Faber.

FOX, A. (1976), 'The Meaning of Work', Block 3, Unit 6, *People and Work*, OU Course DE351, Milton Keynes, Open University Press, pp. 9–60.

FRANCIS, A. (1977), 'Families, Firms and Finance Capital: The Development of UK Industrial Firms with Particular Reference to their Ownership and Control', revised edition of a paper presented at the EGOS Symposium on Power, Bradford University, 6–7 May 1976.

FRANK, A. G. (1973), 'Functionalism and Dialetics', in W. J. Chambliss (ed.), *Sociological Readings in the Conflict Perspective*, Reading, Mass., Addison-Wesley, pp. 62–73.

FRANKEL, B. (1978), *Marxian Theories of the State: A Critique of Orthodoxy*, Melbourne, Arena Publications Association Monograph No. 3.

FRASER, R. (1969), *Work: Twenty Personal Accounts*, Harmondsworth, Penguin.

FRENCH, J. R. P. and RAVEN, B. H. (1959), 'The Bases of Social Power', in D. Cartwright (ed.), *Studies in Social Power*, Ann Arbor, University of Michigan Press, pp. 150–67.

FREYSSENET, M. (1974), *Le Processus de dequalification-surqualification de la force de travail*, Paris, C. Sill.

FRIEDMANN, A. (1977), 'Responsible Autonomy versus Direct Control over the Labour Process', *Capital and Class*, 1, pp. 43–57.

FRIEDRICH, C. J. (1952), 'Some Observations on Weber's Analysis of Bureaucracy', in R. K. Merton, A. P. Gray, B. Hockey and H. C. Selvin (eds), *Reader in Bureaucracy*, New York, Free Press, pp. 27–32.

FRUCHTER, B. (1954), *Introduction to Factor Analysis*, Princeton, N.J., Van Nostrand.

FUSSELL, G. E. and FUSSELL, K. R. (1953), *The English Countrywoman: A Farmhouse Social History 1500–1900*, London, Andrew Melrose.

GADAMER, H.-G. (1975), *Truth and Method*, London, Sheed & Ward.

GALBRAITH, J. K. (1969), *The New Industrial State*, Penguin.

GALBRAITH, J. K. (1973), *Economics and the Public Purpose*, New York, Houghton Mifflin.

GAMBLE, A. and WALTON, P. (1976), *Capitalism in Crisis: Inflation and the State*, London, Macmillan.

GARDINER, J. (1975), 'Women's Domestic Labour', *New Left Review*, 89, pp. 47–58.

GARDINER, J. (1977), 'Women in the Labour Process', in A. Hunt (ed.), *Class and Class Structure*, London, Lawrence & Wishart, pp. 155–64.

GARFINKEL, H. (1956), 'Some Sociological Concepts and Methods for Psychiatrists', *Psychiatric Research Report*, 6, pp. 181–95.

GARFINKEL, H. (1967), *Studies in Ethnomethodology*, Englewood Cliffs, N.J., Prentice-Hall.

GARFINKEL, H. (1974), 'The Origins of the Term "Ethnomethodology"', in R. Turner (ed.), *Ethnomethodology*, Harmondsworth, Penguin, pp. 15–18.

GARFINKEL, H. and SACKS, H. (1970), 'On the Formal Structures of Practical Actions', in J. C. McKinney and E. A. Tiryakian (eds), *Theoretical Sociology: Perspectives and Developments*, New York, Appleton Crofts, pp. 337–66.

GEORGIOU, P. (1973), 'The Goal Paradigm and Notes Towards a Counter-Paradigm', *ASQ*, 18, pp. 291–310.

GERTH, H. H. (1952), 'The Nazi Party: Its Leadership and Composition', in R. K. Merton, A. P. Gray, B. Hockey and H. C. Selvin (eds), *Reader in Bureaucracy*, New York, Free Press, pp. 100–13.

GIDDENS, A. (1971), *Capitalism and Modern Social Theory*, Cambridge University Press.

GIDDENS, A. (1973), *The Class Structure of the Advanced Societies*, London, Hutchinson.

GIDDENS, A. (1974), 'Elites in the British Class Structure', in P. Stanworth and A. Giddens (eds), *Elites and Power in British Society*, Cambridge University Press, pp. 1–22.

GILBERT, M. (ed.) (1972), *The Modern Business Enterprise*, Harmondsworth, Penguin.

GINTIS, H. (1972), 'Activism and Counter-Culture', *Telos*, 12, pp. 42–62.

GLASER, B. and STRAUSS, A. (1968), 'Awareness Contexts and Social Interaction', *ASR*, 29, pp. 669–79.

GLYN, A. B. and SUTCLIFFE, B. (1972), *British Capitalism, Workers and the Profit Squeeze*, Harmondsworth, Penguin.

GOLDTHORPE, J. H., LOCKWOOD, D., BECHOFER, F. and PLATT, J. (1968), *The Affluent Worker: Industrial Attitudes and Behaviour*, Cambridge University Press.

GOLDTHORPE, J. H., LOCKWOOD, D., BECHOFER, F. and PLATT, J. (1969), *The Affluent Worker in the Class Structure*, Cambridge University Press.

GOLDWASSER, J. and DOWTY, S. (1975), *Huan-Ying: Worker's China*, New York, Monthly Review Press.

GOODEY, C, (1974), 'Factory Committees and the Dictatorship of the Proletariat (1918)', *Critique*, 3, pp. 27–47.

GORDON, D. M. (1972), *Theories of Poverty and Underemployment*, Lexington, Mass., D. C. Heath.

GORDON, D. (1976), 'Capitalist Efficiency', *Monthly Review*, 28, pp. 19–39.

GORZ, A. (1972), 'Technical Intelligence and the Capitalist Division of Labour', *Telos*, 12, pp. 27–41.

GOULDNER, A. W. (1954), *Patterns of Industrial Bureaucracy*, New York, Free Press.

GOULDNER, A. W. (1955), 'Metaphysical Pathos and the Theory of Bureaucracy', *Am. Pol. Sci. Rev.*, 49, pp. 496–507.

GOULDNER, A. W. (1957), 'Cosmopolitans and Locals: Towards an Analysis of Latent Social Roles', *ASQ*, 2, pp. 281–306.

GOULDNER, A. W. (1959a), 'Organizational Analysis', in R. K. Merton, L. Broom and C. Cottrell (eds), *Sociology Today*, New York, Basic Books, pp. 400–28.

GOULDNER, A. W. (1959b), Introduction to E. Durkheim (1959), *Socialism and Saint-Simon*, London, Routledge & Kegan Paul, pp. V–XXVII.

GOULDNER, A. W. (1965), *Wildcat Strike,* New York, Free Press.

GOULDNER, A. W. (1967), 'Reciprocity and Autonomy in Functional Theory', in N. J. Demerath and R. A. Peterson (eds), *System, Change and Conflict,* New York, Free Press, pp. 141–70.

GOULDNER, A. W. (1971), *The Coming Crisis of Western Sociology,* London, Heinemann.

GOULDNER, A. W. (1973), 'Metaphysical Pathos and the Theory of Bureaucracy', in W. Chambliss (ed.), *Sociological Readings in the Conflict Perspective,* Reading, Mass., Addison-Wesley, pp. 337–52.

GRAMSCI, A. (1957), *The Modern Prince and Other Writings,* translated by L. Marks, New York, International Publishers.

GRAMSCI, A. (1971), *Selection From The Prison Notebooks,* edited and translated by Q. Hoare and G. N. Smith, London, Lawrence & Wishart.

GRAMSCI, A. (1975), *Letters from Prison,* selected, translated and introduced by L. Lawner, London, Cape.

GRAMSCI, A. (1977), *Selections from Political Writings (1910–1920),* selected and edited by Q. Hoare, translated by J. Matthews, London, Lawrence & Wishart.

GRAY, J. (1974), 'The Two Roads', in S. Schram (ed.), *Authority, Participation and Cultural Change in China,* Cambridge University Press, pp. 109–57.

GREENWOOD, R. and HININGS, C. R. (1976), 'The Comparative Study of Local Government Organizations', *Policy and Politics,* 2, pp. 57–65.

GROSS, E. (1969), 'The Definition of Organizational Goals', *BJS,* 20, pp. 277–94.

GROSS, E. (1978), 'Organizations as Criminal Actors', in P. R. Wilson and J. Braithwaite (eds), *The Two Faces of Deviance: Crimes of the Powerful and Powerless,* St Lucia, University of Queensland Press, pp. 119–213.

GROSS, N., MASON, W. S. and MCEACHERN, A. W. (1958), *Explorations in Role Analysis,* New York, Wiley.

GULICK, L. and URWICK, L. (1937), *Papers on the Science of Administration,* New York, Columbia University Press.

GUTKIND, P. C. W. and WALLERSTEIN, I. (1976), *The Political Economy of Contemporary Africa,* London, Sage.

GUTMAN, H. G. (1977), *Work, Culture and Society in Industrializing America,* Oxford, Basil Blackwell.

GUTTMAN, L. (1950), 'Scaling Methods', in S. A. Stouffer (ed.), *Measurement and Prediction,* vol. 4, New Jersey, Princeton University Press.

GVISHIANI, D. (1972), *Organization and Management,* Moscow, Progress Publishers.

HAAS, J. E., HALL, R. H. and JOHNSON, N. J. (1963), 'The Size of the Supportive Component in Organizations', *Social Forces,* 42, pp. 9–17.

HAAS, J. E., HALL, R. H. and JOHNSON, N. J. (1966), 'Towards an Empirically Derived Taxonomy of Organization', in R. V. Bowers (ed.), *Studies on Behaviour in Organization,* Athens, Ga., University of Georgia Press, pp. 157–80.

HABERMAS, J. (1971), *Knowledge and Human Interests,* translated by J. J. Shapiro, London, Heinemann.

574

HABERMAS, J. (1974), *Theory and Practice*, translated by J. Vietal, London, Heinemann.

HABERMAS, J. (1976), *Legitimation Crisis*, translated by T. McCarthy, London, Heinemann.

HAGE, J. (1965), 'An Axiomatic Theory of Organizations', *ASQ*, 10, pp. 289–320.

HAGE, J. and AIKEN, M. (1967), 'Program Change and Organization Properties: a Comparative Analysis', *AJS*, 72, pp. 503–19.

HAGE, J. amd AIKEN, M. (1969), 'Routine Technology, Social Structure and Organizational Goals', *ASQ*, 14, pp. 366–76.

HAGE, J. and AIKEN, M. (1970), *Social Change in Complex Organizations*, New York, Random House.

HALL, R. H. (1962), 'Intraorganizational Structure Variation: Application of the Bureaucratic Model', *ASQ*, 7, pp. 295–308.

HALL, R. H. (1963), 'The Concept of Bureaucracy: an Empirical Assessment', *AJS*, 69, pp. 32–40.

HALL, R. H. (1972), *Organizations: Structure and Process*, Englewood Cliffs, N.J., Prentice-Hall.

HALL, R. H. (1977), *Organizations: Structure and Process*, 2nd edition, Englewood Cliffs, N.J., Prentice-Hall.

HALL, R. H., HAAS, J. E. and JOHNSON, N. J. (1966), 'An Examination of the Blau-Scott and Etzioni Typologies', *ASQ*, 12, pp. 118–39.

HALL, R. H., HAAS, J. E. and JOHNSON, N. J. (1967), 'Organization Size, Complexity and Formalization', *ASR*, 32, pp. 903–12.

HALL, T. D. and NOUGAIM, K. E. (1968), 'An Examination of Maslow's Need Hierarchy in an Organizational Setting', *Organizational Behaviour and Human Performance*, 3, pp. 12–35.

HAMILTON, R. (1978), *The Liberation of Women: A Study of Patriarchy and Capitalism*, London, Allen & Unwin.

HAMPTON, R. (1978), 'The Position of Women in a Capitalist Economy and the Reserve Army Theory', paper presented at SAANZ Conference, 18–21 May, University of Queensland, Brisbane.

HARASZTI, M. (1977), *A Worker in a Worker's State*, introduced by H. Boll, Harmondsworth, Penguin.

HARMAN, H. H. (1967), *Modern Factor Analysis*, University of Chicago Press.

HARRINGTON, M. (1977), *The Twilight of Capitalism*, London, Macmillan.

HART, H. L. A. (1960), 'The Ascription of Responsibility and Rights', in A. Flew (ed.), *Logic and Language* (First Series), Oxford, Blackwell, pp. 145–66.

HARVEY, E. (1968), 'Technology and the Structure of Organizations', *ASR*, 33, pp. 247–59.

HAWLEY, A., BOLAND, W. and BOLAND, M. (1965), 'Population Size and Administration in Institutions of Higher Education', *ASR*, 30, pp. 252–5.

HEARN, F. (1978), 'Rationality and Bureaucracy: Maoist Contributions to a Marxist Theory of Bureaucracy', *Sociological Quarterly*, 19, pp. 37–54.

HEATH, A. (1976), *Rational Choice and Social Exchange*, Cambridge University Press.

BIBLIOGRAPHY

HECKER, D., GREEN, D. and SMITH, K. U. (1956), 'Dimensional Analysis of Motion: Experimental Evaluation of a Time-Study Problem', *J. Applied Psychology*, 40, pp. 220–7.

HEGEL, G. W. F. (1967), *Philosophy of Right*, New York, Oxford University Press.

HEIDEGGER, M. (1967), *What is a Thing?*, translated by W. B. Barton, Jr. and V. Deutsch, Chicago, Henry Regnery.

HEISE, D. R. (1972), 'How Do I Know My Data? Let Me Count the Ways', *ASQ*, 17, pp. 58–61.

HERBST, P. G. (1962), *Autonomous Group Functioning*, London, Tavistock.

HERZBERG, F. (1966), *Work and the Nature of Man*, Cleveland, World Publishing.

HERZBERG, F. (1968), *Work and the Nature of Man*, London, Staples Press.

HERZBERG, F., MAUSNER, B. and SNYDERMAN, B. (1959), *The Motivation to Work*, New York, Wiley.

HEYDERBRAND, W. (1977), 'Organizational Contradictions in Public Bureaucracies: Toward a Marxian Theory of Organizations', *Sociological Quarterly*, 18, pp. 83–107.

HICKSON, D. J. (1966), 'A Convergence in Organization Theory', *ASQ*, 11, pp. 224–37.

HICKSON, D. J., ASTLEY, W. G., AXELSSON, R., BUTLER, R. J. and WILSON, D. C. (1978), 'Strategic Decision-Making in Organizations: Concepts of Process and Content', mimeo., University of Bradford Management Centre.

HICKSON, D. J., BUTLER, R. J., AXELSSON, R. and WILSON, D. (1976), 'Decisive Coalitions', paper presented to an International Conference organized by NATO on Co-ordination and Control of Group and Organizational Performance, Munich, West Germany, July.

HICKSON, D. J., HININGS, C. R., LEE, C. A., SCHNECK, R. E. and PENNINGS, J. M., (1971), 'A Strategic Contingencies Theory of Intra-Organizational Power', *ASQ*, 16, pp. 216–29.

HICKSON, D. J., MCMILLAN, C. J., HININGS, C. R. and SCHWITTER, J. (1974), 'The Culture-Free Context of Organization Structure: A Tri-National Comparison', *Sociology*, 8, 1, pp. 59–80.

HICKSON, D. J., PUGH, D. S. and PHEYSEY, D. C, (1969), 'Operations Technology and Organization Structure: An Empirical Appraisal', *ASQ*, 14, pp. 378–97.

HIGGIN, G. N., JESSOP, N., BRYANT. D., LUCKMAN, J. and STRINGER, J. (1966), *Interdependence and Uncertainty: A Study of the Building Industry*, condensed and edited by C. Crichton, London, Tavistock.

HIGLEY, J., FIELD, G. L. and GRØHOLT, K. (1976), *Elite Structure and Ideology*, Oslo, Universitetsforlaget.

HILL, C. (1964), *Society and Puritanism in Pre-Revolutionary England*, London, Secker & Warburg.

HILL, C. (1969), *The Century of Revolution: 1603–1713*, London, Sphere.

HILL, M. J., HARRISON, R. M., SARGEANT, A. V. and TALBOT, V. (1973), *Men Out Of Work*, Cambridge University Press.

HILL, S. (1976), *The Dockers: Class and Tradition in London*, London, Heinemann.

HILTON, G. (1972), 'Causal Inference Analysis: A Seductive Process', *ASQ*, 17, pp. 44–54.

HIMMELWEIT, S. and MOHUN, E. (1977), 'Domestic Labour and Capital', *Cambridge Journal of Economics*, 1, pp. 26—44.

HINDESS, B. (1977), *Philosophy and Methodology in the Social Sciences*, Hassocks, Sussex, Harvester Press.

HINDESS, B. and HIRST, P. Q. (1975), *Pre-Capitalist Modes of Production*, London, Routledge & Kegan Paul.

HININGS, C. R., HICKSON, D. J., PENNINGS, J. M. and SCHNECK, R. E. (1974), 'Structural Conditions of Intraorganizational Power', *ASQ*, 9, pp. 22–44.

HININGS, C. R. and LEE, G. L. (1971), 'Dimensions of Organization Structure and their Context: A Replication', *Sociology*, 5, pp. 83–93.

HINTON, J. (1973), *The First Shop Stewards Movement*, London, Allen & Unwin.

HIRST, P. Q. (1975), *Durkheim, Bernard and Epistemology*, London, Routledge & Kegan Paul.

HOBSBAWM, E. J. (1969), *Industry and Empire*, Harmondsworth, Penguin.

HOBSBAWM, E. J. (1975), *The Age of Capital, 1848–1875*, London, Weidenfeld & Nicolson.

HOBSON, J. A. (1926), *The Evolution of Modern Capitalism*, London, Walter Scott.

HOFSTEDE, G. (1977)), 'Humanization of Work: the Role of Values in a Third Industrial Revolution', Working Paper 77–16, EIASM, Brussels.

HOLDAWAY, E. A., NEWBERY, J. F., HICKSON, D. J. and HERON, R. P. (1975), 'Dimensions of Organizations in Complex Societies: the educational sector', *ASQ*, 20, pp. 37–58.

HOLLAND, S. (1976), *Capital vs. the Regions*, London, Macmillan.

HOMANS, GEORGE C. (1950), *The Human Group*, London, Routledge & Kegan Paul.

HONIGSHEIM, P. (1968), *On Max Weber*, New York, Free Press.

HOPKINS, T. K. (1966), Review of *Industrial Organization* by J. Woodward, *ASQ*, 11, pp. 284–9.

HOPKINS, T. K. and WALLERSTEIN, I. (1977), 'Patterns of Development of the Modern World-System', *Review*, 1, pp. 111–45.

HORTON, J. (1966), 'Order and Conflict Theories of Social Problems as Competing Ideologies', *AJS*, 71, pp. 701–13.

HOUSE, R. J. and WIGDOR, L. A. (1967), 'Herzberg's Dual-Factor Theory of Job Satisfaction and Motivation: a review of the evidence and a criticism', *Personnel Psychology*, 20, pp. 369–89.

HOXIE, R. F. (1915), *Scientific Management and Labor*, New York, D. Appleton.

HUGHES, E. C. (1945), 'Dilemmas and Contradictions of Status', *AJS*, 50, pp. 353–9.

HUGHES, E. C. (1958), *Men and their Work*, Chicago, Free Press.

HUGHES, E. C. (1971), *The Sociological Eye: Selected Papers*, Chicago, Aldine.

HUNNIUS, G. (1973), 'Workers' Self-Management in Yugoslavia', in G. Hunnius, D. D. Garson and J. Case (eds), *Workers' Control*, New York, Vintage, pp. 268–321.

577

HUNNIUS, G. (1977), 'On the Nature of Capitalist-Initiated Innovations in the Work-place', presented at Conference on the Possibilities for the Liberation of Work and Political Power, Dubrovnik, 31 January–3 February.

HUNT, A. (1968), *A Survey of Women's Employment*, London, HMSO.

HUNT, A. (1975), *Management Attitudes and Practices Towards Women at Work*, London, HMSO.

HUNT, A. (ed.) (1977), *Class and Class Structure*, London, Lawrence & Wishart.

HUSSERL, E. (1967), *Ideas*, London, Allen & Unwin.

HUSSERL, E. (1969), *Formal and Transcendental Logic*, The Hague, Martinus Nijhoff.

HYMAN, R. (1975), *Strikes*, London, Fontana.

HYMAN, R. (1978), 'Strikes', in P. Worsley (ed.), *Modern Sociology* (2nd edition), Harmondsworth, Penguin, pp. 329–40.

ILLICH, I. (1973), 'The Professions as a Form of Imperialism', *New Society*, 13 September, pp. 633–5.

ILO (International Labour Office) (1977), *Bibliography on the Major Aspects of the Humanization of Work and the Quality of Working Life*, Geneva, ILO.

INKSON, J. H. K., HICKSON, D. J. and PUGH, D. S. (1970), 'Organization Context and Structure: an abbreviated replication', *ASQ*, 15, pp. 318–29.

JACOBY, H. (1973), *The Bureaucratization of the World*, translated by E. Kanes, Berkeley, University of California Press.

JAMES, W. (1925), *The Principles of Psychology*, New York, Henry Holt.

JAMES, W. (1948), *Psychology*, Cleveland, World Publishing.

JAQUES, E. (1951), *The Changing Culture of a Factory*, London, Tavistock.

JAQUES, E. (1967), *Equitable Payment*, Harmondsworth, Penguin.

JEPHCOTT, P., SEEAR, B. N. and SMITH, J. H. (1962), *Married Women Working*, London, Allen & Unwin.

JOHNSON, T. (1977), 'What is to be Known? The Structural Determination of Social Class', *Economy and Society*, 6, pp. 194–233.

KALLEN, H. M. (1973), Introduction to M. Natanson, *The Social Dynamics of George H. Mead*, The Hague, Martinus Nijhoff.

KAPLAN, A. (1964), 'Power in Perspective', in R. L. Kahn and E. Boulding (eds), *Power and Conflict in Organizations*, London, Tavistock, pp. 11–32.

KARPIK, L. (1972), 'Les Politiques et les logiques d'action de la grande enterprise industrielle', *Sociologie du Travail*, 1, pp. 82–105.

KARPIK, L. (1973), 'The Politics and Logics of Action of the Large Industrial Enterprise', mimeo.

KARPIK, L. (1977), 'Technological Capitalism', in S. Clegg and D. Dunkerley (eds), *Critical Issues in Organizations*, London, Routledge & Kegan Paul, pp. 41–71.

KARPIK, L. (1978), 'Organizations, Institutions and History', in L. Karpik (ed.), *Organization and Environment: Theory, Issues and Reality*, London, Sage, pp. 15–68.

KASARDA, J. D. (1973), 'Effects of Personnel Turnover, Employee Qualifications and Professional Staff Relations on Administrative

Intensity and Overhead', *Sociological Quarterly*, 14, pp. 350–8.

KATZ, D. and KAHN, R. L. (1966), *The Social Psychology of Organizations*, New York, Wiley.

KERR, C., DUNLOP, J. T., HARBISON, F. and MYERS, C. A. (1973), *Industrialism and Industrial Man*, Harmondsworth, Penguin.

KERR, C. and FISHER, L. (1957), 'Plant Sociology: the élite and the aborigines', in M. Komarovsky (ed.), *Common Frontiers of the Social Sciences*, Chicago, Free Press, pp. 287–309.

KHANDWALLA, P. N. (1977), *Design of Organizations*, New York, Harcourt, Brace Jovanovich.

KING, A. Y-C. (1977), 'A Voluntaristic Model of Organization: the Maoist version and its critique', *BJS*, 28, pp. 363–74.

KNIGHT, P. (1974), *The Successful Applicant Will be a Man*, London, British Humanist Association.

KOLAJA, J. (1965), *Workers' Councils: The Yugoslav Experience*, London, Tavistock.

KOOT, W. (1976), 'Sociological Analysis of Organizational Power: comment to Stewart Clegg', *Mens en Maatschappij*, 30, pp. 201–10.

KREINER, K. (1976), *The Site Organization: A Study of Social Relationships on Construction Sites*, Copenhagen, Danmarks Tekniske Hojskole.

KRUPP, S. (1961), *Pattern in Organization Analysis: a critical examination*, New York, Holt, Rinehart & Winston.

KULA, W. (1977), *An Economic Theory of the Feudal System*, London, New Left Books.

LACLAU, E. (1975), 'The Specificity of the Political: the Poulantzas-Miliband Debate', *Economy and Society*, 1, pp. 87–110.

LAND, H. (1976), 'Women: Supporters or Supported?', in D. L. Barker and S. Allen (eds), *Sexual Divisions and Society: Process and Change*, London, Tavistock, pp. 108–32.

LANDSBERGER, H. A. (1958), *Hawthorne Revisited*, New York, Cornell University Press.

LANDSBERGER, H. A. (1961), 'Parsons' 'Theory of Organizations', in M. Black (ed.), *The Social Theories of Talcott Parsons*, New Jersey, Prentice-Hall, pp. 213–9.

LASLETT, P. (1965), *The World We Have Lost*, London, Methuen.

LASSMAN, P. (1974), 'Phenomenological Perspectives in Sociology', in J. Rex (ed.), *Approaches to Sociology*, London, Routledge & Kegan Paul, pp. 125–44.

LAWRENCE, P. R. and LORSCH, J. W. (1967), *Organization and Environment: Managing Differentiation and Integration*, Boston, Harvard University Press.

LAZARSFELD, P. F. and MENZEL, H. (1961), 'On the Relation between the Individual and Collective Properties', in A. Etzioni (ed.), *Complex Organizations*, New York, Holt, Rinehart & Winston, pp. 422–40.

LENIN, V. I. (1947), 'The State and Revolution', in *Collected Works*, vol. 25, Moscow, Foreign Languages Publishing House.

LENIN, V. I. (1956), *Selected Works*, vol. 2, Moscow, Foreign Languages Publishing House.

LENIN, V. I. (1965), *Collected Works*, vol. 27, Moscow, Progress Publishers.

BIBLIOGRAPHY

LENIN, V. I. (1969), *Selected Works*, London, Lawrence & Wishart.

LEVINE, J. H. (1972), 'The Sphere of Influence', *ASR*, 56, pp. 777–87.

LEVINE, S. and WHITE, P. E. (1961), 'Exchange as a Conceptual Framework for the Study of Interorganizational Relationships', *ASQ*, 5, pp. 583–610.

LEVY, P. M. and PUGH, D. S. (1969), 'Scaling and Multivariate Analyses in the Study of Organizational Variables', *Sociology*, 3, pp. 193–213.

LEWIN, K. (1969), 'Group Decision and Social Change', in H. Proshansky and B. Seidenberg (eds), *Basic Studies in Social Psychology*, New York, Holt, Rinehart & Winston, pp. 29–47.

LEWIN, K., LIPPITT, R. and WHITE, R. K. (1939), 'Patterns of Aggressive Behaviour in Experimentally Created "Social Climates"', *J. Soc. Psych.*, 10, pp. 271–99.

LEWIS, J. (1975), *Max Weber and Value-Free Sociology: a Marxist Critique*, London, Lawrence & Wishart.

LIKERT, R. (1959), 'Management, Measurement and Motivation', in F. E. May (ed.), *Increasing Sales Efficiency*, Ann Arbor, University of Michigan Press, pp. 67–82.

LIKERT, R. (1961), *New Patterns of Management*, New York, McGraw-Hill.

LIPPITT, R. (1940), 'An Experimental Study of the Effect of Democratic and Authoritarian Group Atmospheres', *University of Iowa Studies in Child Welfare*, 16, pp. 43–195.

LIPSETT, S. M. (1960), *Political Man*, Garden City, Doubleday.

LIPSEY, R. G. (1963), *An Introduction to Positive Economics*, London, Weidenfeld & Nicolson.

LITTLER, C. (1978), 'Understanding Taylorism', *BJS*, 29, pp. 185–202.

LOCKWOOD, D. (1958), *The Black-Coated Worker*, London, Allen & Unwin.

LOCKWOOD, D. (1964), 'Social Integration and System Integration', in G. K. Zollschan and W. Hirsch (eds), *Explorations in Social Change*, London, Routledge & Kegan Paul, pp. 244–57.

LODAHL, T. M. (1964), 'Patterns of Job Attitudes in Two Assembly Technologies', *ASQ*, 8, pp. 483–519.

LUKES, S. (1973), *Emile Durkheim: His Life and Work*, London, Allen Lane.

LUND, R. (1976), 'Power and Participation: The Danish Experience', paper presented at the EGOS Symposium on Power, Bradford University, 6–7 May.

LUPTON, T. (1963), *On The Shop Floor*, Oxford, Pergamon.

LUPTON, T. (1971), *Management and the Social Sciences*, Harmondsworth, Penguin.

LUPTON, T. and CUNNISON, S. (1964), 'Workshop Behaviour', in M. Gluckman (ed.), *Closed Systems and Open Minds*, Edinburgh, Oliver & Boyd, pp. 103–28.

MACCIOCCHI, M. (1972), *Daily Life in Revolutionary China*, New York, Monthly Review Press.

MCCONNELL, G. (1966), *Private Power and American Democracy*, New York, Vintage.

MCCULLOUGH, A. E. and SHANNON, M. (1977), 'Organizations and Protection', in S. Clegg and D. Dunkerley (eds), *Critical Issues in Organizations*, London, Routledge & Kegan Paul, pp. 72–85.

MCEWEN, W. J. (1956), 'Position Conflict and Professional Orientation in a Research Organization', *ASQ*, 1, pp. 208–24.

MCGREGOR, D. (1960), *The Human Side of Enterprise*, New York, McGraw-Hill.

MCGREGOR, D. (1966), *Leadership and Motivation*, Cambridge, Mass., MIT Press.

MCHUGH, P. (1968), *Defining the Situation*, Indianapolis, Bobbs-Merrill.'

MCIVER, R. N. (1936), *Community: A Sociological Study*, New York, Macmillan.

MACKIE, A. (1976), 'The Scottish Daily News', in K. Coates (ed.), *The New Worker Co-Operatives*, Nottingham, Spokesman Books, pp. 109–40.

MACKIE, L. and PATTULLO, P. (1977), *Women at Work*, London, Tavistock.

MCLELLAN, D. (1968), *The Thought of Karl Marx*, London, Macmillan.

MCMILLAN, C. J. (1973), 'Corporations Without Citizenship: The Emergence of Multinational Enterprise', in G. Salaman and K. Thompson (eds), *People and Organizations*, London, Longman, pp. 25–44.

MCMILLAN, C. J. (1974), 'The Multinational Enterprise', Block I, Unit 2 of OU Course DT352, *People and Organizations*, Milton Keynes, Open University Press, pp. 33–50.

MCMILLAN, C. J. (1976), 'A Cross-National Comparison of Organizational Control', unpublished PhD Thesis, University of Bradford.

MCNEIL, K. (1978), 'Understanding Organizational Power: Building on the Weberian Legacy', *ASQ*, 23, pp. 65–90.

MACPHERSON, C. B. (1962), *The Political Theory of Possessive Individualism*, Oxford, Clarendon Press.

MACPHERSON, C. B. (1973), *Democratic Theory: Essays in Retrieval*, Oxford, Clarendon Press.

MAGUBANE, B. (1975), 'The Native Reserve (Bantusans) and the Role of the Migrant Labour Systems in the Political Economy of South Africa', in H. Safa and R. M. Du Toit (eds), *Migration and Development*, Paris, Mouton, pp. 225–69.

MAHER, J. R. (1971), *New Perspectives in Job Enrichment*, New York, Van Nostrand Reinhold.

MAIER, C. S. (1970), 'Between Taylorism and Technocracy: European Ideologies and the Vision of Industrial Productivity in the 1920s', *Journal of Contemporary History*, 5, pp. 27–61.

MANDEL, E. (1975), *Late Capitalism*, London, New Left Books.

MANN, F. C. and HOFFMAN, L. R. (1960), *Automation and the Worker*, New York, Holt, Rinehart & Winston.

MANUEL, F. E. (1956), *The New World of Henri Saint-Simon*, Cambridge, Mass., Harvard University Press.

MARCEAU, J. (1976), 'Marriage, Role Division and Social Cohesion: the case of some French upper-middle class families', in D. L. Barker and S. Allen (eds), *Dependence and Exploitation in Work and Marriage*, London, Longman, pp. 204–23.

MARCEAU, J., THOMAS, A. B. and WHITLEY, R. (1978), 'Business and the State: Management Education and Business Elites in France and Great Britain', in G. Littlejohn, B. Smart, J. Wakeford, and N. Yuval-Davis (eds), *Power and the State*, London, Croom Helm, pp. 128–57.

BIBLIOGRAPHY

MARCH, J. G. and OLSEN, J. P. (1976), *Ambiguity and Choice in Organizations,* Oslo, Universitesforlaget.

MARCH, J. G. and SIMON. H. A. (1958), *Organizations,* New York, Wiley.

MARCUSE, H. (1955), *Reason and Revolution,* London, Routledge & Kegan Paul.

MARCUSE, H. (1964), *One Dimensional Man: Studies in the Ideology of Advanced Industrial Societies,* London, Routledge & Kegan Paul.

MARCUSE, H. (1971), 'Industrialisation and Capitalism', translated by K. Morris, in O. Stammer (ed.), *Max Weber and Sociology Today,* Oxford, Blackwell, pp. 133–70.

MARGLIN, S. A. (1974), 'What do Bosses Do? – the origins and functions of hierarchy in capitalist production', *Review of Radical Political Economics,* 6, pp. 60–112.

MARSHALL, D. (1954), 'The Old Poor Law 1666–1772', in E. M. Carus-Wilson (ed.), *Essays in Economic History,* London, Edward Arnold, pp. 295–305.

MARSHALL, G. (1964), 'Sovereignty', in D. Gould and W. L. Koulb (eds), *A Dictionary of the Social Sciences,* London, Tavistock, pp. 686–7.

MARTIN, R. (1977), *The Sociology of Power,* London, Routledge & Kegan Paul.

MARTINELLI, A. and SOMAINI, E. (1973), 'Nation States and Multinational Corporations', *Kapitalistate,* 1, pp. 69–78.

MARTINS, H. (1974), 'Time and Theory in Sociology', in J. Rex (ed.), *Approaches to Sociology: An Introduction to Major Trends in British Sociology,* London, Routledge & Kegan Paul, pp. 246–94.

MARX, K. (1959), *Capital,* vol. 3, Moscow, Progress Publishers.

MARX, K. (1966), *The Civil War in France,* Peking, Foreign Language Press.

MARX, K. (1969), *Theories of Surplus Value,* vol. 2, Moscow, Progress Publishers.

MARX, K. (1969–72), *Theories of Surplus Value,* vols 1–3, London, Lawrence & Whishart.

MARX, K. (1970), *Critique of Hegel's Philosophy of the State,* edited by J. O'Malley, Cambridge University Press.

MARX, K. (1973), *Grundrisse: Introduction to the Critique of Political Economy,* translated and with a foreword by M. Nicolaus, Harmondsworth, Penguin.

MARX, K. (1974), *Capital,* vol. 1, London, Dent, Everyman.

MARX, K. (1975), 'A Contribution to the Critique of Hegel's Philosophy of Right', in L. Colletti (ed.), *Karl Marx: Early Writings,* Harmondsworth, Penguin, pp. 243–58.

MARX, K. (1976), *Capital,* vol. 1, Harmondsworth, Penguin.

MARX, K. and ENGELS, F. (1965), *The German Ideology,* London, Lawrence & Wishart.

MARX, K. and ENGELS, F. (1969), 'The Communist Manifesto', in L. S. Fleur (ed.), *Marx and Engels: Basic Writings on Politics and Philosophy,* London, Fontana, pp. 43–82.

MASLOW, A. (1954), *Motivation and Personality,* New York, Harper & Row.

MATHIAS, P. (1969), *The First Industrial Nation, an Economic History of Britain 1700–1914,* London, Methuen.

MAYER, J. P. (1956), *Max Weber and German Politics*, London, Faber & Faber.

MAYNTZ, R. (1964), 'The Study of Organizations', *Current Sociology*, 13, pp. 94–156.

MAYO, E. (1933), *The Human Problems of an Industrial Civilization*, New York, Macmillan.

MAYO, E. (1975), *The Social Problems of an Industrial Civilization*, London, Routledge & Kegan Paul.

MAYO, E. and LOMBARD, G. F. (1944), *Teamwork and Labour Turnover in the Aircraft Industry of Southern California*, Cambridge, Mass., Harvard Business School.

MEAD, G. H. (1934), *Mind, Self and Society*, edited by Charles Morris, Berkeley, University of California Press.

MEAD, M. (1935), *Sex and Temperament in Three Primitive Societies*, London, Routledge & Kegan Paul.

MEAD, M. (1962), *Male and Female*, London, Allen Lane.

MECHANIC, D. (1962), 'Sources of Power of Lower Participants in Complex Organizations', *ASQ*, 7, pp. 349–64.

MELDEN, A. I. (1961), *Free Action*, London, Routledge & Kegan Paul.

MERRINGTON, J. (1968), 'Theory and Practice in Gramsci's Marxism', *Socialist Register*, London, Merlin, pp. 145–76.

MERTON, R. K. (1940), 'Bureaucratic Structure and Personality', *Social Forces*, 18, pp. 560–8.

MERTON, R. K. (1949), *Social Theory and Social Structure*, Chicago, Free Press.

MEYER, M. W. (1972), 'Size and the Structure of Organizations: a Causal Analysis', *ASR*, 37, pp. 434–41.

MICHELS, R. (1949), *Political Parties*, Chicago, Free Press.

MILIBAND, R. (1969), *The State in Capitalist Society*, London, Quartet.

MILLER, E. J. and RICE, A. K. (1967), *Systems of Organizations*, London, Tavistock.

MILLS, A. J. (1974), 'Factory Work-Ins', *New Society*, 22 August.

MILLS, C. W. (1948), 'The Contributions of Sociology to Studies of Industrial Relations', *Proceedings of the Industrial Relations Research Association*, 1, pp. 199–222.

MILLS, C. W. (1956), *White Collar*, New York, Galaxy.

MILLS, C. W. (1959a), *The Power Elite*, New York, Oxford University Press.

MILLS, C. W. (1959b), *The Sociological Imagination*, London, Oxford University Press.

MINDLIN, S. and ALDRICH, H. E. (1975), 'Interorganizational Dependence: a review of the concept and a re-examination of the findings of the Aston Group', *ASQ*, 20, pp. 382–92.

MITCHELL, J. (1971), *Women's Estate*, Harmondsworth, Penguin.

MITZMAN, A. (1970), *The Iron Cage: An Historical Interpretation of Max Weber*, New York, Alfred Knopf.

MOHR, L. B. (1973), 'The Concept of Organizational Goal', *Am. Pol. Sci. Rev.*, 67, pp. 470—81.

MOMMSEN, W. J. (1974), *The Age of Bureaucracy*, Oxford, Blackwell.

MONDS, J. (1976), 'Workers' Control and the Historians: a New

Economism', *New Left Review*, 97, pp. 81–100.

MONTGOMERY, D. (1974), 'The New Unionism and the Transformation of Workers' Consciousness in America, 1909–1922', *Journal of Social History*, 7, pp. 509–29.

MOONEY, J. D. and REILEY, A. C. (1931), *Onward Industry!*, New York, Harper.

MOORE, W. E. (1948), 'Industrial Sociology: Status and Prospects', *ASR*, 13, pp. 382–91.

MORSE, N. and REIMER. E. (1956), 'The Experimental Change of a Major Organizational Variable', *Journal of Abnormal Psychology*, 52, pp. 120–9.

MORTON, P. (1972), 'Women's Work is Never Done', in *Women Unite!*, Toronto, Women's Educational Press, pp. 46–68.

MOUZELIS, N. (1967), *Organization and Bureaucracy*, London, Routledge & Kegan Paul.

MOUZELIS, N. (1975), Introduction to 1975 edition *Organization and Bureaucracy*, London, Routledge & Kegan Paul, pp. XI–XXXIV.

MULDER, M. (1974), *Power Distance Reduction Tendencies: Problems of Power and Power Relations*, Delft, Foundation for Business Sciences.

MÜLLER, R. (1976), 'The Political Economy of Global Corporations and National Stabilization Policy: a diagnostic on the need for social planning', in D. E. Apter and L. W. Goodman (eds), *The Multinational Corporation and Social Change*, London, Praeger, pp. 179–99.

MUMFORD, E. and BANKS, O. (1967), *The Computer and the Clerk*, London, Routledge & Kegan Paul.

MYERS, C. S. (1921), 'The Efficiency Engineer and the Industrial Psychologist', *Journal of the National Institute of Industrial Psychology*, 1, pp. 168–72.

NAVARRO, V. (1975), 'The Political Economy of Medical Care', *International Journal of Health Services*, 5, pp. 65–94.

NEE, V. and PECK, J. (1975), *China's Uninterrupted Revolution – from 1840 to the present*, New York, Pantheon.

NICHOLS, T. and ARMSTRONG, P. (1976), *Workers Divided*, London, Fontana.

NICHOLS, T. and BEYNON. H. (1977), *Living with Capitalism*, London, Routledge & Kegan Paul.

NISBET, A. (1965), *Emile Durkheim*, New York, Prentice-Hall.

NYMAN, S. and SILBERSTON, A. (1978), 'The Ownership and Control of Industry', *Oxford Economic Papers*, 30, pp. 74–101.

OAKLEY, A. (1972), *Sex, Gender and Society*, London, Temple Smith.

OBRADOVIC, J. (1975), 'Workers' Participation: Who Participates?' *Industrial Relations*, 14, pp. 32–44.

O'CONNOR, J. (1973a), *The Fiscal Crisis of the State*, New York, St Martins Press.

O'CONNOR, J. (1973b), 'Summary of the Theory of the Fiscal Crisis', *Kapitalistate*, 1, pp. 79–83.

O'CONNOR, J. (1974), *The Corporation and the State: Essays in the Theory of Capitalism and Imperialism*, New York, Harper Colophon.

OFFE, C. (1973a), 'The Abolition of Market Control and the Problem of Legitimacy' (I), *Kapitalistate*, 1, pp. 109–16.

OFFE, C. (1973b), 'The Abolition of Market Control and the Problem of Legitimacy (II)', *Kapitalistate*, 2, pp. 73–6.

OFFE, C. (1975a), 'The Theory of the Capitalist State and the Problem of Policy Formation', in L. N. Lindberg, R. Alford, C. Crouch and C. Offe (eds), *Stress and Contradiction in Modern Capitalism*, New York, D. C. Heath, pp. 125–144.

OFFE, C. (1975b), 'Introduction to Legitimacy versus Efficiency', in L. N. Lindberg, R. Alford, C. Crouch and C. Offe (eds), *Stress and Contradiction in Modern Capitalism*, pp. 245–60.

OFFE, C. (1976a), *Industry and Inequality*, translated and with an introduction by J. Wickham, London, Edward Arnold.

OFFE, C. (1976b), 'Crises and Crisis Management: Elements of a Political Crisis Theory', *International Journal of Politics*, 6, pp. 29–67.

OFFE, C. (1976c), 'Political Authority and Class Structures', in P. Connerton (ed.), *Critical Sociology*, Harmondsworth, Penguin, pp. 388–421.

OFFE, C. and RONGE, V. (1975), 'Theses on the Theory of the State', *New German Critique*, 6, pp. 137–47.

OUTHWAITE, W. (1975), *Understanding Social Life: The Method Called Verstehen*, London, Allen & Unwin.

PAGGI. L. (1977), 'Gramsci's General Theory of Marxism', *Telos*, 33, pp. 27–70

PAHL, R. E. and WINKLER, J. T. (1974), 'The Economic Elite: Theory and Practice', in P. Stanworth and A. Giddens (eds), *Elites and Power in British Society*, Cambridge University Press, pp. 102–22.

PALLOIX, C. (1976), 'The Labour Process: from Fordism to Neo-Fordism', in CSE Pamphlet No. 1, *The Labour Process and Class Struggle*, London, Stage I, pp. 46–67.

PALUMBO, D. J. (1969), 'Power and Role Specificity in Organizational Theory', *Public Administration Review*, 29, pp. 237–48.

PARETO, V. (1935), *The Mind and Society*, Cambridge, Mass., Harvard University Press.

PARKIN, F. (1972), *Class Inequality and Political Order*, London, Paladin.

PARKIN, F. (1976). 'System Contradiction and Political Transformation: The Comparative Study of Industrial Societies', in T. R. Burns and W. Buckley (eds), *Power and Control: Social Structures and their Transformation*, London, Sage, pp. 127–46.

PARKINSON, C. N. (1957), *Parkinson's Law*, Boston, Houghton Mifflin.

PARRY, G. and MORRIS, P. (1974), 'When is a Decision not a Decision?', in I. Crewe (ed.), *British Political Sociology Yearbook: Elites in Western Democracy*, vol 1, London, Croom Helm, pp. 317–36.

PARSONS, T. (1937), *The Structure of Social Action*, Chicago, Free Press.

PARSONS, T. (1951), *The Social System*, Chicago, Free Press.

PARSONS, T. (1956), 'Suggestions for a Sociological Approach to the Theory of Organizations', *ASQ*, 1, pp. 63–85, 225–39.

PARSONS, T. (1957), 'The Mental Hospital as a Type of Organization', in M. Greenblatt, D. Levinson and R. H. Williams (eds), *The Patient and the Mental Hospital*, Chicago, Free Press, pp. 108–29.

PARSONS, T. (1960), *Structure and Process in Modern Societies*, Chicago, Free Press.

PATEMAN, C. (1970), *Participation and Democratic Theory*, Cambridge University Press

PEEL, J. D. Y. (1971), *Herbert Spencer, The Evolution of a Sociologist*, London, Heinemann.

PENNINGS, J., HICKSON, D. J., HININGS, C. R., LEE, C. A. and SCHNECK, R. E. (1969), 'Uncertainty and Power in Organizations: a strategic contingencies model of sub-unit functioning', *Mens en Maatschappij*, 23, pp. 418–33.

PERROW, C. (1961), 'The Analysis of Goals in Complex Organizations', *ASR*, 26, pp. 854–66.

PERROW, C. (1965), 'Hospitals: Technology, Structure and Goals', in J. G. March (ed.), *Handbook of Organizations*, Chicago, Rand McNally, pp. 910–71.

PERROW, C. (1967), 'A Framework for the Comparative Analysis of Organizations', *ASR*, 32, pp. 194–208.

PERROW, C. (1968), 'Organizational Goals', in *The International Encyclopaedia of the Social Sciences*, 11, New York, Macmillan, pp. 305–16.

PERROW, C. (1970), *Organizational Analysis: A Sociological View*, London, Tavistock.

PERROW, C. (1972), *Complex Organizations: A Critical Essay*, Glenview, Ill., Scott Foresman.

PETTIGREW, A. (1973), *The Politics of Organizational Decision-Making*, London, Tavistock.

PHILLIPSON, M. and ROCHE, M. (1971), 'Phenomenological Sociology and the Study of Deviance', paper presented at the *1971 Annual Conference of the British Sociological Association*.

PICCONE, P. (1976), 'Gramsci's Marxism: Beyond Lenin and Togliatti', *Theory and Society*, 3, pp. 485–512.

POLANYI, K. (1957), *The Great Transformation*, Boston, Beacon Press.

POLLARD, S. (1965), *The Genesis of Modern Management*, London, Edward Arnold.

PONDY, L. R. (1969), 'Effects of Size, Complexity and Ownership on Administrative Intensity', *ASQ*, 14, pp. 47–60.

POULANTZAS, N. (1973), 'The Problem of the Capitalist State', in J. Urry and J. Wakeford (eds), *Power in Britain*, London, Heinemann, pp. 291–305.

POULANTZAS, N. (1975), *Classes in Contemporary Capitalism*, London, New Left Books.

POWER, E. (1965), 'The Position of Women', in C. G. Crump (ed.), *The Legacy of the Middle Ages*, Oxford, Clarendon Press, pp. 401–33.

PRESTHUS, R. V. (1961), 'Weberian *v.* Welfare Bureaucracy in Traditional Society', *ASQ*, 6, pp. 1–24.

PUGH, D. S., DONALDSON, L. and SILVER, P. (1976), 'A Comparative Study of Processes of Organizational Decision-Making: A Preliminary Report', Working Paper, London Graduate School of Business Studies.

PUGH, D. S., HICKSON, D. J. and HININGS, C. R. (1969), 'An Empirical Taxonomy of Work Organizations', *ASQ*, 14, pp. 115–26.

PUGH, D. S., HICKSON, D. J. and HININGS, C. R. (1971), *Writers on Organizations*, Harmondsworth, Penguin.

586

PUGH, D. S. and HICKSON, D. J. (1972), 'Causal Influence and the Aston Studies', letters to the editor, *ASQ*, 17, pp. 273–6.

PUGH, D. S. and HICKSON, D. J. (1976), *Organizational Structure in its Context: the Aston Programme I*, London, Saxon House.

PUGH, D. S. and PAYNE. R. L. (1977), *Organizational Behaviour in its Context: The Aston Programme III*, London, Saxon House.

RAMSAY, H. (1977a), 'Cycles of Control: Worker Participation in Sociological and Historical Perspective', *Sociology*, 11, pp. 481–506.

RAMSAY, H. (1977b), 'Magnitoogrsk, Zenica, Ansham: State Form and Workers' Control', paper presented at 2nd International Conference on Participation, Workers' Control and Self-Management, Paris, 7–10 September.

RAPOPORT, R. and RAPOPORT, R. (1971), *Dual Career Families*, Harmondsworth, Penguin.

REISSMAN, L. (1949), 'A Study of Role Conceptions in Bureaucracy', *Social Forces*, 27, pp. 305–10.

RENNER, K. (1949), *The Institutions of Private Law and their Social Functions*, London, Routledge & Kegan Paul.

RENNER, K. (1969), 'The Development of Capitalist Property and the Legal Institutions Complementary to the Property Norm', in V. Aubert (ed.), *The Sociology of Law*, Harmondsworth, Penguin, pp. 33–45.

REX, J. (1971), 'Typology and Objectivity: a comment on Weber's four sociological methods', in A. Sahay (ed.), *Max Weber and Modern Sociology*, London, Routledge & Kegan Paul, pp. 17–36.

RICE, A. K. (1958), *Productivity and Social Organization: the Ahmedabad Experiment*, London, Tavistock.

RICE, A. K. (1963), *The Enterprise and Its Environment*, London, Tavistock.

RICE, M. S. (1938), *Working Class Lives*, Harmondsworth, Penguin.

ROETHLISBERGER, F. G. and DICKSON, W. J. (1939), *Management and the Worker*, Cambridge, Mass., Harvard University Press.

ROGERS, J. T. (1920), *The Industrial and Commercial History of England*, London, Fisher Unwin.

ROSE, M. (1975), *Industrial Behaviour: Theoretical Developments Since Taylor*, London, Allen Lane.

ROWBOTHAM, S. (1975), *Hidden from History: 300 Years of Women's Oppression and the Fight Against It*, Harmondsworth, Penguin.

ROWTHORN, B. (1974), 'Neo-Ricardianism or Marxism?', *New Left Review*, 86, pp. 63–87.

ROWTHORN, B. (1976), Review article: 'Late Capitalism', *New Left Review*, 98, pp. 59–83.

RUBINSTEIN, W. D. (1974), 'Men of Property: some aspects of occupation, inheritance and power among top British wealthholders', in P. Stanworth and A. Giddens (eds), *Elites and Power in British Society*, Cambridge University Press, pp. 144–69.

RUS, V. (1970), 'Influence Structure in Yugoslav Enterprise', *Industrial Relations*, 9, pp. 148–60.

RUSSETT, C. E. (1966), *The Concept of Equilibrium in American Social Thought*, Yale University Press.

RUTIGLIANO, E. (1977), 'The Ideology of Labour and Capitalist Rationality in Gramsci', *Telos*, 31, pp. 91–9.

RYLE, G. (1949), *The Concept of Mind*, London, Hutchinson.

SALAMAN, G. (1974), 'Classification of Organizations', in *Structure and System: basic concepts and theories*, Milton Keynes, Open University Press, pp. 37–51.

SALAMAN, G. and THOMPSON, K., eds (1973), *People and Organizations*, London, Longman.

SALAMAN, G. and THOMPSON, K. (1978), 'Class Culture and the Persistence of an Elite: The Case of Army Officer Selection', *Sociological Review*, 26, pp. 283–304.

SAMPSON, A. (1973), *The Sovereign State: the secret history of ITT*, London, Hodder & Stoughton.

SAVILLE, J. (1969), 'Primitive Accumulation and Early Industrialization in Britain', in R. Miliband and J. Saville (eds), *Socialist Register*, London, Merlin Press, pp. 247–71,

SAYLES, L. R. (1958), *Behaviour of Industrial Work Groups*, New York, Wiley.

SCHEIN, E. H. (1965), *Organizational Psychology*, New York, Prentice-Hall.

SCHMITTER, P. C. (1974), 'Still the Century of Corporatism?', *Review of Politics*, 36, pp. 85–131.

SCHNEIDER, E. V. (1950), 'Limitations on Observations in Industrial Sociology', *Social Forces*, 28, pp. 279–84.

SCHNEIDER, E. V. (1971), *Industrial Sociology: the social relations of industry and the community*, New York, McGraw-Hill.

SCHROYER, T. (1972), 'Marx's Theory of the Crisis', *Telos*, 14, pp. 106–25.

SCHULTZ, G. P. and CRESARA, R. P. (1951), 'Worker Participation on Production Problems', *Frontiers of Personnel Administration*, Department of Industrial Engineering, Columbia University, June, pp. 77–88.

SCHUTZ, A. (1962), *Collected papers*, vol. 1, ed. by M. Natanson, The Hague, Martinus Nijhoff.

SCHUTZ, A. (1964), *Collected Papers*, vol. 2, ed. by A. Broderson, The Hague, Martinus Nijhoff.

SCHUTZ, A. (1966), *Collected Papers*, vol. 3, ed. by I. Schutz, The Hague, Martinus Nijhoff.

SCHUTZ, A. (1967), *The Phenomenology of the Social World*, translated by G. Walsh and F. Lehnert, with an introduction by G. Walsh, Evanston, Ill., Northwestern University Press.

SCOTT, F. G. (1959), 'Action Theory and Research in Social Organization', *AJS*, 64, pp. 386–95.

SCOTT, J. and HUGHES, M. (1976), 'Ownership and Control in the Scottish Economy: a discussion from Scottish data', *Sociology*, 10, pp. 21–41.

SCOTT, W. J., BANKS, J., HALSEY, A. H. and LUPTON, T. (1956), *Technical Change and Industrial Relations*, Liverpool University Press.

SECOMBE, W. (1974), 'The Housewife and her Labour under Capitalism', *New Left Review*, 83, pp. 3–24.

SECOMBE, W. (1975), 'Domestic Labour – a reply to critics', *New Left Review*, 94, pp. 85–96.

SELZNICK, P. (1943), 'An Approach to a Theory of Bureaucracy', *ASR*, 8, pp. 47–54.

SELZNICK, P. (1948), 'Foundations for a Theory of Organizations', *ASR*, 13, pp. 23–35.

SELZNICK, P. (1949), *TVA and the Grass Roots*, Berkeley, University of California Press.

SELZNICK, P. (1957), *Leadership in Administration*, New York, Harper & Row.

SELZNICK, P. (1960), *The Organizational Weapon*, Chicago, Free Press.

SENSAT, J., JR. and CONSTANTINE, G. (1975), 'A Critique of the Foundations of Utility Theory', *Science and Society*, 39, pp. 157–79.

SHIBBLES, W. (1967), *Wittgenstein, Language and Philosophy*, Dubuque, Iowa, Tendall/Hunt.

SHOR, E. L. (1960), 'The Thai Bureaucracy', *ASQ*, 5, pp. 66–86.

SHORTER, E. (1976), 'Women's Work: What Difference did Capitalism Make?', *Theory and Society*, 3, pp. 513–28.

SHULTZ, G. P. and WEBER, A. R. (1960), 'Technological Change and Industrial Relations', in J. Heneman (ed.), *Employment Relations Research*, New York, Harper & Row, pp. 199–221.

SILLS, D. L. (1957), *The Volunteers: means and ends in a national organization*, Chicago, Free Press.

SILVERMAN, D. (1968), 'Formal Organizations or Industrial Sociology: Towards a Social Action Analysis of Organizations', *Sociology*, 2, pp. 221–38.

SILVERMAN, D. (1970), *The Theory of Organizations*, London, Heinemann.

SILVERMAN, D. (1972), 'Some Neglected Questions about Social Reality', in P. Filmer, M. Phillipson, D. Silverman and D. Walsh (eds), *New Directions in Sociological Theory*, London, Collier-Macmillan, pp. 165–82.

SILVERMAN, D. (1974a), 'Speaking Seriously: The Language of Grading', *Theory and Society*, 1, pp. 1–15.

SILVERMAN, D. (1974b), 'Speaking Seriously: Part II', *Theory and Society*, 1, pp. 341–59.

SILVERMAN, D. (1975), 'Accounts of Organizations: organizational "structures" and the accounting process', in J. B. McKinlay (ed.), *Processing People: Cases in Organizational Behaviour*, London, Holt, Rinehart & Winston, pp. 269–302.

SILVERMAN, D. and JONES, J. (1976), *Organizational Work*, London, Collier-Macmillan.

SIMMEL, G. (1971), *On Individuality and Social Forms*, edited and with an introduction by K. H. Woolf, London, Collier-Macmillan.

SIMON, H. A. (1952), 'Decision-making and Administrative Organization', in R. K. Merton, A. P. Gray, B. Hockey and H. C. Selvin (eds), *Reader in Bureaucracy*, New York, Free Press, pp. 185–94.

SIMON, H. A. (1957), *Administrative Behaviour*, New York, Macmillan.

SIMON, H. A. (1964), 'On the Concept of Organizational Goal', *ASQ*, 9. pp. 1–22.

SMELSER, N. J. and DAVIS, J. A. (1968), *Sociology*, Englewood Cliffs, N. J., Prentice-Hall.

BIBLIOGRAPHY

SMITH, A. (1937), *The Wealth of Nations*, New York, Random House.

SMITH, J. D. and FRANKLIN, S. D. (1974), 'The Concentration of Personal Wealth 1922–1969', *American Economic Review*, May, pp. 162–67.

SMITH, J. H. (1975), 'The Significance of Elton Mayo', foreword to E. Mayo (1975), *The Social Problems of an Industrial Civilization*, 2nd edition, London, Routledge & Kegan Paul, pp. IX–XLII.

SMITH, M. A. (1977), 'Organizations', in S. R. Parker, R. K. Brown, J. Child and M. A. Smith, *The Sociology of Industry*, 3rd edition, London, Allen & Unwin, pp. 75–84.

Social Trends (1974), London, HMSO.

SOEMARDJAN, S. (1957), 'Bureaucratic Organization in a Time of Revolution', *ASQ*, 2, pp. 182–99.

SOHN-RETHEL, A. (1976), 'The Dual Economics of Transition', in CSE Pamphlet no. 1, *The Labour Process and Class Strategies*, London, Stage 1, pp. 26–45.

SOHN-RETHEL, A. (1978), *Intellectual and Manual Labour: A Critique of Epistemology*, London, Macmillan.

SORENSON, R. C. (1951), 'The Concept of Conflict in Industrial Sociology', *Social Forces*, 29, pp. 263–7.

SPENCER, H. (1893), *Principles of Sociology*, London, Williams & Norgate.

SPRIANO, P. (1975), *The Occupation of the Factories, Italy 1920*, London, Pluto Press.

STANWORTH, P. and GIDDENS, A. (1974) *Elites and Power in British Society*, Cambridge University Press.

STANWORTH, P. and GIDDENS, A. (1975), 'The Modern Corporate Economy: Interlocking Directorships in Britain 1906–1970', *Sociological Review*, 23, pp. 5–28.

STELLING, J. and BUCHER, R. (1972), 'Autonomy and Monitoring of Hospital Wards', *Sociological Quarterly*, 13, pp. 431–46.

STINCHCOMBE, A. L. (1959), 'Bureaucratic and Craft Administration of Production: a comparative study', *ASQ*, 4, pp. 168–87.

STINCHCOMBE, A. L. (1965), 'Social Structure and Organizations', in J. G. March (ed.), *Handbook of Organizations*, Chicago, McNally, pp. 142–93.

STONE, K. (1974), 'The Origins of Job Structures in the Steel Industry', *Review of Radical Political Economics*, 6, pp. 113–74.

STRAUSS, A., SCHATZMAN, L., BUCHER, R., EHRLICH, D. and SATSHIN, M. (1963), 'The Hospital and its Negotiated Order', in E. Friedson (ed.), *The Hospital in Modern Society*, Chicago, Free Press, pp. 147–69.

SUDNOW, D. (1973), 'Normal Crimes: sociological features of the penal code in a public defender office', in G. Salaman and K. Thompson (eds), *People and Organizations*, London, Longman, pp. 346–57.

SUTHERLAND, E. H. (1961), *White Collar Crime*, New York, Holt, Rinehart & Winston.

SUTTON, R. L. (1974), 'Culture, Context and Change-Agent Organizations', *ASQ*, 19, pp. 547–62.

SWINGEWOOD, A. (1975), *Marx and Modern Social Theory*, London, Macmillan.

TALACCHI, S. (1960), 'Organizational Size, Individual Attitudes and Behaviour: an empirical study', *ASQ*, 5, pp. 398–420.

TANNENBAUM, A. S. (1966), *Social Psychology of the Work Organization*, London, Tavistock.

TANNENBAUM, A. S. (1968), *Control in Organizations*, New York, McGraw-Hill.

TAYLOR, A. J. (1972), *Laissez-faire and State Intervention in Nineteenth-century Britain*, London, Macmillan.

TAYLOR, F. W. (1903), *Shop Management*, re-published in *Scientific Management* (1947), New York, Harper & Row.

TAYLOR, F. M. (1907), 'On the Art of Cutting Metals', *Transactions of the American Society of Mechanical Engineers*, 28.

TAYLOR, F. W. (1911), *Principles of Scientific Management*, New York, Harper.

TAYLOR, J. C. (1976), *Experiments in Work System Design: economic and human results*, Berkeley, University of California.

TAYLOR, L. and WALTON, P. (1971), *Images of Deviance*, Harmondsworth, Penguin.

TAYLOR, I., WALTON, P. and YOUNG, J. (1973), *The New Criminology: for a Social Theory of Deviance*, London, Routledge & Kegan Paul.

TERKEL, S. (1975), *Working*, London, Wildwood House.

TERRIEN, F. W. and MILLS, D. L. (1955), 'The Effect of Changing Size upon the Internal Structure of Organizations', *ASR*, 20, pp. 11–13.

THERBORN, G. (1976), *Science, Class and Society*, London, New Left Books.

THERBORN, G. (1978), *What Does the Ruling Class Do When it Rules?* London, New Left Books.

THOMAS, A. B. (1978), 'The British Business Elite: The Case of the Retail Sector', *Sociological Review*, 26, pp. 305–26.

THOMASON, G. F. (1972), 'Organizational Analysis', mimeo, Department of Industrial Relations, University of Wales, Cardiff.

THOMPSON, E. P. (1968), *The Making of the English Working Class*, Harmondsworth, Penguin.

THOMPSON, J. D. (1956), 'Authority and Power in "Identical" Organizations', *AJS*, 62, pp. 290–301.

THOMPSON, J. D. (1967), *Organizations in Action*, New York, McGraw-Hill.

THOMPSON, J. D. and BATES, F. L. (1957), 'Technology, Organization and Administration', *ASQ*, 2, pp. 325–43.

THOMPSON, J. D. and MCEWAN, W. J. (1958), 'Organizational Goals and Environment', *ASR*, 23, pp. 23–31.

THOMPSON, V. A. (1961), 'Hierarchy, Specialization and Organizational Conflict', *ASQ*, 5, pp. 485–521.

THURLEY, K. E. (1975), 'Some Limitations of the Late Development Thesis: Industrial Relations, Organizational Behaviour and Social Structure', paper presented at BSA Conference on Industrial Societies, University of Kent at Canterbury, April.

TÖNNIES, F. (1971), *On Sociology*, Chicago University Press.

TORNQUIST, D. (1973), 'Workers' Management: the intrinsic issues', in G. Hunnius, G. D. Garson and J. Case (eds), *Workers' Control*, New York, Vintage, pp. 374–94.

TOSI, H., ALDOG, R. and STOREY, R. (1973), 'On the Measurement of the Environment', *ASQ*, 18, pp. 27–36.

591

BIBLIOGRAPHY

TOURAINE, A. (1962), 'An Historical Theory in the Evolution of Industrial Skills', in C. R. Walker (ed.), *Modern Technology and Civilization*, New York, McGraw-Hill, pp. 425–37.

TRIBE, K. (1975), 'Capitalism and Industrialization', *Intervention*, 5, pp. 23–37.

TRIST, E. L. and BAMFORTH, K. (1951), 'Some Social and Psychological Consequences of the Longwall Method of Coal-Getting', *Human Relations*, 4, pp. 3–38.

TRIST, E. L., HIGGIN, G., MURRAY, H. and POLLOCK, A. (1963), *Organizational Choice*, London, Tavistock.

TURNER, A. N. and LAWRENCE, P. R. (1967), *Industrial Jobs and the Worker: an investigation of response to task attributes*, Boston, Harvard University Press.

TURNER, B. A. (1971), *Exploring the Industrial Subculture*, London, Macmillan.

UDY, S. H. (1959), 'Bureaucracy and Rationality in Weber's Organization Theory: an empirical study', *ASR*, 24, pp. 791–5.

UDY, S. H., (1961), 'Technical and Institutional Factors in Production Organization', *AJS*, 67, pp. 247–60.

URE, A. (1835), *The Philosophy of Manufactures*, London, Charles Knight.

URRY, J. and WAKEFORD, J., eds, (1973), *Power in Britain: Sociological Readings*, London, Heinemann.

URWICK, L. F. (1947), *The Elements of Administration*, London, Pitman.

VAN DER BERGHE, P. L. (1973), 'Dialectic and Functionalism: toward a theoretical synthesis', in W. J. Chambliss (ed.), *Sociological Readings in the Conflict Perspective*, Reading, Mass., Addison-Wesley, pp. 41–61.

VANEK, J. (1972), *The Economics of Workers' Management: a Yugoslav case study*, London, Allen & Unwin.

VEBLEN, T. (1965), *The Theory of Business Enterprise*, New York, Augustus Kelley.

VENESS, T. (1962), *School Leavers*, London, Methuen.

VERNON, R. (1973), *Sovereignty at Bay: The Multinational Spread of US Enterprise*, Harmondsworth, Penguin.

VERNON, R. (1976), 'Multinational Enterprise in Developing Countries: issues in dependency and interdependence', in D. E. Apter and L. W. Goodman (eds), *The Multinational Corporation and Social Change*, London, Praeger, pp. 40–62.

VILMAR, F. (1973), *Menschenwurde in Betrieb*, Hamburg, Rowolt.

WACHTEL, H. M. (1973), *Worker's Management and Workers' Wages in Yugoslavia: the theory and practice of participatory socialism*, New York, Cornell University Press.

WADSWORTH, A. P. and MANN, J. D. (1931), *The Cotton Trade and Industrial Lancashire*, Manchester University Press.

WALKER, C. R. and GUEST, R. H. (1952), *The Man on the Assembly Line*, Cambridge, Mass., Harvard University Press.

WALLERSTEIN, I. (1974a), *The Modern World System: Capitalist Agriculture and the Origins of the European World-economy in the Sixteenth Century*, London, Academic Press.

WALLERSTEIN, I. (1974b), 'The Rise and Future Demise of the World Capitalist System: Concepts for Comparative Analysis', *Comparative Studies in Society and History*, 16, pp. 387–415.

WALLERSTEIN, I. (1976a), 'A World System Perspective on the Social Sciences', *British Journal of Sociology*, 27, pp. 343–53.

WALLERSTEIN, I. (1976b), 'Semi-Peripheral Countries and the Contemporary World Crisis', *Theory and Society*, 3, pp. 461–83.

WARNER, M. (1975), 'Whither Yugoslav Self-Management?', *Industrial Relations Journal*, 6, pp. 65–72.

WARNER, W. L. and LOW, L. O. (1947), *The Social System of the Modern Factory*, Yale University Press.

WARREN, B. (1972), 'Capitalist Planning and the State', *New Left Review*, 72, pp. 3–29.

WARWICK, D. (1974), *Bureaucracy*, London, Longman.

WASSENBERG, A. (1977), 'The Powerlessness of Organization Theory', in S. Clegg and D. Dunkerley (eds), *Critical Issues in Organizations*, London, Routledge & Kegan Paul, pp. 86–98.

WEARMOUTH, R. F. (1937), *Methodism and the Working Class Movements of England, 1800–1950*, London, Epworth.

WEBER, M. (1923), *General Economic History*, translated by F. H. Knight, London, Allen & Unwin.

WEBER, M. (1947), *The Theory of Social and Economic Organization*, translated by T. Parsons and A. M. Henderson, with an introduction by T. Parsons, New York, Free Press.

WEBER, M. (1948), *From Max Weber: Essays in Sociology*, translated, edited and with an introduction by H. H. Gerth and C. Wright Mills, London, Routledge & Kegan Paul.

WEBER, M. (1949), *The Methodology of the Social Sciences*, translated and edited by E. A. Shils and H. A. Finch, New York, Free Press.

WEBER, M. (1951), *Gesammelte Aufsätze zur Wissenschaftslehre*, Tubingen, Mohr.

WEBER, M. (1968), *Economy and Society: An Outline of Interpretive Sociology*, 3 vols, edited and with an introduction by G. Roth and C. Wittich, New York, Bedminster Press.

WEBER, M. (1976), *The Protestant Ethic and the Spirit of Capitalism*, translated by T. Parsons and with a new introduction by A. Giddens, London, Allen & Unwin.

WEDDERBURN, D. (1972), 'Inequality at Work', in P. Townsend and N. Bosanquet (eds), *Labour and Inequality*, London, Fabian Society, pp. 174–85.

WEICK, K. E. (1969), *The Social Psychology of Organizing*, Reading, Mass., Addison-Wesley.

WESTERGAARD, J. (1977), 'Class, Inequality and "Corporatism"', in A. Hunt (ed.), *Class and Class Structure*, London, Lawrence & Wishart, pp. 165–86.

WESTERGAARD, J. and RESLER, H. (1976), *Class in a Capitalist Society*, Harmondsworth, Penguin.

WHITEHEAD, T. N. (1938), *The Industrial Worker*, London, Oxford University Press.

BIBLIOGRAPHY

WHITLEY, R. D. (1973), 'Commonalities and Connections Among Directors of Large Financial Institutions', *Sociological Review*, 21, pp. 613–32.

WHITLEY, R. D. (1974), 'The City and Industry: the directors of large companies, their characteristics and connections', in P. Stanworth, and A. Giddens, (eds), *Elites and Power in British Society*, Cambridge University Press, pp. 65–80.

WHYTE, M. K. (1973), 'Bureaucracy and Modernization in China: the Maoist Critique', *ASR*, 38, pp. 149–63.

WHYTE, W. F. (1964), 'Parsons' Theory Applied to Organizations', in M. Black (ed.), *The Social Theories of Talcott Parsons*, Englewood Cliffs, N.J., Prentice-Hall, pp. 250–67.

WIEDER, D. L. (1974), 'Telling the Code', in R. Turner (ed.), *Ethnomethodology*, Harmondsworth, Penguin, pp. 144–72.

WILAVSKY, A. (1964), *The Politics of the Budgetary Process*, Boston, Little Brown.

WILENSKY, H. L. (1967), *Organizational Intelligence*, New York, Basic Books.

WILENSKY, J. L. and WILENSKY, H. L. (1952), 'Personal Counselling: the Hawthorne Case', *AJS*, 57, pp. 265–80.

WILLER, D. and WILLER, J. (1973), *Systematic Empiricism: A Critique of a Pseudo-Science*, Englewood Cliffs, N.J., Prentice-Hall.

WILLIAMS, G. A. (1960), 'The Concept of "Egemonia" in the Thought of Antonio Gramsci: Some Notes on Interpretation', *Journal of the History of Ideas*, 21, pp. 586–99.

WILLIAMS, G. A. (1975), *Proletarian Order: Antonio Gramsci, Factory Councils and the Origins of Communism in Italy 1911–1921*, London, Pluto Press.

WINKLER, J. T. (1977), 'The Corporatist Economy: theory and administration', in R. Scase (ed.), *Industrial Society: Class, Cleavage and Control*, London, Allen & Unwin, pp. 43–58.

WINNER, L. (1977), *Autonomous Technology: technics-out-of-control as a theme in political thought*, Cambridge, Mass., MIT Press.

WITTE, E. (1972), 'Field Research or complex decision-making processes – the phase theorem', *International Studies of Management and Organization*, pp. 156–82.

WOLFE, A. (1974), 'New Directions in the Marxist Theory of Politics', *Politics and Society*, 4, pp. 131–59.

WOLFF, J. (1977), 'Women in Organizations', in S. Clegg and D. Dunkerley (eds), *Critical Issues in Organizations*, London, Routledge & Kegan Paul, pp. 7–20.

WOLIN, S. (1960), *Politics and Vision*, Boston, Little Brown.

WOODWARD, J. (1965), *Industrial Organization: Theory and Practice*, London, Oxford University Press.

WOODWARD, J. (1970), *Industrial Organization: Behaviour and Control*, London, Oxford University Press.

WRIGHT, E. O. (1978), *Class, Crisis and the State*, London, New Left Books.

YUCHTMAN, E. and SEASHORE, S. (1967), 'A System Resource Approach to Organizational Effectiveness, *ASR*, 32, pp. 891–903.

ZEITLIN, I. (1968), *Ideology and the Development of Sociology*, Englewood Cliffs, N.J., Prentice-Hall.

ZEITLIN, M. (1974), 'Corporate Ownership and Control: The Large Corporations and the Capitalist Class', *AJS*, 79, pp. 1073–119.

ZIMMERMAN, D. (1971), 'Record-Keeping and the Intake Process in a Public Welfare Organization', in S. Wheeler (ed.), *On Record: Files and Dossiers in American Life*, New York, Russel Sage Foundation.

ZIMMERMAN, D. (1973), 'The Practicalities of Rule Use', in G. Salaman and K. Thompson (eds), *People and Organizations*, London, Longman, pp. 250–63.

ZIMMERMAN, D. and POLLNER, M. (1971), 'The Everyday World as a Phenomenon', in J. Douglas (ed.), *Understanding Everyday Life*, London, Routledge & Kegan Paul, pp. 80–103.

Author index

Subject index

Routledge Social Science Series

Routledge & Kegan Paul   London, Henley and Boston

39 Store Street, London WC1E 7DD
Broadway House, Newtown Road,
Henley-on-Thames, Oxon RG9 1EN
9 Park Street, Boston, Mass. 02108

Contents

*Authors wishing to submit manuscripts for any series in
this catalogue should send them to the Social Science Editor,
Routledge & Kegan Paul Ltd, 39 Store Street,
London WC1E 7DD*

●*Books so marked are available in paperback
All books are in Metric Demy 8vo format (216 × 138mm approx.)*

International Library of Sociology

General Editor John Rex

GENERAL SOCIOLOGY

Barnsley, J. H. The Social Reality of Ethics. *464 pp.*
Brown, Robert. Explanation in Social Science. *208 pp.*
● Rules and Laws in Sociology. *192 pp.*
Bruford, W. H. Chekhov and His Russia. *A Sociological Study. 244 pp.*
Burton, F. and **Carlen, P.** Official Discourse. *On Discourse Analysis, Government Publications, Ideology. About 140 pp.*
Cain, Maureen E. Society and the Policeman's Role. *326 pp.*
●**Fletcher, Colin.** Beneath the Surface. *An Account of Three Styles of Sociological Research. 221 pp.*
Gibson, Quentin. The Logic of Social Enquiry. *240 pp.*
Glucksmann, M. Structuralist Analysis in Contemporary Social Thought. *212 pp.*
Gurvitch, Georges. Sociology of Law. *Foreword by Roscoe Pound. 264 pp.*
Hinkle, R. Founding Theory of American Sociology 1883-1915. *About 350 pp.*
Homans, George C. Sentiments and Activities. *336 pp.*
Johnson, Harry M. Sociology: *a Systematic Introduction. Foreword by Robert K. Merton. 710 pp.*
●**Keat, Russell** and **Urry, John.** Social Theory as Science. *278 pp.*
Mannheim, Karl. Essays on Sociology and Social Psychology. *Edited by Paul Keckskemeti. With Editorial Note by Adolph Lowe. 344 pp.*
Martindale, Don. The Nature and Types of Sociological Theory. *292 pp.*
●**Maus, Heinz.** A Short History of Sociology. *234 pp.*
Myrdal, Gunnar. Value in Social Theory: *A Collection of Essays on Methodology. Edited by Paul Streeten. 332 pp.*
Ogburn, William F. and **Nimkoff, Meyer F.** A Handbook of Sociology. *Preface by Karl Mannheim. 656 pp. 46 figures. 35 tables.*
Parsons, Talcott, and **Smelser, Neil J.** Economy and Society: *A Study in the Integration of Economic and Social Theory. 362 pp.*
Podgórecki, Adam. Practical Social Sciences. *About 200 pp.*
Raffel, S. Matters of Fact. *A Sociological Inquiry. 152 pp.*
●**Rex, John.** (Ed.) Approaches to Sociology. *Contributions by Peter Abell, Sociology and the Demystification of the Modern World. 282 pp.*
●**Rex, John** (Ed.) Approaches to Sociology. *Contributions by Peter Abell, Frank Bechhofer, Basil Bernstein, Ronald Fletcher, David Frisby, Miriam Glucksmann, Peter Lassman, Herminio Martins, John Rex, Roland Robertson, John Westergaard and Jock Young. 302 pp.*
Rigby, A. Alternative Realities. *352 pp.*
Roche, M. Phenomenology, Language and the Social Sciences. *374 pp.*
Sahay, A. Sociological Analysis. *220 pp.*

Strasser, Hermann. The Normative Structure of Sociology. *Conservative and Emancipatory Themes in Social Thought. About 340 pp.*
Strong, P. Ceremonial Order of the Clinic. *About 250 pp.*
Urry, John. Reference Groups and the Theory of Revolution. *244 pp.*
Weinberg, E. Development of Sociology in the Soviet Union. *173 pp.*

FOREIGN CLASSICS OF SOCIOLOGY

● **Gerth, H. H.** and **Mills, C. Wright.** From Max Weber: *Essays in Sociology. 502 pp.*
● **Tönnies, Ferdinand.** Community and Association. *(Gemeinschaft and Gesellschaft.) Translated and Supplemented by Charles P. Loomis. Foreword by Pitirim A. Sorokin. 334 pp.*

SOCIAL STRUCTURE

Andreski, Stanislav. Military Organization and Society. *Foreword by Professor A. R. Radcliffe-Brown. 226 pp. 1 folder.*
Carlton, Eric. Ideology and Social Order. *Foreword by Professor Philip Abrahams. About 320 pp.*
Coontz, Sydney H. Population Theories and the Economic Interpretation. *202 pp.*
Coser, Lewis. The Functions of Social Conflict. *204 pp.*
Dickie-Clark, H. F. Marginal Situation: *A Sociological Study of a Coloured Group. 240 pp. 11 tables.*
Giner, S. and **Archer, M. S.** (Eds.). Contemporary Europe. *Social Structures and Cultural Patterns. 336 pp.*
● **Glaser, Barney** and **Strauss, Anselm L.** Status Passage. *A Formal Theory. 212 pp.*
Glass, D. V. (Ed.) Social Mobility in Britain. *Contributions by J. Berent, T. Bottomore, R. C. Chambers, J. Floud, D. V. Glass, J. R. Hall, H. T. Himmelweit, R. K. Kelsall, F. M. Martin, C. A. Moser, R. Mukherjee, and W. Ziegel. 420 pp.*
Kelsall, R. K. Higher Civil Servants in Britain: *From 1870 to the Present Day. 268 pp. 31 tables.*
● **Lawton, Denis.** Social Class, Language and Education. *192 pp.*
McLeish, John. The Theory of Social Change: *Four Views Considered. 128 pp.*
● **Marsh, David C.** The Changing Social Structure of England and Wales, 1871-1961. *Revised edition. 288 pp.*
Menzies, Ken. Talcott Parsons and the Social Image of Man. *About 208 pp.*
● **Mouzelis, Nicos.** Organization and Bureaucracy. *An Analysis of Modern Theories. 240 pp.*
Ossowski, Stanislaw. Class Structure in the Social Consciousness. *210 pp.*
● **Podgórecki, Adam.** Law and Society. *302 pp.*
Renner, Karl. Institutions of Private Law and Their Social Functions. *Edited, with an Introduction and Notes, by O. Kahn-Freud. Translated by Agnes Schwarzschild. 316 pp.*

Rex, J. and **Tomlinson, S.** Colonial Immigrants in a British City. *A Class Analysis. 368 pp.*

Smooha, S. Israel: Pluralism and Conflict. *472 pp.*

Wesolowski, W. Class, Strata and Power. *Trans. and with Introduction by G. Kolankiewicz. 160 pp.*

Zureik, E. Palestinians in Israel. *A Study in Internal Colonialism. 264 pp.*

SOCIOLOGY AND POLITICS

Acton, T. A. Gypsy Politics and Social Change. *316 pp.*

Burton, F. Politics of Legitimacy. *Struggles in a Belfast Community. 250 pp.*

Etzioni-Halevy, E. Political Manipulation and Administrative Power. *A Comparative Study. About 200 pp.*

●**Hechter, Michael.** Internal Colonialism. *The Celtic Fringe in British National Development, 1536–1966. 380 pp.*

Kornhauser, William. The Politics of Mass Society. *272 pp. 20 tables.*

Korpi, W. The Working Class in Welfare Capitalism. *Work, Unions and Politics in Sweden. 472 pp.*

Kroes, R. Soldiers and Students. *A Study of Right- and Left-wing Students. 174 pp.*

Martin, Roderick. Sociology of Power. *About 272 pp.*

Myrdal, Gunnar. The Political Element in the Development of Economic Theory. *Translated from the German by Paul Streeten. 282 pp.*

Wong, S.-L. Sociology and Socialism in Contemporary China. *160 pp.*

Wootton, Graham. Workers, Unions and the State. *188 pp.*

CRIMINOLOGY

Ancel, Marc. Social Defence: *A Modern Approach to Criminal Problems. Foreword by Leon Radzinowicz. 240 pp.*

Athens, L. Violent Criminal Acts and Actors. *About 150 pp.*

Cain, Maureen E. Society and the Policeman's Role. *326 pp.*

Cloward, Richard A. and **Ohlin, Lloyd E.** Delinquency and Opportunity: *A Theory of Delinquent Gangs. 248 pp.*

Downes, David M. The Delinquent Solution. *A Study in Subcultural Theory. 296 pp.*

Friedlander, Kate. The Psycho-Analytical Approach to Juvenile Delinquency: *Theory, Case Studies, Treatment. 320 pp.*

Gleuck, Sheldon and **Eleanor.** Family Environment and Delinquency. *With the statistical assistance of Rose W. Kneznek. 340 pp.*

Lopez-Rey, Manuel. Crime. *An Analytical Appraisal. 288 pp.*

Mannheim, Hermann. Comparative Criminology: *a Text Book. Two volumes. 442 pp. and 380 pp.*

Morris, Terence. The Criminal Area: *A Study in Social Ecology. Foreword by Hermann Mannheim. 232 pp. 25 tables. 4 maps.*

Podgorecki, A. and **Łos, M.** *Multidimensional Sociology. About 380 pp.*

Rock, Paul. Making People Pay. *338 pp.*

● **Taylor, Ian, Walton, Paul,** and **Young, Jock.** The New Criminology. *For a Social Theory of Deviance. 325 pp.*

● **Taylor, Ian, Walton, Paul** and **Young, Jock.** (Eds) Critical Criminology. *268 pp.*

SOCIAL PSYCHOLOGY

Bagley, Christopher. The Social Psychology of the Epileptic Child. *320 pp.*

Brittan, Arthur. Meanings and Situations. *224 pp.*

Carroll, J. Break-Out from the Crystal Palace. *200 pp.*

● **Fleming, C. M.** Adolescence: Its Social Psychology. *With an Introduction to recent findings from the fields of Anthropology, Physiology, Medicine, Psychometrics and Sociometry. 288 pp.*

● The Social Psychology of Education: *An Introduction and Guide to Its Study. 136 pp.*

Linton, Ralph. The Cultural Background of Personality. *132 pp.*

● **Mayo, Elton.** The Social Problems of an Industrial Civilization. *With an Appendix on the Political Problem. 180 pp.*

Ottaway, A. K. C. Learning Through Group Experience. *176 pp.*

Plummer, Ken. Sexual Stigma. *An Interactionist Account. 254 pp.*

● **Rose, Arnold M.** (Ed.) Human Behaviour and Social Processes: *an Interactionist Approach. Contributions by Arnold M. Rose, Ralph H. Turner, Anselm Strauss, Everett C. Hughes, E. Franklin Frazier, Howard S. Becker et al. 696 pp.*

Smelser, Neil J. Theory of Collective Behaviour. *448 pp.*

Stephenson, Geoffrey M. The Development of Conscience. *128 pp.*

Young, Kimball. Handbook of Social Psychology. *658 pp. 16 figures. 10 tables.*

SOCIOLOGY OF THE FAMILY

Bell, Colin R. Middle Class Families: *Social and Geographical Mobility. 224 pp.*

Burton, Lindy. Vulnerable Children. *272 pp.*

Gavron, Hannah. The Captive Wife: *Conflicts of Household Mothers. 190 pp.*

George, Victor and **Wilding, Paul.** Motherless Families. *248 pp.*

Klein, Josephine. Samples from English Cultures.
  1. Three Preliminary Studies and Aspects of Adult Life in England. *447 pp.*
  2. Child-Rearing Practices and Index. *247 pp.*

Klein, Viola. The Feminine Character. *History of an Ideology. 244 pp.*

McWhinnie, Alexina M. Adopted Children. *How They Grow Up. 304 pp.*

● **Morgan, D. H. J.** Social Theory and the Family. *About 320 pp.*

● **Myrdal, Alva** and **Klein, Viola.** Women's Two Roles: *Home and Work. 238 pp. 27 tables.*

Parsons, Talcott and **Bales, Robert F.** Family: Socialization and Inter-action Process. *In collaboration with James Olds, Morris Zelditch and Philip E. Slater. 456 pp. 50 figures and tables.*

SOCIAL SERVICES

Bastide, Roger. The Sociology of Mental Disorder. *Translated from the French by Jean McNeil. 260 pp.*

Carlebach, Julius. Caring For Children in Trouble. *266 pp.*

George, Victor. Foster Care. *Theory and Practice. 234 pp.*

Social Security: *Beveridge and After. 258 pp.*

George, V. and **Wilding, P.** Motherless Families. *248 pp.*

● **Goetschius, George W.** Working with Community Groups. *256 pp.*

Goetschius, George W. and **Tash, Joan.** Working with Unattached Youth. *416 pp.*

Heywood, Jean S. Children in Care. *The Development of the Service for the Deprived Child. Third revised edition. 284 pp.*

King, Roy D., Ranes, Norma V. and **Tizard, Jack.** Patterns of Residential Care. *356 pp.*

Leigh, John. Young People and Leisure. *256 pp.*

● **Mays, John.** (Ed.) Penelope Hall's Social Services of England and Wales. *About 324 pp.*

Morris, Mary. Voluntary Work and the Welfare State. *300 pp.*

Nokes, P. L. The Professional Task in Welfare Practice. *152 pp.*

Timms, Noel. Psychiatric Social Work in Great Britain (1939-1962). *280 pp.*

● Social Casework: *Principles and Practice. 256 pp.*

SOCIOLOGY OF EDUCATION

Banks, Olive. Parity and Prestige in English Secondary Education: a Study in Educational Sociology. *272 pp.*

● **Blyth, W. A. L.** English Primary Education. *A Sociological Description.* 2. Background. *168 pp.*

Collier, K. G. The Social Purposes of Education: *Personal and Social Values in Education. 268 pp.*

Evans, K. M. Sociometry and Education. *158 pp.*

● **Ford, Julienne.** Social Class and the Comprehensive School. *192 pp.*

Foster, P. J. Education and Social Change in Ghana. *336 pp. 3 maps.*

Fraser, W. R. Education and Society in Modern France. *150 pp.*

Grace, Gerald R. Role Conflict and the Teacher. *150 pp.*

Hans, Nicholas. New Trends in Education in the Eighteenth Century. *278 pp. 19 tables.*

● Comparative Education: *A Study of Educational Factors and Traditions. 360 pp.*

● **Hargreaves, David.** Interpersonal Relations and Education. *432 pp.*

● Social Relations in a Secondary School. *240 pp.*

School Organization and Pupil Involvement. *A Study of Secondary Schools.*

● **Mannheim, Karl** and **Stewart, W.A.C.** An Introduction to the Sociology of Education. *206 pp.*
● **Musgrove, F.** Youth and the Social Order. *176 pp.*
● **Ottaway, A. K. C.** Education and Society: An Introduction to the Sociology of Education. *With an Introduction by W. O. Lester Smith. 212 pp.*
  Peers, Robert. Adult Education: *A Comparative Study. Revised edition. 398 pp.*
  Stratta, Erica. The Education of Borstal Boys. *A Study of their Educational Experiences prior to, and during, Borstal Training. 256 pp.*
● **Taylor, P. H., Reid, W. A.** and **Holley, B. J.** The English Sixth Form. *A Case Study in Curriculum Research. 198 pp.*

SOCIOLOGY OF CULTURE

Eppel, E. M. and **M.** Adolescents and Morality: *A Study of some Moral Values and Dilemmas of Working Adolescents in the Context of a changing Climate of Opinion. Foreword by W. J. H. Sprott. 268 pp. 39 tables.*
● **Fromm, Erich.** The Fear of Freedom. *286 pp.*
●   The Sane Society. *400 pp.*
  Johnson, L. The Cultural Critics. *From Matthew Arnold to Raymond Williams. 233 pp.*
  Mannheim, Karl. Essays on the Sociology of Culture. *Edited by Ernst Mannheim in co-operation with Paul Kecskemeti. Editorial Note by Adolph Lowe. 280 pp.*
  Zijderfeld, A. C. On Clichés. *The Supersedure of Meaning by Function in Modernity. About 132 pp.*

SOCIOLOGY OF RELIGION

Argyle, Michael and **Beit-Hallahmi, Benjamin.** The Social Psychology of Religion. *About 256 pp.*
Glasner, Peter E. The Sociology of Secularisation. *A Critique of a Concept. About 180 pp.*
Hall, J. R. The Ways Out. *Utopian Communal Groups in an Age of Babylon. 280 pp.*
Ranson, S., Hinings, B. and **Bryman, A.** Clergy, Ministers and Priests. *216 pp.*
Stark, Werner. The Sociology of Religion. *A Study of Christendom.*
  Volume II. *Sectarian Religion. 368 pp.*
  Volume III. *The Universal Church. 464 pp.*
  Volume IV. *Types of Religious Man. 352 pp.*
  Volume V. *Types of Religious Culture. 464 pp.*
Turner, B. S. Weber and Islam. *216 pp.*
Watt, W. Montgomery. Islam and the Integration of Society. *320 pp.*

SOCIOLOGY OF ART AND LITERATURE

Jarvie, Ian C. Towards a Sociology of the Cinema. *A Comparative Essay on the Structure and Functioning of a Major Entertainment Industry. 405 pp.*

Rust, Frances S. Dance in Society. *An Analysis of the Relationships between the Social Dance and Society in England from the Middle Ages to the Present Day. 256 pp. 8 pp. of plates.*

Schücking, L. L. The Sociology of Literary Taste. *112 pp.*

Wolff, Janet. Hermeneutic Philosophy and the Sociology of Art. *150 pp.*

SOCIOLOGY OF KNOWLEDGE

Diesing, P. Patterns of Discovery in the Social Sciences. *262 pp.*

● **Douglas, J. D.** (Ed.) Understanding Everyday Life. *370 pp.*

Glasner, B. Essential Interactionism. *About 220 pp.*

● **Hamilton, P.** Knowledge and Social Structure. *174 pp.*

Jarvie, I. C. Concepts and Society. *232 pp.*

Mannheim, Karl. Essays on the Sociology of Knowledge. *Edited by Paul Kecskemeti. Editorial Note by Adolph Lowe. 353 pp.*

Remmling, Gunter W. The Sociology of Karl Mannheim. *With a Bibliographical Guide to the Sociology of Knowledge, Ideological Analysis, and Social Planning. 255 pp.*

Remmling, Gunter W. (Ed.) Towards the Sociology of Knowledge. *Origin and Development of a Sociological Thought Style. 463 pp.*

URBAN SOCIOLOGY

Aldridge, M. The British New Towns. *A Programme Without a Policy. About 250 pp.*

Ashworth, William. The Genesis of Modern British Town Planning: *A Study in Economic and Social History of the Nineteenth and Twentieth Centuries. 288 pp.*

Brittan, A. The Privatised World. *196 pp.*

Cullingworth, J. B. Housing Needs and Planning Policy: *A Restatement of the Problems of Housing Need and 'Overspill' in England and Wales. 232 pp. 44 tables. 8 maps.*

Dickinson, Robert E. City and Region: *A Geographical Interpretation. 608 pp. 125 figures.*

The West European City: *A Geographical Interpretation. 600 pp. 129 maps. 29 plates.*

Humphreys, Alexander J. New Dubliners: *Urbanization and the Irish Family. Foreword by George C. Homans. 304 pp.*

Jackson, Brian. Working Class Community: *Some General Notions raised by a Series of Studies in Northern England. 192 pp.*

● **Mann, P. H.** An Approach to Urban Sociology. *240 pp.*

Mellor, J. R. Urban Sociology in an Urbanized Society. *326 pp.*

Morris, R. N. and **Mogey, J.** The Sociology of Housing. *Studies at Berinsfield. 232 pp. 4 pp. plates.*

Rosser, C. and **Harris, C.** The Family and Social Change. *A Study of Family and Kinship in a South Wales Town. 352 pp. 8 maps.*
● **Stacey, Margaret, Batsone, Eric, Bell, Colin** and **Thurcott, Anne.** Power, Persistence and Change. *A Second Study of Banbury. 196 pp.*

RURAL SOCIOLOGY

Mayer, Adrian C. Peasants in the Pacific. *A Study of Fiji Indian Rural Society. 248 pp. 20 plates.*
Williams, W. M. The Sociology of an English Village: *Gosforth. 272 pp. 12 figures. 13 tables.*

SOCIOLOGY OF INDUSTRY AND DISTRIBUTION

Dunkerley, David. The Foreman. *Aspects of Task and Structure. 192 pp.*
Eldridge, J. E. T. Industrial Disputes. *Essays in the Sociology of Industrial Relations. 288 pp.*
Hollowell, Peter G. The Lorry Driver. *272 pp.*
● **Oxaal, I., Barnett, T.** and **Booth, D.** (Eds) Beyond the Sociology of Development. *Economy and Society in Latin America and Africa. 295 pp.*
Smelser, Neil J. Social Change in the Industrial Revolution: *An Application of Theory to the Lancashire Cotton Industry, 1770–1840. 468 pp. 12 figures. 14 tables.*
Watson, T. J. The Personnel Managers. *A Study in the Sociology of Work and Employment. 262 pp.*

ANTHROPOLOGY

Brandel-Syrier, Mia. Reeftown Elite. *A Study of Social Mobility in a Modern African Community on the Reef. 376 pp.*
Dickie-Clark, H. F. The Marginal Situation. *A Sociological Study of a Coloured Group. 236 pp.*
Dube, S. C. Indian Village. *Foreword by Morris Edward Opler. 276 pp. 4 plates.*
India's Changing Villages: *Human Factors in Community Development. 260 pp. 8 plates. 1 map.*
Firth, Raymond. Malay Fishermen. *Their Peasant Economy. 420 pp. 17 pp. plates.*
Gulliver, P. H. Social Control in an African Society: a Study of the Arusha, Agricultural Masai of Northern Tanganyika. *320 pp. 8 plates. 10 figures.*
Family Herds. *288 pp.*
Jarvie, Ian C. The Revolution in Anthropology. *268 pp.*
Little, Kenneth L. Mende of Sierra Leone. *308 pp. and folder.*
Negroes in Britain. *With a New Introduction and Contemporary Study by Leonard Bloom. 320 pp.*

Madan, G. R. Western Sociologists on Indian Society. *Marx, Spencer, Weber, Durkheim, Pareto. 384 pp.*
Mayer, A. C. Peasants in the Pacific. *A Study of Fiji Indian Rural Society. 248 pp.*
Meer, Fatima. Race and Suicide in South Africa. *325 pp.*
Smith, Raymond T. The Negro Family in British Guiana: *Family Structure and Social Status in the Villages. With a Foreword by Meyer Fortes. 314 pp. 8 plates. 1 figure. 4 maps.*

SOCIOLOGY AND PHILOSOPHY

Barnsley, John H. The Social Reality of Ethics. *A Comparative Analysis of Moral Codes. 448 pp.*
Diesing, Paul. Patterns of Discovery in the Social Sciences. *362 pp.*
● **Douglas, Jack D.** (Ed.) Understanding Everyday Life. *Toward the Reconstruction of Sociological Knowledge. Contributions by Alan F. Blum, Aaron W. Cicourel, Norman K. Denzin, Jack D. Douglas, John Heeren, Peter McHugh, Peter K. Manning, Melvin Power, Matthew Speier, Roy Turner, D. Lawrence Wieder, Thomas P. Wilson and Don H. Zimmerman. 370 pp.*
Gorman, Robert A. The Dual Vision. *Alfred Schutz and the Myth of Phenomenological Social Science. About 300 pp.*
Jarvie, Ian C. Concepts and Society. *216 pp.*
Kilminster, R. Praxis and Method. *A Sociological Dialogue with Lukács, Gramsci and the early Frankfurt School. About 304 pp.*
● **Pelz, Werner.** The Scope of Understanding in Sociology. *Towards a More Radical Reorientation in the Social Humanistic Sciences. 283 pp.*
Roche, Maurice. Phenomenology, Language and the Social Sciences. *371 pp.*
Sahay, Arun. Sociological Analysis. *212 pp.*
Slater, P. Origin and Significance of the Frankfurt School. *A Marxist Perspective. About 192 pp.*
Spurling, L. Phenomenology and the Social World. *The Philosophy of Merleau-Ponty and its Relation to the Social Sciences. 222 pp.*
Wilson, H. T. The American Ideology. *Science, Technology and Organization as Modes of Rationality. 368 pp.*

International Library of Anthropology

General Editor Adam Kuper

Ahmed, A. S. Millenium and Charisma Among Pathans. *A Critical Essay in Social Anthropology. 192 pp.*
Pukhtun Economy and Society. *About 360 pp.*

Brown, Paula. The Chimbu. *A Study of Change in the New Guinea Highlands. 151 pp.*

Foner, N. Jamaica Farewell. *200 pp.*

Gudeman, Stephen. Relationships, Residence and the Individual. *A Rural Panamanian Community. 288 pp. 11 plates, 5 figures, 2 maps, 10 tables.*

The Demise of a Rural Economy. *From Subsistence to Capitalism in a Latin American Village. 160 pp.*

Hamnett, Ian. Chieftainship and Legitimacy. *An Anthropological Study of Executive Law in Lesotho. 163 pp.*

Hanson, F. Allan. Meaning in Culture. *127 pp.*

Humphreys, S. C. Anthropology and the Greeks. *288 pp.*

Karp, I. Fields of Change Among the Iteso of Kenya. *140 pp.*

Lloyd, P. C. Power and Independence. *Urban Africans' Perception of Social Inequality. 264 pp.*

Parry, J. P. Caste and Kinship in Kangra. *352 pp. Illustrated.*

Pettigrew, Joyce. Robber Noblemen. *A Study of the Political System of the Sikh Jats. 284 pp.*

Street, Brian V. The Savage in Literature. *Representations of 'Primitive' Society in English Fiction, 1858–1920. 207 pp.*

Van Den Berghe, Pierre L. Power and Privilege at an African University. *278 pp.*

International Library of Social Policy

General Editor Kathleen Jones

Bayley, M. Mental Handicap and Community Care. *426 pp.*

Bottoms, A. E. and **McClean, J. D.** Defendants in the Criminal Process. *284 pp.*

Butler, J. R. Family Doctors and Public Policy. *208 pp.*

Davies, Martin. Prisoners of Society. *Attitudes and Aftercare. 204 pp.*

Gittus, Elizabeth. Flats, Families and the Under-Fives. *285 pp.*

Holman, Robert. Trading in Children. *A Study of Private Fostering. 355 pp.*

Jeffs, A. Young People and the Youth Service. *About 180 pp.*

Jones, Howard, and **Cornes, Paul.** Open Prisons. *288 pp.*

Jones, Kathleen. History of the Mental Health Service. *428 pp.*

Jones, Kathleen, with **Brown, John, Cunningham, W. J., Roberts, Julian** and **Williams, Peter.** Opening the Door. *A Study of New Policies for the Mentally Handicapped. 278 pp.*

Karn, Valerie. Retiring to the Seaside. *About 280 pp. 2 maps. Numerous tables.*

King, R. D. and **Elliot, K. W.** Albany: Birth of a Prison—End of an Era. *394 pp.*

Thomas, J. E. The English Prison Officer since 1850: *A Study in Conflict.*
258 pp.
Walton, R. G. Women in Social Work. *303 pp.*
Woodward, J. To Do the Sick No Harm. *A Study of the British Voluntary
Hospital System to 1875. 234 pp.*

International Library of Welfare and Philosophy

General Editors Noel Timms and David Watson

● **McDermott, F. E.** (Ed.) Self-Determination in Social Work. *A Collection
of Essays on Self-determination and Related Concepts by Philosophers
and Social Work Theorists. Contributors: F. B. Biestek, S. Bernstein,
A. Keith-Lucas, D. Sayer, H. H. Perelman, C. Whittington, R. F.
Stalley, F. E. McDermott, I. Berlin, H. J. McCloskey, H. L. A. Hart,
J. Wilson, A. I. Melden, S. I. Benn. 254 pp.*
● **Plant, Raymond.** Community and Ideology. *104 pp.*
  Ragg, Nicholas M. People Not Cases. *A Philosophical Approach to Social
Work. About 250 pp.*
● **Timms, Noel** and **Watson, David.** (Eds) Talking About Welfare.
*Readings in Philosophy and Social Policy. Contributors: T. H.
Marshall, R. B. Brandt, G. H. von Wright, K. Nielsen, M. Cranston,
R. M. Titmuss, R. S. Downie, E. Telfer, D. Donnison, J. Benson, P.
Leonard, A. Keith-Lucas, D. Walsh, I. T. Ramsey. 320 pp.*
●   (Eds). Philosophy in Social Work. *250 pp.*
● **Weale, A.** Equality and Social Policy. *164 pp.*

Primary Socialization, Language and Education

General Editor Basil Bernstein

Adlam, Diana S., *with the assistance of Geoffrey Turner and Lesley
Lineker.* Code in Context. *About 272 pp.*
Bernstein, Basil. Class, Codes and Control. *3 volumes.*
●   1. *Theoretical Studies Towards a Sociology of Language. 254 pp.*
    2. *Applied Studies Towards a Sociology of Language. 377 pp.*
●   3. *Towards a Theory of Educational Transmission. 167 pp.*
Brandis, W. and **Bernstein, B.** Selection and Control. *176 pp.*

Brandis, Walter and **Henderson, Dorothy.** Social Class, Language and Communication. *288 pp.*

Cook-Gumperz, Jenny. Social Control and Socialization. *A Study of Class Differences in the Language of Maternal Control. 290 pp.*

● **Gahagan, D. M** and **G. A.** Talk Reform. *Exploration in Language for Infant School Children. 160 pp.*

Hawkins, P. R. Social Class, the Nominal Group and Verbal Strategies. *About 220 pp.*

Robinson, W. P. and **Rackstraw, Susan D. A.** A Question of Answers. *2 volumes. 192 pp. and 180 pp.*

Turner, Geoffrey J. and **Mohan, Bernard A.** A Linguistic Description and Computer Programme for Children's Speech. *208 pp.*

Reports of the Institute of Community Studies

Baker, J. The Neighbourhood Advice Centre. A Community Project in Camden. *320 pp.*

● **Cartwright, Ann.** Patients and their Doctors. *A Study of General Practice. 304 pp.*

Dench, Geoff. Maltese in London. *A Case-study in the Erosion of Ethnic Consciousness. 302 pp.*

Jackson, Brian and **Marsden, Dennis.** Education and the Working Class: *Some General Themes raised by a Study of 88 Working-class Children in a Northern Industrial City. 268 pp. 2 folders.*

Marris, Peter. The Experience of Higher Education. *232 pp. 27 tables.*

● Loss and Change. *192 pp.*

Marris, Peter and **Rein, Martin.** Dilemmas of Social Reform. *Poverty and Community Action in the United States. 256 pp.*

Marris, Peter and **Somerset, Anthony.** African Businessmen. *A Study of Entrepreneurship and Development in Keyna. 256 pp.*

Mills, Richard. Young Outsiders: *a Study in Alternative Communities. 216 pp.*

Runciman, W. G. Relative Deprivation and Social Justice. *A Study of Attitudes to Social Inequality in Twentieth-Century England. 352 pp.*

Willmott, Peter. Adolescent Boys in East London. *230 pp.*

Willmott, Peter and **Young, Michael.** Family and Class in a London Suburb. *202 pp. 47 tables.*

Young, Michael and **McGeeney, Patrick.** Learning Begins at Home. *A Study of a Junior School and its Parents. 128 pp.*

Young, Michael and **Willmott, Peter.** Family and Kinship in East London. *Foreword by Richard M. Titmuss. 252 pp. 39 tables.*

The Symmetrical Family. *410 pp.*

Reports of the Institute for Social Studies in Medical Care

Cartwright, Ann, Hockey, Lisbeth and **Anderson, John J.** Life Before Death. *310 pp.*

Dunnell, Karen and **Cartwright, Ann.** Medicine Takers, Prescribers and Hoarders. *190 pp.*

Farrell, C. My Mother Said. . . . *A Study of the Way Young People Learned About Sex and Birth Control. 200 pp.*

Medicine, Illness and Society

General Editor W. M. Williams

Hall, David J. Social Relations & Innovation. *Changing the State of Play in Hospitals. 232 pp.*

Hall, David J., and **Stacey, M.** (Eds) Beyond Separation. *234 pp.*

Robinson, David. The Process of Becoming Ill. *142 pp.*

Stacey, Margaret *et al.* Hospitals, Children and Their Families. *The Report of a Pilot Study. 202 pp.*

Stimson G. V. and **Webb, B.** Going to See the Doctor. *The Consultation Process in General Practice. 155 pp.*

Monographs in Social Theory

General Editor Arthur Brittan

● **Barnes, B.** Scientific Knowledge and Sociological Theory. *192 pp.*

Bauman, Zygmunt. Culture as Praxis. *204 pp.*

● **Dixon, Keith.** Sociological Theory. *Pretence and Possibility. 142 pp.*

Meltzer, B. N., Petras, J. W. and **Reynolds, L. T.** Symbolic Interactionism. *Genesis, Varieties and Criticisms. 144 pp.*

● **Smith, Anthony D.** The Concept of Social Change. *A Critique of the Functionalist Theory of Social Change. 208 pp.*

Routledge Social Science Journals

The British Journal of Sociology. *Editor – Angus Stewart; Associate Editor – Leslie Sklair. Vol. 1, No. 1 – March 1950 and Quarterly. Roy. 8vo. All back issues available. An international journal publishing original papers in the field of sociology and related areas.*

Community Work. *Edited by David Jones and Marjorie Mayo. 1973. Published annually.*

Economy and Society. *Vol. 1, No. 1. February 1972 and Quarterly. Metric Roy. 8vo. A journal for all social scientists covering sociology, philosophy, anthropology, economics and history. All back numbers available.*

Ethnic and Racial Studies. *Editor – John Stone. Vol. 1 – 1978. Published quarterly.*

Religion. Journal of Religion and Religions. *Chairman of Editorial Board, Ninian Smart. Vol. 1, No. 1, Spring 1971. A journal with an inter-disciplinary approach to the study of the phenomena of religion. All back numbers available.*

Sociology of Health and Illness. *A Journal of Medical Sociology. Editor – Alan Davies; Associate Editor – Ray Jobling. Vol. 1, Spring 1979. Published 3 times per annum.*

Year Book of Social Policy in Britain, The. *Edited by Kathleen Jones. 1971. Published annually.*

Social and Psychological Aspects of Medical Practice

Editor   Trevor Silverstone

Lader, Malcolm. Psychophysiology of Mental Illness. *280 pp.*
● **Silverstone, Trevor** and **Turner, Paul.** Drug Treatment in Psychiatry. *Revised edition. 256 pp.*
Whiteley, J. S. and **Gordon, J.** Group Approaches in Psychiatry. *256 pp.*

Printed in Great Britain by
Lowe & Brydone Printers Limited, Thetford, Norfolk